The Ancien Régi...
A History...
1610–

D0912081

A History of France will, in five volumes, provide an account of
1,000 years of French history. The authors are among the most distinguished French historians, and the reception given to the first three
volumes when they appeared in France in 1987 and 1988 suggests that
this will be the standard history of France for many years to come.

France in the Middle Ages 987–1460
Georges Duby

The Royal French State 1460–1610
Emmanuel Le Roy Ladurie

The Ancien Régime, A History of France 1610–1774
Emmanuel Le Roy Ladurie

Revolutionary France 1770–1880
François Furet

The French Republic 1879–1992
Maurice Agulhon

The Ancien Régime
A History of France
1610–1774

EMMANUEL LE ROY LADURIE

Translated by
Mark Greengrass

BLACKWELL
Publishers

First published as *L'Ancien Régime 1610-1770* by Hachette, 1991
First published in English 1996
First published in paperback in English 1998

2 4 6 8 10 9 7 5 3 1

Blackwell Publishers Ltd
108 Cowley Road
Oxford OX4 1JF
UK

Blackwell Publishers Inc.
350 Main Street
Malden, Massachusetts 02148
USA

British Library Cataloguing in Publication Data
A CIP catalogue record for this book is available from the British Library.

Library of Congress Cataloging-in-Publication Data

Le Roy Ladurie, Emmanuel.
[Ancien Régime. English]
The Ancien Régime: a history of France, 1610–1774 / Emmanuel Le
Roy Ladurie; translated by Mark Greengrass.
p.   cm. – (A history of France)
Includes bibliographical references and index.
ISBN 0–631–17028–6
ISBN 0–631–21196–9 (pbk)
1.   France – History – 17th century. 2. France – History – 18th century. 3. France –
Civilization – 17th century. 4. France – Civilization – 18th century. I. Title. II. Series.
DC121.L4713 1996
944'.03 – dc20
95–43602
CIP

Typeset in 10½ on 12pt Plantin
by Best-set Typesetter Ltd., Hong Kong
Printed in Great Britain by T. J. International, Padstow, Cornwall

This book is printed on acid-free paper

Contents

List of Illustrations

1

Temperate Monarchy in its Last Incarnation

The beginning of the century was truly auspicious. Henry IV's reign, which inaugurated the Bourbon monarchy, placed France for over a decade under the influence of a political constellation open to talent and new ideas. Henry of Navarre, a distant cousin of the Valois kings who had ruled France from 1328 to 1589, was a legitimate descendant of St Louis. By the normal genealogical rules governing the dynastic game, he had acceded to the throne; yet it was also thanks to his great personal qualities that he gradually succeeded in imposing his will as sovereign in the two decades from 1590 to 1610. He had first to conquer or win over his adversaries who, from 1584, had regrouped their forces, most notably in Paris, into a 'League'. Violent, ultra-Catholic and sometimes populist, the League was a dangerous opponent for Navarre. For the first time, France's urban populations were mobilized by an ideology which was both religious and civic. In some respects the process foreshadowed the sans-culottes and radicals of the French Revolution although their political motivations rested on altogether different foundations.

Henry IV pacified these semi-fanatical stirrings by a combination of brute force and conciliation. He thus brought to an end the cycle of civil wars, sometimes called the wars of religion, which had engulfed France and the continent of Europe, and to which the enduring and profitable stability of Elizabethan England proved such a contrast. By the edict of Nantes (1598), Henry IV laid the foundation for a peaceable contiguity between those of different religious beliefs. This was the first time it had been attempted in one of Europe's large states for, although a similar confessional pluralism also existed at this time in Germany, it was on the basis of a multiplicity of different states. It was also far from kindling the kind of toleration which would be foreshadowed in the Enlightenment. In 1600, a 'right of conscientious objection' was hardly recognized for its own sake. In essence, however, priests and pastors learnt to live together in France without attacking one another or (at the very least) without the one openly persecuting the other. In the villages of southern France, the Protestant minister was sometimes even to be found participating in a cordial game of *boules* with the *curé*.[1] Neither Spain, with its anti-Protestant, anti-Jewish, anti-Islamic tendencies, nor yet the fundamentally anti-papist England, was able to measure up to such a pattern of coexistence. Its equivalent was only to be found in relatively small states, such as the Netherlands, or in distant Poland. The revocation of the edict of Nantes in 1685 would, of course, put an end to the fruitful French experiment in confessional coexistence – but this was after it had lasted for a full 80 years.

Henry's reign also consolidated the influence of a class of office-holders who, finding themselves for the most part a leisure class, the owners of châteaux, constituted a nobility of conscious creation and defined dignity (as opposed to a nobility which was innate, well-born and gentle-bred).[2] Historians have long called them the *noblesse de robe*. In the state, they were proprietors of their posts (sometimes no more than sinecures), owners of their offices. In some respects they were more fortunate than modern state functionaries, for they enjoyed not merely the passing entitlement to office, as nowadays, but also its hereditary disposition. They could pass it on to their descendants or sell it at will, always providing that whoever acquired it could, at least in principle, display a modicum of competence. As a result, a kind of hereditary grouping of dignitaries in public office emerged. By the second third of the seventeenth century, this had progressively coalesced into some 40,000–50,000 families with the title to an office which was passed on through the family line. It amounted to no more than about 1 per cent of the 4–5 million households in the kingdom. This small but influential élite was not always a paragon of administrative virtue when it came to the routine government of the country. Yet the entrenched stability of the office-holding élite acted as a counter-balance, at least in part, to the possible absolutism and arbitrary authority of the Bourbon monarchy. It constrained the excesses of ministerial or monarchical despotism and was linked to the two key features in the progressive elaboration of the French state which we have already delineated for the period from 1595 to 1610.[3] These two features, *viz.* renewed growth and openness, would not last long. Growth was implicit in the administrative mechanisms of a state whose central conception was still that of the 'tree' of justice.[4] The 5,000 state officials in 1515 increased to some 50,000 in 1661 and the 'little' state of the young Valois king, Francis I, became the more substantial state, albeit still fairly modest in bureaucratic scale, of the young Louis XIV.

---

[1] According to Marc Venard, *Réforme protestante, réforme catholique dans la province d'Avignon – XVIe siècle* (Paris, Editions du Cerf, 1993).

[2] A 'dative' noblesse 'de dignité', as opposed to a 'native' noblesse 'de gentilité'; see C. Loyseau, *Cinq livres du droit des offices* (Paris, 1610) and Brigitte Boisdevant-Gaudemet, *Aux origines de l'Etat moderne, Charles Loyseau, 1564–1627, théoricien de la puissance publique* (Paris, Economica, 1977).

[3] E. Le Roy Ladurie, *The Royal French State, 1460–1610* (Oxford, Blackwell, 1994), p. 229 *et seq.*

[4] Ibid., pp. 200–4.

The greater openness was the major achievement of Henry IV and Sully. It was not entirely of their own making; indeed, it developed tendencies similar to those already present in the French state under Charles VIII, Louis XII and Francis I before the Day of Placards in 1534. These were still discernible after the reign of Henry II (who had been for the most part an apostle of intolerance) during the age of Catherine de Médicis and Henry III. Openness manifested itself in the reign of Henry IV in three major ways. There was, firstly, a pacific coexistence with the Protestant minority within the kingdom. Secondly, there was a solid alliance with the Protestant powers to the north and east, such as the Netherlands, England and the Protestant Swiss cantons. Finally the instruments of state gave positive backing to an economic environment which for the two or three decades following 1595 would be favourable to economic growth. The attempts of Henry IV and Sully to stimulate economic production and commercial development should not be overestimated but they were far from insignificant. They relied on mercantilist perceptions which stressed the importance of encouraging native manufacture and the export of finished products, and discouraging the export of raw materials. But the famous 'chicken in the pot' was not put there by the application of rigidly pursued state-enforced ideologies and there was still room for the semi-liberal empiricism of pot-luck.

The assassination of Henry IV on 14 May 1610 did not put an end to these tendencies and their durability is, in retrospect, worth stressing. Coexistence with the Protestants, begun at the pacification of Nantes in 1598, lasted officially more or less until 1661. Although Richelieu would destroy by military force the Huguenot party, he let the French Protestant churches survive and they were only gradually suppressed in the period from 1661 to 1685. The second component of Henrician 'openness' – the close entente with the Protestants beyond the northern and eastern frontiers of France – also survived long after his death. Despite some fluctuations, the diplomatic alliances with 'heretic' states were reinforced by the cardinal-ministers in order to strengthen France's hand against its Spanish adversary. Finally, the encouragement given to economic enterprise and manufacture would continue to be amongst the preoccupations of French ministers, whether Sully, Richelieu or (still more) Colbert. The results of such endeavours would be patchy and would depend largely on changes in an economic climate which the state was incapable of altering. Indeed, after 1635, the state made matters worse for the economy through the effects of the increased levels of its borrowing.

★　★　★　★　★

We may now examine the various symbolic aspects of the French monarchy such as they were manifested in the aftermath of Henry IV's death. The months following the king's assassination are interesting in that the pace towards a more absolute monarchy quickened at the time of the coronation of Louis XIII.

The coronation took place on 17 October 1610 and did not follow the established order of events, as in the days of Francis I or Henry II. Normally the funeral service for Henry IV would have taken place first. With it would have come the moment when the effigy of the dead king would be placed on public display, the representation of the continuity of royal dignity.[5] This would then have been followed by a formal session of the Parlement of Paris in a *lit de justice* which would then be seen in the eyes of the law-officers as inaugurating the reign or, as in 1610, the Regency. Only then would the king's coronation take place. In 1610, however, this established order of events was reversed. The *lit de justice* took place in the Parlement of Paris on 15 May 1610, the day after the assassination, and well before the funeral. In one sense, this was a response to urgent necessity; the new king had to be proclaimed speedily because the situation was fraught with danger. In another, however, it encapsulated an essential change of perspective. The transmission of royal dignity was no longer dependent on the effigy as the incarnate representation of a mortal monarch. Instead its transmission was dependent upon the individual blood lineage which linked Henry to his son Louis, passing directly from one to the other without any mediating element. Changing the metaphor to one which was current at the beginning of the seventeenth century, the clouds of death had but for a moment obscured the sun of sovereign authority from the leading figures in the kingdom. 'The king never dies' was a phrase used more frequently in France at this time in place of the older and more abstract formula: '[Royal] dignity dies not' (*Dignitas non moritur*). The mystique of the blood royal became of greater significance than the office of monarchy itself. This shift was a logical development of the concept of 'indivisible sovereignty' which had been advanced by Jean Bodin in 1576. As a result of this change it was inevitable that the 'legislative autonomy of His Majesty the King', with all its absolutist overtones, would be in the ascendant in comparison with the preceding centuries when the full panoply of royal *Majesty* amassed constitutional limits around the monarchy and restricted the personal authority of an individual king.[6]

Tradition had to be respected, however. Even the coronation rituals of 1610 were readily organized around the 'three functions' of traditional authority proposed by Georges Dumézil. These provide a means to understand the fundamental nature of such authority. Although it would be possible to trace the origins of this threefold pattern back to its distant Indo-European origins, its functional rationale is independent of its remote ancestry. The first function proposed by Dumézil concerns religion,

---

[5] Ibid., pp. 132–3. See also the works of the school of American historians of royal ceremonial, especially R.E. Giesey, *Cérémonie et puissance souveraine* (Paris, A. Colin, 1987) and *Le Roi ne meurt jamais* (Paris, Flammarion, 1987).

[6] For this subject, see R.A. Jackson, *Vive le Roi! A History of the French Coronation from Charles V to Charles X* (Chapel Hill, University of North Carolina Press, 1984) and, more especially, Marina Valensise, 'Le Sacre du roi', *Annales ESC*, 41 (1986), 547.

justice and sovereignty, conceptions with which a group of clergy identified themselves to a certain degree, not to mention (amongst the laity) the office-holders and (still more) the chancellor. The latter believed himself (and they themselves) to represent not merely 'Justice' but also 'sovereign Majesty'. The second function is military and orientated towards the nobility. The third is more difficult to define because it relates in large measure to all that is not encompassed in the first two. It refers to the basic problems of fertility, fecundity, prosperity and productivity. In terms of social identity, this part of the monarchy's functioning rationale was devoted to the Third Estate.[7] The latter was made up of all who were ruled and commanded, commoners alike since the other orders (priests, public officials and aristocrats) had easily identified themselves with the 'first' and the 'second' functioning rationales.

The coronation was prepared with great care. Immediately after the arrival of the queen and her son at Reims, and during the days leading up to the central ceremony, the young king was escorted on a visit of the various monasteries, churches and holy relics preserved in the city. On Saturday 16 October he received confirmation at nine years of age at the hand of the Cardinal de Joyeuse who, on the following day, would be responsible for the coronation rites.

On Sunday 17 October, following on from the early scenes (the wakening of the 'sleeping king' and the processions of the holy ampula and crown jewels and regalia to the cathedral), the ceremonies of the coronation itself began. They commenced with the promises and were followed by the coronation oath, sworn by the boy-king upon the Bible. The various phrases of these promises were concerned with the first function of traditional authority. He swore before God to preserve the rights of the bishops and the church, to prevent violence, to be just and merciful in his judgements and to expel all heretics from all the lands and jurisdictions of the crown. The final part of the promises was pregnant with potentially perverse consequences; but this would only be true if monarchs applied its terms faithfully, as would Louis XIII (partially) and Louis XIV (completely). For his part, Henry IV only committed himself to this oath at Chartres in 1594 in order to break it four years later in the edict of Nantes.

---

[7] For Georges Dumézil – see, for example, his *Mitra-Varuna* (Paris, PUF, 1940) – these three functions involve juridical/political and magical/religious sovereignty, physical and military force and, finally, fecundity. According to Dumézil, these distinctions originate in the ancient ideology of the Indo-Europeans. It is perhaps, however, the case that this schema was more or less implicit in the history of vast tracts of Eurasia, in zones whose ethnic origins (Indo-European, Semitic, etc.) were very varied. See, for example, the interesting passage from the Old Testament in *Jeremiah*, 51, vv. 20–35. But this difficult question of its origins is not of significance here. The tri-functional ideology, dear to the heart of Dumézil, inspired numerous institutions and writings in ancien régime France, amongst which are to be found the 'three estates' and many other complex entities. We shall have occasion to return to this convenient means of classification in later chapters.

In between the moment when these promises were made and the coronation oath, which consecrated them, lay a simulated 'elective' ceremony in which the lords bishops of Laon and Beauvais asked the assembled multitude if they accepted Louis XIII as their sovereign. In the cathedral at Reims in 1610 there was an expression of ready consent, a vast collective rumble of approval. The importance of this flattering approval should not be overestimated. Such an 'electoral formality' only dated back to the coronation of Henry II in 1547. It had no integral part in the old medieval *ordo* which, from 1250 onwards, was squarely based around the all-powerful king. At the same time, it should not be entirely dismissed from account. Unanimous 'elections' in modern non-democratic states have been more specious, and eventually more dishonest, than the assent granted Louis XIII by the several thousand spectators who witnessed his coronation in October 1610.

The second act of the coronation invested the king with the symbols of chivalry (gold spurs, sword, etc.). Within the unfolding ceremonies this was a brief, but indispensable, 'excursus' in the direction of the military roles of the king.

In the third act, that of holy unction, the religious dimensions of the ceremony returned to the centre of the stage. The Cardinal de Joyeuse applied the holy unguent to the king's head, his stomach, his shoulders and arms. By this time, even before the holy oil had beem smeared over the palms of his hands, the child Louis was already considered fully as a king. The grand chamberlain helped him into a series of three vestments which made him the equivalent of a sub-deacon, a deacon and a priest. After these religious rites, the king was invested with the objects representing justice and sovereignty (a ring, a sceptre and the hand of justice) by the presiding cardinal. Sovereignty thus proceeded from God via the bishop at the high altar. Finally came the moment of crowning itself when the 12 peers of the realm (six lay peers and six ecclesiastics) placed their hands on the crown and conferred on Louis the power which would henceforth be his to exercise. It is a remarkable fact that, in the English coronation ceremony, the act of coronation itself (the best embodiment of the conceptual perpetuity of the royal office, independent of any individual person) was far more central to the ceremony than in France. The French rite, at least as it was enacted in 1610, initially laid emphasis on the personal and nominal continuity of a succession of human beings, a continuity incarnate in 1610 in the young Louis at the moment of his father's death. The dual, 'sacral-sovereign' nature of the first function in French kingship is readily identifiable, however, in the French coronation rite. The chancellor, a lay officer who was the trunk of the tree of justice, was the one who called on the 12 peers each to place their hands collectively on the crown which the presiding cardinal, one of the 12 peers, set upon the king's head whilst the other peers kept a finger on the crown.[8] This group, led by the constable carrying

---

[8]   For all this paragraph, see R.A. Jackson, *Vive le Roi!*, p. 157.

the coronation sword, conducted the king to his throne, the physical and symbolic embodiment of royal majesty. This was the moment of climax and the acclamations of 'Vive le Roi' rang out in Latin and French. Commemorative coins and medallions were distributed around the people crowded into the sanctuary. About 750 sparrows, goldfinches and small birds were released from cages into the rafters of the cathedral, probably a foreshadowing of the amnesty of various prisoners which would shortly take place on the orders of the new sovereign. Then the king participated in a Mass, in the course of which Louis offered the cathedral in Reims a golden vase, some gold and silver 'loaves' as well as 13 gold coins.

Once the Mass had been said, the king made his confession and communicated in both kinds (bread and wine), thus emphasizing once more his affiliation to the clerical order above the mass of laity. The finale took place in the episcopal palace. A day or so later, Louis received the collar of the Order of the Holy Spirit. At the sanctuary of St Marcoul outside Reims, he touched about 850 scrofula victims. After the freeing of some prisoners (we do not know how many), Louis XIII returned to the Louvre, his Paris residence.

It is noticeable how the apparently immanent divine and transcendent features of the ceremonies appeared at every stage. No element escaped being immersed in them, even those components which concerned the vitally important prosperity or economic life of the king's subjects, or those which touched on his warrior function. The martial element in the ritual was far from negligible but, apart from some solemn processions of the coronation sword before and after the anointing of the king, this 'military section' was limited to the chivalric investiture sequence, which was, itself, sacral. As to the features concerning the third functional element (fructiferous, prosperous, popular and commoner-orientated) they only made an occasional appearance. Collected together in one component of the ceremony, there was something artificial about the way they sought to be convincing. They allow us (and this is the point of this analysis) to put the coronation into some kind of perspective. This was not completely or entirely a religious ceremony with some chivalric attachments. Rather we should accept that, in the cathedral in Reims, the 'people' (for the congregation was not made up entirely of those from the first two estates of the realm) were asked summarily to approve the coronation of the new king; then, finally, the people were invited to acclaim the act. For their part, the monarch and his entourage used numerous gestures to evoke in a variety of ways, some more oblique than others, the kingdom's prosperity, or referred in different, and highly symbolic, ways to the wealth (and sustenance) of the realm. Hence the distribution of money and the gift of golden 'loaves'. Other gestures were made towards the dangerous elements in society (the freeing of prisoners) or the suffering in its midst (the Royal Touch). By these symbolic means, the sovereign was displayed as in rapport with the humble and disadvantaged at the very bottom of the Third Estate.

Many of the ceremonies we have just described were surreptitiously slanted or modified in the course of the coronation of 1610 in comparison with previous enthronements. They tended to emphasize more clearly the sacred incarnation of the king's physical embodiment and, through it, subtly put to one side the traditional perception of a constitutional transmission of an abstracted monarchical 'Dignity' from one king to his successor. Take, for example, the morning levee of the young Louis XIII, the 'dormant king', on the morning of his coronation. With the doors of his bedchamber closed, the king feigned an arousal from sleep by the third knock from the bishop who, from this moment onwards, no longer addressed him as 'son of Henry the Great' but as 'Louis XIII whom God has given us for king'. This was but one way of indicating that, before the coronation, and from the moment of Henry's death, his scion manifested the royal quality which God had fundamentally infused in him.

A further innovation marks the coronation of 1610 off from those which had preceded it. For the first time in the history of the lineage, the king exercised, even *during* his coronation, his classic right of granting pardon to certain convicted criminals. In this instance, too, the chronological contiguity between taking the royal oaths, being anointed, crowned and acceding to the power of exercising the royal pardon marks a conceptual enlargement of the authority of the king in the direction of a personalized absolutism which constitutes the objective, sought after although never completely realized, of the French monarchy from 1614–27. Despite the regular practice of issuing amnesties, exercised by modern presidents at the moment of their appointment, we should be aware of the 'absolutist' innovation which the exercise of the royal pardon represented in 1610.

There was one further sign of a reinforced Bourbon dynasticism with its absolutist pretensions. The princes of the blood were given a more prominent place and confirmed in their rights of precedence amongst the lay peers of the realm (who were, as we have seen, required to hold the crown above the head of the little Louis XIII during the coronation). This precedence was to the detriment of other peers of the realm who did not enjoy the privilege of being of the blood royal. This increased status for the royal family (narrowly defined) had been foreshadowed for some time. An edict of Henry III in 1576 had already pronounced it as a fact. He had intended it, as had the statements of his mother before him, in order to enfeeble the House of Guise. These were princes of the House of Lorraine and they did not enjoy consanguinity with the Capetian royal line. In any case, the ultra-Catholic members of the Guise family were a considerable threat to the royal lineage in the course of the second half of the sixteenth century.

The granting of such rights of precedence among the lay peers to the descendants of St Louis alone in October 1610 favoured the mystique of the blood royal at the expense of the juridical limits which had, for so long, held in check the royal office. In the light of this absolutist tendency, the quasi-electoral component of the coronation ceremony, or at least the acquiescence in the ceremony solicited from the crowd in the sanctuary of the cathedral, should not be overestimated. Of course, the proponents of elective monarchy during the wars of religion, made great play of this point. Supporters of such 'Frankish' traditions of election, supposedly practised by the barbarian kings of the French past, included the Protestant 'monarchomachs' (or 'king-haters') such as Hotman and Beza. In due course, they were joined by Catholic League adherents such as Jean Boucher as well as some of those who participated in the League estates general of 1593.[9] After 1594, however, the 'pro-absolutist' thought of Bodin (as formulated in 1576) became predominant. He held that the king 'did not accept his sceptre . . . from the people, but from God alone'.[10] Contemporary disciples of Bodin, such as Pierre de Belloy, Nicolas De Thou, André Puchasse, Guy Coquille or Jean Baricave advanced similar views. The ritual of popular assent, which was continued in the coronation of 1610, became ever more insignificant.[11] As Richard Jackson has noted, 'the writers (Bodin, Coquille, etc.) who denied that there was any value to popular consent and elective monarchy, were thus weakening the theretical limitations on the power of the monarchy. In the elaboration of absolutism, they played an essential role.'[12]

The absolutism which was heralded by the 1610 coronation was in no way comparable to the monstrous totalitarian regimes of the twentieth century.[13] Theoretically, the second Bourbon king would become a 'quasi-absolute' king when he attained his legal majority after the Regency of Marie de Médicis. Yet he would exercise his authority within the context of a temporal monarchy on this earth and not in some divine ether, conserved by the church. Thus the French monarchy was what we might describe as a 'relative absolutism'. Besides, although the king was theoretically quite powerful, in practice he was constrained in a variety of ways. He was limited by existing rights. Nowadays, albeit anachronistically, we might call these the 'rights of man'. They embraced the divine and natural law – the latter including amongst its 'human rights' the right to property, the right to civil liberty (i.e. the right not to be a slave or a serf). It placed a duty of responsibility towards the public interest and the well-being of his people upon the ruler. There were other significant limits upon his power, too, such as the Estates General which would be convened for the last time in 1614, and the fundamental laws of the kingdom, such as the law of succession to the throne through the male line only. *De facto*, the king was also limited by the autonomy of the office-holders. Proprietors of their

[9] On these monarchomachs and Catholic theorists who had imbibed crypto-democratic notions, see Le Roy Ladurie, *The Royal French State*, pp. 189–91; 217.

[10] Bodin, *République*, VI, 5 (2). Jackson, *Vive le Roi!* p. 118 (French edition).

[11] Jackson, *Vive le Roi!*, pp. 114–19.

[12] Ibid., p. 119.

[13] In principle, totalitarianism exercised power without limits, which was not the case with absolutism.

posts, they could not be removed from office or easily manipulated to suit the whim of a prince.

The autonomy of the office-holders had been clearly demonstrated by a sequence of events some months before the 1610 coronation. The Regency of Marie de Médicis owed its origins, in fact, to a series of sessions of the Parlement of Paris, one of which (at least), that of 14 May 1610, boldly sketched out a 'government of the magistrates'. The 'justice-state' made its appearance on the scene with renewed aspirations. By a swift decision of the court, immediately following Henry IV's death, the Parlement of Paris proclaimed that same day the Regency of Marie de Médicis.[14] The queen mother let this pass, although the powers which they had exercised did not fall with their normal competence. Normally, the Parlement would have been expected only to acclaim *post festum* the inauguration of the new king who would then himself have announced, in a child's voice, the beginnings of the Regency and handed over his authority to his mother. This was what subsequently would happen, but only during the *lit de justice* convoked in the normal fashion by the royal authorities on the following day, 15 May.[15] Should not the minor *coup d'éclat* which anticipated this event on 14 May be seen as reflecting the growing consciousness of the office-holding classes? The Parlement was at the acme of these classes; it was their incarnation. And it was in the same year, 1610, that the major work of Charles Loyseau, *On Offices*, devoted to defending and defining office-holding practice, appeared.

★   ★   ★   ★   ★

Henry IV's assassination left the kingdom in the hands of his widow, Marie de Médicis. This would last until 1614, when the boy-king Louis XIII attained his legal majority, and, in reality, until 1617 when he became fully involved in the direction of state with the murder of Concini, the queen mother's favourite.

Marie was born in Florence in 1573, home of the Médicis, a family of rich and recent *parvenus*.[16] Yet she was also the daughter of an archduchess of Austria and was thus, via her mother, a Habsburg. She put to good use both her bourgeois self-reliance and her imperial pride, and the resulting exalted sense of her own standing was sufficient in this period of relative social elasticity (1610–14) to command the respect of most people, though not, perhaps, the aristocratic grandees. From the various contemporary texts and the writings of subsequent historians it is possible to piece together the main features of a negative, pejorative portrait of Marie de Médicis. She was, they say, plump and upright, greedy for power, for

[14] Sarah Hanley, *The* Lit de Justice *of the Kings of France: Constitutional Ideology, Legend, Ritual and Discourse* (Princeton, NJ, Princeton University Press, 1983), p. 232.
[15] Ibid.
[16] Michel Carmona, *Marie de Médicis* (Paris, Fayard, 1981).

jewels and for gratifications – the latter raked in by her confidante, Leonora Galigai. The Regent amassed a personal fortune which put her in the league of the great fortunes of seventeenth-century 'state servants'; but Sully, Concini, Richelieu, Mazarin and Colbert all enjoyed fortunes far in excess of Marie de Médicis' 6 million *livres*. Against such reputed rapacity, Marie also knew how to be generous to a fault. She showered gifts on those in her entourage, many of whom were Italians. Although there were some who earned their disgrace, on the whole they displayed a sincere loyalty towards her. She was capable of strong emotional commitments and of tender love, especially towards her daughter Henrietta, who became queen of England, and also, to a lesser degree, towards her son, Gaston. This was in contrast to the scant regard in which she held Louis XIII, who never enjoyed his mother's affections. The Virgin Mary was the object of the Regent's most spectacular devotions, typical of the kind of Italianate, Hispanic, ultramontane, Catholic piety which would attract the criticisms of some commentators who doubted the depth of the queen mother's convictions, and even their sincerity. Yet she enjoyed close contacts with the key figures in what would become the 'century of saints'. She regarded Bérulle and Marillac, the spiritual heirs to the Catholic League, as amongst her circle. They were the leading advocates in the long-heralded French counter-reformation.[17] Captivated by the prospects of real power as Regent, she showed that, on occasions, she was not bereft of political talents. Towards the Huguenots, at least in the early years of the Regency, she displayed a forbearance which arose more from political expediency than genuine conviction. Few were impressed, however, by her intelligence. Mentally, she was as lumpish as she looked. Things did not go badly during the Regency; but, once it was over, she handed over the reins of power to her favourite, Concini, and then to the adolescent Louis XIII who showed the desire, the will, and even the capacity, to maintain, if not to strengthen, the royal prerogative. Eventually, Marie had to submit to the authority of Richelieu, her one-time servant (*créature*). He was brilliant, however, once he had arrived, at kicking away the ladder up which he had climbed to prominence. Perhaps frigid, certainly cantankerous, she was demeaned by the amorous adventures of Henry IV and she detested having to put up with living in what she regarded as his seraglio. Yet throughout her life, Marie was able to call on an ample degree of Florentine dissimulation, an accumulation of resentments and jealousies, and a reserve of sometimes remarkable obstinacy. Against Richelieu she would deploy secret agents and deadly spells which would epitomize the destiny of a queen mother who was, after 1631, in exile, frustrated and increasingly out of touch with the realities of French national life.

---

[17] One of the best portrayals of her is to be found in the delicate brush-strokes of Pierre Chevallier, *Louis XIII* (Paris, Fayard, 1979), p. 64 *et seq*. See also A. Lloyd Moote, *Louis XIII the Just* (Berkeley, California University Press, 1989), p. 27 *et seq*.

Plate 1 Marie de Médicis Under the Regency of Marie de Médicis, the quasi-constitutional monarchy of Renaissance France reached its finale. Here, at the beginning of the Regency (c.1610) the Regent is portrayed by Franz II Pourbus ('Pourbus the Younger').
Paris, Musée Carnavalet

Such are the components of a caricature, viewed with hindsight, of the queen mother. She was less fortunate than Anne of Austria, whose friendship with Mazarin finally transformed her into a figure of consequence. Marie de Médicis, by contrast, enjoyed all that power could offer before finding herself consigned to a perpetual political wilderness until her death. The political consequences of the rule of the 'second French Médicis' Regency, which lasted *de jure* and then, latterly, *de facto*, from 1610 to 1617, were, however, far from negligible. After 1617, however, and (above all) after 1630, Henry IV's widow was defeated at every turn and condemned to look back nostalgically to the power which she had lost for good.

At the beginning of the second decade of the seventeenth century, this was well in the future and Marie enjoyed real authority which, in the short-term, she deployed with some ability. Amongst the various opposing political groups in contention at the highest échelons of power there was a narrow circle of close confidants and intimate advisers around the Regent herself. Amongst these was the lawyer Dolé, the physician Duret and, above all, the Italian duo Concini-Galigaï. The latter were husband and wife, both Florentines and, like the queen mother, avaricious. They were thus cordially detested although, on occasion, they could act decisively in the national French interest against Spain. Then there was the group of ministers and their entourage which the queen mother had inherited from Henry IV's régime. They were not as close to the queen mother, but they were active and influential. Senior figures in office, they had served their turn, often as moderate adherents to the League, before passing on to official positions under Henry IV and then Marie. By then they were ready to put their weight behind a rapprochement with Madrid. Ennobled through office, or on the way to being so, they emerged from the great clans of secretaries of state (such as the Brulart, the L'Aubespine and the Villeroy). They occupied the chancellorship (Sillery), financial affairs (Jeannin) and foreign affairs (Villeroy). The latter was hispanophile and in receipt of a pension from the Spanish; his influence in council remained predominant over foreign matters from 1611 until the end of 1614. There were finally some foreign diplomats, notably the papal nuncio and the ambassadors of Spain and Florence, who were part of the groups determining policy under the Regency. Henry IV would never have allowed them to be amongst the inner cabinet of his close advisers. Marie, however, associated them in various ways with her rule and demonstrated her rapprochement towards Hispanic and Mediterranean Catholicism. The various groupings which we have thus defined are typical of the strategic realignment which was undertaken by the French government at the behest of Marie de Médicis and her advisers. This realignment recognized the new lines of force in European politics brought about by the death of Henry IV, itself one more reason to adopt a lower profile in external affairs during the Regency.

Once the Jülich-Cleves affair had been sorted out there was no other issue to cloud relations with Spain; on the contrary, France sought to maintain its good standing at the Spanish court – not least because it neutralized the influential clerical group at the French court whose aspirations (and even their intrigues) were orchestrated by

Marillac.[18] To the south-east, the Savoyard alliance with France, which had been constructed with some difficulty by Henry IV, was sacrificed without a moment's thought by Marie de Médicis in order to secure favour at Madrid. At the beginning of 1612, the Spanish marriages were announced. These had been mooted for a long time but, by this date, they coincided perfectly with the new strategic imperatives of the Regency. They conjoined inexorably Louis XIII and Anne of Austria, the daughter of Philip III and, in the opposite direction, they also united the young Elisabeth, daughter of Marie de Médicis, with the inheritor of the Spanish throne, the future Philip IV. By increasing the possibilities of lasting peace both within the kingdom and without, this double union was by no means a fatuous proposal. It represented something of a departure, however, from the diplomatic patterns established under Henry IV. He had sought to bolster France's Protestant alliances to the north and the north-east whilst avoiding too close a rapprochement with France's Ibero-papist southern neighbours. Although Marie was more hispanophile, she nevertheless ensured that she maintained her links with England, even signing an alliance with the English in September 1610. A further marriage was envisaged between Madame Christine, another daughter of Marie, and the young Henry Stuart, Prince of Wales.

There remained, however, the enormous problem of the higher nobility – the princes of the blood, the princes of foreign extraction and the powerful French aristocracy, the Huguenot and Catholic grandees. The authority of Henry IV and Sully had held them in check without ever intending to humiliate them or domesticate them entirely, as would Richelieu and Louis XIV. Henry IV's assassin, Ravaillac, had reawakened old appetites for rebellion and Marie, aware of the fact, distributed gifts and pensions totalling millions of *livres* to the grandees to secure their loyalty. The budgetary surplus accumulated by Sully, although far from inexhaustible, found the funds to pay for it for the first few years and, since it proved impossible to line the pockets and coffers of the aristocracy *ad infinitum*, the Regent invited the most eminent and most noted amongst the grandees to join the royal Council, threatening to transform it into a talking-shop whilst real power retreated into the hands of an intimate and dynamic inner-group composed only of the Regent's close friends and current favourites (Concini, Dolé, the nuncio, the Spanish ambassador, etc.).

It would be wrong, however, to consider the higher nobility as an integral group. Although its members enjoyed some common aspirations, tending always in the direction of wanting something more (whether of power or favour), they were also profoundly split over issues, especially religious ones, which divided the whole of French society. The grandees

---

[18]   The Jülich-Cleves affair had begun in 1609 over the disputed succession of the duchy of Cleves, following the extinction of the ducal lineage, and it brought France and Spain to the brink of conflict. The death of Henry IV, followed by an agreement in 1614, provided a provisional settlement to the question.

both shaped and mirrored public consciousness and their individual conflicts reflected the diversity of ideas and political options at large within the French kingdom.

The grandees began by losing one of their luminaries, a key representative figure from amongst the Protestant aristocracy. There was little love lost between the Regent and Sully. The latter was politically isolated after the death of Henry IV and left the government. Marie remained, however, on tactically good terms with the other leading and powerful Protestant nobles such as Bouillon and Lesdiguières. She also took good care to ensure that good relationships were maintained with the reformed churches. The Regent confirmed their security strongholds (*places de sûreté*) and the payment of the salaries of their ministers from royal funds. The fall of Sully was, nevertheless, an event of some significance. It signalled the first beginnings of the political demise of the Huguenot party which would reach its ultimate stage in the revocation of the edict of Nantes in 1685.

The moderate misfortunes of one grandee provided, of necessity, a welcome opportunity for others. The Guise clan, which had been in eclipse after the defeat of the League, regained some of its former influence. Henry III and Henry IV had suffered a good deal in the last two decades of the sixteenth century from the affronts to their authority from these Lorraine princes whose ultra-Catholic loyalties were fundamentally at odds with the last Valois' moderation and the first Bourbon's heresy and subsequent ex-heresy. By contrast, Marie was benevolent towards both the papal curia and Madrid. She regained the loyalties of the Guise who had for so long been the pensionaries of the Spanish court. There were other grandees, too, who made common cause with the Guise clan around a shared Catholicism and a conjoined clientage network. Amongst these were the *grand écuyer* Bellegarde, and the duke d'Epernon. The army was directed by the *maréchaux* of France, such as Brissac, and led by the young Charles de Lorraine, Duke de Guise (son of the leader of the Catholic League under Henry III, Henri de Guise). The army remained basically loyal to the Regency.

By contrast, amongst the 'establishment aristocrats' there was (at the opposite end of the spectrum) the disloyal Condé clan. They merit our attention, not because of the personality (reputedly effete) of their leader, Henry II, Prince of Condé, father of the Great Condé, but because of the older issues represented by the Condé faction or, more simply, the whole Bourbon wing. For more than 60 years, the Valois had successfully repressed the 'factional' engagements of those within the royal family, supported from outside the royal lineage by various noble coteries. If one looks at the period before 1494, from Charles VII's reign to that of Charles VIII, there was the Praguerie (i.e. the future Louis XI in opposition to his father, Charles VII), followed by the League of the Public Weal (i.e. the younger brother, Monsieur Charles, against the elder brother and crowned king, Louis XI). Finally there was the stupid conflict between the uncle

(Louis d'Orléans, the future Louis XII) and his nephew, the ruling King Charles VII. But the evil spell was broken between 1490 and 1560. Four successive Valois kings, Charles VIII, Louis XII, Francis I and Henry II, demonstrated that they were masters in their own house. They nipped in the bud the fratricidal and parricidal conflicts which had, in the past, concerted the contradictory forces and aspirations of various kinds of political groupings around a grandee from the Capetian royal line and close to the king himself. Of course, the Italian wars had played a part in this process by directing the turbulent French nobility towards the Italian peninsula. In this perspective, the revolt of the Constable de Bourbon in 1523 was an event whose significance should have given pause for thought, for it was a kind of 'alarm signal' or advance warning of what was to transpire 40 years later. The constable was from the powerful Bourbon family, who traced their descent back to St Louis. After 1560, they would be the incarnation of political opposition (through Antoine de Navarre and Louis de Condé, both Protestants). After 1594, they would be the incarnation of royal power (in Henry IV). Then, after 1610, they represented both royal power (Louis XIII, through Marie de Médicis as intermediary) and the opposition to it (in the Condé branch of the Bourbons, the close cousins of both Henry IV and Louis XIII). The bizarre amorous adventure of Henry IV for Charlotte de Montmorency, the newly-wed princess of Condé, in 1609 complicated matters. The cuckolded Condé clan threw in their lot with those who were 'against' the king. Henry IV's death made things more difficult still. Henry II de Condé, Charlotte's husband, had been brought up a Catholic. Unlike his father and his grandfather, the leaders of the Huguenots, he could not put himself at the head of the Protestant party. This responsibility would shortly fall to the duke de Rohan, an able strategist and scion of the Breton aristocracy. But some clientage connections remained, albeit erratically, at the disposition of the prince of Condé. They made their appearance from time to time in the decade of the 1610s amidst the more politically engaged Huguenots and those Catholics opposed to the state. However the Condé never succeeded in mustering the grand 'politique' alliance between Calvinists and centrist-Catholics formed under the aegis of the Montmorency which had been the characteristic feature of the French Midi in the decades of the 1570s and '80s. The Catholic counter-reformation was already too influential and such liaisons were seen as unnatural or sacriligious unless they were for purely short-term reasons.

To understand the contentious spirit of the Condé trio (Condé, Conti and Soissons) after 1609–10, one must return to the problems of the royal succession. Condé, the first prince of the royal blood, would accede to the throne if the male successors to Henry IV and Marie de Médicis – Louis XIII or Gaston d'Orléans – were to die. In official ceremonies, the precedence of the princes of the blood was straightway given greater prominence, directly after the immediate members of the royal family. This enhanced precedence for the Capetian princes was in conformity with the new 'blood' mystique which upheld royal ideology to an ever greater degree after 1600 in contrast with a less 'genetically' perceived Renaissance monarchy, more limited in its authority and more 'constitutional' in its scope. What was upsetting, from the point of view of 'their Highnesses', the princes of the blood, was that their power did not live up to the prestige implied in these rituals. In terms of real authority, Condé was, as the Cardinal de Retz would put it, a 'nothing who can only be multiplied into something because he is a prince of the royal blood', with his nominal prestige the only multiplying factor. The prince was acutely aware of this and, with a degree of spite, or perhaps we should accord him a measure of political perspicacity, he took up various general grievances. Some of the causes he espoused were amply justifiable. They included the need to control royal expenditures better than they had been from 1610–11 by Marie de Médicis, the Concini and others. He called for some participation in the nomination of nobles to posts as provincial governors, and in decisions concerning the king's marriage. He wanted to restrict the authority of a chancellor who had become too excessively dominant in government to judicial matters alone and to limit the powers of the over-powerful secretaries of state to the execution of decisions alone. Above all, there was the central demand for the summoning of the Estates General, which would have the effect of placing the monarchy under the yoke of a form (albeit imperfect) of national representation. The ultimate objective was surely to ensure the princes of the blood and the great offices of the crown of France an active, even a dominant, voice in the councils of state. As regards the latter, Condé was to some degree isolated from the power-élite. Marie, her circle of intimate advisers, the *robins* in council and some of the grandees (around Guise) acted as a 'political entity' and kept Condé out of power. Yet the isolation was less complete than one might imagine because the prince was echoing the widely-held aspirations shared by the leading figues amongst the nobility, the office-holders, even the *bourgeois*. The end result was a princely revolt which was not without support from the provinces. The revolt was begun under the direction of Condé and Nevers (Catholic grandees) as well as Bouillon (a Protestant) in eastern France. Vendôme, Henry IV's illegitimate son, led the revolt in Brittany. The rebellion lasted from January to May 1614. For the first time since the end of the wars of religion, the Protestants were restive, and this gave those in power cause for concern. The leaders of the revolt, with Condé at their head, demanded a less pro-Spanish policy, a return (in essence) to the direction of affairs under Henry IV, and the convocation of the Estates General. The fact that the royal armies remained loyal to Marie was absolutely vital in preventing the revolt becoming a civil war. In May–June 1614, Condé's mini-revolt was pacified. This recognition of reality was still more evident in that the Regent accepted, at least superficially, major concessions to Condé on the vital point of the summoning of the Estates General, something which proves, incidentally, that the monarchy was not yet entirely 'absolutist' in the strict sense of term, since it was still susceptible to control (albeit not for very long) by the (more or less) authentic representatives of the king's subjects. By operating like this, Marie struck a double blow since she expected to be able to manipulate the Estates to prolong her own authority after the proclamation of Louis XIII's majority, which would occur in the autumn of 1614. Marie de Médicis and Condé were seeking entirely different goals; the latter would be the one who was disappointed.

The calling of the Estates General proved that, despite the impression of improvisation, the Regent sometimes had nerves of steel. The election of delegates to the Estates was carefully orchestrated by the government. What a difference between 1588 and 1789! The result amongst the Third Estate, where one might have feared that those of an aggressive political standpoint would have been elected, was that those deputed to the national assembly were, in the main, office-holders who were fairly compliant towards the established régime. As it was, the basic popular demands and other views expressed in the traditional *cahiers* drawn up (in principle) by the electors, remained moderate in tone. Of course the peasantry complained about taxation. But one has to bear in mind that taxes, in terms of their monetary volume, were not at the dizzy heights to which they would rise under Richelieu and Mazarin when, from 1630 or, still more, 1636 onwards, the ritual petitions of the *cahiers* would be replaced by open revolts amongst tax-payers against the taxes they were being asked to pay. In 1614, the same peasantry reflected the beginnings of the French counter-reformation when they expressed the desire to have well-trained priests and a diligent and pious church. Their demands were legitimate but they were hardly revolutionary – the Catholic League had been defeated 20 years earlier. Even the proceedings of the Estates, near the Louvre in Paris and at the convent of the Grands-Augustins, worked to the advantage of the Regent and, paradoxically, in support of the latent absolute monarchy. The Third Estate, Gallican and pro-*parlementaire* in its sympathies, aspired to reinforce the independence of the monarchy as against antimonarchical excommunications which might, as in the past, issue forth from Rome. Their desires are readily comprehensible and even profoundly national. But in the context of the period, they could only serve to assist the prerogatives of the sovereign. Towards those nobles who spoke out against the venality of offices to annoy the representatives of the Third Estate, the latter had an effective reply. They evoked the burden and inequity of the pensions which the royal Treasury showered on 'parasitic' aristocrats. Raising the level of the discussion somewhat, Henri de Mesmes, the *lieutenant civil*,[19] acting as the spokesman for the Third Estate, offered a discreet snub to the nobility in his speech of 24 November 1614 when, under the guise of showering them with compliments after an altercation, he declared: 'The three orders are brothers, children of a common mother,

---

[19]   I am paraphrasing the text cited in Roland Mousnier, *La Vénalité des offices sous Henri IV et Louis XIII* (Rouen, Fayard, 1946), pp. 575–614.

France. The clergy is the eldest, the nobility the next and the Third Estate the youngest. The nobility should recognise the Third Estate as a brother and not as something to be despised. There are many individual families where the elder children have snatched the property but where it is the youngsters who have rescued the family name and given it its lustre.'[20]

Each of the orders at the Estates of 1614 tried to ensnare the other but they were held in check by the ties which bound them inextricably to the destinies of a monarchy which had positioned itself above the rest of society. Venality of office for the senior commoners (*roturiers*) – mostly already well on the way to joining the nobility of the robe – constituted the ties which restrained the Third Estate, just as the pensions for the nobility, and particularly for the courtiers, held in check the noble order. In such circumstances, the Estates were dissolved in February–March 1615 without having quarrelled amongst themselves but without having achieved very much. Condé had been paid what was due to him. But could much by way of the eventual enfeeblement of royal power have ever been expected from an assembly whose members dutifully turned up on parade to Mass and presented themselves before the altar six at a time to receive communion? The clericism of the League had contained an anti-royal component to the degree that the monarchy had refused to give in to the demands from the integrists amongst the Catholic clergy. By contrast, the clericism of the Estates in 1614, even to a degree the Gallicans amongst them, worked for Marie. The Estates also supported established authority in the sense that both were now reconciled with Rome or Spain and retained few of the personal Protestant ties of Henry IV. There had been significance to Sully's resignation, even if the religious coexistence between Huguenots and Catholics continued to be a concrete reality in the France of the decade of the 1610s.

The Estates of 1614 resolved nothing. They did, however, reaffirm – by the simple fact that they had been summoned – the continuance (albeit not for long) of a pre-absolutist monarchical system limited both as to its objectives and the means by which to achieve them. The magistrates of the Parlement of Paris took up where the three estates had left off and, encouraged surreptitiously by Condé, forcefully registered their opposition to financial malversation, to foreigners holding places in government (in fact, to the Concini duo), to the abandonment of France's Protestant allies abroad (this particular complaint was also voiced by Condé), to the incompetence or worse of the administration and to the proven corruption of ministers of state.

---

[20] The theme of the (delicate) fraternity of the three functions under the same father or the same mother, was already to be found in currency in the Middle Ages, for example in the *Chanson de gestes des Narbonnais* – see Joël H. Griswart, *Archéologie de l'épopée médiévale, structures tri-fonctionnelles et mythes indo-européens dans le cycle des Narbonnais* (Paris, Payot, 1981). It was taken up again (independently of these sources, of course) by Henri de Mesmes in 1614 and by the seventeenth-century dramatist, Piron, in his play entitled *L'Ecole des pères* (A. Piron, *Oeuvres* (Amsterdam, 1764), vol. i).

The alliance of the Parlement with Condé, cemented for the first time in 1615, was the harbinger of a similar coalition which would be realized (albeit not without problems) a generation later during the Fronde. An unwritten pact united the senior magistrates (who were discontented with ministerial government) with the princes – Condé senior under the young Louis XIII, Condé junior under the young Louis XIV. In both cases, they shared similar views to those of the senior magistrature, although their motives were very different in each case. The complete eclipse of the Estates General as a force for national representation from 1615 until 1788 is, nevertheless, a historical fact of considerable significance. It provided the definitive basis for the absolute monarchy and left the remnants of its representative role to the Parlement. Was this sovereign court a suitable vehicle for expressing the wishes of the king-dom's subjects? We should note, by way of reply, that it had no elective component, and that it tended to arrogate to itself the role of tribune of the people. For want of a better solution, the Parlement would retain the attributes of a people's tribune – or perhaps a senate – until the first tremors of the French Revolution. In the meantime, the Parlement's magistrates would have to come to terms with a period of enforced quasi-silence on their part during the particularly authoritarian rule of Louis XIV. The Parlement aspired to embody in every respect the legiti-macy of the rule of law and did not let slip any occasion to remind others of the fact.

The years 1616–17 witnessed the final and flamboyant rise of the Concini and then their rapid eclipse. Rightly or wrongly, the Regent saw in them the best guarantee of her authority. In opposition to her, during new moves of confrontation (the latent, princely, civil wars of this period were endemic) Condé was finally arrested in September 1616. The old ministers of Henry IV (Jeannin and those from the Brulart-Sillery-Puisieux family grouping) were removed from power despite their long years of docile service towards the Regent. She dismissed them in order to have them replaced with her own team. Gradually a ministry of *créatures* de-voted to Marie and Concini was put in place in 1616 – Barbin, Mangot and . . . Richelieu. But this would not be for long. The government would be replaced in April 1617 when Concini was put to death on the orders of Louis XIII.

★   ★   ★   ★   ★

Something, finally, should be said of the king, Louis XIII, who (whilst still an adolescent) seized power or, at least, took it away from Concini in the spring of 1617. The birth of Louis in September 1601 had been a moment of great joy for his father, Henry IV. Immediately 'the tears ran down his face as large as *petits pois*.' These tears are one piece of evidence (amongst many) to dispel the historiographical myth, cherished by Philippe Ariès, of the indifference of parents towards their new-born children.[21] This emotional commitment and love was reciprocated; Louis adored Henry, and this affection was to have consequences in the later developments of the reign. For the fact that the child had known and loved a father who was formerly a Huguenot, coupled with the fact that he was closely cared for by a physician, the famous Héroard, who remained a Protestant for many years, were amongst the 'preliminary' influences which would determine in due course what would be the religious standpoint of Henry IV's successor. He would be inevitably hostile to the Protestant party as a military force but not at all ill-disposed to the maintenance of the French Protestant reformed churches. A gentleman, and a monarch's son, Louis was strongly aware, from the age of seven, of the exalted position which he enjoyed. 'My rank prevails in all places' he replied to his illegitimate brother, 'Féfé Vendôme', who wanted him to join in a court ballet at Fontainebleau.[22] But Louis XIII would never be a willing courtier. The spectacle of being surrounded by other courtiers, his like, or (rather) his inferiors, bored him. He wanted, nevertheless, to be seen to be playing his part, part of the hierarchy and (by definition) at the summit of that hierarchy. A month after Henry IV's assassination, the child appeared already very well aware of the duties of a king, as these were traditionally perceived. 'To give the people something to celebrate, to fear God, to do justice, such is the manifold function of His Majesty' was the substance of what he told his tutor on 25 June 1610. More striking were the phrases he used at the closing stage of the Estates General in February 1615: '*Messieurs*, I will make plain the desire which I have to serve God, bring comfort to my people, protect and render justice to each and every one in such fashion as will content you all.' These two texts come from the mouth (with, or without, some prompting from others) of a 10-year-old boy (in 1615, a 15-year-old). It is not difficult to read into them the various functions of archetypal, pre-Colbertian monarchy. Firstly, came religion and justice. Secondly there was protection (especially military protection) of subjects. Thirdly there was the concern for the welfare and contentment of the people – i.e. their prosperity.

Louis was profoundly religious. He was brought up to an austere pattern of virtue, in which the security and well-being of the people mattered, as did justice (if not clemency, for the king's sense of justice was tinged with a touch of spite). He attended Mass every day and knew the key parts of the litany, the Pater Noster and the Credo, from an early age. He was not an ultramontane Catholic; his religious consciousness was not drawn from south of the Alps or the Pyrenees. Nevertheless, he demonstrated a certain hostility towards the extreme Gallicanism of various individuals in his

---

[21] Against this myth, see *Poésie lyrique latine du Moyen Age*, ed. Pascale Bourgain (Paris, collection 'Bibliothèque médiévale', 1989), p. 122.
[22] Chevallier, *Louis XIII*.

Plate 2   The majority of Louis XIII   The majority of Louis XIII was declared in early October 1614. In this allegorical portrayal by Rubens, painted between 1622 and 1625, Marie de Médicis hands over the helm of the ship of state, energetically rowed by the four Virtues ('Strength', 'Valour', 'Justice' and 'Religion'), to her son Louis. Standing by the mast is the figure of France (and not Pallas Athene as sometimes asserted).
Paris, Musée du Louvre

entourage. He regarded them as Huguenot in tendency, even though not members of the party.

Was it not this kind of piety, deep in his heart and his upbringing, which prevented Louis from pursuing the forced conversion of the Huguenots? He well understood that it would lead to all manner of sacrilege among Protestants forced to partake in the Mass when they were viscerally sceptical towards the Real Presence in the Eucharist. In comparison, Louis XIV was both more pious and more ideologically inclined than his predecessor. Operating in a very different political climate, he shared none of these scruples. He would force the Huguenots to abjure by the use of the *dragonnades*.[23] By this means, the Sun-King thought it appropriate to make his Protestant subjects bear the brunt of his gestures of penitence for the sins of his youth and mature years. It was a problem which never bothered Louis XIII, whose attitude towards women was always irreproachably Catholic. His religious consciousness was a way of life, a moral obligation. Outside marriage, Louis XIII was chaste, in conformity with the injunctions of the Catholic church.[24] Like his *dévot* subjects, he took these injunctions literally. We should put to one side the false myth – often cited, even now – that the kings of France had to display a super-virility, surrounded by a full complement of mistresses, in order to win the respect of their subjects.

Respectful towards the moral code and the Ten Commandments, Louis XIII also nurtured a strong prejudice against women. His childhood was marked by a precocious liberality of talk and gesture which was then followed by the stricter sexual morality urged on the king from the age of six or seven by *père* Coton, his Jesuit confessor. Liaisons outside marriage, which he had witnessed all too often in the seraglio of his father's court, were abhorrent to him. Even as a child he referred to his father's mistresses (despite his affection for his father) as whores. His father's illegitimate offspring he despised, above all his illegitimate half-brothers whom he once said mattered to him 'less than a turd (*sic*)' and this contrasted with his attitude towards his legitimate sister Elisabeth, for whom he showed nothing but genuine affection. To complete the picture, we should add the king's disillusionment at his marriage with the seductive Anne of Austria, a marriage whose main, and tardy, achievement was the birth of the Sun-King and his brother Philippe. Should we explain this in terms of Louis XIII's homosexual tendencies, and (more questionably still), homosexual acts which were referred to by the gossip writer of the period,

---

[23] See below, chapter 6.
[24] See the remark by the nuncio Corsini, reported on 27 October 1623: 'Amidst a court given over to pleasure and subject to so much change, I hold the king's virtue uniquely immutable. . . . In the flower of youth, having become absolute King in France, he has given no occasion to expect in him any of those vices or licentiousness which are ordinarily inseparable from those who enjoy great power. Neither a love of gambling nor affairs with women, not even the excesses of anger distract him from the path of innocence' (Chevallier, *Louis XIII*, pp. 180–1).

Tallemant des Réaux? His evidence is not to be trusted but it is not inconceivable. At all events, it would only have strengthened a frigidity towards the opposite sex which had its roots both in his religious background and personality.

These, and other matters, to one side, Louis XIII was a mature individual, typical in his attitudes of a certain kind of French noble of the period. He had put up with the harsh, abrasive affections of his father. He had endured, for the good of his soul, the subtle and engaging education in the style of Montaigne offered by the physician Héroard, his schoolmaster and companion throughout his childhood years. A soldier to the core, Louis wanted early on to be both commanding officer and combatant, able both to execute a military manoeuvre as well as order one to be carried out. He loved the open air and was a noted huntsman of blackbirds and butterflies, wolves and young stags. At the age of nine, he had already killed eight deer. He benefited from the physical education of his youth, showed signs of nervous depression, and did not take care to wash overmuch. Yet he enjoyed a robust constitution although his health was poor from about the age of 11. He ate chicken and wine, rode well with the pack of hounds which he himself had trained and, after a tiring day, generally slept soundly and for a good long time.

The king also trained falcons, merlins and vultures for hunting at its toughest and most exquisitely demanding. All the favourites of Louis XIII came from amongst his hunting companions – Luynes, Baradas, Toiras, Saint-Simon (the father of the diarist) and Cinq-Mars. The king had a lively interest in flora and fauna. He did not merely hunt animals but also collected them, dead and alive, from rabbits to monkeys, from chameleons to chamois. Louis was good with his hands. He played *jeu de paume* (an early form of tennis) and *palemail*. He was a qualified craftsman, a polymath. He made armour, he was a metallurgist, a printer, a wheelwright, a stable-hand, a farrier, a coachman, a chef and a pastrycook. Henry IV, both in his childhood and later, was close to the peasant world. Louis XIII's contacts, in a society which was becoming more urbanized, were markedly more technological, with those from the artisan and working classes. In this way, although he was much respected by his soldiers, he sustained the 'popular front' of the French monarchy which one ancien régime author identified as one of its distinctive traits.[25]

Yet less 'vulgar' activities also attracted the king's attentions. Louis XIII was an artist, a musician, a lute player, a violinist and a drummer. He organized ballets, he drew and painted. Of the four preoccupations which were expected to be found in a monarch – his state, warfare, hunting and, lastly, women – Louis XIII neglected the last, concentrated on the second and third and gave the first a reasonable share of his attentions.[26]

---

[25]   F. Funck-Brentano, *L'Ancienne France et le roi* (Paris, 1912).
[26]   According to Chevallier, *Louis XIII*. See also, for all the preceding details, M. Foisil, *Journal de Jean Héroard* (Paris, Fayard, 1989).

Intellectual matters were not his strong point. He had a speech impediment, he gave his tutors little encouragement and he showed little talent as a Latinist. Yet, in the context of a French culture which was pre-Cartesian and which had not yet cultivated the notion of pure thought, this type of individual, substantial and sensible, was the embodiment of the average noble. He was well in tune with the times, baroque or, at least, pre-classical.

One of the notable aptitudes of Louis XIII, a jealous and sulky child with temper tantrums, was his capacity for keeping a secret, his impassive dissimulation and sang-froid. The existence of these aptitudes was demonstrated when he removed Concini from power in April 1617. In this incident was reflected, albeit in a more brutal fashion, the later episode of the seizure of power by Louis XIV in 1661, when he organized the arrest of Fouquet. Both were part of the swift, classic process by which a new and young king imposed his will and installed his own team in government. As a result, the preceding team was eliminated even if it was that of one's own mother, the Regent Marie.

Concini, the *maréchal* d'Ancre as he had become, the one in whom the queen mother had placed all her confidence, was an adversary not to be underestimated by the young king. As we have seen, he could reflect feelings of French identity (or, rather, anti-Spanish sentiments). He was obsessed with power – although, in this respect, he was not alone – but he had the misfortune to be an Italian. He wanted this power for himself and for the queen mother, his patron. He thus attempted successively to eliminate all those who attempted to stand in his way – Condé, first (arrested in September 1616), then the former ministers of Henry IV (dismissed from Marie's service), and finally Guise. The method was that of paring away the opposition, like slicing a salami sausage. Concini relied on the army, or a branch of it, and on some of his fellow marshals, including Brissac and Lesdiguières. But in a 'just' rectification, Louis had the *maréchal* d'Ancre assassinated in the course of an ambush in April 1617. More central to the plot than Luynes, the king's confidants and favourites were his companion conspirators from the *robe* – Déagent and Tronçon – as well as the baron de Vitry, a veteran soldier and willing hand. Marie found herself powerless after the coup. In theory, Louis XIII was captain of his own ship. In a macabre pogrom, on the evening of 24 April, the body of Concini would be torn apart by a riotous mob. The mutilation elevated Concini to the classic role of being the diabolic scapegoat at the end of the Regency. The bodies of Coligny and Ravaillac before him had been similarly profaned, in different circumstances but under the impulse of an analogous collective exasperation.

Louis XIII was $15\frac{1}{2}$ years old. Beginning with his mother, he undertook a series of family estrangements which would alienate him from his wife, his brother, his illegitimate half-brothers and his cousins. He had to look for support and collaborators outside his own family. Already active and asserting himself in the corridors of power was the controversial figure of Armand-Jean du Plessis who would become, in 1624, Cardinal de Richelieu.

PART I

Absolutism in its True Grandeur

2

Reason of State and its Irrationalities

Armand-Jean du Plessis de Richelieu was born in 1585 of a line of Poitevin nobility which had not always kept to the straight and narrow. His father, one of Henry III's favourites, had occupied the post of *grand prévôt* (the head of the royal court's police and justice) at the last Valois court. Richelieu's ancestor died in his 80s in 1590 and had remained, throughout his life, a loyal royalist, hostile to the League, to Spain and, to the extent that it represented ultramontane Catholicism, to Rome. In this respect, the career of the future cardinal, although more spectacular, was mapped out in that of his father – determined, unstinting (which created its own problems), and featuring high ambition and Gallican patriotism. From the age of 20, Richelieu prepared himself for his ultimate roles. He would prove to be a good Catholic but a mediocre papalist. His mother, born a La Porte, was descended from a bourgeois family of Parisian advocates. The future prelate was a brilliant student during his secondary education at the *collège* de Navarre and he then had the benefit of an equestrian and military training as befitted a young nobleman. The death of his elder brother in 1602 and the withdrawal of another brother from the career, pushed Richelieu (who had not anticipated it) towards an ecclesiastical career. He had to reclaim the bishopric of Luçon, attributed (in principle) to members of his family from 1584. Enthroned in 1606 in a diocese which was partly Huguenot, Richelieu was there able to confirm by personal experience what he already knew of the Poitevin mentality. It would not do to re-Catholicize the Protestants by force. So he tended to the spiritual needs of his flock but he rejected all forms of extremism, whether from ultra-*dévots* or, later, from Jansenist enthusiasts. A long-meditated ambition for an impressive career, coupled with a firm desire to overcome the lack of means and financial inadequacy which had hung over his family since his father's death, led him from an early date to be a client and protégé of Marie de Médicis. He then came to prominence as one of the leaders of the French church at the Estates of 1614 and became a minister of Marie and Concini in 1617. Louis XIII disgraced him and, compelled to change tack, Richelieu eventually threw off the protection of Médicis

Plate 3 Portrait of Cardinal Richelieu The famous full-length portrait of Cardinal Richelieu by his protégé, the Flemish painter Philippe de Champaigne, was painted in 1634. It depicts the cardinal in his study overlooking the Palais Royal (as it would later be known). In the background lies Montmartre with the Benedictine convent and the Church of the Martyrs. The cardinal's magnificent scarlet *cappa magna* is covered with a simarra, an exquisite chamber robe; and although the cardinal is wearing his cardinal's hat (a red biretta), it is the insignia of the Order of the Holy Spirit which occupies a centrality in the painting. Richelieu himself has the air of a man of state and royal servant. Portraits from the later years of his ministry depict him in an obviously more majestic fashion.
Paris, Ministère des Affaires étrangères

patronage and was propelled once more towards the *Conseil d'en haut*, becoming first minister in 1624. His career was a brilliant ascension towards the top; it was the more remarkable for the number of reverses he suffered on the way, although these never turned out to be critical.

At the heart of any great career such as this there lies inevitably a personal genius, the 'most outstanding of the century' as one of his adherents put it in 1627. Its characteristics drew on the initial tensions between the (restricted) means at his disposal and the scale of his dreams and desires. His lineage was honourable but the family had fallen on hard times. The cardinal sought to revenge the latter. He dreamt of re-establishing himself close to the heart of affairs amongst the king's servants. This was where his father had made his reputation; but the cardinal had hardly the health or the fortune to sustain such ambitions. Hence the cardinal's dominant preoccupation with the acquisition of money; hence, too, his *parvenu*'s taste for conspicuous expenditure, demonstrated by his ducal stables staffed by 180 servants and with 140 horses and mules (as against 166 and 32 respectively for his counterpart in Spain, Olivares).[1] Richelieu, the gentleman of modest beginnings, set his sights on the Louvre and surrounded himself with a 'mafia' of Poitevin compatriots, relatives and neighbours (the Bouthillier, *père* Joseph, Théophraste Renaudot, Razilly, La Porte). From the end of the reign of Henry IV he attempted to propel himself to the court and made no secret of his desire one day to be at the heart of affairs. To achieve this objective, he brought an indomitable will, a capacity for long-term decision-making, resilience coupled with a sense of responsibility, and a sense of timing and destiny. Once a decision was taken, and not without mature reflection, this was someone who was a stickler for implementing it in every way. He kept his grip on everything, displaying an almost sadistic attention to detail in matters of repression. He was aware of the limited forces which France could command, however powerful it might seem, and was thus prepared, when it seemed necessary, to adjust his aims to suit what was possible, redefining in the process his tactical (sometimes, even, his strategic) objectives.[2]

Confronted by the emotive issues which threatened to engulf France in disorder and by the emotions within himself in particular (his upbringing was certainly more tempestuous than it has been painted and he never entirely detached himself from female company), Richelieu learnt to impose a strict self-control upon his own temperament. He did not raise his voice; he only allowed himself to shed tears when he intended to do so. Reason became his touchstone – i.e. his native wit coupled with his prudence which allowed him to adjust to circumstances. His reason, for example, dictated that the sale of royal offices should be stopped; his prudence told him he should leave well alone. His sense of self-discipline

[1] J.H. Elliott, *Richelieu and Olivares* (Cambridge, Cambridge University Press, 1984), p. 19.
[2] William Church, *Richelieu and Reason of State* (Princeton, NJ, Princeton University Press, 1972), p. 295.

and of masculine virtue drew on the neo-stoic and Christian traditions to be found in the works of Tacitus, Charron and Justus Lipsius. He adopted a luxurious lifestyle as preeminent minister for the purposes of display and ostentation. But in his personal life he remained austere. He readily displayed a cruel streak to a degree matched in French history only by Louis XI and Robespierre (who was infinitely worse). But this judgement only holds for the means which he adopted to pursue his objectives. Although the means were hardly edifying in many instances, the ends he pursued were what one might regard as laudable, namely the establishment of divine and human order. It just so happened that their attainment happened to be to Richelieu's advantage. Thus he was more of a Tiberius than a Nero. He worked for the prosperity of the king, inseparable from the cardinal's own greatness and a great burden for the kingdom to bear. Yet this prosperity was also inseparable from the safety of the state and the country at large. The cardinal was 'for King and Country' (as they would say in eighteenth-century England) but the first part of the phrase counted for much more with him than the second. He was a good Catholic, but unlike his brother (who became a Carthusian monk), he was no contemplative. He liked action, wanted to make things happen, and to leave his mark on events. He made his influence felt as much by the force of persuasion as the persuasion of force, by the strength of his convictions – such as when (but it was a vain hope) he sought to bring the Huguenots within the body of a reunified church, or when he harangued the Estates General of 1614. Richelieu had many facets – he was a statesmen, a prelate, a writer, a soldier. He was at one and the same time a bibliophile, a builder and an art-collector. Ultimately he risked trying the patience of the most even-tempered. Rather than seeing him launching out on so many (especially military) fronts, they would have preferred to see him concentrate more, and by choice, on the more pacific paths of stability and ensuring the well-being of his subjects.

Richelieu's religious ideas were of a piece with his attitudes towards the Huguenots. True to his Poitevin background, where the two religions lived in coexistence, he knew that such coexistence was an inevitability. They could only be converted by the force of persuasion. They should be assuaged, not affronted. In his penitential and confessional policy, the bishop of Luçon did not require a perfect contrition and remorse for sin along with a firm declaration that the sinner had repented and would sin no more. He differed from his rigorist or *dévot* colleagues by requiring attrition only – i.e. the sense of repentance based on the sinner's fear of eternal damnation, a fear which was the starting-point for a kind of repentance and which was accepted by lenient confessors like Richelieu. The distinction was well understood by those who had to undertake confession and it marked out the great distinction between Richelieu and Bérulle. Richelieu was a pastoral prelate and not a mystic. His faith was not in doubt, but its well-springs lay in a reasonable religion; he did not surrender himself to the seductive logic of the heart. Richelieu was antagonistic, of course, to the political aims of the Protestants, despite his tolerance of their rights to exercise their religion. He was allergic to the incredulity of the *libertins* yet he found the *dévots* no more attractive. He rejected the bigotry of 'the extreme right' as well as the atheism of 'the extreme left'. He was a theologian of the just mean, reconciling the acts of grace by God with the liberty of conscience of individual human beings. In this respect he set himself apart from extreme Jansenism, which took as its starting point a divine omnipotence which excluded the possibility of mankind's free will, believing instead in the 'bondage of the will'.[3]

As the holder of a doctorate from the Sorbonne, Richelieu took his lineage from that ancient faculty, founded by the king (St Louis) in 1257 and later confirmed by the pope (Alexander IV) in 1259. Drawing on the traditions of the Sorbonne and his own convictions, Richelieu retained an essential duality in his thought: God and the kingdom, the papacy and the crown; neither should be underestimated, short-changed or asphyxiated by the other. The Vatican had its role to play but it should not interfere with the temporal prerogatives or religious responsibilities of the monarchy.

The cardinal's political thought was novel in its applications but entirely traditional in its starting-points. Richelieu was an absolutist. He did not summon the Estates General (they would be 'absent' for 175 years thereafter); nor, after 1627, did he consult an assembly of notables. He constrained or suppressed some of the provincial estates such as those of Provence (1639) and Dauphiné (1637), leaving to Mazarin the task of putting an end to those in Normandy in 1655.[4] Yet he persisted in thinking of France as made up of three orders (nobility, clergy and Third Estate) and there thus followed three functional components or essential elements for political activity. Whatever demonstrated the kingdom of God and the sovereignty of the state, as indivisible as a point in Euclidean geometry, should be reinforced. Similarly whatever related to human reason and the reputation of the prince, to the capacity and fidelity of a minister of state, to the good conduct of justice, and to the necessary superiority of the church and authority had to be sustained in comparison with the Huguenots, whose activities would be no more than tolerated.

Secondly, the cardinal turned his attentions towards the military, the grandees and the lesser nobility (with their courage and masculine sense of virtue) who had to be disciplined and rendered loyal rather than destroyed – although some heads would have to roll and some castles would have to be brought down to size. He reflected on the exalted sense of functional importance enjoyed by the military and which he had further inflated (Richelieu would deploy an army of 150,000 men in wartime). Finally, Richelieu allowed his attentions to turn to the common people, all those

[3]   Pierre Goubert, *Mazarin* (Paris, Fayard, 1990), pp. 368–90.
[4]   All that follows is taken from the *Testament politique*, the best edition of which is that by Louis André (Paris, Laffont, 1947).

who were not noble, clergy or sovereign. They should be governed according to what was in the public interest and what would maintain harmony. They should be required to obey for their own good. They should be able to support themselves and enjoy that security of tenure which would enable them to do so. At the same time, they would be able to pay their taxes and sustain the royal treasury (in order to support the army) whilst ensuring that the minister himself was reimbursed with an 'honest return' (20 millions . . .) in proportion to his just deserts. By his noble acts and by propaganda of a high order the king would win the hearts of his people, both in Paris and in the provinces, in the towns and the countryside as well.

From this elevated perspective, the cardinal took his standpoint from a consideration of the kingdom of God, the fount of wisdom and nature. The Catholic church was close to his heart. He resisted the anti-Gallican efforts of the papacy; yet he believed that it was Italy, the centre of the world, and particularly the Holy See, which made and unmade princely reputations. Contrary to the Parlement of Paris, which wanted to subject ecclesiastical authority to lay control, Richelieu set great store by the independence and dignity of the French church, even (and especially at these moments) when he wanted to harness it to his grand designs. When he evoked the clerical estate, he did so in terms of a clerical ideology and a similarly triumphalist tone to that used by the abbé Sieyès towards the Third Estate in 1789. 'When the church finds itself in the dilapidated condition in which it is at present, what is to be done to restore it to the condition in which it ought to be?' He was a Thomist in the sense that he correlated reason, that light of nature with which he found himself abundantly endowed, with justice and merit. This explains his attitude towards the favourites. Concini, Luynes, even Olivares, were perceived by him as favourites, inferior beings to his own exalted person, for whom reason was able to be the master of his emotions, having the responsibilities of neither a wife nor children (even though there were nephews and nieces to look after).

To Richelieu, what was reasonable and just should be given some backbone; reason had to be reinforced by power, if possible in negotiations, but if necessary by military confrontation. It did not need to be unnecessarily ferocious, but there was no need to be squeamish about the use of force. His view of princely virtue demonstrated the governing first principles of the exercise of power. A prince must be faithful to his allies; other sovereign princes should be convinced that they can count on him; and this conviction was worth more to him than a large army in the field. Reason, to Richelieu, was coterminous with prudence, the art of the possible, that sense of timing which Richelieu's *Testament politique* would ascribe to Louis XIII. All these rational components were, however, viewed within a perspective which was fundamentally pessimistic about human nature. Here was, underneath his Thomism, a bedrock of Augustinianism in his thinking. Although reason was to be found operating everywhere, so too was the force of original sin; and there were more people that were wicked or foolish than were wise, and the evil would outnumber the good. Hence his refusal to contemplate almost any idea of national representation. For the majority of mankind cannot recognize what is best for it, and it was wisest not to reveal the mysteries of state to all and sundry lest it let the genie of revolt escape from the bottle which had been kept carefully sealed up until then.

Richelieu's legitimacy in such conditions as these drew its strengths from the future.[5] He was a minister who anticipated a post-war world, only engaging in armed conflict (with rational detachment) in order that it might eventually be concluded to the benefit of the people at large whose advice could not at that moment be sought on the matter since they were incapable of formulating their views in an intelligent fashion. The system of carrot and stick, which played its part in the making of Richelieu's private fortune, was directed *a priori* towards the elaboration of a glorious national identity of the future, in the achievement of which the discomforts of the past and the present were distasteful necessities. The future belonged with God. It would be the inspiration for a prince; and also the 'voice' of sane opinions in council, and especially to the ministers and the councillors of state – i.e. to Richelieu himself, whom the king had chosen to conduct his affairs of state since (unlike Louis XIV) he chose not to assume that burden himself.

The state, however, was not to be confused with the king, with the blood royal, with the sovereign majesty of the king, still less with the minister of state, even if it was inseparably connected with all of them. The state was a larger entity than a monarch. In certain respects, it was to be identified with the three estates, or with the whole of corporative society (which the absolute monarchy had a tendency to fragment). The state established a link between the royalty of Louis XIII and the realization of this corporative society which was nothing other than a national identity voiced through a common language whose moment of glory had arrived. Reason and the state were henceforth to be consubstantially united. Was there not an (albeit rather crude and somewhat tenuous) 'reason of state'?

If there was, it should not be termed 'Machiavellian'. Both Protestants and Catholics had reserved their strongest criticism for Machiavelli in the sixteenth and seventeenth centuries on account of his unsavoury reputation as a cynic. A cardinal, even one called Richelieu, would have found it hard to make the Florentine Machiavelli's views palatable, even if some of the cardinal's more extreme or exotic supporters made occasional and prudent use of the maxims to be found expressed in 'The Prince'.

Those at the centre of affairs under Louis XIII tended, however, to go beyond the royal state formulated by the Valois (with its customary, regulated and moderate foundations). They moved in the direction of an

---

[5] *Testament politique* (1689 edition), pp. 257 and 269. Cf. the edition of Louis André, pp. 334 and 345.

administrative apparatus which was at once more expansive, more absolute, and apparently less scrupulous. In the process, however, they stressed
that the objectives which would be realized through this absolutism had to
be justifiable on Christian grounds. Even if the means adopted in each case
did not always stand up to scrutiny, there was an attempt to square the
circle as between religion and secular authority – the latter in faithful
conformity with the former but never in subjection to it. The excessive
rigidities of Augustinian theology were thus left to one side. It was altogether too concerned with making sure that things had been properly
carried out. It would ensure that all those in power had clean hands, but
also that they had no power either. The intellectual circle around Richelieu
thus had every encouragement to look instead towards the 'Tacitean' ideas
which had been advanced by the humanists in the years from 1550 to
1625. According to their formulations, politics should not be shrouded in
mystery and it should not have to bend the knee before the authoritarian
injunctions of the clergy, whose legitimacy remained, but was restricted to,
the kingdom of moral and spiritual ends.

Amongst the Renaissance humanists who furnished the arguments
exploited by the advocates of Reason of State under Richelieu there
were the Italian intellectuals of the first generation of the counter-
reformation – Botero, Ammirato and Frachetta.[6] There were also the
leading lights of late sixteenth-century French thought – Montaigne
and Du Vair. The theoretical ideals of the Bourbon monarchy can
be summarized under three headings – liberty, property and public
utility. The first implied the right of subjects not to be slaves, the
second a respect for landed wealth and the third a serviceable state
working for the common good (which Richelieu would define as the
public interest). Yet the pathways towards the public good were not always
to be found laid out in the fashion of a neat, formal French garden. There
were back alleys and winding paths barely cut out through the undergrowth. They had, nevertheless, to be followed for the common, Christian,
good.

It is clear that the French monarchy was ready for a step forwards
towards a more modern state. The first sign came when, in the period of
Henry IV and the young Louis XIII, Béarn (which was the last feudal and
Protestant principality) was removed from the map as an independent
state and coalesced with the French state. Having passed through these
straits, 'plus ultra' – much more lay in store. The twin poles of Richelieu's
thought provided every justification along the way. For this was the man
who, on his death bed, would state objectively that he had followed no

---

[6]   Giovanni Botero was the author of *Della Ragione di Stato* (*Of Reason of State*), published
in Venice in 1589. Scipione Ammirato produced an edition of *Discorsi supra Cornelio Tacito*
(*Discourses upon Cornelius Tacitus*), published in Florence in 1594. Girolamo Frachetta was
more moderate in his views, expounded in his *Discorso della Ragione di Stato* (*Discourse on
Reason of State*) which appeared in Venice in 1592.

other aim than the good of religion and of the state.[7] These two inseparable objectives – even if sometimes in contradiction with one another – were the pursuit of divine grace and human liberty. These twin goals, at once religious and strongly secular, befitted a prelate with a strong secular streak in him. He justified them with reference to the past – thanks to his deep sense of history. He projected them on to the future in a search for his own glory as well as that of his sovereign and the dynasty which he represented.

It was in the conflict with the Habsburgs that the issues were placed in the clearest focus and where the rhetoric of 'Reason of State' (*Ragione di Stato*) had to be called upon to defeat the counter-propositions of the *dévots*.[8] It did not prove too difficult to mount strong arguments against them. In the Indies, they pointed out, Spanish hypocrisy had justified the most bloody enterprises under the pretext of religion. At the same time, it was impossible to prevent the more particular argument being advanced that, since Europe had evidently lost all sense of a shared religious unity, this was a reality to which one had to adapt. After all, it was Francis I who had not shocked the contemporary theologians of his day too much by forging alliances with the Turks and the German Lutheran princes. The austere Capuchin, *père* Joseph, was hardly any different when, from around 1635 onwards, he advocated a realistic French diplomacy not based on confessional lines.[9] He could hardly be accused of being a Machiavellian. We should add, however, that the *de facto* alliance which Richelieu entered into with the Protestants of Sweden and Germany guaranteed a certain latitude to the French Protestants and underwrote the continuation of a measure of openness which contemporaries found more disturbing than we can readily imagine.

There was no shortage of advocates cultivated and rewarded by the

---

[7]   See the description of Richelieu's death in Henri Griffet, *Histoire du règne de Louis XIII*, 3 vols (Paris, 1758), iii, 576; cited in L. Lalanne, 'Un récit inédit de la mort de Louis XIII' in *Revue historique*, 55 (1894), 302–8 (cited p. 305).

[8]   Church, *Richelieu and Reason of State*. The *dévots*, whose pattern of daily life was fixed by St François de Sales in his *Introduction à la vie dévote* (1609), sought to infuse every episode of their daily life with religious significance and God's love. They became a political force under the influence of Bérulle and Marillac and were pro-Spanish (in accordance with their Catholic commitment) until they were forced from influence by Richelieu (and Louis XIII) at the time of the celebrated Day of Dupes of November 1630. Their influence amongst the élites of France was, nevertheless, to remain considerable.

[9]   *Père* Joseph Le Clerc du Tremblay, known as *père* Joseph or *l'éminence grise* (1577–1638), was an elderly Capuchin (and *a priori*, therefore, of no great tolerance) who became involved in Catholic projects for a holy war against the Turks. Was it the case that, in these circumstances, he could envisage it as an ecumenical project, carried forward in accord with a degree of Protestant assistance? At all events, he was, from 1611 onwards, a friend and then a devoted agent of Richelieu. He became the enthusiastic executor of the cardinal's anti-Habsburg strategy and showed no hesitation in advocating, and then carrying out, the policy of allying with the Protestant (and thus 'heretical') states of Europe such as Sweden.

cardinal to defend his point of view, which was one with plenty of good sense to commend it when looked at from one perspective. Both the most eminent and those from less exalted backgrounds were nurtured, or even nursed to the task. This was not the moment for a great genius, a Bodin or a Bossuet, able to take the initiative on every issue of state, every political question of the day. It was rather more the case of several hack writers willing to take up the cudgels by 1630 on behalf of an issue which was apparently patriotic and not overtly anti-religious. Once Richelieu's position in authority was cemented, he was able to call upon the services of a Béthune (the theoretician of the treatise on *The Counsellor of State*) or of a Noailles, for whom Louis XIII, albeit the heretics' accomplice, was a new Moses. Also ready to serve was Le Bret, offering a kind of condensed (and more rigid) version of Bodin's views upon sovereignty, as well as Guez de Balzac, a willing chameleon for the cardinal. The Parlement and the Sorbonne, true to their Catholic but Gallican traditions, provided the first minister with groups of allies who were ready to cross swords with the papal nuncio or with Spanish Jesuits.

After 1639, it was the turn of four academicians to enter the fray: Silhon, La Mothe Le Vayer, Priézac and Balzac. There were also some mavericks working away at the margins: Dupleix, for example, compared the ministerial panoply to a form of presidency, directly placed under the orders of God. Machon (who changed tack after Richelieu's death) advanced a scarcely disguised Machiavellianism, albeit curiously reworked and Christianized, on behalf of his patron. It is easy to understand why, when confronted with Richelieu's more compromised allies, some of the old guard who remained hostile to His Eminence, chose to rechristen him 'Rochelieu', the cardinal of La Rochelle, the Huguenot's fellow-traveller.

They made too much of their criticism for, in reality, the principle of Reason of State drew on a whole armoury of mutually sustaining ideas and concepts. At its heart lay the image of the 'state Catholic' or the 'Catholic statesman'. Such a phrase would have otherworldly overtones which would be manifest these days. In those days, however, it linked certain Christian fundamentals, which no one had any doubts about, to the selfish purposes of a voracious government. Divine right, articulated in a monarchy which was necessarily secular, and during a period when its structures were in the process of elaboration, posed intractable problems for the harmonization of immoral means to ethical ends – or, rather, for the definition of a particular morality for the exercise of power, different from the morality of everyone else. Royal justice 'never died'; instead, in the age of Richelieu and Louis XIII its dimensions substantially altered and enlarged. His Majesty encroached more and more on the powers of the Parlement, itself reinforced by the rising values of royal offices. From a conflict along these lines would emerge the Fronde, 15 years later. This encroachment did not require much of the king since he possessed military force against which the magistrates, in the last analysis, had little means of resistance. How many regiments did the Parlement possess? Louis 'the Just' or Louis 'the just Arquebusier'? His critics held that, at the siege of the Huguenot stronghold of Montauban in 1621, the just despatch of rebels to prison had become rather too closely intertwined with the just process of shoot to kill.

Each individual Christian exercises the virtue of clemency towards others because, by virtue of his Christian charity, the way to Paradise beckons. The state, however, has no need to be so restrained. A political collectivity, it has no immortal soul to save. It has nothing to lose by exercising all the severity which it judges to be necessary when dealing with rebels, delinquents or the ideologically subversive. Such, at least, was the official line of the cardinal, manifest in the examples made of the executions of Chalais and Cinq-Mars.[10] Loyalty to the sovereign king was coterminous with loyalty to the state; a Montmorency would lose his head for having cultivated feudal loyalty (to Gaston d'Orléans rather than loyalty to Louis). Those who professed to be shocked or who were sceptical about such events could only stand by and watch, thus indicating how little they had understood about the scale of the affairs being wagered. But in the sycophantic and apologetic literature, there were examples aplenty, drawing especially on the Bible, which exalted Louis XIII to become a God and Richelieu to become one of the Prophets. It reminds one, albeit in different contexts, of the canonical status of the Emperor and the Shogun amongst the Japanese or, closer to home, of the Pope and the cardinal-nephew, the omnipotent adjunct of His Holiness.[11]

Before enjoying the anticipated benefits there were some real hardships to endure in the meantime – a heavy burden of taxation, some controversial deals with heresy, including even the Turks. Straightway, the propagandists run the gamut of the relevant metaphors. Mercury is a poison; but, in small doses, it cures syphilis. The sun burns; yet its rays are the source of life. It hardly mattered whether it was the Sun-King Louis or the mercurial Richelieu who was tackling the Habsburg cancer. Dissimulation, that royal quality, even (at times) deceit, a refusal to honour one's word – these were all doubtless regrettable, but formed the almost unavoidable downside of the loyalties owed to the state. To sustain a good conscience in such matters, the church was always to hand to lay out the authoritative guide to salvation; and, so far as the powers on this earth were concerned, the church enjoined subjects to passive obedience without qualification. When the occasion required it, Richelieu was prepared to frighten Catholics with the spectre of a French schism, although he did not regard it as a serious threat himself. At this point it is worth recalling that all these

---

[10] On Cinq-Mars, see below, p. 54.
[11] It was customary for popes in the seventeenth century to make use of the services of one or several of their nephews, ecclesiastics who were *ipso facto* promoted to be cardinals and who became something like first ministers to His Holiness. This was the case, for example, with Pope Gregory XV (pontiff from 1621 to 1623) and his nephew (Lodovico Ludovisi). The arrangement had its advantages but it also invited numerous abuses.

attempts to reassert order under the beguiling banner of Reason of State, however highly visible they were, could only have a limited effect. Richelieu was the master (and that only to a limited degree) of 45,000 civil servants, or rather 'office-holders' – as against the army of 1,990,010 functionaries to be found in the France of 1986.[12] He did not have the means to control, in any fundamental way, a population of 20 million. So much for 'internal affairs'.

As for his foreign policy, the cardinal's stance, whilst being bellicose in tone, was far from being wholly uncompromising. The German historian Fritz Dickmann has convincingly shown in research which attracted criticism[13] that Richelieu was keen to secure a measure of European security for the smaller states of Europe against the predominance of the Habsburgs. He sought mutual guarantees to maintain peace, legal obligations bilaterally arrived at, but each one arranged under the protective 'umbrella' of French hegemony. The cardinal did not seek to advertise at every juncture French demands for territorial expansion. When they were advanced, backed up by military force, there was always a sense that they were amply justified by legally valid claims.

The ideal of a Christian monarchy remained, therefore, still of manifest importance to Cardinal Richelieu. Anything else would have been anathema to the piety of a king such as Louis XIII, assisted by such a princely prelate. For such a Christian monarchy to become the seat of a *Realpolitik* agenda created a host of ambiguities. Amongst the opposition to Richelieu, various pamphleteers sought to denounce the contradictions or to exploit them, to highlight the yawning gap which they had opened up with traditional Catholicism. Amongst the cardinal's adversaries should be included Bérulle, Marillac, Jansen, Morgues and St-Cyran.[14] Many of these figures emerged, like Richelieu himself, from the stable of Marie de Médicis' service in the years from around 1620 to 1626, which goes to show that the Regent Queen was not such a poor judge of talent after all.

These were the fundamental notions of Richelieu when it came to the primary bastions underlying the social role of government – religion, sovereignty and reason. When it came to the military, Richelieu sought (and arrived at) a significant expansion in its role. To achieve this, he wanted the nobility to become in reality what in theory it already was supposed to be, a service order. At the same time, however, he wanted it

---

[12]   The 1988 report of the *Cours des comptes* (in respect of the years immediately preceding it), quoted in *Le Monde*, 26 July, 1988; to this figure should be added the 287,564 agents who were not in a civil servant post.

[13]   Fritz Dickmann, 'Rechtsgedanke und Machtpolitik bei Richelieu, Studien an neu entdeckten Quellen' in *Historische Zeitschrift*, 196 (1963), 265–319.

[14]   For the *dévots* Bérulle and Marillac, see above, p. 11. Saint-Cyran (1581–1643) was the early French exponent of Jansenism. Mathieu de Morgues, also a theologian, was *abbé* of Saint-Germain-des-Prés and a client of Marie de Médicis before he put his talents to good use as Richelieu's servant. After the Day of Dupes, he would become one of the cardinal's opponents alongside his patron Marie de Médicis.

shorn of its tendencies towards private feud and political influence. However, he was to discover that the 'second order' had a different agenda of its own. The nobility as a whole were less interested in their old martial valour and more concerned with their family lineage and the standing which it brought them within society. Here were the beginnings of a division between the absolute monarchy and a gentry which drew its inspiration from its ancestral lineages, the blue blood which flowed from father to son, rather than the blood which was spilled on the field of battle. Yet, putting the Fronde to one side, the origins of a genuine separation between the crown and the old nobility would only occur much later in the course of the eighteenth century with the emergence of a liberal-minded nobility, inspired by the ideas of the *philosophes*.[15]

Finally, beyond the monarchy, with its essentially religious origins, albeit buttressed by a quasi-lay conception of sovereignty, and outside the circle of the nobility which might become a more militarily conceived order of society, there lay (in third place), the rest of society. Those who were neither clerics nor officers nor nobles nor soldiers but producers and tax-payers composed more than 90 per cent of French men and women (by today's frontiers) – 19 million individuals. Richelieu conceived of this as a nation – something which he perceived in the rather aggressive sense of the 'French nation' in contrast to the 'Spanish nation'. He also saw it as a population: the most numerous and thus, objectively, the most powerful in Europe (he was right to imagine that the population of Spain was substantially less than that of the French realm). Each manifestation of authority required its own particular quality of rule. Thus, the sovereign monarchy was to draw upon the quality of *Reason*. The same ruler, when acting as the soldier-king, should be governed by the quality of decisiveness, of strength of will, of manly *valour*. When it came to displaying the qualities of the king who was father to millions of his people, he should take as the guiding principle, *public interest* – although this would often be something which would be barely understood by the population at large, since it lacked the necessary wisdom. For their part, the people had to show their respect and obedience. In peacetime, the essential qualities a ruler should display to the common people were 'repos' (civil peace), 'règlement du royame' (the remedying of grievances), and finally 'épargne' (the ever-desirable lowering of taxes). In wartime (i.e. after 1630, and particularly after 1635), it proved necessary to abandon some of these sweet dreams and concentrate on the more straightfoward 'survival of the realm in its greatness and in its glory'. Of course, the war abroad should not *a priori* be set against the quest for internal peace. The subjects of the realm had to finance the armies by means of heavy fiscal burdens which had increased in huge measure; nevertheless, and here the cardinal drew on the image of the familiar Poitevin mule, they should not crushed under

---

[15] Ellery Schalk, *Ideas of Nobility in France in the Sixteenth and Seventeenth Centuries* (Princeton, NJ, Princeton University Press, 1986), p. 212 *et seq.*

the weight of an excessive burden – yet the author of the *Testament politique* does not explain how such an excess should be defined.

The widespread misery which resulted from increased taxation was denounced by the cardinal's opponents (Gaston d'Orléans) and by their apologists. The revolts which ensued were (in principle) punished by the authorities to ensure that discipline was restored over the ignorant multitude, a restoration of civil peace which was often far from easily achieved. The cardinal's picture of the world had no place for the political representation of the second estate, let alone the third – which is why Richelieu is rightly seen as the architect of absolutism. But the king should attempt to win the hearts and minds of his subjects, and this was a way of providing them with a role, even though it was only one of offering the king their praise and admiration. Finally, there were Richelieu's views of women, whom he regarded as a kind of fourth estate, a dangerous herd. One should steer clear, he wrote drily, 'of factions which have their roots in the feebleness of the opposite sex' – regent queens constituted, above all, an 'open invitation' to such goings-on: Catherine de Médicis, Marie de Médicis (and, in due course, Anne of Austria) would not enjoy the cardinal's approbation.

Beyond such different orders of society and orders, clearly defined and strictly justified, Richelieu formulated an audacious government strategy, burdensome and innovative in its military and financial aspects (Louis XIII, he once said, always took pleasure in doing what his predecessors had never dared to). The strategy was more reformist than revolutionary, for to have tried to change everything at once would have been suicidal, the equivalent of wild beasts in the lord's vineyard, destroying his vines and crops. It was better, as he put it, to bring some degree of order within the existing disorder, an order which could, in time, be further adjusted but not destroyed. The prodigious and enduring elaboration of the state which was achieved in under two decades under Richelieu was undertaken by changes to political life and without overturning the social fabric. When the cardinal invoked reason, valour and the public interest (with their basis in reward, fiscality and internal peace), his opponents sought to invert the three qualities and accused him of ambition, violence and cupidity. Under his leadership, the patronage state, beloved by Renaissance monarchs, was replaced (and with a sense of religious piety) with the predator state, founded on modern fiscal exactions and with a patriotic agenda. This was the kind of state which thought of itself as, and that has been taken to be, absolute.

*   *   *   *   *

As a bishop, and shortly a cardinal, Richelieu belonged to what might be described as the political wing of the Catholic counter-reformation, thus drawing a distinction from the *dévots* although the separation between these two tendencies in the movement did not really take place until around 1630, after the final break between Spain (which was presented as religious fervour personified) and France (which became the home of religious opportunism). Richelieu's religion was thus coextensive with his administrative and lay responsibilities. The state, like the church (or almost to the same degree) was a divine creation; as such, it had to be protected at any price, which meant, if necessary, opposing the Papacy if it seemed to threaten the French church. The clergy should on no account try to set themselves up in opposition to the monarchy as they had done to such ill effect during the League. And, even if it was not to the liking of Rome, they should be submissive in the temporal domain to the secular powers that be, since they should have both royalist and Gallican affiliations – doubly consecrated, as it were. Here, within a Christianity which had been only a little adapted for lay purposes, lay one of the profound roots of absolutism.

Richelieu, the adherent to Bodin and his views on sovereignty, was fervently committed to becoming a grandee in every sense. Yet he resolutely opposed the illegitimate revolts of major aristocratic figures against the king (apart, that is, from his rather lukewarm support for the rebellion of his fickle patron Marie de Médicis shortly after which he would make his peace with Louis XIII and desert her).[16] In normal circumstances, Richelieu preferred to work in a society which could be conceived (even if the reality was not always to reflect it) in terms of a harmonious subordination of the various elements, even though his perception of this hierarchy short-circuited its traditional components as manifested in the Estates General (although he was a spokesman at the Estates of 1614) and ignored the other elements of feudal authority.[17] His royal anti-feudalism (which, however, did not prevent Richelieu from becoming a powerful landowner and thus purchasing many seigneuries) was part of the ideology of the period. The same attitude was reflected in the works of Charles Loyseau in 1611, the writer who whilst he defended royal office-holding was often critical towards seigneurial authority. Those in positions of authority had to submit to the sovereign's will just as children had to obey their father, the faithful to accept the injunctions of the church and students the

[16] In July 1620, Richelieu felt that he had no other choice than to follow Marie de Médicis in one of the 'conflicts between mother and son' against Louis XIII. After her defeat at Ponts-de-Cé in August 1620, he put together the reconciliation between Marie and Louis from which, in due course, he would benefit. He thus laid the groundwork for his transfer of loyalties from the party of the mother to that of the son, a transition which was completed with unedifying skill during the years from 1624 to 1630.

[17] As a general rule, Richelieu remained faithful to the notions of aristocratic hierarchy which the painter Philippe de Champaigne, working under Richelieu's instruction, would evoke in the gradation of the celestial hierarchy in his paintings. Seraphims were charged with the love of God. Dominions had the oversight of the sovereignty and territorial aggrandizement of the kingdom. Principalities saw to the prosperity and tranquillity of France. See Bernard Dorival, 'Richelieu, Philippe de Champaigne et la décoration de l'église de la Sorbonne' in *Bulletin de la société de l'histoire de l'art français* ([1972]1973), 95–103.

authority of their teachers, etc. Was the severity of the punishments accorded those who transgressed the fundamental rule of obedience not directly contrary to the needs of Christian charity? As a priest and as a faithful Catholic he supported the latter whilst at the same time demonstrating that, in personal affairs, he could be particularly vindictive. But when it came to the state, the whole question had to be seen in a rather different light. As a collective entity the state had a lifespan beyond that of simple mortals; as a result, neither eternal life nor damnation awaited it in the life hereafter. It was therefore excused the necessity of treating its enemies in accordance with the forgiving injunctions of the Gospels to charity. Instead the state chose to draw upon the image of the wrathful God of the Old Testament, a God who thirsts for justice and avenges the wrongs committed by the great and small. In this light, it is legitimate to punish with the greatest rigour such infractions (duelling, conspiracies, etc.) as take place amongst the 'régnicoles', no matter how powerful or privileged.[18] Here was the particular force of Reason of State.

Politics is, however, all about knowing how to adjust to the prevailing circumstances. These meant that, in around 1620, it appeared impossible to imagine an elimination of the Huguenot 'religion' in France. The most that could be achieved was to raze Protestant fortresses to the ground and outlaw their military levies and to pray, but not always with much conviction, for their conversion back to orthodox Catholic doctrine. Although Richelieu had initially had no ecclesiastical vocation, in time he came to be an excellent priest and cleric, understanding the degree to which the flames of eternal damnation were always a weapon which had to be kept in reserve in the conduct of human affairs. As a confessor of penitents who came to him as he exercised his priestly duties, he displayed a considerable flexibility. He did not ask them for a demonstration of absolute contrition but only required a sign of its beginnings in the simpler and much less perfect attrition.[19] When the moment was right, he seized the initiative and set himself apart from the *dévots* of the Bérulle-Marillac clan, who had been his close associates. Thereafter, the cardinal put himself at the head of a party of *Bons Français*,[20] whose adherents expected God to make use of true patriots like themselves for his own immanent purposes and greater glory, even though they might risk at some stage offending (albeit for good reasons) the supreme pontiff. Richelieu had little of the ample generosity

---

[18] 'Régnicoles' – i.e. the natural inhabitants of a country, defined in terms of the legal rights and responsibilites which they possessed (see M.A.P. Littré, *Dictionnaire de la Langue Française*, 7 vols (new edition) (Paris, 1956–8) vi).

[19] Church, *Richelieu and Reason of State*, p. 52.

[20] In comparison with the Catholic League, which looked to Rome and Spain for its political direction, the 'Politique' party of the period of the wars of religion defined its political orientation as essentially national, although many of its adherents were Catholic. In a similar way, the *Bons Français* under Richelieu were outspokenly critical of those *dévots* within the Catholic church whom they accused of being in cahoots with the Austrian and Spanish Habsburgs as well as the Vatican.

and tolerance of the Chancellor Michel de l'Hôpital nor the chivalry which inspired Bayard. Yet he shared their willingness to be persuaded to engage both with the Habsburgs and with anti-Calvinist persecution within France. The latter implied some concessions with the 'heretics' and Richelieu was, in reality, less ideologically committed on the issue than Louis XIV would be later on. But it is also the case that Louis XIV would be more strongly tempted to assume the mantle of ultra-Catholicism once Spain had been defeated, taking it from the shoulders of the declining power and brandishing it to prove that he was indeed the Most Christian King. The circumstances bred the later intolerance

Richelieu's politics can thus be defined and clarified best in comparison with those of Henry IV. The First Bourbon, albeit moving in an absolutist direction, left a good deal of freedom of manoeuvre in the hands of the nobility and, *a fortiori*, in the hands of the Huguenots. In external affairs, he allied with the Protestant states of Europe (England, the Netherlands and the North German princes) against the Habsburgs, and especially against Spain. Finallly, he assisted by the return of peace a spontaneous economic expansion which the government, with the patronage of Sully, attempted to stimulate still further by measures favourable to growth, some of which were purely symbolic and others of which had a demonstrable effect.

In comparison, the cardinal's measures towards the Huguenots, accused on some occasions of being a 'state within a state'[21] were, at first sight, much cruder, even though they provided the pretexts which he was able to turn into justifications for his actions. In July 1627, the English, anxious to protect their Calvinist co-religionists in La Rochelle, and keen at the same time to curtail French maritime and commercial ambitions, led an expedition to the Ile de Ré. Through the powerful Rohan-Soubise family, they established an alliance with the Rochelais. But, as in Béarn a decade earlier, the Huguenot initiative merely invited the full weight of repression. The siege of La Rochelle, which lasted from August 1627 until October 1628, proved to be extremely arduous. The town was eventually seized and it lost its ramparts and its municipal liberties, although Protestant rights to worship there were maintained. It was the same story in the following two years during which the cardinal led a victorious military campaign against the Huguenot Midi, against Privas and the Protestant-dominated towns of Languedoc and Guyenne which culminated in June 1629 in the Grace of Alais. In imposing this treaty upon the defeated party,

---

[21] The estimated Protestant population in France, in the light of which Richelieu's policy was developed, was over 904,000 at the beginning of the seventeenth century out of around 20 million Frenchmen, taking into account the contemporary frontiers – 'to which there should be added the 100,000–125,000 inhabitants of Béarn, Protestants by law established if not by conviction'. The comparable figure for around 1630 would be about 830,000, which was during, or on the eve of, a steady but persistent flow of conversions and emigration. See Philip Benedict, 'La Population réformée au XVIe siècle', in *Annales ESC*, 42 (1987), 1453–4.

Richelieu embodied the plans which he had outlined only weeks before to foreign ambassadors at the French court. 'We have to give serious consideration to the Huguenots. I hope and I am convinced that shortly . . . we shall achieve our objectives . . . It is essential that all the fortifications of [their] towns are dismantled. Once that is done, they will discover that the king will show them very great beneficence. They will enjoy their goods and possessions intact, freedom of conscience, and their privileges [such as their rights to tribunals for the implementation of the edict of Nantes] . . . But His Majesty requires them to behave as his subjects and no longer to have the means to raise a rebellion or to refuse him the duty they owe him of obedience. They must return to that obedience, either by agreement or by force . . . In four or five months time, I am confident that the issue will be resolved.'[22]

The rigorous maintenance of the authority of the state which is the essence of Richelieu is echoed in these few lines. Yet this preoccupation did not extend so far as to impose upon religious minorities the requirement of subscribing to the confession of the majority since religious unity, according to the cardinal, would only arise with a return of the Huguenots to a form of Christianity eventually orchestrated under the aegis of the clergy of the Catholic church, a return to which the Huguenots freely consented.

In general, Richelieu thus remained true to the plan which he had proposed in 1615, and which differed markedly from the legalized violence and forced conversion practised later by the Sun-King. It was in his closing speech on behalf of the clergy before the Estates General that he had proposed: 'As for the Protestants, all our concerns are directed towards their conversion, which we must encourage by means of our example, our teaching and our prayers. These are the only forces with which we should seek to combat them.' To this singular statement of objective, Richelieu remained broadly consistent for the remainder of his career. The Protestant churches should be induced to be 'reunited' with the Catholic world by negotiation and by doctrinal concessions (however distasteful to the Vatican). They should be won over by proposals, conferences and summit meetings, as well as by the rather less elevated (but far from inhuman) dispersal of handsome payments to pastors prepared to switch to the Catholic side.[23] This was not far removed from the politics of coexistence practised by Henry IV. In reality, once the turbulent years of the La Rochelle and Languedocian campaigns were over, the Huguenots found themselves entering calmer waters and were no longer officially hounded by the king's ministers. They were still subject, however, to some degree of official harassment as in the marginalization of the bi-partisan tribunals or *chambres de l'édit*, the interference in the composition of Protestant municipalities (which were constrained to allow more Catholics into their council

[22] Pierre Chevallier, *Louis XIII* (Paris, Fayard, 1979), p. 346.
[23] This follows Pierre Blet, 'Le Plan de Richelieu pour la réunion des Protestants', in *Gregorianum*, 48 (1967), 100 *et seq.*

chambers), and various obstacles put in the way of the pastors' organizing Protestant worship.

Richelieu's temporary hostility towards French Protestants around 1628–9 was surely of a piece with his equally brief alliance with the Catholic *dévots*. But these short-lived excursions contrast with the cardinal's persistent and stubborn hounding of the higher aristocracy, or of certain of its scions. Yet this did not prevent this extraordinary figure from aspiring to join the higher aristocracy himself. Every conceivable means, both of financial and other kinds, he set to work to achieve this objective and to such good effect that the nephews (and nieces) of the cardinal all, in due course, joined the ranks of the aristocracy and became critics of the government of the day. Some historians have been surprised by this paradox but it is more apparent than real and corresponded closely with the contradictions and realities of contemporary experience. The monarchs who were, even more than their ministers, the protagonists of centralization, spawned powerful cadet princely lineages (Condé, Vendôme, Orléans . . .) who proved to be the harbingers of revolt.

One of the first incidents which typified this repressive stance was that of the unfortunate Chalais, who was executed in 1626 upon Richelieu's order.[24] The authority of the cardinal, with that of Louis XIII as its close ally, spoiled for a fight not merely with Chalais but also with members of the royal family, some closer to the Bourbon lineage than others. Amongst the closer were the Bourbon-Condé, like the count of Soissons and the two Vendôme, the illegitimate half-brothers of Louis XIII. There was worse to follow. Gaston and Anne, the king's brother and his wife, committed treason against him. It is easy to imagine that, in this litany of affairs, things had reverted to the situation in France a century and a half previously when conflicts between royal and princely factions had put the Dauphin, later Louis XI, in opposition to his father, his brother, and finally his nephew. The motives for the plotting in 1626 are not difficult to discern. It was an anti-ministerial conspiracy put together by a group of great nobles. They sought to prevent the marriage of Gaston d'Orléans since, and Gaston shared their views, once he was married off to some titled descendant, he would no longer be in a position to marry Anne of Austria, supposing that Louis XIII were to die (and he was forever poorly) and she become a widow. The execution of Chalais inaugurated a lengthy sequence of aristocratic executions, to the extent that Richelieu became the aristocrats' executioner – more markedly so than Louis XI but way behind St Just. Nothing in the seventeenth century would serve to equal the displays of the 'Lords High Executioners' of the Committee of Public Safety in 1794.

Following the execution of Chalais,[25] the death sentences passed on Montmorency-Bouteville and Des Chapelles, the inveterate duellists, are

[24]   Henri de Talleyrand, Count de Chalais.

[25]   The following paragraph owes a good deal to the substantial work by François Billacois, *Le Duel dans la société française des XVIe et XVIIe siècles* (Paris, Ecole des Hautes Etudes, 1986).

also revealing affairs. During the three decades from 1607 to 1637, duelling had become much more widespread. Through it, the 'second order' (the nobility) attempted to define its own identity in the face of a growing absolutism. A noble who found himself engaged in a duel counted the challenge as the equivalent of an archive full of legal titles to nobility. The deaths which resulted confirmed or gave early testimony of an aptitude for a great military career which might be expected to be followed by any gentleman worthy of the name. In one single bloodthirsty gesture the duellist defied the authority of the prince, which so constrained some amongst the nobility. The presence of seconds at duels as assistants who were equally sworn to a fight to the death at the sides of the principal protagonists, reawakened the archaic ethics of the vendetta. In 1643, a Coligny would once again issue a challenge to a Guise; the hostility which existed between these two families since the previous century would be cited, in a more or less sincere fashion, by way of justification.

The young noblemen who tore into one another also lay down the challenge to the grey-beards amongst the *noblesse de robe* who periodically would stand in Parlement to condemn the survivors from such encounters, or their corpses. The existence of a 'generation gap' should also not be ignored. The numbers of deaths which resulted from this 'detestable habit' were not huge, and certainly not (despite the perdurable legend to this effect) sufficiently large to threaten any decrease in numbers amongst the nobility. Even so, the problem was evidently serious, and particularly well-advertised, during the years from 1620 until the outbreak of war in 1635 which deflected the aggressions of the old nobility away from their tendencies towards fratricidal assassination.

Faced with the problem, royal policies displayed a certain ambiguity. It was axiomatic that the monarch and his close relatives could in no way be seen to engage in a duel, unless it was with the emperor or another sovereign prince, and this, in reality, would never again occur.[26] As the first gentleman of the realm, Louis XIII should, in any case, seek to prevent the nobility from foolishly sacrificing itself in internecine strife. Such was the chivalric duty which the young Bourbon king had to shoulder. The fount of sovereignty, he was also the guardian of justice. This had a great levelling effect and prevented the aristocrats from assuming a bloodthirsty preeminence over the other orders of society and required them to behave peaceably towards others. As God's Lieutenant on this earth, Louis required each of his subjects, even the most mighty, to observe the Commandment: 'Thou shalt not kill.' But, from another perspective, it appeared altogether more paradoxical; for the occupant of the throne and his first minister, both of them nobles, could hardly resist a sneaking admiration for the bravura of these duellists, which might have been put to better purpose. From this point of view, one can well appreciate the full

---

[26] Ibid., p. 33; also V.G. Kiernan, *The Duel in European History. Honour and the Reign of Aristocracy* (Oxford, Oxford University Press, 1989), p. 44.

sense of the public involvement in the combat of Montmorency-Bouteville and Des Chapelles against other duellists in 1627 at the *Place Royale*, recently constructed in Paris by Henry IV. By settling their differences in the midst of the capital and in one of the show-case pieces of Bourbon civic reconstruction, rather than deep in the heart of the countryside, Des Chapelles and his colleague set themselves in spectacular fashion against the process of the reconstruction of monarchical authority which had so occupied the king's and his minister's attentions. Bouteville was an immature young man, dancing with death, a 'baroque mixture of Don Quixote and Don Juan'.[27] He conformed to the typology of the 'libertine' aristocrat, with some of the religious scepticism which this implied. He had solid and well-established relations with Gaston d'Orléans, the eternal conspirator, but he was not personally driven by a desire for revolt. The subsequent repression was a case of the swashbuckler confronting the cardinal. The sentence of death pronounced against Des Chapelles and Bouteville was criticized by the nobility but broadly approved of by the office-holders and by the merchant community. It was far from signalling the end of duelling, the cases of which would only start to decrease ten years later, from 1637 onwards, under the combined impact of the war abroad, the cardinal's attempts to outlaw it, and the beginnings of the collapse in the baroque ideological framework which had supported it. The moment in June 1627 when these two swaggering noblemen were executed might well be taken to mark, in a symbolic way, the birth of absolutism, within which nobility was not to be annulled but to become gradually integrated, domesticated and rendered loyal – at least this was what Richelieu proclaimed even if it was not always to be reflected in reality. The year 1627 was also that when the last assembly of notables took place . . . until 1787. This, too, was the moment, *a contrario*,[28] for the birth of the full majesty of absolutism, that which denied the necessity for 'representation' or for a nationally organized participation in government.

Up to 1628–9, the centralizing endeavours of Richelieu were directed against the aristocrats and their allies (Gaston and Chalais respectively) or against the Huguenots (at La Rochelle and Privas). A radical change in this overall direction took place in 1630, the year of the 'great storm'. The latter had been brewing for some time. In December 1627, the death of Duke Vincent of Mantua without a direct successor led the government of Louis XIII into opposition to Savoy, Spain and the Emperor – in the end against the determination of Catholic Europe from Habsburg Vienna to Madrid. The future direction of French affairs was starkly presented. Should France continue its war against the Huguenots, whose aggression showed little signs of decreasing; or, on the other hand, should France follow the logic of its national and dynastic imperatives and oppose the Austro-Hispanic-Savoyard bloc, and its Catholicism?

[27] Billacois, *Le Duel*, p. 270.
[28] Jeanne Petit, *L'Assemblée des notables de 1626–7* (Paris, 1936).

This was the essence of the problem which pitted Richelieu against Marillac, the *Bons Français* against the *dévots*. As the Superintendent of Finances from 1624 onwards, and Keeper of the Seals from 1626, Marillac[29] found his political influence on the increase; at times, it was even decisive. He belonged to the group of mystics who owed their principal inspiration to Bérulle. Marillac participated (after his own fashion) in the '*dévot* upsurge' to which France succumbed in the seventeenth century, a century which is still called by some the 'Century of Saints' and which was dominated by the Catholic reformation, otherwise known as the Tridentine counter-reformation. The future adversary of the cardinal was, however, both a creative and realistic politician. He wrote numerous plans for reform which have been the subject of exhaustive studies. He was haunted by the problem of the people's suffering, the danger of antifiscal revolts, of the imperative need to 'relieve the suffering of the people' which entailed the need for effective state regulations – and the latter could only be achieved by a period of peace. He had no difficulty, of course, in reconciling these philanthropic and generous sentiments with a cast of mind which was ultra-papal, pro-Spanish and anti-Huguenot; not to fight a war in Italy would mean keeping taxation at a low level and retaining good relations with Spain, which happened to share his Protestant-phobia. Such an alliance thus served further to motivate the need to 'cut off the head and tear the heart' (*sic*) out of the Calvinist hydra, and particularly within France itself.

Marillac's conceptual framework was inspired by a certain logic but it led to unforeseen consequences. Ultra-Catholicism had been bellicose during the League and committed to the extermination of the Huguenots, and even of moderate Catholics. To the extent that the battleground had shifted outside France's territory and against Spain, this aggressive stance was replaced in ultra-Catholic circles by a more pacifist attitude. Marillac's attitudes can be mirrored by those, later on, of Archbishop Fénelon, the resolute adversary of Louis XIV's wars and the instigator of a certain kind of pacifism. For most of the time, Marillac had the backing of the inner council (the *Conseil d'en haut*) since he enjoyed the support of the queen mother, Marie de Médicis who was herself equally hispanophile, and who at various instances from 1627 to 1630 acted in fact as Regent. But events would, in this respect, overtake her.

In March and April 1629, French forces invaded Casale[30] in accordance with Richelieu's wishes. This was one of the strongholds of Montferrat, a dependency of the duchy of Mantua. In September, Marie de Médicis began a 'cold war' against the cardinal and in support of Marillac. A factional struggle ensued in which the Bourbon and Lorraine princesses,

---

[29]   Georges Pagès, 'Autour du grand orage', *Revue historique*, 174 (1937).
[30]   Casal, or Casale.

along with the duchess d'Ornano,[31] urged the queen mother to wage a bitter offensive against her titled and mitred opponent. In March 1630, Pignerol, the fortress which held the key to the plain around Padua – and thus to Italy itself – fell to the French forces. Richelieu wanted to continue the war. For him, it was a matter of 'banishing all thought of repose, retrenchment and reform within the kingdom'.[32] This was pure anti-Marillac. By September, the sickly Louis XIII came close to death; but he made a miraculous recovery and thus saved the cardinal from certain disgrace and possibly from assassination. In October, France took advantage of its military advantage to install Charles de Nevers as duke in Mantua. The climax came in the Day of Dupes (in fact the crisis lasted for two days, 10–11 November 1630) in the following month after which Marie, the duper who was duped, found herself excluded from power and soon neutralized.[33] The same fate befell to various degrees Anne of Austria and Gaston d'Orléans. In opposition to his mother, his wife and his brother, and against the advice of the numerous friends whom this trio could call on amongst the aristocracy and the senior office-holders, Louis XIII chose to support Richelieu and the party of military engagements (limited at first; then without limits) abroad. Richelieu was a master-strategist who had first delivered a left-hook, which had left the Protestants weakened but not eliminated; he then followed this up with a serious of punches aimed at the Catholic *dévots* and the pacifists – two groups who had for some time tended to become one and the same.

The defeated were forced to withdraw and lick their wounds. The crisis of the Day of Dupes led to the exile of Marie for the remainder of her life. Gaston, on the other hand, only retired for a brief period; after all, he remained the heir to the throne until the birth of Louis XIV. Accused of support (albeit somewhat shaky) from amongst the higher nobility, from the Guise, the Bourbon-Condé, the Bouillon, and above all the Montmorency, sustained by Spain and by Lorraine, 'Monsieur' (the title generally given at this period to the younger brother of the king) would not

---

[31] They formed the kernel of a female opposition to the establishment in power, an opposition emanating from amongst the aristocratic élites. Such a phenomenon had already made its appearance under the League and would be very visible during the Fronde.

[32] Cited by George Pagès, 'Autour du grand orage', pp. 82–5; cf. Pierre Grillon, *Les Papiers de Richelieu* (7 vols in prog., Padua, Monumenta Europeae Historica, 1982), v, 212 (doc. 196).

[33] The 'Day of Dupes' lasted, in fact, for at least two and a half days: *Sunday afternoon 10 November 1630*: the session of the *Conseil d'en haut* was concluded and Marie de Médicis told Richelieu that she would have no more dealings with him and forbade him to have anything in future to do with her household affairs. *Monday morning 11 November 1630*: after a violent altercation, Marie believed herself to have won the day against Richelieu. However Louis XIII (who, in fact, continued to support Richelieu) and Richelieu both withdrew from the court leaving the 'duped' courtiers to applaud Marie's victory. *The night of 11–12 November 1630*: Louis XIII renewed his confidence in Richelieu and disgraced the Marillac bothers who would shortly be arrested. Marie fell from power.

be deterred from leading a small rebel army into France from the north-east in June 1632. He was to be deceived. No support was forthcoming from Burgundy despite having been a province which had demonstrated its hostility towards the increasing taxation which had been imposed to pay for the preparations for war by Richelieu. Hyper-fiscality, the inevitable consequence of the rejection of Marillac's pacifism, was the dominant theme of the 1630s since it produced a kind of involuntary allergic reaction in the body of French society in the shape of popular revolts. These were fomented from beneath by a rejection of over-burdensome taxation and manipulated from on high by aristocratic conspiracies.[34]

After his naive misreading of reactions in Burgundy, Gaston made his way southwards to Languedoc where he made common cause with those who took a dislike to the new taxes imposed from the Louvre and looked on his arrival with favour. Richelieu wanted to replace the provincial estates of these southern regions with office-holders, known as *élus*, who would levy the increased *taille* on their own authority.[35] This illustrates how little progress the cardinal's reforming efforts had made; he merely intended to institute *élus*, i.e. office-holders who owned their offices, rather than administrative officials at the beck and call of the government. Languedoc was far from unanimous, however, in welcoming the 'rein-forcements' to its cause provided by Gaston and his faction. Throughout the 22 civil dioceses of the province, Gaston could count on the loyalty of its governor, Montmorency, and some of the élite of the provincial estates. But convinced Protestants, suspicious of the hispano-papal connections of Gaston and his mother, did not lift a finger for him, and nor did the Parlement of Toulouse. Defeated by a tiny royal army at Castelnaudary in 1632, the Gaston-Montmorency axis fell to bits. Monsieur, courageous as always, beat a hasty retreat from the uprising which he had instigated. Montmorency was condemned and executed in October 1632, following the fate already meted out to the *maréchal* de Marillac, the Keeper of the Seals' brother, who had been put to death in May 1632 after a travesty of a trial.

Richelieu was careful, however, to set limits to his vengeance. The rebellious province of Languedoc was pardoned, even acquitted. The *élus* were suppressed and the province was given permission to hold its estates again – a device which held in some check the galloping fiscality of

---

[34]   Antifiscal revolts in France during the reign of Louis XIII have long been considered, particularly by English historians, as 'savage', the work of 'primitive rebels' and other such pejorative and unsympathetic terms. The emergence in highly-developed modern England in February–March 1990 of a series of antifiscal demonstrations against the poll-tax (a variation on the old French *capitation* of the seventeenth century) should provoke some reassessment of this 'anglo-chauvinist' perspective towards the continent.

[35]   The provincial estates were representative assemblies, composed of the three estates of the realm, and which continued to exist in certain peripheral provinces of the kingdom such as Languedoc, Brittany, etc.

Richelieu and his ministers. It would be difficult to imagine a government acceding to the requests of a trades union whose leader had just been hanged or decapitated; and yet this was by analogy what had happened in the French Midi in 1632 and the following years. The precedent had already been set, however, by a rather similar sequence of events in 1548 by the 'Pitauts' revolt in Aquitaine.[36]

After 1632, the procession of conspiracies, agitations and uprisings followed a similar 'twin' pattern. Networks of grand seigneurs would emerge to embody the diffuse (or sometimes more precise) reactions of clans of *robins*, clerics and pacific-minded gentlemen (the latter posing as anti-authoritarian, and anti-dictatorial *junkers*). Each group came together to condemn with sincerity the people's suffering, the continuation of the war and fiscal oppression, and, above all, the alliance of their government, Catholic (not to say cardinal) in principle with the Protestant princes in Germany and elsewhere. It is difficult in clandestine movements of opposition like this to disentangle the part played by liberal and pacifist principle from that of straightforward intrigue.

To the fore amongst the opposition was Anne of Austria. During the summer of 1637 she was discovered passing information to Spain. A century later, Saint-Simon wrote some prejudiced and inexact pages on the incident, describing the young queen being searched and investigated 'even internally'[37] by the Chancellor Pierre Séguier, who had been provided with a roving commission to look for compromising letters by the cardinal. Towards the close of that same year, *père* Caussin, Louis XIII's confessor, let his own hispano-Catholic inclinations be known. He attempted to bring some influence to bear upon his confessee in favour of peace and the relief of popular distress and against the compromising 'friends' with whom France was allied, who were non-Catholic (such as Sweden) and even, in one instance, not Christian either (the Turks). In this instance, Richelieu had only himself to blame. He was the one who had brought the confessor 'wolf' into the 'fold' of the confessional monarchy. In desperation, the cardinal would find it necessary to dismiss the priest whom he had wrongly considered as his 'creature' and replace him with someone who would be evidently more docile.

After Caussin, it was the turn of Soissons. Louis de Bourbon, Count of Soissons, invaded France with a small force and support from the duke of Bouillon, who was prince of Sedan, and confronted the royal army at La Marfée on 9 July 1641. However, Soissons had a stupid habit of raising the visor of his helmet in warm weather with the butt of the pistol. The result was that he died in battle – but accidently, the result of his shooting himself in the temple. This did not stop Richelieu's agents from being accused of having orchestrated this 'providential' death. Where the cap fits . . . .

[36] E. Le Roy Ladurie, *The Royal French State, 1460–1610* (Oxford, Blackwell, 1994), p. 147.

[37] Saint-Simon, *Mémoires*, ed. A. de Boislisle, 45 vols (Paris, 1879–1930), i, 189.

The most spectacular affair was that surrounding Cinq-Mars. He was the young favourite of Louis XIII who became involved in a pro-Madrid conspiracy and in order to take a stand against despotism. In due course this was discovered by Richelieu and his agents, and possibly with the assistance of Anne of Austria. The latter, having toyed with both sides, hoped to reconcile herself to her husband the king and to the omnipotent cardinal by means of a squalid denunciation. Cinq-Mars and his accomplice de Thou were executed in due course on 12 September 1642. It seems clear that, before the death of his favourite, the king had become compromised in plots which had as their objective the political or physical elimination of the cardinal, seen as the only obstacle towards the conclusion of a peace. Such a revelation, albeit in shadowy terms, that the king had entertained the possibility of peace, even of assassination, put him in a difficult position in terms of his relationship with Richelieu, who was thereafter able to make the king, ill at ease with his conscience in the matter, do whatever he chose. At the end of the reign, the minister exercised a complete domination over the prince and found himself in a position to lay down the law. In the complex triad of relationships between Anne, Louis and the former bishop of Luçon there is an 'awful certainty' in the reaction of Louis to Anne's treason and in that of Richelieu towards his sovereign's wholly equivocal attitude towards him. In the end these would all turn to the advantage of Richelieu who, little by little, was able gain the upper hand over his two associates, king and queen, who found themselves gradually transformed into the junior partners of the cardinal-minister.

Beyond the bare chronology of events, outlining the crude repression meted out to some of the aristocracy and nobility, it is possible to delineate any major strategic considerations which motivated the cardinal to execute those such as the *maréchal* de Marillac, Chalais, Montmorency-Bouteville, Montmorency, Cinq-Mars and de Thou. Richelieu ordered some blue blood to be spilled but it did not flow in torrents. There was no desire to exterminate the nobility, which would be the task which the Montagnards would set themselves in 1794; rather he wanted them to honour their obligations. Only a small number of individuals were executed. Yet he confronted clans and dynasties, branches of princely houses or the royal family; kinsmen of Marie de Médicis, Anne of Austria, Gaston d'Orléans, the count of Soissons, the duke of Bouillon. . . . His campaign would be continued, albeit in a more restrained fashion, by Mazarin (a disciple of the 'Great Cardinal') and then in his turn by the young Louis XIV, Mazarin's follower. The results would be striking in the sense of the discipline, or self-discipline of the great nobles which would be instilled from one generation to the next. They would be controlled, punished and made to toe the line – but they would also be bought and cajoled into compliance. Thus Montmorency-Bouteville, the duellist who was executed in 1627, would be the father of the *maréchal* de Luxembourg, the '*tapissier* of Notre-Dame' – so numerous would be the captured enemy flags which his soldiers would bring back and which would hang in the cathedral of Paris like tapestries. Despite some remarkable false moves, particularly during the Fronde and the 'affaire des poisons' of 1679–80, Luxembourg would be one of the great military leaders of Louis XIV's army. He exemplified the service nobility (in the full sense of the term) of the kind which would make its appearance in the rationalized monarchy which wanted to see itself, and projected itself at the time of the League of Augsburg, as 'absolute'. The same could be said of the duke of Bouillon who wanted to frustrate Richelieu's purposes at every turn; yet his younger brother was none other than Turenne, who would also have his moments of rebellion and desertion, but who would nevertheless ultimately become the loyal servant of Louis XIV. The La Rochefoucauld provide us with a further family to compare across the period from 1640 to 1700. La Rochefoucauld the elder, author of the *Maxims*, greatly despised Richelieu and became an anti-Mazarin *frondeur*. His son would become simply the *grand veneur* of Versailles, the Sun-King's lap-dog, always waiting at the servants' door to answer the king's call. We may also compare the services which they performed; Cinq-Mars, for example, whom Louis XIII executed for conspiracy in 1642, was his *grand veneur*. The count d'Armagnac, a prince from the House of Lorraine, who would be his successor in the post under Louis XIV, was only one obsequious courtier amongst many.

When one examines what motivated the noble adversaries of the cardinal, they drew upon, but not uniquely so, the defence of traditional values. For them it was a question of preserving the ideological and affective 'patrimony' of gentlemen,[38] aristocratic freedoms. They wanted to maintain the old limited, balanced or 'mixed' monarchy which was being hammered into oblivion by the cardinal, the founder of the modern French state. Some of the conspirators were nothing more than valorous d'Artagnans. Others, however, resembled Aramis – deeply pious, profoundly secretive. Amongst those who entered the lists there were several who were *dévots*, who had felt the influence of the counter-reformation, and whose sympathies lay with Spain.[39] D'Ornano provides a good example. The henchman of Gaston, he found himself incapable of approaching a girl called Marie, such was his veneration for the Virgin Mary, and he embodied this kind of ultra-Catholic opposition, in the style of Marillac, to the cardinal.

The noble opposition did not speak with one voice, however. Many of its most distinguished adherents were tinged with neo-stoicism, in the spirit of Epictetus, Seneca and Plutarch.[40] From such sentiments they

---

[38] Jean-Marie Constant, *Les Conjurateurs. Le premier libéralisme sous Richelieu* (Paris, Hachette, 1987). Arlette Jouanna, *Le Devoir de révolte; la noblesse française et la gestation de l'état moderne, 1559–1661* (Paris, Fayard, 1989), pp. 212–44.

[39] Joseph Bergin, *Cardinal de la Rochefoucauld. Leadership and Reform in the French Church* (New Haven and London, Yale University Press, 1987).

[40] Constant, *Les Conjurateurs*.

imagined that the rulers of a state (and, failing them, their opponents) should cultivate a political climate based upon wisdom, clemency, heroic virtue, constancy, friendship, gentleness, trustworthiness, honour, honesty, lack of interest in material advantage, the good fortune of being able to suffer in a worthy cause, a religious devotion towards a promise made – in short, a politics based upon the Sovereign Good; such ideas and values are already to be found amongst such gentlemen as Campion or Montrésor in Gaston d'Orléans' entourage or that of the count of Soissons.

The final common trait amongst the opposition arose from an anti-despotic libertinism, a harbinger of religious scepticism. Amongst those who were influenced in this way, we may cite Fontrailles, one of Gaston's companions, or Cinq-Mars himself. Then there was Cramail, who owed his loyalties to the Guise. The mention of this great princely House in this context is indicative of a transition. At the end of the sixteenth century, there had been an ultra-Catholic Guisard League, dangerous for established authority. By the decade of the 1630s, this had become an anti-cardinal force (eventually *frondeur*) which was much more heterogeneous. The *dévots*, the direct inheritors of the *Ligueurs*, were still present; but they rubbed shoulders readily enough with the kinds of free-thinkers who would eventually undermine the religious foundations of the Ancien Régime. The familiar scepticism of the eighteenth century might even be seen making its first appearance during the decade of the 1640s. At all events, it is difficult to conceive of an opposition, forged under the regime of one cardinal-minister, followed by another, which did not also encompass some anti-clerical and libertine elements. It would have been impossible to refashion 40 years on the coherence which had marked the ultra-Catholic League.

To elaborate a coherent and united political programme from such elements would eventually become possible, but that day was a long way off. Some common ground was, however, relatively clear; around Gaston d'Orléans, the thinking was that the old corporate structure of society, divided into the four or five orders (nobility, clergy, office-holders, merchants and rural world, whose miserable condition was highlighted) should be emphasized as against the absolutist patina which had been placed over it more recently. Richelieu himself was stigmatized as a despot and as the 'Mayor of the Palace'.[41] The historical comparison was a telling one, although not entirely exact. Finally the Estates General should be convoked to determine whether France should continue the war; and there should be a greater participation of *parlementaire* magistrates in government in order to give a more representative component in political affairs.

---

[41] Under the Merovingian kings, the Mayor of the Palace was the governor of the royal household. It was thus not difficult for someone in that position to exercise *de facto* the functions of a kind of elementary 'prime minister', or even to take over the authority of his sovereign.

This had been quite well thought out and it led in due course, growing out of the conspiracy of the count of Soissons which has already been referred to, to the first manifestation of the conspiratorial projects of the Fronde, or to a 'pre-Fronde'. Those involved in it would include the young Gondi (the future Cardinal de Retz), who already enjoyed a degree of influence upon the clergy and people of Paris, both of which retained a certain nostalgia for the League. Some influential office-holders from the sovereign courts (the *Parlement*, the *Chambre des comptes* and the *Cour des aides*) also made their appearance, as did the bourgeois militia,[42] directed (at least in part) by the office-holders themselves. Then, finally, came the 'people' whom Gondi hoped to win over with massive operations of poor relief after the fashion of St Vincent de Paul. The conspiracy's plan, which had not been badly conceived, came to nought with the accidental death of the count of Soissons in July 1641 at the hollow victory of La Marfée. Gondi and his associates demonstrated, however, a surprising prescience as to the turn of events in the Fronde as it would turn out just over seven years later in 1648. Amongst this rather heterogenous group, Gondi would be one of those rare individuals who had a grasp of opposition strategy, if not (given how anachronistic the term would be) the temperament of a revolutionary leader.

★   ★   ★   ★   ★

The second great axis of Henrician politics was, as we have seen, the friendship and active cooperation with the Protestant states of the North and East. This meant opening up the French kingdom to entities which were fundamentally different from it; but this was seen as a way of balancing the Habsburg menace as well as an implicit complement to the strategy of religious entente within France which had been signified by the edict of Nantes of 1598 (even though this entente was seen by the cardinal through the perspective of an eventual reunion of the churches to the benefit of Catholicism, albeit a reunion achieved by non-violent means).

Richelieu did not renounce the coexistential 'axis' which Henry IV had put in place. This was despite the enormous deflection of the siege of La Rochelle, captured in 1628, Richelieu's moment of Calvinophobia. But

---

[42]   The bourgeois civic guard or Parisian militia was, both before and during the Fronde, commanded in each of the 16 quarters of the city (Saint-Martin, Saints-Innocents etc.) by colonels who had, under their orders, several *dixaines*, the size of whose companies could vary between 50 and 800 'bourgeois'. Each company of the *dixaine* included a captain, a lieutenant and an ensign. During the Fronde, the militia could mobilize up to 50,000 bourgeois who were often out of sympathy with the current régime. The ranks of the companies came, in a descending hierarchy, from the *robe*, the shop-keepers and the artisans. The basic condition which had to be met to be allowed into the militia was to be a resident. The last great 'civic militia' demonstration occured in 1660 and proved to be a highly respectful and legal affair in honour of Louis XIV and Maria Theresa. The bourgeois militia remained, however, suspect to the absolutist authorities.

this spectacular siege looks in retrospect like an isolated event, the detail of which should not obscure from us the main pattern. It is true that the Henrician inheritance in terms of pro-Protestant diplomatic effort would be heavily underlined by the cardinal's bellicist stance, resulting from the war itself, but also emanating from his particular temperament as a statesman. And this, in a sense, would change everything. Whereas Henry IV gently whistled the tune for others to hear, Richelieu would thunder it out for all to hear; but the tune had not changed. Louis XIII became transformed into the arbiter of Christianity, using force because that was what was required, rather than the champion of international Catholicism.

The Thirty Years War,[43] from this point of view, provided the cardinal with a convenient testing ground. In European terms, the war represented the ultimate stage of the great armed conflicts which had occurred because of religious divisions. The tiny and distant remnants of this great struggle amongst Christians are now to be found in the flames of hatred or half-extinguished braziers of contestation to be found in Northern Ireland. The roots of the war were to be located, initially at least, in the crude attempt of the Habsburgs to establish their hegemony, first in Bohemia, then in Germany, and then in the rest of western and central Europe. This was a double hegemony, of Habsburg authority, and also of Catholicism. However Richelieu's reaction to this, in contrast with his predecessor and patron, Marie de Médicis, who had been by inclination more pro-Spanish, was to fight Habsburg imperialism, which he regarded as dangerous, counter to French interests and also to the interests, rightly understood, of Catholic piety:

Christendom [the cardinal wrote in 1632], is afflicted by two powerful forces. One of these is the Protestants, who fight for their *religion*. The other is the House of Austria, which oppresses *liberty* and, by the *subversion of justice* and the other means which they deploy to achieve their goal are *against the Christian religion*. [The means which they use] are ambition, *usurpation*, disguise, the art of sowing *divisions* amongst *the nobility*, *encouraging revolt amongst the lower orders* and seditious remours amongst the *notables* who do not support their party. By such means they overturn *public equity* and those *pious* individuals who are indissolubly *linked* to it. The proof of this double truth lies in the history of the recent and present troubles . . . With the same candour, we can say that *France* has, over the centuries, *repressed* the excesses of *impiety* and *injustice* and that God has used it to sustain his church and the common repose against the greatest attacks of these two monsters and that it is the only force which devotes itself to the task with such ardour.[44]

The cardinal then recalled that whilst Louis was engaged in 'establishing *a pacification in religion and in the state* by the subjection of La Rochelle which was acknowledged by common consent as the most just cause that

---

[43]   Geoffrey Parker, *The Thirty Years War* (London, Routledge and Kegan Paul, 1989).
[44]   The emphasis has been added.

our century had furnished', the House of Austria sought to exploit the king's preoccupations by reopening conflict in Italy under the pretexts of Mantua and Montferrat.

In such remarkable reflections, Richelieu dismissed the charge of an elementary Machiavellianism which has often been laid at his door. Of course, he sought to exploit Reason of State and other similar ruses as means to garner support; for he was all too aware of the forces which could be unleashed from a powerful state, a rampant fiscality and a modern army deployed throughout the territory of France. But the cardinal's objectives (albeit slightly distended) remained those of a Christian commonwealth – piety, inextricably linked with justice; public tranquillity, the public good as St Thomas Aquinas would have called it; the taming (but not the abolition) of the Huguenots and the aristocracy. In the case of the latter, the cardinal himself wanted to become a grandee, and one of the grandest at that. The Habsburgs were thus only to be attacked to the degree that, under cover of the church of Rome, they conducted themselves in an unchristian fashion, one which was manifestly to be condemned as unjust, or even impious.

Hence the tightrope walked by the cardinal who needed to cultivate, in order to sustain the semblance of a heterogeneous alliance, the small or modestly sized Catholic states such as Bavaria which would remain a traditional ally of France. At the same time, without compromising such alliances, the cardinal had to come to the aid of 'heretic' states in order to counter-balance the overwhelming force of the imperial Austrian Habsburgs, sustained by their Habsburg cousins in Madrid. In pursuing this stance, Richelieu was doing no more than continuing the pro-Lutheran diplomacy which had been inaugurated by Francis I in January 1534 when he had signed a secret pact with the (Protestant) Landgrave of Hesse. Of course, the religious divisions in Europe were less firmly delineated in early 1534 than they would be a century later. Francis I could remain true to his Catholicism and, at the same time, seek out a rapprochement with the German Lutheran princes in the name of a sincere evangelism. Richelieu, on the other hand, inhabited a world where the boundaries between the two confessions were clearly mapped out. He therefore had to rely on arguments drawing upon a theology of the common good, of justice and of piety, in order to salve his own conscience. All the same, and despite the protection afforded by these divine graces, the ultimately pro-Protestant drift of his foreign policy, determined by the logic of the political circumstances of the moment, would eventually reinforce in the long term the deeper currents which would eventually lead to the almost entirely secular drift of Europe's diplomatic practices. Richelieu had entered the battlefield with the *Summa* of St Thomas in his knapsack. In the event, and in retrospect, however, he would appear as the progenitor of *Realpolitik*; what has to be dismissed as a manifest nonsense at the time becomes, in retrospect, a reality. So, from 1626, French subsidies went to the army of Ernest of Mansfeld, the ally and coreligionist of Christian IV, King of Denmark, during the first (so-called 'Danish') phase of the German Lutheran resistance to the Austrian Habsburgs in the Empire. From January 1631, however, it was the turn of the king of Sweden, Gustav Adolf, to received subsidies from France to the tune of a million *livres tournois* a year in return for the considerable services rendered by his powerful army against the emperor Ferdinand II, the cardinal's chosen enemy. In return, the Swedish king accorded the cardinal a more or less fallacious promise to respect the Catholic religion in German lands. The cardinal regarded the game as worth the candle since Gustav was attempting in 1631 to put together a vast coalition of 'evangelical' princes. They included the Electors of Brandenburg and Saxony as well as the able mercenary leader Bernard of Saxe-Weimar. In 1632, the French invasion of the duchy of Lorraine, regarded as pro-Spanish in its sympathies, was strongly supported, or rather 'assisted', to the north by the forces of the Calvinist Dutch republic who attacked the Spanish Netherlands and created a useful division. In February 1635, Richelieu made the alliance with the Dutch official through a defensive and offensive coalition which sought to exploit the revolt in the Spanish Netherlands. France could hardly be more anti-papal in its allegiances. In 1635, and then again in 1636, the Swedish Chancellor Oxenstierna also concluded an alliance with the French which was favourable to the Protestants of Germany and which gave Sweden a substantial pension from Louis XIII.

Despite being undermined, if not ruined, by fiscality, France still remained during this period in global terms the richest European country, able to sustain being bled white in order to transfuse sufficient resources to mercenaries abroad. For Richelieu, traumatized by the defeat of the Swedish and Lutheran forces at Nördlingen (6 September 1634), to assist the Protestants became a critical matter for the French state. The logic which led him to declare war upon Spain in May 1635 was ineluctable; for, summarizing what the cardinal wrote on 11 September 1635, 'to let the Protestant party of Germany be destroyed would be to allow the Holy Roman Emperor and Spain in due course to direct all their forces against France. To assist the Protestants, so battered by the Nördlingen defeat, required offering them immediate and material assistance, and the hopes of more to come from a power of renown.'[45] At the same time, in the spring of 1635, Rohan, the veteran Protestant of the Cévenol campaigns against

---

[45] The full text, drawn up by Richelieu, and cited by G. Pagès in *La Guerre de Trente Ans* (Paris, Payot, 1939), p. 204, is as follows: 'Il est certain que si le parti [*i.e. the Protestants*] est tout à fait ruiné, l'effort de la puissance de [*la*] Maison d'Autriche tombera sur la France. Il est certain encore qu'après l'échec arrivé depuis peu, le Parti ne peut subsister, s'il n'est soutenu d'un secours présent et notable, et d'une espérance plus grande, et d'un nom puissant, étant certain que, sans un tel secours, toutes les villes impériales se débanderont, Saxe fera son accord et chacun pensera à ses affaires par des voies qui rendront bientôt ce grand parti une seule ombre de ce qu'il aura été . . . Il est certain encore que le pire conseil que la France puisse prendre est de se conduire en sorte qu'elle puisse demeurer seule à supporter l'effort de l'Empereur et de l'Espagne.'

the cardinal, rallied to his call to arms in the name of national unity and was despatched to the Valtelline with a force of 12,000 to block it off from the Spanish forces massing in the Milanais. To the north, at the end of May 1635, the royal troops, having defeated the forces of the Cardinal-Infant,[46] joined with the Dutch army near Maastricht only to find themselves feebly marching back to France in September. On the eastern front, the army of the Cardinal de la Valette (from the Epernon family) collaborated without difficulty, but also without great success, with the troops of Bernard of Saxe-Weimar to take the war to the duchy of Lorraine. In October 1635, the French exchequer even agreed to the financing of the army of Bernard of Saxe-Weimar along with that of Sweden since the Swedes no longer had the capacity to fund it themselves with their own subsidies.

In 1636, there would be many similar cross-confessional contacts and although they did not end in tears, they left a bitter taste in the mouth. This was the year when the Protestant Dutch under the Stadtholder Frederick Henry danced to the cardinal's tune. The latter, anxious about the military situation which was hardly favourable to France, encouraged Louis XIII to make his famous vow to the Virgin Mary to intercede for divine assistance to aid him. With Calvinists in one hand and the Virgin in the other, Richelieu was clearly taking no risks! The Emperor Leopold would act in exactly the same fashion in 1687–8 when he would call upon his friends in the Vatican as well as Lutheran Germany against the Bourbon monarchy; so the cardinal would not be the only 'papist' to rely upon Protestant assistance in this fashion. On several occasions the Spain of Olivares had also had recourse to subsidies towards or alliances with the Huguenots of the duke of Rohan (during the Cévennes campaign) against Louis XIII, or with the Swiss Protestants of the Grisons. The response of feigned shock which greeted the spectacle of the 'heretical' links of the cardinal from some orthodox Catholics thus needs to be placed in perspective.

Despite a good deal of clever footwork, the French position in the war would only be reinforced slowly. In 1636, it found itself in the classic position of a large state at the beginning of a large-scale war for which it had hardly begun to mobilize its resources. Beyond that, it also suffered from the disadvantage of fighting adversaries whose forces, albeit strategically weaker than those of France, were better prepared and battle-trained by the campaigns which they had already fought. Rectifying this imbalance would require time. Profiting from this temporary advantage, the Spanish penetrated as far as Corbie in April 1636, thus menacing the French capital. This incursion was brought to an abrupt halt thanks to the patriotic response of the Parisians who provided both money and partly the men too with which to put a defending army into the field. The Parisian

---

[46] Ferdinand of Austria, Cardinal-Infant of Spain, was a younger son of Philip II. Born in 1609, he arrived in the Low Countries in 1634 at the head of a Spanish army.

response is psychologically interesting. Half a century earlier, its inhabitants had taken up arms not against Spain but on its behalf, led on to do so by the integrist preachers who pontificated in the name of the pro-Spanish League. By the 1630s, Parisian loyalties had returned to supporting the patriot cause and, after a brief interlude, Richelieu's popularity survived intact at this crucial moment amongst the crowds assembled on the Pont Neuf. Taking into account the changed climate and the retreat from the League radicalism, the cardinal had nevertheless displayed great ability during the previous decade and it was during this critical juncture that he would find his reward. Richelieu knew exactly how to place himself at the centre of the political forces through which he would be able to mobilize the moral and material resources which he would require. Having struck a blow to his 'left' during the siege of La Rochelle, he had clearly demonstrated his determination to smash the spinal column of the military forces of the Protestants (but not to break the Protestants' necks, in contrast with Louis XIV). He could then, relying on the broad mass of Catholic support, strike to his 'right' with all the aggression which it would need against the ultra-Catholic pretensions of the Habsburgs. One historian whose habitual inspiration had deserted him, concluded his biography of the cardinal with the unfortunate expression, 'We see in Richelieu the perfect incarnation of the average Frenchman.'[47] Yet the phrase contains a grain of truth in it; Richelieu was very far from being an average Frenchman but he did put himself at the centre, at the summit, and this dominant position he was able to exploit with determination and talent.

On its own, however, it would not have sufficed merely for Richelieu to have enjoyed a measure of support within France. If he was able to weather the storm of 1636 it was also because the 'heretic' prince of Orange was prepared to respond favourably to the cardinal's proposition and to open up a further war-front to the rear of the Cardinal-Infant upon the Dutch frontier of the Spanish Netherlands. He thus forced the Spanish prelate to scuttle back to Brussels to repel such an attack. In 1637, the defection of the Protestant Grisons in the Valtelline dangerously exposed the local presence of French forces there, and particularly the Protestant general Rohan. But, at the same time, and by way of compensation for Richelieu, a combined Dutch and French operation in the Spanish Netherlands brought the two allies the twin successes of Landrecies and Breda. This campaign also marked the first spectacular success of the young Huguenot military commander Turenne amongst the ranks of the French forces. Like the elderly Lesdiguières before him, it would take a long time, 30 years to be precise, before he was persuaded finally to convert to Catholicism.

It would be easy to rehearse a good many more franco-Protestant joint operations. In the course of the following years, Richelieu would play his alliances with great ability. Sometimes it was Bernard of Saxe-Weimar,

---

[47]   Michel Carmona, *Richelieu, l'ambition et le pouvoir* (Paris, Fayard, 1983), pp. 156–7.

through whose efforts Breisach was captured in 1638. Sometimes it was in conjunction with the Dutch, who claimed a victory over the Spanish fleet off Dover and who would renew their alliance with France at the beginning of 1640. At other times it was with the Swedes who again directed their forces towards the heart of Germany. The initial military reverses were thus overcome. The final victory of Condé at Rocroi in 1643, a year after Richelieu's death, was merely the well-earned reward for a long succession of well-coordinated military campaigns. They were conducted on the basis of a common front with Western European Protestantism directed against the Habsburgs. The cardinal who had appeared almost baroque at the siege of La Rochelle had thus become transformed into the Huguenot hero of the hour in the international arena. The evolution was somewhat bizarre but it also contained a degree of logical progression.

$$\star \quad \star \quad \star \quad \star \quad \star$$

The third essential element in the politics of Henry IV was his encouragement to economic prosperity. The increase in production and commerce after the definitive end to the religious wars in 1595 had inevitably occurred to a degree of its own accord as a simple consequence of recuperation and economic recovery[48] during the first 15 to 20 years of the seventeenth century, both before and after the death of the first Bourbon king. The favourable measures which Sully had promulgated in this respect were, taken on their own and in conjunction with the limited capacities for intervention in economic matters in the hands of those in power, fairly feeble. His efforts might be seen as a kind of supportive homeopathy for this global organism with a population of 20 million which was manifestly becoming more robust. The symbolic effect of these measures was, nevertheless, considerable. They served as an example to be copied in the future.

The political economy of Richelieu (after the interregnum of Marie de Médicis who had little understanding of such problems) should be seen above all as the continuation of that of Henry IV and Sully. To that of the cardinal, however, should be added a touch of warlike aggression and maritime enthusiasm which were not present to the same degree amongst the policies of the two 'model' statesmen of the beginning of the century. As Jean Eon has suggested,[49] 'exploring the utilitarian benefits of trade through his admirable strength of mind' the cardinal sought to set himself certain politico-commercial objectives such as 'to drive pirates from our coasts, extend our frontiers, defend our allies . . . deliver the final blow

---

[48] To which was added the fortunate conjuncture of an increase in silver from Potosi in France in the course of the later 10 to 15 years of Henry IV's reign. See E. Le Roy Ladurie, J.N. Barrabdon, B. Bollins, M. Guerra and C. Morrison, 'Sur les traces de l'argent du Potosi', *Annales ESC*, 45 (1990), 493–5.

[49] Cited by Henri Hauser, *La Pensée et l'action économique du cardinal de Richelieu* (Paris, PUF, 1944), p. 47.

against heresy [La Rochelle]' and finally, having (at least in his mind) won all the necessary military victories, to 'procure an advantageous peace for France and give it the true means by which it could rest content in every respect which was by establishing good and strong companies for the sustenance of trade and navigation'. Peace, repose, contentment, in short, the common good . . . who could refuse to accept such a programme, realized through the creation of effective trading companies! In this respect, Richelieu was very much in the tradition of Sully and the precursor of Colbert. National prosperity was, for Richelieu, a goal but it was also (and above all) a means since by this means the royal treasury would be replenished thanks to the increased revenues which would ensue.

In these texts Richelieu returned to the concept of a 'magic square' or 'protective tetragram'[50] which summarized the structure of thought which, rightly or wrongly, has been called mercantilist. Primary products should be allowed free entry to France and their export should be prohibited. For manufactured goods it was the reverse; their importation should be prohibited and their export encouraged. This was in order to secure a favourable balance of trade since such regulation encouraged the importation of cheap primary goods and the exportation of manufactured goods with a greater added value. In a crude fashion it is not difficult to find the same conceptions of 'political economy' (a term which had been popularized in 1615 by Antoine de Montchrestien)[51] reflected amongst others in the French political élite. Such views are, in reality, to be found amongst the deliberations of the Estates General of 1614 and the assembly of notables of 1626–7. The latter had been thoroughly informed on the problem through a text prepared by Michel de Marillac who was still on close terms at that date with Richelieu. The 'code Michau' (the great royal ordinance prepared by Marillac in 1629) gave such notions official blessing. In particular, it envisaged the creation of a monopoly of French trade in ships which were exclusively of French origin in order to favour economically the French components of its foreign trade. The same political objectives were effectively pursued by Cromwell's England in 1651.

For the rest, it was the 'naval' aspect which marked out Richelieu from Sully, whose horizons were more limited. For his part, the cardinal had a broader perspective and sought to develop a French navy with a twin military and civilian purpose. Up to this period, the French navy had been significant only for its insignificance, despite its strategic possibilities. The realization of his objectives, however, was very far from being outstanding. Having been full of enthusiasms at the beginning, Richelieu was a strong supporter of the development of trading links and a territorial presence in the Atlantic. Despite the best of intentions, however, it was not long before he inflicted huge damage upon the metropolis of French commercial activity in the Atlantic by starving and humiliating La Rochelle into

50 Ibid.
51 *Traité de l'économie politique, dédié au Roy et à la Royne Mère du Roy*, n.p.n.d. [1615].

submission in 1628. Did the right hand know what the left hand was doing? One has to conclude that in the last resort the cardinal's politico-religious strategy took precedence over his more purely mercantilist objectives.

In consequence, and setting aside the regional case of La Rochelle, the high cost of the territorial campaigns against the Habsburgs during the 1630s ('covert' war, followed by 'open' hostilities) constrained the cardinal to put strict limits upon the overseas investment which at the beginning of his government he had hoped massively to expand. There was something to show by way of results, however, in the Antilles, Martinique, Guadeloupe and Dominica. Thanks to the activities of the planters in growing cotton, tobacco and sugar cane (encouraged by the rapidly expanding European demand), the French population (both of slaves and non-slaves) reached some 7,000 in 1642–3. In the case of Quebec, there were hardly more than 300 inhabitants of French origin there at about the same time – scarcely more than the population of a large village back home in France.[52] This statistic serves to give some perspective (even allowing for the significance it would have for the future) to the more romantic ways in which the exploits of the soldiers, colonists, explorers and fur-trappers of French origin who peopled the banks of the St Lawrence seaway have been viewed. Elsewhere, in Africa and Asia, there was little or nothing to show from the efforts of the commercial companies established with the cardinal's blessing.

Hence the temptation among some otherwise admirable historians[53] to view these exploits as nothing more than a smoke-screen with which to mask the ways by which the cardinal sought to enrich himself. As regards the latter, Richelieu certainly wasted no time. He swiftly divested some of the greater nobility (Montmorency, Guise . . .) of their titles to the sought-after posts in the admiralty[54] and appropriated them to himself. To these were added other offices, benefices and maritime profits associated with numerous French 'havens' and ports, mainly along the Atlantic coast, to a lesser extent in the Mediterranean.

In the course of the exceptionally profitable last years of the decade of the 1630s, these possessions and offices were returning to Richelieu's own treasury an annual income of at least 200,000 *livres*.[55] This maritime portfolio was second only to the financial returns from ecclesiastical sources in its importance as a source for Richelieu's fortune. It would be wrong, however, to equate the maritime interests of the cardinal simply to the question of Richelieu's personal gain or 'financial advantage', as one might conclude from a hasty reading of the recent work of the historian

[52] Jean Hamelin, *Histoire du Québec* (Toulouse, Privat, 1976), p. 21.
[53] Joseph Bergin, *Cardinal Richelieu. Power and the Pursuit of Wealth* (New Haven and London, Yale University Press, 1985).
[54] This meant, in essence, sitting in judgement on disputes occurring at sea and in the respective sea-ports.
[55] Joseph Bergin, *Cardinal Richelieu*, 7, p. 243 *et seq.*

Joseph Bergin. For the facts are incontestable and speak for themselves and they show us a statesman with an overall naval policy which lay beyond his lively passion for his own fortune.

From 1630, in reality, the size of the French navy, reconstituted from almost nothing, would be at least 40 ships. All that was lacking was logistical support such as well-equipped ports, supplies, and a skilled labour force on land.[56] The maritime tradition of the French state had begun afresh, and thereafter it would have an uninterrupted history to the present day. In the end, the mercantilist dreams of the cardinal, which were reduced to ashes as a result of foreign warfare and the fiscal disorder which it brought in its wake, were only realized principally in those areas which contributed to the war effort, and particularly the establishment of a combat navy. To these areas, 'honourable commerce', although it was not frowned on, took second place.[57]

Almost the entire history of Richelieu can be written around the financial equivalent of the eating disorder, bulimia. His reputation is inextricably linked to the inexorable logic of taxation, the generator in France, as elsewhere, of the modern state. The state-building process was determined by the financially crippling wars with their vast appetites for centralization and for increased taxation. It was also, however, the result of other independent, endogenetic processes such as the irresistible gravitational pull in Europe towards the creation of the major European powers and the progressive subjection by them of the weaker territorial components. The major powers gradually expanded, absorbed and coalesced in an irreversible process. Such processes have to be seen as having an ineluctable global force, the consequences of which would have occurred with or without Richelieu. But Richelieu did not waste his strengths in trying to stop the pace of change; rather, he worked with it, spurring it on when the occasion seemed to require it. Richelieu might readily have echoed Clemenceau when he said: 'I *wage* war.' To a greater extent than Clemenceau, however, he allowed himself the means to turn this elementary statement into a reality.

The fiscal and financial pressures mounted rapidly during the three years from 1632 to 1635. The first summit was quickly reached and, during the years which followed, this was where fiscality remained for some time. Before 1632, the revenues of the monarchy were invariably below 50 million *livres*, sometimes by a generous margin. After that date, they climbed to 60, 120, even 200 million *livres*. The same also held good for the secret expenses. These were around 10 million before 1631 and two or three times that figure thereafter. Extraordinary expenditures were around 10–11 million in the year from 1607 to 1633. In 1634, they had risen to 67 million, 157 million in 1635, and then settled at around 40 million a year thereafter.[58] One could go on illustrating the impact of the

---

[56] This according to information kindly supplied by Daniel Dessert.

[57] Hauser, *La Pensée et l'action économique du cardinal de Richelieu*, p. 25 *et seq.*

[58] All these figures are taken from Richard Bonney, *The King's Debts. Finance and Politics in France, 1624–1661* (Oxford, Clarendon Press, 1981) – the statistical tables *in fine.*

increase in fiscality during this period. Richelieu (like Louis XI before him) discovered that France had been under-taxed and found that it could pay; he exploited the fact up to, and beyond, the limits. Subsidies were fed through to the Dutch and the Swedes; the much heavier burden of the costs of the French army campaigns were met. The huge fortunes accumulated by the treasurers were acquired on the side from the receipts into the royal exchequer, some of which they filched. The Superintendent of Finances Bullion would leave 8 million *livres* behind him; the Chancellor Séguier 4 millions. As for Richelieu himself. . . . It became normal to anticipate the state's revenues by one or two years in advance; a 'slash and burn' fiscality.

Recent historiography has sought to demonstrate that the politics of rapidly rising fiscality, such as that put in place by Richelieu, brought in its wake a strong popular reaction which involved uprisings and even peasant wars against taxes.[59] Peasant uprisings against the collection of direct taxes as well as the farming of indirect taxes such as the *gabelles*, *traites*, *aides* etc. broke out in many localities during the cardinal's ministry. Other popular movements were directed against the movement of troops and particularly against their forced billeting upon particular localities. There was a lively fear of the ravages, rape and pillage inflicted upon civilians by the soldiery from which they sought to protect themselves by preventing the troops from entering their streets and houses. The most spectacular insurrections took place in the south-west where the Croquants deeply disturbed Richelieu. The research of Richard Bonney,[60] however, has demonstrated nevertheless that the hostile reaction to taxation, which often took the form of an aggressive dislike of the state, was not the prerogative of the south of France, still less of Aquitaine alone. The same reactions can be discovered also, albeit more discreetly expressed, in Picardy, Berry, the Touraine, the Orléanais and in Champagne both during the ministries of Richelieu and Mazarin. The contribution from northern France to this movement was as widespread, although less intense, than in southern France. The pre-Fronde disturbances were spread out throughout France; in this respect they were remarkably similar to the pre-revolutionary agitation which would occur a century and a half later.

The fisco-financial pressures and the discontents which they created are inseparable from the career of Richelieu himself, whose fortune was essentially based upon the rise in taxation which was out of all proportion with what had happened in the past and which his authoritarian measures had helped to sustain. The cardinal collected his share – a tithe here, a money payment there – and invested part of it in land. In this fashion he constructed the wealthiest fortune in France – 20 million *livres*, three times the size of Sully's, almost double that of Marie de Médicis herself. Richelieu

---

[59] B. Porchnev, *Les Soulèvements populaires en France de 1623 à 1648* (Paris, SEVPEN, 1963). R. Mousnier, 'Recherches sur les soulèvements populaires en France avant la Fronde', *Revue d'histoire moderne et contemporaine*, 4 (1958), 81–113.
[60] Richard Bonney, *Political Change in France under Richelieu and Mazarin, 1624–1661* (Oxford, Clarendon Press, 1978), ch. 10.

Plate 4   The beggars   Sébastien Bourdon, a Protestant painter from Montpellier, studied in Italy before making his way to Paris in 1638 at the age of 22 to begin a successful career as a painter. This is a detail from one of his paintings, now in the Louvre. It reveals the influences of the Italian/Dutch school of Van Laer and the French school of the Le Nain brothers on his work. It also reflects some of the characteristics of the period when it was painted in his earlier years in Paris – the problems of fiscality and the impact of war. This fragment depicts beggars in the wake of a carriage of the well-to-do.

Paris, Musée du Louvre

had to move with the times; to maintain his rank – for a first minister must also be a grandee, and possibly even a super-grandee – he needed a fortune which more than matched a duke and peer's, dwarfed that of a mere financier. Only Mazarin with his 38 million *livres* would fare better than his predecessor.[61]

The cardinal was a shrewd investor. He provides an example of the now classic proposition that land but also, more surprisingly, silver and gold (whether in money form or not) belonged above all to the élite groups of the period (nobility, clergy, office-holders) and not to an entrepreneurial bourgeoisie or merchant capitalist class which, in reality, at this date remained in the formative stage of its career. But there were many aspects to Richelieu; he might be compared with the millionaires of the twentieth century who combined immense fortunes with stinginess. Richelieu also played the part of a minor provincial gentleman who, by means of his own shrewdness and intrigue, had finally arrived at the summit of the noble hierarchy. He was a Rothschild and a Rastignac rolled into one. But there was never a hint of the Robespierre in him. He never sought to destroy the noble order whose system of values he completely shared. He merely wanted to see the nobility brought under greater discipline. This erstwhile insignificant prelate eventually rose to become a prince of the church. He united in himself various important and diverse drives; an almost over-whelming sense of sovereignty, the preeminent churchman, noble virtue, the individual with vast lands and huge fortune, all of which were to be carried ever forward by constant endeavour. To find any comparison for this extraordinary career, we should perhaps look to some of the im-mensely wealthy heads of state in the twentieth century. But for the most part they turn out to be, like Goergin or Marcos, repulsive monsters. In the seventeenth century, the model statesman who made his fortune in serving the king kept within certain limits which were honoured more in the breach. In this respect, Sully, Richelieu, Mazarin, Colbert, all of whom made their fortunes to varying degrees, were exceptional and this was broadly accepted apart from a few inveterate critics.

In its exhaustive detail, the inventory of the cardinal's wealth (i.e. 20 million *livres*, accumulated on the strength of an initial fortune which was held to be extremely slender) on his death can be broken down by value broadly as follows: 25 per cent in land, 20 per cent in money; and the rest in public offices, provincial governorships and investments in alienated royal domain, houses and moveables and government debts etc.[62] His main sources of revenue came from his ecclesiastical benefices, from the maritime sector, the royal domain and from his landed investments. De-spite the lengthy law-suits over the succession after his death, the family –

---

[61]   Françoise Bayard, *Le Monde des financiers au XVIIe siècle* (Paris, Flammarion, 1988), p. 416. Richelieu thus acquired the equivalent of 20 million *livres*, and Mazarin almost double that sum. The *fermiers*, *financiers* and *fermiers généraux* were worth less than a million *livres* although one of them was worth two million.

[62]   Joseph Bergin, *Cardinal Richelieu*, p. 248 *et seq.* and *passim*.

the heirs of his nieces and nephews, Richelieu's relatives – continued to cut a substantial figure in France through to the Revolution. There would be a *maréchal-duc* Richelieu and a *ministre-duc* d'Aiguillon etc. It was almost as if the cardinal knew that to establish a lineage and its landed base you had to lay the foundations with a view to the very long-term future.

In Richelieu's lifetime, his financial collaborators were chosen to form a highly prestigious team. They included a prelate with a naval and noble background (Sourdis), a distinguished figure from the higher ranks of the *noblesse de robe* (Nicolas Colbert, the father to the minister), some pure commoners (Le Masle) and some Huguenot financiers (the Tallemant). The group exalted and magnified their lord and master. It is not everyone who can claim the privilege of having hired the Colbert, the Sourdis or the Tallemants to manage their financial affairs.

The financial tourniquet which began to be applied from 1634–5, which had no comparison since the days of Louis XI, created a problem for the state's exchequer as well as for the cardinal. According to the erudite historian Françoise Bayard, the royal treasury acted as the 'pump' for between a third and half of all the money in circulation within France, sucking it in and then circulating it out, recycling the money which the Treasury collected.[63] The effort which an operation on this scale required was impressive, and particularly in a realm which is often presented, and without much exaggeration, as a mosaic of local autonomies. There are other statistics which are equally striking. The budget of the French state during this period of 'war-finance' would be the equivalent in value to over a fifth of the total grain production of France and more than an eighth of the estimated gross national product.[64] To be able to mobilize such a huge volume of precious metal was no small affair, and particularly when the munitioners of the state and its creditors required to be paid in cash – in gold or silver coins. They were suspicious of paper transactions and they were right to be so. The financiers were a socio-economic (or perhaps socio-political) grouping composed of no more than 4,000 specialists, whose main function was to collect the revenues at a time when the state needed them urgently. Any failure on their part brought with it inevitable consequences; it was during Richelieu's ministry that an entire army would disband having not received its pay within the given time.

These thousands of financiers did not belong *as such* to the world of the office-holders, although many of them were the sons of office-holders, or themselves had purchased an office (generally in the financial administration, since this favoured their operations). As financiers, however, they simply acted as private individuals, in exactly the same way as their successors in the nineteenth century would do, save that the latter became involved in all sorts of business enterprises which, for the most part, did not involve the state. The 4,000 financiers of the seventeenth century, on the other hand, acted as agents for the state alone, uniquely for the king and his agents. The private financiers of the seventeenth century – those who were employed outside the state sector, were termed 'bankers' or 'merchant-bankers'. The financiers who were servants of the state were termed 'projectors'[65] because they presented the state with proposed ventures in return for a percentage of the receipts generated or hidden source of revenues accounted for by the Exchequer. Thus there were projects for a new way of selling salt, for the sale of offices for the payment of wages to the *trésoriers de France*; or a projector might offer to take up the farm of indirect taxes on which they take a reduced profit and offer to pay the king the difference as the sovereign to whom all taxes should theoretically be paid, whether from *gabelles, aides*, etc.

Other financiers acted as *traitants*; they operated in an *ad hoc* fashion in accordance with a particular 'treaty' which they had negotiated with the king's Council. Through these arrangements they became responsible for the levy of the *tailles* in a particular region, or for a loan, or for a tax on some individual offices, etc. There was a particularly large number of substantial deals struck during the years from 1630 to 1646. They characterized the years of crypto-war, and then of open warfare during which the state had recourse to whatever expedient it could find to raise liquid cash and by a variety of routes.

Amongst the same large group there were also *prêteurs*.[66] They advanced huge sums to the state in order, for example, to pay for the subventions to the Swedish and Dutch allies of Louis XIII or to build up the navy. They would be reimbursed, with the king's permission, in due course upon a specified regional or national revenue stream (the *aides de France*, the *gabelles* of Languedoc . . .). This arrangement spent the revenues of the state in advance of their receipt which merely increased the eventual deficit still further.

These financiers, mainly of French origin, had taken over from the Italian bankers of Lyon and other foreigners who, 85 years previously, had financed the Valois campaigns. They also included a certain number of Huguenots although, after 1630, they were increasingly drawn towards the *dévot* currents of the Catholic reformation. They were all rich but, albeit with some exceptions, they were not amongst the very rich. Their origins were often lowly, sometimes fairly modest; so they took it upon themselves to acquire letters of personal nobility as a step towards hereditary nobility. Such social ascension rendered them detested, sometimes discriminated against. Yet they were as essential to the functioning of the monarchical system as the royal armies. They provided the means whereby it could function efficiently and thus overawe its neighbours.

For Richelieu, the objectives of power remained traditionally the same: to maintain royal service, including military service, to govern with justice

[65] I.e. 'donneurs d'avis'.
[66] Bayard, *Le Monde des financiers au XVIIe siècle*, p. 228 *et seq.*

and order, to keep the peace if possible, to maintain internal harmony, all in the name of the state, an artifical abstraction. The means to achieve these ends was, above all, a vastly increased military force. Therein lay the essence of a renewal, or at least a profound change, in the state. Taxation 'for the war' was much more burdensome than before and, of necessity, inflicted damage upon the economy of the realm. This taxation sustained the militarized state as well as the country's élite with a cardinal at its head who was a millionaire 20 times over. The resulting centralization was very far from removing or suppressing local initiatives, whatever Tocqueville may have claimed two centuries later and with some exaggeration. The nobility of the Cotentin, however, were not wrong to feel the burdens as 'heavy'. Centralization and, with it, absolutism, took shape in a noticeable way from around the period 1630 to 1635 at the same time as the institution of the *commissaires départis* or 'intendants' became more widespread alongside the increase in taxation and the accompanying wartime pressures.[67]

The monarchy had sent such individuals into the province for over a century. But until the entry of France into the Thirty Years War, first by stealth and then by storm, they had only been employed in a minority of provinces. After 1635, by contrast, they were to be sent for the first time throughout the kingdom to be the eyes and ears of the regime. They were delegated by the cardinal and given the responsibility of overseeing the collection of taxes and the repression of antifiscal rebellion. They were to use judicial means generally, but there could be a recourse to military force if it proved necessary. The intendants bore witness to the centralizing direction of the French state.[68] Violence is not always the harbinger of change but the Thirty Years War certainly gave birth to the administrative monarchy in France and it provided the opportunity for the cardinal to recruit the individuals who would be the intendants from amongst the stable of the *noblesse de robe*, which was still called the *noblesse de dignité* in contrast with the nobility which saw itself as *noblesse d'épée*, of gentility and ancient extraction, whom the state saw fit to command on the battlefield and be killed there.

By selecting the state's agents in this fashion, Richelieu followed in the pattern of his predecessors; he merely had a larger number to find than

---

[67] For the slightly later period, one must have recourse to the great work of Anette Smedley-Weill, *Correspondance des intendants avec le contrôleur-général des finances (1677–1689). Naissance d'une administration* [Sous-série G7 (Archives Nationales), Inventaire analytique] (Paris, Archives Nationales, 1989).

[68] According to F-X. Emmanuelli, *L'Intendance du milieu du XVIIe siècle à la fin du XVIIe siècle* (Aix, Université de Provence and Champion, 1981) [esp. the conclusion], the intendant was a 'decentralizing' agent which made the institution rather different from the later prefects. But Emmanueli draws too heavily upon the rather special case of the intendant at Aix. Elsewhere, it is rather the classic conception of the intendant as a mediator but also a centralizer which seems to fit the case better. See, e.g., Maurice Bordes, *L'Administration provinciale et municipale en France au XVIIIe siècle* (Paris, SEDES, 1972), pp. 116–59. Cf. V.R. Gruder, *A Governing Elite in Eighteenth-Century France* (Ithaca and New York, Yale University Press, 1968).

they did. It was no longer a mere handful of commissioners that were sent out from Paris in the years after 1630–5. Instead they formed a coherent group whose size equalled or surpassed the number of regions they had to serve – which amounted to about two dozen generalities whose areas were often different in various ways from the old provinces of France. As nobles of recent origin, the intendants had not acquired their status in fighting, their sword in hand, against the enemies of the realm. In reality, they owed their nobility to their fathers and grandfather who already occupied offices in the vital judicial or financial institutions of the kingdom. Their families (and the intendants between 1624 and 1661 were chosen from around 115 families) were allied to one another and formed the kernel of a 'political class' or a group of decision-makers who saw it as their vocation to govern the country.

Whatever the arrogance or pretentions which they displayed, the intendants held, in reality, the key to the real functions of both regional and central government. They had received the necessary judicial training both in theory (as university or college students who had studied law, particularly Roman law, the handmaid of the notion of the state) and in practice. They had practical experience in their younger days as magistrates or advocates. The nobility of older lineage, ensconced in their noble domains or in their regiments, could not aspire to such professional competence. In this respect, the French situation differed from the English experience. In England, the nobility, broadly speaking, never surrendered political authority, whether in or outside Parliament. They were often prepared for their official and civil duties by several years of legal training at the Inns of Court in London following on from a degree at Oxford or Cambridge. They paid taxes and they saw themselves as responsible for the state.

The first stage in the process of becoming an intendant[69] was to become one of the 'masters of requests'.[70] There is something extraordinary about the survival of this remarkable group. In the distant medieval past they had transmitted to the sovereign, as their name implied, the petitions of his subjects; hence their presence as *rapporteurs* in the councils of state. They are to be found there today, still with the same name, protected amidst the *Ecole Nationale d'Administration*. From 1624 to 1642, the masters of requests were one of the major adjuncts of the imperialist and protean aspects of the Richelieu régime. Before acquiring the title, the masters of requests had often held an office in the sovereign courts (particularly the Parlement of Paris; then, later on, the *Grand Conseil* or the provincial parlements or the *Cour des comptes* or the *Cour des aides*). They were experienced and, of necessity, rich (their offices were bought and sold for 150,000 *livres* each).[71] They came from the good schools and they had the

---

[69] See Bonney, *Political Change in France*.

[70] *Maîtres des requêtes.*

[71] Such wealth was of use to them since the salaries of intendants were often paid in arrears, if at all. They did not, unlike Richelieu or Mazarin, derive a profit from their service.

right sort of financial security. Their background (which was more judicial than that of the Prefects of present-day France whose background is more in the executive parts of the state) readily led them towards presiding over a provincial law-court, conducting an enquiry in a distant province, and receiving commissions to carry out on behalf of the king. They were thus well prepared for the varied tasks required of an intendant. Their ultimate goal was to enter into the councils of government and they therefore associated themselves during their careers with the '*robins* serving on Council' who shunned, and in turn were shunned by, the *robins* in Parlement. 'The masters of requests are as the desires of the heart; they aspire to be so secret that they do not exist.' In a successful career, the mastership of requests was only a stage in a career which was often curtailed. They became successively (or at least this was what they aimed for and what motivated them) councillors in the Parlement, masters of requests, intendants or commissioners in a generality and then finally councillors of state and, in the most fortunate cases, secretaries of state, ministers, keepers of the Seals, or even the chancellor himself!

One might thus, using modern bureaucratic parlance, speak of the 'pyramid' structure of their career options in government; the path to the top was certainly not, like a cylinder, straight-sided and roundly distributed. In reality, many of the masters of requests fell by the wayside, or remained in the lower echelons of the group. Only a small handful, for obvious reasons, made it to the top. In the despatch of their duties in the provinces, the intendants often displayed an acute sense of the sovereignty of the king and the state, and one of their number, Cardin Le Bret, a latter-day Bodin and an expert in both the theory and practice of intendancy, presented such notions as axiomatic.[72] His starting-point was a pessimistic view of the nature of sinful man who needed to be shown how to behave well and not abuse his freedom of choice. This should guide the actions of the intendants as they approach their tasks and seek to justify their actions. When faced with a choice between the privileges and proprietorial rights of subjects on the one hand and the strategic and political imperatives of the state on the other, they readily opted for the latter, particularly when, as during the years after 1630–5, France found itself on a war-footing and in a 'state of emergency', many of the aspects of which would subsequently become the normal state of affairs, even during peacetime, under Louis XIV.

It is significant that it was after the period 1628–35 that many of the intendants acquired the powers to supervise not merely 'justice' and 'finance' (which almost went without saying) but also 'police' (i.e. 'administration'). This configuration of the administrative age (1653–1789) seems so elementary to us. Yet the triptych of functions ('justice', 'finance' and 'police') took shape in a dramatic fashion after 1630 amidst the

---

[72] Cardin Le Bret, *De la Souveraineté du Roy* (Paris, 1632).

thunderclaps of the 'great storm' which was the prelude to a hardening of political attitudes around the cardinal which would become enduring and which coincided with the consecration of an absolutism which would be announced with a fanfare of warlike trumpets.

In financial matters, the intendants were more and more given the task of repartitioning the tax burden after 1637–42. They acted as substitutes for the office-holders who had specialized in this task. These were the treasurers of France (in reality, responsible for the accounts) in each generality and the *élus* (who were responsible for judicial decisions relating to the *tailles*) in the *élections* (the areas of jurisdiction below the generalities). These two categories of office-holder, the treasurers and the *élus*, were more or less up to the task in peacetime but inadequate to run a system of war-finance. Hence the establishment or proliferation of intendants who were more efficient. They would continue to be in place, even after the war and beyond 1659.

When it came to the more classic question of the relationship between the intendants (and Richelieu) and the provincial governors, the position was ambiguous. Several intendants were put in place to counteract the influence of the local governor (for example in Brittany against the troublesome Vendôme). Others, on the other hand, became practically the right-hand men of the governors. As regards the latter, the cardinal had frustrated the ambitions of some of them (d'Epernon) and decapitated those who stood in his way (Montmorency). He was content to make use of those who, like the elder Condé,[73] were prepared (albeit after some hesitation) to rally obediently to the royal banner. Once again, there was no intention of destroying the higher nobility (no more than there was of eliminating the Huguenots) but of domesticating them. The racehorses had to be trained, not sent to the knackers' yard or put out to graze.

The same approach, more subtle than has been appreciated, governed the attitude of the twin cardinalcy (Richelieu, then Mazarin) to the provincial estates. Although the latter evidently constrained monarchical sovereignty they nevertheless had their uses providing they agreed loyally to raise the taxes required of them by the state. 'The estates of Normandy and Dauphiné disappeared for good at the juncture but those of Brittany, Burgundy and Languedoc survived and even prospered.'[74] In Languedoc, this was despite the severe crisis provoked by Montmorency's rebellion in 1632. In this area, as in others, Richelieu exploited his capacity for 'organizational empiricism'. The examples of Normandy and Dauphiné, on the other hand, where the estates were suppressed, demonstrated that in those provinces, and elsewhere, there was a progression towards a certain absolutism.

[73] I.e. Henri II de Bourbon, Prince of Condé (1588–1646) and the father of the Great Condé.

[74] Bonney, *Political Change in France*, p. 382.

The cardinal's authority was also reflected in the entourage of half-servants, half-ministers around him. These included, institutionally, the chancellor, often supplemented by the Keeper of the Seals as well as the four secretaries of state who were at the head, so to say, of the embryonic ministerial departments of war, finance and foreign affairs. The superintendent of finances prepared the budgets, supervised the officers of accounts and authorized expenditures. The intendants of finance were roughly the equivalent of the under-secretaries of state at the Treasury today. The office-holding *robe* (Bullion, Sublet and the Bouthilliers) and the clerical *robe* (*père* Joseph, Mazarin) were preeminent in the *Conseil d'en haut*, the supreme governing council of the state. The *noblesse de race* were notable by their absence and, in Paris, their role was formal and they were there merely to put in an appearance. Where they had a useful part to play was in the armies and the government of the provinces. Considered *en bloc* the true blue blood of the 'authentic' aristocracy counted for less in the state than the half-blue blood of the *robe* in council and office. Amongst the latter, those of proven competence included a Bullion as Superintendent of Finance, who enriched himself by taking his portion from the king's coffers, with the indulgent approbation of the cardinal, himself a goldsmith.[75] The Bouthilliers came from a family of advocates who had family connection since the sixteenth century with the maternal ancestors of Richelieu. Sublet des Noyers became a Secretary of State for War after a career in state finance – pen and purse at the same time. He was as sharp as mustard, capable of dictating 18,000 letters in the space of seven years. He manipulated the marshals of France like a military operation – there was something of a Louvois in him. In 1635 the realm entered into a fully fledged war without sufficient preparation.[76] Sublet's task was to rectify the situation. He was partly responsible for the beginnings of the strategy and the construction of an armed force which would assure the French victories after 1640. Of these various individuals, Claude de Bullion was one of the most representative. Loyal to Richelieu, involved up to his neck in the wartime economy, the inventor of the Louis d'Or coin, he would leave behind him when he died in 1640 a fortune worth over 8 million *livres tournois*. Thanks to the war situation, this office-holder had become a 'man of substance' (financially speaking) and also a man of discernment since

[75] Cf. Jean-Pierre Labatut, 'La Fortune de Bullion', *XVIIe Siècle*, 60 (1963), 11–39.
[76] According to Bonney, *The King's Debts*, p. 173, the French army was composed of 9,500 cavalry and 115,000 foot at a cost of 27 million *livres* a year in 1634–5 – but the figures for the size of the army are debatable. A slightly higher estimate in 1635 gives 12,250 cavalry and 132,000 foot. A still higher estimate for 1636 would give figures of 27,000 cavalry and 172,000 (?) horse. According to Bonney, this should be compared with the 300,000 men that Philip IV (of Spain) supposedly had under arms in the 1620s. It is also much less than the 300,000 or more which Louis XIV had at his disposal in around 1710 (André Corvisier, *Armées et sociétés en Europe de 1494 à 1789* (Paris, PUF), p. 126). Beyond these troops, however, Richelieu utilized the army of Bernard de Saxe-Weimar.

he was the patron of the architect Le Vau and the painters Vouet and Blancard.[77]

*   *   *   *   *

The military context is not the only one. Richelieu's contributions to France's intellectual life were far from negligible, although they were 'orientated' towards various directions.[78] In the realms of literature, or at least of manuscripts, the cardinal stimulated the reform of some of the Benedictine abbeys in France from 1626 to 1636. He thus developed the congregation at St Maur, with all the glory of having established the nursery of French archival scholarship. In this respect, the analysis of Joseph Bergin, who seeks to explain all the changes that the cardinal-minister sought to carry forward in monastic structures (and thus of St Maur) merely in terms of his usual rapacity, is too reductionist.

In the area of publishing, Richelieu established from around 1639–40, in company with Sublet des Noyers, the royal printing house. It specialized in typographical work with oriental characters and in the publication of works of divinity and the Latin classics. This was of a piece with Richelieu's personal library. A third of the collection were theological works but the rest were works in French, Hebrew verses and books in Latin. His collection of 6,000 volumes, although substantial, pales in comparison with the 50,000 volumes of the central library of the congregation of St Maur by the turn of the century. Placed at the centre of the 'Gutenberg galaxy', Richelieu had no qualms about 'bending the press' in the service of his politics and his personal reputation. In order to do this, he operated with three groups of collaborators, all of whom were either sycophants or intellectuals. The first circle embraced his close servants (Bullion, *père* Joseph . . .). A second, rather more distant from him, incorporated propagandists who were politically less committed (Péréfixe, Mathieu de Morgue, Fancan . . .). Guarding the flanks of his reputation were the cardinal's historians, a clutch of compliant, even boot-licking, writers such as Dupleix and Sorel (though the latter was a good novel-writer). By his establishment of this three-fold entourage the cardinal was taking account of the formation of the world of European letters and intellectuals. Under the impact of the Thirty Years War and other longer-term trends, the latter was a world which was abandoning

---

[77] According to Abel Poitrineau in François Bluche, *Dictionnaire du Grand Siècle* (Paris, Fayard, 1990), p. 249.

[78] See *Richelieu et le monde de l'esprit*, a catalogue of the Sorbonne exhibition (Paris, Chancellerie des Universités de Paris et Académies françaises, Imprimerie Nationale, 1985); also *Richelieu et la culture. Actes du colloque international en Sorbonne*, ed. Roland Mousnier (Paris, CNRS, 1987).

the universality of Latin in place of the vernacular languages, in particular French. Richelieu was, in any case, doing no more than following the example set by the 'crown cardinals' of the Roman church or by the leading aristocrats of his day (Condé, Orléans, Montmorency . . .), all of whom had a camarilla of clerics and intellectuals in their service.

Yet the cardinal-minister operated on a larger canvas and he could act to censor printed works which he disliked. Between 1630 and 1642 the cardinal made use of the services of his client and fellow Poitevin, the clever medic Théophraste Renaudot. Between them, they invented the French newspaper as an organ for directing the flow of information, and also disinformation. The idea of an official newspaper was perhaps in the air at the time but the *Gazette* of Renaudot provides an example of the beginning of political journalism, if not of journalism itself which, in France at least, developed alongside a state which was itself becoming more authoritarian. It would be a long time before the 'gazettes' of Paris, Lyon and Toulouse would be synonymous with a pluralist concept of liberty. The slow beginnings of the journalism of the future remained highly personalized. Richelieu and Louis XIII did not hesitate to take up their pens and write things themselves for the *Gazette* which they subsidised. Yet this too was a sign of the absolutist state still in its infancy. It is difficult to imagine Louis XIV playing the pen-pusher.

The cardinal also sought to envelop with his favour the developing world of intellectual sociability and he established the *Académie française* in 1634, a society of distinguished men of letters. It provided a link between the court and the city. Richelieu hoped in his usual fashion that he would be able to manipulate it. But the Academy, which was the inspiration for a proud declaration of independence from Guez de Balzac, would escape *post mortem* from the clutches of its creator. It became the touchstone for a new sense of legitimacy for the autonomous, independent writer. What had been established to become the intellectual organ of state would gradually become transformed in the course of a century and a half to be the route by which, through authentic works of literature, the government of men and women could be torn down, reshaped and redirected.

Richelieu was no ordinary churchman and he removed the stigma of shame and ill-repute from the theatrical world and the acting profession (a stigma that Bossuet would attempt to reimpose once more). For several decades, thanks to Richelieu, dramatists and actors would enjoy a period of repose and fairly extensive freedom. Richelieu himself wrote stage-plays or commissioned paid writers to develop them on the basis of plots which he had devised. They attacked Anne of Austria fairly openly or heaped praises on the European strategy of the cardinal, the links which had been forced with Protestant states and his hostility towards the hispanico-Austrian Habsburgs, despite their Catholicism. As literary works they were mediocre. They were a way of trying to influence the stage but they hardly affected its development as an institution which was already inured to patriotic and state-building pedagogy of the Corneille kind following the first stage performance of the *Cid* in 1636, at precisely the same moment as the great national crisis of Corbie. That year the dangerous and seductive power of Spain seemed to be everywhere, both on the banks of the Somme and on the stages of the theatres where Spanish themes were enjoying a great popularity . . . .

Richelieu's intentions were generally heavily directive, although he was not always able to substantiate this with resources or realize it in practice. Only one aspect of intellectual life attracted criticism from Richelieu and this was the domain of secondary education, which was then enjoying one of its most productive periods. There were 65,000 students in this branch of education studying at any one time in the first half of the seventeenth century, which was a record in comparison with any other period in the Ancien Régime.[79] This was a remarkable achievement and it should be noted that it coincided with the increased number of office-holders and the construction of absolutism. The cardinal complained, in particular, about the over-production of young Latin scholars. But the cardinal's complaints did nothing to stop the fathers of bourgeois families, and nobles, and sometimes the sons of artisans and peasants too, from sending their offspring to the Jesuit colleges or (later) the Oratorians. His sentiments reflected, with some ill-grace, the huge numbers of students in these colleges; but this would eventually level off in the course of the following century.

In the realm of the plastic arts, Richelieu's taste sometimes deserted him (he preferred the mediocre Cesari to Rubens, for example). Yet, like Henry II, Montmorency, Louis XIV or Colbert, he judiciously chose the best artists – Vouet to some degree and, above all, Philippe de Champaigne and Poussin. The galleries of statues and portraits which he collected exalted the glories of war and the dignity of justice; the themes were of military might but, still more, of administrative, judicial, scientific and religious sovereignty. Thus, in his palaces, there were series of paintings of Roman generals, tolerant (even religiously heterdox) humanists such as Erasmus and Savonarola, and a solemn procession of statesmen who might be seen as the cardinal's precursors (Abbot Suger, the Cardinal d'Amboise . . .). Richelieu also had himself sculpted as a fully standing figure in marble or bronze. There was a triple innovation here. Such forms

---

[79] This figure should be set alongside the 48,000 pupils in French colleges on the eve of the Revolution and it even stands comparison with the pupil numbers recorded in 1842! (M-M. Compère, *Du collège au lycée (1500–1850)*, pp. 89–157. See also R. Chartier, M. Compère and D. Julia, *L'Education en France du XVIe au XVIIIe siècle* (Paris, SEDES, 1976), p. 190. Should we imagine that it was the case that the process of élite formation in ancien régime France had thus reached its 'natural limits' under Louis XIII? However, one should bear in mind that there was a degree to which the colleges had lost their grip of the education market after this date and that there were new establishments of primary or junior education which tend progressively to be under-recorded in the statistics after 1650 or 1700.

of statuary were generally reserved for kings, emperors and lay statesmen or for generals who had victoriously conquered the enemy. In addition, Richelieu arranged for himself to appear in the iconography alongside Louis XIII, one single entity represented in two persons, the Hercules of this Atlas, the Mentor of this Ulysses, the Moses of this Yahveh; or, more humbly, as the good gardener who picks the caterpillars and grubs off the *fleur de lys*! Before smiling, however, we should remember that the duo of monarch and prime minister would have a long future before it. A collector of works of art who had to exercise self-restraint, Richelieu would let Montmorency give him his artistic collection just before he put his head on the executioner's block. The duke rather hoped, by this expensive gift, to protect his family and inheritors from the cardinal's revenge. The cardinal created museums of sculpture, particularly at the château of Richelieu, which would be visited in later centuries by tourists. This was a step towards the more formal establishment of a structure of public museums which would eventually be established in Paris in the eighteenth century.

Louis XIII's minister took to architecture as did every statesman of the Ancien Régime, following in the footsteps of Francis I or Henry II; and, after the sterile decades of the wars of religion, like Henry IV, Sully and Marie de Médicis. She had been the cardinal's patron and she inculcated in him a passion for building. He constructed, or reconstructed, the important church at the Sorbonne (itself sited in a highly symbolic place). He built a sovereign palace, called the Palais-Cardinal and a little later the Palais-Royal, on a site at right angles to the Louvre. Fortifications were constructed, as at Brouage, and others were begun on the western and northern flanks of the kingdom. Richelieu thus continued the work of Sully and prefigured that of Vauban. It was a matter of fencing off the 'square field' of the realm. In so doing, he reinforced his defensive foreign policy, one which would avoid risky and far-off military adventures to the East. The cardinal also conceived of a project for a town: Richelieu. Geometrically laid out in the Italian fashion it was a successor, historically, to the city of Henrichemont which had been close to Sully's heart. After the death of its inceptor, however, this new creation would be almost stillborn, little more than a small walled town. The cardinal also constructed buildings with a social purpose such as a hospital for the war-wounded, although these would be eclipsed by the end of the century by the great palace of the *Invalides* built by Louvois. He erected great country houses (at Rueil, and then at the château of Richelieu itself). Throughout the expanse of his gardens he laid out sandy walkways in geometric patterns according to classical tenets and the better to suppress weeds and the noise of walking on stone. He proliferated the fountains and water-devices, as Henry IV had done at Saint-Germain-en-Laye and as Le Nôtre would do at Vaux-le-Vicomte and Versailles. And all this was realized in the most complete confusion between the public and the private, between the revenues of the state, the budgets for its departments, and the cardinal's own treasury. There was no distinction to be made between building for France, for the glory of it . . . and for the family of the princely prelate whose family would, in due course, be among the dukes and duchesses of the kingdom.

3

France and the Fronde: the Age of Anne of Austria and Mazarin

Richelieu had died on 4 December 1642 and Louis XIII followed him to the grave on 14 May 1643. His death was one more testimony to the rise of absolutism. On the 18th May following, a *lit de justice* took place in the Parlement at which the infant Louis XIV, scarcely five years old, was carried into the chamber by the High Chamberlain, the duke de Joyeuse and the Captain of the Guards, the count de Charost.[1] Before the assembled magistrature, the muttered words of the boy-king were taken to be his consent to what the chancellor would shortly pronounce. Louis XIII's will was set aside and instead the authority of the state was vested in the Regent Anne of Austria. In exchange for their willingness to ratify this decision, the *parlementaires* would shortly receive, 18 months later, the privilege of hereditary nobility.

In this novel circumstance, there was no further recourse to the ceremonies of the royal effigy fabricated in the image of the dead monarch. Under Francis I, and even up to the reign of Henry IV – albeit by then in a more restricted way – this effigy had symbolized the continuum of royal dignity. But the old proverb 'Royal dignity never dies' was replaced, as we have already said, by the more recent maxim 'The King never dies.' The biological and mystical continuum of the blood line from father to son counted for more – and to a greater extent even than it had done following Henry IV's death – than the legal transmission of an office within a particular lineage. From the death bed to the divan (or *lit*) of justice – the practical and theoretical sovereignty of a given monarch and his heirs counted for more than the perennial institutions of the kingdom which, at all events, contained far fewer representative elements than in the past.[2]

From 1630 to 1642, Jules Mazarin had enjoyed the high favour of, firstly, Richelieu, and then Anne of Austria. This ensured that, following the death of the first cardinal-minister and that of the king, he would be

[1]   François Bluche, *Louis XIV* (Oxford, Blackwell, 1990), p. 19.
[2]   Ralph Giesey, *Royal Funeral Ceremony* (Geneva, Droz, 1960), p. 231.

Plate 5 Portrait of Louis XIV, King of France, with Anne of Austria, Queen of France, his mother This portrait of the young Louis XIV with his mother, Anne of Austria, was painted before Louis XIII's death, probably in c.1642 in the studios of the cousins Henri and Charles Beaubrun, an *atelier* which was active in the years from 1630 to 1675 and which specialized in paintings of the royal and Parisian élites. The picture does full justice to Anne of Austria, who was then in her prime. *Versailles, Musée national du château*

promoted to the rank of the first minister in charge of the affairs of the kingdom from the second half of 1643.

Giulio Mazzarini was born in 1602 from a family of gentry from Rome, whose nobility was genuine but which had fallen on hard times. They were clients of the great Colonna family and the young Mazarin was a good pupil of the Jesuits before frequenting the fleshpots of Rome without hopes of much more by way of a career. He then followed his friend and protector Giromamo Colonna on a trip to Spain before making a start on a military career. Then, in a further change of direction, he joined the pontifical diplomatic service before emerging in classic fashion as an ambassador's secretary. Mazarin's sisters were well-placed in marriage to the Martinozzi and Mancini families and this in due course gave him nephews and nieces in family relationships which encompassed many of the princely lines of Western Europe: the Nevers, Bouillon, Mercoeur (Lorraine), Soissons (Savoy-Carignan), Conti (Bourbon-Condé) . . .[3]

Mazarin's career had its beginnings in Rome and he relied on the patronage there of several aristocratic houses. Besides the Colonna, the patrons of his father, there was the Cardinal Sacchetti and, above all, the Barberini. Amongst the latter figured Pope Urban VIII himself, and then Cardinal Barberini, and eventually his younger brother Cardinal Antonio, an essential base for Mazarin's launch into the wider world. Other cardinals would be in time his 'equals', friends rather than former patrons. This would be true of Bentivoglio, for example, and Bagni (known as 'The Dame' – not a comment on his personal life). Bagni was an open-minded individual who would introduce Mazarin to the free-thinker Gabriel Naudé who would become his librarian. We should also mention Cardinal Bichi (known as the 'Great Dame' – same remark – or 'Bichi the Red' for his military exploits). These prelates formed with Mazarin the French lobby at the pontifical court in Rome. The more menial tasks were carried out for Mazarin by *abbés* such as Benedetti, his agent for works of art, and Ondedei, a trusted servant whom His Eminence would in due course transfer to Paris. Ondedei would be the go-between for Mazarin with Anne of Austria during the Fronde. He would eventually become bishop of Fréjus in 1654.

Mazarin's homeland was the original seat of the church, the land of prelates and priests. France, his adopted country, was the land of the state. In January 1630, Mazarin, the mere envoy of the Holy See, met Richelieu for the first time. He conceived an instinctive attachment towards him, a filial 'adoration' which was, at least at the beginning, unreciprocated.

---

[3] For this point and what follows see Georges Dethan, *Mazarin, un homme de paix à l'âge baroque, 1602–1661* (Paris, Imprimerie Nationale, 1981), p. 20 and p. 345, n. 41. Cf. Madeleine Laurain-Portemer, *Etudes mazarines* (Paris, Boccard, no date) and also 'Un mécénat ministerériel: l'exemple de Mazarin' in *L'Age d'or du mécénat 1598–1661*, presented by R. Mousnier and J. Mesnard with an introduction by M. Fumaroli (Paris, CNRS, 1985), pp. 89–106. Simone Bertière, *La vie du cardinal de Retz* (Paris, De Fallois, 1990) provides useful points of comparison 'between the one cardinal and the other'.

However, in October 1630, Mazarin was able to be of service to the French cause. He proved a tireless negotiator at Casale and, crying '*Pace, Pace*' managed to negotiate a truce between the French royal troops of Schomberg which were outnumbered there by the Spanish soldiers of the marquis of Santa Croce. He thus avoided a combat which would have been certainly lost by the French and earned Richelieu's gratitude.

The 12 following years saw Mazarin's gradual integration into the smart governing élites of the kingdom. The motives which drove him onwards were various and complementary. He was hispanophobe (and therefore francophile) – like his predecessor Concini. The court at Rome, although it was prestigious, only afforded him modest diplomatic employment, despite the grandiose titles ('extraordinary nunciature', etc.). Mazarin was a person of considerable intelligence, presence, charm and human warmth who wanted nothing better than to be integrated amongst Richelieu's 'creatures' and amongst France's military and financial élite. He achieved this by means of small steps, intimate contacts . . . and military expeditions. Some military chiefs such as Créqui, Schomberg and Toiras above all, kept in close contact with him. Some of the secretaries of state, particularly the War Secretaries (Servien, Chavigny) also became his intimate acquaintances and useful contacts. From the beginning Mazarin had understood entirely that in the France of 1635 warfare was a fundamental component of power. With Richelieu (to whom he was known as *frère Coupe-Chou*) he knew how to amuse and also when it was important to keep a straight face. He behaved gallantly when he was called upon to do so, as in the company of the duchess d'Aiguillon, the cardinal's niece and family friend. Smaller and less rewarding tasks did not deter him. We find him acting as a political adviser, as it were, in Savoy or in a more distasteful role as police investigator in the nasty Cinq-Mars affair. He gave ample proof of his competence. He was an agent of the Bourbon government from 1636 onwards, a naturalized French subject in 1639, and a cardinal in 1641, thanks to Richelieu's protection. With his circle of friendships, and the strong emotional attachment[4] which Anne of Austria had already formed towards him, he was one of the two or three possible candidates for the post of first minister.

In reality, the death of Richelieu, and still more that of Louis XIII, thrust Mazarin under the gaze of the future Regent. He already had experience of women destined to be heads of state. He had long enjoyed the confidence of the engaging Chrétienne de Savoie, Henry IV's daughter, whom France had manipulated to the point of oppression, and her amour Count Philip of Savoy. According to Walter Montague, the English Cavalier of lost causes, Mazarin had enjoyed a liaison with the seductive Henrietta Maria,

---

[4] Pierre Goubert writes amusingly (*Mazarin* (Paris, Fayard, 1990)) that two out of three *chartistes* (G. Dethan and M. Laurain-Portemer – research students at the Ecole des Chartes) considered this a purely platonic affair whilst the third (Claude Dulong) concluded that she had a brief physical love-affair with the cardinal following his return from exile during the Fronde.

Plate 6 Cardinal Mazarin Philippe de Champaigne's painting of Cardinal
Mazarin captures the prelate in the classic pose for a prelate, cardinal or pope.
In the background the medieval fortress of Vincennes, close by Paris, is featured
and this provides some evidence by which the painting may be dated to around
1653, for it was not until October 1652 that Mazarin acquired the governorship of
the citadel after the death of the previous incumbent, Léon Le Bouthillier, Count
de Chavigny, the former secretary of state under Louis XIII.
Chantilly, Musée Condé

another daughter of Henry IV – her husband, King Charles I of England, had been executed in 1649.

What constituted the 'Mazarin coalition' which functioned more or less continuously from 1643 to 1648, and which the various crises of the Fronde would disrupt but which would be reconstituted in a modified form afterwards? Anne of Austria was the decisive figure amongst the cardinal's new alliances. That she was emotionally attracted to seigneur Jules was important. For all that we know it was a purely platonic relationship but she knew she could count on his loyalty in any circumstances since he was not related to any of the other faction leaders amongst the royal family. Vendôme-Beaufort, Condé and Gaston d'Orléans – the cardinal was beholden to none of them. He had his eyes on a distinguished patron and she was almost within his grasp.

Independence from other factions did not exclude various forms of cooperation. Mazarin would have the greatest difficulties with the illegitimate branch of the royal family, the Vendôme-Beaufort. But he tried to keep on good terms with the legitimate line. From 1643 to 1649, his relationships with the king's cousins (Gaston d'Orléans, the brother of the late king, and the Condés (brother and son)) remained cordial and evenly matched. Mazarin was thus able to accumulate various of the more senior and substantial offices at court without incurring their enmity. He was the young King Louis XIV's godfather. As the superintendent of his education, the king became his disciple and friend. He was also entrusted with the household of the queen. He continued to live in the Palais Royal, adjacent to Anne of Austria's apartments, which was enough to set the gossipers to work.

In military and administrative affairs, Jules Mazarin saw to it that, in an informal way, he surrounded himself with efficient and, still more important, loyal clients. Turenne, in particular, would remain loyal to him through thick and thin despite one temporary lapse during the Fronde. Other *maréchaux* such as Gramont, du Plessis-Praslin and Fabert were loyal to him. Amongst the commissioners for war (*commissaires des guerres*) and the military intendants (*intendants d'armée*) he had numerous essential supporters, many of whom were destined for careers in high office. They included Le Tellier, Particelli d'Emery, Fouquet and Colbert. They would provide a secretary of state for war and then chancellor, and then three superintendents of finance and a *contrôleur général des finances* respectively. It was as though the blossoming of administrative responsibilities around the chiefs of staff of the army would eventually be transcended by the possibilities of even more exalted posts in central government. Mazarin retained the heavy fiscal expenditure and taxation which Richelieu had initiated. Using their clients lower down, both cardinals presided over the destinies of a military state which lay, however, fundamentally in the control of the *robe* on the royal Council and which never lay in the authority of the professional soldiers.

Once installed in the heights of power from the spring of 1643 onwards,

Mazarin consolidated his grip by means of this group which was part network, part faction and part cabal. Several members of the royal Council or secretaries of state could have put up some resistance to him but they were gradually removed from power, in some cases some months before Louis XIII's death (in the case of Sublet des Noyers), and in others by Anne of Austria afterwards. She did little to resist the cardinal's entreaties and it did not take long for Chavigny to be removed (like Sublet, one of Richelieu's clients), followed by the influential Bishop Potier, who held posts both in church and state, and who was disgraced in October 1643 at the time of the *cabale des importants*. This cabal had the support of the illegitimate Vendôme royal branch of the Bourbon, both father and son, and particularly of the duke of Beaufort, a real ninny who enjoyed playing to the gallery. It also drew support from the three great aristocratic houses of Rohan, Luynes and Guise, brought together in the person of the seductive charms of the duchess of Chevreuse, the celebrated *chevrette*, who was a Rohan by birth, and then successively a Guise and a Luynes by marriage. She imagined that the former friendship which she had enjoyed with Anne of Austria gave her the door to power and gave her the authority to dispose of all policy in favour of Spain. Finally, the cabal had the support of a group of noble intellectuals of a neo-stoic tendency (amongst whom Saint-Ibar would be one of the prototypes).[5] This gave Vendôme a degree of cultural respectability. The arrest of Beaufort in September 1643 and the exile of Madame de Chevreuse from the court nipped this growing movement of opposition in the bud. It would surface again, however, during the Fronde. The cabal was very much of its period, however, and coincided with the emergence of a female opposition in aristocratic circles which sought to promote the opposite sex. Its dissolution also reflected Mazarin's relatively mild response in comparison with Richelieu. '*Frère Coupe-Chou*' imprisoned and exiled, but he did not execute his aristocratic opponents.

In certain respects, Mazarin was more flexible and more likeable than his predecessor under Louis XIII. Yet in the essentials he perpetuated Richelieu's foreign policy. This was with the agreement of Gaston d'Orléans, Condé and, above all, Anne of Austria, now that she was purged of her pro-Spanish inclinations. The alliance with the Protestant powers to the north and east of France against Habsburg hegemony remained a pivotal axis of strategy for the kingdom's future. On 3 April

---

[5]   Henri d'Escar de Saint-Bonnet, seigneur de Saint-Ibar, was from the entourage of the count of Soissons and would become later one of the *fidèles* of the future Cardinal de Retz. Saint-Ibar, an enemy of favourites and tyranny, was attracted to the stoic and Christian elements current in the seventeenth century. Louis de Bourbon, Count of Soissons (1604–41), called 'Monsieur le Comte', was a prince of the blood and a willing plotter against Richelieu who died accidentally (or not, as the case may be) at the battle of la Marfée in 1641. He was born into the cadet branch of the Bourbon-Condé whose elder scions carried the titles 'Monsieur le Prince' or 'Monsieur le Duc'. It was from the elder branch of the family that the Great Condé ('Monsieur le Prince') was descended, the grand-nephew of 'Monsieur le Comte'.

1645 the allied forces of Sweden, Hesse and France under the overall command of the Huguenot Turenne defeated the Catholic army of the duke of Bavaria, the emperor's ally, at Allerheim in Swabia.[6] Pope Innocent X did not take kindly to this defeat. Yet it was precisely the clarity of objectives pursued by Mazarin which enabled him to react to this victory in a relatively moderate fashion. Having once secured his fundamental aim he wanted to negotiate a reasonable peace treaty with the Empire. His aim was to diminish, rather than destroy, their authority. There were occasions, of course, when the cardinal allowed such military victories free rein over his fevered imagination.[7] In 1646, he even seriously contemplated the annexation of the Spanish Netherlands! But it would be a mistake to imagine that he entertained any dream of reaching out to the natural frontiers of a notional Gaul. He simply wanted, following in the traditions of the defensive perspectives of Richelieu, to ensure that Paris had a large fortified and protected zone to its north and east. The capital would thus come to occupy a more central position in the kingdom and be at its true heart.[8] The pro-Protestant policy adopted by Mazarin was a two-edged sword. In one respect, its logic guaranteed a measure of 'acceptance' if not of 'tolerance' to the Huguenots within the kingdom. It thus placed Mazarin in the political traditions of Henry IV's acceptance of the Protestant minority and, in a longer perspective, he would even claim to be the heir of the politics of coexistence adopted towards the heretics within and without the realm by Francis I and then by his Italian predecessor Catherine de Médicis.

Such pluralist, even multi-confessional, attitudes did not bring much comfort to the majority of France, or at least to its tax-payers. Under Mazarin, the increased fiscal exactions instituted by Richelieu, the most savage seen in the kingdom since the days of Louis XI, were continued, sustained and legitimized for the rest of the century. The total of military or militarily-related expenditures, composing loosely what one might term the twin heads of 'war' and 'extraordinary expenses', were held below the level of 20 million *livres tournois* during the prosperous years of Henry IV's reign from 1600 to 1610. Despite various ups and downs, this figure gradually crept upwards in the course of the two decades following Henry IV's death. Then, during the period of declared warfare from 1635 to 1642, Richelieu had increased the figure to an average of 82 million *livres* a year. This four-fold increase was made necessary by the demands of war, but also by the process of sudden extension in state power, both civil and military, which the creation of the modern state entailed. Mazarin (or those who ran the finances during his preeminence) increased the total of these two heads of expenditure to 123 million *livres* between 1642 and

[6]   Geoffrey Parker, *The Thirty Years War* (London, Routledge and Kegan Paul, 1989), p. 176.

[7]   Georges Pagès, *La Guerre de Trente Ans* (Paris, Payot, 1939), p. 254.

[8]   Madeleine Laurain-Portemer, 'Questions européennes et diplomatie mazarine', *XVIIe Siècle*, 42 (1990), 48.

1647, and without provoking any devaluation in the currency[9] – i.e. without undermining the values of the fixed investments in *rentes*. It would, however, be the *rentiers* who would accuse him of endangering their revenues during the pre-Fronde years and in the Fronde itself. In the circumstances, Mazarin was hardly a 'man of peace'[10] even though he demonstrated an impressive ability in putting together various diplomatic compromises. The latter were achieved through Mazarin's having two strings to his bow. His key negotiators were Abel Servien and Claude de Mesmes (the count d'Avaux), both from the *robe* nobility, and they were by turns respectively unyielding and conciliatory, and both under the continual instruction of their master. Louis XIV would employ the same tactics in the following generation with Croissy and Pomponne.

The positive links with the reformed powers of Europe have already been alluded to. They were embodied in the anti-Spanish treaties concerning trade (1655) and military alliance (1657) with 'Protestant' England. Should this also be interpreted as opening up the kingdom to the full participation of its own Protestant minority, geographically concentrated within the Huguenot 'crescent' which, running via the Gironde, the Garonne, and across the Cévennes to the Rhône valley, fertilized the southern third, or perhaps half, of France? In general terms, there was an opening, or, at the least, a small chink of light. Under Mazarin, just as had been the case under Richelieu, at least since 1629, French Protestants had enjoyed a relative degree of coexistence with the Catholic majority. There had been periods of conflict but these were different from the difficult times of the sixteenth century, and those which would occur once more after 1661. During the Mazarin years, the *Conseil d'en haut* confirmed the edicts of pacification, protected the rights of the Chambers of the Edict (*chambres de l'édit*) and recognized the fiscal privileges of Protestant pastors and their rights to preach. In May 1652, the royal authorities relaxed their stance even further. To prevent the spread of the southern Fronde movements extending to the Protestant 'crescent' a royal edict annulled the restrictions which Louis XIII had enacted upon various aspects of the civil and religious life of the Protestant minority. It did not take much imagination for Protestants to feel that the clock had been turned back (save in respect of the Huguenot fortress *places de sûreté*) to the first decade of the seventeenth century and the golden age of confessional coexistence. The need to preserve public order and prevent any outbreak of religious strife whilst the Fronde lasted was of greater importance in 1652 than the need to maintain a confessional uniformity in the kingdom. Mazarin already had enough of a revolt on his hands and even the *dévot* Chancellor Séguier had

---

[9] G. Frêche, *Prix des grains à Toulouse* (Paris, PUF, 1967), pp. 126–7. In fact, France's currency retained its value. The *livre tournois* remained *grosso modo* stable under Mazarin in comparative terms. It declined slightly in 1636 and then again later on in 1693. It would seem that the French economy retained its vigour both before and after the Fronde and despite the crises. Colbert was able to build upon relatively solid foundations.

[10] Despite the title of the excellent work of George Dethan, *Mazarin, un homme de paix*. . . .

to admit the inevitability of some concessions to suit the needs of the moment.

However, the picture should not be presented in too rosy a light. In Catholic circles, anti-Calvinist elements set to work against these 'disconcerting' developments (for the Protestants remained aggressively hostile to the papacy, although they did not have the decisive factor of force on their side). Successively, the national assemblies of clergy, the parlements and the intendants (some of whom were strictly devout) sought to frustrate and halt the progress of heterodoxy. They tried to limit the powers of the Chambers of the Edict (which were hated by the magistrates of the parlements). They introduced Catholics into the municipal governments and consulates of southern towns which, up to that date, had been Huguenot dominated. There was no reason why there should not be a Catholic presence on such bodies but it was all a matter of timing, of degree, and of the excessive authority exercised by the Catholic majority. Here and there, there were restrictions introduced in respect of the rituals of the *religionnaires* and upon mixed marriages. A Breton Protestant church was moved; a number of pastors were ordered not to preach outside their place of residence; and, although this was a rare occurrence, some artisan guilds introduced restrictions upon entry to the guild on ground of 'heresy'. Protestants were limited in their rights of assembly or national convocation over and above their national synods. The appointment of pastors was restricted to those native to France, and foreigners (e.g. from Geneva) found themselves excluded. Finally the recently-founded devout congregations of laity such as the Company of the Holy Sacrament and that for the Propagation of the Faith tried to convert, but also to spy and to denounce . . . for there were some Tartuffes in their midst. In his final years, Mazarin seemed to associate himself with such a policy of repression, at least in what he said. On the one hand he ordered the dissolution of the Company of the Holy Sacrament with the attendant loyalty from Catholic extremists which it enjoyed, in order to reinforce the authority of the episcopacy. On the other hand, he began once more to harass the Huguenots. So it was decided that the national synod of 1659, when it was finally allowed to meet, should be the last. The Protestant academy at Montauban was transported to the 'back of beyond' at Puylaurens.[11] More ominous still than these irritating gestures was the royal declaration of 1656 which envisaged the despatch of commissioners around the provinces to supervise a strict enforcement 'to the letter' of the edict of Nantes among the Huguenot minority. In reality, however, this edict of 1656 was only put into practice after 1661, the critical year of the beginning of real repression, and the year of Mazarin's death.

In retrospect it is clear that everything was already in place by 1661 for the cycle of repression which Louis XIV would unleash when he began his

---

[11]   The academy at Montauban was a prestigious educational establishment for the offspring of Huguenots.

personal rule. But it is wrong to write history from a teleological standpoint and it may be said as a simple statement of fact that, from 1630 to 1660, French Protestants enjoyed one of the least unpleasant moments of their long and often far from happy history under the Ancien Régime. Such a brief flowering of latitudinarian attitudes at the heart of French culture was a social fact which went beyond merely political considerations. But it would be right to credit some of it to Mazarin and his collaborators. The cardinal did not have to constrain his considerable talents towards this end; on the contrary, he distrusted the ultra-devout Catholics in any case and, had the *dragonnades* existed, they would have horrified him.[12] Finally the Fronde had given him pause for thought, and had forced him to make concessions – and in this respect it had performed some service.

The war waged alongside the Protestant states brought with it as its logical extension some degree of comprehension of Protestant heterodoxy within France but, at the same time and in a contradictory fashion, it also implied the permanency of centralization and of royal authority. The absolutism which had been put in place from 1624 onwards was consolidated. During the six years from the death of Louis XIII to the Fronde the costly campaigns and interminable anti-Habsburg war required the continuous presence of effective authority (i.e. the intendants) to oversee the collection of the heavy burden of taxation. The older ranks of officeholders who normally carried out the task (the *élus* and *trésoriers de France*) had neither the power nor the determination to carry it through. And so the war dragged on. Condé had some remarkable victories such as that at Rocroi in 1643 but he failed in the siege of Lérida in Catalonia in 1647. Fortune turned its back on him, contemporaries would say: 'Son dada demeura court à Lérida.'[13] In 1645 a huge loan of 115 million *livres* anticipated, or already began to eat into, the state taxes due in 1647.[14] It would take the Fronde of 1648 onwards to bring to a temporary standstill the twin ratchets of fiscality and administrative centralization and even reduce taxation. But once the Fronde had been contained and was over, the process of centralization would begin again as if nothing had happened

[12] On all this, see Richard Bonney, *Political Change in France under Richelieu and Mazarin, 1624–61* (Oxford, Clarendon Press, 1978); Janine Garrisson, *L'Edit de Nantes et sa révocation, histoire d'une intolérance française* (Paris, Seuil, 1985); Elisabeth Labrousse, *Essai sur la Révocation de l'édit de Nantes, une foi, une loi, un roi* (Paris, Geneva, Labor and Fides-Payot, 1985).

[13] 'His nag stopped short at Lérida' – an expression which would become a proverb used by Madame de Sévigné about the temporary impotence of her own son in the company of la Champmeslé (Madame de Sévigné, *Lettre à Madame de Grignan*, 8 April 1671). Mazarin briefly hoped that he might be able to exchange Catalonia for the Spanish Netherlands and integrate the latter into the French kingdom. This, writes the good Lavisse in lyrical vein, 'would have changed the ethnic character of France' (*Histoire de France . . . à la Révolution*, lx vols (Paris, Hachette, 1900–11), vii (part i), 12). He nevertheless wanted control of Catalonia. However, Condé failed at the siege of Lérida in June 1647 and would only recover his 'attack' in the victory at Lens the following year (August 1648).

[14] Bonney, *Political Change in France*, p. 52.

in the intervening period, as though there was a certain established routine within absolutism itself. That routine would, from time to time, dull the wits through an excessive penchant for the cult of the personality and through a selective rewriting of history.[15]

One of the aims of the revolt of the senior magistrates and office-holders during the Fronde was to suppress the intendants, dangerous and efficient rivals in the exercise to the holders of office. The *parlementaire* Fronde of 1648 obtained their removal, at least in part. But as soon as it seemed possible to do so, Anne of Austria and Mazarin reinstated their faithful agents. In November 1649 Particelli d'Emery was reinstated as superintendent of finances and, from that moment onwards, the government felt itself under no constraints from despatching individuals into the province who, under the various assumed guises of *commissaire*, *intendant des finances*, *maître des requêtes*, or *intendant de l'armée* were nothing other than carbon copies of the provincial intendants of the period from 1633 to 1648. Sometimes they were even one and the same individuals. Equally, following the final return of Mazarin from exile at the end of the Fronde, his principal collaborators (Servien, Fouquet, Le Tellier, Séguier) were, as one might imagine, strong supporters of a return to this firm resolution of things. It was during the decade of the 1650s, and even before the advent of Colbert as a minister, that the tradition of intendants serving for a long period of time and having responsibility for large provinces began. Bazin de Bezons would hold the Languedoc intendancy from 1653 to 1673; Bouchu that of Burgundy from 1656 to 1683 – a fact which also underlines the continuity between the Mazarin and Colbertian periods which has been emphasized in Pierre Goubert's recent biography of Mazarin.[16] The *trésoriers de France* and the *élus* had been pushed to the sidelines by the considerable financial powers of the intendants and their protests at what had happened were in vain. The state took no account of them and it was almost as though the Mazarinism of the post-Fronde years no longer had any time for the office-holders. It would be more precise to say, however, that he sought to retain their presence whilst domesticating them and teaching them to be loyal. He treated them just as he dealt with the aristocracy and upper nobility. He did so with a degree of scrupulousness because the intendants were responsible for carrying it through and they acted as functionaries of the state, or rather honest commissioners for it. They did not prevaricate and they did not seek to advance their own interests (unlike their grand patrons (Richelieu, Mazarin and, in the near future, Colbert) who tended to pocket a good deal on the way). But although the trio were financially not above suspicion they did not belong to the world of the masters of requests – the nursery of the future

---

[15] See the inspired and brilliant pamphlet of Marc Suriano, *La Brosse à reluire sous Louis XIV* (Paris, Nizet, 1989).
[16] Goubert, *Mazarin*.

intendants – whose professional integrity was often of a remarkably high standard.

The Mazarin years were thus relatively open towards Protestant Europe and towards heterodoxy at home and abroad. They were also years of administrative burden with not much that was positive to report on the economy and standards of living either. The economic climate during the years from 1640 to 1661 was particularly difficult and this was something which was independent of any particular minister, however gifted. The volume of precious metal arriving from Spanish America in Europe was especially disturbed during these two decades, and notably during the years 1653–4 and 1659.[17] The European wars and above all the excessive taxation which accompanied them did nothing to help matters. Levels of consumption began to decline, thus aggravating the crisis. This decline was particularly registered in northern and central France in the purchase of salt; from 1646 to 1664 the volume of purchase was down by 7 per cent in comparison with the levels immediately preceding that period. The decline was of the order of 17 per cent in comparison with the 'base' level of 1621–3. As for grain production, the register of the degree of vitality in the agricultural sector, it also declined by varying amounts around and during the Fronde years, particularly in north-eastern France, the Parisian region and the northern provinces of the Massif Central. The rural population had also reached its peak in the years from 1630 to 1640 and then seems to have slipped back during the war years and the Fronde when plagues and death were particularly rife, above all during the terrible years of crisis from 1649 to 1652.[18] Whatever criteria one chooses to examine, it is clear that France was a long way off the good old days of the '*poule au pot*' which was the image for the golden age of the first quarter of the seventeenth century.

Faced with the difficulties which made France sometimes 'a field of human suffering' during these years, neither Mazarin nor Anne of Austria nor their ministers had an economic policy worthy of the name. It is true that, in his *Carnets*,[19] the cardinal noted his concern for the shortage of food with its effects on army supplies as well as public order. On his death bed, Mazarin asked the young Louis XIV, 'by virtue of the duties of a good king . . . to succour his people not only by reducing the taille but also all

---

[17] Michel Morineau, *Incroyables Gazettes et fabuleux trésors* (Cambridge and Paris, Cambridge University Press and Editions de la Maison des sciences de l'homme, 1984), pp. 105–18, notably p. 112.

[18] Jacques Dupâquier, *Histoire de la population française, de la Renaissance à 1789* (Paris, PUF, 1988), vol. ii, 67–8 and 203. Fernand Braudel and Ernest Labrousse (dirs), *Histoire économique et sociale de la France* (Paris, PUF, 1970), ii, 726–30.

[19] The note-books of Mazarin (*carnets*) were published by Victor Luzarche (Tours, Péricart, 1893); cf. Victor Cousin, 'Carnets autographes du cardinal Mazarin', *Journal des savants* (1854), pp. 457–521, 600, 687, 753; (1855), pp. 19, 84, 161, 217, 304, 430, 525, 622, 703; (1856), pp. 48, 105. André Chéruel, 'Les Carnets de Mazarin pendant la Fronde (septembre–octobre 1648)', *Revue historique*, 4 (1877), 103–38.

the other impositions of whatever shape or form, providing always that he could sustain the necessary and indispensable expenditure for the general preservation of the state . . .'.[20] This allusion to taxation is the more pointed since Mazarin was responsible for two further ratchets to the tax-burden, one before the Fronde and one afterwards, both more considerable than the already considerable increase under Richelieu. What is striking in what Mazarin wrote is the absence of any personal reflections on agriculture, industry or French trade, even from the narrow point of view of the interests of the state treasury. He is a world away from the mercantilist and naval thought of a Richelieu who had grasped, in his *Testament politique*, the essential lines of force and weakness in the economy of his day.

The object-lesson in such matters which Richelieu had presented would pass the next generation by, or rather would by-pass the next cardinal, and become the direct legacy of the man from Reims, Colbert, who had immersed himself from early in his career in commercial, colonial and maritime considerations which owed their origins expressly to Richelieu. In the interim, Mazarin was certainly a brilliant disciple of his immediate predecessor in matters of state, the equal of his master when it came to the practice of war and diplomacy, but without any particular views on the patterns of production and trade. He thought a good deal more about how to line his own pockets, and in this respect he exceeded even Richelieu. The increasing fiscal burden was not a disaster for absolutely everyone. Seigneur Jules Mazarin managed his own domestic affairs to perfection without giving a second thought to the broader perspective of the French economy and its trade.

The wealth acquired by the ostentatiously acquisitive Mazarin was truly astounding – much greater than that of Sully, Concini, Marie de Médicis, Richelieu, or later, Colbert or Talleyrand. The results defy the imagination. When he died, Richelieu's successor owned 35 million *livres* of assets and an overall fortune of 38.5 million *livres*. This should be compared with the 20 to 22 million *livres* of Richelieu, or the 15 million *livres* of Henry II de Condé, the father of the Great Condé; or the 4 million of Chancellor Séguier. The multi-millionaires of the eighteenth century would find it hard to match the fortune of Cardinal Mazarin. The Condé family with its 31.5 million *livres tournois* (now worth 30 per cent less than it had been in 1661) was the equivalent in real terms of only about 60 per cent of Mazarin's fortune. What is more, Mazarin was not the scion of a princely house but a *parvenu* and one who had not always had luck on his side. The Fronde had been his ruination. Yet, thanks to his indomitable capacity to recover his position, he recovered his wealth (at the expense of tax-payers) in under a decade. The disposition of the Mazarin fortune can be reconstituted thanks to the post-mortem inventory of 1661 and it was made up

[20] Pierre Clément (ed.), *Lettres, instructions et mémoires de Colbert*, 10 vols (Paris, Didier, 1861–71), i, 535.

of land (5 million *livres*), loans (10 million), regalian rights alienated from the state, of provincial governments (but did these really constitute his 'property'?), and, to a total of 8,700,000 *livres*, liquid wealth in the form of silver and gold coins. This was more than that contained in the vaults of the Bank in Amsterdam!

The geographical distribution of his various landed, governmental and ecclesiastical properties was mainly within the western and northern half of France, particularly in Alsace, the northern and western frontier regions, and the western Atlantic seaboard, from Mayenne to Brouage.[21] The annual revenues enjoyed by the cardinal from this capital (amongst other sources) amounted to 1,700,000 *livres*. This included 573,000 *livres* from his ecclesiastical benefices, 300,000 *livres* from Alsace (a good prize), 1,600,000 *livres* from his estates, etc. With the assistance of his acolyte in such matters, Colbert, the cardinal acted like a tax-farmer, a fiscal broker like no other. He was the living incarnation of the first, untamed generation of absolutism when notions of service, however eminent, rendered to king and country were interlarded with those of reward on a hugely inflated scale, largesse distributed in underhand ways as well as, sometimes, above board. Once again the first minister sought to cut a figure as a grand, in this instance a quasi-monarchical, aristocrat. Its fulfilment was on a prodigious scale but the mentality which lay behind it was not exceptional for the period.[22] One of Mazarin's claims for greatness was to have collected together, and at great expense, a remarkable library of 35,000 volumes and opened it to the public. The *parlementaires* of the Fronde chose singularly the wrong moment to disperse it in 1652.

★   ★   ★   ★   ★

Mazarin occupied the corridors of power more or less (and generally more than less) from 1642 to 1661, from the death of Richelieu until his own demise. These two Mazarine decades were divided in half by the equivalent of a geological fault. Known as the Fronde, it lasted for six years from 1648 to 1653. It was a violent episode in French political history which warrants close attention.

The Fronde was primarily a problem of the office-holders and of the capital city. The number of officers increased enormously in the period

[21]   All this follows Daniel Dessert, 'Pouvoir et finance au XVIIe siècle: la fortune du cardinal Mazarin', *Revue d'Histoire moderne et contemporaine*, 23 (1976), 160 *et seq*. See also Daniel Dessert, *Argent, pouvoir et société au Grand Siècle* (Paris, Fayard, 1984), p. 292 and Françoise Bayard, *Le Monde des financiers au XVII siècle* (Paris, Flammarion, 1988), p. 416. Cf. Claude Dulong, *La Fortune de Mazarin* (Paris, Perrin, 1990).

[22]   Richelieu and Mazarin's colossal fortunes served certain necessary objectives. They both pursued policies which were not particularly Catholic, and particularly in their alliance with Protestant powers. As a result, and in order to resist the Vatican and the greater part of the French clergy, they both needed all the influence they could muster. The considerable wealth which they both accumulated served for both as a kind of guarantee of their influence against resistance to their policies which was far from negligible.

from 1515 to 1665, by which date there were a minimum of 46,047 royal officers of whom almost 9,000 were judicial magistrates, 5,000 financial officials, and the rest, i.e. over 30,000, were various lesser officials such as court ushers (*huissiers*), notaries and inspectors of weights and measures etc.[23] By comparison, in around 1515, there had only been 4,041 officials at most. The 'accumulated momentum' of the office-holding classes had thus vastly increased in this period of substantial growth in administration and in state apparatus over the century and a half. The office-holders, and particularly the *parlementaires*, 'constituted a social group which tended to become a political class with political ambitions, hungry for power'.[24] This was demonstrated in the increase in their ranks, their greater wealth, the growth of their patrimonies (in land and other assets), and above all in their exercise of their rights of registration, verification and remonstration of royal edicts.

In addition, the explosion of official resentments could count in Paris on the existence of an unstable urban population which was often discontented and which had also vastly increased in numbers during the first half of the seventeenth century. The capital had a population of 275,000 in around 1571 and this had decreased to less than 200,000 in the aftermath of the siege of 1590; but, by 1637, this had risen to the already enormous figure of 430,000, and it would reach half a million by the end of the seventeenth century.[25] Paris lay at the heart of a state whose fiscal voraciousness drained vast sums of money from the kingdom and which thus generated employment and purchasing power in the city which housed the seat of royal and ministerial authority.

The judicial officials found their best expression in the Parlement of Paris, the epitome of the kingdom's judicial institutions. An institution of this kind was not far removed from the important English courts of King's Bench and Common Pleas, which also had an exalted sense of judgeship. The very concept of Justice as something which transcended the person of the French king and which would be independent of the assemblies legitimately representative of the kingdom (such as the Estates General, etc.) would become of enormous significance at a later date. It would correspond to the central tenets of Kant's philosophy, desirous of creating categorical imperatives and universal values independent of arbitrary will or popular caprice. In a more concrete fashion it would inspire, with the assistance of Montesquieu, Jefferson and Madison, the creation of a number of lasting institutions of arbitration such as the Supreme Court in the United States and, by a process of imitation of it, various Constitutional Councils and similar bodies, both in France and elsewhere.

[23] Roland Mousnier, *Le Conseil du roi* (Paris, PUF, 1971), ch. 1.

[24] Jean-Marie-Constant, 'La Noblesse et la Fronde', *L'Histoire*, no. 115 (October 1988), p. 29.

[25] E. Le Roy Ladurie, *The Royal French State, 1460–1610* (Oxford, Blackwell, 1994), p. 276; Roland Mousnier, *Paris au XVIIe siècle* (Paris, CDU, 1961), fascicule 1.

The Parlement of Paris already enjoyed some far from negligible advantages.[26] It was situated close to the heart of sovereignty, if not to the crown itself. Of course it lacked any degree of representation such as was the case for the House of Commons in England or, more spasmodically, the Estates General in France. Nevertheless it was the incarnation of the highest principles of justice. In principle at least, it came close to the monarchical will. It could, depending on the circmstances, either reinforce that will or disable its decisions by the simple fact of its rights of registration, verification and remonstration. The Parlement also enjoyed good contacts with the younger and more dynamic judges through its Chamber of Inquests (*Chambre des enquêtes*), with the nobility (the peers sat in its midst), and with the people, especially the Parisian multitude, over which it had responsibilities for policing the food supplies in situations of grain shortage.

It is easy to understand why there might be a conflict between this tribunal with such exalted pretensions and a more administratively-directed state. From its origins until the beginning of the sixteenth century, the state had been packed with judicial officials of one sort or another (bailiffs, seneschals and lieutenants, etc.). This had constituted no problem for the parlements, either in Paris or the provinces. Later, royal administration had fallen more into the hands of financial officials (*trésoriers de France*, as well as *élus* under the later Valois, and even during Henry IV's reign) and this already created some antagonism with the parlements.[27] Eventually it passed to the *commissaires* and intendants whose authority Richelieu had, if not created, at least multiplied and reinforced. Yet the very principle of a 'commission' was considered as arbitrary, taxing and burdening the people at will, and it was opposed by the councillors of the sovereign courts both in the provinces and in Paris who sought to defend the concept of an 'office' as essential to their *raison d'être*.

There was an element of ambiguity in Richelieu's attitude towards the Parlement of Paris. In principle, he resisted the temptation to cultivate an attitude of sustained hostility towards the sovereign court. He needed it for his own purposes and he knew that it was the defender of a Gallicanism which was close to his own heart. Nor was he likely to ignore the fact that it represented one of the most essential ways by which royal power was legitimized. And yet His Eminence was quite prepared in particular circumstances to treat the magistrature harshly. He restricted their influence by appointing special commissions reserved for the masters of requests. In 1641, he limited their rights of remonstration. He subjected them to a continuous, or at least frequent, game of blackmail over whether the

---

[26] A. Lloyd Moote, *The Revolt of the Judges. The Parlement of Paris and the Fronde, 1643–1652* (Princeton NJ, Princeton University Press, 1971).

[27] See George Pagès, 'Essai sur l'évolution des institutions administratives en France du commencement du XVIe siècle à la fin du XVIIe siècle', *Revue d'histoire moderne*, 7 (1932).

paulette, the tax which office-holders paid to ensure their rights to transfer their office to their descendants or to another purchaser, would be continued or not. All these measures, however, were carefully considered. The cardinal was well aware of the fact that this was an area where he could not go too far. The concerted opposition of the senior judges, drawing on their formidable legalism for the issue in hand, would be more difficult to counter and repress than an elementary uprising of the high and mighty nobility or the people which could easily be dealt with by the decapitation of some and the hanging of the rest. And when it came to the power of Paris, Richelieu drew what lessons he needed to know from the experience of the League which he had learnt in his infancy. It was decided that the capital city should be managed gently and not overwhelmed with taxes. Paris, it seems, was the equivalent of the untouchable ox. Mazarin, younger than Richelieu and fresh from papal-dominated Rome, was less aware of Parisian idiosyncracies and he was prepared to challenge its favourable treatment.

There were already some premonitions, however, which should have been enough to dissuade Mazarin and Anne of Austria from a policy of excessive confrontation with the forces of disorder and revolt. From 1640 to 1651, uprisings or revolutions against excessive fiscality and the authority of the state broke out in Portugal, Naples, England, and eventually in the Netherlands.[28] The pursuit of war had provoked this explosive set of circumstances, since it was as voracious in devouring the tax revenues of Spain as in France.[29] The result would be a greater degree of assymetry in the common pursuit of wealth between the king, promoter of a level of taxation which had never been envisaged previously, and the nobility, office-holders and aristocracy, who were equally kept at a greater distance from the king by the cardinal-ministers.

In 1644 the *toisé* edict was promulgated which sought to exploit the demographic and physical growth of urban Paris. It created a new tax, equivalent to a year's worth of rent, on all proprietors of dwellings illegally constructed on the outskirts of the capital. The tax was expected to raise

[28] The Fronde formed one of the 'six contemporaneous revolutions' analysed by R.B. Merriman in his *Six Contemporaneous Revolutions* (Oxford, 1938 – photocopy from UMI, Ann Arbor, Michigan, 1972) and also in a shorter printed conference paper given at Glasgow on 22 April 1937 as the 7th Lecture of the David Murray Foundation at the University of Glasgow (Glasgow, Jackson and Sons, 1937).

[29] The authority of the Spanish monarchy was compromised, either temporarily or permanently depending on circumstances, in Catalonia (1640), Portugal (1640) and Naples (1647). The opposition they faced was often for fiscal reasons, especially in Catalonia and Naples. It was the same for the Fronde (1648–55). The English civil war began with a revolt against Ship Money and the authoritarianism of the Stuarts, culminating in the execution of Charles I in 1649. Finally, there was a Dutch revolution in which the Stadtholders from the House of Orange (with its monarchist and centralizing tendencies) had to give way to the more 'decentralized' government of the grand pensionary Jan de Witt (1651). In each case, therefore, there was a 'rearguard' action being waged against absolutism, and against excessive fiscality. Everywhere, too, there were the problems created by an economic crisis, by poverty, and by misery in the years from 1640 to 1660.

between 4 and 10 million *livres*.[30] In 1645, the holders of portions of alienated royal domain which they had purchased at inflated prices to assist the hard-pressed Treasury and expand their property also faced a tax on it. In 1646 and 1647, a sales tax was introduced on meat and wine. At the beginning of 1648, the brinkmanship over whether the *paulette* would be suppressed or not began to oppress the Parlement of Paris. Hence the discontent of a goodly number of Paris property-owners and *parlementaires*. The scene was being set for the Fronde with its often baroque, even burlesque moments. But there would be some bloodthirsty ones as well. Mazarin, for all his maladroitness, was an acutely political animal and he was better able to survive and bounce back than Charles I in London or Olivares in Madrid.

The Fronde was not a single movement, any more than the French Revolution was, or still less the Russian Revolution, the latter being classically divided up between the February and the October revolution. The first Fronde took place between 1648 and 1649 and it revolved around the revolt of the judges and, more broadly, the office-holders whose significance had increased in late Valois and early Bourbon France. We should therefore properly begin to analyse the Fronde from January 1648, when disturbances in Paris against taxation on 11 January involving popular, merchant and bourgeois elements took place against ministerial 'oppression'. Some days later, the *lit de justice* of 15 January reawakened opposition amongst the judges who had up to that date been more frightened of the possibility of popular disturbances becoming uncontrollable. Anne of Austria and Mazarin did their best to shelter behind the puppet authority of the child-king Louis XIV during the *lit*. They proposed to enregister under various new guises the taxes which had been introduced in the recent past. There were new sales-tax 'tariffs' proposed; the new tax on alienated royal domain, a new franc-fief tax,[31] and then finally 12 new masterships of requests were created. The Parlement replied with a set of prudently-worded remonstrations which did not set out to challenge in principle the royal will. However these *parlementaire* criticisms weakened the credibility of the government. They demonstrated the existence within the Parlement of a conservative group (albeit critical of various aspects of the exercise of royal authority) and which was represented by Molé, one of its *présidents*, who had a talent to flatter his fellow-judges and persuade the sovereign king. This group coexisted, however, with a more radical group, more openly hostile to royal power, and one which encompassed the younger magistrates of the Chamber of Inquests (*Enquêtes*) and the old *conseiller* judge Broussel, who was a good deal less senile than contemporary writers and subsequent historians have suggested. By creating the new offices of masters of requests the market in offices would be saturated and

---

[30] Moote, *The Revolt of the Judges*, p. 98; cf. Ernst Kossmann, *La Fronde* (Leiden, University of Leiden, 1954).
[31] *Franc-fief* was an often burdensome tax exacted from commoners who acquired noble property.

Anne of Austria thus alienated those individuals who were already in place and who formed the essential components of executive decision-making amongst the intendancies and commissioners amongst the provinces, etc. The Regent thus threatened to cement a link which had not existed previously between the *noblesse de robe* in Council (such as the previously loyal masters of requests) and those in the Parlement (who had always been prepared to take up a negative attitude towards royal authority). Once begun, this *parlementaire* and *officier*-led opposition was legitimized. Far from proposing a revolutionary agenda, it pointed towards a middle route, a reforming *via media* which would lay out the path for reform in the following summer of 1648.

At that point the open struggle between the sovereign courts and the Regency took a further turn. During March and April 1648, Mazarin and Anne of Austria, forever short of money and frustrated by the resistance demonstrated by the Parlement following the *lit de justice*, put into force various vexatious measures such as suppressing the wages of the office-holders or the *paulette*. The *parlementaires* replied in turn on 13 May 1648 by the court order (*arrêt*) uniting the various sovereign courts, a development which, with a good deal of imagination, might be compared with the Tennis Court Oath.[32] The edict brought together the four sovereign courts (the *Grand Conseil*, the *Cour des aides*, the *Chambre des comptes* and the Parlement itself). In defiance of the various taunts of the Regent, this conjoint entity, which became known as the *Chambre Saint-Louis*, published its legislative manifesto in 27 articles which displayed a degree of distaste (though not outright hostility) towards absolutism. By the way in which it was drafted, the magistrates hoped to recover some or all of the prerogatives which they felt had been trampled on during the disordered 30 years of rule by cardinal. They demanded the abolition of legal cases being heard before intendants, extraordinary commissioners or by appealing such cases directly before masters of requests, all of which they held to be outside the law. At the same time, they proclaimed the sovereign rights of equity jurisdiction, including an abolition of detention without trial beyond 24 hours after arrest (a clause which would have a particular effect on later historians who would see this as the abortive beginnings of a French version of Habeas Corpus). In the same fashion, the four courts wanted to become the arbiters of consent to taxation. No new tax should in future be imposed without having first been verified in due form, which was tantamount to meaning having secured their approval. Their corporate interests were very clearly demonstrated in the clauses. There was to be no new creation of offices which would debase the value of those offices already in existence. The salaries of officials were not to be tampered with. At the same time, the Parlement proclaimed itself the protector of tax-payers whose discontent had been spectacularly manifested as fomenting

---

[32] The famous oath of the Third Estate on 20 June 1789 at the beginning of the French Revolution.

the urban uprisings and peasant revolts. As a result they required the reduction of the *tailles* by a quarter and the abolition of the various new property and urban taxes such as the *toisé*. The 27 articles openly attacked the tax-farmers and financiers who had become the principal supports of the 'finance state' as opposed to the 'justice state'. The sovereign magistrates wanted to revoke the extraordinary deals which these individuals had struck with the state and to reduce the rates of interests which they enjoyed on the loans which they had made to it. They also wanted to put the financiers through the Caudine Forks of a Chamber of Justice which would investigate their activities. Such propositions would be followed in due course by Jean-Baptiste Colbert. They even sought to exclude financiers and their relatives from any post in the sovereign courts – for, in reality, they were often related to, or had married into, the families of sovereign court judges. They were particularly exercised to outlaw the much-disliked practice of using the *comptants* to make irregular payments to the profit of the financiers in a way which avoided any degree of serious scrutiny such as would normally have been exercised by the *Chambre des comptes*. Once the 27 articles had been launched, the various courts cast around for allies whose support they could court. The Parlement sprang to the defence of the merchant community which, despite Mazarin's involvement in an attempt to woo them through the Parisian *Hôtel de Ville* and its *Prévôt des Marchands* (acting under instructions), had never been strong supporters of the cardinal-ministry. The magistrates were also particularly solicitous of the *rentiers*, those who had lent the state small amounts of money in the form of *rentes* and whose interest payments could be a ready target for a treasury short of revenue if the moment seemed right. Finally the *parlementaires* reasserted their own role as the magistrates reponsible for the markets of the capital, for overseeing its essential food supplies and policing the streets. They paid lip-service to the continuing needs of the warfare but it was inevitably the case that a policy of fiscal relaxation such as they envisaged would sit more readily alongside the ending of hostilities.

Overall, these demands were fairly moderate and they were certainly less radical than those proposed in the more far-reaching writings of the Catholic priest Claude Joly in 1652. Invoking the Almighty, Joly linked the duties of a king to the interests of the people. He conferred power upon the Parlement but he also invested it in the Estates General, the representative body of the three orders of the realm. But the Parlement rejected the call to summon the Estates General and sought to retain its own monopoly of the role of representing the nation (or whatever passed for it at this period) before the king. So the resolutions of the *Chambre Saint-Louis* were more typical of a *via media* rather than a revolutionary set of demands. They envisaged the restoration of a justice-state which would be pacifically inclined and temperately ordered and where royal absolutism was kept within limits and attenuated by the existence of councils composed of members of its judiciary rather than pouring out directly the pure and unadulterated arbitrariness of its favour upon its subjects. In this respect, the strategy of the Parlement of Paris was more reasonable than that of the English Long Parliament which, after several years of turmoil, pushed its radical stance towards political suicide and the eviction, and then the execution of the Stuart king in 1649.

The attitudes of the French magistrates had, nevertheless, their utopian aspects, for the government by the judges which they envisaged, and which was the foreseeable result of their 27 articles, had never truly existed independently of the monarchy and would not do so in the future. Such a governing judicature was a useful device for affirming certain underlying principles of equity which ought to govern each and every individual but it was not a realistic way of proceeding in the routine administration of a state. The historical trend of the seventeenth and eighteenth centuries was either towards pure absolutism or towards the development of representative Estates General such as in the Netherlands or in the English House of Commons. At best the judges could only exercise a restraining influence, such as happened during the Fronde or during the eighteenth century. It would be obliterated as soon as a true revolution occurred to resurface later as an auxiliary instrument of state in its North American form of Supreme Court or in the European constitutional courts of justice.

The radical populism of the Paris Fronde worked outwards from the moderation of the magistrature and became manifest in the days of barricades from 26 to 28 August 1648. The first signs of trouble began on 26 August when the *conseiller* Broussel was arrested by a detachment of militia and guards from the Queen's retinue whilst the Te Deum was being sung at Notre-Dame to celebrate the recent victory at Lens. Anne evidently hoped to retrieve some of the concessions which she had been forced into making under the pressure of the *Chambre Saint-Louis* and which she regarded as excessive. Then came the great day of barricades of 27 August when 1,260 were erected in the city. Anne was immediately forced to agree to the Parlement's demand, itself under pressure from the populus, that Broussel should be released. In the course of the following days, calm was gradually restored, although not without incidents. Beyond the details of what happened in the short-term, however, there are some underlying characteristics to these days of barricade. Firstly, although it hardly seems a central issue, there was economically-based discontent. Rents in Paris in fact decreased during the three-year period from 1645 to 1647, a sign of weakness in the market and the number of transactions.[33] In addition, the fiscal innovations of Mazarin (the *toisé*, the new sales-tax tariffs, the increased dues on alienated royal domain) were badly received by that fraction of the Parisian population which was accustomed to paying few taxes. The disquieting and disturbing effects of overt affront to privilege during the Ancien Régime are well known. The privileged, whether rich or poor, tended to revolt more readily than their underprivileged and desti-

---

[33] Cf. E. Le Roy Ladurie, *Territoire de l'historien* (Paris, Gallimard, 1973), vol. i, 128.

tute counterparts. Secondly, there were chains of influence which mobilized individuals from the bottom right up to the top of society but the merchant classes, the artisans and the people were at the heart of those who were actively engaged. The Parlement found its hand forced by the crowd to take up a role, and a spectacular one, during the days of barricades. Paul de Gondi, the coadjutor of the archbishop of Paris (and the future Cardinal de Retz) acted as an intermediary if not already as a leader. He had contacts with some of the *parlementaires* of lesser rank who, besides their offices as judge, were also captains of the civic militia in their residential districts and thus partakers in the brief rebellion alongside merchants of various descriptions. A man of the world, and perhaps even of large horizons too, Gondi discreetly constructed and eventually took part in cabals against Cardinal Mazarin which would soon become notorious. They included highly-placed *parlementaires* such as Novion, the *président* Viole, the *conseiller* Blancmesnil, besides the inevitable figure of Broussel himself.[34] They also enjoyed the participation of former ministers such as Chavigny and Châteauneuf and a gathering coterie of grand seigneurs variously recruited from among the three branches of the Bourbon family – i.e. that of Orléans, the king's brother, the Condé-Conti, his cousins, and the Vendôme-Beaufort, the illegitimate branch. Amongst the grandees who joined the Fronde cause, there was to be found the duchess of Longueville, the sister to the Great Condé (who, for the present, remained loyal). Joining it at the end of 1648 in the name of anti-Mazarinism was Condé's brother, Armand de Conti, along with the duke of Longueville and then the prince de Marcillac, the duchess of Longueville's suitor, and who would become more famous later as a writer and as duke de la Rochefoucauld. These families were well-entrenched in the provinces. Longueville was governor of Normandy, Conti in Champagne, whilst the Marcillac-La Rochefoucauld had estates in Aquitaine. Overall, the Fronde opposition crossed the boundaries of classes as well as orders and ranks in society at large. It had a potential leader in Retz who was held in low esteem and had been rejected by the courtiers around Anne of Austria.[35]

When it comes to those who actually manned the barricades during the three critical days of August 1648, it is no longer possible to imagine them as vagabonds, the dangerous elements in society, the mob, the riff-raff, etc.[36] It was the commercial élite as well as the Parisian craftsmen, particularly based on the Ile de la Cité, mobilized through the craft guilds,

---

[34]   On the preceeding and succeeding sections, see the essential articles of Roland Mousnier, 'Quelques raisons de la Fronde: les causes des journées révolutionnaires parisiennes de 1648', *XVIIe siècle*, 1 (1949), 33 *et seq.* Augmenting and correcting Mousnier, cf. Jean-Louis Bourgeon, 'L'Ile de la Cité pendant la Fronde, structures sociales' in *Paris et Ile-de-France. Mémoires publiés par la Société historique et archéologique de Paris et de l'Ile-de-France*, 13 (1962), 122 *et seq.*

[35]   See Simone Bertière, *Le Cardinal de Retz* (Paris, Klincksieck, 1978).

[36]   Bourgeon, 'L'Ile de la Cité'.

confraternities and civic militia, who provided the basic components of the so-called 'popular', and generally armed, bands which had assembled with great clamour in an apparently unpremeditated way. Those social elements generally considered to be 'inferior' (such as valets and servants etc.) were content to follow and reinforce an uprising which was controlled by the city's master-craftsmen, tradesmen and shop-keepers. In other words, the lower and lower-middle elements of Parisian society imitated the middling strata once they had themselves been galvanized to action.[37]

Psychologically, those who manned the barricades were mobilized by the classic phenomenon of finding a scapegoat and turning it into the 'devil incarnate' and thus a good reason for 'political engagement'. Mazarin provided a ready target for his opponents. He was Italian, and therefore allogeneously un-French, he had made a fortune by unscrupulous means, and it was easy to turn Mazarin into a hated figure. By contrast, the young king (Louis XIV was only about ten years old) had their respect; but they wanted to shelter him from the intrigues which Mazarin wove around him. Mazarin, who enjoyed the affections if not the physical love of Anne of Austria, was hated rather in the fashion that some of the consorts of the eighteenth-century Bourbons would become popularly detested, whether their mistresses (Madame Du Barry) or their wives (Marie-Antoinette). At all events, the myth of the king's wicked counsellor and evil friend was widespread. The image of Broussel, on the other hand, was a more positive way by which popular energies were polarized. A venerable father-figure, he was accorded a degree of spontaneous affection; and, beyond his years, he would have earned his standing amongst the bourgeoisie and the people of Paris because of his resourcefulness as a politican. Fear, however, would remain as an essential component of civic unrest in this traditional society. The 'rush to arms' of the bourgeois, artisans and merchants was on the pretence of a fear of disorder amongst the populace at large and of an ensuing pillage by the city's vagrants. Such fears justified the arming of its citizenry, however much that was contrary to the good order and peaceable composure which the royal government sought in the capital. As the fateful days of the barricades wore on, however, the groups which had organized the uprising began to fear the reprisals which the royal army might exact upon them. Although it was far from a strong force, it was stationed not far from their barricades and such fears, as so often is the case, merely reinforced the aggressive determination of their leaders and more militant supporters in the midst of the Parisian rebellion.

The Fronde and the anti-Fronde proceeded by repeated fits and starts. Not for the last time, Anne of Austria was tempted to give away with one hand what she took back with the other. Outraged by the boundaries

---

[37] In various publications, Maurice Agulhon has stressed the concept of 'inter-social imitation'.

which the Parlement wanted to place upon the absolute authority of the king, the queen and the royal family recided to leave Paris. A French king or Regent needs to know exactly when to vacate the capital. There were other moments of popular unrest or religious fervour when Catherine de Médicis, and then, later, Henry III, were forced to confront the problem, just as Louis XVI, Charles X and Louis-Philippe would have to in the future. It was a delicate matter which had to be tried, but which was by no means certain of success. If it failed, then the fate of the monarchy at Varennes would await the vanquished.[38] On 13 September 1648, the royal family left Paris without too much difficulty to take up a new residence at Rueil, a location which was made the more symbolic by the fact that Richelieu often spent his time there. This stay outside the capital did not last long. Anne of Austria and Mazarin did not have the means to support their political endeavours and, on 22 October, the queen signed a declaration which was a capitulation in all but name to the *parlementaire* demands, such as they had been formulated in the 27 articles drafted a few months earlier. Some of its formulations were toned down so that there emerged a 'reginal' version of the text with a monarchy still vaguely absolutist but henceforth (at least in principle) trammelled by the initiatives of a Parlement. The *via media* was thus the more developed and embellished. In such circumstances it could hardly serve matters to stay away from the capital much longer. So, towards the end of October, the queen and the royal court returned to Paris. The period at Rueil and then at Saint-Germain had lasted barely six weeks in total, a false exit worthy of a Feydeau farce which brought to an end the Shakespearian tension of the first nine months of the year.

At all events, the die had been cast, at least for the immediate future, in July 1648. D'Emery, the Superintendent of Finances and financiers' friend, was dismissed for what would turn out to be a period of 16 months. He was replaced by La Meilleraie whose principal merit in the eyes of the Parlement was his incapacity to come to a deal with the *traitants* and to see eye-to-eye with the financiers, which was disastrous from the point of view of the royal Treasury. Meanwhile, other important problems remained undecided. The Peace of Westphalia bringing to an end the war in the Holy Roman Empire was lavishly publicized in October 1648. But the *parlementaires* were preoccupied with domestic issues and the war between France and Spain continued. The problems of heavy taxation and the funding of war, all those which had caused the Fronde in the first place, remained as acute as ever for the following year.

On the night of 5–6 January 1649, to coincide with the feast of Epiphany (the *jour des rois*), Anne of Austria, Louis XIV and the remainder of the royal family left Paris whilst Condé, still loyal to the government, envisaged a siege of the city in the name of the Regent with a force of 12,000

---

[38]   Varennes-en-Argonne [Meuse] where Louis XVI and the royal family were captured on 20 June 1791 as they sought to reach the French frontier.

troops – evidently inadequate against a city with a population of more than 430,000. In reality, this exodus was a response to an increasingly hostile, anti-Mazarin climate in which urban resistance to taxation was fomented by the *parlementaires*. The royalist faction and the court hoped to finance the expenses of the war against Spain (to which they attached a high priority) by heavy taxation. This was the reason behind the continuing heavy fiscal exactions; and the latter were only possible to conceive and apply, or at least this was how it seemed, if the royal government left Paris in order to protect itself from *frondeur* aggression.

Anne of Austria and Jules Mazarin did not leave the capital without making sure that they retained some loyal friends and numerous partisans to the royal cause, both active and passive, within Paris. Its municipal government, made up of the *échevins* and the city Provost (*Prévôt des Marchands*), was full of government agents who had been more or less co-opted into power by the crown; the *Hôtel de Ville* was more or less at the cardinal's behest. Many of the city's goodly merchants, the grand (and sometimes not so grand) bourgeoisie, preferred civil peace and hated the prospect of civic unrest. They had their eyes on the commissions to supply luxury goods, financed by the royal Treasury and by courtiers. They missed the Mazarin years and, although they did not make their sympathies public, they were content to make preparations for the return of the one individual whom the *frondeurs* regarded as their quintessential enemy. There was therefore no question of the city being completely in the hands of a Cardinal de Retz or a Mazarin, just as it would not be universally behind Pétain or overwhelmingly for de Gaulle in 1944. The *parlementaires* themselves were not all of one mind either. There were some Mazarinists in their ranks just as there were, on the other side, many determined *frondeurs* – Viole, Novion, Broussel and such like. But the majority of opinion in the Parlement was fairly conservative and supportive of the *via media*. It had entered into conflict with Mazarin, who had been vilified in one of its edicts; but, at the same time, it negotiated with the (royal) financiers, the (royalist) *Hôtel de Ville*, and with the Regent herself. It swiftly disassociated itself from the execution of King Charles I in England on 30 January 1649. The Parlement wanted to reform the absolutist structures of the state and it sought to twist them until they were almost unrecognizable; but it did not seek to overturn them and did not see itself as a revolutionary body. It wanted a peace ministry to replace the war-mongers and a régime which governed by ordinary, rather than extraordinary, means. However, as the state fragmented and disintegrated for a period, it opened the door to pressures from the upper nobility, who were more unpredictable than the *parlementaire* gentry and more amenable to Hispanic temptations of the kind which would have horrified Richelieu. For their part, the magistrates were inured to such temptations by virtue of their Gallican, anti-Jesuit, Jansenist and anti-Vatican stance which made them suspicious of *dévot* Madrid. The close relatives of the king – i.e. Gaston d'Orléans (his uncle) and the Great Condé (his eldest cousin) –

remained at this stage loyal to the court. By contrast, Conti (Condé's younger brother), the duke de Longueville (his brother-in-law), the prince of Marcillac-La Rochefoucauld, the duke de Bouillon (Turenne's brother), the duke de Beaufort and the illegitimate line of the Vendôme princes already mentioned, the duke d'Elboeuf (the Guise pet from the Lorraine family), the *maréchal* de la Mothe-Houdancourt and many others joined the leading rebels in Paris. There, they met up with a clutch of elderly conspirators who had managed to evade the imprisonment or banishment to which Richelieu had consigned them. Although the leading *frondeurs* of the Parlement (Viole, Le Coigneux, Broussel, etc.) were linked by numerous bonds to the Paris bourgeoisie and its populace, in another light they were also connected or had bonds of loyalty to both the greater and the not so great nobility who provided the military muscle for the whole opposition enterprise. Such groups were nevertheless fickle, unreliable and hot-headed. They had to hand over the political direction of the revolt to the Parlement, the stronghold of the moderates of the *via media*. The Fronde was too important a matter for it to be left in the hands of the soldiers. The blue-scarved and theatrical feminism which made its first highly visible appearance during the Fronde on 11 January 1649, and which was the contemporary counterpart of the more pacific *précieuses*, wove a web around the red robes and soldiers' spurs. This feminine declaration emanated from the young scions and their elders amongst the loyalist aristocrats such as the Chevreuses (mother and daughter) and the duchesses of Longueville and Bouillon. Their amorous intrigues had time to weave their way into and around the factions which were directed by Gondi, Conti and La Rochefoucault-Marcillac in company with their aristocratic consorts.

Other actors also took up lesser parts in the drama. In the provinces, the parlements of Aix and Bordeaux actively contested the authority of their provincial governors. In Paris, the populace sometimes took on the aspect of a seething mass of shop-keepers and street-salesmen organized into guilds and militia companies; at other times it played the part of a rabble, roused into action against Mazarin or against the pro-cardinal stooges encamped in the *Hôtel de Ville*. Sometimes they behaved like a strike-force which could be spontaneously activated by its anti-tax or anti-financier sentiments. At other times, they seemed at the behest of the grandees, docile enough so long as they were directing their hostility towards Mazarin. Amongst the villages around Paris, the peasantry had to put up with a good deal of violence and devastation inflicted by Condé's soldiers and by mercenary troops. The military forces of the state created a battle-zone in the countryside around Paris to overwhelm the *frondeurs* within the capital. It was in this zone that the conditions for the crisis would simmer until they eventually erupted in the terrible demographic crisis which afflicted its villages in 1652.[39] Yet the regular troops of Condé's army were

---

[39] Dupâquier, *Histoire de la population française*, ii, 203.

able to do no more than trounce the Paris opposition in a series of suburban skirmishes in February 1649.[40]

It was towards the close of winter and the beginning of spring, during February, March and April 1649, that a rapprochement began to take place between the *parlementaires* and the supporters of Mazarin. The Parlement had no wish to become the instrument of the grandees who wanted to get their hands on the provincial governorships and the instruments of power and who would willingly make common cause with Spain to achieve their ends. However, as we have already indicated, the Spanish alliance was unthinkable to many magistrates since it conflicted fundamentally with their political and religious convictions. In addition, the Parlement was afraid of the people, especially the noisy meetings of advocates who claimed an affinity with them, and who had become very exercised against, and very determined to oppose by force, the financiers and the cardinal. The latter, albeit there was no longer the military threat of the Austrian Habsburgs (because of the peace of Westphalia), feared Spanish intervention towards which Turenne was making crude overtures. Where one Habsburg threat had been replaced by another, Cardinal Mazarin was prepared to make concessions. At the beginning of April 1649, the Parlement accepted the peace accord which would bring the first civil war of the Fronde to a close. Each party to it took care to protect itself from hostile criticism from its own side. Mazarin assuaged the queen's anger and Molé that of his colleagues in the Parlement. In essence, however, the peace represented a victory for the moderation of the magistrates. The 27 articles of June/July 1648 were to be maintained, the Fronde rebels were to be granted an amnesty, and rights of assembly were granted to the *parlementaires*. Those in power baulked at the proposition of one Dubois-Montandré which sought to take over royal absolutism from within by requiring royal government to submit to the equally absolute and manifestly equitable wishes emerging from parlements and people, wishes which (with those of the prince himself) should be synthesized by the Parlement of Paris. No doubt such a synthesis would have been contentious and the *parlementaires* showed every sign of being satisfied with the pacification which had been arrived at, and the more so since it avoided the immediate risk that they would become dominated by the grand seigneurs who had joined the Fronde. Yet the aristocrats could at some stage always choose to make common cause with the 'people' and begin the civil war once more in their own interests. By retiring from the field of battle, the magistrates unmasked the redoubtable forces of the princes and other Condés who could each turn into a Cromwell.

A relatively short period of peace succeeded the accord reached at Rueil. On 18 August 1649, Louis XIV, 11 years and 11 months old, made a triumphal entry into his capital of Paris. As an object of affection amongst the crowds, the king had retained their loyalty despite some trace elements

---

[40] Pierre Georges Lorris, *La Fronde* (Paris, Albin Michel, 1961), p. 81.

Plate 7   Louis XIV as Jupiter, vanquisher of the Fronde   In this painting from the French School, painted between 1653 and 1661, the young Jupiter/Louis is presented with a smile of innocent satisfaction, brandishing lightning in his right hand. His left foot rests on the hateful Gorgon's breastplate and scattered around the lower half of the picture are the dispersed trophies of victory. Meanwhile, in the background, Vulcan and his assistants are forging further dissuasive thunder-bolts for the sovereign Jupiter/Louis to direct against his enemies if necessary. The Latin text at the bottom reads: 'An approving Jupiter cedes his weapons to Louis: the world witnesses the appearance of a new Jupiter.'
Versailles, Musée national du château

of republicanism imported from England in small homeopathic doses. Yet no one should be deceived by such routine displays of enthusiasm. In July 1649, the execution of the printer Morlot[41] – who was condemned to be hanged for having published various rather amusing, but scurrilous, anecdotes against Anne of Austria and Mazarin and who had been rescued at the last moment by the Paris mob – gave the measure of the violent anti-Mazarin forces amongst Parisian public opinion.

In these circumstances, two factions gradually crystalized into being at either the national level or that of Paris itself. These two factions channelled such discontents and sought to divert the flow of patronage, places, pensions and favour which would accompany their eventual victory towards them and their respective faction-leaders. One found its support initially in the milieu of the church (Gondi) and close to royalty. The latter was represented in the faction by Beaufort who enjoyed close proximity, albeit from an illegitimate line, to the monarch as well as support amongst former *robe* ministers from the royal Council (Châteauneuf) or senior figures in the Parlement (Charton and, above all, Broussel). These four or five individuals and their friends are the historic leaders of the 'old Fronde' – i.c. the opposition which had taken its stand in 1648 and the early months of 1649. They relied for their support in the capital on the *rentiers* who, since the Treasury was exhausted, no longer received any return on their investment. The same faction associated itself with the demands from various elements of the capital city's bourgeoisie and populace although the latter were not slow to conclude that some of their leaders, especially Gondi and his followers, had let them down and might even be suspected of Mazarinism. The 'old Fronde' leadership was thus fairly easily separated from its basis of support. Gondi and his partisans had neither the demagogic determination nor sufficient by way of armed force to contemplate the beginning of another civil war without qualms. Retz, the coadjutor,[42] was willingly to put his weight behind the *via media* of 1648 which the crowds in Paris, with the experience of rebellion behind them, now considered too moderate. A good cardinalcy expedited from Rome at the behest of the Regent would be sufficient to keep Retz quiet.

The other faction was more directly related to the military and army leaders and was therefore more dangerous. It included the leading army commanders of the period such as Condé and Turenne. Neither of them found that they could always rely on the support of the regiments which in principle they commanded. It was at this point that Condé, who had been the Regent's right-hand man during the first Fronde, turned against his

---

[41] See the excellent work of Christian Jouhaud, *Mazarinades, la Fronde des mots* (Paris, Aubier-Montaigne, 1985), p. 158.

[42] A *coadjutor* was a cleric nominated to assist a bishop or archbishop in the exercise of his episcopal duties and to succeed him in the see after his death. This was the post which Jean-Paul François Paul de Gondi, the future Cardinal de Retz and leader of the Parisian 'movement' during the Fronde, exercised alongside his uncle Jean-François de Gondi, Archbishop of Paris.

former patron Anne of Austria. He joined forces with the men and women from his own family (Conti, Longueville) and their associates (La Rochefoucauld) who had put their weight behind the Fronde in 1648. Condé's own ambitions had conflicted with Mazarin's in the autumn of 1649 and created a fundamental incompatibility. As for Turenne, finding that he was unable to secure the support of his own soldiers, he mobilized the Bouillon clan and the peasantry of his viscounty of Turenne. The former 'military commanders' of the old Fronde, the nobles who had placed themselves at the disposal of the *parlementaires*, also joined up with the new noble Fronde. Military experience amongst the leadership of this new Fronde was to prove far from a universal panacea, however, and Turenne and Condé, finding themselves lacking supporters precisely because of the inner logic of the central authority which they had deserted, were unable to secure a decisive victory over the remaining royal army.

The lesser nobility often found the princely ambitions of the Condé camp distasteful. Yet, for those actively involved in the march of events, Condé's faction had the great advantage of not being tainted by an exclusively Paris dimension of the kind which would limit the possibilities for someone like Gondi of having a wider impact and intervening on a broader stage. It has to be said against this, however, that Condé, who had directed the siege of Paris between January and April 1649 in the name of the crown before joining the rebels, was the object of lively opprobrium thereafter in the capital, a fact which Mazarin would play on in due course.

In the provinces, Condé's supporters were well-placed, thanks both to the provincial governorships which several of them held as well as their clienteles amongst the squirearchy and the office-holder groups who were beholden to the prince. Such favourable factors were particularly noticeable in Burgundy (thanks to Condé himself), in Normandy (where opposition would, however, be swiftly quelled), and in the south-west (thanks to Turenne, La Rochefoucauld, etc.). The *parlementaires* of Rouen, Bordeaux and Aix were sufficiently aroused to provide the military force of the grandees with, alongside the anti-fiscal agitations in the Midi, particularly in Aquitaine, the combustible elements necessary to generate a social consensus amongst the opposition. Urban oligarchies, however, were more reticent since they were more beholden to royal authority and because they represented a certain respect for order which was naturally present amongst the merchant notables of the larger towns. Unrest simmered in the provinces within a national and regional anarchy which was a symptom of a kingdom which was internally weakened to the point of disintegration. Order was very far from being restored throughout France in the period from April 1649 to January 1650. The Mazarin ministry was certainly the flagship for good or ill of the Regency and of legitimate government, and ministerial and military decree. It retained the critically important facility of playing a balancing role between the two factions which were its adversaries, the former old *frondeurs à la* Gondi and the new Condé *frondeurs*. However, following some miserable moments at the beginning of December 1649, the coadjutor Gondi recovered sufficiently by the end of the year for the Regent and Cardinal Mazarin to coax him into supporting them by dangling the possibility of a cardinal's hat before him. Even the presence of a well-meaning and committed reformer like Broussel amongst the ranks of the old *frondeurs à la* Gondi was not sufficient to frustrate the political manoeuvrings of Anne of Austria and Jules Mazarin.

Once the ministerial team had thus secured their position in Paris, they turned the full weight of their hostility against Condé whose grand manner, bizarre intrigues and voracious demands for provincial governorships and pensions touched a raw nerve and irritated Anne of Austria and Mazarin. The latter's disillusionment with the prince was quickly shared by the minister's henchmen, principal amongst whom was the figure of Le Tellier, the Secretary of State for War. On 18 January 1650, Condé, his brother Conti, and his brother-in-law Longueville were arrested and imprisoned. This was the day which marked officially the beginning of the princely Fronde, the more bitterly contested now that their family heads were incarcerated – and somewhat unjustly as well. The case against Condé was far from overwhelming – apart, notably, from his bold attempts to seize Le Havre and Normandy from Mazarin's control. Richelieu, in his day, had not spared the executioner's axe when it served the turn. Mazarin, less ferocious, handed his opponents over to the efficient, but not blood-stained, hands of a gaoler. Although imprisonment remained, execution in such matters was a thing of the past. It was a mark of progress.

This is a moment to take stock of where things had progressed to in France, or that assemblage of people who spoke in the name of France and which was so divided in the immediate aftermath of the imprisonment of the princes. On the one hand there was a 'Mazarin' party dedicated to resisting any threat towards, or retaining and maintaining the brutal extension of, state authority which had prevailed in the periods from 1624 to 1630 and then again from 1642 to 1648. Secondly there was an 'outerwing' of Condé's supporters, a dynamic and military element which attempted rather late in the day to overturn the growth in state power which had occurred over the preceding two decades; or rather it sought to take control militarily, Cromwell-style, of the summits of power. Between the two one can make out a centre group – very Parisian, made up of the leaders of the old Fronde, with Gondi to the fore. The terms adopted by English historians of 'court', 'country' and 'city' might well sum up the divisions between Mazarin, Gondi and Condé; and, indeed, a close observer of the kingdom, La Bruyère would use them without qualification: 'la cour', 'la province' and 'la ville'.[43]

After the abortive attempts by the princes to raise the provinces of Normandy and Burgundy, their efforts were concentrated on the south-

---

[43] La Bruyère, *Caractères* (Paris, Garnier, 1962), 'Des femmes', para. 30 (1), p. 119.

west and on Bordeaux. They sought to exploit the latter's political divisions which had become apparent by June 1650. The divisions were threefold. Firstly, there were the local (Mazarinist) supporters of the provincial governor d'Epernon, in due course supported outside the city by the royal army. Then there was a moderate, anti-Epernon *parlementaire* group. Finally the forces of the sometimes extreme and adventurist grand Fronde assembled around the princess of Condé,[44] who had taken up refuge in the city and who acted as her husband's political surrogate during his imprisonment. They included the middling and lower ranks of society with support also amongst the councillor-judges of the Parlement – though not from amongst the *présidents* of the court who were moderates.

The strategy of Mazarin and the Regent remained valid. To defeat the supporters of the imprisoned Condé, whom he believed to be a dangerous adversary, Mazarin openly sought allies amongst the Fronde leaders from the (dare one say 'soft'?) 'centre'. Various posts, particularly in government and including the superintendency of finance, were distributed in Paris to members of Gondi's faction. When it came to re-establishing peace in the Bordelais in the autumn of 1650, it was achieved after mediation, following which the friends of the *parlementaires* and of Gondi were put into positions of influence – and to such an extent that it risked upsetting the clients of both Mazarin and Condé at one and the same time. The Parlement of Bordeaux was restored to its authority. Condé was not released even though an amnesty was granted to the other princes and princesses who had become compromised during the rebellion. This was a rebuff for the politically active and extremist *condéens*, and also for Mazarin; by contrast, however, it was a victory for the centrist group of old *frondeurs* of the *via media* which His Eminence the cardinal had, acting like a sorcerer's apprentice, conjured into prominence in order to draw support from this faction by distributing senior posts (including ministerial portfolios) to them.

So was the coadjutor Gondi on the thresholds of power? Things were not that simple and Mazarin was not that naive. It was rather more the case that the *parlementaire* group in Paris (which was, incidentally, rather divided) and Gondi's various willing and not so willing 'friends' enjoyed something of a reflected glory in the period from 1648. From May through to the peace of Rueil[45] – i.e. until April 1649 – they had imposed a revolution on the French government, or at the very least a judicial and legal evolution which gave the monarchy an assumed patina of enlightened absolutism whilst imposing upon it a series of checks and divisions. From

---

[44]   Claire Clémence de Maillé-Brézé, the daughter of Urbain de Maillé-Brézé, *maréchal* de France, and of Nicole du Plessis-Richelieu, was Cardinal Richelieu's niece. In 1641 she married the duke d'Enghien, the future Great Condé. During the Fronde Claire, despite being the niece of the architect of absolutism, would demonstrate at Bordeaux and elsewhere her active support for her *frondeur* husband whilst in prison, and again after his release. The marriage did not turn out to be a happy one in the years after the Fronde.

[45]   Moote, *The Revolt of the Judges*, p. 210.

April 1649 (the peace of Rueil) through to January 1650 (Condé's arrest), the *parlementaires*, whose median and central role is evident, remained the leading moderate figures, relying (albeit only tangentially) on Mazarin against the revival of a powerful *condéen* opposition which would be provincial and/or popular in the nature of its support, and princely in its forms. From January 1650 to October 1650, the supporters of Gondi moved progressively and inexorably (in accordance with their political instincts) towards the centre of the political stage and their attitudes began to correspond more and more closely to the concept of the *via media*. This move put them in amongst the Mazarinists who were in the process of trying to restrain the militant and militaristic *condéens*. The fruits of their labour were to be found in the Peace of Bordeaux (October 1650). The resulting sequence of events would indicate, however, that this move of the moderates towards a watchful centre and then, in due course, towards a military left-leaning stance was in accordance with a certain logic, that of the revolutionary radicalization of the Fronde which was to a degree independent of the wishes of its principal actors. We should note in passing that these topological analogies (*via media*, 'leftward leaning' etc.) are not inappropriate as ways of indicating the political lines of force, or perhaps the 'vectors' of politics during the Fronde. They should certainly not be confused with the terms 'right' and 'left' in their modern connotations.

The process of radicalization appeared, firstly, at the level of political vocabulary, even though one should not take it too much at face-value. The terms of abuse which were current, albeit unjustifiably so – such as Republics, Fairfax, Cromwell (the latter, horror of horrors, a regicide in power) – became more prominent in the rhetoric of the Mazarinists and used to calumniate the coadjutor and his (albeit moderate) allies amidst the Parlement. The magistrates of this august assembly were far from pleased to become the target of such frightful vilifications which tended to present them also as regicides in power. The indignation on their part was one of the motives which contributed to their process of enlargement of the increasingly bitter rifts in Paris during the first three months of 1651. Thus the *parlementaires* found themselves wrongly represented (by Mazarin's supporters) as anti-royalist and, in due course, some of them would begin to live up to their reputation. Give a dog a bad name. . . . Contemporary commentators also noted a hardening of attitudes and of actions. There were numerous provinces where resistance to taxation became something of a guerilla war. Meanwhile, at the other end of the political spectrum, the cardinal-minister Mazarin, Anne of Austria's friend, was preparing, whether he liked it or not, for a new rupture with Gondi. The cardinal-minister stood in the way of Gondi's ambition to receive a cardinal's hat from the pope. Given the tensions already present and the anti-Mazarin sentiments which had made an impact everywhere, this rupture was, in any case, an inevitable occurrence.

In the event, the winter of 1650–1 saw the forging of an alliance between *condéens* and old Gondi *frondeurs*, a union which would have been almost unimaginable in the preceding years. From this 'union of the two Frondes' all sorts of consequences flowed. At the beginning of 1651, the Parlement sought the official dismissal of Mazarin and the freeing of the remaining princes from prison. In fact, the princes from the Condé family were liberated and, a few days later (on 16 February 1651), they made a triumphal entry into Paris. Mazarin left the capital, and then the kingdom, and Anne of Austria and Louis XIV were practically prisoners of the Parisian militias in the Palais-Royal. Popular agitation increased amongst the clergy and the nobility and the latter began to come together in order to summon the Estates General. Such agitation, however, gave scant comfort to the Parlement, which had little respect for institutions which might become competitors to it; and the Estates General could easily challenge the *parlementaire* pretension to represent the wishes of the country. For these few weeks, these various developments created a situation which one might readily describe as revolutionary, if that adjective had any meaning in this context for contemporaries. But they were revolutionaries without a Revolution! It was precisely for this brief moment that there was a coincidental coming together of the seizing of the initiative by the *parlementaires* alongside the newly manifested political initiatives of the nobility. In other words, besides the absolutism *tertius gaudens*[46] developed or reinforced in France by the Thirty Years War (and which would survive these years of conflict to become the basis of the centralized modern state which meant so much to Louis XIV and his successors) there were now at least two other rival or alternative models on offer of a temperate monarchy. One emanated from the political engagement and accompanying pretensions of the Parlement at the beginning of the Fronde in 1648 which were still matters of active political discussion. The other was implied by the actions of the nobility in proposing the reactivating of the Estates General, a body which might compete with the Parlement and the summoning of which they sought to frustrate.

Of the two assemblies of the nobility, that of September–October 1649 (which was dissolved by the Court) and that of February–March 1651 (also dissolved in due course), it is the latter which will merit our further attention. It was legitimately summoned on 6 February 1651 by Gaston d'Orléans, Lieutenant-General of the kingdom. He hoped to use it as a way of putting pressure on the Court to release the Condé princes (in fact, they would be freed from prison on 13 February). The assembly produced an 'act of union' which carried the signature of over 400 participants. Its leaders, Montrésor, Fiesques, and the moderate Escoubleau, marquis de Sourdis, pressed for the reunion of the Estates General, the respect for the law and for proper consideration of the need of the provincial élites (the 'country'). This stood out in contrast to the essentially Parisian demands ('city') of a Gondi which were formulated in opposition to the Court

---

[46] A third party which took pleasure from eventually displacing the other two.

('court') and based essentially around the Parlement and the *Hôtel de Ville*. . . . The several hundred noblemen convoked in these assemblies could not envisage a separation of powers of the kind outlined in Locke's *Two Treatises of Government*, the inseparable components of the Glorious Revolution of England in 1688; or of the kind proposed by Montesquieu in the *Esprit des Lois*. Instead, the assembled gentry had a vision of 'harmony, concord, affection and balance' – in short the political virtues of antiquity, practised within a Stoic context. Affect, friendship, political conduct envisaged as baroque theatre, all transformed the noble leaders into characters out of a stage-play, barely capable of facing the hard and cold realism of a Richelieu, a Mazarin or a Colbert who was discreetly building up his influence in the shadow of Cardinal Mazarin's soutane.

As it turned out, the assembly of nobility decided to disband in March 1651 under the influence of the Parlement as well as Gaston d'Orléans and even Condé. Louis XIV's majority was declared on 7 September 1651 once he had reached the age of 13 and this brought to an end the dream of holding an Estates General, a dream which had exercised imaginations in the winter and spring of 1651. The overspill of *parlementaire* agitation into the convocation of a 'national' assembly from the three orders of the kingdom – the achievement of which would be the great 'success' of the years 1788–9 – was thus one possibility which was aborted almost as soon as it was advanced in 1651. This is one of the objective reasons why the Fronde did not become a radical revolution. At the same time, it is also the case that the major contributory components to the implosion of the Ancien Régime in 1789 were also conspicuous by their absence during the Fronde. The emergence of developed élites with a conscious sense of their own identity; an egalitarian ideology; a new political culture; circles of enlightened thinking; the militant autonomy of the people and the Third Estate (or its active and engaged minorities); the peasant semi-revolution; and finally the international situation set up beforehand by the War of American Independence – nothing, or almost nothing, of any of these components can be identified in 1651.

It was in March–April 1651 that the Condé-Gondi axis which had easily intimidated the monarchy, an alliance of fish with fowl, began to collapse. The hostility of the *parlementaires* to the promotion of cardinals to ministerial posts (Mazarin) and also to the advancement of future or possible cardinals such as Gondi and Châteauneuf, marginalized these two leading figures from the old Fronde which would thenceforth be divided against itself. In April, Anne of Austria disgraced Châteauneuf and gave the seals to Molé who was a moderate figure and entirely royalist in his leanings. From May, Gondi foreswore his *condéen* leanings and made his peace with the Regent. In August he escaped (he claimed) an assassination attempt following a dramatic altercation with the convinced *condéen* La Rochefoucauld – a remarkable quarrel between these two great writers whose works, however, would only be known to the public at a much later date. In September 1651, Condé arrived in Bordeaux. He began to make

preparations for a civil war which Mazarin was seeking in the circumstances to launch him into, such was the cardinal's anxiety to use this route
as one way of restoring the credentials of a régime which would thus
become absolute. The grand coalition between robe and sword against the
full exercise of authoritarian royal authority fractured. Was it not the case
that the French monarchy, having never really faced the full negating
consequences of a revolution *à l'anglaise*, had weathered the worst of the
storm? What strengths could the French monarchy muster in the face of
the *condéen* Fronde?

The *condéen* Fronde was to be a highly combative affair which, from
the autumn of 1651 until the following autumn, would be bloody and
destructive. It represented in its own fashion a synthesis of the various
preceding *parlementaire*, noble, princely, and popular Frondes. The
Fronde was never a monolithic movement but its disparate elements
seemed eventually to come together, and against it (or them) during its last
phase, and standing for embattled authority, was a Mazarin who had
himself experienced an eclipse. But he had returned from exile to find
Anne of Austria more enamoured of him during the winter of 1651–2. His
return threatened to widen the scope for civil war, so intense was the
hatred towards the Italian in France. In fact, the cardinal would undertake
a further personal period of exile in August 1652 under pressure from the
parlementaires. This would be designed, however, as a ruse to provide a
breathing-space, encourage Parisian pacifist sentiments, reassure the
parlementaires, bring the civil war to a close, and isolate Condé. It was a
calculated risk which, whether fortuitously or not, would turn out to have
been worthwhile.

Against the cardinal and the royalists stood Condé himself, an aggressive figure, full of resentments for having been ousted from the heights of
national authority. In direct conflict with the monarchical government, he
directed his rebel troops with courage and intelligence, albeit generally
without much success. A newly loyal Turenne led the combat against him
without overwhelming difficulties but with high casualties on both sides.
Once again the already-stated rule was demonstrated, that a strategic
genius, a Condé or a Turenne, could only have his full effectiveness when
reinforced by the fiscal and military apparatus of a great state. Condé
could rely, as always, on the princes of his family (Conti, Madame de
Longueville) and the nobility in arms for his cause (La Rochefoucauld,
Tavannes, Marsin). He also had the support of fragments or elements of
the solid bourgeoisie (albeit a minority within the bourgeoisie as a whole)
as well as the urban masses (who also were far from always the majority of
the population of Bordeaux, or Paris). Amongst the motivations which
drove them onwards there was, to recapitulate, their mutual hostility to
the fisc and the state which they accused (not without exaggeration) of
elephantiasis. They opposed absolutism even though Condé would eventually become transformed into an absolutist prince of the first importance
– a Cromwell or even a Bonaparte. Finally they were united by a certain

sense of communal justice which could in certain extreme circumstances become infected by vague republican notions. They shared an acute awareness of the current economic crisis, of dearth and of misery, itself the result in large measure of the civil wars which ravaged the provinces and particularly Aquitaine and the Ile de France. Finally they were mutually subordinated, both in civil and military matters, to the situation of clientelism which held together the leading rebels and more particularly bound them to the prince of Condé in person, who could exploit these ties to be in a position to levy some of his troops from his *fidèles* and dependants.

Condé, the generalissimo of the revolt, chose Bordeaux as his first base for operations in September 1651, an explosive city whose internal disputes during this period testify to its surprising dynamism. Then, after a difficult campaign northward from April 1652, the victor of Rocroi established himself in and around Paris. From 4 July a bloody putsch in the capital gave the prince the supreme authority in the capital for several months. The three individuals who acted as his lieutenants in the city – Broussel as *Prévôt des Marchands*, Beaufort as the governor of Paris, and Gaston d'Orléans, *alias* Monsieur as the Lieutenant-General of the kingdom – enjoyed at one and the same time real power and symbolic authority. In terminology, but also in reality, they covered exactly (in their theoretical titles) the functions of trade, of the army, of sovereignty. Gaston d'Orléans' presence was a particular reminder of the rooted opposition of the preceding decades to the unbridled absolutism set in train by Richelieu. The rash and dashing Beaufort, a pretty-plumed numbskull, focused the demands of the lower orders who invested a good deal of loyalty in him. Broussel, finally, represented *parlementaire* reformism, the left-wing of the senior judges. This elderly magistrate did not share in the extremism which was manifested in pamphlets and deeds by the *condéen* faction with its solid roots in Paris. Broussel retained his links with his colleagues in Parlement who had not been deflected from seeking a middle road between Mazarinist absolutism on the one hand and the illegality of the princes (for the Parlement regarded them as being guilty of having drawn their sword against the king). Of course, the Condé party did not always leave the *parlementaires* much freedom to develop their centripetal 'moderantism' during the summer 'communard' of 1652 as they would have liked and following their own deeply-held convictions. If their authority was sometimes compromised it was because the red-robed magistrates had to capitulate on more than one occasion to the pressures which were unleashed during these turbulent months to the crowds manipulated by the prince. In some cases, these crowds contained a goodly number of *condéen* soldiers disguised as civilians. But there were also any number of ordinary folk (stevedores, boatmen, vagabonds etc.) enrolled (even paid) by Beaufort. Also turning out to demonstrate their support were the bourgeoisie and merchants of the *quartier* Saint-Martin or Saint-Nicolas-des-Champs, who had taken against their fellow bourgeoisie and a

Parlement which they judged too soft and which they suspected at every turn of Mazarinist leanings.

Condé's final defeat[47] would be manifest in October 1652 with his departure from Paris for Flanders and the return of the king to the capital, and in February–March 1653 by the return of Mazarin himself. The latter had been kept in renewed exile for six long months because of the mazarinophobe and anti-*condéen* sentiments of the Parlement and, taking into account the fact that there was a good deal of bluff in the cardinal's actions which were designed to disarm by his departure the Parlement's rebuff, it remained the case that the centrist strategy of the *parlementaires* had paid off. It allowed them to maintain during the final years of Mazarin and into the age of Louis XIV important political space, real or imagined, which they would demonstrate with considerable efficiency during the *Unigenitus* affair in 1713. At all events, this was to be one of the less immediately apparent successes obtained by the *frondeurs* and despite the fact that their effort had been seemingly rewarded by a resounding defeat. They succeeded in setting some sort of limits to absolutism, forcing it to exercise power with prudence for over a decade and thereafter to endow it during the Colbertian period with a more seductive public image that Louis XIV would never entirely shake off.

When Mazarin returned to Paris in February 1653, he had the support of the queen and the young king. He utilized the services of the superintendents Servien and Fouquet in financial affairs. Chancellor Séguier was responsible for justice and authority and Secretary of State Le Tellier looked after war. In 1654, the submission of the *frondeurs* to royal authority took place logically enough with the marriage of the cardinal's niece, Anne-Marie Martinozzi, with the prince de Conti, the leading rebel in the Bordeaux Fronde. It was a reconciliation but the opposing factions were not dissolved. The Fronde would only finally be put to rest in 1679–80 with the almost simultaneous deaths of the two great impressarios of the age, La Rochefoucauld and Fouquet, the rebel and the minister.[48]

Mention of Conti takes us back to Bordeaux where perhaps we can speak of an *après*-Fronde just as, in the following century, there are *après*-Robespierres – the latter-day Jacobins and Montagnards after Thermidor. Following the Parisian dénouement of October 1652 there would be the curious and fascinating phenomenon in the provinces of a half-popular, half-bourgeois Fronde under princely auspices which would only be brought to a close in July 1653. Known as the

---

47   The *condéen* entourage would remind us somewhat of the noble revolt of 1788–9 if the latter had not taken place in circumstances which were unique to the end of the eighteenth century, as a result of which the Revolution would become a fundamentally anti-aristocratic movement.

48   Madame de Sévigné, *Lettres* (letter to Guitaut, 25 August 1670, recording the death of Retz; and to Madame de Grignan, 3 April 1680, recording that of Fouquet).

Ormée[49] of Bordeaux it developed (more clearly than in Paris) out of the local *parlementaire* Fronde. This *parlementaire* Fronde had lasted from April 1648 through to June 1650 and it would seek to install in the provinces, as in the centre of the realm, a monarchy closely controlled by the parlements, including that of Guyenne in Bordeaux. Then came the *little Fronde* in Bordeaux from June 1650 to May 1651. It was a moderate *via media* movement led by the *présidents* of the local parlement and by the notables of Bordeaux. This Fronde was *a priori* ill-disposed towards *condéen* exaggeration and it would have been readily contented with a temperate monarchy, purged of its absolutist excesses. At the same time there developed at the local level after June 1650 a 'great Fronde' with the backing of the princess of Condé. It had the support of the councillors in the Parlement who were much more radical than their *présidents*, and this grew in time into the Aquitaine princely Fronde after May 1651. Both these Frondes sought the return of a limited monarchy, such limits being defined by the participation of the higher aristocracy in the corridors of power. The only exception was that the best-placed seigneur, Condé for example, would become in his turn fully absolutist and certainly militarist when he occupied a position in government, a possibility that Condé's final defeat denied him the possibility of experimenting with. Although it existed before March 1652, the Ormée in Bordeaux only became fully formed at that date. Historians see in it something of a revolutionary movement. In fact it was inspired by an idealized and vague notion of a fiscally benign monarchy and one which was, moreover, 'popular'. It was a beneficent and highly idealistic vision based on a tradition which flattered *a posteriori* the reigns of Louis XII and Henry IV. Such a popular monarchy meant at least the favouring of urban autonomy and the municipal privileges of the great Gironde port. The Ormée drew its support from the *rentier* bourgeoisie rather than the *parlementaires*, as well as from the ranks of the commercial and artisan classes and even the lesser nobility. It organized itself on the basis of the local militias not as a party but as a company or a confraternity after the fashion of the League of the past stripped of its religious extremism which had no place in the France of 1652. This confraternity took care to look after the welfare of its members. At the same time it provided the rebel princes (Conti and the rest) a supply of what we would call nowadays sherpas or *harkis* – the military and civilian supplementary forces for street demonstrations and fights, etc. The grandees used these voluntary auxiliary forces without any scruples and

[49] The Ormée owed its name to an alley of elm trees situated close by the church of Sainte Eulalie in Bordeaux where the *robins*, artisans and merchants of the movement frequently met – for example in April 1651. The result was the creation of a slightly disorganized uprising which became known as the Ormée. See Charles Higounet, *Histoire de l'Acquitaine* (Toulouse, Private, 1971), p. 295; Eckart Birnstiel, *Die Fronde in Bordeaux, 1648–1653, Schriften zur Europäischen Sozial- und Verfassungsgeschichte* (3 vols, Frankfurt-am-Main, Peter Lang, 1985), iii, 38.

rejected them once they had exploited the Ormée for all that it was worth. Amongst the Ormée we find the remnants of various ancient clientèles. Amongst the latter there were (paradoxically) the local clients of Richelieu who had long manifested their rooted opposition to Epernon Senior, the cardinal's great adversary in the region . . . and his son would become subsequently the hated pro-Mazarin stooge of the *frondeurs* of the southwest. In the ranks of the brave *ormistes* of 1652 were the defenders of a revived monarchy (on a temperate, limited, controlled and divided basis) and a scrupulous moral attitude. According to Christian Jouhaud, they made up the populace of this city of virtue. They would rather be allowed an increased degree of upward social mobility in a way that the élite notables of the parlement and of the city of Bordeaux, the defenders *de facto* of heredity of offices, would only contemplate with extreme reluctance. The *ormistes* were critical of, but not destructive of, the old order; they were not sans-culottes.[50] The movement was, however, a substantial one and it provides us with a way to understand rather more fully how urban populations, whether from the civic notability or not, were able to complement movements of rebellion wherever they arose in France, whether their origins lay with the *robe* or with the higher nobility.[51]

In the Gironde, as in the Ile de France, these various opposition manifestations are evident and reflected in the anti-Mazarin pamphlets that are properly known as *mazarinades*. Their critique was far from revolutionary – the most daring of them restricted themselves to the familiar Bodinian distinction between a monarchy worthy of the name (good, moderate) and a tyranny or despotism. They did not go far down the road towards the execution of a legitimate monarch. The English pattern, with its deflection towards a militant and military republican solution, is not reflected in the French treatises and pamphlets. What they lacked in the depth of their critical analysis, they made up in the vehemence of the style in which they were written.[52]

The successive Frondes of the judges, the princes, and the nobility have been each considered in succession. The latter would continue in some measure from the 'forest conspiracies' through to the last years of the 1650s, plots in which the gentry of the west of France played a leading part. They sought to limit, or at least to frustrate, the prerogative rule of absolutism just as they had when they toyed with representative assemblies and advanced the noble principle.[53] Finally, we have mentioned the popular Fronde and that of the pamphleteers.

There remains the Fronde amongst the clergy. Their rebellions were

[50] Despite what Roger Chartier says in 'L'Ormée de Bordeaux', *Revue d'histoire moderne contemporaine*, 21 (1974), 279–83 – a rare moment when inspiration deserted him.
[51] The most recent synthesis is that of Eckart Birnstiel, *Die Fronde in Bordeaux, 1648–1653*. This has been used considerably for this passage.
[52] Cf. Jouhaud, *Mazarinades: la Fronde des mots*, upon which this section greatly relies.
[53] Pierre Goubert, *Mazarin*, ch. 15: Arlette Jouanna, *Le Devoir de révolte; la noblesse française et la gestation de l'etat moderne, 1559–1661* (Paris, Fayard, 1989), p. 273 *et seq.*

Plate 8 Mazarinade According to Christian Jouhaud, this Mazarinade engraving depicts a true and tragic story, no doubt embellished for the occasion, of two sisters from a noble family of the region around Bordeaux. The elder married a noble of the sword (*Poulidor* – the name had associations with beauty in Occitan). The younger married a valorous *robin* (*Fortunat* – 'The Fortunate') and she was much influenced by her Capuchin Friar, by definition a *robin*, and a Frondeur. In the course of a baroque duel between the two sisters (centre lower panel) the younger Frondeuse sister kills the elder with a stone from a sling (a *Fronde*). The final panel of the pro-*parlementaire* Mazarinade presents her supporters as including noblemen of the sword as well as of the robe.
Paris, Bibliothèque nationale, cabinet des Estampes

non-violent but they were the more significant as a result. They began to appear following the imprisonment of Gondi. He had been granted his cardinalcy in February 1652 and henceforth he would be known by his title as the Cardinal de Retz. His arrest took place on 19 December 1652 on the orders of the monarchical government which was back in power. Clerical disaffection would last well beyond 1653, however, and thus after what is properly called the Fronde.[54] It took on new life in particular after August 1654 when de Retz succeeded in escaping from his imprisonment. His vicar-general Chassebran, hidden in the church-tower at the Paris

[54] Richard Golden, *The Godly Rebellion* (Chapel Hill, University of North Carolina Press, 1981).

church of Saint-Jean-en-Grève, stoked up the flames of opposition
amongst the secular clergy against Mazarin. The parish priests, or a good
number of them, had been influenced by Richerism[55] and set themselves
up against both royal authority and the French episcopacy. The Jansenists
amongst them declared a war of words (albeit a vicious one) against the
regular orders[56] of clergy, particularly the Company of Jesus. They were in
the latter-day tradition of clerics who already played a part in the Fronde
'contestations' from 1648 to 1653, writing *mazarinades* or other sulphur-
ous satires. Amongst them were Arnaud d'Andilly, Claude Joly and
various other 'politically engaged intellectuals'.[57] The anger of these ecclesiastics persisted well beyond the years of the Fronde. Some of the Paris
clergy became latecomers to the anti-Mazarin coalition composed of the
various 'estates' in the Ancien Régime (or a minority from each of them)
– the 'princely' nobility, the judges (themselves of the *noblesse* too), and the
people. At various points during the Fronde they had raised the standard
against the absolutist state whose growth had been possibly too rapid and
which constituted the legacy of Richelieu and the early years of Mazarin to
the French kingdom.

★　★　★　★　★

Such an analysis of the clerical Fronde suggests two further general remarks by way of conclusion. Firstly, the Fronde (including the clerical
après-Fronde) was far less fanatically inspired and religious than the
Catholic League. There is no doubt, as we have just demonstrated, that it
had its ecclesiastical aspects, and especially in the years from 1654 and
1655. But there is no comparison between this and the processional and
frenzied extremism of the period from 1585 to 1595. In this respect, we
are faced with the real beginnings of an overall positive process of the
secularization of collective attitudes even if not of laicization, pure and
simple. It would be wrong to see in the Fronde a purely reactionary and
feudal phenomenon in comparison with the radicalism of a French Revolution which was orientated towards emancipation and progress. In reality,
even in the history of the mentality of political opposition, the years of the
Fronde represent a clear evolution and (why should we not use the word?)
'progress' in contrast with the League. The Fronde directed itself at targets
which were far more down-to-earth even if the next world continued to
have an influence, and a particularly indispensible one when called upon
by Gondi and his supporters. For France remained a solidly Catholic
kingdom; so it was something that the *frondeurs* had clearly renounced the

[55] *Richerism* was a set of doctrines inspired by the ideas of the theologian Edmond
Richer (1560–1631). It envisaged a stronger position of the parish clergy within the
church.
[56] The 'regulars' were the members of the 'regular' clergy (monks etc.) in contrast with the
'secular' clergy in the parishes (who lived in the world or 'siècle').
[57] According to the expression of Christian Jouhard in *Mazarinades*.

dévot (and intolerant) exhibitionism which had characterized the Catholic League.

Secondly, to the extent that the Fronde engaged, in various degrees, the full range of social groups within France, from the people to the clergy via the magistracy and the nobility, it constituted not a united social front but a movement which engaged the totality of French society. In this sense the Fronde did have something in common with the French Revolution which also would involve the parlements, the liberal-minded nobles and eventually the patriot clergy. The coming of 1788, and even the events of spring 1789 should be seen from the points of view of these three social groups as leading on directly from the Fronde of 1648–55. But the social composition, and the ideas, which were manifested at the end of the eighteenth century were of an entirely different kind and degree. In retrospect they would give the Fronde *a posteriori* the feel of a great series of failed revolts in contrast with the immense uprising which would sweep up the Ancien Régime in the declining reign of Louis XVI and carry all before it.

At the same time, the Fronde was not as radical as the English Revolution during which the Stuart monarchy would be overthrown by a coalition (albeit not always one whose members saw eye to eye) of the English Parliament and the army. In France, the divison which rapidly appeared between the Parlement (which was an entirely different institution from the English House of Commons at Westminster) and the princely *frondes* (noble and *condéen* in their inspiration) ensured that the Bourbon monarchy survived intact. At their most radical, the *frondeurs* tried to unravel the absolutist accretions of the French state and moderate its exercise of power by regulating it through the use of judicial, customary, and even representative, checks. The degree to which the young King Louis XIV was the object of acclaim during and after the Fronde shows the degree to which antimonarchical sentiments had no place in France at this date. There was no comparison with England in 1649, and still less with France at the end of the eighteenth century.

We should note, finally, that the Fronde contained one element of quite remarkable modernity in it, a feature which was a foretaste of the future. In 1648, the leading element of public service in the state (the Parlement) sought, and for the first time to this extent, to put itself at the head of a consciously organized movement of disobedience against established authority. This would emphasize the fact that the governing élite of the kingdom and at the heart of the state had been unable to secure the obedience not just of the aristocracy (which had thrown off the bridle at an early date) but also the traditional servants of the king who were from the *robe* and amongst the office-holders. As we shall see, this was not the best of examples to set for the future and the lesson would not be lost on future generations, and it would find itself being emulated more frequently in the eighteenth century.

4

The Snake and the Sun

On 26 August 1660, Louis XIV made his solemn entry into the French capital.[1] Carried on a throne, he entered from the east by the *faubourg* Saint-Antoine, the site of the skirmishes with Condé's forces in July 1652. The inscription beneath the throne carriage evoked the good counsels of Anne of Austria, the military accomplishments of the young king, and his marriage to his Spanish bride Maria Theresa. Justice, force of arms, fecundity . . . an accord with Spain (a prelude to hostility towards the Huguenots?) and military themes, dressed up with the emblems of his sovereign predecessors – were these not all harbingers of the new reign's future direction? On the morning of 26 August, the city's clergy, the university of Paris, the city corporation and the craft guilds paraded before the sovereign, with members of his family and the chancellor in attendance. In the afternoon, his ministers – i.e. the chancellor once again and Mazarin's entourage (taking the cardinal's place for he himself was indisposed) led the detachments of household guards and other troops along with the *grand maître de l'artillerie* and the *grand écuyer*. The king and the queen brought up the rear of the procession. Thus the main 'estates' of the kingdom (the state itself, those serving God, the city, the craft guilds etc.) demonstrated in a highly visible way their loyalty to the king in his presence, and then in his company.

Louis XIV, 21 years of age, the son of Anne of Austria and Louis XIII, was on parade. His genealogical procession was as prestigious as that taking him inside the city walls, half a millennium of ancestry stretching back ten generations. It was made up of men and women whose origins were French or (more commonly) Latin – Italian principally – with the addition of a few German ancestors and others of different backgrounds. By both his mother and his father, Louis was at once Habsburg and Bourbon, but by his own volition he was much more Bourbon than Habsburg. The schooling and intellectual training which he had received

---

[1]   René Pillorget, *Nouvelle Histoire de Paris: Paris sous les premiers Bourbons* (Paris, Hachette, 1988), p. 634 *et seq.*

from his tutors and governors was adequate without being more than that. Throughout his long life, the king would sometimes foster the view that he was something of an ignoramus. This was an affectation which the king had in common with the *noblesse d'épée* who wanted to distance themselves from the pedantry of the *robins* and the common pedants.[2] The young king pretended – it was a pardonable indulgence – to have only a modicum of knowledge about anything. He never claimed to have developed a particular understanding of any special category of learning or knowledge, whether it be religious or purely lay. During his childhood and adolescence, Anne of Austria and, above all, Mazarin provided powerful object-lessons in competency which, when combined with the practical survival skills taught by the trials and tribulations during the Fronde, educated the young Louis, who was still only king in name. His native intelligence, his rapid and often sure-footed intuition (with some notable 'exceptions' such as the revocation of the edict of Nantes) provided the rest. His capacities for expressing himself were well-founded too. The king's use of language was clear and well-judged, free and easy, precise and full of sense. What was also noticeable in someone who had been timid before he had gained rapidly in self-confidence as a young man was his complete identification with the role of sovereign king that destiny and lineage had decreed for him. The characters created by Molière and La Bruyère were not more clearly identified with their respective characteristics of avarice, distraction or misanthropy than Louis XIV with the characteristics of kingship.

He reigned with a natural and professional accomplishment, without any apparent effort. This was the triumph of his family training rather than anything which had been satisfactorily imparted to him by his tutor. The unfortunate counterpart of this generally favourable upbringing was a haughty extrovertness, unaccompanied by overweening pride it is true, but a distended ego which made him adept at appropriating to himself the most varied actions of his ministers, his army and his diplomacy. If Colbert had founded a manufactory, it was the Sun-King who believed – and wanted others to believe – that he himself had been behind such an industrial initiative, who had laid the first stone. Making do with a little was not his forte – at least not until the years from 1690 to 1695 when he had to cut his coat according to his cloth.

Louis XIV was the conscious or unconscious inheritor of the theoreticians of the preceding three generations. They had adumbrated the notion of *imperium* in its plenitude which had gradually[3] become absolutist. All the young king had to do to become a disciple of such apostles was

---

[2] On the education and upbringing of Louis XIV see the recent summary by Marc Fumaroli in his communication to the conference on *Les Monarchies*, dir. E. Le Roy Ladurie (Paris, PUF, 1986).

[3] The key dates so far as the establishment of absolutism as a fact is concerned are to be found in 1439 (when the fiscal *taille* became independent of the Estates General) and, of course, 1614 and 1627 (the last meetings until 1787–9 of representative assemblies, i.e. the Estates General and the assemblies of notables).

to listen as a child and an adolescent to what was said and discussed around him in the circles of the court, absorbing their basic attitudes without having read a word of Bodin or Cardin Le Bret. Their standpoints filtered through to him via his entourage and successive ministers, the latter being responsible for communicating the basic tenor of such notions to the new king by what they said and how they behaved towards him. The range of absolutist doctrines was thus filtered through to him by a process of daily distillation adapted to his personal needs. Louis sought to restore to its unique status the sovereign entity of kingship which had been carved up between king or regent on the one hand and successive cardinal-ministers on the other, not to mention the *frondeurs* as well. Taking account of this desire to reunify supreme authority in himself, it is readily comprehensible why Louis should have taken to himself the mythological symbolism which had, in the preceding generation, been pressed into service by the Barberini pope, Urban VIII, Mazarin's first master. For Anne of Austria's son, it was a question of exploiting with enthusiasm the luminescent images of Apollo, the Sun-God, with all the logical and aesthetic possibilities imaginable, just as the gardens at Versailles demonstrate. There, the Sun-God stole silk-thread moments of nocturnal pleasure in the Grotto of Thetis. When he woke up he charged about the continents of the earth spreading heat and light in his chariot. As a child in the arms of Latona he transformed the revolting peasants of Lycia into frogs just as Anne had mastered the grandees at the close of the Fronde on behalf of her son.

The Louis XIV of this earlier period of his personal rule presented a kind of enlightened despotism before the astonished eyes of the rest of Europe. He projected around himself the refracted light of divine wisdom, rational but not yet entirely lay. Catholic, royal culture made a point of its Prudence, its Reason and its Good Sense, but this was in place of (and understandably so) the strict and secular (even anticlerical) rationalism of the eighteenth-century philosophes. A rationalist after his own fashion, Louis XIV was a kind of Frederick II of his own generation, more devoted to the church than his Prussian counterpart and more influenced by Jesuit teaching than the Hohenzollern Frederick who made a point of taking his teaching from Voltaire. Each owed his inspiration to sources appropriate to his generation; but each practised an authoritarianism which sought to avoid obscurantism.

The *Mémoires*[4] of Louis XIV provide us with a means to locate and to bring together the various stages by which their 'author' had arrived at his political and moral points of view. Coming at the top of the intellectual hierarchy proposed by the king or his amanuensis were itemized, as with

---

[4] Jean Longnon (ed.), *Mémoires de Louis XIV* (Paris, 1927). This text and edition has been the subject of some criticism. See, in this respect, Edmond Esmonin, *Etudes sur la France des XVIIe et XVIIIe siècles* (Paris, PUF, 1964), p. 203 *et seq.* (republished from his article in *Revue d'histoire moderne* (1927), pp. 449–54 to which Jean Longnon replied in the same journal the following year (1928): 'A propos des mémoires de Louis XIV', pp. 136–41.

Richelieu,[5] the cardinal virtues. These included, of course, piety, but also the virtues more appropriate for civil society – grandeur (a virtue in itself), equity, compassion, liberty and natural beauty of spirit, moral rectitude, vigilance, a concern for reputation, a search for respect, a mention of judicious advice, foresight, authority, fidelity towards the state, moderation, probity, clemency and a taste for good order.

At the centre of this intellectual hierarchy, the level classically occupied by the warrior and noble virtues, the *Mémoires* locate the power of armed force, vigour, nobility (of course), honour, the exalted or cruel destiny of the aristocracy, blue-blooded and blood-spent, the glory of his kingly ancestors and of the king himself, military professionalism, a resolute soul and, when appropriate, a sense of peace as the *a priori* complement to the acts of war.

In third place in the hierarchy of royal values came those of use and utility, whether it was the indispensable sweat of the labouring masses or an aptitude, if possible, in matters of business and its encouragement. The *Mémoires* express the king's interest in such matters, in the conscientious endeavour of entrepreneurs and constructors, in the delights of the simple pleasures of the craft of kingship when undertaken wholeheartedly. The indispensable treasures of a Prince such as Louis XIV were the industry of the people, the interest of future kings in the kingdom (a complement to the glory of his ancestors), his subject people in general, the vagaries of the king's own fortune, the simple pleasures (or absence of evil) in the world of work or the world in general, including (without being too rigorous about it) the repose of the governed which Mazarin's godson regarded as essential, just as Richelieu had already done.

Louis XIV had, at least in his younger years, an undeniable preoccupation with the welfare of his people, with their 'well-being', their happiness. Even the concept of a necessary battle against unemployment can be found, albeit very discreetly expressed, here and there in the *Mémoires*. But the priorities laid down by the king and his entourage were religious and military, although these were not to the exclusion of the (somewhat platonic) theme of the battle against the social evils afflicting his subjects, against their misery. Yet the most important agendas were Catholic conversion and territorial consolidation, the latter readily capable of becoming a justification for pure and simple conquests of new provinces. But Louis XIV was more interested in piecing together his lands like a modest peasant or notary. His patent ideology was the advancement of the Catholic religion and Louis was not, emphatically never, an insatiable conqueror with a messianic or totalitarian mission. He knew his limits. There was nothing of the 'furious fool'[6] to him and, in this respect, he was totally different from (for example) Charles XII or Napoleon, who were both

[5] See above, chapter 2.
[6] This was the expression which would be used by Cardinal Fesch at the time of the Empire about his nephew Napoleon whose unlimited territorial ambitions he (with some reason) feared.

individuals who were viscerally committed to limitless expansion, to ever-widening geo-political hegemony. Louis XIV was first and foremost a first-class, modern administrator.

Tensions inevitably emerged amongst his various and diverse objectives. They were sometimes resolved in the long-term in favour of the needs of the church or the defence (i.e. the aggrandisement) of the realm and to the detriment of his imperative to protect the well-being of the public, since the latter paid for the other desiderata.[7] In addition, the ecclesiastical, political and military establishments tended to close in on themselves to the point of providing their own *raison d'être*. In the end, 'dominance is only sustained by the capacity to maintain and develop the system of hegemony in its entirety and the interests which underpin it.' The interests of state became less related to those of its subjects,[8] even though some of its subjects (aristocrats, senior clergy, merchant notables and, above all the office-holders and *commissaires* who were comfortably ensconced within the apparatus of state itself) could call on influence *in situ* and thus receive personal rewards from the state greater than those which ordinary mortals might expect to receive or to exercise rights to.

Reinforcing these tendencies, Louis XIV was able to undertake a minor administrative 'revolution' in 1661. Revolution is perhaps too strong a word for what was, in reality, simply an administrative shift and one which reinforced trends which had been evident from the first half of the century, certainly from the Richelieu period and possibly from the more distant days when Sully began to show his great talents as a financier and establish his preeminence over the chancellory. In short, financial matters had already, on occasions, taken precedence over judicial affairs. This was a vital step and one which became definitive after 1661. In this perspective the former *frondeurs* of the high judicature were on the way to being humiliated, even though Louis XIV would treat them with circumspection for a dozen years thereafter.

The administrative change dated from March 1661. Mazarin had died during the night of 8–9 March 1661 and Louis, following in the footsteps of his father after the death of Concini, was able to establish immediately his personal rule. From 10 March, the king excluded the princes of the blood from the *Conseil d'en haut* as well as the prelates and cardinals, the marshals of France – all the cohorts of aristocrats and clergy who had

---

[7]   The studies of Anette Smedley-Weill, (*La Correspondance des intendants avec le contrôleur général des finances, 1667–1689. Naissance d'une administration* [Sous-Série G⁷ (Archives Nationales), Inventaire analytique (Paris, Archives Nationales, 1989)]) demonstrate, in any case, that, for the period to which she refers, the desire for the well-being, or the least ill-being of the people is never absent from the consciousness of the provincial intendants who, at this point, no doubt reflected the preoccupations of their master, the king and the *contrôleur général*. However, a desire, however sincerely felt, is not always a priority.

[8]   Herbert Marcuse, 'Trieblehen und Freiheit' in *Freud in der Gegenwart. Frankfurter Beiträge zur Soziologie*, 6 (1977), cited by Jürgen Habermas, *La Technologie comme 'idéologie'* (Paris, Denöel-Gonthier, 1968 and Gallimard, 1975), pp. 6 and 52. See also Jean-Marie Domenach, *Des idées pour la politique* (Paris, Seuil, 1988), p. 24.

infiltrated the council chamber under Anne of Austria and Mazarin. In the long-term history of the taming of the greater nobility in France, a history which would only end in the French Revolution and the wicker baskets next to the guillotine, the Louis XIV phase was significant but not necessarily an irreversible set of changes. After 1715, the grandees would recover under Louis XV some of the trappings of political power which they had lost in the preceeding reign. At all events they lost none of their fortune or their rank under the half-century of the Sun-King's rule.

So the supreme power which was no longer theirs to exercise fell into the hands of the absolutist system in its pristine state. They were excluded from the deepest and most hidden recesses of power which henceforth would include only a selection of ministers of state, especially those whose loyalty had already been tried and tested in their clientage links with Mazarin – whose network became Louis XIV's. These were Lionne, Le Tellier and Fouquet (who would shortly be replaced by Colbert). They came from the *robins* on Council. They were well-to-do, technocratic and of recent nobility, from families who had not long left the bourgeoisie behind. In the *Conseil d'en haut*, Louis met them several times a week in regular sessions, discussing with them the secrets of state, especially in matters of religion (the organization of the church), diplomacy and war. The individuals attending the *Conseil* would change in the course of the 55 years of the reign; but the principles would remain, save for the moments when Louis, who had excluded his mother, brother and his cousins from this powerful and select committee, would introduce his son to its deliberations in 1691, or his eldest grandson in 1702 – both on the logical grounds that as inheritors of the throne they should thus become co-partners in the essential decisions which were taken there.

The most marked excusion from the *Conseil* was the chancellor, the figure who had in the past been the general secretary of the monarchy, whose office was at the head of the judiciary and who was intimately involved with financial affairs, with war, and with the administration through the intendants. Taking advantage of the advanced age of Chancellor Séguier, who had nevertheless remained loyal to the basic interests of the monarchy throughout the Fronde, Louis and Colbert gently marginalized him and his office without destroying its *raison d'être* completely.

The essential ministerial post, and the one which would remain so more or less until the end of the Ancien Régime, was that of General Controller of Finances (*contrôleur général des finances*). It would soon be in Colbert's hands, through whom the administrative post would be conjoined to the reality of the huge influence he would wield. The *contrôle général* was, in modern terminology, the Ministry of Finance and the Ministry of the Interior rolled into one. *Ipso facto*, the 'finance-state' (with its decision-making and its policing functions) was reinforced and the 'justice-state' correspondingly diminished. The latter would, however, retain many important aspects until the Revolution, particularly under the auspices of the provincial parlements and the Parlement in Paris. The chancellor continued, of course, to play a part in the *Conseil des dépêches* where matters relating to the provinces were discussed. But this was a committee which became increasingly sapped of real authority by the *Conseil d'en haut*, and fell into comparative desuetude as the reign progressed. It would be resurrected by Louis XV. More resilient and persistent was the Council of Finance (*Conseil royal des finances*). It is said that, in this council, Colbert decided on the facts of the matter in question and that the king signed the necessary papers, it being the case that the king believed that he was doing well by entertaining the belief that he did everything. It was an illusion which the powerful minister Colbert did everything to sustain. But is it not the case (as we have discovered in more recent times, for example in the inter-war years), that the equivalents of Colbert, the ministerial figures of the time, were inevitably manipulated by their senior civil servants and political advisers? The Council of Finance was from time to time flanked by a Council of Commerce – for, without business prosperity there would be less tax to collect. In an analogous fashion, the Council of Dispatches (*Conseil des dépêches*) spawned a micro-council of religious affairs, destined to take care of (and how!) the Huguenot question. One should add, just to complicate things still further, that when Louis XIV came to choosing bishops destined to be 'instituted' by the papacy, he took advice from a Council of Conscience (*Conseil de conscience*) which would in due course be reduced to its constituent elements only, being made up (after the deaths of others who sat on it) of the king himself and his Jesuit confessor, either *père* Annat for the beginning of the personal rule or *père* Le Tellier at the end of the reign, with several others in between.[9]

'Jesuitization' in the distribution of the great diocesan benefices – or such were the grumblings to be heard amongst the senior clergy! Yet thanks to this arrangement, Louis put together little by little an episcopacy owing loyalty to him. This episcopal 'corpus' would be fully operational after about a quarter of a century, in 1685, at the crucial moment of the Revocation. We should add to this polysynodie (for such it was) by way of completeness a mention of two further councils, composed of councillors of state (*conseillers d'état*) and masters of requests (*maîtres des requêtes*). One dealt with contentious legal business and was known as the Privy Council (*Conseil d'Etat privé*; also known as the *Conseil des parties*); and the other was the Council of State and Finance (*Conseil d'Etat et des finances*) whose names indicate their specialism.[10]

This is sufficient in this context to indicate the collective or 'conciliar' character of the way by which council decrees and decisions (*arrêts*) were arrived at within government. In the light of all these various committees, absolutism, even though decisions were eventually made by the great

[9] François Bluche, *Louis XIV* (Oxford, Blackwell, 1992), p. 107.
[10] On the council structure, see Michel Antoine, *Le Conseil du roi sous le règne de Louis XV* (Geneva, Droz, 1970), p. 43 *et seq.*; also François Bluche, pp. 104–6. On the 'corps épiscopal' from 1661 to 1685, see Michel C. Peronnet, *Les évêques dans l'ancienne France* (Université de Lille III, 1977).

arbitrator himself (the king), were very far from being simply the result of his royal will. They emerged from a kind of collective kingship, unpacked, discussed, and then finally decided upon. The 'justice state' was far from being defeated; shown the front door, it immediately entered again by the back. The very act of deliberative decision-making, which remains today the typical pattern of tribunal panels and assize courts, was the daily work of these various conciliar bodies.

If one were to look for the true processes of executive action in the modern sense of the term, but within the absolutist framework, one finds it most in the activity of the *liasse* which occurred in the course of the afternoons or evenings when the king met with one of his ministers or with a secretary of state[11] to prepare for the decisions which would be made in council, or to take them there and then under executive powers on matters relating to the navy, fortifications, finance etc. This way of working retained a familial or even 'patrimonial' sense to it since many of these *liasses* (the term which was used for the dossier on which the particular minister was working) occurred, during the last 20 years of the reign, in the chamber of Madame de Maintenon, the semi-clandestine spouse of the Sun-King.

Amongst the most significant sovereign acts of Louis XIV, taking place after the 'purge' of the *Conseil d'en haut* in March 1661, was the 'coup' at Nantes in September of the same year. This 'coup' was the arrest of Nicolas Fouquet, the Superintendent of Finances. He had become for a brief while, following Cardinal Mazarin's death, one of the leading political figures. However, those who do things on a large scale can also achieve things on a smaller scale. So, having already reformed and 'slimmed down' the *Conseil d'en haut* at the end of the winter of 1661, it was not difficult to go one stage further at the end of the summer of 1661 and replace it with a small group of leading decision-makers to improve the workings of the new ministerial team. Louis XIII and Richelieu had already confronted the same problem – in 1610 and 1630 respectively – of taking over the old machinery of government whilst wanting to change one or two of its operatives. For Louis XIV, as for his father, the method remained the same. It meant creating a scapegoat who could be blamed for all the errors and crimes of the past and the destruction of whom might serve as an expiation for them. The sacrificial lamb in this instance was Nicolas Fouquet. Did he deserve to be treated in such an ungrateful fashion?[12] Certainly his protégé, the steadfast poet La Fontaine[13] who stood by him long after his disgrace, did not think so. And the king did not rebuke the poet's loyalty (but then the Louis XIV régime knew how to be indulgent towards the 'lesser fry').

[11]   Bluche, *Louis XIV*, pp. 106–8.
[12]   Daniel Dessert, *Fouquet* (Paris, Fayard, 1987). On the theory of scape-goating, the best recent analysis is that of Yves Chevallier, *L'antisémitisme* (Paris, Editions du Cerf, 1988), pp. 90–182.
[13]   See Roger Duchène, *La Fontaine* (Paris, Fayard, 1990).

Well before his imprisonment, the origins of the Fouquet 'clan' (for such there was) had taken on a classic pattern. The Fouquet were descended from a family of merchant textile notables from Anjou in the sixteenth century whose offspring over several generations arrived in due course amongst the magistracy of the Parlement (the red robe) and then finally in the royal Council (the black robe). Nicolas Fouquet's personal misfortunes did not stand in the way of his family's canonical progression towards the old nobility, for his direct descendant would be the valorous *maréchal* de Belle-Isle under whom the sword of office would be substituted for the pen.

Fouquet's personal career also began in a familiar fashion. The family already enjoyed the protection of Cardinal Richelieu (here was yet another individual owing his future to the cardinal's favour!) and he became a provincial magistrate, then a master of requests, then finally an army intendant. In due course, Mazarin was struck by the young man's intelligence and charm. In November 1650, he chose him as his *procureur général*, as a result of which the ministerial team could call on the services of an able and loyal agent amidst a Parisian Parlement which was still enthralled by Fronde sentiments.

In 1653, Fouquet became superintendent of finances and thus became a dominant (though not the sole) figure in the 'fisco-financial' system of the monarchy. Things being what they were, the system was dominated by the need to satisfy the monetary demands of the armies, the court . . . and Mazarin himself. Having enriched himself through the exercise of high office during this financially exacting period, Fouquet had the wherewithal to construct himself a palatial residence at Vaux-le-Vicomte. With Le Vau as architect, it would be the inspiration for the architectural projects of the Sun-King. Imprisoned in 1661, the unfortunate Fouquet narrowly escaped execution but was condemned to spend the rest of his days until his death in March 1680 in the gloomy fortress of Pignerol.[14] The huge debts which he had built up and which afflicted his own financial position on the eve of his arrest go towards supporting the proposition that, at least from 1650 onwards, he had been relatively honest. At all events, he had, like a loyal subject, lent a lot of money to the state, even to the extent of risking his own personal bankruptcy as a result of such profligate loans. The same could not be said of Richelieu, Mazarin or Colbert, who proved to be canny managers of their financial affairs, so that their debt levels as proportions of their vast fortunes remained small, and their operating reserves much larger than their dispersed loan capital.

All of which may well have been the case; but Daniel Dessert, Fouquet's talented recent biographer, goes one step further and turns Fouquet into a Dreyfus-figure and Colbert into a less than attractive stooge. Yet to present Fouquet as a national hero is tantamount to turning a *baudruche* into a *montgolfiere*. At all events, once Fouquet became the

---

[14]   Bluche, *Louis XIV*, p. 972 [of the French edition, Paris, Fayard, 1986].

prisoner of Pignerol, it left the field wide open to the ambitious energies of Colbert.

Colbert, too, owed a good deal to his family. The Colbert had been farmers in Champagne and masons in Rheims in the second half of the fifteenth century. But they did not keep their noses in the plaster and there was a Colbert who was a good architect at the beginning of the sixteenth century, and then Colberts who were traders or 'wholesale mercers' amidst the urban élites of Reims. They traded wholesale in luxury goods, cloth, food products, construction materials and military munitions both locally and over a wider scale in both France and northern Italy. The legend of the flourishing 'draper' who was the ancestor of the great minister is thus oversimplifying the picture. With Oudard Colbert de Villacerf (1560–1640), the clan began to have wider horizons both in Troyes and in Paris. Trade and manufacture remained part of his activities, but added to it were banking, financial dealings with the state, the marriage of daughters to the young offspring of people in high places, and appearances at court . . . the financial and social world was thus in place from which the personal career of the greatest Colbert would take off two generations later. Under the Ancien Régime, it was not possible to rise from nothing; there were very few 'self-made men' but rather more 'self-made families'.

Nicolas Colbert de Vandières (1590–1661), the father of Jean-Baptiste Colbert (the future minister) also made the transition, following in the family traditions, from being a merchant *bourgeois* of Rheims to being a *payeur de rentes* based in Paris and (more or less clandestinely) a *partisan* caught up in the fisco-financial dealings of the realm. His honesty did not always stand up to scrutiny (and neither did his son's!) and his success in strictly monetary terms (interrupted by a bankruptcy which did not prove fatal to him) remained modest. He only left 225,000 *livres* in capital of various kinds to his numerous children. A relatively small fortune was not, however, *a priori* a handicap; the fact that Nicolas had after all been able to establish himself solidly in the capital enabled the young Jean-Baptiste to put his first foot on the ladder to power.

Born in 1619, Jean-Baptiste Colbert had a good education from the Jesuits in Rheims. He also benefited significantly (even though he did not have any period of higher education) from the influence of the social milieu around the *robins* amongst which he grew up. In due course, his father placed him in an apprenticeship with a Lyon banker, and then with a Parisian notary, and then with a Paris solicitor (*procureur*). Eventually Colbert became a junior clerk for a munitioneer, and then a commissioner for war (*commissaire des guerres*) – and thus already an office-holder. He spent some time travelling with the military intendants to regions close to the war-fronts and combat zones. At length, he was lucky enough (and he knew how to exploit his good fortune) to become a clerk for the Secretary of State for War, Le Tellier, whose brother-in-law and senior clerk was another Colbert, called Saint-Pouange. In 1648, he married (still within the milieu of the army financiers)[15] Marie Charron de Ménars, and also was made a *conseiller du roi*, at which point the young man's career definitively 'took off'. He thus emerged at the beginning from the Le Tellier stable, along with the Le Tellier-Louvois clan which would provide, in the years from 1660 to 1690, Colbert's collaborator, later his rival.

In June 1651, Colbert ostentatiously (if not officially) abandoned his responsibilities at the war ministry under Le Tellier to become the manager of Mazarin's huge fortune. He would find himself exiled for a few months, but the cardinal would repent later for having sometimes 'turned his back' on someone who in due course would become his right-hand man and whom he had formerly snubbed. After several years of dedicated work, Colbert could afford to let himself be carried upwards with the sovereign destinies of his boss, once he returned to France and to power in 1653. He was thenceforth in the best possible position to advance his own career. Risking being regarded as one of the 'wicked rich' after Mazarin's death, he took his cut from the financial wheeling and dealing around Mazarin. Whilst he added to His Eminence's treasury, he invested his own wealth and advanced his own relations, the Colbert clan, in their financial dealings and by placing them in important government posts. In 1657 he began his dispute with Fouquet and he had some justice on his side. The kind of Breton conspiracy which the superintendent seemed to be putting together had something of the Fronde about it, despite the various mitigating circumstances.[16] Condé had been arrested for a good deal less in January 1650. It also foreshadowed the various inter-ministerial conflicts which would be the subject of debate for years, even decades, to come. Colbert versus Fouquet was a preliminary eliminating round; Colbert versus Le Tellier would go on, in a variety of ways, for over quarter of a century.

As for Colbert's indiscretions, they are not sufficient to make him into a rodent, eating his way into the state like a mouse making holes in a gruyère cheese, any more than we should see those of Richelieu and Mazarin in a similar light, despite the chorus of scholarly works to the contrary from Daniel Dessert and Joseph Bergin. To regard these statesmen as 'the greatest of thieves from the monarchy' is equally superficial.[17] Dishonest they certainly were; but they were also powerful political figures in their own right, especially Mazarin and Colbert, and they did not separate the major theme of serving the king (or the state) from the minor theme, albeit more alluring, of increasing their own, and their family's wealth. The pleasures of wealth were inseparable from the utility of power.

[15]   Inès Murat, *Colbert* (Paris, Fayard, 1980), p. 24; Daniel Dessert, *Argent, pouvoir et société au Grand Siècle* (Paris, Fayard, 1984), p. 326.
[16]   One would need the disarming charm of Daniel Dessert (see his *Fouquet*, p. 254 and appendix 4) to be unconscious of it.
[17]   'Les plus grands voleurs de la monarchie' – the expression is drawn from the revue *L'Histoire*, no. 60 (October 1983) – a special issue devoted to Colbert.

Plate 9 Portrait of Jean-Baptiste Colbert This water-colour portrait of Jean-Baptiste Colbert drew its inspiration from the work of the Flemish painter and Jesuit, Daniel Séghers, who specialized in portraits embellished with garlands of flowers. The cold and slightly melancholic austerity of Colbert – copied with modifications from a painting attributed to Claude Lefebvre and dated to 1666 – is balanced by the floral surrounding made up of simple flowers which might well be taken to symbolize the economic resurgence and release of France's natural riches which Colbert was setting in train.

Paris, Musée de la Marine

The ordering of their priorities, which excludes the notion that they were cynical manipulators of deals to their private benefit alone, can be clearly demonstrated in the case of Mazarin, despite the fact that he often mixed up his exercise of power with his personal buying-power. Was it not the case that he actively dissuaded Louis XIV from courting his niece Mancini, despite the success of this projected royal love-affair and despite the benefit it would have brought to the dynastic lineage of Mazarin himself? This was because it would defeat the grand design of a Spanish marriage, the linchpin of Mazarin's diplomacy, which was closely correlated with the advancement of the grandeur of France relative to the Madrid court. There was the same resolution of the conflict of interests when Colbert wrote to his brother Charles (appointed intendant in Alsace in 1655): 'I avow to you my burning passion to see our family ascendant by the ways of *honour* and *virtue*, and that everybody should be in accord as to the *fortune* which is due to us.' He made it evident that he understood fortune to be one of the pinnacles of a triangle of family values. Virtue, and the desire to do well, to put oneself at the service of the public and to adopt those austere, perhaps even rigid, values which were current in professional daily life, were all equally important.[18] Finally, the cult of honour gave an aristocratic flourish to these Colbertian sentiments; and it was the case that various descendants and sons of the great minister became officers in the royal armies, accepted into the military nobility, and would perish on the 'field of honour' during the interminable Louis XIV wars.[19] They would demonstrate their loyalty to the lesson in fundamental values which they had received from their father Jean-Baptiste Colbert. He himself, of course, had been a commissioner for war during his younger years. It was a profession where he would discover the opportunity to exercise his patriotism and not merely his undeniable taste for making money.

The various stages in Colbert's ministerial career reflected in a broad context his assuming authority over various sectors of the state under the control of Louis XIV. Yet this authority did not become total; the land armies and foreign affairs would almost entirely escape his clutches (although his brother Croissy would be in charge of foreign affairs after 1679). The war ministry was in the hands of Le Tellier, with Louvois, who would succeed him in due course, at his side. Foreign affairs were controlled by Lionne, and then Pomponne. With the title of Minister of State (1661), the superintendency of Buildings and Arts (1664), the Grand Treasury of the Royal Orders of Chivalry (the *Grande Trésorerie des ordres du Roi*) (1665), and the secretaryship of state for the king's household (1668), Colbert acquired considerable authority over the sovereign domains of the state, cultural affairs, the noble and meritocratic hierarchies (the 'Orders' of France), and finally of administration, to which should be

---

[18]   Jean Meyer, *Colbert* (Paris, Hachette, 1981), p. 191 *et seq.*
[19]   See Roland Mousnier (dir.), *Un nouveau Colbert. Actes du colloque pour le tricentenaire de la mort de Colbert* (Paris, SEDES-CDU, 1985), p. 88 (the contribution of Charles Engrand).

added his duties for overseeing justice following the announcement of the *Grands Jours* of Auvergne in 1665. The secretaryship of state for the navy (1669) also gave Colbert in some respects some responsibilities for war – or what would now be called Defence. Finally, Colbert enjoyed *de facto* control over the new Royal Council of Finances (*Conseil royal des finances*) from 1661 onwards, which was the period when he sponsored the creation of the Companies of the West and East Indies (with mixed success) and 20 manufacturing concerns. In 1665 came his accession to the post of *contrôleur général des finances* – a post which would be of the first importance for the remainder of the Ancien Régime – followed by his purchase of the office of Grand Master of French Mines (*grand maître des Mines de France*) in 1669. These made Colbert not just the veritable 'patron' of state finance but also of the French economy, albeit there were considerable restrictions in respect of the economic influence he could wield, given that production was dispersed in small-scale enterprises and that state economic influence remained small, despite its growth from 1635 onwards. Guglielmo Ferrero would say of Bonaparte that 'it was never a question of being a sleeping partner when it came to establishing the power of the First Consul. He seized the reins of power totally, without allowing any controls over them.'[20] One might say the same of Colbert once he was established as supremo after 1665, with the sole proviso that he did not control absolutely everything, but only almost everything, and that he remained under the overall direction (generally benign, but occasionally irksome) of Louis XIV for his exercise of power.

It is strange that, although Colbert is still pictured as an economic technocrat (either as a great innovator in that domain or merely an imitator of others, according to the preferences or prejudices of historians), he was also, and perhaps primarily, a minister of applied scientific rationality. We should perhaps remind ourselves of the quartet of primordial values to which Louis XIV subscribed, and which were, in descending order: religion, reason, good order and hierarchy.[21] Of these various concepts it was the second which preoccupied Colbert from an early date; for he was, like Louis XIV, a rationalist. This should come as no surprise for someone in the age of Spinoza, the generation after Descartes. In 1666, Colbert founded the Academy of Sciences; with an illustrious future before it, the Academy specialized in principle in mathematics, astronomy, cartography, botany, anatomy and chemistry. Some years later came the costly construction of the Paris Observatory, a Colbertian establishment in every sense of the word, and which was accompanied by a museum of machines and mechanical models.[22] The number of printed books in the Royal Library increased from 11,000 to 36,000 under the stimulus of an

[20]   Guglielmo Ferrero, *Pouvoir; les génies invisibles de la cité* (Paris, Librairie Générale Française, 1988), p. 10.
[21]   Saint-Simon, *Mémoires*, ed. A. de Boislisle, 45 vols (Paris, 1879–1930), vii, 177.
[22]   Charles Frostin, 'L'éveil scientifique de la France' in *l'Histoire*, no. 60 (October 1983), pp. 44–52.

individual who, at the same time, devoted much enthusiasm to the development of his own Colbertian collection. In fact the number of manuscripts in the Royal Library grew at a rather slower rate precisely because the shrewd and somewhat unscrupulous bibliophile kept the best pieces for his own collection, his nature having for once the upper hand.[23] At the same time Colbert invested significant resources in encouraging what we would now call a 'brain-drain' into France. The Italian Cassini, the author of a spectacular map of the moon's surface and father of France's cartography, was lured to Paris; so too was Huygens from the Netherlands, Leibniz from Germany and Oläus Römer from Denmark. The latter used an observation of the satellites of Jupiter to measure the speed of light in 1675. Thus was established, in the age of Newton himself, one of the basic reference points for Einstein's theory of relativity.

The research which Colbert favoured was far from being for its own sake. The astronomical and mathematical quests were inseparable from other initiatives to understand the earth's space, particularly its maritime space around France and across the globe. There was the measurement of coastal shelves, the degree of the meridian, the attempt at geodesic triangulation,[24] all of which resulted in the topographical maps of France produced by Cassini Junior. To have one minister as secretary of state for the navy and superintendent of Buildings and Arts allowed the development of multidisciplinary investigations at both pure and applied levels in naval matters.

A shift from a world where scientific research was hardly stimulated at all on any rational grounds to one where there was a scientific strategy, is generally attributed to the thinkers of the nineteenth century – to Proudhon, Saint-Simon, Jean-Baptiste Say, Marx, Madame de Staël, Taine or Renan.[25] This movement would come to dominate a whole section of the intellectual world and, eventually, influence the politicians as well. Colbert, however, assisted and protected by Louis XIV, had already developed, as we have seen, just such a programme and ambition in which scientific rationalism was developed for the service of the state. Despite Colbert's empiricism, in many respects he was also often systematic and innovative. Of course Colbertian rationality, thus defined, was always within the limits defined by Religion, Good Order and Hierarchy,

---

[23]   Simone Balayé, *Histoire de la Bibliothèque nationale des origines à 1800* (Geneva, Droz, 1988), p. 71 *et seq.*

[24]   Joseph Konvitz, *Cartography in France, 1600–1848* (Chicago, University of Chicago Press, 1987). In fact, Colbert provided the key stimulus, with the assistance of the astronomer Jean-Dominique Cassini, for French cartography, the latter having remained somewhat under-developed under Henry IV and Louis XIII until that date. Terrestrial cartography and also maritime charting were developed, a necessary adjunct to the development of the navy. The enterprises of Riquet equally resulted in detailed maps concerning the construction of the canals.

[25]   Jacques Julliard, François Furet and Pierre Rosanvallon, *La République du centre* (Paris, Calmann-Lévy, 1988), pp. 128–9.

and it differed considerably from the scientific rationality of the eighteenth-century philosophes. In both cases, however, the ambitions or pretensions to knowledge are equally vaunting; but the Reason of the Enlightenment tended to be the harbinger of Revolution and the destroyer of the established order, whilst the Reason of its forebears remained philosophically and politically prudent, conservative in many ways, certainly Catholic. In this latter respect, Colbert was from the same stable as Louis XIV.

It should be added that even the most distinguished intellectuals of the day, when they venture out from their narrow specialism, are vulnerable to the grossest of political and practical errors whilst they more or less shelter under the mantle of their prestige. The same was true for the quasi-scientific rationalism which Colbert was attempting to put into practice. His ministerial initiatives were too abstract and schematic in many instances, and flawed in their practical application, especially in the commercial and manufacturing spheres.

It was only one step on from applied science to legislation. Colbertian initiative thus had a double edge to it; there was innovation stimulated from on high, patronized by the Prince; and 'systemic' spontaneity from below. As the minister in charge of finance, Colbert theoretically had nothing to do with the problems connected with the theory and practice of law which were the domain of Chancellor Séguier. However, with nudges in this direction from Louis XIV, coupled with his exploitation of the enormous legal talents of his uncle Pussort, a highly professional and formidable jurist, Colbert was once more in a position to impose his stamp on an area of government which was not his responsibility. When it came to legal codes and ordinances, the Colbert–Pussort team set to work with a strategy which was organized along logical as well as chronological lines. The ordinances on *Eaux et forêts* (Water and Forest resources – the latter providing the raw materials for ships) led on to those on the *Marine* (Navy) and *Commerce* (Trade). These three in due course provided the linchpins of the two ordinances on *procédure criminelle* and *procédure civile* (Criminal and Civil Legal Procedures) – a total of five great law codes. The team of draftsmen under Colbert and Pussort had no recourse to the Estates General (in desuetude since 1614) nor to the parlements (which were irritated not to have been consulted). However, in the wake of the Fronde, these law-courts were not held in the highest esteem even though they had retained many of their former privileges. In their place it was councillors of state, masters of requests and advocates specially selected for the task who drew up the five great juridical texts. The method and the choice of personnel would be similar to those employed by Bonaparte when it came to the drafting of the *Code civil* (Civil Code). The whole drafting process emanated, in the final analysis, from the pure sovereignty of the king, 'no more divisible than a geometric point' and as capable of generating legislative light as the executive or judicial organs of government.

'Reason asleep, out creep the monsters.'[26] In one respect, the ordinance on criminal procedures of 1670 marked the exorcism of one nightmare; it 'eliminated from the judicial system' the legal prosecution of witches. This was progress towards a Christianity which was increasingly infused with rationality. Colbert in legal affairs, Malebranche in theological matters, are both enlightened representatives of the same new tendency. In other respects, the Colbertian legal initiatives met with varied success. Some of the clauses in these law codes survive today, such as those which still define the sea-coast as public property despite the wishes of the promoters of mass beach-tourism that it be made private property.[27] In other respects, however, the Colbertian ordinances (like, albeit to a lesser degree, Napoleon Bonaparte's Civil Code) remained a dead letter in various respects, testimony to the difficulties which scientific rationalism in government would experience, even when it was underwritten by absolutism. It found it difficult to 'bite' into the twisted, baroque, real world of associations and guilds which formed the fabric of daily life under the Ancien Régime. In this respect, the route taken by the Renaissance monarchy which involved simply collecting together in writing all the local customs without trying to change them too much was more empirical and more realistic than that chosen by Colbert; and more empirical too than Marillac and *président* Brisson's[28] efforts to encodify law, which were also more suitable to the stratosphere of jurisprudence than applicable in the real world.

How was this wave of legislative innovation, or new tradition of legislation, to become implanted in the provinces when executive authority was felt so relatively feebly there? Recent historiography has tended to underline Colbert's empiricism, which was supported by Louis XIV. At the beginning of his ministry, Colbert made use of the services of a roving court of judges from the Parlement of Paris to see justice done in the Massif Central against a host of petty criminal elements of all kinds, seigneurs, lesser office-holders etc. This court, the *Grands Jours d'Auvergne* (1665), gave the Parlement of Paris an Indian summer of influence before the prolonged winter of exclusion which was inaugurated in 1673 when its rights of remonstrance were strictly limited.[29] In a complementary fashion, however, the provincial intendants (rivals in influence to the office-holders) returned in strength across the realm at the close of the civil wars after having been abolished by the *frondeurs*. Their periods of stay in the same location tended to become longer after the years from 1666–9.[30] This was

[26] 'Le sommeil de la Raison engendre des monstres' is the legend on a famous engraving by Goya, reproduced (for example) on the cover of *Cahiers rationalistes*, no. 186 (March–April 1960).

[27] Marguerite Boulet-Sautel, 'Colbert et la législation' in *Un nouveau Colbert*, ed. Mousnier, p. 119 *et seq.*

[28] Ibid.

[29] R. Bonney, *Political Change in France under Richelieu and Mazarin, 1624–1661* (Oxford, Clarendon Press, 1978), p. 420.

[30] Ibid., p. 427.

already a way for them to consolidate their position. After 1681–3, they had powers to prevent local towns and villages becoming indebted to ensure that tax-payers paid royal taxes rather than the interest payments on municipal debts. This had the effect of establishing administrative control over expenditure and the issuing of loans by these local authorities, thus developing a new form of centralization. But this should not be regarded in too tragic a light. The 'tutelage' of public bodies by central administration would remain a constant feature of modern French history . . . until as recently as the 1970s.

The intendants also entrusted themselves with the 'designation' of nobles. The authentication of their title of 'knight', formerly a matter of word of honour, was now to be scrutinized much more closely. As always, it was inspired by the fiscal objective of preventing fraudulent tax evasion by individuals claiming to belong to the nobility. The unforeseen result, however, was that it favoured the *noblesse de robe* whose titles of nobility and parchments were much better preserved (and thus susceptible to verification) than the *noblesse d'épée*. At the same time there was a gradual and gently progressive fusion between the two nobilities to the benefit of the former. In the end there arose an increased legalism amongst the old nobility, which had resisted it for so long, but whose essential nobility was now defined and constrained by state decree. The ancient oaks of aristocracy gradually became the roses of a nobility whose rationale was ever more clearly subordinated to the preponderant sovereign will of the prince. This was one of the numerous processes which prepared, underpinned and supported the 'absolutization' of the political system. In this respect, of course, Colbert had done nothing new. The 'searches for false nobles' (*recherches de faux nobles*) had already begun under the earlier Bourbons (the Valois having been much more relaxed about such matters) – such as in 1598 by Henry IV and Sully, or, in their turn, in 1634 and 1640 by Louis XIII and Richelieu; and again in 1655 (by the young Louis XIV and Mazarin). But Colbert, as always, demonstrated his tenacity. He undertook such matters on a grand scale and with considerable care whilst his predecessors had become discouraged or diverted and only innovated by expedient fits and starts when it was a matter of pursuing false nobles.

Generally speaking, the provincial intendants under the cardinal ministers had been part of a war-machine, or (at least) instruments destined to facilitate the financing (by extracting revenues, often in a somewhat brutal fashion) of the costly anti-Habsburg wars. But, after 1659, the intendants rapidly became part of a 'peace-machine', retaining all their energies and a good deal of their fiscal initiatives but deploying them as instruments for centralization in the scarcely war-time conditions of the 12 years from 1661 to 1672. The 'military state' of Richelieu and Mazarin, developed to deal with the huge frontier tensions of that period, thus became by a process of relatively painless transition, the administrative monarchy of the 1660s, destined to last well beyond that period and to engender by a copycat process (although there would be differences) the consular and prefectoral networks which would rule France in the nineteenth and twentieth centuries. Thus did the war years from 1635 to 1659 affect the political structure of France after 1661.[31] Around the intendants developed (tautologically) the intendancies, whose bureaucratic tasks did nothing but increase with so many town and village accounts to survey!

Hence, also, the trend towards a kind of 'conceptualization' of authority; or, at the very least, a more abstract sense of the state than had existed in the past. The provincial governors, grand military figures, were physically, personally and in every way representative of the king's presence in the province.[32] For his part, the intendant was the presence of the state in the province.[33] But a greater degree of abstraction introduced a chiasmus, a possible schism, between the king and the state. 'I depart, but the State goes on for ever'[34] declared Louis XIV on his death bed – the exact reverse of the ludicrous formula: 'l'Etat c'est moi', which has so often been ascribed to him. The Sun-King spoke better than he knew. After his death came Louis XV, less conscientious than his immediate predecessor and less concerned to identify himself with every single state initiative. The state, if it can be regarded as a self-consciously separate identity, could thus begin to realize that the monarchy was no more than a figure-head or a figurine on top of a superstructure, and one which could be detached from the underlying hull of public functions supporting the ship of state.[35] Its crew (office-holders, servants of the state, the creatures of the Enlightenment) could envisage a world where they were liberated from their royal captain. Prancing Pegasus did not need a Zeus or an Aurora for a mount. And once it was free of its rider, free to leap into the unknown, was it not the Revolution which beckoned?

Louis XIV stood as guarantor of good order after the disastrous Fronde years when civil war had brought ruin to the realm. At the same time, the king caught the *dévots* napping and swiftly snatched from them their programme of anti-Huguenot repression. He regarded them as Tartuffes,[36] makers of intrigue, who mixed piety with politics. He had virtually no objection (despite their representations to him) to giving his final authorization to Molière to put on his famous play (1664–9): at the same moment, La Fontaine was holding the sexual misdemeanours of monks and

---

[31]　Ibid., p. 419 *et seq.*

[32]　As Michel Antoine has amply demonstrated in 'Colbert et la Révolution de 1661' in *Un nouveau Colbert*, ed. Mousnier, p. 109 *et seq.*, this applied to the governors but not, as Lavisse thought, to the intendants.

[33]　Ibid.

[34]　François Bluche, *Louis XIV vous parle* (Paris, Stock, 1988), p. 269; Philippe de Courcillon, Marquis Dangeau, *Journal . . . avec les additions inédites du duc de Saint-Simon* (Paris, F. Didot, 1856–1860), xvi, 128.

[35]　This is the perennial 'Tocquevillian' question of the administrative and centralized state, over and above the changing compositions of dynasties, then (post 1789) of republics.

[36]　'Tartufo' was the false *dévot* hypocrite from Italian comedy who formed the subject of Molière's famous play of 1664.

nuns up to public derision. Meanwhile Louis intensified the hostility towards Calvinism which would lead ultimately to the complete suppression of the heresy and the Revocation of the edict of Nantes. To establish moral and religious order in the realm, the king made use of the Catholic church, the Le Tellier clan, and the parlements. Colbert and his clients were, on the other hand, distinctly more reserved in such matters. Pragmatic, systematic, but not ideologically directed, Colbert would not, if left to his own devices, have launched any offensive against the Huguenot *temples*. He had the measure of the important economic role played by the Huguenots; and, in any case, the politics of exclusion held out no allure for him. For example, the senior administrators assigned to the Navy were all from the Colbert clan and they let the homosexuals aboard the galleys alone, more concerned that the male crews aboard these floating hulks should be good rowers rather than with their sexual orientation. By contrast, the *dévot* Provençal intendant, Arnoul, adopted a repressive policy towards them.

In a similar fashion, the *contrôleur général* did not adopt anything of a 'racist' attitude (as one would say now) towards the Canadian Indians. He wanted to see them convert to Christianity and marry their daughters to the new migrants from France. For Colbert, the demographic success of the colony was all-important and, in comparison with that, the question of the racial purity of the Whites was of lesser significance, and he paid little attention to it. More importantly, the exportation of Christianity to the banks of the St Lawrence river came second place to the trade in beaver-fur in Colbert's priorities. Left to his own devices, Colbert would doubtless have preferred not to have wined and dined with infidels. He was a conventionally pious man, with a simple religion, austere, restrained and with a marked absence of zeal. He would doubtless have let the church continue, as under Richelieu, to heap obloquy upon the heads of heretics; but that was where the matter would rest. The specific logic which drove Louis XIV towards the total extinction of the minority churches was a much stronger statement than the relatively relaxed attitudes of Colbert. This logic did not lack force (in both senses of the word), either in terms of the reasoning which it implicitly embodied or in terms of the judicial force which reinforced and carried it through. In the battle between the Protestant pipkin and the massive Catholic pumpkin, Colbert found that, despite all his own inclinations perhaps, he was obliged to take sides.

The success of Colbert (and of Louis XIV) in the years following 1661 still requires an explanation. The ending of the turbulence of civil war (from 1653 onwards in fact), the contagious effects of a new stress upon discipline and order, and the appearance of new, rather efficient, social networks – all these forces operated without the effects of royal constraint, for it would be ludicrous to explain everything post 1661 in terms of royal repression. The social order reconstituted from the *membra disjecta*, the fragments of which had been too often pushed in different directions, now found itself in greater harmony.

In general, there was a greater willingness to accept the initiatives and edicts emanating from central government. At worst they were greeted with friendly irony rather than the Homeric invective which had been their reception in the years from 1630–50. Respect for Bourbon royal legitimacy was apparently effortlessly associated with the respect accorded to God. The chains of command were solidified and this reinforced the sense of social hierarchy which satisfied the social élites. A sense of French nationhood was also more prominently voiced ('I am French as well as King' Louis XIV would declare in 1703; 'Whatever harms the glory of the nation is felt by me over and above every other interest.'[37]) In fact, in the absence of national will or popular sovereignty, both of which were democratic concepts which had yet to make their appearance, patriotic glory and a vigorously Gallican conscience acted as the cement for the collective basis of absolutism. Louis XIV understood all this perfectly whereas Louis XV, whose reign was plentiful in military defeats and anti-Gallican invective, chose rather to forget it. In the years from 1665 to 1670, this nationalism *style louis-quatorzien* was the more influential because, at least in the provinces which still had local estates (Languedoc, Provence, etc.), it remained compatible with a pronounced regionalism which was perhaps less flaunted but more effective than before. At the same time, the symbols of authority became more demonstrably visible. Episcopal palaces were constructed or reconstructed at great expense during the Colbertian 'Indian summer' for the French economy. Portraits of consuls appeared in town halls. And quarrels over rights of precedence between the various privileged elites were settled by the arbitration of the royal Council or on the instructions of the *contrôleur général* addressed to the intendant, rather than (as in the past) by challenges to a duel.

The intendants already played an essential role in government under Richelieu and Mazarin but they still remained roving and somewhat isolated commissioners, tethered like a goat to a particular region for a few years. However, in the second half of the century, the intendants became institutionalized as the 'intendancy' with the latter acquiring writing clerks and subdelegates around the official in post, many of them recruited from amongst the local notables who served without remuneration from the king and purely for the honour and the prestige which was involved. For its part, the intendancy could not deliver all its benefits (which would always be limited in nature) save to the degree and extent to which they acted as brokers for the vigorous local entities and élites rather than agents of command and direction from central government.

Historians have concentrated their attentions on the *pays d'Etats* when examining the interactions between national politics and local influential élites. In Languedoc, the active obedience of the region was more and

---

[37] Cited in François Bluche, *Louis XIV vous parle*, p. 92; this whole paragraph owes much to William Beik, *Absolutism and Society in Seventeenth-Century France* (Cambridge, Cambridge University Press, 1985).

more guaranteed by the provincial estates. Theoretically representative of the three orders, in reality, they were closely controlled by the 22 bishops of the vast province, the 22 uncrowned viceregents of its dioceses who sat in the estates. They were often remarkable individuals, personally chosen by the king increasingly as vacancies arose and selected on ground of piety (naturally) but also (and above all) for their élite connections, their administrative competence and their loyalty to His Majesty. At all events, these prelates were committed to the anti-Huguenot direction of government policy and they rallied the Catholic lower clergy behind it. An interactive system was put in place in which a cult (in many respects rather unedifying) of monarchical personality emerged from the provincial estates themselves, a sincere admiration for the king. Whether his image was consciously cultivated or not,[38] each sovereign king had his own style and the Sun-King was better than the cardinal-ministers in involving the regional assembly of Languedoc in the exercise of power, including matters of purely material interest such as the collection of taxes.

The estates of Languedoc were in fact in charge of the collection of taxation in the province. They then handed over a portion of the taxes collected to the royal Treasury, retaining a significant amount for themselves in the hands of the estates' treasurer (the *trésorier de la Bourse*). This money was destined to pay for local expenditure which had been deemed necessary by the provincial élites, and also to pay for the sometimes illicit profits which some highly placed individuals in the provincial élites had assigned to themselves. Since the provincial estates were thus running their own administration, they made themselves professionally competent by employing permanent syndics. Herein lay the secret of the lack of conflict between the king and provincial representatives in the estates. The governor and the intendant manipulated these syndics, not with the threat of the executioner's axe but a simple stick (a menacing *lettre de cachet*) and an equally generous measure of carrot (monetary gratifications, grants of 'cash' pensions to the most influential and most pliable of regional figures). Rather than use crude menaces or resort to brutal reprisals, those up in Versailles or Paris preferred to forge *in situ* in Toulouse and Béziers the elements of a political consensus. They dangled before the bishops and their fellow delegates at the Languedoc estates the Colbertian prospect of a flourishing regional economy, a prospect whose enticements their predecessors in Louis XIII's time, more obsessed with questions of the distrbution of authority, had declared themselves incapable of appreciating.

As for the Chamber of Accounts (*Chambre des comptes*) in Montpellier, with its regional responsibilities (at least in principle), the intendant Baltazar had accused it under Mazarin, not entirely wrongly, of rebellion. During the succeeding period, it was 'retained' and recompensed. It took its share from the fiscal receipts of the 22 dioceses which were themselves

---

[38]   Marc Suriano, *La Brosse à reluire sous Louis XIV* (Paris, Nizet, 1989).

shared out between the king and the estates. It did so the more readily because a number of the councillors of the chamber were the ones who did not take too much trouble to disguise the fact that they were behind speculation and profitable deals in the royal finances. Absolutism, or what one now means by that term, implies thus, then as now, a good dose of reciprocity without which it could never function properly.

When it came to the municipal consulates, the town halls of the larger villages and towns of Languedoc, Colbert ensured that they were more closely scrutinized by the intendancy; they could no longer incur debts as and when they liked. To the west of the province, the Parlement of Toulouse had proved to have an aggressive attitude in the 1630s and 1640s towards the financiers of the royal fisc, towards those who purchased recently-created offices, intendants, and extraordinary commissioners. A generation later, however, the magistrates in this sovereign court had become much more compliant and cooperative towards the king. Those in power consulted them when it was reasonable to do so. It entrusted them, following the example of the Parisian Parlement in Auvergne, with holding the *Grands Jours* in the Cévennes in 1666. They suppressed the Chamber of the Edict (*Chambre de l'édit*) on their behalf; partially staffed by Huguenots, they disliked it because it competed with their jurisdiction. Monarchical authoritarianism could sometimes appear like a crown of thorns to the *parlementaires* but more often than not it was a bed of roses in which the magistrates made themselves comfortable.

The American historian William Beik has written of absolutism having a 'common programme' (it is for him to justify the anachronism of such terms) in which the peripheral élites and central power recognized their mutual interests. But he is evoking the same notions of reciprocity. The primary point of this 'programme' in those regions where Protestants were numerous was precisely the common battle against heresy. It spoke most readily to the clerics and Catholic laity who, in many instances, demonstrated a degree of mental rigidity, bigotry even, in respect of the Protestant problem.

In this respect, the history of those provinces with Calvinist minorities such as Languedoc is very revealing. Beginning in 1660 when the Toulousains celebrated the marriage of Louis XIV by burning an effigy representing 'heresy' (nothing would be gained by waiting), it would reach a climax in 1685 when the intendant Lamoignon de Basville arrived in triumph with a small and vigorous army which would be entrusted with the completion of the former Huguenots' 'conversion'. The approbation for the arrival of Basville's army is significant since it neatly indicates the synthesis which had been put together between local interests and centralizing desires felt by the majority of Languedocians. By satisfying the former, the 'absolutist' régime ensured itself a support-base among the élites and the robust affections of the peoples of the Midi between 1661 and 1685.

Such a solution to the problems of sovereignty and spirituality applied in the first decades of Louis XIV's personal rule (after 1661) were unilaterally imposed but only after mature consideration by a good number of people. Nor was it the only way by which the pro-absolutist consensus might be reinforced. In Languedoc, as elsewhere, the 'new model' monarchy of the Colbertian years eventually found a remedy for the thorny problem of the presence of military forces in the provinces, and particularly the garrisoning of troops on local populations. During the Thirty Years War, this had been an inexhaustible source of irritation, friction and frequent popular uprising when localities were faced with unpaid or badly paid soldiers who shamelessly looked to the local inhabitants to recoup their losses. From 1659 to 1672, the (relative) peace began to heal the wounds caused by the military garrisoning of the previous years. After 1672, when military conflict returned, the proper reimbursement of the 'billeting expenses' of the regiments on the move and the regular coordination put in place between the Ministry for War, the military commanders, and the estates of Languedoc made the soldiery a much less troubling burden for local communities. In a further development, the intendants actively sought after 1682 to procure places in the army for young gentlemen from the province, a measure which was greatly appreciated amongst the gentry, or those that considered themselves as such. The 'searches for false nobility' (*recherches des faux nobles*) had created a good deal of resentment (in Languedoc it had begun in 1668 under the intendant Bazin de Bezons) but in the end it provided the true nobility (i.e. all those who had passed the test successfully) with an impression of security and legitimacy which could only increase the nobles' desires for loyalty above all towards the king, and even towards an absolute king. It is true, however, that this dependence on the state would have its disadvantages and, in the long-term, it would increase the unpopularity of the nobility which would find itself lastingly damaged by absolutism; but such difficulties did not reveal themselves clearly before the following century.

The neo-loyalism of the French élites also emerged from the reconstruction of the financial system. The weight of taxation remained high but it ceased to grow beyond all measure. In fact the burden of direct taxation began to decrease under the first 12 years of Colbertian predominance as a result of the external peace which *de facto* diminished the fiscal appetites of the state. At the same time, the revenue from indirect taxation increased but this was a result of better management of the tax-farms which governed the collection of the *gabelles*, the *traites* and the *aides* by Colbert and his collaborators. Such an increase in the long-established 'indirect' tax revenues was also a consequence of an increase in consumption, which was itself the result of the (relative) peace in the 14 years from 1659 to 1672 and the resulting return (albeit not necessarily long-lasting) of a degree of prosperity. This was a period of a relatively benign economic climate and it was felt as such by contemporaries. After 1672, and through to the end of Louis XIV's reign, the fiscal burden began to increase once more, spasmodically, as a consequence of the major military conflicts, but it never exceeded the (already very considerable) fiscal levels set for the first time under Mazarin.

However, and here the example of Languedoc is once again instructive, this fiscality, which remained a heavy burden despite its ups and downs, acted powerfully to stimulate a class of local financiers who became an integral part of the local élites. They were much more accepted, much better received in local society than their equivalents in Paris. The experience would foreshadow the fusion amongst the élites which would occur in Paris in the eighteenth century. The Languedoc financiers occupied the posts of receivers-general (*receveurs généraux*), diocesan tax-collectors (*receveurs diocésains*), treasurers for military 'billeting' and treasurers of the estates' *bourse*. Some of them, such as Penautier, Riquet, Sartre and Crozat were nobles or about to become nobles. They mixed effortlessly amongst the cream of the cream of the provincial notability and even amongst the leading financial figures of the Ile de France around Paris. The 'links' which were thus established with Paris were one component of a process of nationalization of the regional élites which can also be traced amongst the higher nobility. The Grignan family from Provence, the Castries from Montpellier were now to be found at the Versailles court, fish swimming in a larger pond . . . thus would emerge new supporting and integrating forces for the French Ancien Régime in the substructure of Louis XIV's absolutism.

Such forces were not merely 'social', or purely platonic in their effects. They corresponded to a real consolidation of the various parties engaged in tax collection in which, instead of all taxation being directed towards Paris, a portion was transfused back to the province itself. A third of the tax collected in Languedoc remained *in situ* and this was a percentage which seems to have increased from 1647 to 1677. This went to servicing the regular interest payments to the various local institutions, whether individual municipalities or the province itself (the total level of such indebtedness had risen to 9,964,000 *livres* by the death of Colbert on the basis of direct taxation from the 22 dioceses of Languedoc which was estimated at 3,800,000 *livres* a year). The creditors – *parlementaires*, bourgeois, advocates, financiers, rich widows, nobles, clerics, convents, sometimes even artisans – enjoyed the benefits of their loan entitlements, and, once verified, these *rentes* could be bought and sold on. Why should such individuals, ensconced in their *rentes*, envisage any sort of challenge to the established order and oppose the Apollo in Versailles who had guaranteed the security of their investments?

Even the *canal du Midi* which was initially greeted with hostility by the Languedocian estates was eventually to evoke some enthusiasm from its notables. The architectural splendour of the canal enticed them, as did the economic returns which resulted from the enterprise and the size of the capital, guaranteed from fiscal sources, which it mobilized. All these various benefits flowed profitably through and around the coffers of the assembly of the three estates of the province. There would be numerous spin-offs, including the payments to the workforce on the new waterway and compensation to the former possessors of expropriated property on its route. In the end it was a remarkable success to have provided, by means of the canal, an object-lesson in mercantilism to an assembly led essentially by 22 prelates who might have been thought of as no more than reactionary placemen. Yet there was an underlying trade-off which governed the reactions of the regional episcopacy. The bishops voted the essential funds for the canal linking the Mediterranean and the Atlantic, but with the implied condition that they would obtain the destruction of the reformed religion's churches. 'You give me the Huguenots; I will give you the canal' was, without too much subtlety, the underlying message and it had been completely grasped by the king's provincial agents.

Thus, the Colbertian period which marked the first phase of Louis XIV's personal rule had the remarkable effect not of suppressing (which would have been impossible) the chronic splits which tore apart the élite groups in French society, but of exorcising their divisions. It acted in an emollient way – for instance on the splits in the urban world of Languedoc, between the consulates and the parlement, the estates and the Chamber of Accounts, the Huguenots, the artisans, the intendancy, etc. where these various institutions and 'constituted bodies' had a long tradition of mutual entrenched hostility – and its effects were felt not just upon the élites. Under Louis XIII and Mazarin, the 'enforcers of law and order' were endlessly trammelled by such disputes. Under Colbert, however, the *gens de bien* (as those who were the successors and inheritors of law enforcement would henceforth be termed) took the places of the previously turbulent and divided élite. They would accept the centralizing direction of the government and, in return, it would defend their decentralized privileges. The sovereign would govern; the local notables would accept that exercise of power but they would not be excessively humiliated by it. The grandees had merely to stand in the sunlight of the Astrea whose rays daily shone out on Versailles and the rest of the kingdom. The Protestants provided a convenient scapegoat until the day when they would find their beliefs sacrificed on the altar of religious and national unity. The hegemony of *Un Seul* was self-sustaining and mutually reinforcing. The infantile squabbling of the dominant élites which had existed in the time of the cardinal-ministers, and even more so during the Fronde, was firmly in its place. Where Richelieu had decapitated his opponents, Louis XIV charmed them, subjugated and dominated them in a way which was both symbolic and real. In Languedoc, the clientage networks were regrouped into one meridional synthesis under the distant direction of Colbert but under the more immediate patronage of the intendant d'Aguesseau, of the Cardinal de Bonsy (*alias* Bonzy), *président* of the estates, and of his brother-in-law the marquis de Castries, Lieutenant-General of the province of Languedoc and the acknowledged leader of the provincial nobility. In many respects, this province was typical of similar processes which were at work in the other provinces, both north and south, in the kingdom.

The Colbertian period coincided in various ways with a substantial increase in monarchical sovereignty, even in circumstances where the latter came up against, for whatever reason, the irreducible components (sometimes sizeable areas) of local, corporate or regional autonomy. Colbert also played a leading part in this period in forging a considerable addition to the military force of the kingdom through the creation, almost from scratch, of a navy – the colonial and commercial objectives of which were almost completely obscured by its overwhelmingly military purposes. After the fall of Fouquet, Colbert took in hand the development of the fleet, gradually building up his dominance over naval matters until he was made Secretary of State for the Navy in 1669. The twin objective was to imitate the Dutch without attempting immediately to overtake them, since their naval power, ships of the line and merchant marine had been been built up since the beginning of the seventeenth century. In 1672, the objective of 120 French ships of the line was reached. This would be the figure which would be sustained *grosso modo* throughout the remainder of the reign (a six-fold increase on the 18 vessels in existence in 1661). To these ships should be added the 30 or so galleys, a force which was gradually retrenched, beginning in Colbert's latter years. The galleys were essentially concentrated in the Mediterranean and very slow (five kilometres an hour without working the rowers to death); they formed a force of dissuasion,[39] which could cut communications between Barcelona and the Spanish possessions in Italy. In sum, the galleys were apparently a show-force with little overall effectiveness, of decorative value only, but very cheap to crew (the galley-slaves came for nothing).

This rise in naval power was inseparable from the rise of 'Far-West' Brittany since the days of Duchess Anne of Brittany into the specialist 'flagship' naval provider of the majority of the front-line crews for the kingdom's new maritime power. France's future lay, in part, on the oceans; and the same was also true for the merchant marine which increased of its own accord (although there were also some Colbertian subsidies towards naval construction). Between 1660 and 1680 it increased from 200 to 500 ships and from 150,000 tons to 240,000 tons. There was thus an increase registered in ships of all kinds, both for civilian and military purposes. At Toulon, Marseille, Rochefort, Lorient, Brest, Le Havre and Dunkirk, there appeared the modern concept of an arsenal, bringing together in one port (old-established or newly created) all the workshops necessary for the fitting out and re-fitting of ships. These constituted the premier industrial sites of the period. Seen in this light, Colbert's efforts were of greater consequence in this area than Richelieu's since the latter, by sheer necessity, had launched a fleet without thinking through all the logistical problems which would result.

---

[39] André Zysberg, *Les Galériens, vie et destin de 60,000 forçats sur les galères de France, 1690–1748* (Paris, Seuil, 1988).

Other features of modernity, of varying degrees of attractiveness, also began to make their appearance. Military service as a national obligation, the end-results of which would be all too clear during the French Revolution and Napoleonic Empire, stealthily emerged during the remarkable decade of the 1660s on the coasts of France. The principle of a general census of the seamen, which would eventually be replaced by a 'maritime enlistment', had been proposed 40 years earlier by Colbert's great precursors in naval matters, Montmorency and Richelieu (the former having been executed by the latter, but not before he had 'borrowed' some of his ideas in naval affairs). But the principle was finally put into practice by Colbert's agents, following ministerial initiative, on the Atlantic coast from 1665 onwards. Thus was instituted a forced recruitment of enlisted seamen in rotation by 'successive classes'. And although it would only gradually take shape, there was a significant anticipation of what would become, over a century later, the norm in the civilized states of Europe who, one after another, would enlist conscript armies. In fact the Sweden of Gustavus Adolphus, well before Colbert's day, had provided an example to follow with conscripted land armies.

Further, in the Navy Office, Colbert tended to employ 'commissioners' (*commis*) or 'scribes' in place of office-holders. The latter were proprietors of their office which they could sell or dispose of at will whereas the former were merely the holders of a title *de facto* which was not transferable (in precisely the same way as contemporary civil servants occupy their posts). These *commis* were nominated by the secretary of state (and not by the chancellor). There were rules governing their promotion. The ministers acted in a similar fashion in other administrative areas under his authority such as the colonies, the royal manufacturies, the road and bridges department. Thus, under the stimulus of absolutism, was created a bureaucracy, comparable with those of our day, but one which remained very much a minority, an embryo within the royal state. It would become considerably developed during the eighteenth century, especially in the area of the farming of indirect taxes. An office had characteristics both of the fief (a delegated power; or a power delegated to a succession of holders of a particular office) and of the market (the office-holder could sell it or acquire it for a price). The posts of *commis*, or functionary, by contrast, were above and beyond the market. They would preserve this 'modern' characteristic right up to the late twentieth century, including particularly the 'socialist' states which tried to free themselves, at least for a period, from the laws of the market. . . .

There were also other supplementary and enduring features of modernity which would later become widespread in other instruments of authority. There was, for example, the use of individual filing-cards (rather than registers) in the administration of the galleys. There was also the creation of an invalidity fund for the navy, supported by regular payments both from the state and from the seamen themselves. At the same time, the officers of the navy became more professional, even though they remained essentially recruited from amongst the nobility, which thus became a true 'service nobility'. Incompetent grand seigneurs like the Vice-Admiral Jean d'Estrées, who single-handedly lost a whole squadron of 17 ships on the rocks in 1678,[40] gave way to first-rate specialist naval officers like Duquesne, Tourville and, later, Jean Bart. The navy's sole significance for Colbert and his collaborators lay in the creation and protection of long-distance commercial trade, complemented by transoceanic colonies. The examples of the Netherlands and Spain respectively remained powerful in this respect. It was particularly frustrating, therefore, that the long-distance trading companies founded by Colbert should all have failed, save that of the West Indies which proved to be an excellent long-term investment that, after a slow start, would have a brilliant future before it in the eighteenth century. But various outposts were created or developed at Pondichérry and Réunion. Important footholds were established in Canada (which had 20,000 inhabitants of French origin in 1700 as compared with the 7,850 in 1675 or the 2,500 in 1660). The same was also true for the Antilles where slave plantations devoted to the production of tobacco and cane sugar were also set up. In the Caribbean it was also a case of establishing the 'bridgehead' of a transatlantic France which would be developed in the eighteenth century. In the Far East, Colbertian policies were concerned with the learning of oriental languages and the encouragement of exploratory expeditions, such as was realized in the publication of the accounts of discoveries of Thévenot, Bernier and Tavernier in, respectively, the Levant (at the court of the Great Mogul), Turkey, Persia and the Indies.

In many respects, the economic and colonial politics of Colbert was for several years indistinguishable from that of Louis XIV and it followed the directions mapped out by Richelieu; but this was the relatively pacific Richelieu and, by definition therefore, not the cardinal of the Thirty Years War phase. Hence the accusation often levelled against Colbert that he was nothing other than a carbon copy or a filcher of his predecessor's ideas. It was undoubtedly true that Colbert would, over and above the clientage ties which linked him as a younger man to his patron Mazarin, be prepared willingly to acknowledge before the *Conseil d'en haut* his sincere admiration for 'this great cardinal' (Richelieu) who would also be the master of the rising young Mazarin. So the genealogy of influence was complete: Richelieu *le Poitevin*, Mazarin *le Romain*, Colbert *le Rémois*. The second cardinal had, in his own way, been a talented and somewhat unscrupulous executor, without much by way of great personal originality, of the basic ideas of Louis XIII's first minister.

Colbert's various projects involved the development of the navy, the colonies, French manufacture and the subjection of the nobility to a much stricter code of discipline imposed by the state; the hand of Richelieu, whose ability to conceptualize was so remarkable, appears at every turn.

---

[40]   Etienne Taillemite, *Histoire ignorée de la marine française* (Paris, Perrin, 1988), p. 113 *et seq.*; Saint-Simon, *Mémoires*, xv, 81 *et seq.* and sidenote.

However, Richelieu was able to theoretize on problems but he did not always have the spare time or the necessary resources which a peace alone would have given him and which would have been indispensable to bring the schemes which he sketched out in the *Testament politique* to fruition. Colbert, on the other hand, would have the opportunity, for a good stretch of his ministry, to realize them, and particularly in the area of the economy.

*   *   *   *   *

Continuities from the days of the first cardinal-minister to the young Louis XIV can also be found in diplomacy. The traditional alliance of France with the United Provinces, an alliance of established importance to Henry IV and Richelieu, was maintained for several years more (albeit not without hitches). It corresponded to the old monarchical global strategy of sustaining certain Protestant powers in Europe, a strategy directed against the Habsburgs. In the fratricidal war between the Protestant England and the equally Protestant Netherlands from 1665 to 1667 the French government sided (albeit with a bad grace) with the latter and against the former.[41] In similar circumstances, Louis XVI would lend support to the American colonies against the English in 1778. However this configuration of alliances was not uncommon. Richelieu had been a loyal ally of the Netherlands and at least once declared war on the Stuart king. In external affairs, the first years of Louis XIV's personal rule were thus hardly distinguishable from the lengthy preceding phase under the cardinal-ministers. All that changed was a rather stronger emphasis on initiatives 'for glory'. There were, for example, the famous 'preludes to the politics of magnificence' by virtue of which the Sun-King sought to humiliate the diplomatic representatives of the kings of Spain, of England, and above all of the Sovereign Pontiff over questions of etiquette in respect of some Barbary brawls and the precedence of carriages at court. Historians of this century from Lavisse to Goubert have long criticized the aproach of the Sun-King. The fact is, however, that these 'preludes' now appear somewhat ridiculous; and, as Ragnhild Hatton has demonstrated in works which have generated some comment, in his punctilious and formalist attention to such niceties, Louis XIV did not differ greatly from the attitudes in similar circumstances of the other crowned heads of Europe, whether they were tsars, emperors or just monarchs.

Over and above these petty squabbles over prestige (which sometimes concealed important political or strategic manoeuvres) the anti-Habsburg direction of French policy remained in force for the following years, and particularly during the War of Devolution (1667–8). Louis XIV sought to exploit the opportunities afforded by the death of his father-in-law Philip

---

[41] The Anglo-Dutch war of 1665–7 was caused by English interference with Dutch interests in Africa and North America. In this affair, France reluctantly sided with its old allies in the Netherlands. It would be the last time before the 'wholesale revision' of this traditional political alliance took place six years later.

IV of Spain in 1665, and also the delicate health of Philip's son and heir, the little Charles II, the child of his father's second marriage. The traditional and enduring French hostility towards the dynastic house which governed in Vienna and Madrid is readily recognized in the event, a hostility which had remained dominant in the Louvre, and later at Versailles, from Francis I onwards. The Sun-King used some specious legal arguments against the young King Charles, drawing on the legal inheritance customs of Hainaut. By the custom of devolution, in these regions, certain lands 'devolved' to the children of the first marriage (Maria Theresa) rather than the children of the second (Charles). It was a poor quarrel but a classic and effective way of starting a fight. The systematic invasion of the southern Netherlands, half open warfare, half siege-campaigns, allowed Louis in 1667 to overwhelm the Spanish troops garrisoned there, cut off from their Spanish base and much inferior to the French troops both in numbers and in fire-power. The overall effects of the campaign could be justified on the grounds of defence which, however open to criticism it was, was not entirely without 'value', at least when judged on its own terms. The occupation and subsequent annexation of substantial amounts of territory, corresponding to the present French *départements* of the Nord and the Pas-de-Calais as well as a substantial slice of present-day Belgium, would enable the king, with the assistance of Vauban, to protect *ipso facto* Paris on its northern flank by means of an 'iron curtain' of fortresses at Lille and elsewhere. The unpleasant surprise of finding a foreign invasion menacing Paris, such as had occurred to Richelieu in 1636 (the year of Corbie), would in future be banished. But Louis XIV's conquest was also seen as deeply offensive by others, and this was the other side of the coin. Such an annexation, so quickly carried out, of a sizeable part of the southern Netherlands raised the gravest reservations in England and great fears in the northern Netherlands. It was French imperialism and they were absorbing new territories; by the treaty of Aix-la-Chapelle (in May 1668), after a short campaign, the French kingdom gained Charleroi, Douai, above all Lille, and then Armentières, Tournai. . . .

Louis XIV's reputation as, according to Sir William Temple, 'the great comet which is arisen over Europe', was henceforth well-established. His personal charm and his equitable disposition were well recognized and so too was his conciliatory attitude towards his own subjects. But, at the same time, whatever the motives with which he sought to justify his actions in terms of the necessary territorial protection of the state, he was readily preceived by France's neighbours as 'the gobbler-up of lands and states whenever and wherever'. And that, following the very logic implied by France's recent annexations, led to a complete revision in French foreign policy.

From 1672 onwards, the Netherlands became the focal point for these huge changes. The territorial annexations undertaken by Louis XIV in the Spanish Netherlands were provocative for the Netherlands. They menaced its frontiers to the south-west in precisely the region where Richelieu, with greater prudence, had been happy to envisage a buffer-state, a 'Belgian' republic as we would now call it. For his part, Louis would recognize later in his life that the Dutch War of 1672–9 was one of the great errors of his life, one which he excused on the not unreasonable grounds (as he pretended) that he was a young king, still obsessed with his own standing in the world.

'Rationality' was indeed not entirely absent from Bourbon calculations. Globally, the Netherlands stood in the way of French aggrandizement, just as England would at a later stage, and not only for geo-political reasons. Economic, maritime and commercial considerations were also important. From 1664 onwards, initiated by France, both countries had engaged in a tariff war against one another. Restrictive customs duties were imposed on Dutch goods in 1667, 1671. . . . The habitually nonchalant Colbert allowed himself to be carried away by the utopian vision of a hugely enriched kingdom, once the Netherlands had been conquered, either completely or in part, and its long-distance maritime trades diverted towards France. The newly rebuilt French navy, developed by Colbert, was waiting to attack the Dutch naval fleet; and, in reality, the French navy had an important part to play and would secure victories in 1672, 1673, and (finally) in the Mediterranean in 1676.[42] Moreover, the Netherlands was a Calvinist republic, both features being profoundly distasteful to the Sun-King. There was, therefore, a series of reasons, political and religious, which deepened the predetermined conflict between France and the Netherlands and contributed to the realignment of French diplomacy.

At first, the United Provinces were isolated, an 'easy' prey in 1672 to the armies of Louis XIV and Louvois. But, in reality, the Netherlands was a world power and France's first flush of success was brought to an end not far short of Amsterdam by the determination of well-armed Batavians opening their dykes and determined to make a last stand. Louis' victories had a boomerang effect, resulting in the dismissal from power in the summer of 1672 of the moderate bourgeois régime of De Witt. Political dominance passed into the aggressively francophobe and anti-papal hands of William of Orange. It had not been many years previously that the *via media* beloved of the Parlement of Paris had, in a similar fashion, given way to the more violent engagements favoured by the prince of Condé during the Fronde.

France's military intervention failed to defeat the United Provinces directly and its efforts were thus transferred from 1673 onwards to neighbouring territories to defeat the Dutch coalition which had taken on a continental dimension. Hence the brilliant military campaign of Turenne in Alsace (1674–5) against the coalition, or, equally, the successful block-

---

[42] In 1672 and 1673, the English and French fleets, then in alliance, fought indecisive battles against the Dutch fleets at Sole Bay (May 1672) and at the Texel (August 1673). From January to April 1676, Duquesne led (often successful) naval operations against the Dutch admiral De Ruyter in the Bay of Messina.

ing move, albeit at heavy cost, undertaken by Condé at Seneffe in August 1674 against the combined armies of the coalition (Spain, the Dutch and the Holy Roman Empire) who were attempting to make inroads into the southern Netherlands. It was here that, returning to its starting-point, the war finished with the impressive attack on Ghent executed by Louis XIV's generals in 1678 in order to force the enemy to the peace table, having failed decisively to win the war. Meanwhile, the Sun-King would willingly have foregone his Dutch objective (which was well beyond his grasp) and settled for routing Spain, a debilitated enemy and one which (on reflection) was ripe for attack given the preceding defeats inflicted upon it. But by then a grand alliance had formed against the Bourbon king, including both the Protestant and Catholic powers of Europe which together were worried by French expansionism. France knew (but did these powers care to admit it?) how to limit its ambitions when it was important to do so, when to negotiate and give way; in some respects, Louis XIV was an ideologue, particularly against the Huguenots within his own kingdom. But in external affairs, he did not behave like an armed conqueror inspired by a messianistic goal *à l'outrance* – the kind of messianism which is to be found at various times in Europe from the end of the eighteenth century through to the twentieth century. France's neighbouring states, both big and small, were not, however, aware of the nuances which are picked up by the historian.

From 1673–4, almost all Protestant Europe (England, Brandenburg, and the other Protestant German princes) and a good proportion of the Catholic powers of Europe (the Empire, Spain) drifted into hostility towards France or, in the case of England, which had been the enemy of the Dutch, into positive neutrality towards them, a shift registered in 1677 by the marriage of William of Orange with the daughter of the future James II. In 'Germany', France could only rely with any degree of frequency upon Catholic Bavaria. The ideological division began to harden. Left to his own devices, the English king Charles II would have happily cooperated with the French who paid him substantial pensions; but popular and parliamentary animosities against the calvinophobe France became more pronounced, despite the efforts of King Charles. The Test Act of 1673 excluded 'papists' from public office. In France, the vaguely 'liberal' period in which the king had backed the performance of *Tartuffe* against the *dévots* tended to become a distant memory. It was not that Louis XIV had personally become a member of the *dévot* cabal, for he had never had any time for it.[43] But he became more prominently engaged, along with his bishops, in the aggressive defence of the Catholic, apostolic and Roman

[43] The *dévots*, who mixed ardent religiosity and political ambition, grouped themselves around the former Company of the Holy Sacrament, Anne of Austria, the prince de Conti, the Archbishop of Paris Hardouin de Péréfixe. They attempted, and not without success, to prevent the public staging of Molière's play *Tartuffe* in 1664. Louis XIV, at this moment anti-*dévot*, would eventually ensure its performance in 1669.

religion. The hegemony of the 'true faith' constituted one of the progressively more predominant concerns of Louis XIV after 1661.

Louis had no cause to complain, however, for the Peace of Nijmegen in 1678–9 had ceded Franche-Comté to him from Spain. Thus a new 'province of the rising sun' was added to the hexagon, taking its place after that of Alsace, conjoined to it by the cardinal-ministers, and before those of Lorraine and Savoy which would be annexed under Louis XV and the second Bonaparte respectively. Yet the northern Netherlands, more than ever united in the Calvinist spirit, held firm and rallied around them the continental and insular adversaries of France. After his costly 'victories' Louis XIV could pose as the arbiter of Europe and savour a period of real apogee. But, in reality, Europe became more than delicately poised in its relations with Louis XIV; it became clearly hostile. With the exception of the Swiss cantons, who still provided mercenary troops for France, and Sweden, which remained a loyal ally to Bourbon France (albeit militarily disqualified by Prussia following its defeat of the Swedish army at Fehrbellin in 1675), all the Protestant princes deserted Louis XIV. Those upon whom, from the reign of Francis I onwards, the Valois and then the Bourbons had generally relied for support had turned their backs (openly or secretly) on Louis XIV. Despite the overt flattery of the Prussians towards the Sun-King, they considered themselves as his secret or declared enemies. In this respect, the diplomatic system which the cardinal-ministers had inherited from Henry IV was partially dismantled. France remained the adversary of the Habsburgs but it no longer stood suitor to the 'heretic' states of Europe – rather the reverse. Although unconquered, it was undoubtedly the case, however, that the Netherlands felt the strain of war, at least in terms of its economy and demography. The golden age of maritime expansion and financial and commercial predominance came to an end for them in 1672 as a result of a war burden which was too heavy for a country which was economically extremely robust but territorially modest, a great country which lacked continental space and which was required to fight on two fronts, on land and at sea. In this respect, Colbert had won the battle, or at least part of the battle that he had entered into in collaboration with Louis XIV.

But was France in much better shape? The great revolts of Bordeaux and then of Brittany of 1674–5 are proof that, for some of the French population, the burden of taxation was hurting. Warfare eroded Dutch prosperity but the French *contrôleur général* could not afford to rejoice at the difficulties of his adversaries and quasi-neighbours. For the economic situation affected the whole continent and the military conflicts both past and future gravely compromised the success of his own commercial and industrial initiatives. They even risked, through excessive taxation, doing considerable damage to agriculture, whose fortunes Colbert observed with the closest attention.

And yet French agriculture still seemed to have a reasonably buoyant and robust sense of prosperity. It afforded a solid basis (by means, once more, of fiscal exactions) for the various initiatives undertaken by the state. Even the notion of a relative rural prosperity during the Colbertian years (after the Fronde crisis and the famine of 1661) might surprise some historians since they have become habituated to think of the period in terms of a 'seventeenth-century economic crisis' and to apply it specifically to the long cycle of depressed grain prices which coincided with the first decades of the personal rule of Louis XIV. In fact, if one were to follow Simiand, whose ideas long constituted an orthodoxy, this period constituted a 'phase B' which was particularly characterized by low grain prices which had a negative effect on profits and investment – in short the long-term tendencies were towards a crisis. No doubt such an approach retains some value for the 1930s or for the last third of the nineteenth century. But when it is applied to the Louis XIV period it barely stands up to a sustained examination of the realities which lie behind a superficial analysis based on a simple reading of price trends. The level of cereal prices was certainly relatively low from 1663 to 1690, i.e. during the Colbertian period and afterwards. Yet this corresponded to a favourable state of affairs which was not necessarily perceived as unwelcome. For France, and Europe more generally (particularly western and central Europe) had just survived a brutal period during the middle of the seventeenth century, called the 'time of troubles' in some places; a period of civil wars and military conflicts, revolutions, epidemic catastrophes and agricultural disasters. Thereafter came the 'time of ripe ears of corn' which would be located in the collective memory in the Colbertian years. The latter were marked out by the completion of a phase of economic reconstruction or reconstitutive stimulus of the rural ecosystem. After one or two difficult decades, the harvests became after 1662 or 1663 henceforth sufficient, sometimes plentiful, generally adequate to national demand. Grain production (and other forms of rural production) increased to such a degree that prices were depressed and farmers had some difficulty in making a profit from the surplus which they offered to the market. The last civil war had been brought to a close in 1653, the Franco-Spanish phase of the Thirty Years War was ended in 1659 and the last of the famines took place in 1662. Thereafter came a 'post-war' situation favourable to economic stimulus and reconstruction which has numerous historical parallels. Amongst the latter, we might cite the long period of agricultural and demographic recuperation after the Hundred Years War during the flourishing 'Renaissance' period beginning *circa* 1450. Then there were the good years under Henry IV and Sully, a period which lasted well beyond the regicidal act of Ravaillac until around 1620. Then again, after the Colbertian period, there was the striking eighteenth-century expansion coinciding with the Peace of Utrecht (1713) and the new departures following the death of Louis XIV (1715). This list could be 'supplemented' in more recent times; other good periods of 'post-war' prosperity can be isolated after 1815; after 1918 (the 'ten glorious years' from 1919 to 1929); and again after 1945. The 'models' pursued during these various phases were doubtless very different one from another, given the differences in circumstances and centuries which separated them. To maintain for the moment an analysis on the basis of differing chronological periods, we may discern various distinct chronological frameworks for post-war growth. In some cases it could give the signal for a phase of long and sustained growth (1450–1560; 1713–70) or for a quick burst of expansion (the '30 glorious years' from 1945 to 1973). On the other hand, 'post-war' growth could take the form of a rather more limited and modest period of economic recuperation and welcome growth. It is in this 'minor' mode that we should place, as we have already noted,[44] the Sully phase which had none of the sustained vigour of the 'Renaissance' period or of 'eighteenth-century expansion'. The Colbertian phase also fits into this mode.[45] It was an 'Indian summer' which would be rapidly interrupted, or at all events constrained, by the successive trials and tribulations and hyper-fiscality of Louis XIV's later wars (the War of the League of Augsburg, and the War of Spanish Succession).

In more specific detail, having survived the brief and disastrous famine of 1661, the two or almost three succeeding decades were marked by high levels of cereal production[46] in Languedoc, Provence, the Bordelais, the Périgord, Auvergne and Upper Normandy. Elsewhere there was a sustained recovery over longer than a decade following the disasters of the Fronde or after the miseries of the Thirty Years War (definitely over by 1659) in the Ile de France, Picardy, Cambrésis, Alsace, Burgundy. Recent research in Maine-Anjou and Lower Normandy, the Beauce, Poitou, Brittany, Savoy and on the southern estates of the Knights of St John of Jerusalem fully confirm this chronology.[47] In sum, a period of relatively high cereal production levels was experienced for most of the decades of the 1660s, 1670s and even 1680s. It is true that the record levels for cereal production recorded during the latter part of the *beau* sixteenth century (before 1560) were rarely surpassed under Colbert. But the relative abundance of the harvest recorded during Colbert's ministry and even after his death, put an end to famine for close on 30 years (from 1663 to 1691). For

---

[44] See the closing pages of E. Le Roy Ladurie, *The Royal French State, 1460–1610* (Oxford, Blackwell, 1994), and the beginning of this present volume.

[45] We should note in passing that this is not to ascribe a determining role to the acts of great men, such as Sully or Colbert. Their names are acting simply as chronological 'frontier-posts'.

[46] E. Le Roy Ladurie and Joseph Goy, 'Première esquisse d'une conjoncture du produit décimal et domanial; fin du Moyen Age – XVIIIe siècle' in Joseph Goy and E. Le Roy Ladurie, *Les Fluctuations du produit de la dîme* (Paris/The Hague, Mouton, 1972), p. 362 *et seq.*

[47] Joseph Goy and E. Le Roy Ladurie, *Prestations paysannes, dîmes, rentes foncières et mouvement de la production agricole à l'époque préindustrielle* (2 vols, Paris, Mouton, 1982), ii, 491; 521; 529; 557; 553; 583; 607; 693. Also fundamental, despite the ideological tenor of the work, is Guy Lemarchand, *La Fin du féodalisme dans le Pays de Caux* (Paris, CTHS, 1989), pp. 114–15 (and for demographic confirmation, p. 98).

the moment cereal prices remained fairly low (although this was an international trend, or at least a west-European phenomenon). In these circumstances it was not too difficult to feed the workmen engaged in constructing Versailles or the *canal du Midi*, or to provision the soldiers of the French army. The Dutch War was thus financed more readily by the royal Treasury during a period of relatively low prices than the wars of the League of Augsburg and of the Spanish Succession which coincided awkwardly with years of high prices for grain.

The down-turn in grain production levels which began at varying dates (depending on the region) either slightly before or slightly after 1690, and which would overshadow the last 25 years of Louis XIV's reign until 1713–15, would transform the nature of the problem. However, Colbert and his immediate acolytes were able to work, imagine, build and conceive projects within an agricultural environment which continued to serve as the 'pack-horse'.

The fiscal politics of Colbert – let us say more broadly those of Louis XIV and of the state – was established around a general background of relative prosperity, or at least a degree of economic resilience. In return, Colbertian politics played its part, by a judiciously restrained fiscal burden, in preserving the vigour of the productive sector of the economy and the favourable conditions which prevailed at least for the first decade of Colbert's ministry and even beyond that. Doubtless the case that the hyper-fiscality of Richelieu and Mazarin and the vastly increased scope for the apparatus of the state which had begun from 1635 onwards remained henceforth an established fact. We follow Alain Guéry[48] in defining the net revenues of the monarchy as what remained of the gross revenues after all the expenses charged against them have been deducted (briefly, those state revenues remaining *in fine* to assign to expenditures save for the times when the latter were so burdensome as to result in a deficit at the end of the year). We should note that these net revenues, from 1600, an initial date which has been arbitrarily chosen, to 1636 (that is to say, *grosso modo* up to the moment when open war was declared) were always at a level below, and sometimes well below, 26 million *livres*.[49] From 1637 to 1656, the same budgetary category went up to 42 million *livres* with points when it reached 63 or even 70 million *livres*. The Thirty Years War was obviously the cause of this vicious fiscal spiral. Yet it is noticeable that during the first decade of Colbert's ministry and well beyond that period the state continued to extract a king's ransom. There was never any likelihood of a return to the frugal habits which had prevailed in the period before the phase of brutal increase, fiscally and in other respects, of absolutism. From 1661 to 1671, the net annual revenues of the state still amounted to 58

[48] Alain Guéry, 'Les Finances de la monarchie française sous l'Ancien Régime', *Annales ESC*, 33 (March–April 1978), 216–39.
[49] Ibid., to which has been added a roneotyped file which the author has kindly supplied.

million *livres*. However, Colbert had radically decreased the weight of direct taxation (i.e. the *tailles*), to the great relief of France's rural population. But, by way of compensation, the volume of indirect taxation on salt, wine, tobacco and customs dues was increased by more than an equivalent proportion. This increase was the result of better fiscal management which entailed the financiers being more efficiently controlled by the state. It was also (and above all) the effect of a rise in national consumption during the favourable post-war climate in the wake of the Peace of the Pyrenees (1659), the latter paving the way to over a decade of good years (for the War of Devolution was only an epiphenomenon, a military expedition which did not really disrupt, or not yet, the 'profound' period of peace from 1660 to 1672).

Despite the decrease in the *taille* just referred to, the overall net revenues from taxation had thus increased after 1661 in comparison with the former period of more fortunate fiscal frugality (before 1635) and even in comparison with the first turns of the tax screw caused by the major military engagements and initiated by Richelieu. These high levels in the tax receipts under Colbert might be regarded as somewhat onerous but, in fact, they represented a healthy position both in terms of the economic climate, already presented, and in terms of fiscal management.

For there was some comfort in the fact that expenditures had been restored to much more reasonable levels. To make one further comparison, during the phase of the modest pre-Richelieu state before the cardinal's 'turn of the screw' up to and including the year 1633, global expenditures incurred by the state remained consistently (and sometimes well) below 60 million *livres*. From 1634 to 1656 (following which date there is a gap in the accounts) the equivalent figures for expenditure were whipped up by the demands of war to reach close to 114 million *livres* a year. Even taking account of a certain degree of depreciation in the purchasing power of money which was occurring at the same time, the excessive fiscal pressure appears evident. The extraordinary levels of expenditure in the period from 1634 to 1656, which were clearly way beyond the net receipts of the state, were only made possible by supplementary borrowing, which would eventually become a burden, one way or another, on the tax-payers. Such expenditures would, at all events, be translated into considerable deficits which would amount on average annually to 73 million *livres* from 1634 to 1656, i.e. three times the annual deficits recorded in the relatively pacific years from 1635.

It is at this point that one begins to appreciate the scale of Colbertian fiscal purification. The latter would have remained unrealizable despite the minister's prodigious talents, without the underlying support provided by the favourable direction of the economy to the process, by the pacific and dynamic movement for economic reconstruction during the decade of the 1660s and after. From 1662 to 1671, the average annual expenditures of the state did not go higher than 66 million *livres*, i.e. no more than 58 per cent of the previous levels during the period of the great wars (1635–59). Expanding receipts; shrinking expenditures – the recipe for the deficit![50] The latter did not rise higher during the 'glorious decade' from 1662 to 1671 than 4.5 million *livres*, an insignificant amount. And in some years (who would have believed it?) the Colbert budgets were even in surplus (in 1663, 1665, 1666, the good years). The Dutch War would witness the return of the spectre of deficit finance, but at a level much less onerous than during the Richelieu or (even more) the Mazarin years.

Colbert's financial management was therefore not at all bad; even declared opponents of the minister such as the historian Daniel Dessert, do not contradict that.[51] Where Fouquet negotiated rates of interest with financiers of 33 per cent or even 40 per cent for the *affaires extraordinaires*, Colbert brought them down to 16.6 per cent. Thanks to this, the record levels of rates of interest under Fouquet never returned and throughout the reign of Louis XIV they would oscillate within the range of 16.6 per cent and 24.5 per cent. In all this, there is no point in transforming Fouquet into a warrior-financier, without fear and without reproach, whilst turning Colbert at the same time into a sinister manipulator. Colbert, who undoubtedly had the benefits of a favourable economic climate, did improve things financially and economically. The period of peace and relative prosperity from 1662 to 1672 gave France the opportunity of exploiting her considerable capacities for regeneration and reinvigoration to rebuild her reserves from which Louis XIV would draw in quantity during the Dutch War without ruining the country. During the Colbertian period and sometimes as a result of his effort, the 'Great King' and his subjects enjoyed many good and some excellent years.[52]

During this phase of wealth-creation, albeit on a moderate or gentle scale, France remained a country of vast and numerous resources. The Colbertian state stocked up in it, like in a gigantic money-box, the vital resources to finance wars or more pacific endeavours.[53] In 1683, the total stock of money in public and private hands was the equivalent of at least 500 million *livres*,[54] or 10.3 per cent of the overall money in Europe. The following decades would witness a decline in the national monetary stock. From 1661 to 1683, the financiers acted like 'gold-seekers' (or silver-hunters) who sought to enrich the Treasury in any way possible, and to enrich themselves on the way. In this respect, the majority of the important individuals who were close to the levers of power – be they Richelieu, Mazarin, Fouquet, Colbert or Louis XIV himself – acted as financiers

---

[50] This is according to the remarkable unpublished research of Alain Guéry; research report to the CNRS (1981), p. 52.

[51] Daniel Dessert, *Fouquet*, p. 63. These figures alone speak volumes against a good number of the polemically presented conclusions which Dessert's otherwise excellent work contains.

[52] Ibid.

[53] Ibid.

[54] Ibid., p. 175.

whose individual enrichment was not perceived as completely scandalous by contemporaries; at most there was 'a little abuse'. Fouquet himself once wrote: 'I have never understood how it could be a crime for men of business or other persons of great quality to draw *all the advantages which they could* (*sic*) by their industry or under cover of the favour of those whom they approach [*for protection*]. If it is the case that there is a crime in that, M. Colbert and those who have the confidence of M. le Cardinal would all be criminals too, for the name of their master has been worth a lot to them in gratifications.'[55]

On this basis, the directions of Colbert's financial strategy were towards conducting things more rationally than in the past. The farms of indirect taxes were progressively unified. They took on already the aspect of a great capitalist concentration. There was an attempt, not entirely unsuccessful, to reconstitute the royal domain which had been much reduced by alienations. But the wind turned against such strategies and the Dutch War from 1672 required there to be a return to traditional expediencies, albeit better managed than previously. A public debt was created by the mechanism of the 'constitution of *rentes*'; and, as in the days of Richelieu and Mazarin, further *affaires extraordinaires* (as the sale of new offices, or taxes of office-holders already in post were called) were set in train.

Such was the fiscal climate when Colbert, for better or worse, went into the Dutch War with his master Louis. At the structural level, however, the idea of a 'group',[56] which might be more loosely diluted into a kind of 'holding', is nonetheless revealing to the extent that it describes the 'money men, the grand seigneurs, the office-holders, not to mention the important agents of the state' who surrounded Jean-Baptiste Colbert as their unchallenged leading figure. One thinks in this respect of the career of one Nicolas de Frémont, born of a *robin* family, first an agent, and then one of Colbert's leading financiers, a friend and collaborator. His son and daughters, children and grandchildren alike, were related by marriage to the great ministerial, military and aristocratic families of the period, to the Lorge (linked to the Turenne), to the Catinat, the Chamillart, the Lauzun and the Saint-Simon. . . .

Colbertians and Colbert-ites – the great minister's relatives and friends had to paddle their way through dangerous waters. The Chamber of Justice (*Chambre de justice*) that the king and Colbert instituted in 1661 heavily penalized a number of former financiers who were accused of having profited too much from their handling of monarchical revenues. The Colbertians and Colbert-ites who were aggressive men of business

---

[55] Cited from ibid., p. 316.
[56] It would be absurd to become paranoid about this 'Colbert group'. 'Group' perhaps; 'Holding Company' maybe; 'Mafia' no. As Anette Smedley-Weill has demonstrated in a great thesis which is still partially unpublished on 'l'Administration française de l'entre-deux-guerres (1678–1689)', Colbert's clients were nominated to the posts of provincial intendant on the grounds of their merits and not only because of their factional connections.

seized on the opportunity it presented to oust their disgraced colleagues, temporarily deprived of powerful protectors, and who were seen by them as competitors or adversaries less fortunate than themselves. The end-result of this process of removal, this cleaning-up operation, did not involve individuals facing the death-penalty, but the financiers who were its victims were *de facto* dismissed in favour of their colleagues who were currently high in favour.

Amongst those individuals who were 'in the ascendant' and who enjoyed success under Colbert we may mention by way of one example Prosper Bauyn, an agent of the Treasury who specialized in fiscal dealings involving south-west France. He was responsible for 'recovering monies' from the generality of Montauban. Over and above other responsibilities which he undertook there, he was the owner, along with certain other members of his family, of the offices of general receivers of finance (*receveurs généraux des finances*) in his Montauban 'department'. He also enjoyed (an important resource and respected position) a share in the general tax-farm of the *gabelles*. The attractive position he occupied would not long survive the death of his patron in 1683.

It has been claimed that there was a 'Colbert group' functioning around the great minister. This is the thesis particularly of the historian Daniel Dessert who has rightly elaborated the careers of some of Colbert's faithful collaborators. The list of the latter is numerous; by way of example, we may cite that of François Berthelot, responsible for gunpowder and saltpetre; or, again, Samuel Daliès de la Tour, a former Protestant now dedicated to Catholic conversion and even a *dévot*. A farmer of the *gabelles* and a receiver of the *tailles* in Dauphiné, Daliès was charged with the supplies of wood and other *impedimenta* for the royal navy, for which Colbert was the minister. He managed a defined 'hinterland' for the navy account which embraced Provence, Dauphiné, Forez, the Lyonnais, Auvergne, Bourgogne and the Nivernais. He was particularly involved with the exploitation of forest resources and the assembly of arms manufacture and artillery for the construction and equipping of ships. But should we speak of a 'holding-company' rather than a 'group'? Pierre-Paul Riquet, the inventor and constructor of the *canal du Midi* was not purely and simply a 'creature' of Colbert's 'nepotism', which is how Dessert describes him, who (in addition) 'systematically exploited a carve-up in Languedoc' for himself.[57] In fact, this established Languedocian who had emerged from the business of *gabelle* administration was a true 'creator' – very far from being a 'creature'! In order to achieve the vast enterprise which he had begun, he shrewdly put himself under the patronage of a statesman with vision who operated out of Versailles. Far from 'carving up' the Midi for himself, Riquet 'carved out' of the land, out of the bare rock even, the canal which brought fertility to the whole province. This new watercourse would, in due course, add to the fortune of its constructor, and legiti-

---

[57] Dessert, *Argent*, pp. 328, 331, 394.

mately so after all the heavy and risky investments which it had involved – or rather to the fortunes of his descendants, for Riquet himself was (at least temporarily) financially ruined by the operation.

We have just described the 'cleaning-up' operation which was carried out at the expense of some of the financiers. But the golden calf of state finance had lost none of its force and money still had its allure. Looked at objectively, the institution of state finance, albeit fissured into various cabals, continued to prosper, if not to grow. As a result of the Chamber of Justice, it had the opportunity to improve its methods of operation and become rather less open to abuse than in the past. After a selective excision of some (but not all!) of the gangrenous individuals in its midst, it took on a new aspect – 'Colbert-factionalized' rather than 'Mazarin-factionalized'. Should all this be a matter for criticism? A state bureaucracy, the weight of which is a matter of daily complaint in our own day, would no doubt have been equally inefficient at the collection of indirect taxation in c.1665. In these circumstances, the private sector, or semi-private (i.e. the financiers of this period) were not so badly placed to fleece tax-payers without it costing too much. For his part, the king only wanted to collect his share. It hardly mattered to him whether millions of 'taxable' heads of families were 'handled' by public tax-collectors rather than by semi-privatized excisemen (*gabelous*), the latter proving eventually to be more efficient than the former.

Loyal whenever possible to those in power, practically all Catholic, the financiers were also nobles. It was not a secure sense of nobility, however. There were those whose nobility was old-established; more often it was more recently established; for half of them, however, their nobility was newly created in the lifetime of the title-holders, although inheritable by their progeniture. The financiers were multi-faceted individuals who skilfully played a part in the three roles which traditional society assigned to the leading 'estates' of the Ancien Régime. They chose the 'good' religion. They aped, not without attracting some mockery, the aristocracy. They pursued activities which, if they were not economic, were at least 'monetary' or 'fisco-financial' in nature.

Besides, they enjoyed the support of many various representatives of the wealthy and refined upper strata: the grand seigneurs *d'épée*, the senior *parlementaires* of the *robe* class, the widows with a substantial rental income, and many others, magistrates and others, did not shy away (clandestinely) from investing their wealth in 'deals' (*traités*) which the financiers struck with the king for the levy (for example) of indirect taxes, and from which they hoped for a profit. The gentlemen and ladies of polite company did not make a song and dance of such involvements. At all events, the privileged classes were sleeping-partners who put up the money for the financiers and for the political system. In the end, the excisemen, tax-gatherers and other 'publicans' whom the 'true' nobility affected to despise, acted as names (*prête-noms*) or straw-men (even if the latter had money to place on their own account as well) who acted, at least for part of their operations, as intermediaries *vis-à-vis* the 'shadow financiers' or participants from the upper-classes. They were, in short, intermediaries for the *Participes* (as they were called by contemporaries) originating from the court nobility or the higher magistrature. This was an additional reason for the financiers to rally to the support of Catholicism, or to remain its faithful adherents. They were more than willing to offer their services to the French church. They often managed, and in a profitable fashion, the vast landed estates (farms, domains, mills etc.) owned by abbeys and bishoprics.[58]

The financiers were not closely connected with the mercantile world, despite the fact that some of them had tried their hand at commerce in their youth or were simply the sons of merchant-traders. Colbert attempted, albeit with limited success, to introduce the world of the tax-gatherers into the great companies which he founded to handle international trade and manufacture etc. In fact, these 'intruders' or these 'exogens' from the world of the *gabelles* and elsewhere amongst royal financial administration succeeded overwhelmingly in arms manufacture and in certain of the spear-head industries such as mirror manufacture. The world of finance (in general) retained a quasi-aristocratic flavour; it tended to be snobbish towards the men of commerce . . . in order to avoid being treated with disdain by the authentic titled nobility.

Some historians,[59] including some eminent ones, have gone beyond this conclusion about the 'cascade of disdain' and presented a more critical analysis in which the world of finance did not merely disdain but *paralysed* the economic, industrial and capitalist development of France. In short, the public sector (the state) and the semi-pubic sector (the financiers) rendered the economic sphere of the 'private sector' relatively impotent. It is a paradoxical assertion given the constant care with which Colbert nurtured craft-skills, industries and mercantile activity. In reality, during the first 12 years of his ministry, and more generally throughout the whole Colbertian phase, this paralysing effect is nowhere proven to have existed.

Later, on the other hand, post 1690, during the period of the great wars of the League of Augsburg and of Spanish Succession, the extraordinary burden of taxation, as before under Richelieu and Mazarin, would effectively constrain (a less emphatic word than *paralyse*) numerous sectors of the economy, particularly agriculture, but by no means all of them. To the degree that the tax-collectors were responsible for collecting the heavy fiscal take, there was no relaxation in the grip of the régime of the financiers. But, via the simple route of the neo-pacifism of the monarchy, they became relatively less exacting, or (more precisely) less predatory than in the wartime period. One thus has a set of two relatively independent variables: finance and economy. The latter was only restricted by the former in the particular wartime conditions of exceptional intensity. For

---

[58] Ibid., p. 382.
[59] Ibid., pp. 413–430. Françoise Bayard, *Le Monde des financiers au XVIIe siècle* (Paris, Flammarion, 1988), p. 375.

the rest of the time, France industrialized (or not, depending on the period) from the eighteenth century through to the twentieth century; and the way in which taxation was 'managed' had no great effect on the process. Fiscality could be placed in the hands of semi-private financiers (as was the case in the eighteenth century) or in the hands of public tax-collectors (as during the nineteenth and twentieth centuries). But the economy followed its own path and, from 1600 to 1800, it flourished *grosso modo* during periods of peace and was only gravely jeopardized (at least in certain sectors) during the periods of war when these affected the main body of the country either from the fiscal or, *a fortiori*, from a demographic point of view.

This proposition is more strongly reinforced when we measure the economic and monetary management of Colbert as well as his immediate successors (and not merely his financial management[60]) against the contemporary indicators which show it to have been very impressive, taking account (it is true) of the socio-historical environment in which Colbert was working. The figures speak for themselves. There was price stability from 1662 to 1692;[61] and there was monetary stability too, for there was no devaluation between 1 April 1654 and 31 December 1689.[62] What twentieth-century minister of finance would not envy such stability over a period of 30 years or more, and signifying a total absence of any inflation either in prices or money, even during the Dutch War? That these remarkable results had been achieved in the context of rather depressed popular living standards and in a context where no trade union pressure or threats of serious strikes would occur to unleash the infernal cycle of salaries and prices is undoubtedly true. But the richer elements in society were not the only ones to profit from Colbert putting the demon inflation to sleep. The point is easily established *a contrario*; for the demon set to work once more in the years between 1692 and 1713, during which period there was a serious deterioriation in the living conditions of the 'inferior' classes in numerous respects.

Colbert was not merely a great financier; he was also a paragon industrial strategist, creating new manufacturing industries and stimulating those which already existed. In this respect, the stimulus coming from above was inseparable from the results obtained on the ground. In other words, the actions of one highly placed individual should only be judged in terms of the processes of development which, in fact, were already under way. Such processes, above all at this early date, only depended partially upon the action of the state, *a fortiori* only partially upon those of a minister, however important he might be.

Unfortunately we have no reliable data on the growth of French industry during and immediately after the Colbertian period. There is, however,

---

[60] See above, p. 162.
[61] Micheline Baulant and Jean Meuvret, *Prix des céréales extraits de la mercuriale de Paris*, 3 vols (Paris, SEVPEN, 1960), ii, 135.
[62] Ibid., iii, 157.

one exception to this, which is the woollen industry. The growth of the latter from 1666–72 to 1692 was 2 per cent per annum (according to the figures published by Markovitch in 1971) but according to the latest statistics (modified by the same author in 1976) was only of the order of .58 per cent per annum between the same dates. It was a moderate, but already substantial rate of growth, almost the exact equivalent to the average annual increase in the same industry in France throughout the *beau dix-huitième siècle* (1708–87), this being considered a remarkable period in the long-term for French manufactured industry. In comparison, the Colbertian period is not to be underestimated.[63] In other words, in terms of the textile industry, the 1660s, 1670s and 1680s witnessed a significant increase in level of production.

If we turn to the other fundamental industry of the period, the building industry, the graphs produced by Micheline Baulant demonstrate that, in Paris, the salary of masons reached a maximum figure and remained at that fairly modest level for the two and a half decades from 1664–5 to 1691. This is hardly surprising since it was the period when Versailles was under construction and various other examples of Louis XIV architecture. It was an age also when the capital city was growing in population, and thus in buildings too.[64] Where buildings go. . . .

Sector by sector, however, the learned and often-cited studies of Charles W. Cole,[65] alongside the quantitative research of T. Markovitch as well as the monographs of other historians, allow us to arrive at a detailed judgment of the various results of Colbert's industrial initiatives; or, at least, the results of the solid articulation of his governmental voluntarism reacting with the processes (spontaneously generated or otherwise) of manufacturing growth such as took place in France from 1661 until the beginning of the War of the League of Augsburg.

Turning first, or rather, returning to the woollen industry, remarkable or at least very encouraging results were obtained at Abbeville (thanks to the Dutchman Van Robais), at Sedan, Louviers, Elbeuf and Dieppe in fine drapery manufacture. During the last few years of his life, Colbert led a firmly-directed move, with the assistance of the senior provincial figures (the duke de Noailles, its governor, the intendant d'Aguesseau, the Cardinal de Bonsy, archbishop of Narbonne and *président* of the estates of Languedoc), to encourage cloth manufacture at Clermont-Lodève and (in what is now the Aude department) at Saptes and Carcassonne. These installations were, depending on the local circumstances, concentrated in

[63]   Thomir Markovitch, 'Le triple centenaire de Colbert', *Revue d'histoire économique et sociale*, 49 (1971), 312; and, above all, see the later modifications in his *Histoire des industries françaises: les industries lainières de Colbert à la Révolution* (Geneva/Paris, Droz, 1976), pp. 486–7 and *passim*.
[64]   Micheline Baulant, 'Les Salaires des ouvriers du bâtiment à Paris de 1400 à 1726', *Annales ESC*, 26 (1976), 478.
[65]   Charles W. Cole, *Colbert and a Century of French Mercantilism*, 2 vols (New York, Columbia University Press, 1959).

vast warehouses, factories of a kind, or again dispersed under the aegis of merchant factors into the capable hands of home-based cottage industry. This extremely shrewd Colbertian stimulus to industry turned in superb results a decade later (and beyond, towards the end of the century). Thus the ground-work was laid for the great wave of exports, varying in volume but growing in scale, of Languedoc cloth to the Levant from 1690 up to the Revolution.

Perhaps we may be permitted to make an incidental comment on the basis of the Languedocian lands and their industrial history. The English historian, James Thomson, has elucidated in learned fashion the minutiae of the birth and development of the drapery enterprises which were founded at Villenouvette, near Clermont-Lodève, typical of those founded under Colbert. He has also taken careful note of the initial appearance and subsequent growth in the powerful 'export'-led cycle of cloth from southern France to the Levant. But in all this, no matter how long-term the development, he sees only an archaic phase of industrialization, and even a 'negative barrier'[66] (*sic*) which was inevitably going to end up on the scrap-heap of history when faced with the true industrial revolution of the kind which occurred in Great Britain in the last third of the eighteenth century and which alone provided the appropriate method by which continental industrialization would proceed in the following period. There is no doubt that, at this point, erudition gives way to ideology; and the weaknesses of a historical method which is excessively monographic, like attempting to forecast the weather from one's back garden, begin to be apparent. It is true that Thomson can claim to be part of an outstanding school of English historians working on France who generally show little by way of bias towards the extraordinary (as they were) developments which took place industrially across the Channel in England. Instead, they tend to adopt a protective tone towards the French experience during the Ancien Régime. At this point, one thinks of the great work by William Beik on the political structures of Louis XIV's France which he finds at once fascinating, efficacious . . . and 'feudal'! We might also mention the somewhat unilateral work of Joseph Bergin on Richelieu's great malversations or, indeed, that of Macfarlane on English individualism in comparison with the so-called 'primitivism à *la polonaise*' (*sic*) of the French peasantry.[67] And this is only to select the most distinguished by way of example.

It would be easy to answer Thomson with reference to the fact that French manufacture, at least to judge by the evidence of its woollen

---

[66] J.K.L. Thomson, *Clerment de Lodève, 1633–1789* (Cambridge, Cambridge University Press, 1982), p. 459 and *passim*. Despite our divergent views in one particular respect, I take this opportunity of expressing my great admiration for this superb work.

[67] Beik, *Absolutism and Society*; Joseph Bergin, *Cardinal de la Rochefoucauld. Leadership and Reform in the French Church* (New Haven and London, Yale University Press, 1987); Alan Macfarlane, *The Origins of English Individualism: the Family, Property and Social Transition* (Oxford, Blackwell, 1978).

industry, continued to do well through to the end of the Ancien Régime, by which time the industrialization of Lancashire and of the Midlands was already well under way. From 1777 to 1787, the French woollen industry experienced its greatest period of growth, i.e. of 1.8 per cent per annum, much greater than the rather lower rates of growth registered for the same sector between 1666 and 1776.[68] The reply to James Thomson could easily be along the lines of: 'Those whom you are supposedly killing off are, in fact, doing quite nicely, thank you.' In reality, what retarded the French textile industry to some degree, sometimes forcibly restraining it, was not its Colbertianism. The latter would eventually become archaic; but it would have been easily overcome in the longer-term, just as all sorts of anachronisms of a similar kind would be overcome in a large country which would become wedded to industrialization sooner or later. What really held it back apparently was rather more the 'national catastrophe' (which is the bold expression of Lévy-Leboyer) of the French Revolution for France's industrialists and merchants, accompanied by and then followed on by extremely costly wars, the disruption of commercial networks and markets, etc. The Revolution, however productive it was from other points of view, would see the loss of 20 or 25 years of growth and development for the national economy in comparison with the sustained growth which continued to be demonstrated in the case of Great Britain. This was independent of the structural (technological) backwardness which evidently marked off the French hexagon from England to the former's detriment from around 1760 onwards.

From this digression we can now return briefly to the woollen industry once more. Again, the developments concerned products which were rather more commonly employed than luxury fabrics. Colbert succeeded in establishing various cloth manufacturies, particularly at Seignelay (on his own lands) as well as Abbeville, in the prestigious wake of Van Robais. Then the annexing of Valenciennes to France in 1679 secured it several additional units of production. Valenciennes was in fact a great centre for the manufacture of camlet – cloth mixed with goats' or camels' hair. There is within this acquisition a theme worthy of more general consideration since the territorial annexations which were achieved by Louis XIV in the north, north-east, and to the centre-east, quite substantially increased the developed – i.e. the industrialized – regions in proportion to the more economically 'sluggish' areas such as the Massif Central and the Midi, which had long been part of the Capetian domain. The Sun-King thus acquired a stake in the manufacturing axis of Europe which had long run from England down to northern Italy through Flanders, the Rhineland, the upper Rhône/Saône basins and the Swiss regions.

The true Colbertian triumph was with silk production and silk manufacture. In fact it was sufficient, as it turned out, for him merely to 'push the door open' since the demand for such luxury products was strong once the

---

[68] Thomir Markovitch, *Histoire des industries françaises*, p. 486.

volume of imported silk from Italy had decreased. The industry of silk spinning developed at Lyon under Colbert as well as in the Vivarais, spreading into the small towns of the region, and at Nîmes. The latter saw the number of its silk looms double between 1661 and 1681. Although the Nîmois were in large measure Huguenots, the Revocation did not stop this growth from continuing – indeed rather the reverse. Some opportune 'conversions' sufficed to deflect the storm. Those who suggested to the Nîmois of the period that there was a general crisis in the seventeenth century during the personal rule of Louis XIV would have made them laugh, even supposing that they had any notion of an economic situation which was not widespread at the time. As for silk manufacture, Lyon constituted the focal point for an extraordinary development. The fabrication of silk at Lyon had stagnated from 1621 to 1660; but it then tripled its production from 1661 to 1690, and the process was set to continue and grow in the following century. It had a spin-off effect in the surrounding region, an economic zone which included Saint-Chamond and, above all, Saint-Etienne. They were involved either at the first stages of production (spinning) or in the latter stages (ribbon manufacture) of the 'silk chain'. The high-quality products (gold and silver thread and capes) were henceforth manufactured at Lyon which broke the monopoly of Milan. The initiative of the local élite and of the urban population combined with the protective tariffs and import restrictions which the minister had introduced. Printing in the sixteenth century; silk manufacture in the second half of the seventeenth century: this hugely active economic centre at the Saône-Rhône confluence was in the process of growth and adaptation.

Less convincing, no doubt, are Colbert's excursions, sometimes muddle-headed, sometimes astute, into the dyeing, bleaching (the 'royal bleach-works' naturally), and above all into the manufacture, of cloth, an ancient French speciality into which he sought to infuse a wholly new dynamism. This gave him yet another occasion to demonstrate his habitual empiricism. Colbert, the one who is accused of strict corporatism, is to be found dissolving, by decision of the royal Council, the guild of cloth weavers at Le Mans in order to open up their craft to all the new-comers from the rural parts of Maine and the Alençonnais.[69] This is no longer Colbert; it is Bertin or even Turgot. Colbert as the precursor of the physiocrats – who would have believed it! But there is much to be expected of someone who, in his own way, is the very reverse of doctrinaire. The following year, in 1667, he equally opened up access to silk manufacture in the Lyonnais to the Huguenots.[70] He thus contradicted, and in the pursuit of his manufacturing objectives, the anti-Protestant politics of Louis XIV and the Malthusian or calvinophobe reactions of the silk-workers of Lyon who, in principle, had endeavoured to be unanimously, or almost unanimously, Catholic.

[69]   Charles Cole, *Colbert*, ii, 198.
[70]   André Latreille, *Histoire de Lyon et du Lyonnais* (Toulouse, Privat, 1975), p. 235.

The one who can do the least can also do the most. Colbert took a big gamble equally with the manufacture of silk hose on a loom, making use of royal protection, ministerial subventions, and still more of the atmosphere of the day. The loom itself was a 'machine' invented at the end of the sixteenth century and which was composed of 3,500 metal parts. It involved the most advanced technologies of the period. Such kinds of manufacture barely existed in France around 1655. During the 35 years which followed it was developed in Paris of course and in the Ile de France. But it was, above all, in Lyon, and in Nîmes where it was put into service. In Nîmes there were 350 looms of this type in use by 1692 operated by 109 master-craftsmen, often Huguenots or ex-Huguenots.

The Rhône axis and its Cévenol rim were the harbingers for the start of the southern 'boom' which characterized the eighteenth century. At the same time, the bulk of the cloth industry – old-fashioned hand-knitted woollen stocking manufacture, often localized in the Paris basin – also made progress, albeit in a less spectacular fashion than that exhibited by the 'machine'-made silk stocking. These developments took place during the two or three Colbertian decades, before and just after the minister's death. He attempted, without much success, to interest the general hospitals, where the poor were housed, in the production of these 'woollen' stockings.

The minister also became involved in lace-making. A female occupation, particularly undertaken in towns, it existed above all, and with the exception of the lace-makers of Aurillac, in northern France. The privileged company established by Colbert to teach French ladies the Venetian, or Flemish, style of lace-making, was a failure except at Sens and perhaps at Alençon. It had an influence, nevertheless, on the evolution of the aesthetic tastes of producers and consumers, both of which had become too exclusively French. And the interventions of the minister (by correspondence) with the tutors and other folk who chivvied the young lace-makers into action in the provincial centres is somewhat amusing. Governmental centralization was not always an easy ride.

In the so-called 'royal' workshops producing tapestries, furniture and *objets d'art* (the Gobelins and *galerie du Louvre*) Colbert was at least able to show what he was capable of. Under the stimulus of the painter Le Brun at the Gobelins they fashioned the décor of Versailles, and then shortly of Marly too. . . . Other (also royal) manufactures devoted themselves to the production of tapestries only; the most northerly was situated at Beauvais; the most southerly, in fact 'central', was at Aubusson, divided up into various workshops.

The metallurgical industries for military and maritime purposes (cannon etc.) inevitably strongly inspired Colbert's activity. But it was the production of mirrors, desired both by the court and by the urban worlds, which constituted one of the most remarkable successes of industrial Colbertianism (which had numerous failures in the various and diverse industrial activities which he sought to activate or stimulate). Nothing was spared to make this glass venture a success, of which the *galerie des Glaces* at Versailles remains today as a testimony. Highly qualified craftsmen were imported from Venice, causing as much commotion in the French capital as profit. A privileged company was founded in 1665, protected by customs duties and the grant of a monopoly with investment coming from financiers from the fiscal sector, progenitors of industrial capitalism. This company was integrated, thanks to the involvement of Seignelay, Colbert's son, into a previously independent manufactury founded at Tourville in the Cotentin and which had glass-makers of great skills. Thus were laid the foundations of a great firm which would, in due course, demonstrate its continuing vitality. In the nineteenth century it would take on the name of Saint-Gobain, which is now a household name. Colbert's methods in the manufacturing area were thus sometimes to stimulate by means of competition, and more often by means of privilege. They had their periodic failures; but there were also, or they laid the ground-work for, undoubted successes, some of which were huge. In the specific case of the royal glass Manufactury (the future Saint-Gobain), the return on capital in 1670 was already of between 26 and 30 per cent. Yet this was a company which had cost the state very little to establish and its initial financial capital had come essentially from the semi-private share-holders from the world of state-finance – not far removed, of course, from the centre of power. The capital of the Manufactury nevertheless grew five-fold between 1667 and 1680, rising from 112,500 *livres* to almost 500,000 *livres*.[71]

Colbert's industrial strategy was not concerned merely with this or that sector of the metallurgical, textile or glass-making industries. It was inspired by a vision, by a sense of overall strategy. He therefore set on foot the collection of the first industrial statistics in 1664. The survey would provide an explicit model for the famous provincial enquiries undertaken from 1697 onwards for the instruction of the duke of Burgundy. The statistics which Colbert thus acquired were of high quality. In the localities, the effort was completed by the creation of a corps of industrial inspectors.[72] In this respect, it is completely wrong to follow many historians in presenting Colbert as merely a replicator who realized in practice the ideas long ago expressed by his 'great elders', older and more outstanding than he was, such as Louis XI, Sully or Richelieu. Industrial statistics, an industrial inspectorate: these are very much the personal brain-child of Louis XIV's appointed collaborator.

The Colbertian mania for industrial regulation has, however, been much criticized, in contrast to the vaunted liberalism, supposedly of greater efficiency, which was practised from time to time in this period in England and the Low Countries and of which Adam Smith was the

[71] All this follows Claude Pris, *La Manufacture royal des Glaces de Saint-Gobain, 1765–1830. Une grande entreprise sous l'Ancien Régime* (Université de Lille III, 1975), ii, 870. See also Claude Pris, 'La Manufacture des Glaces de Saint-Gobain avant la révolution industrielle', *Revue d'Histoire économique et sociale*, 52 (1974), 161–72.

[72] Thomir Markovitch, 'Le triple centenaire de Colbert', p. 305.

theoretician. But the activists of the industrial party in France, the inspectors and others who were created by Colbert's endeavours, were more conscious of the marked differences between English entrepreneurs and their French counterparts in this respect, the latter being somewhat negligent when it came to maintaining the 'quality' of their products. The vital regulations imposed on the Languedoc producers concerning the quality of the cloth which they made were a powerful stimulus to the increase in the Languedoc textile exports to the Levant, whose consumers had proved themselves to be very exacting. This would constitute one of the latter-day benefits for which Colbert should have the posthumous credit, having laid the basis for one of the great successes in the Mediterranean politics of the French kingdom in economic matters in the eighteenth century.

Here, however, was a great national paradox. France under Louis XIV, in the guise of Colbert, was soon the beneficiary of his resolute actions and (whatever one may say) also from his being a strategist capable of shaping at critical moments the industrial system. The physiocrats under Louis XV also provided a group of thinkers whose competence was particularly evident in rural matters; but, unlike Colbert, they were not well-disposed towards craftsmen as a group; they regarded them, without justification, as a sterile class. The result was a hemiplegic France whose best-known economists in the eighteenth century were incapable of envisaging in one and the same moment the two essential pillars of production, agriculture and industry. The English, on the other hand, excelled at the task of providing an overall, and at the same time two-sided, picture. Once more, it was Adam Smith who would apply the concepts which he regarded as essential – free enterprise and a desirable freedom of the market – to crofts and farms as much as to shops and factories.

And yet . . . Colbert and his agents in various different circumstances recognized the need to keep both agriculture and manufacture in the picture at one and the same time.[73] In this respect, the minister would demonstrate that he could abstract himself from the detailed regulatory approach which distinguished later theoreticians so reproach him for. We have already provided an important example from Maine. Here is another, this time from the year 1673, when Colbert[74] suspended the application of a regulation requiring top-quality products from the producers of Languedocian cloth. He promulgated this liberal-minded and exceptional 'stay of execution' with the 'factors' producing the caddis and *burattes*[75] in the Gévaudan, the Velay, the Cévennes 'and other surrounding locations'.

---

[73]　This was particularly true of the intendants, half of whose interventions in local economic affairs concerned, either directly or indirectly, the agricultural sector (food supplies etc.) – at least according to the research of Anette Smedley-Weill, *La Correspondance des intendants*.

[74]　Markovitch, *Histoire des industries françaises*, p. 214.

[75]　Woollen goods, produced and sold very cheaply.

These were, for the most part, peasants or merchant-factors who employed a large cottage-based workforce in the villages during the leisure of the cold season. Yet this was one of the main areas of proto-industrialization in traditional France. At the beginning of the eighteenth century, when the inspectors of manufacture condescended to estimate the lower-quality textile production in the south-east quarter of the Massif Central, they discovered that it represented a sixth, or perhaps even a fifth of the output of woollen goods *throughout the kingdom*, a truly staggering figure and one which gives the lie to too much talk about the under-development of the south of France, an under-development which is worth stating from time to time without making too much of it. Although Colbert was not a countryman in the strict sense of the term, he was nevertheless (amongst many other characterizing features) a country 'proto-industrialist', something which made him a child of his time. With the assistance of his collaborators, he knew how to size up situations, intervening when it was the right moment in the major trends for growth, and even innovation, both in the town and the countryside.

Viewed in the longer-term, the years from 1661 to 1683 form a united but contradictory whole. Of the three panels in the political altarpiece of Henry IV, two had been, or were in the course of being, obliterated. Firstly, an authoritarian 'holist' régime in which the part played by absolutism was much more considerable, strongly reduced the possibility for the kind of open pluralism which the first Bourbon had granted the Huguenots and the grand seigneurs. The former, still respected in the intervening period of the cardinal-ministers, found themselves persecuted after 1661 before the period of the Babylonic captivity which awaited them in the 15 last years of the century. The latter had already been persecuted under Richelieu before finding themselves definitively and lucratively tamed and domesticated under Louis XIV's personal rule.[76] As a result, his 'absolute' regime in a paradoxical fashion introduced an egalitarian leavening, or at least a decrease in and limitation of aristocratic power, into French society. The lesson would not be lost when it came to preparing the revolutionary events of a century or so later on. Secondly, the Protestant alliances had also disappeared from France's diplomacy. They had formed the corner-stone of the strategy of the later Valois and early Bourbons. With the Dutch War they evaporated or rather were quickly transformed into the reverse.

Economic openness seemed, nevertheless, to retain every chance of success. Colbert was a new Sully, more bourgeois, more of a realizer than his model predecessor. He was carried along by a favourable economic climate which had the merits of encouraging a certain degree of industrial,

---

[76] Arlette Jouanna, *Le Devoir de révolte; la noblesse française et la gestation de l'état moderne, 1559–1661* (Paris, Fayard, 1989), p. 396 and *passim*; and William Beik, *Absolutism and Society*. They both insisted on the notion that the aristocracy was integrated into the absolutist system rather than brutally domesticated by it under Louis XIV.

commercial and colonial expansion, which Colbert claimed the credit for when the need arose. He began to realize the great productive schemes of Richelieu which had remained mere sketches, albeit sometimes richly suggestive, or never left the drawing-board. From this point of view, the work of Colbert was already pre-determined, not least because, as we have seen, only part of the achievement was his, the rest being the result of the favourable circumstances in which he was operating. Colbert's achievement was the meeting of chance and genius, of *Fortuna* and *Virtus*. On the other hand, some twentieth-century historians[77] have accused Colbert of having only wanted to fill the king's coffers through the additional taxes raised from the wealth created on the basis of a prosperity fostered from above. 'The treasure of princes, more than the wealth of nations' say these critics. But how can one separate the intention from the result, the fiscal consequences which were realized from the equally concrete increase in the manufacturing base? And then, at the heart of the question, a deep study of the mentality of Colbert's agents (the intendants) indicates clearly that, however obsessed they might be by the fisco-financial tasks which they had, they also were preoccupied sincerely with the welfare of the people, or at least limiting the 'ill-fate' which might befall them.[78] In this respect they were certainly at one with the preoccupations of their masters, and not least with Colbert and Louis XIV.

Colbertianism marks the beginning of an 'industrial party' in France. This was of considerable significance. But, when it came to Colbert himself, however active and talented he was, the worm was already in the apple. To want at all costs to catch up with and overtake the highly developed Netherlands was an economic and military objective which, when put into effect, was to put in place a strategy which would have an inevitably anti-Protestant tendency to the degree that it was conceived upon an anti-Dutch phobia; and one which, as it became more radically orientated, for this reason among others, would also be hostile to a certain kind of Calvinism. Thus, in the decade of the 1670s was laid the groundwork for the later phase, the second 'intercycle'[79] of the Louis XIV years, the period from 1683 to 1700, with its strongly authoritarian and 'organic' tendencies which were so opposed to the spirit of critical enquiry. The latter, however, remained a lively force upon which, in the intellectual

---

[77]   This was one of the favourite themes of Jean Meuvret in his seminars at the Ecole des Hautes Etudes consecrated to economic history in the seventeenth century.

[78]   Such is one of the essential conclusions that one can draw from the research of Anette Smedley-Weill, *La Correspondance des intendants*.

[79]   Ernest Labrousse christened periods of 15 to 20 years in length 'intercycles' to distinguish them from the classic seven-year or eleven-year cycles of traditional economic analysis. The word is readily applied here, especially in relation to the sequence of events in political terms, to the periodization of the whole phase of Louis XIV's rule: (1) Colbertian years (1661–83); (2) *fin de siècle* with the Revocation and the War of the League of Augsburg (1683–1700); (3) the end of the reign which often (but not always) coincided with moments of great difficulty (1700–15).

world, the elements of a 'crisis of European conscience'[80] at the end of the century were already being laid down.

[80] Paul Hazard, *La Crise de la conscience européenne (1680–1715)* (Paris, Bovin, 1955).

5

Gallican Extremism

The ten years following the Peace of Nijmegen in 1679 are interspersed with a series of significant dates – the death of Colbert (1683); the Revocation of the edict of Nantes (1685); and the beginning of the great conflict known as the War of the League of Augsburg (late 1688). This 'inter-war decade' was characterized by a hardening, a 'closure' of Louis XIV's 'system'. His aggressive strategy was evident on three fronts. In the first place the Revocation of the edict of Nantes asserted the increasing rigidity, religious and political, of the structures of monarchy and Catholicism. At the same time measures were taken against the Protestant powers, maritime and continental, which for their part became more and more hostile to the Sun-King. In their eyes Louis the Bourbon became 'Lewis the Baboon'. France stood powerful but alone or almost alone. Catholic nations, and even the papacy, were bullied by the Versailles government in exactly the same way as their 'heretical' counterparts. As the century drew to its close Louis XIV maintained Richelieu's hostilities against the Habsburgs of Vienna and Madrid, whilst abandoning the cardinal's pro-Protestant strategy by attacking towards the north and the east. He was therefore faced with new, more intractable adversaries.[1] Louis XIV's foreign policy represents a remarkable change of direction. As long as Spain was the leader of the Catholic world, France under Richelieu, despite being Catholic herself, allied with the Protestant powers against Madrid. With Spain duly humiliated, it became possible for Louis XIV to assume the mantle of leader of international Catholicism. From the peculiar perspective of *Realpolitik* this change of objective was not necessarily illogical. But the excess of enemies led to armed conflict on a European

---

[1] The foreign policy of Louis XIV represents a remarkable example of substitution. Whilst Spain was the leader of the Catholic world, Richelieu's France, despite being also Catholic, led the Protestant powers against Madrid. Having, in due course, weakened Spain, it became possible for Louis XV to take up on behalf of the French kingdom this rewarding role of being leader of international Catholicism which Spain no longer had the power to sustain, a role which was therefore 'for the taking'. From a rather particular *Realpolitik* perspective, this was not entirely absurd.

scale, giving rise to massive increases in taxation. In time these would throw whole sectors of the economy, notably agriculture, which had enjoyed a relative prosperity under Colbert, into crisis. The impulse towards more uncompromising policies during the 1680s needs to be explained. The last doves are scattered, the hawks soar and dominate. Why? Or at least how? Before refining our analysis, the phenomenon of the Revocation should be viewed in overall perspective.

Its roots lie long in the past. Looking only at the previous quarter of a century, systematic discrimination against the Huguenots had begun with the Peace of the Pyrenees in 1659 and especially with the beginning of the personal rule of Louis XIV in 1661. The interplay of individual initiatives and socio-political forces producing intolerance may be seen in all its harshness during the 25 years preceding the final act. These phenomena, like the links of a chain one following on the other, are a matter of both 'intentionalism' and 'functionalism'.[2] *Intentionalism* would explain the Revocation as deriving from the personal will of Louis XIV. The fact is that, unlike his predecessors and successors, Valois and Bourbon alike (with the single exception of Henry II, whose reign was shorter and whose judgements were more impressionistic), Louis XIV had always harassed and oppressed his Huguenot subjects. Things got worse in this respect at the end of the 1670s. In the rather salacious Affair of the Poisons,[3] the official royal mistress of the moment, Madame de Montespan, had been compromised by a series of insidious accusations, true or false. In order to seduce, dominate, even kill her royal lover, she was said to have employed magic, black masses, provocative dress, and so on. Louis XIV, more astute in such matters than the unfortunate Louis XVI was to be in the Necklace Affair, defied (like Louis XV in the trial of d'Aiguillon) any publicity which would be awkward for himself and the woman he loved or had loved. Justice, under His Majesty's orders, nevertheless bore down mercilessly: several dozen people were executed, a score worthy of Richelieu. Louis arranged matters so that his beloved would be neither exposed nor condemned. But with the wisdom of advancing age, he broke with her. After a few final dalliances (typified by the silly and charming Marie-Angélique de Fontanges), he settled down. He forgot Nausicaa (Louise de la Vallière), rebuffed the charms of Circe (la Montespan), and dwelt at last under the wing of Penelope (Madame de Maintenon), marrying her clandestinely in 1683, after the decent interval imposed by the death in the same year of his first wife, Maria Theresa, as the result of a boil in the armpit which developed into septicemia. La Maintenon, 'the universal abbess', as Saint-Simon called her, long delivered from the Calvinist 'errors' of her girlhood, could refuse the church nothing. And what a woman wants . . . .

---

[2]   See, in this context, the annotations of Philippe Barrin in *L'Histoire*, no. 118 (January 1989), 27–30.

[3]   Jean-Pierre Labutut, *Louis XIV, roi de gloire* (Paris, Imprimerie Nationale, 1984), p. 243 *et seq.*

Plate 10   Mademoiselle de La Vallière   Louise de la Vallière (1644–1710) was the first of Louis XIV's 'three glorious' extra-marital liaisons. His passion for her began in around 1661 but, in 1667, she found her place in his affections beginning to be shared by Athénaïs, marquise de Maintenon, who gradually assumed prominence in the period from 1667 to 1674. It was in respect of Mademoiselle de La Vallière that the king declared the necessity of 'keeping the tenderness of a lover separate from the decisions of a sovereign king', a separation which he was able to uphold with greater consistency than his successor.
Maintenon, Fondation du château

Louis XIV had always been religious, but not excessively so, and he knew little of the subtleties of theology. But little by little he fell into line and became assiduous in the performance of his pious duties. In the flush of his youth in 1664, he had, together with Molière, encouraged the staging of the *Plaisirs de l'Ile enchantée*. He had tolerated the production of *Tartuffe* against the *dévots,* whom he considered his adversaries (but not

Plate 11   The marquise de Maintenon and her niece Madame de Maintenon
(1635–1719), the last of the '*trois glorieuses*' mistresses of Louis XIV, was also the
most strong-willed and intelligent. She succeeded in persuading the king to marry
her in 1683; his subsequent fidelity towards her demonstrated her ability to retain
the king's affections. She is depicted here with her niece in a painting after Louis-
Ferdinand Elle.
Maintenon, Fondation du château

against the bishops, whom he turned into his clients). But all that now lay
in the past. Soon he would be more interested in the creation of *Esther*, the
exterminator of the heterodox,[4] the actors in which would be the noble
young ladies of Saint-Cyr, pupils of the establishment founded by Madame de Maintenon, alias the widow Scarron, a new and devout Anne of

---

[4]   *Esther*, 9 on the 75,000 or so killed at the behest of this heroine.

Austria. This *vieille Ripopée*,[5] as la Palatine called her, cannot be held responsible as such for the Revocation of the edict of Nantes. But there is no reason to reject out of hand the precious testimonies of contemporaries and memorialists, great writers or simply great wits, like Saint-Simon, Ezechiel Spanheim,[6] Robert Challe, or, again, the Princess Palatine. They insist upon the yearning for personal and collective repentence emanating from a sovereign turned apostle, desirous of performing penitence on the far from complaisant backs of his Calvinist subjects. The memorialists bear witness also to the ambience surrounding the royal spouse, the seraphic prude, flanked by an *ad hoc* entourage with whose help the act of 1685 was contrived in the conscience of the king. This would be the intentionalist version of the affair, an account difficult to refute so far as it goes. But voluntary intentions, even emanating from the king, were not all there was to it. The 'functionalist', or simply 'global' aspect of things also needs to be considered. With or without Louis XIV, a set of socio-cultural conditions apparent between 1660 and 1680 'functioned' or predisposed things towards the Revocation, even though it needed someone, the king, to apply the final touch.

The Catholic church had been pursuing its counter-reformed transformation for more than half a century. Self-confident and imperious, it would have no qualms about the idea of suppressing, or at least absorbing, anti-Vatican heresy (even if on a personal level many priests of all grades rejected the concept of forcing consciences). The state apparatus, with the Le Tellier-Louvois clan in the *Conseil d'en haut*, possessed the network of intendants ready to get to work in the provinces: with Colbert dead, they would become the agents of a 'conversion state'. The parlements had for more than a century been eager hunters of pastors; they asked only to get their sights on the same game once more. Finally, the army was large, battle-hardened and disciplined, at its head numerous officers excited by the prospect of ridding the country of the Huguenots once and for all. Since 1679 no foreign war, capable of diverting the soldiery, the dragoons in particular, from their sacred mission within the kingdom, had flared up outside French borders. So a union of the sword and the three *robes* (clergy, royal Council and parlements) was forged against a common enemy, a despised minority. A two-headed nemesis, royal and corporative,

[5] This was the somewhat unkind sobriquet coined by the translators from the original German, using the French word *ripopée* (old 'rehash' or old 'molasses') to render the word used by la Palatine in her correspondence to insult la Maintenon whom she could not stomach (*Lettres de Madame, duchesse d'Orléans, née princesse Palatine* (Paris, Mercure de France, 1981), p. 114 [letter of 6 February 1695]). We should recall that Elisabeth Charlotte of Bavaria, the Princess Palatine, daughter of the Elector Palatine, was the second wife of Monsieur, the duke d'Orléans, Louis XIV's brother. The letters from this colourful bilinguist constitute an essential source for a good understanding of the court of the Sun-King at Versailles.

[6] Ezechiel Spanheim, *Relation de la Cour de France en 1690* (Paris, Mercure de France, 1973), p. 51; Saint-Simon, *Mémoires*, ed. A. de Boislisle, 45 vols (Paris, 1879–1930) xxviii, 226–7.

individual and global, menaced French Protestantism. It remains to be seen in detail how this open conspiracy against the weak worked itself out over the timescale of a generation or even a century, the apparently final signal only being given in October 1685 by the edict of Fontainebleau, signed by Louis XIV and Chancellor Le Tellier.

The anti-Huguenot measures from the 1660s onwards emanated from the *arrêts* of the *Conseil du roi*, which functioned more as an administrative tribunal than as a council of ministers. They proceeded also from the wishes of the parlements (Toulouse) or the votes of regional assemblies (estates of Languedoc). The *Conseil du roi* did not always act in a spontaneous manner: it had often been solicited beforehand by clerical authorities, such as general assemblies or agents of the clergy, or syndics of dioceses. Protestantism was attacked by a dual entity: ecclesiastical, but also state and monarchic. The latter, which would soon get the bit between its teeth, was compliant and attentive to the suggestions of the former. The alliance established at the summit between a group of leading prelates (Le Tellier, Harlay, Bossuet[7]) and the organs of state justice (king, chancery, secretaries of state) was reflected at the base in anti-Protestant militancy. The ideologues preparing the Revocation could be Jesuits, sometimes Gallicans against the wishes of the Society, such as *pères* Meynier and Maimbourg, or else they emerged from the lower reaches of provincial justice, like *maître* Pierre Bernard, councillor in the *présidial* of Nîmes and author in 1666 of an *Explication de l'édit de Nantes*,[8] violently hostile to the Huguenots of Languedoc and elsewhere. The measures taken against the minority religion were not always applied or even applicable. They identified its adherents as schismatics, destined for pure and simple reintegration, while in reality they were a 'heretical' group, extremely resistant to reconciliation about fundamental differences over rites and dogmas. The repressive measures handed down from Versailles undermined the legal functioning of the Protestant churches and more generally of Reformed communities at all levels. They abolished, immediately or gradually, the Huguenot national synod and the *chambres mi-parties*.[9] They induced the destruction of temples, whether attached to fiefs, the one permitted in each *bailliage*, or those attested as existing since 1598. They limited, with mixed success, the numbers of Protestants attending sym-

---

[7] Charles Maurice Le Tellier (1642–1710), the younger son of Chancellor Le Tellier and the brother of Louvois, was archbishop of Reims from 1671 until his death. He was one of the leaders of the French episcopacy in the last third of the seventeenth century, along with François Harlay de Champvallon (1625–95), who became archbishop of Paris in 1671.

[8] The *Bibliothèque nationale* possesses the re-edition of this text in 1683 as well as various works by the same author.

[9] The synod brought together ministers and 'elders', representatives of the reformed churches; it could be called 'national' when it was constituted of delegates coming from such different provinces of the kingdom as included Huguenot communities in their population. The *chambres mi-parties* included magistrates recruited from amongst the 'two religions' and thus offered the best guarantees of justice being accorded to the Protestants, notably when the latter were involved in litigation with Catholics.

bolic acts in the street or the open air, such as processions or funerals. They obliged Protestants outwardly to respect Catholic manifestations, such as the displaying of the Holy Sacrament or the cult of the Virgin. The anti-Huguenot policy also put into practice a form of professional exclusion, a *Berufsverbot*. This was an inverted mirror image of the measures enacted by the London government against English and, more rigorously, Irish papists, at least as far as public employment was concerned. The *Conseil du roi* barred Protestants from sitting on town councils and from acquiring royal or seigneurial offices. In the private or semi-public sector, the *métiers jurés* of the artisanate (linen workers, pewter makers) and the liberal professions (medicine, the law) were closed to Huguenots. The individual's life cycle was placed under surveillance at each successive stage. On his or her entering the world, the midwife was, in theory, a Catholic, even if the mother was a Protestant. Huguenot education was banned. Protestants were even robbed of their deaths, being visited on their death beds by judges trying to obtain the hoped-for last-minute conversion. Purely theoretical clauses went completely over the top, like those which forbade Muslims from embracing the doctrine of Geneva!

These measures did not spring fully armed from the forehead of Louis XIV. They appeared in an escalating sequence over a quarter of a century, marking out a chronology of repression. They show the strategy[10] of the authorities who hatched them and reveal the gestation of the final Revocation. It was not meant for purely external consumption. The purpose was not simply the elimination of an irritating, deviant or atypical minority for the benefit of a monopolizing clergy. In fact the monarch and his people made a present of doctrinal unanimity to the clergy. In exchange they obtained from the priests a more complete obedience to the sovereign power. The secular authorities thus got what they wanted. Order was less and less threatened by revolt, as the population became better controlled by a clergy now loyal to the state. This was the result obtained by opportunist politicians; they did not foresee the long-term dangers created by this vast exercise in intolerance, dangers from which the persecuting church would also suffer. In the century to come, despite becoming less intolerant over time, it would be all the more easily open to criticism on account of its long and profitable complicity with the governing élite. Thus weakened, 'papist' clerics would be even more appetizing targets. All in all, the principles espoused by Louis and his ministers were close to the religious absolutism of a James I of England or a Hobbes, closer still to Cromwell, the violent oppressor of Irish papism, or the partisans of Erastianism, so called after Thomas Erastus (1524–88), the Swiss theolo-

---

[10]   An attempt to expel the Jews from south-west France failed to match anti-Protestant repression (*AN* G⁷134 – May 1688; in particular 13 May 1688). The authorities abandoned this measure in the light of the danger which it presented to the Bordelais economy (reference kindly provided by Anette Smedley-Weill).

gian who contested the autonomy of the church and proposed its strict submission to the state. Catholics and Protestants, when in power, converged strangely in this manner.

You scratch my back, I'll scratch yours. This simple principle of mutual exchange could be illustrated, well before the Revocation, by the assembly of the clergy of 1670. This meeting granted the king a considerable *don gratuit*, expecting in return the energetic measures 'necessary' to deal with the Protestants. Later, the picture is more ambivalent, not always being simply a question of such petty bargaining. The Peace of the Church in 1669 had dispensed with the Jansenist question for 30 or so years, and in this situation of newly restored, if temporary Catholic unity, complicity between church and monarchy was free to develop. Between the quarrel over the *régale* in 1673 and the assembly of the clergy to discuss the Four Articles in 1682 a three-headed and sometimes contradictory Gallicanism (monarchical, ecclesiastical and *parlementaire*) was inextricably associated with anti-Huguenot persecution. Oppression was stepped up after 1678–9, when the Treaties of Nijmegen, with Spain in November 1678 and the Emperor in February 1679, put an end to foreign war. Louis now had a free hand within his kingdom.[11] He could now defer more completely to the desires of the church, and even become fanatically militant in settling accounts with his heterodox subjects. Playing the glorious Cornelian hero, he would be Constantine reborn, a second Theodosius, champion of the sole official religion against all other beliefs, devotee of absolutist integration, absorbing the non-conformist minority.

From the time of the Dutch war this new status as champion of Catholic dogma, acutely deferential to the wishes of the clergy, had given the king an excellent hand in bargaining with the French priesthood, the principal beneficiaries of his attentions. Louis did not even have to wait for the pope himself to be convinced about the pious necessities of a rigidly anti-Calvinist French policy. The prelates, by virtue of the conditions of their appointment, were clients of the Sun-King. Authentically Christian, they doubtless were able to hang on to a degree of autonomy from their exacting master, at least in the spiritual sphere. But this only made them more determined, for example over the *régale*, the king's right to collect for himself the revenues of vacant bishoprics and nominate to benefices dependent on them, to concede to Louis XIV what they would have energetically refused to Henry IV, former Huguenot and son of Jeanne d'Albret.

The *régale* affair, occurring as it did during the Dutch War, illustrates in a piquant manner this current of mutual sympathy established between the state and the clergy, for reasons of self-interest on both sides, and directed against both the Protestants and the pope, who paradoxically did duty as the twin targets against which royal policy was directed. By a declaration

[11] France made peace with Spain at Nijmegen in September 1678 and with the emperor, also at Nijmegen, in February 1679.

of 1673, Louis XIV extended the *régale* to the southern dioceses, where coincidentally the Protestant population was at its strongest. They had up to then been exempt from the *régale*, which had by contrast been generally applicable in the north. But from then on the king could collect certain revenues and make appointments to certain benefices during vacancies in the south. The losses thus suffered by the bishops would be compensated for by the persecution of local Protestants. The link between Gallicanism and anti-Protestantism continued to be evident. When Louis XIV took possession of Strasbourg in October 1681 he re-established Catholicism in the city, much to the displeasure of the local Lutherans. Now he wanted to profit from the services he had rendered to the papist cause by obtaining from the pope an *indult* or special grace acknowledging the justice of French demands over the *régale*. Should the pontiff refuse (as he did) to grant this *indult*, the combined authority of the king and a special assembly of the clergy would refute papal pretentions. So, de-Lutheranization (up to a point) of Strasbourg; bi-fold Gallicanism, episcopal and monarchical; and suspicion of Rome: the triple or quadruple strategy of the French church and the absolutist state, advancing hand in hand, is clear and active. Protestants had no choice but to hang on and try to behave themselves.

The illustrious clerical assembly of 1681–2 in no way diverged from this by-now canonical arrangement. When Bossuet, good Gallican as he was, addressed this learned assembly in November 1681, he proposed limiting the power of the pope in relation to the church and monarchy of France, but he was careful at the same time to underline the Catholic credentials of Louis XIV, that is to say 'Calvinists converted, temples thrown down, the cathedral of Strasbourg seized from the Lutheran sectaries'. Tit for tat, once again? A few days later, Harlay, Archbishop of Paris, joined in the chorus raised by Bossuet and Le Tellier. 'Louis XIV', said Harlay, 'has rendered such service to the church that all the treasures of this church would not suffice to recognize it; the archbishop hopes, therefore, that the pope will come to terms with this (by recognizing and rewarding royal services) rather than undermining the liberties of the Gallican church.' The implicit terms of the bargain appear clearly once again. In the same month at the same assembly, the *promoteur* Chéron, a subordinate of the archbishop of Paris, brandished anti-Protestant rhetoric and praised the success of the sovereign against heresy, combining this with the exaltation of a monarchical Gallicanism (the king-priest) and episcopal Gallicanism ('the bishops re-established in their sees'). Such citations could be repeated endlessly, so let us simply reiterate that the Gallicanism of Mgr Le Tellier, Louis XIV and their acolytes emerges from it all as an affair between Frenchmen, an exchange of good and loyal services between the bishops and the king, whom it helped to make more 'absolute'. The pope is left on the sidelines and the Huguenots under the whip of persecution. The same people who hurled invectives at the pope at the same time wrung the necks of the Protestants.

Plate 12   The King in his Council, the arbiter of Peace and War   This cleverly executed engraving by Nicolas Langlois from an almanac of 1682 is an able piece of propaganda of the kind which had become common in France from c.1610. Louis XIV is shown surrounded by his son, the Dauphin, his brother, and by Condé, the first prince of the blood. Also there to offer advice are his ministerial clans, the Colbert (Jean-Baptiste Colbert and Colbert de Seignelay), the Le Tellier (the chancellor and his son, Louvois) and the Phélypeaux (La Vrillière). In the lower inserts are presented the annexation of Strasbourg (Louvois) and the canal du Midi (Colbert). The almanac was not far from the truth for 1682, the year of the king's Gallican triumphs and France's 'European hegemony'.
Paris, Bibliothèque nationale, cabinet des Estampes

The remainder of the debates and decisions of the 1682 assembly revolved in the same spirit around two fundamental and complementary texts: the Four Articles drawn up by Bossuet and the Pastoral Injunction to Protestants. Yet the Bossuet of the Four Articles was exactly the same man who converted[12] the Protestant Turenne in 1668 and wrote the *Exposition de la doctrine catholique* for the purpose. Long before 1682 he had rejected papal infallibility, because it prevented *a priori* the return of the Reformed to the True Church. The declaration of the Four Articles in 1682 arose originally from the claims of the state over the *régale*. But it reflects nevertheless the position of the secular power as well as the anti-Roman mentality of the episcopate, under the guidance of Bossuet and Le Tellier. It fits in also with the anti-Protestant strategy of an uncompromising Gallicanism, offering the Huguenots the choice between a gilded cage or the iron bonds of a nationalist church extracting a high price from the Vatican and which it was hoped could be more to their taste. The Articles affirmed: first, the independence of the secular power from the church; secondly, the superiority of an ecumenical council over the pope; thirdly, the respect owed by the Vatican to the privileges of individual churches; and fourthly, the denial of the personal infallibility claimed by the Holy Father. Did this represent, then, in Bossuet's judgement, the price to be paid for the return of the lost sheep to the fold, encouraged of course by the judicious use of *dragonnades?* It is only in such a perspective that the celebrated Pastoral Injunction (the *Avertissement pastoral de l'Eglise gallicane assemblee à Paris à ceux de la RPR pour les porter à se convertir et à se réconcilier avec l'Eglise*) can be properly understood. This text is tied on the one hand to the resolutions of the assembly of 1682, obediently exalting the power of the monarchy, and which it was hoped would render the church, suitably 'depapalized', more attractive to the Huguenots.[13] On the other hand, it was bound up with the demolition of numerous Protestant *temples*, at the time and later, with which the temporal authorities rewarded the clerical lobby for its docility, consolidating the union of Throne and Altar, with the former in the driving seat. The combination of Gallicanism and repression represented by the assembly of 1682 was to have serious repercussions in the months and years to come: the Protestant revolt of June 1683, organized by the Huguenot lawyer Brousson, is significant here.

The most noteworthy rebellions up to 1675, date of the last insurrections in Brittany and Bordeaux, had taken place in predominantly Catholic areas. Without disappearing entirely, these uprisings among the 'papists'

---

[12] For all this, see Pierre Blet, 'Louis XIV et le Saint-Siège', *XVIIe Siècle*, 31 (1979), 137–54. See also Pierre Blet, *Les Assemblées du clergé et Louis XIV (1670–1693)* (Rome, 1972) as well as 'Le Conseil d'Etat et les protestants, de 1680 à 1685', *in Bibliothèque de l'Ecole des Chartes*, 130 (1972).

[13] For a full picture of our views concerning the Revocation, see E. Le Roy Ladurie, 'Longue Durée et comparatisme: Révocation de l'édit de Nantes et Glorieuse Révolution d'Angleterre', *Revue de la Bibliothèque Nationale*, no. 29 (Autumn, 1988), pp. 3–17.

died down in the era of escalating anti-Protestant repression. French Catholics, by a miracle of obedience, calmed down and fell back into line, dazzled by the 'divine surprise' of 'decalvinization', culminating soon in the almost total 'conversions' of 1685.

In the short-term 1683 prepared the way directly for 1685. Brousson's aim was simply to organize reprisals against the destruction of the Protestant churches. But the massive success of the popular Huguenot demonstrations which he provoked in June 1683 triggered or 'justified' the infernal cycle of ever harsher repression. They instigated the development of the military actions and campaigns of destruction for which Louvois would bear the responsibility. After legal harassment, the Protestants now faced the *dragonnades*, designed to convert Huguenots by lodging dragoons and other soldiers in their houses. Inaugurated by the intendant René de Marillac in Poitou in early 1681, with the encouragement of the government, they were to continue in Protestant areas between 1683 and 1686 and up to 1698 and beyond. The entire process culminated in the final act at Fontainebleau in 1685. Regardless of factors and actors, aims and consequences, any overall assessment of the Revocation should obviously, following the example of a recent work by Elisabeth Labrousse,[14] seek to avoid anachronism.

We should first state the obvious: in terms of abstract morality the Revocation is clearly indefensible. It was already so in 1685 for a thinker like Bayle,[15] capable of transcending the miseries of his age and formulating a theory of tolerance such as would be eventually handed down from the Enlightenment to our own times. The Revocation does, however, become 'defensible', even if this 'defence' seems odious to us today, when placed in the context of the demands imposed by the unity of faith, king and law, a unity seen as necessary for guaranteeing and reinforcing the cohesion of the kingdom and the state. The absolutist contract between the monarchy and the overwhelming Catholic majority was reinforced by the Revocation; the alliances with Spain and France's other Catholic neighbours were consolidated. In the 1700s the French army would operate in Spain like a duck in water: the contrast with the cruel fate suffered by Napoleon's troops, seen as impious atheists by the Spanish church, is eloquent in this respect. The compromise between church and state implied by the act of 1685 would last at least until 1762, when the dissolution of the Jesuits, promulgated by the parlements, was accepted by the executive power. Together with other stabilizing factors, imposed from above by the state and accepted by the great mass of its subjects, though not of

---

[14] Elisabeth Labrousse, *Essai sur la Révocation de l'Edit de Nantes; une foi, une loi, un roi* (Paris-Beneva, Labor et Fides-Payot, 1985). See also Janine Garrisson, *L'Edit de Nantes et sa révocation, histoire d'une intolérance française* (Paris, Seuil, 1985).

[15] Much more than Jurieu, Locke and even Voltaire, the Protestant Pierre Bayle (1647–1706) proposed in his writings a true theory of toleration which recognized 'the rights of the errant conscience', in other words the (legitimate) right to dissenting error, including theological dissenting error.

course unanimously, such a compromise helped to bestow on the country a social peace. There is no reason to go into ecstasies about this, but this peace had been unknown in the years of the ultra-Catholic Holy League, and during the long period of internal wars and plebeian revolts, the 'time of troubles' or perpetual Fronde between 1620 and 1675. The Revocation, it is worth repeating, despite a few exceptions which proved the rule, put an end to large-scale rebellion among the Catholic masses, and this was no mere coincidence. It also put an end in the long-term to Protestant revolts, but only after 1710. *De facto* Gallicanism, even if checked by the papacy[16] to an extent after 1693, constituted from 1682–5 onwards the backbone of the two swords, spiritual and temporal, clerical and royal.

Joined together in this way, the two authorities were dissuasive or persuasive enough to make their subjects, almost all of them faithful to the established church, acquiesce in a code of submission and discipline such as Henry III and even Louis XIII, ruling a country still divided by questions of faith, would have been incapable of imposing. While not creating prosperity, the Revocation produced a consensus from which only heterodox minorities were *ipso facto* excluded. Their misery acted as a foil and functioned, to the benefit of the régime, as a factor making for the religious and national integration of a majority which was far from being always silent. The bishops and *curés* were all the more motivated in preaching social and even patriotic concord to their parishioners by their appreciation of the religious zeal of the king. The Catholic petty bourgeoisie, as represented by the *Souvenirs* of the notary of Nîmes, Borrelly,[17] bled themselves dry to pay their taxes to a monarch who had proved in spectacular fashion his favourable disposition towards the 'true' faith. Only an innovative thinker, like the Huguenot Bayle, smitten (despite Bossuet or Jurieu) by a tolerant and unconventional modernity, could express indignation, in the name of the 'rights of straying conscience', against the 'unanimism' of the agents of the Revocation. Similarly, only historians blessed with the benefits of hindsight can see how, by revoking the edict of Nantes, the ancien régime state, egged on by the church (and vice versa), was injecting itself with the deadly germs of accumulating hatreds: Huguenot hatred first, then wider anticlerical hatred, and finally (at a surprisingly early date) 'anti-despotic' hatred against a religious and governmental system which could in retrospect be accused of all the sins of intolerance

[16] It was in 1693, in fact, that Louis XIV, in the midst (incidentally) of famine in the kingdom and 'cornered' by the League of Augsburg, began to retract upon the requirement that French clergy should accept the Gallican Four Articles of 1682. He wanted to undertake a rapprochement with Rome and, for its part, Pope Innocent XII put an end to the papal boycott upon the canonical institution of bishops chosen by Louis XIV. This 'patching-up' of their quarrel was the distant harbinger of the concessions which the French monarchy would make to ultramontanism following the *Unigenitus* bull, in 1715, concessions which were not eventually well received by public opinion in France and which, in consequence, would destabilize royal sovereignty.

[17] E. Le Roy Ladurie, *Les Paysans de Languedoc*, 2 vols (Paris, Manton, 1966) i, 611–12 and 642.

and made into a scapegoat for all ills. In 1685, this settling of scores lay far in the future, but when it came the church of France would inevitably be implicated, given its willing complicity in the acts of that year.

Moreover, during the early modern period France was far from alone in the imposition of religious uniformity and the formation of an historic bloc between church and state at the expense of minorities and for the benefit of a possibly absolute system of government. The examples of Muslims, Jews and Protestants in Spain, the Old Believers in Russia, Christians in Japan, Catholics in Scandinavia, among many others, are enough to prove the point.

Closer to home, the English case is particularly interesting, involving as it does a Protestant power whose behaviour towards its 'papists' may be compared with that of a Catholic kingdom like France towards its 'heretics'. Everything is there: penal laws aginst the Roman church under Elizabeth I; imprisonment and executions of Catholic priests between 1581 and 1586; fiscal discrimination against Catholics under Charles I; the so called Popish Plot, invented in 1678 by the hoaxer Titus Oates; revival of the penal laws and excessive taxation after the Revolution of 1688; diminution and almost complete expropriation of Catholic landholdings in Ireland by William of Orange and his successors.

The Infamous Revocation of 1685; the Glorious Revolution of 1688. The two events, despite appearances, are not totally different in essence one from the other. Both affirmed the logic of the state church, Gallican on one side, Anglican on the other, ideological steam-rollers crushing all that was different, in the interests of what was fondly imagined to be the religious, moral and political unity of the French and English peoples.[18] About the Revocation itself, the edict of Fontainebleau of October 1685, almost everything that needs to be said has been said: the fear and panic of the Huguenots, abjuring in their tens of thousands to escape the *dragonnades*, the military occupation of Protestant homes and the atrocities and threats which followed. In reality, many Protestants converted out-

---

[18] For a more detailed comparative analysis, see Le Roy Ladurie, 'Longue durée et comparatisme . . .', also, on English and Irish developments, see A. Dures, *English Catholicism, 1558–1642: Continuity and Change* (Harlow, Longman, 1983); also T.W. Moody and F.X. Martin, *The Course of Irish History* (Cork, Mercier Press, 1977). In 1641, before the expropriation of Catholic land, Catholics still owned 59% of Irish land; in 1688, after the expropriation, it was 22% and, following the expropriations carried out by William of Orange, it was 14%. The percentage fell to around 5% in 1778. This dramatic fall was the result, amongst other reasons, of discriminatory legislation and the conversion of a number of noble land-owners, often for self-interested reasons, who had determined to abandon, or resigned themselves to quit 'popery'. The fundamental data of Moody and Martin's work are to be found on p. 201 (the relevant maps) and pp. 202–20, especially pp. 219–20 for the eighteenth century. See equally John Kenyon, *The Popish Plot* (London, Heinemann, 1972) and M. Ashley, *James II* (London, J.M. Dent, 1977); Louis M. Cullen, *An Economic History of Ireland since 1660* (London, Batsford, 1972); Daniel Dessert, *Argent, pouvoir et société au Grand Siècle* (Paris, Fayard, 1984), p. 197; E. Léonard, *Histoire générale du protestantisme* (2 vols, Paris, PUF, 1982), vol. ii.

wardly in the hope (not unfounded) of being able one day to return to the
more or less open practise of their 'heretical' worship.

The edict of Fontainebleau, signed on 18 October 1685, was the work
of the aged Le Tellier along with Louis XIV. It recorded, with a minimum
(or maximum?) of bad faith, the massive abandonment of Huguenot
beliefs by their adherents, declared the edict of Nantes to be therefore
irrelevant, and abrogated it. Another 'panic' movement on the Catholic
side is also evident, corresponding to the enthusiasm felt by the vast
majority of the people, and expressing, sincerely or insincerely, un-
bounded admiration for the sovereign who had overthrown the Protestant
hydra. After 1685 Louis XIV enjoyed a considerable revival of popularity.
This collective aberration by the Catholic population is not surprising.
There was now no reason to fear, as there had been at the time of the
League a hundred years previously, the dangers of a divorce between the
king and the church, between the state and the Catholic people, henceforth united like the fingers of the hand. But this was too good to be true,
pregnant with repercussions to come in the following hundred and two
hundred years; anticlericalism, with Voltaire's help, would soon be in the
air.

The final act was the painful exile of 200,000 Protestants, 20 per cent of
the Huguenot population, 1 per cent of the national population. The
consequences were not totally disastrous for France, but ambivalent. Exile
created a diaspora which turned out on occasion to be useful for the
kingdom. It ruined certain industries, at Millau for example, while sparing
others, such as silk at Nîmes. Huguenot demography was undermined, the
category most affected being artisans, rather than the peasantry, for one
cannot carry landed property, however small, away on the soles of one's
boots.[19]

The period around the Revocation saw the growth of international
tension, culminating, after four years of cold war, in hot war, the conflict
known as the War of the League of Augsburg, from 1688 onwards. The
preparation for war, and the war itself, between 1679 and 1697, are
inseparable from the initiatives of Louvois who, though he died in 1691,
left behind a military heritage which shaped strategy and tactics, often
remarkable, at times open to criticism, until the end of the century.

François-Michel Le Tellier, who became the marquis de Louvois whilst
still very young, was born in 1639. The Le Telliers were by origin a

---

[19]   A good deal of space has been given over in this analysis to the Revocation. It should be
remembered, however, that the number of acts dealing with Protestantism constitute only
3 per cent of the overall administrative correspondence of the intendants across the whole
realm in Series G7 of the *Archives Nationales* for the inter-war years (approximately) from
1677 to 1689 which embrace the Revocation. The proportion was much greater, of course,
in those provinces such as Languedoc which contained solid Huguenot minorities (Anette
Smedley-Weill, *Correspondance des intendants avec le contrôleur-général des finances (1677–
1689). Naissance d'une administration* [Sous-Série G7 (Archives Nationales), Inventaire
analytique] (Paris, Archives Nationales, 1989)).

Plate 13 François-Michel Le Tellier, Marquis de Louvois François Le Tellier,
Marquis de Louvois was, at the time that this was painted (1689) by Antoine
Hérault, at the height of his powers. The son of the chancellor, Michel Le Tellier,
he had become progressively secretary of state for war (in succession to his father),
superintendent of posts (1668), minister of state (1672) and superintendent of
royal buildings (1683).
Versailles, Musée national du château

peasant family, installed in the early sixteenth century at Chaville, not far from Paris. They founded a line of merchants and lawyers. Michel Le Tellier, Louvois' father, was an important officer in the civil administration, before becoming intendant of the Army, secretary of state for War, and finally chancellor of France. Through marriage to Elisabeth Turpin, the niece of another chancellor, Le Tellier took the first steps in a brilliant career for which he was destined by talent, origin and the unfailing patronage of Mazarin and then of Louis XIV.[20]

Louvois lacked the breadth of vision of a Colbert: like Bismarck he was sceptical about colonial expansion. But at a time when war was already too serious an affair to be left to the generals, Le Tellier Junior represents the prototype of the ideal functionary, hard-working, without 'excessive' scruples, hard on himself and on his enemies. He promoted the interests of his family and his clients, proving to be demanding and protective towards both. He had many mistresses, and would have been a real ladies' man if he had not been kept too busy by the duties he imposed upon himself every day. He was to leave a considerable fortune, nine million of his own, more than twice that for the clan as a whole, acquired in the same manner as those of Richelieu, Mazarin and Colbert.

Among the many bureaucratic and technical reforms introduced in the army by Louvois, the most important was probably the principle of seniority in the promotion of officers. This did not mean that personal merit was ignored. High birth remained grounds for advancement, but not so crucial as it had been up to now, though this was enough to raise cries of horror and alarm from the duke de Saint-Simon. Louvois did not invent the idea of military seniority. It had already been applied by his father, Michel Le Tellier, when he had been secretary of state for War. But Louvois decreed its systematic application after 1675, when he extended it to the marshals of France, a decision which seems to have displeased the courtiers of Versailles.[21] This initiative by the Le Telliers seems to anticipate the similar procedures which would be adopted by a civil administration enamoured of the principle of seniority in the nineteenth and twentieth centuries.

French foreign policy in the inter-war decade between the Peace of Nijmegen in 1678–9 and the beginning of the War of the League of Augsburg in 1688 displayed a *sui generis* combination of annexationist expansionism, pursued step by step, and an anti-Protestant ideology, inflexible but not necessarily bent on conquest. Despite this surprising element of relative 'moderation', the brutal approach associated with Le Tellier solved nothing. It was even compounded by the conduct of Colbert's younger brother, Croissy, Secretary of State for Foreign Affairs,

[20] André Corvisier, *Louvois* (Paris, Fayard, 1983); see also Louis André, *Michel le Tellier et Louvois* (Paris, 1942; reprinted Slatkine, Geneva, 1974); and C. Rousset, *Histoire de Louvois* (Paris, Didier, 1973).
[21] Corvisier, *Louvois,* pp. 137 and 337.

an uncouth individual, though more subtle than Louvois.[22] The dominant ideology in these various domains was of course impregnated with Catholicism. Louis XIV did not intend to relaunch the religious wars which had raged in the past. But, sustained by the considerable forces represented by the French church, élite and people, he persisted in harrying the Protestant states to the north and east when they opposed his schemes. He remained, therefore, on bad terms with Holland, where his foremost adversary, William of Orange, though not wielding absolute power, exercised considerable influence. The Revocation set Louis at odds with the Lutheran states of Germany, the most influential of which was Brandenburg. In 1688 the Glorious Revolution toppled the Stuarts and propelled England into the camp of Louis' enemies. The king of France miscalculated: he thought, wrongly, that William would have his hands full in England and therefore be incapable of intervening on the continent. But the speed with which events in England rushed to their conclusion gave the lie to this judgement, which had not seemed so foolish at first. The Protestants of Europe were now united against Louis XIV. He had underestimated his adversaries. Furthermore, Louis, with his usual intransigence, decided upon the eradication of heresy in Savoy, which he treated roughly as if it were a satellite state; in reality, though, the Duke of Savoy, Victor Amadeus, bridled at this arrogance. All in all, Louis XIV and his entourage made no exceptions: the pro-Protestant diplomacy and strategy of Francis I, the early Bourbons and the cardinal-ministers was abandoned lock, stock and barrel.

In the wake of religious ideology came rampant annexationism. Louis XIV jettisoned Richelieu's old 'heretical' friends, like Holland, turning them into committed adversaries, while at the same time retaining the cardinal's traditional enemies, the Habsburgs of Vienna. This double collection of hostile entities multiplied the dangers faced by the kingdom all around its borders to a degree that Louis XIII and Anne of Austria could never have imagined. It is true that French military power had grown considerably since 1661, but the expense of maintaining it had increased accordingly. The 'reunions', that is to say annexations, and more far-flung incursions of French troops into the southern Low Countries and Germany, towards the Palatinate and the Cologne region, could not but irritate and infuriate the rulers of Vienna and Madrid. They remained as badly disposed towards Versailles as they had been for the previous half century. Thus the danger of encirclement hung over a heavily defended but isolated France. In this intractable state of affairs offensives by the French were furbished with 'defensive' pretexts, sincere for some, specious

---

[22] Charles Colbert, Marquis de Croissy (1625–96), the younger brother of Colbert, was *commissaire* in the armies, and then an army intendant, *conseiller* in the Parlement of Metz (1656) an intendant in a *généralité*, a master of requests (1663), a *conseiller d'état* (1669) and a diplomat who in 1679 succeeded Pomponne as secretary of state for foreign affairs and Louis XIV's minister.

in the eyes of adversaries. Nevertheless, possibilities for manoeuvre 'along the inner lines' did enable the king of France to resist the encirclement for which he was himself largely responsible. Under such conditions, can a case be made in Louis' defence, either in contemporary terms or by historians, those makers and breakers of the royal image? Did his behaviour in the 1680s deserve a gratitude based on Catholicism and nationalism?

Religion first. Many people after 1685 viewed the king of France as a steadfast champion of the established church. And yet such gratitude had its limits. Pope Innocent XI, relatively moderate, far from uncompromising, and above all a friend of Habsburg Austria, disapproved of the violent aspects of the Revocation. At the same time the ecumenical title of defender of Christendom, Catholic and Protestant, against the infidel was reserved for the emperor, and not the king of France, for all his zeal and militancy. Leopold I, at the head of a heterogeneous empire made up of Lutheran and Catholic principalities, faced up to and drove back the Turks, the sworn enemies of the religion of Christ in all its forms, so earning himself the admiration of Berlin and the Vatican, Amsterdam and Munich.

As far as nationalism is concerned, the national feeling espoused by a succession of French historians of the Left and the Right, from Lavisse to Bluche, has led them to credit Louis with the almost total perfection of the north-eastern flank of the hexagon, achieved in part thanks to the 're-unions', especially Strasbourg, effected by his soldiers and jurists after 1678. The basis of these reunions was often morally dubious. But what great nation in its struggle for self-realization has ever been bound by such scruples? The divorce between ethics and politics is flagrant here. As Ragnhild Hatton has written: 'in France [historians] have expressed both total condemnation of Louis as an impenitent warmonger and an equally total justification of his wars, either as having been defensive or as having succeeded in establishing the present frontiers of France.' And the Anglo-Scandinavian historian adds among the principal motifs of the glory of Louis XIV, 'quite as much as the literary, artistic and scientific flowering of France during his reign . . . the fact of having attained almost entirely a strongly defensible eastern frontier'.[23]

This interpretation allows us to soft-pedal the accurate but too clear-cut judgements which we have reproduced or proposed up to now. Crude Catholicism and rampant annexationism by Versailles at the height of its glory? Certainly. But this did not mean, as Ragnhild Hatton again points out, that Louis XIV and his team were incapable of keeping their given

---

[23]   Ragnhild Hatton, 'Louis XIV et l'Europe; éléments d'une révision historiographique', *XVIIe siècle*, 31 (1979), 109. In a more general way, the considerable work of Ragnhild Hatton on Louis XIV, on Swedish history, the Hanoverians, on George III and Charles XII, on Anglo-Dutch diplomatic history, and on Europe in the Louis XIV period, on the history of ideas, of absolutism, on warfare, and on William III throws a completely new light on the Louis XIV period. Sadly her work remains almost unknown in France!

word or acting through third-party mediators or negotiators, as indeed they did on several occasions. Much of the behaviour for which Louis and his advisers have been vehemently criticized was in fact typical of the age throughout Europe. We have already evoked the persecution of Catholics in Ireland alongside the persecution of Protestants in France, even if the contexts of the two cases were very different one from the other. As for the devastation of the Palatinate in 1689, for which Louvois was responsible, it was indisputably repellent, but was to find its counterpart in 1704 in the pillage of areas of Bavaria on the orders of the highly civilized duke of Marlborough, not to mention the destruction wrought by a Charles XII or Peter the Great. Louis XIV, all the more exposed to criticism because of his longevity, behaved like a village notary, peasant or land-grabber eager to enclose his domain, extend it if possible, and barricade the doors or gates of his holding. But a door can be open and closed at the same time! The conquest of Strasbourg in 1681 closed the opening on the Rhine which had allowed the invasion of Alsace by Imperial forces, but it also made possible excursions by the French through the breach thus created towards German territories to the east. It is true that the spirit of conquest did not carry Louis very far over the Rhine. His programme of acquisition was open to question, but in the end was relatively modest, and this at the very moment when Catholic Austria was beginning to absorb without hesitation a large part of Protestant Hungary by putting spokes in the wheels of the former Ottoman occupation. In this way the extent of the hereditary lands of the Austrian monarchy would be doubled in size, without the western powers, with the exception of Louis XIV, becoming unduly alarmed. This only served to exacerbate the complex of encircle-ment by the Habsburgs, based on the Ebro and the Danube, suffered by the subjects of the Sun-King. But Leopold I was cast in the hero's role, because he was killing Turks with the blessing of the pope, while Louis XIV was eliminating Protestants under a crossfire of execration from London and Amsterdam. Anglo-Dutch anger was justified, but unmindful of the suffering endured by Ottoman Islam, far from the shores of the Channel.

Such reflections, formulated by European and American historians, permit the development of a less rebarbative image of Louis XIV in the last 20 years of the seventeenth century than the sometimes anachronistic picture portrayed by the committed adherents of two perfectly respectable historical schools, British Protestant and French Republican, both for perfectly good reasons sworn enemies of the Sun-King, at the time and ever since.

In chronological detail: whatever refinements may have to be made to the traditional picture, it is clear that tension was mounting during the six or seven years following the Peace of Nijmegen as a result of the policy of 'reunions'. Among the most memorable of these annexations were those of Luxemburg, Strasbourg and Montbéliard. The names may be glorious, but the amount of territory acquired was in each case only modest. Louis

XIV, Croissy and Louvois proceeded, under one legal or military pretext or another, with these seizures, which all aroused opposition from the other powers. The national territory of France was thereby increased, to a not inconsiderable extent overall, on the frontiers of Flanders, Lorraine, Franche-Comté and Alsace.

Another cause of hostility was provided by the fortresses built by the king's engineers on the banks of the Rhine and the Moselle, at the edge of German-speaking territory. According to German opinion, these violated the accepted boundaries of the kingdom of France. Anti-French feeling to the east of the rivers was greatly increased, creating from 1687 onwards a situation of diplomatic crisis between Versailles and the states of the Empire.

We should be clear about these twin initiatives of the French policy-makers: 'reunions' and construction of fortresses. They were, it would be claimed, defensive measures,[24] though not perceived as such outside the kingdom. The aim was to consolidate the north-eastern frontiers of France by getting rid of the gaps and inconsistencies which made them vulnerable. The annexation of Montbéliard, for example, 'drew a line' between Alsace and Franche-Comté, so reducing the risk of invasion. As for the fortresses, they were by definition meant for defence or deterrence, though again liable to create among potential adversaries the feeling of being victims of provocation.

The decision-makers (Louis, Louvois, Chamlay[25]) wanted above all by these means to protect the kingdom against incursions from the north and east. They were aware of a deterioration in the balance of forces. Between 1679 and 1688 the military power of France, which had been at its height at the time of the Peace of Nijmegen, gradually declined, while that of the German states was increasing. The Germans were justifiably alarmed by the 'defensive' measures being taken by the French. The impression of expansionism created by these new strongholds, erected beyond the legal frontier, meant that they could not be portrayed as an inoffensive sort of Maginot Line. Furthermore, the way in which the seizures of territory preceding the 'reunions', especially at Strasbourg, were carried out, like the construction of fortresses, could not fail to be offensive to the Germans, the Dutch, and even to the pope, the faithful friend of Catholic Austria. Circumstances were building towards a conflict for which both sides would blame the other,[26] but in which the French would appear as the villains, despite the clear conscience which they loudly and possibly even sincerely professed.

[24] Hatton, 'Louis XIV et l'Europe'.
[25] Jules-Louis Bolé, Marquis de Chamlay, was from a relatively modest background and eventually served as the chief of state of the French armies, notably (but not merely) in the Flanders campaigns, alongside Louis XIV, and then, in Louvois' lifetime, alongside the celebrated secretary of state for war. Highly capable, Chamlay enjoyed a not insignificant role *vis-à-vis* the king (to whom he had ready access) in diplomatic and fiscal matters.
[26] See, in this respect, the malevolent opinions formulated by La Bruyère concerning William of Orange – (*Caractères* (Paris, Garnier, 1962), 'Des jugements', para. 119).

The Palatinate would confirm in indisputable fashion the aggressive nature of the Versailles government's policy. Charles von Simmern, the Elector Palatine, died in 1685, to be succeeded, in theory, by Phillip Wilhelm von Neuburg, 'head of the closest branch', a Catholic, and father-in-law of Leopold I. This imperial alliance, it goes without saying, did not please Louis and his ministers. But could this be said to justify a defensive riposte, which would of course be seen as offensive, by the French?

One marriage could be set against another marriage. Louis XIV was the brother-in-law of a Palatine princess, Liselotte, known as Madame, daughter of the deceased Elector and wife of Monsieur, the Duke d'Orléans. Louis laid claim, therefore, through Monsieur and Liselotte's rights of inheritance, to almost half of the Palatinate in the form of seigneurial rights, fiefs, vineyards, etc. on the left bank of the Rhine. Thus did sovereignty advance under the cloak of feudal legality! This was not as paradoxical as it may appear. Louis' demands would be followed in late 1688 and 1689 by actions destined to have grave consequences: military invasion; and above all, during the retreat which followed almost immediately after the initial advance, the destruction of the towns of the Palatinate on the orders of the secretary of state for war. This was also conceived as a defensive action: the aim was to prevent any future military activity. Like Louis' later actions in the Cévennes, it took the form of the destruction of property more than the killing of people. (The aerial bombardments of the twentieth century would be much worse in this respect.) But it gave rise in Germany to a perfectly comprehensible anti-French reaction which was to last for several generations. Louis XIV's general staff no doubt dreamed about annexing areas across the Rhine, not in a search for natural frontiers, but rather to create a 'frontier of iron' providing strategic depth in the north-east. Even the dovish Vauban let himself be swept up by fantasies of this nature, orientated towards pre-emptive conquest beyond the Rhine. The angry reaction in Germany is not surprising: the Palatinate, with its sizeable Protestant population, preferred to live under the tutelage of Phillip Wilhelm, a Catholic prince, but one who by force of circumstance was inclined towards toleration, rather than under French domination, which they had every reason to fear would bring the Revocation in its train.

Moreover, outside the Palatinate, events in Cologne after 1687 served to darken further an already threatening horizon. This great 'papist' city, situated at the top end of the bend of the Rhine, was surrounded by Protestant territory. It controlled a vital opening towards central Germany and the Low Countries. The wily Archbishop of Cologne, Max Henry von Wittelsbach, a good friend of France, was also prelate of Liège, Münster and Hildesheim. He had put together, in a haphazard fashion, a satellite principality along the north-eastern borders of France, the maintenance of which seemed essential to Versailles. At the Germano-Imperial Diet, Wittelsbach had acted as an agent and devoted friend of the Sun-King.

His death in 1688 created problems. Germany had by now recovered from the ruinous devastation of the Thirty Years War, which would soon be nothing but a painful memory. It was inevitable that Louis XIV's manoeuvrings, aiming at the election of another of his agents, the prince of Fürstenberg, to the see of Cologne, would be badly received. At the risk of being monotonous, it is worth repeating that Louis saw this as a defensive move, aimed at protecting the French position in a legitimate outpost of influence in imperial territory. But the sovereigns and petty princelings of Germany saw the interference of their larger western neighbours in an ethnic and linguistic domain where they had no right to feel at home as degrading and unjustifiable, in the Rhineland even more than in Alsace. For the time of the all-powerful Cardinals Richelieu and Mazarin had long past. Franco-German antagonism was now kindled along borderlands which were now displaying considerable economic dynamism, itself helping to generate strong military and political reactions against invaders from the west. The Palatinate and Cologne became the trouble spots.

Louis went to war in the autumn of 1688 in order to turn his pretentions in these two territories into reality. He refrained from attacking Holland, so avoiding repetition of his blunder in 1672, which he now recognized as such. He launched a localized conflict, which he hoped in vain to keep within narrow limits. His aim was to do no more than seize the chain of strongholds stretching from the borders of Alsace to Cologne. This, he thought, would accomplish his essential objective of securing the eastern frontier.[27] And in fact these citadels were conquered within a few weeks. But Louis had once again underestimated his enemies and miscalculated the disastrous psychological effects of his aggressiveness. He found himself facing a German coalition, assembled piece by piece, of Catholic princes, including the Emperor and Bavaria, and Protestant magnates, headed by Brandenburg, for the Prussian Elector had renounced his friendship with France after the Revocation. Thus was formed in 1686 the League of Augsburg, which evolved into the Grand Alliance, incorporating Holland and then the England of William of Orange. The Empire was gaining more and more solid support on its western flank. To the east the Turkish threat had long kept the Emperor occupied, to the secret satisfaction of Louis XIV. But his pleasure was premature. After the lifting of the siege of Vienna in 1683 a succession of Austrian victories led to consequences which the Sun-King had not foreseen. The Emperor's prestige in the Christian world, Catholic and Protestant, rose to new heights. The German nation united, first against the infidel, then against Louis XIV, now regarded as more Catholic and above all more Gallican than truly Christian.

Louis, bolstered by his military strength and the inexhaustible demographic resources of the kingdom, could be certain from the outset that he would not be defeated. But he no longer held the hand of trumps which, even badly played, had assured him (with difficulty) a certain strategic and even moral ascendancy during the Dutch War. He had lost a major part of his credibility with his adversaries. They suspected his desire to eat away at German territory. Was this realism or paranoia on their part?

---

[27] Hatton, 'Louis XIV et l'Europe'.

Was the situation on the other, non-Germanic frontiers more favourable to Bourbon ambitions as the war which was to involve the whole of Europe began? Spain was now incapable of regaining her former status as a major military power. She too was humiliated by the 'reunions' effected by France after the Treaty of Nijmegen at the expense of the southern Low Countries. In December 1683 the rulers in Madrid attempted a military response to the unilateral actions of Versailles. They were swiftly defeated and forced to cede Luxemburg to the French by the Truce of Ratisbon in August 1684, which also confirmed French occupation of Strasbourg for 20 years. The Spanish rulers were wounded and humiliated by the Luxemburg affair. They could not bring themselves to rejoice at the Revocation, even if it sanctified the triumph of a religious orthodoxy close to their own hearts and those of their subjects. A few years later the War of the League of Augsburg saw a vengeful Madrid joining the anti-French chorus of Christian princes, Catholic, Lutheran and Calvinist. For the first time Louis XIV found himself isolated in Europe. He had no choice but to fall back on a shameful, unavowed collusion with the Islamic Ottoman Empire.

In Italy as well the good reputation of France was collapsing. Pope Innocent XI was offended by the cutting Gallican remarks which Bossuet, as the faithful mouthpiece of the king, had aimed at him at the assembly of the clergy in 1682. His Holiness retaliated by refusing investiture to French bishops, to the considerable detriment of the dioceses of the kingdom! Similarly, the Revocation of 1685 left Innocent XI, like Charles II of Spain, cold. The hopes of the Versailles government, always eager to be as ultra-Catholic as possible, were dashed. The pope had not forgotten Bossuet's caustic utterances of 1682 and only grudgingly congratulated a king who thought he had acquired great merit by his 'definitive' destruction of heresy. To add insult to injury, the French ambassadors in Rome claimed exorbitant privileges known as 'liberties' in the neighbourhood around their palace. These prevented the pontifical police from imposing order in streets plagued by rogues and petty crooks. And yet the diplomats from other countries accredited to the Vatican had willingly given up the said 'liberties'. French arrogance, once again!

The Republic of Genoa for its part had commited the 'crime' of providing supplies for the Spanish fleet. Was this sufficient justification for the devastating bombardment inflicted on the city by the French navy in May 1684, under the personal supervision of Seignelay, son of Colbert? Some historians, including Ragnhild Hatton, think that the inhabitants of Genoa did indeed 'deserve' this punishment because of the maritime aid with which they had equipped the Spanish, or at least that the said punishment was perfectly in keeping with the spirit of the age. And in fact the Genoans did keep their heads down afterwards, 'provoking' Versailles no further. Nevertheless the affair confirmed the negative image created by the severe methods favoured by Louis XIV; methods which turned out to be a double-edged sword, effective in dissuading potential adversaries, but in the long run only serving to generate an accumulating build-up of emnity and bitterness.

From 1686 onwards, French soldiers and envoys in Savoy (D'Arcy, Catinat and others) behaved like forces of occupation. Employing the durable pretext of repression against the local form of Protestantism known as Waldensianism, they succeeded in rallying a good part of the local Catholic clergy to the pro-French camp. But Victor Amadeus did not forget Louis' off-hand treatment of him and would make the French pay for it some years later.

In the north, by contrast, Louis behaved with all the moderation of which he was fully capable when he thought it necessary. At the outset of the conflict he concentrated his forces in attacking the middle Rhine valley, thereby carefully avoiding his youthful blunders of 1672. Holland was not to be provoked. Louis hoped that, grateful for such forbearance, the Dutch would let him wage war unhindered in the Cologne region and the Palatinate. He envisaged a kind of Blitzkrieg, on limited territory of his choosing. He would swiftly be disabused!

William of Orange, as fine a strategist as he was a mediocre tactician, leapt into the breach thus created. To be precise, he took advantage of the opportunity to land without warning[28] on the coast of England and, with the lukewarm compliance of the local élites, dethrone the papist King James II. James' Anglican subjects, having little choice in the matter, nevertheless needed some persuading. But, in the end, they were only too willing to let the Stuart king depart in peace. As the restorer of the rights of England's Catholics, James' reputation suffered a boomerang effect from the Revocation. Popery had shown its capacity for intolerance in France and therefore had no right to claim rights for itself in England. Such was the strange retaliatory logic of the age: no freedom for the enemies of freedom, or those thought to be so. In reality English Catholics, loyal and few in number, posed no threat to the survival of Anglicans and Nonconformists. But the Orangists, through a tit-for-tat mentality and visceral anti-Catholicism, ignored such details.

In 1689, as a war which may be called for the first time in history a world war, for it would embrace oceans and continents, was breaking out in various locations, the French missed the opportunity of restricting it within the narrow bounds that Louis XIV had envisaged. The conflict escalated rapidly, determined by shifting alliances, a succession of skirmishes on various fronts, and accumulated bitterness. It drew in France's powerful neighbours (Orangist England, Holland, the Empire, Spain) as well as a host of minor powers in Germany and elsewhere, all of them at odds with the kingdom of the Bourbons. France had the resources necessary to confront all her adversaries, but because of her splendid isolation she would not be able to pursue the kind of glorious combat she had waged in 1667 and about which Louis and his entourage, headed by Louvois, Chamlay and Croissy, still fantasized. They were eager for a fight, but not

---

[28]   J.R. Jones, *The Revolution of 1688 in England* (London, Weidenfeld, 1972).

in so many theatres of operation. Reality would soon put an end to their delusions.[29]

By 1689 the fronts were established. The east was stabilized following the retreat of the French army after the devastation of the towns of the Palatinate. What could have been the decisive action of the war took place to the north-west: Louis XIV's troops, supported by an effective naval force, landed in Ireland in March 1689, bringing James II with them. In 1690 they were defeated at the Battle of the Boyne by an Anglo-Dutch army supported by Huguenot forces. James had no choice but to retreat back to the continent. The crucial hand had been played. Beaten at sea off La Hougue in 1692, the French lost control over the Channel and with it any serious hope of landing on the English coast. On the other hand, reinforced by her huge population, good logistics and talented leaders, France was impregnable on land, as the convincing victories won by Luxemburg at Fleurus in July 1690 and Steenkerke in July 1692 demonstrated plainly. After these two successes Louis XIV prudently adopted a defensive posture. He did not attempt to follow up his victories by breaking through into Holland and Germany, thereby sensibly ignoring the wishes of Luxemburg, his young officers, and the scatter-brained Saint-Simon, consistently warlike or pacific at the wrong moments.

The war of position pursued its course. France scored some points, but no more than that. Luxemburg was victorious once again at Neerwinden in July 1693 in the course of a summer campaign without any great aggressive intent. Off Lagos in June 1693 Tourville vanquished a large Anglo-Dutch fleet carrying grain from the Levant to a starving northern Europe. The famine of 1693–4 was raging and hampering all the belligerents, France above all. It influenced the character of military operations. Thus the example of Lagos was contagious; piracy and maritime raiding took the place of pitched sea battles. It was the equivalent, on a smaller scale, of the submarine warfare of the twentieth century.

It was also a time for promotions: in 1693 Louis XIV created a contingent of marshals of France, including Tourville, Catinat and Boufflers. Several of them were remarkable commanders, as Vendôme and Villars were also to be. It is unreasonable to talk of a crisis of military leadership at this time,[30] despite the unmerited promotions of nonentities like Villeroy. Moreover, the much-vaunted Turenne and Condé, to whom their younger counterparts were supposed to defer, had been prepared quite shamelessly to betray their homeland. The new and brilliant tacticians of the 1680s, led by Boufflers and Catinat, never behaved like that.

In the same year of 1693 the Sun-King decreed, as a recognition of military valour, the creation of the Order of Saint Louis,[31] with its flame-

[29] On the preparations leading to the conflict of the League of Augsburg, see the important work by Charles Boutant, *L'Europe au grand tournant des années 1680, la succession palatine* (Paris, SEDES, 1985).

[30] Pierre Goubert, *Louis XIV et vingt millions de Français* (Paris, Fayard, 1966), pp. 234–6.

[31] Saint-Simon, *Mémoires*, i, 302.

coloured ribbon, on the same pattern as the Order of the Holy Spirit, with its blue ribbon. Thus was prefigured, by more than a century, the red ribbon of the Légion d'Honneur, which in peace and war was destined to glitter on innumerable chests in the hexagon and elsewhere.

In concrete terms, the great powers were in a situation of stalemate. In attempting to break it, a mirage which gradually faded, they had recourse to new fiscal and financial measures, often costly, but in the long-term creating a sort of modernity in a style appropriate to each individual country. The intendancies had been extended to the whole of France during the Thirty Years War, and they survived without a break in the occasional periods of peace which followed. The War of the League of Augsburg in turn furnished the opportunity for a new tax, damaging in the burden it imposed on individual fortunes, but innovative in theory if not always in practice. The *contrôleur général* Pontchartrain, along with the intendants and provincial notables, prepared the ground for this unprecedented imposition.

The *capitation* came into force during 1695. It consisted of a levy on heads of families, graded according to the 569 social ranks[32] into which the population was divided. The idea had been 'in the air' for some time. The *capitation* had already provoked, by a sort of defensive anticipation, several revolts during the seventeenth century, as a result of rumours (generally false) that the government was going to impose a *per capita* tax on adults, children, hats, sexual acts, etc. In 1694, when the plans were drawn up, and 1695, when it was put into effect, Louis was probably aware of the analogous measures already enacted in Austria for the purpose of financing the same war. The French *capitation* sanctioned the degressive hierarchy of ranks, grades and professions, while saddling them all with conceptual equality before the taxman. We find here once again Louis XIV's usual two-sided comportment: submerging distinctions and privileges in a 'revolutionary' fashion before the state, while at the same time respecting and even reinforcing the 'Jacob's ladder'[33] of the social hierarchy.[34] France was thus able to find money for her armies through taxation (the exact opposite of what would one day be the policy of Necker). In England, where the financial credibility of the monarch and especially of the Parliament was so much greater, the war could be financed by borrowing. The Bank of England, founded in 1694, would outlive the conflict it was created to pay for.

The humdrum routine of military activity, devoid of inspiration on both sides, need not detain us long. William III, finally rid of his old and brilliant opponent Luxemburg by the latter's death in January 1695, took Namur in September. Vendôme, the French commander in Catalonia,

---

[32] François Bluche and Jean-François Solnon, *La Véritable Hiérarchie sociale de l'ancienne France* (Geneva, Droz, 1983).
[33] *Genesis*, 28, v. 12.
[34] It would be in this respect that Louis XIV was, as Lemontey and Tocqueville claimed, a precursor of 1789.

achieved his first success there in June 1696, marking the beginning of a great career. He was soon revealed as a new Turenne, minus the treason, plus homosexuality. In the spring of 1696 the French fleet in Brest busied itself with simulated preparations for a landing in England. Only the English were fooled. In reality, these closing stages of the conflict were marked by negotiations, pursued with intelligence by the Bourbon side, rather than by warfare, now conducted half-heartedly by both sides.

The negotiations had more chance of success because the death of Louvois in 1691 and that of Croissy in 1696 had removed two of the most aggressive ministers, especially the former, from the *Conseil d'en haut*. Their deaths marked the final decline of the old Mazarin-Colbert-Le Tellier team, since Croissy had been Colbert's younger brother and Louvois was Le Tellier's son. The diplomatic Pomponne,[35] favouring a gentler approach, was back in favour from 1691 onwards. Flanked by his nephew Torcy (from the Colbert clan but of a new vintage), Pomponne as secretary of state for foreign affairs took charge of the negotiations with the enemy. Such diplomacy, pursued to its successful conclusion, should help to modify the crude image of an inflexible and arrogant Louis XIV which has been handed down to our own day.

Louis aimed to break the Grand Alliance, which had in December 1689 brought together the Catholics and Protestants of Germany and Austria, the Empire, Holland, Spain, Savoy and England, by employing a combination of firmness and moderation. Between 1690 and 1694 Versailles made use of the linguistic talents and worldly relations of a French envoy, Baron Bidal d'Asfeld. This Bidal was the son of a Parisian silk merchant who had been ennobled and 'baronified' with a fief in the duchy of Bremen by Queen Christina of Sweden for services rendered.[36] Acting as an agent of Louis XIV, he tried to create a neutralist third party in northern Germany against the 'war-mongers' of the Empire. Abundant French subsidies, amounting in all to some two million *livres* a year, filled the coffers of the duke of Hanover, the Catholic bishop of Münster, the protestant king of Denmark and the duke of Wolfen-büttel between 1691 and 1695. At first this had no effect. The German

---

[35] Simon Arnauld, Marquis de Pomponne (1618–99), nephew of the Great Arnauld. Despite his Jansenist tendencies and his friendship for the Fouquet clan, he was employed as an intendant and then on diplomatic missions before becoming, on account of his considerable talents, Secretary of State for Foreign Affairs in 1671, succeeding Lionne. He was disgraced in 1679 following a trifling affair (in reality the result of intrigues by the Colbert and Le Tellier clans who regarded him as too Jansenist and too moderate). He would only return to being minister of state on the death of Louvois in 1691. His son-in-law, Colbert de Torcy, who had been groomed by him, would be secretary of state for foreign affairs under his father-in-law. Pomponne was thus reconciled with the Colbert clan. The Pomponne-Torcy line was a relatively flexible one and sought to infuse a greater degree of suppleness into Louis XIV's diplomacy which on various occasions, but by no means all, appeared more hard-line. For such flexibility, see the negotiating period from 1698 to 1701, directed (it should be noted) successively by Pomponne and then by his son-in-law.

[36] Saint-Simon, *Mémoires*, i, 237.

princes, even the Catholics, happily received French money, but they could not forgive Louis XIV for the 'reunions' and the expansion of his kingdom into the formerly Spanish domains of the Low Countries and Franche-Comté, an expansion which Louis continued shamelessly beyond Alsace into the heart of Germany. Nor could they stomach the anti-Huguenot extremism of Versailles. Since 1685 this had become distasteful to the pan-Christian and Leibnizian ecumenicism with Protestant overtones which was flourishing in German lands of all religious persuasions.[37]

By manoeuvring skilfully, however, Louis XIV and Pomponne scored a first success with the defection of Savoy. In 1696 Victor Amadeus broke with the Emperor and thereby effectively destabilized the anti-French coalition. The famine of 1693–4, caused by rain and cold, bringing disease in its wake, struck Savoy as severely as it did France. Compromise was forced on the two countries. Even the four resounding French victories won by Luxemburg, Catinat and others in 1693 at Neerwinden, Charleroi, Heidelberg and Marsaglia were not in themselves decisive. They merely showed that the Bourbon state was still powerful, even if it could not overturn the balance of forces.

Only a political solution was possible. In 1695 the negotiations undertaken by Tessé for France and Gropello for Savoy took a serious turn.[38] They defined the bases for an agreement. France agreed to the dismantling or restitution of the fortresses of Casale and Pinerolo, once considered as vital by Richelieu. In other words, the investment of French energies in the north-east of the almost completed hexagon was accompanied by almost total disengagement in Italy, a process which had been implicit in but not initiated by the Treaty of Cateau-Cambrésis in 1559. Moreover, by the terms of the same agreement, once diplomatic relations were re-established, Savoyard ambassadors to the court of France were to be accorded the honours due to royal envoys, so preparing the way for the promotion of the subtle Duke Victor Amadeus to fully regal status. The marriage was arranged between Marie-Adélaïde, daughter of Victor Amadeus, and the duke of Burgundy, Louis XIV's grandson (from this union would be born Louis XV). On this basis, Savoy was willing to transfer from the Imperial camp to the French camp. As a consequence of this balancing act, the enemies of the Sun-King would from now on see Victor Amadeus as slippery and treacherous. But only the result counted: after 1696 Savoy had effectively changed sides. Furthermore, Louis XIV became reconciled with Pope Innocent XII, abandoning the old 'Gallican'

---

[37]   This follows the article by Janine Fayard, 'Attempts to Build a "Third Party" in North Germany, 1690–1694' in R. Hatton (ed.), *Louis XIV and Europe* (London, Macmillan, 1976). This had originally been published under the title 'Les Tenatives de constitution d'un tiers parti en Allemagne du Nord, 1690–1694', *Revue d'histoire diplomatique*, 74 (1965), 338–72.

[38]   The capable and useful diplomat Tessé certainly did not merit the spiteful remarks accorded him by Saint-Simon (*Mémoires*, xi, 47 etc.). On Gropello, see Geoffrey Symcox, *Victor Amadeus II* (London, Thames and Hudson, 1983).

insolence he had displayed towards Innocent XI. Italy, caught between the hammer of Turin and the anvil of Rome, was effectively neutralized. The road to peace, eventually signed at Ryswick in 1697, was open. Also on the horizon was the bull *Unigenitus* which in 1715 would strike a new blow against Gallicanism or national Catholicism.

The Treaty of Ryswick was a finely balanced contract, drawn up in the interests of the three leading powers. The exclusive French preponderance recognized by the Treaties of Nijmegen in 1678–9 and to a lesser extent at Ratisbon in August 1684 in the truce that acted as prelude to the Revocation was no more. Thirteen years after Ratisbon, can we say that there were neither victors nor vanquished? The trio of great powers at the end of the seventeenth century comprised Austria, France and the conjoined couple of Holland and England.

First, Austria would soon experience a vast territorial expansion thanks to her incessant and long-lasting struggle against the declining Ottoman Empire. By the Treaty of Karlowitz in 1699 the Turks were to cede almost the whole of Hungary to the Habsburgs. And this was merely the prelude to even greater aggrandizement, confirmed in 1718 and including Belgrade, a part of Serbia, Wallachia and the Banat.

In the west, England and Holland dominated the seas in co-sovereignty with France, which had just acquired Santo Domingo, destined to become the great sugar-producing island in the eighteenth century, so making an enormous contribution to the prosperity of Nantes, Bordeaux and the kingdom in general. In Canada, Pierre Le Moyne d'Iberville[39] had brought Hudson Bay (several million acres of snow and ice) under French control. Above all he had kept the flag flying over Quebec and Acadia and mounted raids into Newfoundland. By 1699 Louisiana was beginning to take shape. The Iroquois made peace in 1700–1. New France was at its apogee. For a nation apparently ruined by Louis XIV, it was not so bad.

On her eastern frontiers, France gave up most of the 'reunions', conquests and claims put forward or realized during the ten years of grandeur after Nijmegen between 1678 and 1688. She kept Sarrelouis, Strasbourg and the whole of Alsace, which was far from nothing. The French had started the War of the League of Augsburg for the sake of Cologne and the Palatinate, prepared to die for some corners of foreign German fields. But by the end of the conflict these goals had been forgotten. Strasbourg, however, had been held and French influence extended in Canada and the Caribbean. War is a chameleon whose intentions change as it follows its course.

All in all, this great conflict was not a defeat (or not only a defeat) for Louis XIV. True, his domination in Europe was no longer unchallenged. He had to face increased competition from two rapidly rising states or

---

[39] Pierre Le Moyne, *Chevalier* d'Iberville (1661–1706) was from the first generation of French Canadians, typical of the naval adventurer and North-American explorer of the Ancien Régime. Known as the 'Canadian el Cid', he was, along with his brothers, one of the artisans of the early grip on what who later become for several centuries francophone Quebec.

groups of states. The costs for France of her modest successes were much greater than they had been in previous conflicts. And this expense was largely responsible for the economic crisis of the final decade of the seventeenth century, overshadowed by wet and unfriendly climatic conditions which played havoc with grain harvests.

★   ★   ★   ★   ★

That there was an economic crisis in the 1690s is undeniable, but its depth and extent are not so evident. In 1694 Archbishop Fénelon, horrified by the famine then raging, wrote vindictively, in a phrase destined to go down in history, that France had become 'nothing more than a great hospital, devastated and without provisions'. But it would be wrong to generalize: this could only be accurately applied to the two 'famine years' of 1693–4. The swan of Cambrai was deliberately blackening a picture which in reality should be rendered in chiaroscuro. Some sectors of the economy, those which would be referred to in the jargon of today as 'ultramodern' or 'avant garde', remained healthy and even showed signs of vigorous development, though they did stand out as exceptions within an overall situation of falling production.

In Languedoc, the silk industry of Nîmes provides an eloquent example. One would have thought, since we are talking about a Protestant city and bourgeoisie, that the Revocation would have been fatal for this kind of activity. But not at all! Nîmes under Louis XIV successfully converted from wool to silk. The woollen industry abandoned the city for the countryside and the mountains of the Cévennes, where labour was much cheaper, while in Nîmes between 1640 and 1680 silk-working moved in to take its place. Hosiery workshops, almost all owned by Protestants, immediately began the manufacture of silk stockings. In the ordinary course of events the Revocation should have destroyed these new enterprises, but this did not happen. Timely conversions to Catholicism allowed those involved to stay in the city and prosper,[40] as the intendant Basville, no friend to the Huguenots, pointed out: 'These merchants of Nîmes are still bad Catholics, but at least they have not stopped being good businessmen.' By the 1700s the workshops of Nîmes reverberated to the sound of a thousand stocking-making looms, where 25 years earlier there had only been a handful. Clearly, the expression 'end of the century crisis' does not apply to this Languedoc city, spared (unlike the Cévennes) from the dangers of Louis' anti-Huguenot policy.

The same point applies to the export of cloth from Languedoc to the Levant. This grew from 2,200 pieces in 1688 to a record figure of 11,962 in 1695. The succeeding years from 1696 to 1698 stagnated between 7,000 and 9,000 pieces, before taking off again to 11,000 or 12,000 between 1702 and 1709. The decade of the 1710s saw the trade soar to

[40]   This follows J. d'Huard, *Histoire de Nîmes* (Aix-en-Provence, Edisud, 1982), pp. 190–1.

new heights: 20,000, then 30,000 pieces,[41] up to 32,240 in 1713. Fénelon's jeremiads, valid for other regions, did not apply at Lodève or Carcassonne.

On the broader front, woollen production in the kingdom as a whole, measured in finished pieces, rose from 670,540 in 1668 to 788,000 in 1692 and 1,009,000 in 1708. In monetary terms, these figures correspond to 20 million *livres* in 1688 and 54 million in 1708. The rate of expansion, as far as finished pieces are concerned, amounts to 0.58 per cent per year between 1666 and 1692 and 1.56 per cent between 1692 and 1708. This last figure is higher than those reached at any time during the eighteenth century, except during the dynamic pre-revolutionary period between 1775 and 1787, equivalent to an annual growth rate of 1.81 per cent. This series of calculations, taken from the work of T. Markovitch[42] is open to question. There were undoubtedly years of crisis between 1692 and 1708, including during the difficult period of the War of the League of Augsburg. But these were not enough to put a stop to a persistent and at times remarkable growth. Similar remarks could be made about the considerable expansion in foreign and colonial commerce and about the silk industry in Lyon, which easily jumped over the crevass opened by the famine of 1693–4. These diverse but convergent variations on an expansionary theme allow us to place the authentic and far more numerous indications of crisis in proper perspective. These concern above all the agricultural sector in the 1690s. They were caused by, among other factors, the pressure of taxation which disfigured the last decade of the century for the sake of financing soldiers, cannon and ships.

On the subject of war taxation, we may consult once again the work of Alain Guéry.[43] The net income of the state, calculated in terms of its equivalent in tonnes of silver, amounted at the height of the War of the League of Augsburg to 800 tonnes. This is the highest figure for the entire seventeenth century. The previous peak during the Thirty Years War had been 520 tonnes. It is a far cry from the mere 200 tonnes during the period of the Frondes, and therefore of tax-payers' strikes, or the 280 tonnes at the time of the Peace of the Pyrenees. The subjects of the Sun-King were still fortunate in the early days of Colbert, say up to 1672. But from then on, from the Dutch War to the conflicts at the end of the century, they had to endure, from the fiscal point of view, the rigours of a war economy. Between 1672 and 1700 there was no real decline in the net revenues of the state, even during the 'inter-war period' of 1679 to 1688. The lowest figure, around 1680, was still equivalent to 600 tonnes of silver. It was as if the state never really disarmed between hostilities, from the Dutch War

---

[41] J.K.J. Thomson, *Clerment de Lodève 1633–1789* (Cambridge, Cambridge University Press, 1982), p. 228.

[42] Thomir Markovitch, *Histoire des industries françaises: les industries lainières de Colbert à la Révolution* (Geneva/Paris, Droz, 1976), pp. 487–9.

[43] Alain Guéry, 'Les Finances de la monarchie française sous l'Ancien Régime', *Annales ESC*, 33 (March–April 1978), 216–37, esp. 227.

to the League of Augsburg. The Revocation was itself, in its own way and in some respects, a declaration of internal cold war by a France which was technically at peace with the world but tense and militarized at home and abroad.

'Budgetary'[44] analysis in turn leads to a similar conclusion. Expenditure was always greater than net income and created deficits. These reached a peak equivalent to 1,300 tonnes of silver during the War of the League of Augsburg, thus easily beating the previous records, themselves painful enough, of between 1,100 and 1,200 tonnes set during the Thirty Years War. By comparison with the 'fin de siècle' conjuncture, which weighed so heavily on the economy, the minimum expenditure of 440 tonnes attained before the Dutch War must have bred nostalgia for the age of Colbert.

Fiscal bulimia and its attendant difficulties for the economy may be observed empirically in the correspondence of the intendants. Up to about 1688 these regional commissioners remained faithful to the instruction of their late master, Colbert. They took a keen interest in the economic well-being of their *généralités* and the prosperity of agriculture, manufacture and hospitals. They showed a proper concern for the scrupulous collection of taxes but also for the economic comfort of the people. There was a philanthropic side to these men. After 1688 by contrast the *commissaires départis*[45] only had one idea, manifestly handed down from above, in their heads. The king ordered them to find money, for the revenue, for war preparations and then for war itself: from taxes of course, whether new taxes like the *capitation*, or by raising the *taille*, as well as from the sale of offices and cutting the salaries of officers who could do nothing to prevent it.

Agriculture, as we have already said, was clearly in crisis, but manufacture was not spared, despite the good performances of certain branches of the textile industry. The true depth of the agricultural depression may be seen in the receipts from tithes and land rents, the 'real' revenue of course estimated in kind or in prices adjusted to take account of fluctuations in the value of money. From this evidence it is indisputable that a period of decline in agricultural production began after 1680 and even more after 1690, a slump associated with the wars of the second half of the reign of Louis XIV, the League of Augsburg and the Spanish Succession, and with the high level of taxation during these years. The fall in tithe receipts is particularly noticeable in Languedoc, Provence, the Bordelais, Périgord, Aquitaine, the Lyonnais and the Auvergne. Here we find a more or less violent repetition of the disasters similarly recorded during the Thirty Years War and temporarily remedied during the Colbertian and post-

---

[44] This term is used with a grain of salt, given that some historians (notably John Bosher) have denied the existence of what might truly be called a detailed 'budget' under the Ancien Régime. For his part, Michel Antoine does not hestitate to speak of a budget for this period.
[45] To describe the intendants, we have resorted to the terms *commissaires régionaux* (for they controlled regions which were often as large as those under the present 'regional prefects') and also *commissaires départis* (which was one of the terms used for them in the seventeenth century).

Colbertian recovery, what we have called the 'Indian summer' of the seventeenth century. The final bitter after-taste of the crisis, at the turn of the eighteenth century, is most noticeable on the frontiers of the kingdom, in the Cambrésis, the Namurois and Wallonia; in the Ile de France as well, but here particularly after 1703 – for Paris, the cosseted centre of economic growth, withstood the crisis thanks to the tax money flooding in from the rest of France and the strong demand created by its wealthy citizens. The capital and its surrounding countryside thus constituted a relatively sheltered zone, escaping the general depression, at least until 1703 or thereabouts.

Recent research in the last 20 years has revealed also the evidence of agrarian crisis in Normandy during the last years of Louis XIV, with the exception of the rich plains around Caen, and also in the Beauce, Poitou and Savoy, where tithe revenues declined by 22.6 per cent between 1680 to 1685 and 1700 to 1715. Finally, in the southern domains or *commanderies* of the Order of Saint John of Jerusalem,[46] tithes and land rents fell by 32.2 per cent in real terms between the 1670s and 1710–20.[47]

As far as agriculture is concerned, the final years of Louis XIV's reign were not completely disastrous, but they were grim almost everywhere, from Cambrai to Narbonne, from Bordeaux to Lyon, and even in Namur. Burgundy and Alsace were nevertheless exceptions. In these two provinces, increases in net agrarian production, propelled by a long process of reconstruction after the Thirty Years War, were still evident at the beginning of the eighteenth century. If we try to estimate the importance of the depression of 1690 to 1715 in quantitative terms, we notice once again that it was relatively mild in the countryside around Paris, where the receipts of land rents, calculated in real terms, fell by only about 15 per cent by comparison with the preceding period. Elsewhere, in both northern and southern France, tithes and rents fell in real terms by between 25 per cent and up to 33 per cent, depending on the region in question, by comparison with the relatively comfortable, even agreeable decades in the quarter of a century or more before 1680–90. This fall after 1680 or 1690 cannot be explained by resistance among the tithe-paying peasants, not during this age of Catholic revival, symbolized by the Revocation and making for docility in rural areas. Cereal production and agricultural production in general was indeed suffering.

---

[46]   The Order of the Knights of St John of Jerusalem dates back to the eleventh century and had a quasi-religious as well as (at least in principle) a quasi-military character. The seat of the order from 1530 was at Malta. The order was immensely rich and possessed vast landed domains, or groups of domains, known as *commanderies*, both in France and in Europe. Their accounts were well-maintained over several centuries and throw much light on agricultural conditions.

[47]   On all of which, see Joseph Goy and E. Le Roy Ladurie, *Les Fluctuations du produit de la dîme* (Paris/The Hague, Mouton, 1972), p. 364 *et seq.* Cf., from the same two authors, *Prestations paysannes, dîmes, rentes foncières et mouvement de la production agricole, à l'époque pré-industrielle* (2 vols, Paris, Mouton, 1982), ii, 491–733 (contributions from B. Garnier, J. Pavart (fig. 11), J-M. Constant, J. Nicolas, G. Gangneux).

Bad harvests could be disastrous for an often archaic peasant economy further weakened by heavy taxation. Moreover, when the level of average harvests fell over the period of a decade then one or two very bad cereal harvests resulting from unfavourable climatic conditions became even more catastrophic, most particularly for small producers and modest consumers, both of whom ran the risk of malnutrition. More simply, the result, in exceptional circumstances it is true, was famine. Such was the fatal chain of events in the last decade of the century, buffeted simultaneously by war, taxes and climatic conditions.

The years between 1687 and 1701 were cold and wet. They constitute one of the low points of the 'little ice age' identified by Christian Pfister. Wheat, by origin a denizen of hot dry countries, cannot stand either hard frost or excessive rain. The extremely cold decade of the 1690s, therefore, witnessed several subsistence crises of an extremely severe kind,[48] among them one in which grain rose to its highest price of the seventeenth century. The failed harvest of 1693 was followed by an apocalyptic famine of almost medieval proportions. It was at its most severe in France, her continental neighbours and Scotland. In England, by contrast, its effects were insignificant, for English agriculture enjoyed higher productivity thanks to technology, mixed farming and fertilizer, while a highly developed maritime trade in cereals allowed imports from the Baltic to make up for the temporary shortages caused by bad harvests around London or Bristol.

In France, a combination of precarious agrarian structures, short-term events and the deteriorating climate lay behind the famines of 1693–4. In the 1680s, warm and dry growing seasons had led to a series of superb harvests in northern France and England. Grain prices fell accordingly,[49] but not for long! From 1687 onwards cold summers, indicated by the late grape harvests of the 1690s, characterized what would be called, albeit with considerable exaggeration, the 'little ice age of the seventeenth century'. The cold was especially destructive for the harvests in the high valleys of the Alps. In these regions cereals, clinging to the mountain-sides at the extreme limits of their habitat, survived the rigours of the climate with difficulty even at the best of times. But in the Alps the springs and summers of 1687, 1688, 1689, 1690 and 1692 were cold and often wet, with disastrous consequences for the harvests. 'Since 1690', wrote a Savoyard official in 1693, 'the greater part of the people of the Tarentaise and the Maurienne have lived on bread made from ground nutshells, mixed with barley and oat flour.'

---

[48]   E. Le Roy Ladurie, *Histoire du climat depuis l'an Mil* (Paris, Flammarion, 1982), i, 82 *et seq.*; Gordon Manley, *Climate and the British Scene* (London, Collins, 1962); Christian Pfister, *Klimageschichte der Schweiz von 1525 bis 1860 und seine Bedeutung in der Geschichte von Bevölkerung und Landwirtschaft* (Bern/Stuttgart, Academica Helvetica [Interdisziplinäre Veröffentlichungen der Schweizerischen Geisteswissenschaftlichen Gesellschaft und der Schweizerischen Naturforschenden Gesellschaft, vol. vi], 1988).
[49]   Le Roy Ladurie, *Histoire du climat*, i, 83.

The year 1692, cold and wet through spring and summer, stands out particularly. The wine harvest was late: in Francophone Switzerland as late as 9 or 12 November! These rainy and chilly summer months damaged products such as chestnuts, buckwheat or wine which provided subsistence and cash sales for the impecunious peasantry. In the autumn of 1692 the intendant Bouville painted a sombre picture of the Limousin: 'All the chestnuts are lost and most of the buckwheat . . . The vines have suffered greatly and there will be very little wine . . . For lack of cereals it is probable that people will be hungry after Lent.' The same pessimistic outlook was expressed in the Ile de France, Anjou, Normandy, Poitou, Béarn and elsewhere.

As an inclement summer gave way to an equally bitter autumn, distress intensified and famine loomed. On 24 October 1692 Maupeou d'Ableiges, intendant of the Auvergne, solemnly and prophetically foretold the famine which would last through the summer of 1693 to that of 1694. 'What is to be feared', he wrote, 'is a great shortage of wheat not only in the year to come but also in 1694. Most of the land in the upper Auvergne has not been sown. This does not mean that they are lying fallow or that there is not enough grain to sow, but the bad weather has so retarded the harvest and new sowing that most of the peasants have not taken the risk, and those who have risked it are certain that they will have no crops . . . The vines, which promised much, have been entirely destroyed by the recent frosts. There is no hope that the grapes will ripen.'

Famine broke out the following year; 1692 was the fatal year that led to the two terrible years. Cold, wet, with late wine harvests gathered in the snow, it jeopardized the current harvest, that of August 1692, and because the planting of grain was delayed or left undone, the crops of 1693 and the daily bread of 1694. The year 1693, not as cold as 1692, nevertheless saw an icy spring and grains attacked by blight. Cereal crops suffered their *coup de grâce*. The harvest of 1693 thus coincided with the start of a famine the likes of which had not been seen since 1661. It is worth pointing out that this gap of more than 30 years represented a fairly good performance which should, despite everything, be mentioned among the positive achievements of Louis XIV's reign. Neither the times of the last Valois, nor the reign of Louis XIII, nor the rule of Mazarin could boast of such a long period without famine such as that enjoyed by the generation of 1662–91, a generation distinctly better off than its predecessors.

Fénelon's murderous metaphor needs, then, to be properly assessed: was France in 1694 a 'great hospital desolate and without provisions'? The historical and geographical demography of death allows us to qualify the bishop's sweeping statement.[50] Famine swept through an enormous diagonal from the north-north-east to the south-south-west, passing through the Paris basin and the Massif Central to the Aude and the western Pyrenees.

---

[50] Our annotations serve as a prelude to the large investigation which Marcel Lachiver is currently undertaking on the famines of 1693 and 1709.

On the other hand, it spared Brittany and the south-east, including the present-day *départements* of the Hérault and the Gard where, as we have seen, the export-orientated textile industry could achieve a considerable prosperity. The existence of such exceptional sectors modifies Fénelon's assertion without contradicting it, because profits made in manufacture, modest though they may have been, did allow many people to avoid the worst consequenes of the great hunger.

In overall terms it is possible that about a tenth of the Sun-King's subjects died during the two years 1693 and 1694, through famine and especially the epidemics it brought in its train. Taking into account a decline in the birth-rate which was not made up for in subsequent years, this would mean a fall in population of at least two million.[51] The equivalent today would be a catastrophe which killed five million French people. And yet once the famine was over the signs of demographic recovery would as usual make themselves evident. Widows remarried, young and older women bore children for the first time or started again. The losses would be compensated for, but the shock had been severe.[52]

The rootless population, beggars and unemployed, proliferated; for potential employers, often short of money themselves, could not afford to hire them. This was known as 'the impotence of individuals'. In bad times the poor had eaten cabbage stalks and a form of 'bread' made from the roots of ferns, which were of no use in resisting disease. The fate of the civilian population was further complicated by grain requisitions and having to provide lodgings for soldiers. Provinces held on to available stocks of cereals, as did parishes which thereby left neighbouring communities to starve. The price of wheat tripled or quadrupled inland while it only doubled in a great, well-provisioned port like Bordeaux. But the invigorating effect of the sea air was only a partial consolation. Contagious diseases imported from the true famine areas killed large numbers of Bordelais. Recurrent subsistence riots tried in vain to fight back against the disastrous weather as well as the machinations of grain hoarders.[53]

In such a situation of crisis, political opposition would have been legitimate or at least comprehensible. Yet only a bare skeleton is evident. The struggle, simple skirmishes perhaps but ominous for the future, was led by a handful of intellectuals from the nobilities of the sword and the *robe*, judges, priests or Protestant pastors, few in number but representing the tip of a sizeable iceberg. The consensus which had operated for the past 30 or so years came to an end. The Revocation had at first been applauded

[51] F. Lebrun, 'Les Crises démographiques en France aux XVIIe et XVIIIe siècles', *Annales ESC* (March–April 1980), 220. J.-P. Poussou, 'Les Crises démographiques en milieu urbain; l'exemple de Bordeaux, fin XVIIe-fin XVIIIe siècle', *Annales ESC* (March–April 1980), 236.

[52] Jacques Dupâquier, *Histoire de la population française, de la Renaissance à 1789* (Paris, PUF, 1988), ii, 206 *et seq.*

[53] Michel Marechal, 'Aspect de la crise de 1693–1694 dans la généralité de Moulins', *Revue d'histoire moderne et contemporaine*, 31 (1984), 537 *et seq.*

willynilly by writers such as Bossuet, La Bruyère and La Fontaine, carried away by religious and nationalist enthusiasm, either spontaneous or manufactured. Nevertheless, different reactions soon came to the surface. Vauban drew up a memoir advocating the recall of the Calvinists, intended for the eyes of Louvois. It did not question the principle of the edict of Fontainebleau, but took note of the unfortunate consequences in the economic, commercial and demographic fields, and the negation of the authentic spiritual values which should have been upheld by the Catholic church.

In a text on warfare, drawn up in 1693, the same Vauban affirmed that the greatness of kings could be measured by the number of their subjects. This was not likely to be easy reading for Louis XIV, at the head of a state the demography of which, despite its population of over 20 million souls, appeared at that moment undermined by war, famine and disease to such an extent that it would be incapable of 'keeping up'. In 1694, the second year of the famine, Fénelon in turn denounced (tautologically) malnutrition, abandoned land, depopulated towns and countryside, unemployment, the decline in commerce, and the futility of military victories. Fénelon's critique was important because a strong oppositional party formed around him at the very heart of the court, a ducal party, comprising Colbert's nephews, allies of the duke de Saint Simon. As another sign of things to come, in 1695 Pierre de Boisguilbert, a magistrate from Normandy, protested against the excessive taxes weighing heavily on peasant landholdings; they were, he said, destroying the very sources of agrarian production, food consumption[54] and the circulation of money.

On the Huguenot side, in 1690 there appeared a pamphlet, *Les Soupirs de la France esclave*, probably the work of pastor Pierre Jurieu (at all events that is the least unlikely attribution). According to these sighs of enslaved France, nothing of fundamental importance should be done in the kingdom without the consent of the estates and the social groups (nobility and clergy to the fore) which together formed the nation. The government of France would on this basis become more aristocratic (after the fashion of the Valois) than monarchical (as in the Bourbon system). Absolutism would be replaced, at Versailles or Paris, by an English-style monarchy tempered by aristocratic influence. This was a long way from the highly authoritarian monarchy defended by Bossuet as well as by some promi-

---

[54] These texts (which I have summarized) and data are to be found in the following works: M.O. Keohane, *Philosophy and the State in France from the Renaissance to the Enlightenment* (Princeton, NJ: Princeton University Press, 1980), pp. 328–55; A. de Rochas (ed.), 'Oeuvres (de charactère politique) de Vauban' in *Journal des économistes*, 4th series, 18 (1882), 169 *et seq.* and 239 *et seq.*; Esmonin, *Etudes sur la France*, p. 373; Pierre de Boisguilbert, *Le Détail de la France* (n.p., 1695) – this book would be republished many times under the title *Le Détail de la France* or *La France ruinée sous le règne de Louis XIV*. See, finally and fundamentally, Fénelon, *Ecrits et lettres politiques*, ed. Charles Urbain (Paris, Bossard, 1920), pp. 142–57. On Fénelonian opposition, Lionel Rothkrug, *Opposition to Louis XIV* (Princeton, NJ: Princeton University Press, 1965), pp. 267–86 may be consulted with profit.

nent members of the Protestant élite, such as Bayle or pastor Jean Claude.[55] The disunited 'opposition' included, therefore, two churchmen, Fénelon and Jurieu, from different churches; a civil officer, Boisguilbert, representing those as yet still rare members of the élite who thought, read and wrote; and Vauban, a soldier in the so-called *armes savantes* of artillery and fortification, who was also one of the most original minds of the age. Unanimous support for the government was no longer the rule among the leading thinkers of the age. But neither can we speak of a vast movement of public opinion of a kind that would be seen later. Opinion, that goddess of the century to come, was still in her infancy or waiting to be born. She would have to wait until 1750.

This breaking of the consensus among the highest élites of the kingdom, however limited it may have been, was not simply the result of a certain disillusion with war and various other major and minor hardships. More positively, the international and conceptual consequences of the Glorious Revolution of 1688 were also taken into account, most notably in the case of Jurieu, by reason of a certain implicit 'Protestant' solidarity which united, despite all their differences, Anglicans, Nonconformists and Calvinists on both sides of the Channel. Can the impact of events in England also be seen in Fénelon's awareness of the importance of representative institutions? Viewed from the continent the second English Revolution had another ideological advantage in that it had shed no blood and therefore wiped out the memory of the execution of Charles I in 1649, which had for so long been used to frighten French supporters of a more limited monarchy. At the same time, the defenders of absolutism, such as Bossuet, held no monopoly rights to right-thinking opinions or automatic superiority in controversy. Proof had now been provided in one of the most important nations of the west, even if geographically separated from the continent, that a monarchy under limited supervision by the 'States General' (the Commons and the Lords in English parlance) could function without disorder or degenerating into anarchy, thanks to cooperation between the 'Estates', flanked for good measure by a charismatic leader, William of Orange.

In this sense the absolutism of Louis XIV had seen its most comfortable years between 1661 and 1687. The glory of the Sun-King was somewhat tarnished by the Glorious Revolution. What had happened in Britain, in combination with the miseries experienced in France in subsequent years, made possible a revival in political thought, which saw itself as independ-

---

[55]   The pastor Claude (Jean) (1619–87) had a southern background before he 'went up to Paris' to become the minister of the Charenton *temple*, itself the preserve of the Huguenot congregation of Paris. He stood, in Paris until the Revocation and then afterwards until his death in exile, one of the uncontested leaders of French Protestantism. But, in contrast to Jurieu, his political thought remained within the limits of absolutism and the respect due to the sovereign monarchy. On Jurieu himself, beyond the *Soupirs* (already mentioned, and which were published in Amsterdam in 1689), see Keohane, *Philosophy and the State*, p. 315.

ent from the absolutist government. The inclination towards submission was broken. The burden had become too heavy and turned into intellectual conformism. Deference had been the necessary complement to those concepts, from Bodin to Cardin Le Bret, from the aftermath of the Frondes to Bossuet, which had reduced all matters concerning sovereignty to the decisions of the prince, hopefully inspired by God and natural law.

★   ★   ★   ★   ★

The treaties of Ryswick, signed in September and October 1697, showed an undeniable spirit of reconciliation on the part of Louis XIV.[56] France made peace (for a few years) with the huge coalition formed by Spain, England, Holland and the Empire. Five weeks later, on 7 December 1697, Marie-Adélaïde, daughter of Victor Amadeus, Duke of Savoy, and Anne-Marie d'Orléans, herself daughter of Monsieur, brother of Louis XIV, was married to her cousin the duke of Burgundy, eldest grandson of Louis XIV and future father of Louis XV. This union was the fruit of peace between France and Savoy. The ceremony and the clothes on display were spectacular: a lady's dress could be weighed down with 21 kilos of gold in finery and thread. Fashionable hairdressers charged their elegant clients up to 20 *louis* an hour on the morning of the marriage. On 11 December, during the ball which extended the ceremonies, the throng was so great that Monsieur, the bride's maternal grandfather, was accidentally battered and thrown to the ground. The dancing, nevertheless, respected the social hierarchy as enumerated by Saint-Simon: the princes and princesses of the blood were followed in correct order by duchesses, ladies and finally unmarried ladies. The festivities ended on 17 December with the staging at the Trianon of *Isse*, an opera by André Destouches, a former musketeer turned court composer. It was one of the great displays by the dazzling but already embittered Versailles described by Saint-Simon.

Versailles remained until the end of the reign the site of court activity and the glittering setting for royal marrying and mourning. The château was a living universe, constantly growing and renewing itself. Its classical regularity only came to dominate after a chaotic series of often uncoordinated alterations. A glance backwards is necessary. The long and complex history of Versailles, the regrets and second thoughts of its architects, the successive phases of its expansion, were determined above all by the very long political and physical life with which a robust constitution had blessed Louis XIV. If the king had seen generations of military leaders come and go, from Turenne and Condé through Luxemburg to

---

[56] This spirit of reconciliation with the king, in contrast with the more uncompromising attitudes which had been signalled in the preceeding 15 or 20 years, is clearly revealed in the fine analysis accorded it by Jean Bérenger in his article on 'Ryswick' in François Bluche, *Dictionnaire du Grand Siècle* (Paris, Fayard, 1990), p. 1369.

Villars and Vendôme, the same applies to the builders and decorators of Versailles. After Le Vau,[57] colleague and follower of Le Brun,[58] came Mansart,[59] who would die only shortly before Louis XIV. Colbert encouraged his master to place the creators of his great buildings on the same level as his military captains as contributing equally to the grandeur and power of princes.

During the first part of the reign, the painter Le Brun, a dilettante protected by Colbert, had established a visual language for the palace based on classical mythology. Courtiers and visitors to the château were thus bombarded with various messages, above all the icon of the Sun-King, Apollo-Phoebus, dominating and Copernican. This heliocentrism relegated the planets, heavenly and courtly, to a subordinate position. Their dependence was made visible by the Paris Observatory, subsidized by the king, and by the stone envelope of the new château: the apartments of the king and queen were decorated with ceilings depicting the planets in their orbits. Apollo was a versatile fellow: when he took a relaxing bath in the grotto of Thetis in the park of Versailles he was, by association of ideas, exalting the navy created by Colbert.

The god played a more central role in the hall that bore his name. There stood from 1682 the royal throne, guarding the great 'apartment' facing the Hall of Mirrors. The throne was of solid silver, eight feet high, made in one single piece. On top of it stood a statue of Apollo, ruling over the figures of Justice and Strength depicted on the back of the seat, the base being flanked by four children carrying flowers. Apollo the just: vigorous, youthful and fertile.

Comparable themes had already been expressed, in a more searching fashion, in a work by Nicolas Mignard which adorned the chamber and antechamber of Louis XIV at the Tuileries. Around a central Apollonian motif, this painting on multiple panels expressed several ideas. Those attacking the glory of the sovereign or neglecting to respect it are ridiculed

---

[57]   Louis Le Vau (1612–70), son of an important masonry contractor and brother to an architect, was the greatest French architect of the period, constructing the Versailles of the first period of Louis XIV's personal rule. This was after he had 'cut his teeth' on the houses built for financiers, on Fouquet's Vaux-le-Vicomte, on the present Institut de France (formerly the 'Collège des Quatre Nations') and on the colonnade of the Louvre.

[58]   Charles Le Brun (1619–90) was both a great painter and founder of a whole school of painting, and also the director of the Gobelins – here and elsewhere, an official artist. He would be (in his case, as with Le Vau, it was after Vaux-le-Vicomte) responsible for designing the overall internal decoration at Versailles and for the painted ceiling of the *galerie des Glaces* in particular.

[59]   Jules Hardouin-Mansart (1646–1708), the grand-nephew of the famous French architect Mansart (d.1666) would, in turn, be the great (royal) architect principally for the second half of the reign, that of Louvois, followed by Pontchartrain or Chamillart. The church of the Invalides with its dome and façade, the marble Trianon and the chapel at Versailles are sufficient testimony of the immense stature of someone whose achievement was recognized in an *équipe* (Robert de Cotte etc.). At the same time, he was a powerful administrator who became almost a minister (he was *surintendant des bâtiments du roi* from 1668); in reality, he developed into one the grand seigneurs of Louis XIV's court.

or destined for disaster (Midas or Niobe); the uncouth characters who make arms for enemies of the monarchy are taking a huge risk (the Cyclops); and presumptuous leaders who wish to take the place of the prince in directing the people are punished (the story of Marsyas). In other words, a glorious monarchy to be respected by all, monopoly of military violence in the hands of the state, obedience of the people.

In certain circumstances Apollo could be replaced by Venus, to whom the 40-year-old Louis, before 1681, rendered frequent homage. The Three Graces crowned the goddess, graceful and naked, in her own salon, so making her all-powerful over other divinities and authorities. On the ceiling she effortlessly dominates Jupiter, Mars, Neptune, Vulcan and Bacchus, representing sovereignty, war, the sea, metallurgy and intoxicating viniculture respectively. This ensemble was inspired by an older salon of Venus, polytheist and planetary, embellished by Pietro da Cortone in the Pitti Palace of Florence between 1640 and 1647. The Tuscan paintings stressed above all the draconian choice made by the Medici between the virtuous wisdom of Minerva and the pleasures of vice represented by Hercules. But at Versailles this ethical theme made way for a multifarious distribution of celestial functions. Apollo, supported by Venus, triumphs over the dionysiac forces of the anarchy of the Frondes, which in reality had never been fully subdued.

A repetitive and encyclopaedic symbolism runs through the iconography created by Colbert and Le Brun: before 1674 the minister had commissioned six groups of four statues each for the park of Versailles. They represented the four seasons, the four elements, the four times of day, the four quarters of the world, the four genres of poetry, and the four humours which governed the behaviour and health of the human body. Physical macrocosm and cultural microcosm were synthesized. Versailles in its first phase, therefore, was a maker of myths. The artists, acting as pedagogues, created a symbolism around the person of the king such as he wished to be seen by present and future generations. Le Brun and his team used the pagan pantheon and Greco-Roman history as a mine for multi-faceted and almost unlimited allegories. The nobles of the court, raising their heads, deciphered the puzzles on the ceiling as we might figure out a crossword. The king, thinly disguised as a hero of legend or antiquity, was revealed as gracious and skilful like Mercury, wise and prudent like Augustus, just and equitable like Trajan or Marcus Aurelius, valorous like Cyrus or Constantine, magnanimous like Coriolanus or Alexander, magnificent in his sumptuous palace like Vespasian or indeed Nebuchadnezzar.

Versailles was, in this first phase of the personal rule, an enchanted island of pleasure and love. As the château grew it became, as we have said, a temple of Apollo and the divinities orbiting around him. From 1678–80 onwards, the style of décor changed. The palace became more theatrical and elevated the personality and person of Louis, stripped of the heroic and mythic rags which had been extracted from the annals of ancient history for his benefit.

Apollo, Hercules and Alexander were expelled from the ceiling. Their place was taken by the great deeds of Louis XIV, depicted openly. The 12 labours of Hercules, originally proposed by Le Brun but rejected by order of the *Conseil d'en haut*, were replaced by 26 glorious royal actions between 1662 and 1678: in order, the improvement of finances, the arts, navigation and justice, and then diverse episodes of the wars in Holland and Hungary or against Spain, when France was victorious (failures were not depicted). Hercules only appeared in the pictures adorning the ceiling as a kind of junior policeman, mercilessly beating up the bearded personage of the Rhine while Louis XIV traverses the river in a flying chariot.

Louis was France, even if the reverse was not true. A historian of statistical bent could count 23 historical figures represented 72 times. Above them the king appears 13 times and France 11 times, almost as often. The sovereign subsumes and organizes the nation.

Le Brun, supported by Colbert, was the herald of the two successive representations of the monarch, the first mythological, the second personal. After Colbert's death Louvois became Superintendent of Buildings. He had a reputation as a philistine in matters of sculpture, but he learned quickly. As efficient in completing a building in Versailles as in destroying a town in the Palatinate, he made sure that everything was finished on time. He quickly pushed Le Brun to one side and recruited Mansart. The latter, if asked, was capable of adapting to the simple military tastes of Louvois, responsible for buildings as for war. Under Richelieu, Sublet des Noyers had performed a similar dual martial and artistic function. Thus Mansart was prompted to build the church of Notre Dame at Versailles, with its squat, heavy lines, and especially, on the side of the château, the new Orangery with its interior arcades, regular and austere like a luxurious barracks. A great spender of money rather than a great Minister of Finance, Louvois increased considerably the annual amounts dedicated to the construction of the palace, passing from an average of 808,000 *livres* per annum between 1664 and 1690 to a maximum of more than ten million *livres* in 1685. The year of the Revocation, therefore, coincided with the highest expenditure on Versailles. This was in fact no coincidence: it illustrates a profound and continuous tendency in Louis XIV's policies. These were often centred around his foreign wars, but in 1685 external relations were in a state of cold war: repression against the Huguenots, undisturbed by extraneous distractions, could go hand in hand with the building of a great palace. Both schemes were underscored by the same conceptual apparatus and also by a certain *hubris* on the part of Louis XIV: after his triumph in the Peace of Ratisbon, the king, who could be so reasonable, even rational, had momentarily lost sight of his limitations.

The long final period of the reign corresponds with the creation of the royal chapel within the palace. This was the logical accompaniment to large-scale and very costly ecclesiastical policies: struggle against the pope in the name of Gallicanism (up to 1693); against the Protestants, from the Revocation to the Camisard war in 1703; against the Augustinianism of the Jansenists, under the pretext of the papal bull *Vineam Domini* condemning the disciples of Port-Royal, promulgated in 1705 by Louis' command. These pious excesses on three fronts demanded a corresponding sanctuary in the palace: it was in any case necessary for royal and courtly devotions.

Mansart got to work in 1688, another significant date, the year in which the first rumblings of the War of the League of Augsburg, pitting France against Protestant and other powers, were heard across Europe. The plan of the new edifice, after some hesitation by the architect, departed from the Roman style, which was perhaps considered too ultramontane by the government, although Mansart did employ it for the dome of the Invalides. The chapel of Versailles was firmly inspired by French royal chapels in the Gothic style, which could after all be seen as Gallican, and which could already be admired in the chapel of the château of Vincennes and, of course, the Sainte-Chapelle in Paris. In this sense the new sanctuary was a revival of a truly French style, under the aegis of Louvois, in contrast to the Italian-influenced conventions which had been dominant, at least to start with, under Colbert and Le Brun.

The financial strains caused by the War of the League of Augsburg slowed down work on the building-sites of Versailles. In 1691 the king sent his magnificent silverware to be melted down into money. To make up for this loss, Louis encouraged his artists to create a décor from substitute materials such as wood and textiles, which they did to remarkable effect in the form of embroideries, silks, Boulle's marquetry, etc. In this time of trial by warfare, the artists of Versailles devised ingenious but effective makeshifts. Finally, despite the War of the Spanish Succession, the trend was reversed. The church was finished between 1706 and 1710. The temporal messages emanating from the château were now complemented, and not before time, by a dose of spirituality, as if the Most Christian King was affirming his confidence in the Almighty at a time when he was waging war alongside the Spanish against the Anglo-German Protestants but also against papist powers such as the Empire and Portugal. On a Gothic plan but realized in a classical, even post-classical spirit, the chapel was inundated by light from transparent windows. The architect rejected the traditional stained-glass windows: worshippers should be able to read their mass books, or in the case of the libertine Philippe d'Orléans their Rabelais, without straining their eyes. The light of Heaven also beamed down from a *trompe-l'oeil* ceiling dominated by God the Father. Saint Louis and Christ stood at the sides of the altar. Towards the galleries, where stood the king during services, were to be found the Holy Spirit, source of religious knowledge, and Charlemagne, the model of a great leader driven and inspired by the tutelary divinity. The organ case, made between 1709 and 1717, is an early example of the rococo style in French art, thus anticipating the splendours of the Regency in the winter of Louis XIV's years.

Looking down on the grand canal from above, the panoramas of Versailles are reminiscent of certain Dutch paintings. To the right, the new chapel rises like a country church above the roof of the château. A central axis is formed by an avenue of green baize down which the king, having descended the steps of the palace, progressed with his equipage and dogs to go hunting in the forests of the park. To the left, we see the orchards, flanked by pot plants from the Orangery, moved outside in summer to delight the eye rather than for eating purposes, around which a horde of gardeners are busily at work. In other words, Versailles, like any village or suburban manor house, was involved in the structures of estates, functions and orders, and also in the cabals which together made up the amalgamated lay and sacred hierarchy of the Ancien Régime, and which Saint-Simon observed with his piercing wit between 1692 and 1723.

The cabals of the château, at the geometrical centre of central government, developed and functioned in the absence of true political parties which would only emerge in a recognizable form after 1770 and the Maupeou coup. Saint-Simon, therefore, confined himself, quite justifiably, to describing the palace cabals in 1700 or 1709 and their three articulations. They formed around the three generations of the royal family and orientated themselves, according to the desires of their members, towards defending the interests of individuals whose fate depended on other members of the group closer to the royal and governmental centres of decision-making and power. They could nevertheless be guided by a certain sense of the general interest if one of the guiding lights of the faction was also an intellectual of the stature of a Fénelon.

The generational divide in the royal family could not be more simple. The first cabal was formed around the reigning couple, Louis XIV and la Maintenon, attaching themselves to the king or his wife through bonds of clientage or friendship. They were counting, justifiably as it turned out, on the longevity of Louis and Françoise. This Faction Number One comprised great nobles (Harcourt), courageous soldiers (Boufflers), comic opera generals (Villeroy), *robins* from the king's councils, ministries and chancellery (the two Pontchartrains, and, later, Voysin), leading gentlemen of the chamber, and high officers of the crown (first equerry Beringhen).

The second 'sodality', meaning a grouping of families, clienteles, ambitions and possibly ideas, was to be found for its part one rung down the Bourbon family tree. It was banking on the theoretically promising future of the Grand Dauphin, Louis XIV's legitimate son, also known as Monseigneur, destined to succeed his aged father unless he died first, as he in fact did in 1711. This second camarilla contained few ministers or *robins* from the royal councils: at most the *contrôleur général des finances*,

Chamillart,[60] would make a brief appearance before his dismissal and comfortable semi-disgrace in 1709. The Monseigneur group, in fact, was especially well endowed with princesses from Lorraine, princes of the blood, males and females from the race of Condé and Conti, and bastard offspring of Louis XIV and his relations, notably Madame la Duchesse, daughter of the king and Madame de Montespan, Monseigneur's half-sister, and with her her legitimate half-brother, d'Antin.[61] To these may be added, blown thither by the winds of favour, Vendôme, a great soldier, but one who found himself from time to time in the king's bad books.

Finally and logically, after the king and his son, the third group was centred around his grandson, the duke of Burgundy. It was made up essentially of the now aged second generation of the Colbert connection: the two nephew-dukes, Chevreuse and Beauvilliers, both ministers, the latter officially, the former *in partibus*, both reformers or at least reformist in relation to the system of the absolute monarchy; and then two supplementary Colbertian offshoots, Desmarets, who, despite a temporary disgrace after 1683, would in the last period of the reign become *contrôleur général des finances*, a role in which he proved expert, and Torcy, Secretary of State for Foreign Affairs. Behind them stood the figure of Fénelon, basically in disgrace after 1699, and teacher of pacifism and plans for representative government, at least for the nobility. He was even the prophet of a kind of utopian socialism, as a reading of *Télémaque* will demonstrate. Fénelon was not devoid of ambition, able in a controlled fashion to bestow on each interlocutor the requisite dose of intellectual, moral, worldly or political honey or gruel; in short a remarkable intellect who would inspire in the long run the strategy and diplomacy of the eighteenth century, based on the semi-pacifism of a Philippe d'Orléans or a Louis XV rather than the almost permanent belligerence of a Richelieu or a Louis XIV. This Faction Number Three sat simultaneously and comfortably in government and in opposition. It accommodated at one and the same time, and often including the same people, a ministerial clan,

---

[60] Michel de Chamillart (1652–1721), from a *robe* family with connections to Mazarin and Colbert, was *contrôleur général des finances* (1699), Minister of State (1700), Secretary of State for War (1701) – in sum, Colbert and Louvois rolled into one. It was a crippling task which finally exhausted him, but not before he demonstrated for over a decade a remarkable record for competence, scrupulousness and hard work. His honesty is a mark of a transition from the 'financial accumulation' of the Mazarin or Colbertian kind and the more frequent integrity of statesmen in the eighteenth century. In 1708–9, the exhausted Chamillart was divested of his ministerial functions. In the meantime, his family had, thanks to him, passed from being *robe* nobility to court nobles (see the excellent biographical *résumé* by L. Trenard in Bluche, *Dictionnaire du Grand Siècle*, p. 293).

[61] From her liaison with Louis XIV, la Montespan had numerous illegitimate children, amongst whom were the duke du Maine, the count de Toulouse, the duchess d'Orléans and Madame la Duchesse (de Bourbon-Condé). From her official marriage to the marquis de Montespan, she gave birth to Louis Antoine, the future duke d'Antin, a model courtier, who would be *Directeur général des bâtiments du roi* at the end of the reign. See Saint-Simon, *Mémoires*, vii, 51.

a circle of noble and intellectual contestation, a school of financial technique, and also two clerical lobbies, hostile one to another. The first was the Jesuit sub-group, supported by *père* Tellier, the king's formidable confessor, the second was the rank-and-file of Saint-Sulpice, who had become through their seminaries the arbiters of truth in the eyes of the minor clergy. The Gallican Torcy added a discreet dose of crypto-Jansenism to a group which did not lack for contradictions.

Cabals Two and Three were gambling, just like Number One, but they had not placed their stakes on the long life-expectancy of the king and his spouse. They had their eyes on the succession or successions which would after Louis XIV's eventual death pass power on to Monseigneur or the duke of Burgundy. Both bets were lost. The son and grandson would both die during the lifetime of the old king, preceding him to the grave by several years. The sodality of the late duke of Burgundy and the Colbertians, in the person of Saint-Simon, one of the last survivors, had no choice but to reinvest their hopes in a last minute convert to Fénelon's ideas, Philippe d'Orléans, who shared certain ideas with the archbishop of Cambrai, even if he drew the line at chastity.

As well as being a nest of cabals the court of Versailles was also a mirror of values, at least those of the aristocratic high society which inhabited the palace. The entourage of Louis XIV, behind the closed doors of the château as on the façade of the church of the Invalides, celebrated the descending chain of social bodies, or more simply the hierarchy, given material form in the ladder of social status, passed on in theory from father to son among princes of the blood, dukes and *pairs*, simple noblemen, *robins* and a sprinkling of commoners. It was manifested also by external signs[62] and even by the seats (armchairs, chairs, stools or standing) which placed individuals at the correct distance from the king or some other personality of high status. In the same spirit, the court insisted upon the separation of the sacred and the profane, more precisely the privileged positions occupied by the king and the high aristocracy in relation to the altar, the communion table and the office during religious ceremonies. Within Versailles, much to the taste of Saint-Simon and some others, a sort of unofficial distinction operated between the pure and the impure, the latter being the illegitimate, the pox-ridden, homosexuals, in short the 'dirty', by contrast with the 'unpolluted' of legitimate birth, healthy in body and heterosexual. Nevertheless, the court was capable of relaxing the rigid divisions in its ranks if necessary. Women were most adept here, using well-tried methods. Girls and ladies, bourgeois, *robines* and most often noblewomen leapt like salmon up the stairs of the waterfall of snobbish contempt, marrying young lords from a higher grade than them-

---

[62] On the remarkable correlation within the hierarchical society of this period between the place of an individual within its institutions and its cabals, see La Bruyère, *Caractères*, 'Du mérite personnel', para. 4.

selves, gentlemen, dukes, even princes.[63] Finally, when one had become, in the technical sense of the term and without pejorative connotations, a courtier, or else the ally or spouse of a courtier, it was possible to break free, if one wished, from the court system. One could do this not through a vain demand for egalitarianism when the hierarchies all of a sudden inspired disgust in a Christian conscience, but simply by renouncing them and retreating away from the world to La Trappe or a simple hermitage or hovel, or possibly to Port-Royal before that monastery succumbed (only to be reborn in people's souls) before the curses of Louis XIV. 'The supreme shock of an act of renunciation is the extreme limit of our power. It is the most powerful and effective force at our disposal.'[64]

Sustaining and representing an aristocratic culture, nowadays long outdated, the court nevertheless deserves great credit for civilizing the nobility.[65] It made noblemen less violent, not in their military role, but in their everyday life as 'civilians', even if a strong dose of hypocrisy was also involved. It created a model for élites outside the court and even for the middle classes, the fashionable Parisians who aped the manners of the court, a model which made for a more peaceful society, less given to the casual shedding of blood. The incorrigible swashbucklers who could not adapt to the new 'softer' manners had no refuge other than in misanthropy and antisocial cantankerousness. Cyranos became Alcestes. Of course, this transformation was only for internal consumption. In relations between states, recourse to bloody combat remained the last resort, accepted as valid, even if it was sometimes delayed, tempered by a more reconciliatory diplomacy. This would soon form part of the spirit of the age, the *Zeitgeist*, but that time had not yet come.

[63] J.-F. Fitou and E. Le Roy Ladurie, 'Notes sur la population saint-simonienne', *Cahiers Saint-Simon*, no. 15 (1987), 89–93. See also the two texts concerning Saint-Simon by E. Le Roy Ladurie in *L'Annuaire du Collège de France* (1975–6), 618–35; (1981–2), 657–85; see also the joint article with J.-F. Fitou in *L'Annuaire du Collège de France* (1989–90), 699–728.
[64] Joseph Conrad in *Sagesse de Conrad* (Paris, NRF, 1947), p. 51.
[65] Norbert Elias, *The Court Society* (Oxford, Blackwell, 1983).

6

Spain in the Heart

The interlude of peace after Rijswijk, between 1697–8 and 1701–2, was filled with activity and contradictions. The principal actors on the international stage were no angels, whether we are talking about Louis XIV (ruling between 1661 and 1715), Frederick IV of Denmark (1699–1730), Augustus of Saxony, King of Poland (1697–1704), Frederick I of Prussia (1701–13), William III of England (1689–1702), or, needless to say, Charles XII of Sweden (1697–1717) and Peter the Great of Russia (1689–1725). The use of armed force in international affairs was not only conceivable but also acceptable. In so far as non-violence in relations between states did exist, it was embodied only in the sick man of Europe, Charles XI of Spain, who was to die in 1700. The other sovereigns of Europe, to the north and east of the Pyrenees, remained faithful, with touches of black humour but not without diplomatic nuances, to the portrait of the rulers of his age given by Thomas Hobbes: 'Kingdoms, for their own security, extend their dominions; they use the pretexts of danger, or fear of invasion, or the help that others could give to invaders; they endeavour, as much as it is in their power, to subjugate or weaken their neighbours, by open force, by secret procedures, for want of a better method, and in all justice; and for these actions posterity will remember them with honour.'[1]

La Fontaine echoed Hobbes: 'Sire, said the fox, you are too good a king. Your scruples show too much delicacy. Well, eating sheep, a low and stupid species, is that a sin? No, no, you do them a great honour by eating them.'[2]

And yet violence and cynicism were not the only features of this brief inter-war period between the wars of the League of Augsburg and the Spanish Succession. Occasionally a desire for peace may be seen on the part of Louis XIV, the short-lived fruit of reflection on the miseries of war deriving from the prolonged conflicts of the Dutch War and the League of Augsburg. A certain mellowing of manners may also be partly responsible.

[1]   Thomas Hobbes, *Leviathan*, part II, ch. 17.
[2]   La Fontaine, *Fables*, book VII ('Les Animaux malades de la Peste').

But it was only putting off the day of reckoning. A fleeting 'pacifism', then, around 1700? It is true that at this precise moment the brutal age of 'hard men' like Louvois had passed out of fashion. The new ministers Pomponne, his son-in-law Torcy, Pontchartrain, Beauvillier, preferred the use of conciliatory language, even and especially when their master above them held ready in his hand the big stick with which he could always beat his enemies if he deemed it necessary. At this time the whole of Europe was preoccupied with the Spanish succession. In Madrid, the ailing Charles XI would soon die without issue, despite the occasional valiant efforts at procreation which he agreed to go through with his queen. Throughout Europe the search was on for an heir to the throne of Castile.[3] There was no shortage of candidates. All the suitable families on the Catholic side – the Habsburgs, the Bourbons, the House of Savoy, and the Wittelsbachs, dukes and electors of Bavaria – were allied to each other and to the languishing Charles XI. Yet paradoxically, the keys to conflict or agreement lay in the hands of a Protestant king, William III, known in the Netherlands as William of Orange. William, at the head of the two maritime powers, England and the United Provinces, was in a position to act as arbiter. Louis XIV was fully conscious of this and behaved with due moderation. Through emissaries and intermediaries he negotiated with William, his once and future principal antagonist. The contact thus established with London anticipated the discussions pursued during the Regency by the *abbé* Dubois, which would in 1717 result in the establishment of good relations with Britain. Only the vaguest outline, however, was discernible in 1698. It was simply a question now of concocting an acceptable proposal for the partition of the Spanish empire, one which it was hoped would be agreeable to the great powers, so avoiding a European war. Louis wanted to spare his people the agonies they had suffered during previous conflicts. A 'first partition' was therefore agreed in 1698. It was a masterpiece of conciliatory diplomacy. On the French side, the Two Sicilies and parts of Tuscany, as well as the Basque province of Guipuzcoa, would go to the Grand Dauphin Louis, son of Louis XIV. The Archduke Charles, younger son of Emperor Leopold I, would receive Milan.[4] Spain herself and her vast American empire would go to the son of the Elector of Bavaria, the young Wittelsbach prince, Joseph Ferdinand. Unfortunately the young Bavarian princeling died in 1699. It was necessary to return to the drawing board.

---

[3] Spain and Castile are certainly not interchangeable. But the former remained the centralizing, federating and identifying component in the latter, just as the little Capetian 'France' served in respect of the larger hexagon of 'France'; or as Prussia would later on in Germany. Besides, the Hispano-American territories would speak Castilian and not Catalan or Galician.

[4] Ragnhild Hatton, *Louis XIV and Europe* (London, Macmillan, 1976); 'Louis XIV et l'Europe, élements d'une révision historiographique', *XVIIe siècle*, 31 (1979); cf. New Cambridge Modern History (Cambridge, Cambridge University Press, 1971), vi, 393.

As a result of the death of Joseph Ferdinand, France and the maritime powers devised a second partition in 1700. Although it could not be put into effect immediately, this agreement underlined once again the momentary conciliatory disposition of the Sun-King. Louis was in effect willing to let a Habsburg, the Archduke Charles, mount the throne of Spain, in return for a promise, which Louis at times did not even insist upon, that the two states belonging to the Austrian and Castilian branches of the family should never be unified. This marked the limits of Louis XIV's anti-Habsburg policy, inherited from Francis I, Henry IV, Richelieu and Mazarin. This anti-Habsburg stance remained fundamental to Bourbon attitudes, but not in a hysterical or visceral way.

Nor was Louis XIV's attitude towards the Netherlands and England, 'married' one to another under William III, without its refinements. To start with, the partition gave important territories in Italy (the Two Sicilies and the Milanais) to the Dauphin Louis, *alias* Monseigneur. Royal morsels indeed, but also consolation prizes for this Louis Junior to whom his father, desirous to maintain concord and peace in Europe, was willing to deny the enormous Spanish succession in favour of a Habsburg. The king hoped that so much self-denial would be pleasing to his own subjects, who still had bad memories of previous wars. But despite all this, the idea that the Versailles government was going to place Italy, dominating the central Mediterranean, under the effective control of Monseigneur made the British and Dutch merchants, anxious to maintain the freedom of their trade with the Levant, see red.

Louis XIV, therefore, overflowing with an unaccustomed amiability, orientated the next phase of the negotiations towards a new French renunciation of her Italian illusions, although compensation would be sought for the kingdom in Lorraine, Savoy, Nice, even Luxemburg. In the mind of an old king endowed with good sense, the idea of active defence of the eastern frontiers of the now almost complete hexagon tended more and more to prevail over the Italian fantasies of the past. The Dutch for their part accepted the idea of a possible French expansion in Lorraine, reassuring themselves with the thought that the southern Low Countries, their barrier against French ambitions, would remain in the hands of Spain or in any case would not fall into those of France. The solid frontier protecting the Netherlands' southern flank against the French would remain in place. The Gaul, as they said in Amsterdam, should be a friend but not a neighbour: *amicus Gallus, sed non vicinus.*

The second partition, like the first a master-work of the maturity and wisdom[5] of Louis XIV, qualities not often associated with his name by posterity, was too neat to come to fruition. It was overturned by the

---

[5] On all of this, see Hatton (ed.), *Louis XIV and Europe*, pp. 37–40 (fundamental); François Bluche, *Louis XIV* (Oxford, Blackwell, 1990), p. 514 *et seq.* For the territorial details of these two treaties of partition, see E. Lavisse, *Histoire de France depuis les origines jusqu'à la Révolution* (Paris, Hachette, 1903–14), viii (part I of the third volume of *Louis XIV*), 60–8.

implicit reservations of William III, who was nevertheless a party to it. Having signed a treaty in order to avoid a European war, William was not burning with desire to go to war to impose the enforcement of the said treaty! Yet Spain, as was to be expected, had reservations about the carving up of her vast empire. Would it be proper to impose it on her by force if necessary, the forces including those of William III, if this was liable to lead to unforeseen and 'perverse' consequences?

Most importantly, the Austria of Leopold I was in a state of high exhilaration. She owed her victories over the Turks and reconquests in Hungary to the military talents of Eugene of Savoy, Mazarin's great nephew and one of the greatest strategists of the age, who had passed from French to Imperial service. Austria had no desire to see the former domains of Charles V chopped into pieces and auctioned off like goods from a market stall. In short, she rejected the ingenious partition prepared by Louis and William. Emperor Leopold did not want to cede an inch of territory in Lorraine, the Basque country or *a fortiori* Italy to the French. At the very most, he tried to tempt his Bourbon brother-in-law with a fine piece of Franco-American nonsense: the utopian, not to say ridiculous idea of granting him Mexico and Peru! In short, the French and the maritime powers had wasted a lot of negotiating skill, their plans ruined by Austro-Spanish opposition. The history of the partition treaties serves only to modify somewhat the one-dimensional and bellicose caricature which has shaped our image of the rulers of this era in general and Louis XIV in particular.

When all is said and done, the king of France had convinced himself, after many painful lessons, that the 'freedom to invade' other people's lands, even 'legitimately' in his own eyes, led to disastrous consequences. He had nevertheless made liberal use of this 'freedom to invade', which remained one of the normal attributes of an absolutist style of sovereignty, from 1667 to 1690 and beyond. Taught a lesson by the sufferings of his kingdom, he chose at the end of the seventeenth century to bend his will towards non-aggression. But would this good will on his part be enough to prevail over the irresistible logic of the power politics of the age, incarnated by Austria, by Spain and *in fine* by France herself?

The clever and non-belligerent arrangements fabricated by the Sun-King with the help of William III came to grief unpredictably against the rocks of a fierce upsurge of Spanish nationalism, springing from a kingdom which was much more vigorous than was thought and buoyed by an economic revival in Catalonia and elsewhere. The ailing body of King Charles II diverted attention from the much more healthy state of the kingdom of Spain. The consciousness of Spanish identity or at least that part of public opinion claiming to speak in its name at Madrid, among the grandees, the prelates and the bourgeoisie, even among the people, could not acknowledge or accept the degrading idea of a partition imposed from outside by the other European powers. New directions for the nation were proposed in Castile and elsewhere, for example by the influential Cardinal

Portocarrero: in future Spain should look towards France, with her powerful fleet and army, rather than towards her old Austro-Germanic ally, papist to be sure, but culturally so distant from Iberia, and above all incapable of providing the Spanish empire with the naval support essential for its survival, something which Louis XIV could do.

It must be admitted that Louis did not push home the advantage granted him by the rising tide of francophilia within the Castilian élite and of which he was informed by Harcourt, the shrewd Norman who was his ambassador in Madrid. Harcourt sought to encourage pro-French feelings, while Louis, as his diplomatic correspondence shows, remained faithful to the rationality of the second partition, which was also supported by William III. He was in fact subscribing to a new idea for Europe: collective security, guaranteeing safe recognized frontiers to each state, as for example in the 'barrier' of the southern Low Countries dividing France from the Netherlands by mutual consent. This way of seeing was not the sole property of the Sun-King. It would have served to secure the mutual interests of the great powers within an international system revolving around four poles – France, Austria, Spain and the maritime powers – successor to the French preponderance of the years between 1678 and 1684. In this context and contrary to the black legend created by historiography, Louis for a while at least managed to keep his cool,[6] until that is he learned about Charles II's will. This news, however, pushed him towards new and more dangerous options. Given the attitudes of the times, which were very different from ours, the outcome would almost certainly be war.

In fact, the announcement of the last wishes of the late king of Spain, received and mulled over in Versailles in November 1700, was enough for Louis, showing the customary flexibility of great statesmen, to do an about-turn. He abandoned the agreeable logic of peace at any price and relief for the peoples of Europe, which had inspired his actions for the previous three or four years. Instead, after a serious but hurried debate in his Council on 16 November 1700, he opted for the acceptance of the will and therefore in all probability for conflict.

At first sight the underlying rationale of the king and his councillors seems faultless. It was best to respect the last wishes of a king who had died childless, proposing the replacement of the deceased Habsburg with a young and sturdy Bourbon. Philip of Anjou, son of the Grand Dauphin, would become king of Spain and sovereign of an empire on which, as in the sixteenth century, the sun never set. His dynasty, once established in Madrid, would last (with interruptions, it is true!) until the present day.

Louis was certainly risking war by his acceptance of the will, but the burden would, he thought, be bearable, because he would enjoy the support of his new Spanish ally, now the fervent friend of a totally Catholic and therefore trustworthy France. Of course, if necessary one would have

---

[6]   Hatton (ed.), *Louis XIV and Europe*, pp. 37–40.

Plate 14 Portrait of Philip V, King of Spain In 1700, the painter Hyacinthe Rigaud drew this portrait of Philip V upon the orders of Louis XIV. Philip V was about to depart to take up the Spanish crown and, in this painting, he is dressed in a traditional, somewhat old-fashioned, Spanish style. This was in order to make the most of the 'local colour' and win the hearts of those Spaniards who would see copies of the work. By his piety and his rapid 'naturalization' into his newly adopted country (20 years later he would only be able to speak French with a strong Spanish accent) Philip V would secure for himself and his successors the loyalties of Catholic Castile and its various dependencies.

Versailles, Musée national du château

to fight, but on only one front, though a very long one, against an enemy (at worst Austro-Anglo-Dutch), 'positioned' outside the ancient Roman *limes*, to the east and north-east of the French domain.

On the other hand, to reject the last wishes of Charles II and accept, whether he liked it or not, the installation of a Viennese archduke in Madrid (this was the second possibility proposed in the will, should the French shy away from involvement) would be to allow the hated Habsburg pincers to surround 'Gaul' on the Rhine and in the Pyrenees.

Let us consider this second scenario for a moment; let us suppose that we wish to make the best of things and accept the 'consolation prizes' to be awarded to France in the Basque country, Italy, Lorraine and Savoy, as foreseen in the treaties of partition. In this case, Louis would have had to use armed force in order to gain effective possession of these juicy morsels, for the tribe of Habsburgs, who had never signed the second treaty of partition, would under no circumstances have handed them over willingly. The result would have been war on two fronts, on the Rhine and in the Pyrenees, even in the Alps, as in the days of Francis I, Henry II, Richelieu and the League of Augsburg.

From a strategic point of view, then, the first alternative, that is acceptance of the will followed by war on one front rather than two, seems acceptable. It is understandable that the dominant faction at the court (the Grand Dauphin, Barbezieux, son of Louvois, and then the duchess of Burgundy, Harcourt, the duke du Maine and Chamillart, followed soon by la Maintenon herself and, from the ex-Colbertian group, Torcy) supported the highly 'fortuitous' option of acceptance. On the other side, the Colbertian, Fénelonian and ducal clan, headed by Beauvillier, remained attached to the treaty of partition, showing a prudence and a certain pacifism, now seen by Louis XIV as having been overtaken by events. Finally, within the dominant faction, Chancellor Pontchartrain showed no particular preference for one choice or the other.

As for the processes leading to the outbreak of war, responsibility cannot be attributed, as historians have done too often, solely to Louis XIV and his advisers, who have been blamed for all the misdeeds and troubles of an early eighteenth century which, pacific as it may have been in other ways, engendered both in abundance. The blame should be shared three ways among the great Catholic powers, lined up two against one. Austria had taken the lead by refusing the treaty of partition which may perhaps have permitted a general reconciliation. Spanish attitudes, during the last days of King Charles and amid the first cries of a newly-born modern nationalism, in turn heightened tensions. Spain refused, quite understandably of course and with fierce Castilian pride, to be cut into slices and divided among the family, like Bernardin de Saint-Pierre's melon.[7] All these Bour-

---

[7]   The writer Bernardin de Saint-Pierre (1737–1814), who regarded the world in purely providential terms and thought that God had created the melon with ribs in order that it could be more easily divided up and eaten *en famille*.

bons, Habsburgs, Wittelsbachs, House of Savoy and *tutti quanti* were brothers-in-law, cousins, uncles and nephews one of another: a veritable House of Atreus. Finally, France, for solid if not always good reasons, put an end to hopes for peace, in the sense that, once she was aware of the tenor of Charles II's will, she executed a sharp about-face so as to claim her rights by dynastic inheritance to the late king's enticing offer. Only the maritime powers, despite their hispanophobia and despite the aggressive impulses of the effervescent warmonger into which William III could transform himself if necessary, remained for a while in a pacificatory mood.

Louis XIV thought he could rely on the support of a Spain which he knew to be powerful (he was not wrong about this), but whose immediate capacity for military action he exaggerated. The alliance with Madrid, he thought, would allow him to avoid a war on two fronts. He balanced the profits and losses of the previous few years between 1698 and 1700, which had been devoted to attempts at closer relations with the Protestant powers. But, fully capable of having more than one iron in the fire, he nevertheless returned to what had been since 1672 one of the main pivots of his policy: the revival of Roman Catholic unity (minus Austria) against the 'heretics.' Despite this, he continued the alliance with Lutheran Sweden, which he hoped would pose a certain threat to the backsides of Austria and Denmark, an ally of the Dutch. In effect, the young Swedish king, Charles XII, was beginning his flamboyant and quasi-Napoleonic career in the extreme north of Europe. However, the demographic resources of the Scandinavian kingdom were incapable of providing adequate support for the slightly crazy military genius at their head. Faced with the vast expanses of Russia he would burn brightly, wear himself out, and destroy himself.

In reality, Louis XIV, though he did not yet fully realize it, was now deprived, or as nearly as made no difference, of all his old allies against the Austro-German Empire. The Swedes were held in check by an ever more powerful Russia; the Turks had been humbled by Prince Eugene and were in no condition to get back on their feet quickly. In more general terms, the preponderance of power in Europe had shifted away from the Iberian peninsula and papal Italy, which latter had nevertheless become once more, during the pontificates of Innocent XII (1691–1700) and Clement XI (1700–21), a good friend of the Sun-King.

As the Age of Reason opened, the major poles of influence climbed northwards and eastwards, towards England, Germany and Russia. They had for a while settled on France alone or almost alone between 1661 and 1687, during the brief episode of the 'French preponderance'. To be sure, they did not then desert the kingdom of the Bourbons. But extending their influence further afield around 1700 they favoured more and more an ever expanding and already semi-liberal England and a Germany without fixed boundaries, strengthened by the tacit benevolence of the autocrat of Muscovy. The galaxy of Germany was now revolving around the two strong points of Vienna and Berlin; the Emperor had deliberately flattered the Elector of Brandenburg by reluctantly bestowing upon him the title of King of Prussia. A stimulating gift for the Hohenzollern! The conflict would therefore be dangerous for the French, much less decisive and clear-cut than the aging though not senile ruler of Versailles had envisaged. He had fallen, without much room for manoeuvre, into the net of the dynastic demands that dominated the age. But he had correctly foreseen that the fragile standard of life of his people could not resist the fiscal and other trials that would be inflicted by the coming war.

His decision taken, the Sun-King still displayed a degree of tact in his dealings with the Emperor. For example, Philip V on the advice of his royal grandfather did not enter his new kingdom of Spain until after the two months' delay foreseen in the second treaty of partition. This would have given Leopold time, should he have so wished, to append his signature to the said treaty, a gesture which would have settled everything, but which did not happen. In other respects, however, Louis XIV, the wise and sensible negotiator of the preceding years, metamorphosed, verbally at least (the time of diplomatic negotiations having come and gone) into an epigone of the Cid Campeador. In a letter in November 1703 to Harcourt, who was made into a duke for the occasion and named ambassador extraordinary to Spain, Louis envisaged joint Franco-Spanish campaigns to drive the Moors out of Ceuta, to defend Catholicism, and to bring the Protestant powers in London and Amsterdam down a peg or two. He affirmed and backed up with action the right of French merchants to get involved in trade with the Spanish colonies, including the *asiento*, the monopoly of the transport and sale of slaves in Spanish Latin America.

This was not to the liking of England and the Dutch, who were anxious to safeguard and protect their transatlantic commerce. In 1701 Louis also held out the possibility for Philip V one day to inherit the crown of France should the Dauphin and his eldest son, the duke of Burgundy, both die before him, which seemed highly improbable at the time. There was nothing to suggest, should this eventuality materialize, that Philip would have 'monopolized' the two crowns for himself, but in the suspicious atmosphere of the age the worst hypothesis was always plausible: pessimistic, gallophobic interpretations were current on the banks of the Thames and the shores of the North Sea. Here the apparently imaginary danger of a fusion between the two Bourbon monarchies was taken very seriously. In February 1701, moreover, Louis XIV, leaving nothing to chance, occupied several strongholds in the southern Low Countries, right at the heart of the 'barrier' with the United Provinces. He was acting in the name of his Spanish allies, the legitimate proprietors of the fortresses in question. But he did not expel the garrisons maintained there by the Dutch, nor take them prisoner: the *casus belli* was not unequivocal. In the end, an understandably annoyed William III took the initiative by withdrawing his garrisons and repatriating them to the Netherlands: the Bourbons had lost nothing by playing a waiting game. Finally, in September 1701 James II, former sovereign of England, died in exile at Saint-Germain-en-Laye and Louis XIV recognized his son, James III, as his legitimate successor. The 'Old Pretender' thus wrong-footed William III, whom he pretended nonetheless to recognize as *de facto* monarch of England. All this greatly irritated English opinion. But the immediate context needs to be taken into account in explaining Louis' behaviour. A few days before the death of James II, Austria and the maritime powers ruled by William, in a spirit of hostility towards France (but the times were creating hostility) concluded at The Hague a 'grand alliance' against Louis XIV. Furthermore, war had already broken out in northern Italy. French forces, badly led by Catinat and Villeroy, had been defeated by an Imperial army, with William pulling the strings and urging the Emperor to action. These circumstances help to explain, though not to justify, the cavalier attitude of Louis XIV towards the king of England, using his Stuart puppets at Saint-Germain for the purpose.

Responsibility for the conflict was shared, as is often the case, but the greater part must be attributed to Louis, ensnared as he was by the problems of succession, decisive at this time. But dynastic scheming and complications were not the whole problem: the reference to the *asiento* on both the French and the Anglo-Dutch sides reveals the economic aspects of imperialist rivalries. The existence of the two imperialisms transcends the arguably false problems of initial responsibility for a particular conflict, for the United Kingdom and France would confront each other on land and sea until 1763 and even 1815. It would be futile to try and determine which of the two adversaries 'started the fight', and unreasonable to try and blame France alone.

$$\star \quad \star \quad \star \quad \star \quad \star$$

At the beginning of the war France possessed considerable forces. Her military strength, according to admittably debatable figures, was to reach 400,000 men, 450,000 if the navy is included.[8] Her demographic resources could produce an inexhaustible supply of soldiers. The nation, even 'depopulated' temporarily by the famine of 1709–10, had by 1715 recovered to a population of nearly 23 million souls within its present-day frontiers, rather more than Vauban had calculated.[9] The naval forces were depleted, even if corsairs 'made up the difference' and brought back American treasure and prizes of war to the home country. Military leadership in the early years was mediocre, piling disaster on disaster under the auspices of comic opera generals from the court and the royal family. Villeroy, La Feuillade, Marsin, the duke of Burgundy, Tallard (a good diplomat but a rotten general) and, among France's rare allies, the Elector

---

[8] François Bluche, *Dictionnaire du Grand Siècle* (Paris, Fayard, 1990), p. 105.
[9] Jacques Dupâquier, *Histoire de la population française, de la Renaissance à 1789* (Paris, PUF, 1988), ii, 54 (on Vauban) and 68 (real statistics).

Max Emmanuel of Bavaria 'brought bad luck' to Louis XIV's armies. It needed several years of catastrophe before a process of natural selection through intelligence brought to the fore capable chiefs like Berwick, Orléans, Tessé and Boufflers, and even military geniuses, like Vendôme and Villars, despite Saint-Simon's maliciousness towards him. Between them this pair would redress a miserable situation, in the Low Countries and Spain and at Toulon.

France's enemies for their part relied on the financial and naval power of Great Britain; on the Austrian army, blooded in conflicts with the Turks; and on the emergence of two generals, Marlborough and Eugene of Savoy, who had learnt from French examples and were fascinated by Louis XIV. Both were to build palaces more or less based on Versailles: Blenheim and the Belvedere in Vienna respectively. A Dutch civilian, the pensionary Heinsius, completed a formidable threesome alongside the two military commanders: his great talents could not be confined within the narrow boundaries of the United Provinces.

The early years of the war in 1702–3 were not too bad for France, except that Louis XIV's strategy failed. He had hoped to take Vienna in a pincer movement, with Vendôme coming from northern Italy, while Villars, flanked by the Elector of Bavaria, advanced along the Danube. But constant disagreement between Villars and Max Emmanuel sabotaged the plan. This fiasco had serious consequences: France's few allies weighed up the new situation. Bavaria stayed faithful, while Spain (in theory) gave strategic depth to the south of the kingdom. But the unpredictable Duke of Savoy, Victor Amadeus, who would not be influenced by his mistress, his ministers, or his confessor, was bridling under the French yoke. As father-in-law of Louis XIV's two grandsons (Burgundy and Anjou, now Philip V) he nevertheless felt that he was being bullied by his son-in-law. In October 1703, Victor Amadeus changed sides, not for the first time, and embraced the cause of the Emperor in exchange for some territorial promises. In the same year Portugal, impressed by the performance of the British navy, also dropped the French alliance and signed the Treaty of Methuen with England. Lisbon would sell wine to the English and buy their cloths, all thanks to Brazilian gold, which was starting to flow promisingly and some of which would now find a home in the cellars of the Bank of England. Above all, the allies now had the option of invading Philip V's Spanish domains through the ports of Portugal. The three years between 1704 and 1706 were disastrous for Louis XIV. In August 1704 Marsin, Tallard and Max Emmanuel were crushed at Blenheim by the superlative duo formed by Marlborough and Eugene. As a result it became more difficult than ever for French troops to operate across the Rhine. In the same year the English seized Gibraltar. The Mediterranean was now a 'swan lake' where British ships could sport themselves without running much risk of Franco-Spanish intervention. In 1705 Archduke Charles von Habsburg established himself in Barcelona, supported by the perennial anti-Castilianism of the Catalans. He now called himself 'Charles III' and was a dangerous competitor for Philip V.

The defeat of Villeroy by Marlborough at Ramillies in May 1706 opened up the road to Brabant and Flanders for the allies. In June, 'Charles III' was in Madrid, but not for long. The very Catholic Philip V would soon recapture his capital from the Habsburg, who, though also a papist, had in the eyes of the devout Castilians committed the sin of being supported by English Anglicans, German Lutherans and Dutch Calvinists. In September the crushing defeat inflicted upon the French by Eugene at Turin confirmed that northern Italy, like Flanders, Bavaria and eastern Spain, was now lost for Louis. Faced with this quadruple setback, in the autumn of 1705 Louis XIV made secret overtures of peace to the Dutch, based on the dismemberment of Spanish possessions, but with Philip V retaining the throne of Madrid. From the beginning of the conflict the Sun-King had realized that partition was almost inevitable. Playing different tunes as the situation dictated, Louis therefore had assumed the various roles of herald of peace (in 1698–1700), territorial hostage-taker (in the southern Low Countries in 1701), and semi-pacifist again (from late in 1705). Louis could be as changeable and variable as circumstances dictated, despite his personal steadfast inflexibility.

After the disasters of 1704–6, 1707 provided some respite for France. Charles XII created a diversion in the Austrian rear, even if few took any notice of it. The French and the partisans of Philip V, thrown out of Italy, regained lost ground in Spain. Villars advanced across the Rhine to Stuttgart. An allied raid on Toulon in August was a fiasco. But matters were to become serious and threatening again from 1708 onwards.

The summer of 1708 was marked, as far as the Versailles government was concerned, by the ordeals inflicted on it by the new master of the game, Great Britain (the union of England and Scotland having been proclaimed in 1707).[10] In July and December Marlborough broke through the northern frontier, first at Oudenarde, then at Lille. The French high command was afflicted by the congenital impotence caused by quarrels between its two chiefs, the inept Burgundy and the more competent Vendôme. It should be noted, however, that the extension of French territory northwards, accomplished 40 years previously, limited the damage. In 1636 Spanish troops had penetrated as far as Corbie, well to the south of Lille. The breach of 1708 was less dangerous.

In the Mediterranean, however, the British effectuated their maritime conquests methodically. By grabbing Sardinia and Minorca they acquired an invaluable line of island bases. Only the Spain of Philip V stood up well amid the tribulations of 1708: the Bourbon venture south of the Pyrenees, costly as it was, now seemed, incredibly, to be paying off. But peace and the offerings to be made to the allies were now uppermost in Louis XIV's mind. He had come to accept that the inheritance of his grandson (who had no say in the matter) would have to be diminished, thereby, he hoped, reassuring the Netherlands, England and Austria.

---

[10]   The Scottish Parliament was absorbed in 1707 into the Parliament of Westminster after negotiations and concessions in favour of the individual interests of the Scottish aristocracy.

France hit her lowest point in 1709. At the beginning of that terrible year a harsh winter destroyed the unripened cereal crops, condemning the people to a sparse and inadequate diet. Famine struck, accompanied by a vague feeling of foreboding as the war continued to go badly. In May 1709 the authorities brought forth and paraded the relics of Saint Geneviéve in the presence of the constituent bodies, regular and secular clergy, sovereign courts and Paris municipality. The various 'poles' of religion, sovereignty and justice performed their allotted duties of intercession with Heaven on behalf of the citizenry. In negotiations with the allies, who were in no mood for compromise, Louis XIV, who now wanted to bring the war to an end, was willing to make sweeping concessions. He agreed to hand back or demilitarize Lille, Strasbourg, Dunkirk and Naples. But he drew the line at the inconceivable, that is to evict his grandson from the throne of Spain, using French troops on behalf of the allies. Louis' enemies seemed determined to humiliate the Sun-King as a punishment for the offensive pride of his youth. But they were wasting their time. Circumstances forced them to return to the model of European equilibrium and collective security which the belligerents seemed to have forgotten since 1701. The Treaty of Utrecht in 1713 would express this ideal, but there was still some way to go. In 1709–10 the allies still preferred to believe that Louis XIV was the master of his family and could dispossess his grandson if he wished to do so. They could not bring themselves to admit that Philip V, now more Spanish than French, had been 'naturalized' by his new country. His grandfather would have found it very difficult to take away a crown which the Castilians thought fitted very comfortably on the head of the young king.

Philip had no intention of relinquishing the crown. Nor was Louis prepared to submit to what would have been an unconditional surrender. In June 1709 he appealed through his bishops and provincial administrators to his subjects and soldiers: neither honour nor justice, he said in essence, would allow acceptance of a shameful peace. It was an appeal, such as Richelieu had previously made in 1636, to a spirit of national feeling, the importance of which was now recognized in the large kingdoms of Western Europe: England in 1688, Spain in 1701, France in 1709. What we are dealing with here, when all is said and done, is one of the first clarion calls of the age of the Enlightenment, the century whose enormous nationalistic charge was to explode between 1789 and 1792.

Furthermore, the famine of 1709 was, as it were, double-edged. Its cataclysmic nature in fact helped greatly to increase the numbers of volunteers for the army, eager to sign up and eat soldiers' rations, more reliable than those available to the rural and urban lower classes.

In the summer of 1709 the French defensive strategy began to gain the upper hand, reversing the trend of the preceding years of desperation. From August onwards the enemy was thrown back in French Flanders, Dauphiné and Spain. In September at Malplaquet Villars and Boufflers were officially 'beaten', being forced to retreat a few kilometres. But the admirable performance of their troops and the heavy losses inflicted on the enemy made it a sort of non-defeat. Not losing was a victory in itself. For Louis XIV who, in his correspondence with his generals, helped by Voysin, showed himself to be an open-minded and understanding chief of staff, Malplaquet marked the beginning of a recovery. It would take several years and the help of Villars and Vendôme for this to be brought to fruition. Like Richelieu after Corbie, Louis, with the nation behind him, prepared to seize the initiative. Great powers can be affected by such delays and only show their true potency after some years of gathering force. But while certain historians are full of praise for the cardinal, the friend of the 'heretic' powers, the same writers have severely condemned Louis XIV, the champion of Catholic southern Europe against Anglo-German Protestantism. Leaving aside such religious problems, the national reawakening of 1709–13 is worthy of comparison with the analogous phenomena of 1637–43, 1792–4, etc.

The resurgence continued. In 1710 France once again put more than 300,000 men into the field. In a brilliant campaign culminating in victory at Villaviciosa on 10 December Vendôme expelled the Austro-British forces from Spain, apart from Catalonia. In the autumn of 1711 Duguay-Trouin's flotilla brought back nearly 1,300 kilograms of gold from an attack on Rio de Janeiro: a victory for the French navy, or what was left of it, in cahoots with the private initiatives of the shipowners of St Malo and other corsairs. On several occasions Latin American gold and especially silver would come to the rescue of the finances of Versailles. In this way Philip V rendered his grandfather a great service. In July 1712 (the extremely slow rhythm of military engagements, year in year out, may be seen here), faced with a new and dangerous incursion by Eugene across the northern frontier, Villars, cutting the Austrian general off from his rearguard and his supplies, broke through at Denain. Villars' tactical skill was here combined with information provided by French agents on the spot and with the simple but resolute instructions provided from afar through the use of a courier system by Louis XIV and Voysin.

Finally, the British about-face, retiring from the front and leaving Eugene to his own devices (but with considerable forces), came opportunely to the aid of the Sun-King, a stroke of luck which historians would say he 'did not deserve.' (But is Frederick II considered any less 'Great' just because the death of Tsarina Elizabeth would allow him to re-establish his position?) From this (as in 1636–43, Rocroi after Corbie) sprang new French military successes: betweeen May and November Villars again vanquished Eugene in the Rhineland, the latter having only 60,000 men, while Villars had 130,000, French and mercenaries. In September 1714 the combined forces of Philip V and the French (commanded by Berwick since the death of Vendôme) captured Barcelona and put an end to Catalan aspirations for independence. This is a far cry from the miserabilist wailing about the exhaustion of the 'end of the reign',[11] even if the prosperity of the nation had been hit hard by 14 years of warfare. In fact, with England having retired from the fray, France in alliance with Spain recovered her 'natural' strategic superiority over her continental adversaries.

At the same time the aged Louis XIV in his role as war leader showed once again the capacity evident since his youth (remember the arrests of Retz and Fouquet) of biding his time, waiting for the right moment, and suffering in silence until things got better.

Louis had more than his fair share of personal suffering at this time. He lost his only legitimate son, who died in April 1711, followed by his grandson, the duke of Burgundy and his duchess in February 1712, and his great-grandson, the duke of Brittany, the following month. All that remained was a three-year-old child, the duke of Anjou, the future Louis XV. But while personal and political misfortunes rained down upon the king, other more fortunate political and diplomatic events provided a welcome contrast.

The key, opening the door to all the others, was the victory in 1710 of the Tory party, the pivotal figure in which was Saint John, *alias* Bolingbroke. Their electoral landslide followed the disgrace of the Marlborough clan, who had by degrees lost the ear of Queen Anne. In the preceding period, largely dominated by Marlborough, the anti-French Whigs had been able to make use of the patriotic and fiscal opportunities provided by the English representative system. Parliamentarians had been motivated by an intense nationalism inspired by the anti-papist chauvinism which had been mobilized by the Revolution of 1688. This gallophobic cycle had lasted roughly 20 years, between 1689 and 1709, but was now waning, running out of steam as people grew tired of war and heavy taxation. The conservative forces of landed proprietors and the Anglican church, less militant than Nonconformist Dissent and supported by pamphleteers like Swift, regained influence against the partisans of maritime imperialism in the milieux of finance and commerce. Great Britain would abandon the hardliners of the Netherlands, just as France, diplomatically at least, repudiated fundamentalist Spain. To each his *ultras.*

In September 1711, following secret French missions in England, Versailles and London reached agreement about a series of basic propositions: French recognition of the royal succession in the Protestant line in England; definitive separation of the two Bourbon crowns of France and Spain; creation or maintenance of a solid territorial barrier in the southern Low Countries acting as a buffer between France and the United Prov-

---

[11]   Daniel Dessert (*Argent, pouvoir et société au Grand Siècle* (Paris, Fayard, 1984), p. 182) points out that the War of the League of Augsburg was much more costly for France than the War of Spanish Succession since, in the former, the realm was fighting alone whilst in the latter it had the support of Madrid and the treasure from the Spanish American empire.

inces. It was a case of divide and pacify, separating and perpetuating national, dynastic and religious entities, thereby better guaranteeing collective security. Each man for himself and each for all. In April 1711 the death of Leopold I radically changed the Austro-Spanish situation. The former puppet 'Charles III', the pseudo-king of Spain opposed to the real king, Philip V, became the Emperor Charles VI, now liable, like his distant ancestor Charles V, to pursue an active policy of domination in Europe and the Atlantic if nothing was done to stop him. The English had no interest in the reconstitution of a new continental or even inter-continental hegemony under the Habsburgs when they just spent a decade at war for fear of its establishment by the Bourbons. This attitude on the part of Britain greatly advanced hopes for peace and with them the prospects of a Louis XIV who no longer appeared as an inveterate war-monger.

It was now up to the diplomats to do their job, and foremost among them Torcy, Secretary of State for Foreign Affairs, son of Colbert de Croissy and therefore nephew of the great Colbert himself. In the last years of the reign, with both his mentors (Croissy, Pomponne) and his rivals for power (Monseigneur, Burgundy, Chamillart) in their graves, Torcy became, as near as makes no difference, the king's first minister. He was backed up, as J.C. Rule has shown,[12] by a highly structured and heterogeneous team, in short by a bureaucracy in the modern sense of the word, salaried, tenured, and with its own hierarchy. For ordinary and extraordinary embassies Torcy employed certain great nobles, such as Harcourt and Tallard, prelates, including Polignac, and *robins* like Mesmes, who were often remarkable diplomats in their own right. One can see how inaccurate it is to present the old nobility as being completely excluded from political power at this time: they could at least console themselves with ambassadorships.

Ministerial work properly speaking, at Versailles and Paris, was in the hands of the chief clerks of the department of Foreign Affairs, who were given heavy responsibilities and well paid for it, aided by subordinate clerks and scribes. A dozen 'offices' dealt with the training of young diplomats and correspondence with ambassadors, as well as with old and recent archives, and payments to secret agents. The so-called *cabinet noir*, finally, did not hesitate to open even the letters of la Maintenon.

Always overtly deferential towards the king, Torcy did on occasions conspire with other ministers behind his master's back; on the other hand he was from time to time short-circuited by Louis' own secret initiatives. Torcy had for a long time occupied the middle ground between war-mongers like Monseigneur and pacifists like Burgundy and Beauvillier. Thanks to him, and with the assurance granted by the fact that the military

---

[12]   J.C. Rule, 'Colbert de Torcy, an Emergent Bureaucracy . . .' in Hatton (ed.), *Louis XIV and Europe*, p. 261 *et seq.*

vigour of the kingdom remained intact, peace was within reach in 1713–14. The personal reign of Louis XIV, which had begun with Colbert, ended, not without finesse or sadness, with the honourable career of another chip off the Colbertian block.

★ ★ ★ ★ ★

The so-called Treaties of Utrecht put an end to the War of the Spanish Succession. They extended from the Peace of April 1713 (the Treaty of Utrecht proper) to the treaty of November 1715 which placed the territory of present-day Belgium under the joint control of the Dutch Republic and Austria. Between the two the Peace of Rastadt, signed in May 1714, ended the conflict between Austria and France. It was drawn up in French, possibly a sign of the cultural hegemony of France at a time when the military domination of the continent exercised by the Versailles government had regressed in relative terms. Be that as it may, the Peace of Utrecht created the basis of a European equilibrium which lasted, despite lesser conflicts, for nearly 80 years, and which would only be destroyed by the earthquakes of the revolutionary and Napoleonic wars. A relative pacification, then, but masterly, comparable to the Treaty of Vienna of 1815 which lasted for nearly a century, until 1914. Of the three French negotiators at Utrecht, Polignac was drawn from the higher clergy; Huxelles, representing the great court nobility, showed undeniable diplomatic talents, despite the hostile portrait presented by Saint-Simon; while Mesnager came from the ranks of commerce and the *robe*. This trio of notable diplomats was thus representative of the dominant groups of the French society of the time.

The government which gained most at Utrecht in 1713 was that of London. The Bourbon kings of Versailles and Madrid ceded to Britain various borderlands and gateways to Quebec (Newfoundland, Hudson Bay and Acadia, from where French settlers would make a painful exodus) as well as extensive commercial privileges in Spanish America, and in the Mediterranean, possession of Gibraltar and Minorca. In the north Louis promised to demilitarize Dunkirk and recognized the Protestant Anne as queen of England. The Stuart pretender was expelled from France.

It is worth noting, as far as the New World is concerned, that the potential still existed for the construction of a French America (Canada, Mississippi, Louisiana[13]) skirting the British maritime colonies on their north, west and south. Louis XIV did not abandon his American possessions, as Louis XV was to do in 1763. But it was already difficult

---

[13] On this subject, see Marcel Giraud, *Histoire de la Louisiane française* (Paris, 1959), vol. i (*Le Règne de Louis XIV (1698–1715)*) and Marc Villiers du Terrage, *The Last Years of French Louisiana* (Lafayette, University of South-Western Louisiana, 1982).

for France to remain a great power on two continents and the oceans. This would lead 50 years later, and quite logically, to the French abandoning Canada and concentrating their influence in Europe and the Caribbean. Britain by contrast reaped the benefits of a single worldwide maritime strategy. The balance of forces in 1713, however, was not yet as unfavourable to France as it was to be in 1763. She was still capable of chasing two hares at once, but only at a very high cost. On the European side of the Atlantic, France kept Lille and its surrounding area, which seems quite natural to us today but was less evident at the time. The southern Low Countries passed from Spain to Austria, with the Dutch obtaining the right to guard against any possible threat from France by maintaining garrisons in various towns, including Namur, Tournai and Ypres.

Thanks to the campaigns of Villars, France kept possession of Alsace and Strasbourg, a much disputed city since the French seized it in 1681. Louis was also able to restore his few German allies to power in Cologne and Bavaria. By way of consolation the Emperor received not only the southern Low Countries but also some choice morsels in Italy: Milan, Naples, and bases in Tuscany and Sardinia. These presents made to Austria, whether in Flanders or Milan, proved in the long run to be precarious. On the other hand, Lille and Strasbourg turned out to be solid acqusitions for France, despite the tragic destiny of Alsace between 1871 and 1944. Neither Italy nor Belgium nor Hungary would remain perpetually Imperial, no more than Quebec would remain French, other than in the form of a large linguistic minority. The Viennese régime, its sap rising in 1713, was nevertheless a great tree with fragile roots. The French hexagon, which attained its near-definitive form under Louis XIV, would remain sturdy for three centuries.

By comparison with the large-scale bargaining of which the Habsburgs appeared to be the chief beneficiaries, the bartering between France and Prussia seems of minor significance. The latter received Neuchâtel in Switzerland; the former gained Orange. It is worth noting also that Britain became a power of some consequence in Germany alongside Prussia and Austria. After the death of Queen Anne, the new dynasty in London would control both the British Isles and Hanover, and this until 1837.

In Italy the map was getting simpler. Leaving aside the papacy, whose power, part temporal, part spiritual, was of a unique nature, there were now only two 'poles' of any significance. Firstly Austria, whose precarious acquisitions have already been discussed; and secondly the House of Savoy, which was casting surreptitious eyes over the islands of the Mediterranean (Sicily, and after 1720 Sardinia), and which regained Nice, Savoy properly speaking, and Piedmont. Victor Amadeus was rewarded for the high-stakes game he had played since the turn of the century as father-in-law of the duke of Burgundy and of Philip V, grandsons of Louis

XIV,[14] and as open or underhand adversary of the Sun-King, the grand-father of his sons-in-law.

Spain for her part lost an assortment of peripheral territories in the north and east, in Flanders and Italy. She kept most of the Iberian peninsula and the Indies. Thanks to the French administrators who arrived in the train of Philip V, their Spanish followers and her own élites, she embarked upon a process of modernization. Philip was forced, however, to renounce any possible succession to the throne of France, a renunciation which hurt his pride and which formed one element among others in the humiliation of the Spanish crown. From a dynastic but also a territorial point of view, Madrid had been sacrificed for and by Versailles, just as the Dutch paid the price for British aggrandizement. The larger states advanced without remorse at the expense of their lesser allies. But the renunciation of the French crown by Philip V, following on the deaths of Monseigneur and the dukes of Burgundy and Berry, left only the young duke of Anjou, the future Louis XV, great-grandson of Louis XIV, as heir to the throne of the Sun-King.

In 1714, therefore, Louis felt forced to legitimize Maine and Toulouse, his bastard sons by Madame de Montespan, making them heirs to the throne in the event of Anjou's death. This preferential treatment, which was contrary to the rules of succession in the Capetian line of the French monarchy, aroused a picaresque and pointlessly verbose protest from Saint-Simon. Louis' action has sometimes been seen by historians as a factor in the monarchy's loss of legitimacy, and its disastrous effects would even be felt, we are told, in the revolutionary crisis of 1789, of which it was one of the innumerable 'causes'. This is a highly extravagant judgement! The dynastic legitimization of his illegitimate sons, that is to say their capacity to succeed to the throne as duly recognized princes of the blood, was decreed by a senile king who would be dead within a year. It was quashed by the Regency and by the Parlement of Paris in a *lit de justice* in September 1715, a few days after the death of the Sun-King, in the session which revoked his will.[15] This 'capacity' would never again be seriously invoked during the eighteenth century. Louis XV, unlike his great-grandfather, never considered elevating his natural children, of which there were many, to the position of potential heirs to the throne. In fact, the momentary 'bastard distortion' which affected the French monarchy in 1714 and 1715 may be compared to the equally irregular decrees which after 1688 reserved the throne of England for the

---

[14]   His 'in-law' status resulted from the marriages of the two daughters of Victor Amadeus: Marie-Adélaïde (who would become the celebrated duchess of Burgundy) with the duke of Burgundy in 1696; and Marie-Louise-Gabrielle to his younger brother, the duke d'Anjou, who had already become Philip V of Spain (the wedding nuptials had been celebrated in 1701). As for Charles, duke de Berry (1686–1714), he was, after them, the third son of the Grand Dauphin, *alias* Monseigneur, himself the only legitimate son of Louis XIV.

[15]   Dom H. Leclercq, *Histoire de la Régence pendant la minorité de Louis XV* (Paris, Champion, 1922), vol. i, ch. 4, p. 5, *passim*.

Protestant lines of succession within the royal family. Bastards or Protestants, we are dealing in both cases with the kind of dynastic sleights of hand which helped hereditary monarchies to overcome difficult situations, allowing them subsequently to return to more regular procedures in the case of Versailles, or in England to establish a precedent which gained the force of customary law.

★ ★ ★ ★ ★

All in all, the Treaty of Utrecht and its succeeding agreements were far from being a total defeat for the French régime: the Bourbons were installed in Spain, where they took root and remained until the present day. In western and central Europe a 'tripod' system was erected with France, Britain and Austria (Russia, though formidable, was still remote) as its three legs. And at the same time the less important powers, the Dutch Republic, Prussia, Savoy and Spain (despite losing ground by comparison with the late seventeenth century) continued to play far from meaningless roles.

Could it be argued that Louis XIV's style of absolutism was now threatened by the rise of representative, if not democratic, régimes? In the long-term this was the case, but contemporaries would have needed to be exceptionally far-sighted to realize it. True, in the Netherlands the government owed its legitimacy to an explicit consensus among the peoples of the United Provinces. But the Netherlands were in decline, hit hard by the hostile pressure exerted by France and the desertion of her British ally. In Great Britain the régime created by the Revolution of 1688 was certainly adorned with the embellishments of representative modernity. A certain number of fundamental freedoms, as well as the Parliament, were guaranteed to British subjects. But it should be made clear that the country was still governed by the various factions of the aristocracy and their clienteles of landed gentlemen, the so-called 'landed interest'. Any 'democratic' model capable of being exported to the continent was very limited. In order to discover a form of government which expressly rejected political inequality it is necessary to cross the Atlantic to the distant and as yet insignificant Massachusetts. Here the Reverend Cotton Mather had in 1636 rejected any idea of creating an upper house like the English House of Lords: God, he said, had not decreed that the political or juridical genius of a father, no matter how great a lord he may have been, would *ipso facto* be inherited by his son. Here Calvinist predestination was being deployed to construct an embryonic democracy imbued with a certain egalitarianism.[16]

It is evident that the seeds of the future, fundamental for times to come, but as yet still marginal, were being sown across the Atlantic. In Europe

[16] George Bancroft, *History of the United States from the Discovery of the American Continent* (Boston/London, Little & Brown/Wiley and Putnam, 1839), vol. i, 385.

absolutism was unscathed.[17] This diagnosis of excellent health applied at Versailles, and even at Cambrai, where Fénelon's dreams of emancipation were only applicable to the nobility, and would have left the Third Estate in its state of virtual political non-existence. The same point is valid for Madrid (despite the Cortes), the Vatican, Vienna, Berlin and Moscow, to mention only the major capitals. One could also cite India, China and Japan, all governed by absolute masters unrestrained by a legal state of the kind which operated, in however authoritarian a manner, in France. In short, rule by one person was the norm over vast areas of Eurasia, only slightly constrained by the representation, often meaningless in practice, of the social orders which made up this kingdom or that empire. In practice, all sorts of gravitational counterweights, not always readily visible, in the heart of society provided a counterpoise to autocracy at the top. These formed a sort of centrifugal force resisting a central power whose absolutist pretentions were more dazzling than really omnipotent.

Louis XIV had made peace, and he had done it without being seduced by the siren voices of angelic irenicism issuing from Beauvillier or Fénelon, who for the moment were frustrated. The king had heard but not heeded the crypto-pacifist entreaties of the aged Maintenon.[18] Moreover, the ruling cabal around Louis, including Voysin and Harcourt, who owed their positions to the old lady, had supported the war and now in 1713 could rejoice in peace with honour . . . but also with economic depression and oppressive taxation. The final agreement signed at Utrecht was centred, as always on the French side, around a state-supported Catholicism, but less Gallican than in 1682. Thus the solid but rough-hewn unity between the administration, the church and the nation, which absolutist governments tried to establish, was preserved in France. Louis XIV had given the royal seal of approval once and for all to an episcopal and militant Catholicism.

In the field of foreign policy Louis continued in 1713–14 to adhere to this unabashed Catholicism, which was so difficult a burden for many of his subjects, as a continuation of war by other means, for after Utrecht the country emerged at last from the tunnel of armed conflict which had been the great concern and scourge of the state for nearly eight decades. In confronting the supposed 'dangers' of Anglo-Hollando-German Protestantism, the king used his ambassadors, Bonnac in Madrid and Luc in Vienna, to try and secure a reconciliation with the Habsburgs of Austria. Political reality made this a necessity. George I, the resolutely Protestant

---

[17]   As to this historical legitimacy of the absolutist 'phase' on the European continent, see the convincing schema of Carl Schmitt, according to which : 'L'Etat (au Moyen Age) est d'abord juridictionnel; à l'âge classique, il est caractérisé par la prédominance de l'Exécutif et se fait absolut: il devient libéral et législateur à l'âge parlementaire' – cf. Jacques Julliard, *Chroniques du septième jour* (Paris, Seuil, 1990), p. 321.

[18]   François Bluche, *Louis XIV*, p. 574, reminds us shrewdly that, in this respect, if France had abandoned its ally Spain, it would have been plunged back into full-scale war with, according to Torcy, an enemy army in Guyenne and Languedoc.

offspring of the crypto-papist or even hyper-papist Stuarts, succeeded Queen Anne on the British throne in September 1714. He thus inaugurated the colourful line of Georges which was to last 116 years. Originally George I was Elector of Hanover, and his new and prestigious status as king of Great Britain did not mean that he ignored the considerable domains he still ruled in northern Germany. He incarnated a sort of living link between Anglicanism and continental Lutheranism. Furthermore, George's daughter, Sophie, born of his tempestuous marriage with another Sophie, had married the Elector of Brandenburg, Frederick William, who became king of Prussia as Frederick William I in 1714. The new sovereign of Great Britain thus established further connections with the bastions of the Reformation in the north of the Holy Roman Empire.

Faced with this Anglo-Prussian Protestant bloc, Louis XIV in 1713–15 inaugurated a new period of Cold Peace. He again modified his diplomatic strategy according to circumstances while remaining faithful to his deeply rooted convictions. He therefore considered seriously the idea of an extension of Catholic alliances to form a counterweight to the 'heretical front'. Such alliances were in any case legitimized by the Divine Will, a useful alibi to which Louis referred endlessly. Habsburg Austria was a vital component of any future coalition: the dangers posed by the Habsburgs throughout the sixteenth and seventeenth centuries had been ended by the successful installation of a Bourbon on the throne of Spain. New developments were in the offing, with their own internal, even perverse, and excessively pro-papist logic. In 1661 Louis had inherited the 'line' of Mazarin, according to which France, the only significant Catholic state to behave in this way, allied herself with the Protestant powers against the papist Habsburgs. Then in 1672 Louis assumed the semi-*dévot* inheritance abandoned by Spain and, as it were, brought it to fruition: France became for a while the only (or almost only) Catholic power facing a Protestant Europe which had gained two important Catholic allies in the Habsburgs and then between 1701 and 1713 the lone remaining Habsburg in the form of the Emperor. Now a new and definitive configuration should be created. Louis XIV, if we are to believe his messages to the French ambassadors in Madrid and Vienna,[19] was trying to bring it about: the Emperor would form part of a tripartite Catholic alliance (France, Spain and Austria) which would stand opposed to the protestant trio of Prussia,[20] England and the Dutch. Each side would have its lesser allies, in Italy on the Catholic side, in Germany for the Protestants. One could go no further in rejecting the ideas of Richelieu and Mazarin, even if the latter had been the undisputed mentor of the young Louis. The anti-Protestant and pro-Austrian orientation embraced with a convert's ardour by the aged Louis

---

[19] Jacques Dinfreville, *Louis XIV, les saisons d'un grand règne* (Paris, Albatross, 1977).
[20] On the rapprochement with the Austrians in April 1715 and a certain degree of frostiness in the relationships with Prussia subsequently (after May 1715), see Dinfreville, *Louis XIV* (*in fine*); also Klaus Malettke, 'Les Relations franco-prussiennes sous Frédéric-Guillaume I', *Critica storica*, 25, no. 3 (1988), 508.

XIV was not lacking in empirical justifications: 40 years later in 1756 France would in effect opt for friendship with Vienna and hostility towards Britain and Prussia in, it is true, a new more secularized climate. In the meantime, the logic of Louis XIV's reign was moving in this pro-Austrian direction, except that the old king's death in September 1715 would be followed in 1716 by a reversal of alliances imposed by Orléans and Dubois, the men of the Palais Royal. The Austro-Latin and Catholic alliance briefly dreamed of by the Sun-King would be forgotten. Priority would be given to different liaisons: Protestant, maritime, liberal, capitalist, British, Dutch. From them would come, and not before time, 25 years of peace.

The militant and fervent Catholicism of the old king and his servants was not directed (within practical limits, of course) only against the heretical powers, who were to remain hostile towards or at least suspicious of France for 45 years, and not without good reason. It was equally aggressive towards the Huguenots within France. Between 1685 and 1715, from the Revocation to his death, the behaviour of the master of Versailles in this respect did not change by one iota. The ideology remained constant. No doubt this belligerent attitude was thought to be justified by the need to respond to the agitation in the Cévennes, which was itself stoked up by the understandable bitterness felt by the Calvinists. The illegal assemblies of Huguenots in the south-east of the Massif Central in 1689 had made the mistake of hoping for military intervention by the prince of Orange. The royal army crushed them brutally.

The much more disturbing agitation, at first convulsionary but soon revolutionary, of the Camisards began in 1700–1. In the Cévennes the prophets who led or incarnated the revolt thought, quite sincerely, that their hysterical convulsions would mobilize the numerous sectaries of the mountains of Languedoc. It is remarkable that, faced with the rigorous religious policy of Louis XIV, opponents of various kinds had recourse to mysticism of one kind or another. On the one hand, the groups of Catholic quietists[21] inspired by Fénelon, in reacting against the narrow chauvinist war-mongering which, they thought, was the policy of the faction in power, embraced the effusions of pure love and direct contact with God as inspiration for the affective unity of the human family. On the other side, the apocalyptic visionaries of the Protestant Cévennes saw the skies open as they were seized by the gifts of the Holy Spirit. Faced with these stubborn southerners, the government alternated harsh measures, such as

---

[21] Quietism was the name given to a theory of divine contemplation and pure love, a solvent (up to a point) of the individuality of dogmas and works. A dangerous force for official Catholicism, quietism had already been the object of a certain degree of Vatican repression in the decade of the 1680s, at the period of the Revocation, in the person of the Spanish theologian based in Rome, Michel de Molinos. Madame Guyon and Fénelon sought to raise this flag and in turn attracted the opprobrium of Bossuet and the sovereign pontiff. Fénelon thus stood condemned both by spiritual and temporal authorities in 1699.

the systematic destruction[22] of 31 parishes in 1703 (though without physically harming their inhabitants), with relative restraint. In 1704 the moderate Villars set about obtaining the provisional defection of the rebel
leader, Jean Cavalier.[23] The Camisard conflict was vicious on both sides.
It represents the last manifestation of religious warfare such as France had
suffered in earlier times, between the reigns of Francis II and Louis XIII.
(In Ireland these 'wars of religion' under various forms, would last much
longer.) But in these early years of the eighteenth century the Huguenots
only had their own human resources, peasants and artisan, to rely on, with
no support from the great nobles, or even from the minor nobility, who
had now embraced either Catholicism or *attentisme*. The fighting dragged
on until 1710, gradually dying down in the course of the decade. Another
indication of the final 'pacification', which was of course anything but
idyllic, is to be found in the sending of Protestants to the galleys: 40, 60,
even 100 per year, starting at the Revocation and lasting through the War
of the League of Augsburg and the Camisard conflict.[24] The numbers fell
to almost nothing in 1711 and succeeding years. Was the coercive power
of the government now turned solely against the Jansenists?

These latter, with their unilateral conceptions of grace and faith, were
suspected of smuggling 'the spirit of Protestantism' into the heart of the
ecclesiastical structures of French Catholicism.[25] In 1713 the publication,
at the instigation of Versailles, of the papal bull *Unigenitus* relaunched the
conflict and coincided with renewed harassment in France against the
partisans of Augustinian theories.

Jansenism had a long history. It first took root at the time of Richelieu
within the high culture of the élite of the *robe* and the *basoche*, exemplified
by the prestigious Arnauld family. This culture expressed itself,[26] avoiding
rhetorical excess, in a language of the heart, not of the court, a language in
harmony with the inspiration coming directly from the Holy Spirit. However, the people who wrote or spoke in this manner did not employ the
physical contortions and convulsions later prevalent among the
Camisards. Jansenist convulsionaries would only appear much later,
around 1730.

From 1700 onwards, and especially after 1713, with Jansenism coming
under fire again, the mania of the lay authorities for interfering in ques-

[22]   Claude Devic and J. Vaissette, *Histoire générale de Languedoc*, 13 vols (Toulouse, 1872–
9), xiii, 799.
[23]   Born of a peasant family close by Anduze in the Cévennes, Jean Cavalier was not much
more than 20 years of age at the beginning of the Camisard war. He was one of its principal
leaders – distinguished, moderate, shrewd and eventually ferocious. He ended his life in
Great Britain, first as the governor of Jersey and then living privately in dignified retirement.
[24]   André Zysberg, *Les Galériens, vie et destin de 60,000 forçats sur les galères de France, 1690–
1748* (Paris, Seuil, 1988), graph on p. 104.
[25]   Catherine Maire. The unpublished text was kindly provided by Catherine Maire and has
been published in Pierre Nora (dir.), *Lieux de Mémoire* (Paris, NRF, 1991).
[26]   Marc Fumaroli, *L'Age de l'éloquence: rhétorique et 'Res literaria' de la Renaissance au seuil
de l'époque classique* (Paris/Geneva, Champion/Droz, 1980), p. 625 *et seq.*

tions of religious discipline and faith was at last given free rein. There was much to do! Existentially and chronologically Jansenism was an exact counterpoint to absolutism.[27] It stalked it like a shadow, contradicting it, dating it, leaving its mark on it. The work entitled *Mars gallicus*, written by Bishop Cornelius Jansen (1585–1638), had denounced France's Protestant alliances, the work of Richelieu, as illegitimate and contrary to the interests of Catholicism. The Jansenist idea was thus, paradoxically, pro-Huguenot in its doctrine of grace, anti-Huguenot in its hatred of 'dishonest' compromises. And in any case the Jansenist stand over Protestant alliances was an implicit condemnation of Reason of State, the doctrine which sought the common good by the unavoidable use of evil means or the choice of the lesser evil. In 1640 as in 1710 the adherents of the Augustinian faction were theoretically apolitical. But in the eyes of the Sun-King, hardly objective it must be said, they constituted 'a republican party in the church and the state'. When Louis thought about them he could not help but recall the poor impression imprinted in his mind by the Fronde and the Cardinal de Retz, a great friend of the disciples of Jansen, *alias* Jansenius. These had no compunction about contesting the principles of authority in two ways: the monarch, they said, could, when necessary, take pride in relinquishing the said principles for the good of the church; the latter in turn, in its visible and hierarchical modalities, should normally, if she was faithful to her mission, move into the background in favour of the invisible church, the only true church embodied in Jesus Christ. For the structures of Catholicism could, like Rebecca, be delivered of the best and the worst at the same time, Jacob and Esau, or the great nephews of Saint-Cyran and 'detestable' Jesuitism. In any case, Divine Right, wrongfully appropriated by the Prince, should be returned to its rightful owner, the Holy Trinity. Furthermore, the Jansenists aroused the suspicions of the lay authorities as well as the clergy in so far as, while habitually voicing such 'deviations', they thought of themselves as good Catholics, and even as the best Catholics of all.

They provided enough evidence to prove the soundness of their Roman orthodoxy, a devotion which by its very excess of zeal could only serve to create greater wariness at the centre of the established church of the kingdom. It is true that, like the Huguenots, they placed great stress upon predestination. But unlike their Calvinist enemies and soul mates they emphasized, in best 'papist' manner, the importance of individual merit, the sacraments and the Eucharist. They proclaimed themselves 'the voices of Christ'. The state therefore considered them all the more dangerous, for they were not outsiders, marginalized by the system as the Huguenots were. They were to be found well and truly in the heart of the régime and the bosom of the church and were capable, if given a free hand, of reforming the clergy in their own way, which was certainly not espoused by the king or even by the pope. Already, they were professing to be a

---

[27] What follows owes much to the analyses of Catherine Maire.

community of saints, male and female, for women, the nuns of Port-Royal, had played an exemplary role in the history of Jansenism.[28] The movement had a European dimension: in England as in the Low Countries they attacked papal infallibility and the combined omnipotence of the throne and the altar, both of which they held to be failing in their respective missions.

In France the conflict had been simmering since the 'Peace of the Church'[29] in 1668. This sweeping of problems under the carpet had restored calm among the episcopate and left Louis XIV's hands free for his battle against the Huguenots. With the Protestant hydra trampled underfoot and France's Jewish communities, in Bordeaux and elsewhere, being too small and too useful commercially for there to be any advantage in bullying them any more than usual,[30] the king's final task was to set about the Catholic champions of all-powerful Divine Grace. This may not appear to have been a pressing issue. But Jansenist ideas were gaining ground among both clergy and laity: they adapted very well to the devout individualism cherished by the Catholic Reformation. Lucid observers like Madame de Maintenon were therefore worried by the quiet and pacific advance of Augustinianism.

The nomination of Noailles, a prelate seen initially as an ally of the royal spouse, as archbishop of Paris in 1695 would belatedly spark off the great altercation. This pious nobleman, still blessed with a baptismal or virginal innocence, was a Gallican with a touch of Jansenist rigour. Madame de Maintenon, whose Sulpician soul kept her immune from Augustinian infection, discovered rather late in the day that her protégé was not the man she had thought he was: the old goose of Saint-Cyr had hatched the swan of Paris, and lived to regret it. Made a cardinal in 1700, Noailles was thus stationed in Paris, at the spiritual and temporal heart of the kingdom, and through his noble family possessed powerful connections at the court. With Bossuet dead in 1704, Noailles, dignified with his cardinal's red hat, personified the Gallican tradition itself going over to the opposition. What a contrast with 1682, when Louis, at the height of his power and prestige,

---

[28] Jacqueline Angélique Arnauld (1591–1661), known as *mère* Angélique, had been, in the reign of Henry IV and the young Louis XIII, the reformer of the convent at Port-Royal, which then turned towards Jansenism under the influence of this extraordinary woman. The cluster of women who became prominent *frondeuses* and *Précieuses* owed a good deal to *mère* Angélique whose nuns would, in the course of the following generations, provide courageous examples of resistance to absolute authority.

[29] The 'Peace of the Church' was established by various statements from September 1668 to January 1669 emanating from the Jansenist doctors and bishops (such as Pavillon from Alet), from the crown and from the pope. They stopped the quarrel between the official Catholic church and the active Jansenist minority. Cf. Bluche, *Louis XIV*, p. 215 *et seq.* Bluche is rightly less severe than Lavisse (*Histoire de France*, viii (part II-2), 6 *et seq.*) on the conditions under which this peace was arrived at.

[30] There were, however, some inclinations towards the forced conversion of Jews (which were quickly abandoned shortly after the Revocation). See, on this subject, my contribution to a colloquy at the Goethe Institute in Paris on Racism in March 1991.

had been able (at a price) to line up the adherents of patriotic Catholicism (the term 'national Catholicism' would be incongruous) under the banners of his Huguenot-baiting and converting legions! In 1711–15 the situation had changed radically: the monarchy was no longer the ally but now the adversary of the very opposition-minded Noailles, who controlled the clergy of Paris and whose position was strengthened by the complicity of a section of the French aristocracy.

One sector of the élites, then, was swinging over into a kind of opposition, actual or existential, though not intentional. In these same years (1715 in particular), pastor Antoine Court[31] was replanting Protestantism in Languedoc, while eliminating the convulsionary frivolities of 1689 or 1703. As a result the future looked bright for the Augustinian coalition, with its dual Calvinist and Jansenist, Huguenot and Catholic roots, despite harassment from the crown and its own internal divisions. The monarchy could not hide the fact that, for all its provocative gesticulating, its attitude vis-à-vis these rising forces was essentially defensive. The aged Louis seemed to have his back against the wall. The Jansenist camarilla would become one of the gravediggers of the system: in the long term it would be among the undertakers wielding pickaxes and spades at the funeral of absolutism.

In whom could Louis, faced with mounting opposition in the church and among the laity, place his trust? He had (and his friends in and around the government could count on) the support, whether silent or vocal, of a significant proportion of the clergy, the Catholic people, the nation. Also favourable were the Society of Jesus in the person of Tellier, the king's confessor, and almost the whole of the court at Versailles, now purged (in theory) of its heterodox elements. Fervent anti-Jansenism created strange bedfellows. Fénelon, a determined oppositionist since the last years of the seventeenth century, could easily be confined, exiled and disgraced, in his diocese of Cambrai. Nevertheless, in this new conjuncture, he flew to the aid of his sovereign, such was his abhorrence of Port-Royal. The Jansenist episode provided an opportunity for the deeply wounded Fénelon to exact posthumous revenge on the Augustinianizing Bossuet, who had humiliated him during the quietist affair. Behind him marched the whole 'Burgundian' coterie, the duke of Burgundy, the inevitable Beauvillier, and others. Fénelon also wished to present himself as a friend of the Jesuits; he desired to re-establish good relations with Rome, which had not treated him well. In any case, his benevolent theory of Pure Love made him a preordained opponent of the hardline partisans of God's Grace.

---

[31] Antoine Court (1696–1760), born in the Vivarais, sought to purge the Protestant churches of Languedoc and Dauphiné from the tendency to convulsionary hysteria from 1715 onwards. He succeeded above all in 're-planting' those churches in conditions of secrecy or semi-secrecy. Royal authority was heavily against them but maintained discreet contacts on occasions with the individual of the first importance, particularly under the Regency, contacts which signified a double degree of moderation – both that of Philippe d'Orléans and that of Antoine Court himself.

Was Louis XIV making excessive concessions to the Jesuits and the Vatican? The fact is that his patriotic image was tarnished by all this, notably in the eyes of the Parlement of Paris which, for the first time in decades, dared in 1714–15 to display a degree of resistance, spurred on by the *procureur général* Henri-François Daguesseau,[32] over the question of *Unigenitus*.[33] Louis' career as sovereign had been based on a direct identification between his person, the state and the nation, and on a direct relationship between God and the king, short-circuiting the pontiff of Rome. The new Jansenist affair could have invalidated the meaning of his whole political life. Between 1700 and 1715 the pope could thus stick his oar into this confrontation among French Catholics, and it was just too bad if Gallican pride was hurt, with the complicity of the king, by Vatican interference. It was enough to make Bossuet turn in his grave.

Against the Augustinophobic 'party' of pontifical and royal conformism were ranged Archbishop Noailles of course, flanked in the wings by certain members of the ruling clique, and not the least among them Chancellor Pontchartrain and Torcy. With them were a large part of the religious orders, whether contemplative, scholarly, mendicant, *rentiers* or teaching (in other words Benedictines, Dominicans, Oratorians). All were united by a visceral anti-Jesuitism: whatever the colour of their frocks, all these monks were jealous of the competition, blessed with success, provided by the followers of Ignatius Loyola. Among the other enemies of the Society of Jesus may be counted the *curés* of Paris and other large cities, dragging along in their wake large numbers of their flocks, all seduced by the glow of austerity and purity emitted by the pious pastors of the Augustinian parishes. That is to say that a good part of the urban bourgeoisie and the petty bourgeoisie in the throws of acculturation was highly receptive to the behaviour as well as the ideas of a party supported by 15 or so bishops and a hundred or so doctors of theology. The towns, whether episcopal or not, were often receptive to Jansenism, and the future would belong to them, demographically and otherwise, during the eighteenth century. The parlements, which had done so much to combat Protestantism, would on the contrary favour Augustinianism with their support. So two of the 'natural' allies used by Louis XIV in the fight against the 'heretics' now passed to the camp of the enemies of the government: the Gallicans in general and the *parlementaires* in particular.

During the twentieth century we have become accustomed to seeing Catholic churches (for example in Ireland, Lithuania, Poland) serve as rallying points for popular opposition to unpopular governments. The situation in France in 1714 could not be compared to these, but the invisible church of Jansenism nevertheless provided a focal point for a broad section of an opposition in search of its soul and defining itself by

---

[32] His family name was, in fact, Daguesseau, one word. A subsequent license accorded him the particle transforming his name eventually into 'D'Aguesseau'.

[33] Saint-Simon, *Mémoires*, ed. A. de Boislisle, 45 vols (Paris, 1879–1930), xxvi, 249.

trial and error, an opposition supported notably, it is worth repeating, by a large number of Jansenist priests, whose rise is in close correlation with the recent spread of seminaries.

Skirmishes began in Paris in 1696, that is to say barely a year after the nomination of Noailles, which in turn coincided with the first reawakenings of an old conflict, a reopening of old rifts. At first Noailles succeeded, with the help of Bossuet, in evading the criticisms levelled against him by the Fénelonians and the Jesuits. For the new archbishop was sympathetic towards the works of Jansenist theorists, in particular the *Réflexions morales* of *père* Quesnel.

The affair sprang to life again with the 'matter of conscience' in 1701–5. Could confessors grant absolution to penitents who claimed to observe a 'respectful silence' about heterodox propositions concerning the real presence supposedly found in a work by Jansenius, a silence equivalent in reality to nagging doubts directed against the Catholic hierarchy? This may seem like hairsplitting, a storm in a font. In fact, however, the sacrament of penitence, much more so than it is today, was one of the cornerstones of eighteenth-century religious practice and religious culture, even among the lower classes. It is easy to understand how it became a question of vital importance in the religious polemics of the time, even if swiftly overtaken by the violence of the resultant debates. With one thing leading to another, the battle of words gradually ascended, with the active complicity of Louis XIV, a part of the episcopate and the king of Spain, to implicate the formidable Pope Clement XI. Clerical 'bi-Bourbonism' had to serve some purpose! Mountains fell to the ground simultaneously: the Alps which protected France from Roman ultramontanism, and the Pyrenees which had rendered possible the many nuances separating Iberian and French Catholicism. The pontiff was given the opportunity, after due reflection, to set about not only Jansenism but also the Gallican pretentions which Louis XIV, less arrogant than he had once been, was now prepared to abandon in part, even if he was thereby unconsciously undermining his own national legitimacy. So in 1705 Clement issued the bull *Vineam Domini*, challenging 'respectful silence' in the matter of conscience: this pontifical text demanded from both confessor and penitent a renunciation in due written form of anything which referred, however remotely, to the work or person of Jansenius. Jansenists were now treated or mistreated as if they were Huguenots. It was almost a second Revocation, 20 years after the first, and with perhaps more impact because it affected the Catholic people, identified at the time with the people of France.

The next step was the destruction of the still-Jansenist convent of Port-Royal des Champs. A handful of heroic and obstinate old nuns remained in what was now virtually a *lieu de mémoire*, not yet recognized as such, but nevertheless the site of a revival of persecution, thereby sowing the seeds of a revived Augustinianism destined to flourish anew. The convent fell victim to an attack led by a peculiarly mismatched trio. Fénelon took the opportunity to be over-zealous in making up for the pacifistic and intelligently anti-establishment attitude he had recently been exhibiting towards the government. The Jesuit Tellier, who became the king's confessor in 1709, was distinctly more harsh than his predecessor, La Chaize: he opened a new chapter in the deplorable history of persecution against the 'sect'. Finally Archbishop Noailles thought it best to cut his losses. He thought that by abandoning the most fanatical of his flock to their sad fate he could preserve the essence of good Augustinian pastoral practice, which was for him in complete harmony with the canons of the true church as he conceived it. The most astonishing aspect of the affair is that the expulsion of the sisters of Port-Royal in October 1709 coincided with the war and famine of one of the worst years of the reign, coming as it did a few months after Malplaquet and before the great frosts of the winter of 1709–10. Louis thus showed that he had lost none of his bite, which he sometimes demonstrated in a most unfortunate manner. The physical destruction of Port-Royal and especially the repugnant exhumation of corpses from the cemetery of the abbey, itself also earmarked for suppression in 1711, constitutes from this point of view a strangely premonitory episode. Eighty-two years later in 1793 the more or less embalmed bodies of the Valois and Bourbon kings, including that of Louis XIV, would in their turn be torn out of the necropolis of Saint-Denis and 'profaned' in a piece of macabre tomfoolery intended to purify the national soil of the relics of the monarchy.[34] The nuns, if they could have seen this from beyond the grave, would no doubt have seen it as a divine Punishment and savoured their revenge.

After the Revocation came the galleys. After *Vineam Domini* came *Unigenitus* in 1713. Was history repeating itself or merely stuttering? Noailles, despite his recent compromise over the first of these texts, had refused, even when urged by the duke of Burgundy, to take energetic action against Quesnel. On the other hand and without worrying about offending the king, the same Noailles banned the Jesuit confessors of his diocese. Louis, his back to the wall, decided to counter-attack and at the same time to raise the stakes. In November 1711 he asked Clement XI to denounce Quesnel[35] and by implication Noailles: in order to please the pope the king disposed of the cast-offs of Gallicanism. The challenges launched by France to the Vatican during the 'affair of the Corsicans'[36] in 1662–4 or the conflicts over the *régale* were now long forgotten. The

[34] Alain Boureau, *Le Simple Corps du roi; l'impossible sacralité des souverains français* (Paris, Editions de Paris, 1988), p. 7 *et seq.* (procès-verbaux des exhumations de Saint-Denis); compare Louis-Ange Pitou, *Voyage forcé chez les anthrophages* (Paris, Sylvie Messinger, 1989), p. 30.

[35] The Oratorian Pasquier Quesnel (1634–1719) was one of the most important theoreticians and leaders of the Jansenists. His *Réflexions morales*, condemned by Clement XI, put the cat among the pigeons.

[36] In August 1662, a quarrel between some drunken Frenchmen and the Corsican guards of the pope produced a rather artificial incident between France and the Holy See. Pope Alexander VI had to despatch his apologies to Fontainebleau through the cardinal-nephew Chigi. But it should be noted that Louis XIV subsequently restored to the Vatican the Comtat Venaissin (pontifical land) that he had unilaterally annexed in 1663.

monarchy of France no longer issued ultimatums, it asked politely. It was prepared to grovel at the feet of His Holiness in order to persuade the said Holiness to 'do something'.

So in September 1713 Clement XI, in the bull *Unigenitus*, condemned Quesnel's *Réflexions morales*. Through the condemnation of this book an entire church, informal but alive and active, felt itself under attack. *Unigenitus* denounced precisely those aspects of Quesnel's work which they considered praiseworthy: the fact of having translated into French and diffused through the teaching of an ever more dynamic clergy both the New and Old Testaments, books of hours and offices, missels, breviaries. The pro-Jesuit and pro-Sulpician faction of the episcopate, dear to the heart of Madame de Maintenon, thus alienated the avant-garde of the laity and the militant lower clergy, the champions of the use of the French language in the liturgy.

As an indirect consequence, the parlements rediscovered the Gallican enthusiasm which they had lost since the Fronde. Following the example shown by a certain number of prelates, they would not accept this powerful new offensive by the 'Vaticano-monarchists'. So, in the last year of his life, Louis XIV, supported by the pope, found a second front of emnity, composed of *parlementaires* and others, opening up against his policy. So had the days of the Fronde returned? The sequence of decisions since the elevation of Archbishop Noailles (misguidedly chosen by la Maintenon) tended to isolate the crown from many of its natural supporters among those who were supposed to make up the two principal 'estates' of the nation and the monarchy. The Colbertian reformation of the nobility from 1668 onwards had duly registered the members of the second estate.[37] The building of the château of Versailles had imprisoned the most distinguished members of the aristocracy in a gilded cage. The Revocation in turn had transformed the official clergy into the accomplices of a totally Catholic state. *Unigenitus*, coming at the end of this road, cut into the very flesh of the church; yesterday the little band of Fénelonians, now (1714) the Augustinian proletariat (endowed, unlike the Huguenots, with powerful leaders, for Noailles was a grand seigneur) were being pushed towards rebellion, even schism, nobility and clergy alike. It is true that the crown could claim that all these measures had been taken in the cause of national integration. The domestication of the great nobility had contributed to the establishment of civil peace. In 1685 the church too had been tied to the wheels of the chariot of state. Now Louis XIV had real motives for combatting the austerity of the Jansenists. For they made great demands on their flocks, frightening them with the prospect of an almost impossible salvation: the Augustinian clerics contributed to the rejection by certain Catholics of a religion which had become too demanding. This was enough to arouse irritation against the sect among more rational and laxist

---

[37] Jean Meyer, *La Noblesse bretonne au XVIIe siècle* (2 vols, Paris, SEVPEN, 1966), i, ch. 2.

theologians, those who advocated indulgence towards sins, as recommended in the eighteenth century by Saint Alphonse de Liguori. The monarchy was not only irritated but suspicious: in the eyes of the secular power it was more than ever a question of right doctrine and the good Christian cause. But even taking into account the crown's various justifications and motives, the fact remains that certain segments of the ruling élites, clerical (the majority of the episcopate) and noble (the aristocracy), either became the puppets of the government or compromised themselves excessively with it, thus cutting themselves off from the most vital elements in the life of the nation and with them from other sections, the most liberal and most activist, of the nobility and the clergy. All this was the bitter fruit of the experience of a child king: Louis XIV still retained bad memories of a Fronde which had given a free hand to the machinations of the great nobility; he had also suspected them of harbouring republican and Jansenizing Augustinian sentiments.[38] From this Louis drew a number of conclusions, often excessive, which remained with him for the rest of his life. And the consequences of his choices, too clear-cut and hasty, would weigh heavily during the eight decades following his death. Absolutism had given new life to the Ancien Régime, but at the risk of precipitating its downfall. In the long term it acted as pallbearer at its own funeral, such as it would be performed towards the end of the eighteenth century.[39] In the medium term, however, *Unigenitus* fits neatly into the overall strategy of Louis's final 15 years – affiliation with the Vatican and a close family alliance with a Spain whose Catholicism was much more baroque and Jesuitical than Augustinian. French Jansenists were given no choice but to behave themselves.

★　★　★　★　★

Cold war against the Jansenist theologians; hot war against the Protestants, whether inside the kingdom or abroad, foreign governments or native Huguenots: this double-edged policy had mixed results. After many ups and downs, it culminated in the establishment of a good defensive situation for France and even in excellent arrangements on her frontiers, but it also sowed the seeds of discord between French Christians. In any case, renewed warfare once again placed a heavy material burden on the nation. The *dépenses engagées* of the monarchy were at their highest during the War

---

[38]　The struggle against Protestantism welded the Gallican church to the régime as well as the anti-Huguenot but Gallicano-Jansenist parlements. The anti-Jansenist sturggle following *Unigenitus* (1713) cut off the monarchy from the Gallicans and the Augustinians in the church as well as the sovereign courts and elsewhere. In this respect, it would enfeeble and isolate the monarchy in the eighteenth century to a much greater degree than the Revocation, even if the latter is viewed in the longer-term perspective of the years from 1685 to 1785, to the eve of the first official emancipation of the reformed churches.

[39]　See, within a completely different context, the interesting reflections on a comparable point of Alain Brossat, *Le Stalinisme entre histoire et mémoire* (Paris, Ed. de l'Aube, 1991), p. 18.

of the Spanish Succession: the equivalent of 1,600 tonnes[40] of silver per
year, as opposed to 1,300 tonnes at the time of the League of Augsburg,
which shows, incidentally, that, despite the black legend, the kingdom had
not been impoverished in the interim. The net revenues of the state from
taxation failed to keep pace with this excessive expenditure. In the worst of
times, 1709, year of the great winter and of great battles, the deficit even
briefly exceeded the equivalent of 1,000 tonnes of silver. A new tax, the
dixième, was therefore created in 1710, to be imposed in theory on all
revenues, noble and non-noble, or merely privileged. War threatened to
bear down heavily on the most diverse social groups, though the degree of
levelling involved, 'the scythe of equality', should not be exaggerated.
Despite the comical fury of Saint-Simon,[41] deploring the fiscal inquisition
carried out in the name of the *dixième* and the 'combustion of families by
this [inquisitorial] lamp shone into their most private parts', the revenues
of the new tax arrived reasonably well. It even convinced England and
certain of her allies that it was time to make peace, since the kingdom of
France was capable of recovering financially to a considerable degree. The
government resorted also to 'cash notes', moderate devaluations, sale of
offices, and loans. The financier Samuel Bernard, on his own account and
along with other lenders, furnished 36 million *livres* to the royal treasury,
that is about twice the annual revenue of the brand new *dixième*, and this
at the very moment in 1709 when this celebrated businessman was himself
about to go temporarily bankrupt. But with Samuel Bernard momentarily
exhausted, the fund presided over by the banker Legendre and supported
from 1710 onwards by the *receveurs généraux*, played, *faute de mieux*, the
role of state bank. A bank in a desperate plight, it is true, but which
nevertheless brought in more than 400 million *livres*[42] to the coffers of the
state between 1711 and 1714, that is several times the annual receipts from
taxation. It is true that Louis and his successor would have one day to pay
back these loans, but with peace re-established this would eventually be
accomplished thanks to John Law's banknotes. The Huguenot bankers of
Geneva and even of Amsterdam, via Legendre, Bernard and so forth, thus
contributed greatly by their loans to the financing of a war effort directed
in theory against international Protestantism. Were the Protestants of
Geneva thereby selling the rope intended to hang them? In fact we should
ask who was fooling whom. Was it the French state, using Calvinist money
to face up to the heretical coalition, or the Genevan financiers, who would
one day be reimbursed at the expense of French tax-payers, especially the
country dwellers, for their money advanced to the Sun-King during the
War of the Spanish Succession?

[40]   Alain Guéry, 'Les Finances de la monarchie française sous l'Ancien Régime', *Annales
ESC* (1978), p. 227.
[41]   Saint-Simon, *Mémoires*, xx, 167.
[42]   F. Braudel and E. Labrousse (dirs), *Histoire économique et sociale de la France*, ii, 274
(contribution of Paul Harsin: 'La finance et l'Etat jusqu'au système de Law').

The nation itself was also reduced to expedients. The heavy weight of taxation drained the resources of individuals or at least of a great number of them. The climatic rigour of a bad year did the rest. The situation of the impoverished peasantry went from bad to worse. In January and February 1709 the famous exceptionally harsh winter destroyed a great part of wheat crops in the ground, on the blade or unripe. It is true that the yields of spring barley, sewn after the great frosts, turned out to be high, profiting from the deaths of weeds and field mice, killed by the cold. But this was a meagre consolation.

Deaths from hunger and especially from opportunist diseases, linked to general impoverishment, were numerous in 1709 and even more in 1710, the second year of dearth, as a result of the bad harvests of the previous year. The Rouergat, Pierre Prion, who bizarrely wrote in the future tense, recounted in his memoirs written under Louis XV:

that he shall see the misery and popular mortality of 1709 when he shall see a great part of the inhabitants [of the village in the Aveyron where he lived] perish through the scourge of poverty. Monsieur the abbot [the churchman who lodged and employed Prion] will every day for four months maintain a great cauldron on the fire to make a gruel with unsieved oat flour to be distributed as charity to the hundreds of poor people dying of hunger who will gather at his door. Families from outside the district will be found dead on the roads and in the stables. Prion will help to carry them on stretchers to be buried in the cemetery, where three at once will be placed in the same grave, all clothed in their miserable rags, as they will be found, and among them old people and young children still with the grass they were eating in their mouths. Although there is nothing more hideous than death, their faces will be seen as like those of angels, which will show that they are true saints, destined for Paradise.[43]

The harvest year 1709–10 was calamitous. Yet the extent of these difficulties should not be exaggerated. Pierre Prion's home village, for example, did not emerge truly depopulated: the annual number of deaths 'merely' tripled or quadrupled, which was serious enough! Overall, however, the catastrophe was less emphatic than in 1693–4, when a totally isolated France was fighting against the whole of Europe, Spain included. The momentary fall in population following 1709 generally speaking spared the coastal regions of the hexagon and also the western regions of the Paris basin, which were better provided for in cereals than the rest of the country.[44] The government, at great expense, imported convoys of grain from the eastern and southern Mediterranean.[45] In 1715 the popu-

---

[43] E. Le Roy Ladurie and Orest Ranum (ed.), *Pierre Prion, scribe* (Paris, Gallimard, coll. 'Archives', 1985), pp. 43 and 153 (the second reference being less 'true to life' than the first).

[44] Following Jes Dupâquier, *Histoire de la population française*, ii, 210; François Lebrun, 'Les crises démographiques en France aux XVIIe et XVIIIe siècles', Annales ESC (March–April 1980), pp. 220–1.

[45] Bluche, *Louis XIV*, p. 535.

lation of France, despite the contagious diseases endemic since 1706,[46] with its 22 or 23 million inhabitants (within its present-day frontiers) was as high as at any previous period.[47] It was even perhaps slightly higher than in the decade 1700–10. The kingdom was demographically vigorous, which itself made possible the resistance shown by Louis XIV's armies, by the simple force of numbers (as well as courage and skill) at Malplaquet or Denain. Louis therefore, like Frederick the Great in 1762, could obtain honourable and even favourable conditions at the Treaty of Utrecht.[48] The impact of the winter of 1709 on the memory of the people was so great as to be misleading. It should not be allowed to distort the reality. Great trees killed by the cold should not be allowed to hide a still-flourishing forest.

It is nevertheless true that the state of the economy was often pitiful. In many of the provinces of France (leaving aside the more sheltered Paris region) agricultural revenues, calculated in supposedly constant prices, thanks to the figures provided by tithes and rents, were declining.[49] This decline was of about a quarter, even a third by the end of the reign, by comparison with the relatively prosperous era of Colbert, the fat years between 1662 and 1683 and even for a short while afterwards. An unavoidable degeneration perhaps. One could not have at one's disposition simultaneously grain, wine and butter or money to pay for grain, wine and butter – and guns.

Other evidence points to an extensive agricultural (and in consequence urban) malaise in the final years of Louis XIV's reign. Consumption of salt, for example, calculated from tax records, may be measured for the northern and central regions of the kingdom in a continuous series from Henry IV to Louis XVI. The figures, stagnant or largely unchanging during the seventeenth century, would rise buoyantly after 1715. Before this, however, they had plunged to a historic low around 1710. Fraud by 'faux sauniers' had some effect here,[50] but more important were the self-imposed restrictions upon consumers, which hit purchases hard. In a conjuncture of real misery, less salt and other food-stuffs were bought. The abandoning of marginal land provides another source of solid evidence.[51] For various reasons this became common after 1700–5, for taxa-

---

[46] Lebrun, 'Les crises démographiques en France'.

[47] Dupâquier, *Histoire de la population française*, p. 68.

[48] The recovery of Prussia under Frederick II after 1762 is as remarkable after its fashion as that of Louis XIV's France after the end of the War of Spanish Succession. But the historiography is more gentle towards Frederick, the Enlightenment king, than to Louis, arbitrarily identified with a retrograde and bigoted obscurantism.

[49] E. Le Roy Ladurie and J. Field-Récurat, 'Sur les fluctuations . . .', *Revue du Nord*, 65 (1972), p. 364 *et seq.*; and *Prestations pay sannes, dîmes, rentes foncières et mouvement de la production agricole à l'époque préindustrielle* (EHESS, Paris, Mouton, 1982, 2 vols), ii, *passim*.

[50] Zysberg, *Les Galériens*, p. 92.

[51] Le Roy Ladurie, *Les Paysans de Languedoc*, 2 vols (Paris, Mouton, 1966), i, 357 and ii, 766.

tion was too heavy; ruined farmers lacked oxen and horses for ploughing and fertilizer; the markets for agrarian products shrank; the demographic pressure exerted in normal times on all possible available land tended to fall, the 'excess' population having decamped to the army, begging, the towns, America or the cemetery. In the 1710s the public authorities, worried by the desertion of the land, carried out large-scale enquiries and tried with meagre resources to encourage potential farmers to start recultivating recently abandoned holdings.

But as with demography a totally black picture should not be drawn of the economy. Farmers were ruined in Languedoc and the Massif Central, but around Paris they survived quite comfortably. In the great trading cities engaged in international commerce the call of the sea made itself heard. In Nîmes and especially Lyon, as we have seen, the silk industry developed and even prospered. Bordeaux benefited from the dazzling expansion of sugar production in Santo Domingo, the western portion of Haiti gained by France at the Treaty of Rijswijk in 1697. By 1714 it was already producing 7,000 tonnes of sugar.[52] Thus this faraway island provided the western façade of the hexagon, at Bordeaux as at Nantes, with the basis for outstanding expansion. We have also already mentioned the Colbertian and especially post-Colbertian rise of cloth exports from Languedoc in the direction of the Levant. This was a symptom among others of the prosperity of sectors of French textile manufacture, at least those orientated towards export, at this time. So between 1688 and 1699 the *généralité* of Montpellier exported an average of 7,684 pieces of 'Occitan' cloth per year through Marseille towards the East. From 1700 to 1710 this rose to 11,406 per year. From 1711 to 1714, in the years customarily depicted as depressed, the statistics show 28,610 pieces,[53] almost four times as many as at the end of the seventeenth century.[54] The economic history of this period full of contradictions between 1700 and 1715 remains to be written. But we know enough to be able to affirm that the sordid picture drawn in all good faith by Fénelon, Vauban, Saint-Simon and several others only showed one aspect, though the predominant one, of the situation.

In a variety of ports and towns and in key and forward-looking industries the forces of renewal were at work, somewhat modifying the traditional schema. All they asked was to be able to reorient the country as a whole towards a period of growth; once that occurred, light would at last counter-balance gloom, and the evidence for such growth emerges after 1715/1720. The historian Ernest Labrousse wrote of misery under Louis XIV, prosperity under Louis XV, an accurate enough assessment in cer-

---

[52] Following Paul Butel in C. Higounet (dir.), *L'Histoire de Bordeaux* (Toulouse, Privat, 1980), p. 160.

[53] Compare this with the figures cited in chapter 5 above.

[54] J.K.J. Thomson, *Clermont de Lodève, 1633–1789* (Cambridge, Cambridge University Press, 1982), p. 228.

tain respects. But it is also true that Louis XIV in the last 15 years of his reign, as in the previous decades, laid the bases, or at least his régime contributed towards laying the foundations of the national vitality which would be deployed in spectacular fashion from the regency of Philippe d'Orléans through to the epoch of Maupeou, Terray, Turgot and Necker.

★　★　★　★　★

The imposing, omnipresent personality of Louis XIV; the length of his reign, comparable to that of Queen Victoria; the enormous influence of the kingdom between 1661 and 1715, when one European in four or five was French: such facts have turned historical debate about the Sun-King, which has now been going on for three centuries, into a private battlefield with, on occasions, no holds barred and in which the winning and most convincing side still cannot be acclaimed with certainty, despite the impartiality of judges disposed in theory to decide the outcome. This is even more true in that since the beginning, and well before Pierre Goubert published his *Louis XIV and Twenty Million Frenchmen* in 1966, any favourable or negative judgement of the illustrious monarch could not be made without looking at his multitudinous subjects, whether the élites or the masses.

Even at the time two schools of thought contended. Bossuet, Molière, Racine and La Bruyère approved of everything and anything accomplished by their master. In praising the person of the king to the skies they lumped together achievements worthy of admiration (the flourishing of the arts, administrative progress, a reasonable extension of national territory) and other highly debatable actions: La Bruyère, at the cost of violating his own principles, celebrated the Revocation in the most sycophantic terms.[55] By his efforts the *vieux solaire* was hoisted up onto the ramparts of the church. But a number of courageous individuals stood up against all the adulation expressed by the men of the first period of the reign. We have already encountered them many times during the second period, stigmatizing the catastrophic consequences of taxation and warfare. Among the most notable were Vauban, Fénelon, Beauvillier, Saint-Simon, Boisguilbert and Jurieu.

The dialogue (often a dialogue of the deaf) between the two sides would continue from generation to generation across the centuries. Voltaire, if

---

[55]   See, for example, La Bruyère, *Les Caractères* (Paris, Garnier, 1962), 'Du souverain ou de la République' *in fine* no. 35 (portrait de Louis XIV). But La Bruyère was less concerned with the fate of the Huguenots, which left him indifferent, than with an evangelical reform of the Catholic church from within (ibid., 'De la chaire', no. 4). And, in any case, La Bruyère was a great writer and past master of the art of *double entendre*, even in the creation of his own two personalities in terms of an intimate and a public self (Compare A. Brossat, *Le Stalinisme*, pp. 98–105).

only to hit back at the régime of Louis XV, from which he had received so many affronts, wrote admiringly of the king in whose reign he was born. In so doing he was, without knowing it, following the intellectual strategy of Saint-Simon who under Louis XV, albeit clandestinely, praised Louis XIII the better to condemn Louis XIV. The two authors implicitly belittled the king whose rule coincided with their public lives (Louis XIV for Saint-Simon, Louis XV for Voltaire) simply by praising his predecessor, a strategy which cost little and avoided any serious risks, especially when done in secret as in the case of the 'little duke.' In his *Century of Louis XIV* (1756), Voltaire presents the reign of his hero as marking an epoch in world history in the same way as those of Pericles or Augustus. A revived and active France, in the forefront of European humanity, after 1661 tore herself free from 'Gothic' backwardness, the repulsive aspects and prolonged ascendancy of which the philosopher deliberately exaggerated. In Voltaire's opinion, however, the nation won renown through its great men: Colbert in administration and industry; Racine and Molière in literature; Bourdaloue in religion; and the *maréchal* de Villars who, following in the footsteps of many other soldiers, extricated the aging Louis from the jaws of defeat.

The Voltairian tradition of eulogizing the Sun-King has continued up to our own time through the works of Madelin and Gaxotte to the recent biography published by François Bluche. This historian by his constant use of the first person plural ('The riposte was not long in coming: once more we took possession of Avignon . . .'[56]) unblushingly inveigles his French readers into identifying with the exploits of the king and the subjects over whom he ruled.

Whatever the peculiarities of his style and this doctoral or nationalistic 'we' and 'us', Bluche's book does have the merit, following Ragnhild Hatton, of stressing an incontestable fact more or less ignored by historians, which is that in 1715 Louis bequeathed to his successors a France which was larger, stronger, better administered and more populous (and not only because of annexations) than the country he inherited in 1643 and even in 1661. The personal role of the king and his close collaborators is not negligible in this achievement, even after giving full credit to the people and the ruling groups who directly or indirectly helped to consolidate the crown and its work.

The Voltairian synthesis was thus relayed across the centuries up to 1987, the year which saw the publication of Bluche's book. Endorsed by the name of the most important French writer of the eighteenth century, this synthesis was able to traverse, not without its ups and downs, the troubles of the Revolution and Empire. It survived and even managed to regain popularity in the nineteenth century. Nevertheless it emerged from the trials of 1789–1815 watered down, holed, even discredited in the eyes of a certain number of scholars.

[56] Bluche, *Louis XIV*, p. 447 (of the French edition).

In fact, the trial of Louis XIV before public opinion, whether flagrant or muffled, had been proceeding for many years, since the time of Fénelon's writings and the English, Dutch and Huguenot pamphlets supporting the League of Augsburg. The indictment did not become systematic, however, until 1788, date of the first publication (though full of mistakes) of extracts from the *Mémoires* of Saint-Simon. In the eyes of their more ignorant readers these *Mémoires* were totally devastating for the Sun-King. How could these readers, knowing little of history, comprehend that Dubois, Villars and Vendôme (for example), all generally dragged through the mud by the little duke, were in reality remarkable servants of the state, the nation and a *fortiori* Louis XIV? The last straw was obviously the almost complete publication of the *Mémoires* in 1829. If this first 'Saint-Simonian cycle' between 1788 and 1829 had not been enough, the 27 years of the Revolution and the Empire between 1789 and 1815 would have provided sufficient inspiration for prejudiced minds to undertake a devastating revision of the reputation of the third Bourbon. Thanks to Voltaire, Louis had enjoyed an Indian summer lasting half a century.

The delicate and brutal role of public prosecutor fell as it happened to Pierre Edouard Lemontey.[57] 1n a work written under Napoleon but not published until 1818, Lemontey was careful to disqualify Voltaire as a witness. The philosopher had, he said, let himself by seduced by Louis' generosity towards writers (generosity which Lemontey, without fear of contradicting himself, tended to deny). Our man set about Louis XIV violently, but in so doing he was thinking above all of Napoleon who, he said, 'only yoked (satellite) kings to his wagon the better to oppress the peoples.' The comparison was very shaky. In reality Louis' ambitions were not at all Napoleonic; barely extending beyond the present-day hexagon. The Sun-King behaved more like a peasant or a notary trying to enlarge and round off his plot of land than a universal conqueror aiming to unify under his control Europe, the Mediterranean world, the Levant, or whatever. The western world since the age of Charles V and without any doubt in the twentieth century has known war-mongers bent on world-wide expansion infinitely more daring, dangerous and ambitious than Louis XIV ever was.

And yet, for all its weaknesses, Lemontey's central intuition remains fascinating: Louis XIV, he says overtly, was a 'revolutionary.' Is this a teleological anachronism? No matter. The long line of historians in the Protestant, republican or liberal traditions, headed by Tocqueville, would throw themselves eagerly into the breach opened up, not without a certain premonitory genius, by Lemontey. Louis XIV, in the opinion of this

---

[57]   P.E. Lemontey, *Essai sur l'établissement monarchique de Louis XIV et sur les altérations qu'il éprouva pendant sa vie de Prince* (Paris, Deterville, 1818).

brilliant and unjustly forgotten essayist, hacked his way through and destroyed the impenetrable jungle of the Gothic constitution of the kingdom. Still according to the same author, he prepared the way, more than a century ahead of the event, for the great upheaval of 1789: with his extreme absolutism, he weakened and isolated the nobility, the clergy, the Parlement and the towns. Until Louis, or at least until Richelieu, these had formed the irregular but durable and solid framework of the ancient and baroque edifice of the old monarchy. In passing Lemontey took pot-shots at the Sun-King's polygamy and then paradoxically his monogamy with Madame de Maintenon, his warlike policy, which proved too heavy a burden for the kingdom, his 'rag paper' diplomacy, his costly obsession with the building of his absurd palace at Versailles, his police state, his maniacal insistence on etiquette, his taste for bagatelles and philandering. In such a perspective, even his undeniable qualities (dignity, consistency, strength of mind, etc.) are laid as charges against Louis because they would help him to divert the course of history towards the whirlpools in which the now rotten ship of the monarchy would come to grief.

Rarely has such an obscure historian left a more influential or brilliant inheritance. A mere mention of the greatest names proves the point. Tocqueville took from Lemontey (without acknowledgement of course!) the model or idea of a centralism established by Louis XIV or the Bourbons in general, by which the 'revolutionary' Louis prefigured the centralization of Tocqueville's own times, under the Convention, Napoleon and the liberal monarchy. Guizot[58] for his part praised the immense contribution of Louis XIV and his ministers to the construction of the state, while, like Lemontey, whose works he had read, deploring the growing isolation of the absolutist edifice. The authoritarian practices of the state had cut it off from the vital forces in the nation, those which if things had evolved differently, in a more 'English' direction, could have become the natural supporters of the monarchical state.

Simonde de Sismondi and Henri Martin, the one from Protestant stock, the other a good republican, also rejected the triumphalism of the Voltairian tradition. They followed in the wake of Lemontey in condemning Louis XIV's foreign policy, which they thought disastrous, while acknowledging some positive aspects of the reign. Michelet, following the example of Lemontey, thought that the fistula which afflicted Louis XIV in 1685–6 was a vital element in explaining the subsequent deterioration in the performance of his régime. Lavisse, whose immense talent has to be acknowledged, managed nevertheless to attack Louis XIV for not annexing the left bank of the Rhine nor the Spanish Low Countries,

---

[58] Concerning what follows, see W. Church, *Louis XIV in Historical Thought; from Voltaire to the Annales School* (New York, Norton, 1976).

present-day Belgium! Equally the same historian,[59] surveying the scene from the heights of the Belle Epoque, criticized the despotic aspects of Louis' reign, among which the violent conquest of these same regions, if it had happened, would have been one of the most debatable exploits!

Lemontey's analyses and the views of Lavisse were taken up again by Georges Pagès, who considered that from the end of the seventeenth century, by reason of insufficient participation in the activities of the state by the different social groups and bodies, 'the pillars upon which the [absolute] monarchy rested were hollow.'[60] Gaston Zeller in turn[61] gives a remarkable exposition on the non-existence of any concern for 'natural frontiers' on the Rhine, which could not obviously have been a motivating factor in the king's policy. Zeller nevertheless accused Louis XIV of showing a considerable degree of aggressiveness[62] in the frantic pursuit of his personal 'gloire'. Philippe Sagnac declares that the Sun-King, at bottom, exploited and subjugated the 20 million French souls exposed to his domination.[63] Finally, two representatives of the *Annales* school in the broadest sense of the term or as we say today 'the new history', Pierre Goubert and Robert Mandrou, may not have strayed too far from the path laid out by the talented succession from Lemontey to Michelet and from Sismondi to Lavisse or Zeller. The attitude of Goubert and Mandrou towards Louis XIV is fundamentally a moral judgement. It implies a condemnation, albeit with qualifications, of Louis' character and of his aggressive and warlike diplomacy, his tyrannical behaviour in the religious field, his 'despotism'. These two historians, especially Goubert,[64] consider that the reign of Louis XIV taken as a whole was characterized by crisis or

[59]   Ernest Lavisse, 'Louis XIV' in *Histoire de France . . . à la Révolution*, 9 vols (Paris, Hachette, 1900–1911), vol. 7.

[60]   Georges Pagès, *La Monarchie d'Ancien Régime en France* (Paris, A. Colin, 1898), p. 215.

[61]   Gaston Zeller, *Aspects de la politique française sous l'Ancien Régime* (Paris, PUF, 1964); and, from the same author, *Histoire des relations internationales*, vol. iii: *De Louis XIV à 1789* (Paris, Hachette, 1955), p. 15 and *passim*; 'La Monarchie d'Ancien Régime et les frontières naturelles', *Revue d'histoire moderne*, 8 (1933), 303–33 (fundamental – the politics of 'natural frontiers' would not be clearly formulated by the French until after 1792).

[62]   Gaston Zeller, 'Politique extérieure et diplomatie sous Louis XIV', *Revue d'histoire moderne*, 6 (1931), 124–43 (an article which is very severe on Louis XIV and Louvois).

[63]   Philippe Sagnac, *La Prépondérance française* (Paris, Alcan, 1935), pp. 58–61; Sagnac pictured above all a violent and terrible humbling of the social 'orders' whereas William Beik, in *Absolutism and Society in Seventeenth Centry France* (Cambridge, Cambridge University Press, 1985), perceives rather an intelligent and able politics of integration on the part of Louis XIV. The same holds true for the other work of Philippe Sagnac, *La Formation de la société française* (Paris, PUF, 1945), pp. 50, 84 etc., in which he insists above all (and not without ulterior motive, of course) on the repressive, even 'inquisitorial' nature of Louis XIV's politics.

[64]   Pierre Goubert, *Louis XIV et vingt millions de Français* (Paris, PUF, 1966), e.g. pp. 112, 223 *et seq.*, and *passim*. Robert Mandrou, *Louis XIV et son temps* (Paris, PUF, 1973 and 1978), pp. 321, 483–7, 532–3 and *passim*.

at least economic recession. This overall judgement is based on a sector-based analysis of prices, which showed a downward or at least stagnant trend from 1662 to 1690. Yet these three decades were in fact relatively prosperous as far as agricultural production was concerned. Furthermore, demographic research has shown the resilience of the French population, despite some undeniably serious crises. Studies of agrarian production, using records of tithes and rents, have given the lie to Boisguilbert and Meuvret, both of whom wrongly dated the crisis of Louis XIV's reign from the beginning of the 1660s and then had it continuing, with more justification, until the king's death. Reality is more on the side of Voltaire and Joseph Goy: these two authors,[65] the latter using the tithe and rent evidence, diagnosed a fall in the volume of harvests[66] and at times a veritable economic debacle (though not in all sectors) between 1690 and 1713. But the first half of the personal reign, from 1661 to 1689, was far from disastrous: in certain regions it could even have been called an age of abundance.

The recent modifications in the image of this key figure in French history and his socio-political environment have, however, come from elsewhere, from Britain, America and Scandinavia. We should refer once again to the work of Ragnhild Hatton[67] of the University of London and her occasional or permanent collaborators. Hatton's purpose, from the beginning of her work, was to destroy the framework of stereotypes and

---

[65] In ch. 30 of Voltaire's *Siècle de Louis XIV* he rightly placed the economic turning-point of the reign of Louis XIV towards crisis in the year 1689, the beginning of the ruinous War of the League of Augsburg. He writes: 'Si l'on compare l'administration de Colbert à toutes les administrations précédentes, la postérité chérira cet homme dont le peuple insensé voulut déchirer le corps après sa mort. Les Français lui doivent certainement leur industrie et leur commerce, et par conséquent cette opulence dont les sources diminuent quelquefois dans la guerre, mais qui se rouvrent toujours avec abondance dans la paix. Cependant, en 1702, on avait l'ingratitude de rejeter sur Colbert la langueur qui commençait à se faire sentir dans les nerfs de l'Etat. Un Bois-Guilbert, lieutenant-général au bailliage de Rouen, fit imprimer dans ce temps-là *Le Détail de la France* en deux petits volumes, et prétendit que tout avait été en décadence depuis 1660. C'était précisément le contraire. La France n'avait jamais été si florissante que depuis la mort du cardinal Mazarin jusqu'à la guerre de 1689; et, même dans cette guerre, le corps de l'Etat, commençant à être malade, se soutint par la vigueur que Colbert avait répandue dans tous ses membres. L'auteur du *Détail* prétendit que, depuis 1660, les biens-fonds du royaume avaient diminué de quinze cents millions. Rien n'était ni plus faux, ni moins vraisemblable. Cependant ses arguments captieux persuadèrent ce paradoxe ridicule à ceux qui voulurent être persuadés. C'est ainsi qu'en Angleterre, dans les temps plus florissants, on voit cent papiers publics qui démontrent que l'Etat est ruiné.' Ignoring the excessive cult of personality towards Colbert, it remains nevertheless the case that, from the chronological point of view (the study of tithes has provided confirmation), Voltaire was right and Boisguilbert was not.

[66] J. Goy and E. Le Roy Ladurie, *Première esquisse d'une conjoncture du produit décimal et domanial. Fin du Moyen Age-XVIIIe siècle* (The Hague, Mouton, 1972), p. 364 *et seq.* See also, by the same authors, *Prestations paysannes*, ii.

[67] Beyond Hatton's frequently cited article in *XVIIe Siècle*, 31 (1979), 109 *et seq.*, the works on *Louis XIV and Absolutism* and *Louis XIV and Europe* which she edited are particularly to be noted.

prejudices which the propaganda of the centuries had built around the figure of Louis XIV, throwing eclipses over the face of the Sun-King. This propaganda stemmed from the resentment, fully comprehensible and justified, of the Huguenots, but also from the less persuasive bias long displayed in British and Dutch historiography and by militant republicanism in France. The partisans of this republicanism sought to obtain an additional but pointless dose of legitimacy for their cause, which in reality had no need for it. They launched an all-out verbal offensive against a dead absolutism, even though this kind of state organization on the continent corresponded in its time with the long-term needs of historical development.[68] One serious historian goes so far as to compare, 'with a good deal of justification', the international Catholicism of the second half of the seventeenth century to Nazism and consequently Louis XIV to Hitler.[69]

Of course Ragnhild Hatton has no problem in summarily dismissing such twaddle. More seriously she reminds us (or demonstrates) that Louis XIV's obsession with ranks and precedence, for which he was so stigmatized after his death, was in fact common to all the European states, great and small, of his age, including the 'liberal' camp of the United Provinces and the monarchs of England. Taking this into account, it is unreasonable to ramble on eternally about the distasteful 'exceptionalism' of the Sun-King. What is more, some of his detractors have criticized Louis, not for being too punctilious about etiquette, but for departing too much from it; such was the complaint voiced by Saint-Simon, lamenting how up to 1715, at the court and elsewhere, the king and his representatives denied to the dukes and *pairs* of France certain signs of deference[70] to which they were conventionally entitled. A little consistency is called for! In reality, as far as the external forms of respect given and received are concerned, Louis, seen in international context, conducted himself in accordance with the times. When he appears exaggeratedly touchy about a symbol or mark of prestige to which he felt himself entitled this is usually because, beyond these trivialities of precedence, there lay some ulterior motive of a more prosaically political kind.

Besides, the attention paid by Louis to formalistic distinctions could make him go too far, by reason of historically based motives which did nevertheless have some rational foundations. Recognizing the young Stuart James III as King of England[71] in 1701 instead of William III undoubtedly dangerously increased the danger of war breaking out, but it was also, Louis thought, a way of avoiding the mistake made by Mazarin

[68] Jacques Julliard, citing Carl Schmitt, in *Chroniques du septième jour* (Paris, Seuil, 1991), p. 321.

[69] Stuart Prall, *The Bloodless Revolution in England, 1688* (New York, Doubleday, 1972), p. 125.

[70] Saint-Simon, *Mémoires*, xxvi, 3 *et seq.*

[71] Ibid., ix, 288 and 291 *et seq.*

when he had ignored (for the benefit of Cromwell) the provisionally dethroned Stuarts, only to pay the price for his blunder after the death of the Lord Protector and the restoration of Charles II. Louis XIV, as a wily politician who liked to think of himself as a profound thinker, rejected the 'anti-Stuart' cynicism of his mentor.

Similarly, it is also traditional, even among well-informed authors, to ascribe to Louis XIV's diplomacy, which so often led to war, one constant motive: *la gloire*. It is necessary, however, to understand the real meaning of this word. *Gloire* often meant nothing more than 'reputation' or 'image' (translating *Ansehen*, the justification for the power of the German princes). Furthermore, *gloire* was not confined to military affairs: it included peaceful achievements which were nothing but honourable (the construction of the Paris Observatory brought the king as much glory as did armed victories). It should also be noted that in most instances Louis' strategic and diplomatic endeavours were motivated solely by considerations of the security of his frontiers or territorial aggrandizement, finely calculated in terms of his interests and the possibilities of the moment. Misplaced vanity had nothing to do with it. In the *Instruction* which he gave to his envoys to Leopold in 1700, Louis told them not to glorify French power and wealth so as to avoid upsetting the Emperor.

The stock image of the *rex gloriosus*, the braggart soldier and blusterer, then, which the young and spoilt Louis XIV had himself lived up to during the first decade of his personal rule, needs to be, if not discarded entirely, then at least toned down. With advancing age Louis was capable of cooling his youthful ardour. This may be seen, for example, in his *post factum*, highly self-critical, judgements on the Dutch War.[72]

But going beyond judgements on an individual, however important he may have been, recent historical writing outside France has tried to take a more objective view of the entire system of absolutism. According to these analyses absolutism should not be seen as establishing a total control over a society which was thereby imprisoned in the net of monarchical power, transfixed by an authoritarianism handed down from above. Absolutism attempted rather to superpose its rationalizing purpose onto a society made up of archaic but living bodies, the *corps* which absolutism wanted to federate but not to destroy. A distinction should be made here between public law and private law.[73] The former was beyond question strongly influenced, in theory, by the 'absolute' power emanating from the sovereign: under Louis XIV the people were not independent political actors, and only made their presence felt through brief and savage uprisings. But private law maintained an autonomous existence between 1661 and 1715, just as it had under Richelieu. It assured the maintenance of civil

[72] Hatton (ed.), *Louis XIV and Europe*, p. 36; and William Church in J.C. Rule (ed.), *Louis XIV and the Craft of Kingship* (Ohio State University Press, 1969), p. 387.
[73] Church in *Louis XIV and the Craft of Kingship*, pp. 364–8 and *passim*.

society[74] and private possessions, whether large or small. In the writings of certain theoreticians,[75] it could be asserted that equity had its source in the unique sovereignty of the ruler. But in reality this pretention was purely theoretical. The dispensation of justice was still diffused, the business of innumerable tribunals which could boast justifiably about their independence, whether at the level of officers who owned their offices or of fief-holding *seigneurs*. In these conditions, absolutism in practice amounted to a process of arbitration, regulating, with varying degress of success, the conflicts that arose within the ruling groups. It was simply not the case that these groups, apart from the courtiers,[76] were merely the humble servants of an all-powerful state.

In his foreign policy Louis XIV's essential aims were to maintain the integrity of the kingdom as it had been defined in previous treaties (Westphalia, 1648) and to protect its territory by controlling the 'gateways' on the frontiers (Alsace, Lorraine, Franche-Comté, etc.), which, if left open, could have allowed hostile armies to threaten the capital, the king's 'house'. This royal residence had to be made secure. Actions to secure control of such 'gateways' and their related guarantees were interpreted by adversaries (and vice versa) as acts of aggression, which in effect they were, beyond all doubt. Yet they cannot be equated with the epic onslaughts of the would-be conquerors of Europe before and since the age of the Sun-King. Louis was simply a powerful piece on the chessboard of the European equilibrium. The aspirations towards a universal monarchy attributed to him by hostile propaganda cannot be taken seriously. At the most, in 1657 and with Mazarin egging him on,[77] Louis had a vague desire to stand as a candidate for Emperor. After this date, a strong concern for a balance of power in Europe underpinned Louis's distrust of Austria, a suspicious attitude greatly increased by the Emperor's success in recuperating Hungarian territory from the Turks.

Furthermore, in a global and comparative perspective, Louis XIV may be relativized to the point of trivialization. Biological fate decreed that he reigned for much longer than his European contemporaries, aided and

---

[74]   The notion of civil society under Louis XIV is not generally formulated as such; but it had already taken shape, although rather un-selfconsciously. It involved an entire social sector which was not controlled in any direct way by the administration directly under the king's authority.

[75]   David Parker is right to stress (in 'Sovereignty, Absolutism and the Function of the Law in Seventeenth-Century France', *Past and Present*, no. 122 (1989), pp. 36–74) the contrast between the pretensions of absolutism to embody a sovereignty which was 'indivisible like a geometric point' and the reality of power in the Ancien Régime which was diffused and dispersed amongst its social groups.

[76]   On the rituals of the court, where the courtiers cut a shabby figure, see, for example, Saint-Simon, *Mémoires*, v, 65–6.

[77]   Georges Livet, 'Louis XIV and the Germanies' in Hatton (ed.), *Louis XIV and Europe*, p. 62 (G. Livet uses notably J. Preuss, 'Mazarin und die Bewerbung Ludwigs XIV um die deutsche Kaiserkrone', *Historische Vierteljahrschaft* (1904)).

abetted by the forces of an over-powerful nation. But in its day-by-day exercise of power the absolutism incarnated by Louis XIV differed very little from the dominant practices of an epoque characterized by a Charles XII of Sweden, a Peter the Great, a Leopold I and, in foreign affairs, a William III of England.

Let us for a moment compare Louis, Charles and William. Of the three, Louis emerges as the most legalist: the Swede and the 'Hollando-Englishman' loved the field of battle, prepared if necessary to pay the ultimate price. Going beyond absolutism *stricto sensu*, Divine Right, on the subject of which so much ironical comment has been directed at Louis XIV, served as the justification for all government in Europe, including the rule of the decidedly non-monarchist States General of the United Provinces. Louis XIV's megalomania, wrongly viewed in later ages as the king taking himself for God in person[78] (in fact for a counterfeit Apollo) did not last long; with advancing age and setbacks it gave way to an attitude of repentant humility.[79] In a more global perspective, absolutism in its full glory undoubtedly represented a necessary rite of passage for the majority of continental states, but also a temporally circumscribed phase in the long history of Europe. This very chronological singularity, which laid him open to attack from political thinkers, helps to explain the focusing of attention on a Louis XIV seen wrongly as the archetypal incarnation of an epoque of authoritarian system-building. Yet this particular variety of authoritarianism, no matter how short-lived it may have been in the overall history of humankind, nevertheless went far beyond the case of a single flesh-and-blood individual.

The Enlightened Despotism of the eighteenth century, in countries other than France, would take a lead from the absolutist tendencies which had flourished in all their ideal purity under Louis XIV and a handful of other rulers. Yet this despotism of the age of Enlightenment was often the work of sceptical or quasi-agnostic monarchs. It would not therefore allow itself to be held in check by the religious scruples which often restrained Louis from going too far down the road to arbitrary power. We know that the Sun-King, once the wars which made them necessary were over, stopped the imposition of certain taxes, such as the *capitation* and the *dixième*. They had only ever been imposed, and even then unwillingly, in order to provide finance for French armies in the field. It is difficult to imagine a Frederick II or even a George II, a great imposer of taxes, acting in this way, in imitation of what was, when all is said and done, a certain moderation. Overweening pride is not always to be found where

[78] François Furet, *Revolutionary France* (Oxford, Blackwell, 1992) distances himself from this *soi-disant* divinization which the recent historiography of the Sun-King sometimes imputes to the king.

[79] Andrew Losski, 'The intellectual development of Louis XIV from 1661 to 1715', in Hatton (ed.), *Louis XIV and Europe*, p. 125. Similarly, Michel Antoine, *Louis XV* (Paris, Fayard, 1989), pp. 596–8; Saint-Simon, *Mémoires*, vi, 245 and n. 5.

simplificatory traditions, passed on through the generations by collective memory and repetitive historians, have said it was.

The French Revolution, moreover, was to mark the beginning of a shift in legitimacy from an almost purely hereditary system to a régime which eventually became representative. England in 1688 had already initiated this shift, almost by chance, as a result of a successful landing due to initiative from the Dutch Republic. The country gave itself a monarch from abroad who, willingly or not, would help the British to become free. In these conditions, who could have foreseen in 1700 that the House of Commons, so submissive under William III, would one day become the mother of parliaments for the entire world? At the beginning of the eighteenth century absolutism was becoming the norm; representative systems, without being exceptional, were or were becoming rare in Europe.[80] To attack the former in the name of the rights which emerged from the latter is to be guilty of anachronism, even if one possesses the extraordinary talent of a Michelet.

The historical image of the Sun-King, it is worth repeating, shifted from Lemontey through Lavisse, to Mandrou.[81] In reality Louis, with all his splendours – ruinous, odious, costly and oppressive, or creative, organizational, rationalizing – was a man of his time. Posterity was to mythologize him as a convenient and caricatured puppet, a target for the darts aimed at him by hatred of despotism, justified in themselves but also anachronistic or teleological.

This 'slippage of image' was already discernible in the work of Saint-Simon, the legitimate or putative father of many future errors. On his death bed, addressing the Dauphin who would soon become Louis XV, the Sun-King had declared, in so many words: 'My dear child, you are going to be the greatest king in the world; never forget the obligations you owe to God, do not imitate me in waging war, try to maintain peace with your neighbours, to relieve your people as much as you can, which I could not always do by *reason of the necessities of the state*. Always follow good advice and remember that all you are you owe to God . . .'. The same text, as revised by Saint-Simon, departs from its initial version that we have just cited and adds some clearly Saint-Simonian interpolations or innovations: 'My child, you are going to be a great king; do not imitate me in my taste for building, nor in my taste for war, try rather to keep at peace with your neighbours, render to God that which you owe Him, recognize your obligations to Him, make him honoured by your subjects, always follow good advice, try to relieve your peoples, which I was unfortunate enough not to be able to do.'[82] The subtle nuances introduced in the *post mortem*

---

[80] Ernst Henrichs, *Einführung in die Geschichte der Frühen Neuzeit* (Munich, C.H. Beck, 1980), pp. 178–9.

[81] On Lavisse's thought concerning Louis XIV, see Jean-François Fitou, 'Comment on récrit l'histoire: Louis XIV de Lavisse à Gaxotte', *Annales ESC*, 44 (1989), 479–96.

[82] On these two texts, see Saint-Simon, *Mémoires*, xxvii, 274–5 and n. 4.

version are evident and even amplified by the little duke who apparently cared little about reproducing accurately the almost last words of the dying king. The *necessities of the state* have disappeared. In the same way the phrase about the king's exaggerated taste for buildings has been added by Saint-Simon, the only chronicler to do so, off his own bat, and yet the confession was thereafter supposed to have been made by Louis himself. It was a shrewd addition. The authentic text straight from the king's mouth signalled the existence of warfare with its attendant *necessities*, from which Louis had certainly drawn what we would consider to be excessive, frankly war-mongering and, ultimately, financially ruinous conclusions. The period between 1713 and 1740 would be very different, characterized by almost 30 years of peace or only limited wars, a perspective which the dying Louis seems to have foreseen when he looked to the future. The Saint-Simonian texts are distorted to perfection: they present the twisted image, which would become dominant in the nineteenth century, of a delirious old king, looking back on his long life and admitting that he had let himself be impelled throughout his reign by an obsession with war and a highly expensive taste for buildings. The idea of unfortunate necessity, for the benefit of the state, was capital in the thought of Louis XIV, yet it has totally disappeared in the interpretative reconstruction by Saint-Simon. The imputation of irrational bellicism and building mania is already in full spate, a double torrent of stereotypes which it would be very difficult to turn back towards its source.

How fortunate by comparison was the Emperor Leopold I! He was clever enough not to reign for as long as Louis XIV and therefore not to offend contemporary opinion or posterity by his interminable rule. He expanded his empire towards the east, but at the expense of the Turks who, luckily for him, hated westerners. He could persecute 'heretics' to his heart's content without his Protestant allies in Western Europe getting too worked up, and with good reason. Luckier on this point than Louis XIV, even several decades after his death, Leopold had no vengeful Saint-Simon nor a Revolution to summon his ghost before the tribunal of History or dig up his corpse. Not everyone is lucky enough to be born and die Emperor of Germany and sovereign of Austria. The scales of historiography 'weigh flies' eggs on plates made of spiders' webs'. Inaccurate and delicate, they are easily upset. In this case hindsight was to be indulgent towards the Habsburg of Vienna if only by paralypsis. But it would not spare the Bourbon of Versailles. He would become the scapegoat for an absolutism which had lost its legitimacy, held up to public obloquy during its dying fall, an absolutism which, however, swallowed up and transcended Louis himself on all sides, and which when all is said and done explains, situates and sometimes justifies the Sun-King in his broad European context and in the long-term perspective of the Ancien Régime.

If we abstract out of our perspectives such *a posteriori* teleologies and ideologies there is, when we look honestly at Louis XIV, something which is beyond the facile and repetitive criticisms aimed at him. It is something on a more elevated plane, 'a subtle and incomparable touch of love and pride, something beyond ability, pure and simple, something which is almost inspirational and which gives to the efforts [of the Sun-King] that refinement which is almost an art, which is an art'.[83]

[83]   Following Joseph Conrad, cited in *Sagesse de Conrad* (Paris, NRF, 1947), p. 39.

PART II

Flexible and Adaptable: The New Absolutism

7

The Overture

Louis XIV died on 1 September 1715. There followed an eight-year period in French politics, the Regency of Philippe d'Orléans (1715–23) which brought with it many surprises.[1] More than most, this period requires careful reconsideration since the history of the Regency has long been written from a rather moralizing and anglophobe perspective which has curiously warped our perception of it. The *abbé* Dubois is criticized with thoughtless severity for having betrayed national interests by signing up to the British alliance. The moral turpitude of the Regent himself is condemned although, in reality, his behaviour was neither better nor worse than many other rulers at various times. Setting to one side the Regency's considerable cultural creativity (Watteau, Montesquieu, Voltaire), the period also presents the historian with the problem of 'conservative change', a question which is far from unique to this period. To define the situation simply, a political system which is tending to become progressively more autocratic under a particular leader or government – Louis XIV in this instance – creates increasing tensions amongst its élites, for its people at large and for neighbouring countries. The causes for this situation may be

---

[1]   The most complete work on the Regency, still unequalled, remains that of Dom H. Leclercq, *Histoire de la Régence pendant la minorité de Louis XV* (3 vols, Paris, Champion, 1921). The studies published by the *Centre aixois d'études et de recherches sur le XVIIIe siècle* as *La Régence* (Paris, A. Colin, 1970) should also be consulted as well as J.H. Shennan, *Philippe, Duke of Orléans, Regent of France 1715–1723* (London, Thames and Hudson, 1979). Frantz Funck-Brentano, *La Régence* (Paris, Tallandier-Brentano, 1931); Jean Meyer, *Le Régent* (Paris, Ramsay, 1985); and, by the same author, *La Vie quotidienne en France au temps de la Régence* (Paris, Hachette, 1979); Michel Chaillou and Michèle Saltiel, *La Petite Vertu, huit années de prose courante sous la Régence* (Paris, Balland, 1980) – an anthology; Arsène Houssaye, *La Régence* (Paris, Dentu, 1875); Maurice Soulié, *Le Régent (1674–1723)* (Paris, Payot, 1980); Claude Saint-André, *Le Régent* (Paris, Tallandier, 1928); Claire-Elaine Engel, *Le Régent* (Paris, Hachette, 1969); Philippe Erlanger, *Le Régent* (Paris, Gallimard, 1938); Jean-Christian Petitfils, *Le Régent* (Paris, Fayard, 1986); Jean-Louis Aujol, *Le Cardinal Dubois, ministre de la Paix* (Paris, Bateau Ivre, 1948); on the system of Law one should refer (besides the brilliant essay by Paul Harsin in Braudel and Labrousse, *Histoire économique et sociale de la France* (Paris, PUF, 1970), ii) to, for example, Edgar Faure, *La Banqueroute de Law, 17 juillet 1720* (Paris, Gallimard, 1977).

numerous: foreign wars, overburdensome taxation, short-sighted despotism, economic crisis, the persecution of this or that minority, etc. Patriotic reasons may exist in good measure to justify why its leadership should have got it into this mess, and such reasons may not have been merely pretexts. Yet the essential problem after the change of the leadership responsible for, or made the scapegoat for, this difficult dilemma is how to resolve the situation without still further damage. Or, to make an anachronistic analogy, how does a state throw off a 'dictatorship'? How does a régime carefully throw off the shackles of the past system of government without destroying itself in the process? Philippe d'Orléans and his collaborators, Law and Dubois to begin with, found a means to resolve the problem in an outstanding way.

How, briefly, should we describe the state of France in 1715? At his death, Louis XIV had left the kingdom at peace with Europe. But pro-Stuart France was not on good terms with England and the Dutch, and France's only ally was the devoutly Catholic Spain of Philip V. The pretensions of the Madrid Bourbons to the throne of France and their territorial claims in Italy and those of the Emperor to the Spanish throne could at any moment endanger European peace. Within the kingdom, the governing classes, or a group within them, felt frustrated and were divided from the rest. The Parlement was half-subdued but it remained more than ever Jansenist in its sympathies because of its fundamental Gallicanism. Like the Huguenots, the Jansenists were excluded from the kingdom by law, despite the tacit support which was afforded them by the Cardinal de Noailles, Archbishop of Paris. The members of the reforming cabal around the duke of Burgundy (Fénelon, Beauvillier, Chevreuse, Saint-Simon) had either died or, like Saint-Simon, found themselves isolated. The situation was not dissimilar for the members of the former cabal of the late Grand Dauphin, various of whom shifted their allegiance and joined the little camarilla around the duke d'Orléans, the rising star of the Palais-Royal and the new Regent. The grandees of the former dominant power grouping around the Sun-King meanwhile clustered round Madame de Maintenon and the duke du Maine. These aristocrats, ministers and military top-brass were frightened of what would follow in the 'aftermath of Louis XIV'.

The public mood is more difficult to read, however, because of the economic crisis and suffering, the reality of which should not be overstated nor completely ignored. There was inevitably an economic recovery of sorts after the Peace of Utrecht in 1715.[2] But vast amounts of agricultural

---

[2]   The speed of the French recovery after the end of the war in 1715, particularly in the leading industrial sectors (glass, external and maritime commerce) also proves, at least retrospectively, the sustained vigour and the capacities for reconstruction which characterized the realm's economy, evidently damaged but not destroyed beyond repair by 12 years of war. At Saint-Gobain, for example, from 1713–14, there was a notable increase in sales of glass and mirrors. At Nantes, the numbers of 'direct' sailings to the Antilles, which were already producing sugar, stood at 42 ships in 1700 (the year before the war began). This

land and farms had been abandoned because of depopulation and depression. The deflationary politics, or rather the considerable appreciation in the value of the *livre tournois*, undertaken by Desmarets, the *contrôleur général des finances* from 1708–15, was harsh on those with debts. A mass revolt, or at least a rising of some elements of the people, which (as in the Fronde) might be complemented by discontents amongst the nobility and the élites, appeared menacingly possible. The situation was not, however, as serious as it had been in 1620 or in 1648. The ambitions of the higher aristocracy had been sufficiently curbed or transformed under Louis for a civil war to seem unlikely. Yet the misfortunes which brought Louis XVI to his tragic end 60 years later are a reminder that a royal, or (later) imperial, succession was, and would remain, in 1559 as in 1870, a difficult transition. Philippe d'Orléans and his advisers would need to display a singular ability to succeed where so many others, regents and regnal monarchs, failed. Louis XIV's rule had been secured by the application of brute common-sense and the good fortune of a long reign. The Regent had to apply more consensual methods. He sought an increased participation in government from France's élite groups and a decreased hostility towards those in power from the lower orders.

The case of Jansenism provides a case-study of the Regency quest for consensus. To woo the Jansenists whom Louis XIV had persecuted meant, in reality, securing the adherence of the *parlementaires*, the universities, the parish priests of the capital city, the mendicant friars and the Benedictines, who always favoured the adept exponents of Augustinian theology. The Jansenist faction was embraced by those in opposition who would have been frightened out of it by new recruits to Protestantism. They had many of the aspects of an opposition political party and strongly opposed the papal Bull *Unigenitus*, promulgated in 1713, which was directed against all over-speculative theories of divine grace. The party included the bishops of

figure remained at an average of 41 ships a year from 1701 to 1706 during the conflict. But, on the return of war, this rose to 71 ships a year from 1713 to 1716. See Jean-Pierre Daviet, *Une multinationale française, Saint Gobain* (Paris, Fayard, 1989), p. 35; Jacques Ducoin, *Naufrages et assurances dans la marine de commerce du XVIIe siècle, le cas de Nantes* (doctoral thesis, University of Paris-IV (Sorbonne), 1989), iii, table 7. This leap ahead takes account of a spectacular rise in the economic fortunes of the French Antilles. The great age of American sugar destined for Europe was taking shape. The evolution in the island populations in the Caribbean is striking; in Martinique, the total population rose from 20,761 in 1702 to 36,229 in 1715, at precisely the same period as the famous Louis XIV 'crisis' which, although its existence is incontrovertible elsewhere, made litle impact here. At Santo Domingo, the overall population literally 'exploded' from 6,688 inhabitants in 1673 to 38,651 in 1722. However great the dynamism of Santo Domingo, it found itself caught up, and then overtaken, by the French population of Haiti. The overwhelming majority of this astonishing expansion, concentrated on a couple of islands, was no doubt the result of slavery, with the trade in black slaves enabling the expansion and the increase in plantations and sugar-mills in the Caribbean. The substantial development of the Atlantic coast at Bordeaux and at Nantes throughout the eighteenth century and up to the French Revolution was to take place on the base laid in Haiti. See J. Meyer, *Histoire du sucre* (Paris, Desjonquères, 1989).

a dozen various dioceses in France as well as the Cardinal de Noailles. The Regent was an able politician, however, and he had the measure of the Jansenist movement in 1714–15, treating it as a potential ally, a willing and cooperative partner. In the crucial session of the Parlement of early September 1715 when the will of Louis XIV was to be set aside, the Regent thus had the backing of the Cardinal de Noailles as well as d'Aguesseau, the pro-Jansenist champion of the Parlement. Philippe would release from the Bastille several Jansenist priests including the elderly homosexual *abbé* Servien. In August 1715, and again in 1716, he let the Cardinal de Noailles ban the Jesuits from preaching in his Paris diocese without any interference. This coincided with the high tide of the Jansenists and their sympathizers under the Regency which came with the nomination of d'Aguesseau in February 1717 to the post of chancellor, a nomination decided by the Regent himself. The Jesuit effort to frustrate their success was, for the present, to no avail. One of their preachers attacked the Regent as a 'little man puffed up with his own pride, without an ounce of wisdom or merit, who is in charge of both religion and the state'. As for Pope Clement XI, the 'prisoner of the Jesuits', he tended to foster this counter-offensive from the disciples of St Ignatius Loyola.[3]

The pendulum would in due course, however, swing in an anti-Jansenist direction. On 28 January 1718, the Chancellor d'Aguesseau was disgraced. He surrendered the seals to the pro-Jesuit d'Argenson. The causes of his disgrace had nothing to do with religion. They were the result of the opposition mounted by the chancellor to the system of John Law which was then at the centre of attention. The fall of someone as politically important as d'Aguesseau signified *ipso facto*, however, a defeat for the Jansenist party (although they did not, it must be said, return to the abyss which the promulgation of *Unigenitus* had opened up beneath the feet of the friends of Port-Royal in 1713). The lack of warmth of Philippe d'Orléans towards Augustinianism is more readily understandable when it is realized that the Regency, although more relaxed in its early days than Louis XIV had ever been, remained very cautious in its attitude towards granting toleration to the Protestants. Philippe was ready to liberate some Huguenots from the galleys; he was not prepared to abolish the revocation of the edict of Nantes. The Revocation would remain, like the destruction of Port-Royal, an irremovable element in the politics of the régime, an unshiftable legacy of his predecessor. This was despite the fact that the committals of Protestants to the galleys from the courts fell to very low levels under Philippe, a sign of a softening of attitudes in comparison with the record numbers consigned to the galleys under Louis XIV.[4]

---

[3]   Clement XI parted company, however, with the Jesuits when he condemned their 'Chinese rites' in 1704 – i.e. the adoption by Jesuit missionaries of certain elements inherent in Confucian ritual in order to encourage the diffusion of Christianity within the Chinese empire.

[4]   André Zysberg, *Les Galériens, vie et destin de 60,000 forçats sur les galères de France, 1690–1748* (Paris, Seuil, 1988), p. 104.

The Jansenist question was linked to the problem of the *parlementaires*. The Parlement of Paris tended towards the Augustinian faction. It represented, however, despite these 'malicious tendencies', a reservoir of legitimacy for Philippe. It was the Parlement which, on 2 September 1715, had recognized the Regency without qualification. He had won them over beforehand by granting them the rights of remonstrance, or rather, he gave the rights of remonstrance, which they had long held, an official status for the first time. At the same time, Philippe secured, by means of a decision in the Parlement, the revocation of the powers which his rival, the duke du Maine, had long exercised as head of part of the army. The Parisian magistrates, in return for the concessions which had been agreed in friendship with their new master, were showered with favours. They were given places on the new 'polysynodical' councils of state.[5] By reintegrating to some extent the Parlement into political life, from which it had been excluded under Louis XIV, it did the Regent's bidding during the honeymoon period of the régime in 1716. Orléans was even willing, when the circumstances required it, to give some additional concessions to these mighty magistrates, even to the extent of allowing them the right of precedence *de facto* in the procession of the Feast of the Assumption on 15 August 1716 which, since he held no great store by religious devotions, he held in contempt.

Around 1716–17, it is possible to map out the various groupings amongst the greater nobility of the kingdom, the magistrates of the Parlement included. *Grosso modo*, they were three-fold. Firstly, there were the *parlementaires* and the princes of the blood, a grouping held together, at least for the moment, by the Regent. Then there were the legitimated bastards of Louis XIV (who were demagogically allied to the non-ducal nobility, which wanted reform but which was not prepared to be snubbed by the peers of the realm). Finally there were the dukes and peers who would eventually be liberal and thus pro-Orléanist. However this latter group refused to take their hats off before the *robins* of the Parlement whose president in turn declined to doff his cap before them. Philippe invariably tried to treat the Parlement with deference but he also attempted to be fair in maintaining the rights of the dukes and peers upon this point of etiquette, especially when they were represented by his friend Saint-Simon. The dukes were held up to ridicule by pro-Parlement pamphlets which accused their ancestors of being no more than scriveners, butchers and fish-mongers. The 'affaire du

---

[5] 'Polysynodie' – i.e. a conciliar system of government in which the aristocracy was heavily represented and which took over from the former secretaries of state and ministerial figures from the *robe* of the Council. The system had been advocated by the group around the duke of Burgundy (Beauvillier, Chevreuse, Saint-Simon, etc.) and it was put into practice by Philippe d'Orléans in September 1715 (Saint-Simon, *Mémoires*, ed. A. de Boislisle, 45 vols (Paris, 1879–1930), xxix, 32 *et seq.*). Not very practical, the polysynodical councils were notable for representing a certain brand of self-sustaining utopia which was specific to the early years of the eighteenth century at the highest social levels.

bonnet'[6] was finally set to rest by a decision (*arrêt*) of the Council of 10 May 1716 which declared their pretensions out of court. The illegitimate sons of Louis XIV also found themselves in contestation. The legitimate princes of the blood, the Parlements and the Regent held them in suspicion after the Louis XIV edict of Marly in July 1714. This had granted his legitimated offspring the innate rights of succession to the crown. The peers, moreover, could not forgive the two bastards, Maine and Toulouse, for having set themselves up as an intermediary rank of the *légitimés* between the princes of the blood and the dukes, thus demoting the latter. Entirely isolated at the pinnacle of the high aristocracy, the bastards thus sought to find for themselves some support from lower down and sought it from amongst the non-ducal nobility. They refused to give precedence to the peers and, in the spirit of reform, they even called for the summoning of the Estates General. Philippe played off these divisions one against another amongst the aristocracy, some of whom were more liberal-minded than others. In July 1717, by now certain of receiving the approbation *a posteriori* of the Parlement, Orléans turned on the bastard Bourbons of Louis XIV and stripped them of their right of succession to the Crown by edict. This represented a triumph for the Parlement, for the dukes and peers, and for the House of Condé, which had long sought their humiliation. Above all, however, it was a decisive victory for the Regent himself. By the fall of the duke du Maine, he consolidated his power-base. The higher nobility, tamed by the places which they had been given as polysynodical councillors, and paralyzed by its own internal divisions, became progressively more amenable to its new master's bidding and objectively, if not subjectively, submissive to his authority.

This half-realized submissiveness presented the Regent with the problem of the old royal court which had so far managed to survive through thick and thin the Philippian rebuffs. The court had been the focus for the heterogeneous coalitions and cabals which had dominated Versailles and even the ministers under Louis XIV. There had been the Maine-Maintenon cabal, composed of grandees and ministers. Then there was Monseigneur's cabal, named after Louis XIV's deceased son. This was made up of princesses from the House of Lorraine, of the Condé-Conti and of the semi-illegitimate sons of Louis XIV. Although their influence had waned, these two groups still carried weight and they regarded Orléans with suspicion. Some of them were ready to rejoin his camp, bag and baggage, so long as he was ready to pay them enough, and in ready

---

6   The 'affair of the bonnet' which preoccupied Saint-Simon in the later years of Louis XIV's reign and at the beginning of the Regency, came down to this: when first presidents of the sovereign courts asked for the opinions (the votes) of those who had the right to speak in the sessions of the Parlement they customarily took off their bonnets when they asked the dukes and peers for theirs. But they had taken to keeping their bonnets on at this point and hence the duke's irritation. The affair is less pointless than it appears since it involved a conflict of precedence and, at heart, of power between the 'native' nobility (the dukes and peers) and the 'dative' nobility (the *parlementaires*) – on this subject, see Saint-Simon, *Mémoires*, xxv, 277 and xxvi, 1–39.

money, for their support. Such was the case especially for the House of Condé, incarnated at court by the young 'Monsieur le Duc'. He would become, for many years, Philippe's willing poodle.

Orléans was obliged to work through these groups and could not immediately introduce his own cabal into the political arena. His friends Dubois and Law, although they were highly intelligent, did not, for the moment, carry much weight – hence Philippe d'Orléans' tactic in the latter third of 1715 onwards of offering posts in the newly created polysynodical councils as seductive and safe sinecures to members of the old court. Although some of them claimed to be his supporters, or at least neutral towards him, many were his natural adversaries and he sought to neutralize them before buying their support out. In the new polysynodical structure, there was to be found, besides the remnants of the *parlementaire* and Jansenist opposition already referred to, the Gotha of the old Louis XIV court.

Amongst the new polysynodical councillors were, in reality, former ministers like Voysin or the Phélypeaux, military chiefs like Villars, and aristocrats like Beringhem. Orléans, here acting in agreement with his councillor Saint-Simon, wanted to make use of the old Maine-Maintenon axis to reinforce the initial stages of the Regency.[7] The polysynodical councils would last from 1715 to 1718 but they would become progressively more vacuous and Orléans disbanded them in the autumn of 1718. He then returned to a more centralized power structure shepherded into place by Dubois. The 'liberal' Regency was at an end; the more autocratic Regency was about to begin. The idea for such synodical councils had been inherited by Philippe d'Orléans when he took on the Regency, notions which had been given him by Saint-Simon. He had no rooted objection to them but neither was he wedded to their existence. He would abolish them in 1718 with the same equanimity with which he had created them in 1715. Only those, such as the *abbé* de Saint-Pierre, who were committed to the idea of political representation, mourned their passing. They, harbingers of the future, had invested the councils with an ideology of aristocratic, even bourgeois, liberalism. Orléans and Dubois, however, were more pragmatic than Saint-Pierre. From their point of view, the polysynodic structure had achieved its historic function by 1718. It had served to provide the old court with the shadow of authority, it had appeased the aristocrats, disarmed the potential for opposition, and allowed Orléans to set in train several enormous diplomatic and financial projects, which would be incarnated by Dubois, and then by Law. Once they were in place, and seen to be working either wholly or partially, these projects became assured of solid support from the élites of France, and

---

[7] Louis de Rouvroy, Duke de Saint-Simon (1675–1755), the unforgettable memorialist, spent the first part of his life at the Versailles court as a discontented courtier and 'closet' memorialist. His military career (1691–1702) was brief and undistingushed. In September 1715, his friend, the Regent Philippe d'Orléans, nominated him councillor to the Council of the Regency. He then became ambassador to Spain (1721–2) and then adopted a studious retirement in 1723 until his death in 1755.

from the country at large. Philippe was then in a position to divest himself of the old court, whose support had always been questionable and which had now no longer any purpose. He would be able to pay them off with Law's new banknotes, or with the money which acted as collateral to them. Hence the dissolution of the polysynody in the autumn of 1718.

In the preceeding year (1717), the new government had faced the normal problem for every regency (for example, that of Catherine de Médicis for the infant Charles IX) and routinely for almost every monarchical succession (as Louis XVI would discover). The new régime had to confront a nobility-focused challenge which, fortunately for the Regent, was politically neutralized by its own internal divisions and ludicrous quarrels over individual rights of precedence *à la* Saint-Simon, and by the dubious patronage afforded it by the bastard sons of Louis XIV. Militarily, this dispute was not on the scale of the Fronde – despite the first publication of the *Mémoires* of the Cardinal de Retz.[8] The seditious activity of the nobility would only result in armed conflict in Brittany where it was limited to the rural squirearchy and only became a problem in 1719, when it would easily be suppressed.

★   ★   ★   ★   ★

During the first years of the Regency, the Jansenists had been appeased, the Parisian *parlementaires* had been successfully seduced, and the upper nobility, henceforth resident at Versailles, had been disarmed. Philippe d'Orléans was now in a position to put in place his foreign policy, and one which would be his most successful creation. He had his hands free at home and there was more time to concentrate on foreign affairs. It was at this point that Dubois, with Orléans' assistance, concluded in the autumn of 1716 a master-stroke in the form of the English and Dutch alliance which, with the support of the Holy Roman Empire, would secure peace in Europe for a quarter of a century. This treaty represented a conceptual shift for the Regency and, along with that of Law's system and the wave of polysynodical liberalization in the post-Louis XIV period already described, was one of the three key developments of the period. The triple and quadruple alliances (England, the Dutch . . .) represented (over and above the intrigues in the chancellories of Europe) a cultural transformation. French foreign policy distanced itself from the Jesuit-style, *dévot* Catholicism which had been so much a feature of their erstwhile allies in Spain. French diplomats, and intellectuals too, aligned themselves with northern Europe, and its maritime, Protestant and capitalist traditions. In people's minds, the Pyrenees had become more of an obstacle and the English Channel or the Rhine less so . . . and not for the first time. The architects of this shift were numerous and the Nonconformists of the

---

[8]   The *Mémoires* of the Cardinal de Retz (1615–79) appeared for the first time in 1717. This initial edition was to have political significance for the opposition at the time of its appearance.

Regency and the Palais Royal entourage congratulated themselves on the paradoxical and productive results which it produced. Against the Stuarts and Philip V would be ranged the dynastic forces of Hanover and Philippe d'Orléans. Amongst them, Dubois was extraordinarily gifted. He was that rare bird in French politics, an anglophile; and although this was appreciated by his British counterparts, it won him few friends in France. In January 1716, Dubois, despite his modest upbringing, was named a councillor of state. He thus became a kind of *ex officio* member of the French power-élite and he had sufficient authority to push the Regent (in a direction he was not unwilling to go) towards the open arms of Great Britain. Here was an alliance between two families which were from the political margins in both cases: the Orleanists were held in suspicion by the French traditionalists from the old court of Louis XIV and the Hanoverians were new arrivals in England. It was an alliance based on self-interest but, as it took shape, its possibilities were considerable. The basis was thus laid for a new European order, based on a French *entente cordiale* with Great Britain, thanks to some small concessions for which, ever since, some unenlightened historians have held Dubois to blame. The groundwork was laid for the definitive renunciation of Spain's claim to the French throne and for the Holy Roman Empire to renounce its claims to the Spanish throne. The peaceful coexistence was thus made possible between the five major powers, England, France, the Dutch, the Holy Roman Empire and Spain.

As always, foreign policy enables us to understand better the networks which cemented those in power and those in opposition and the mutual rivalries which divided them from each other. Firstly, there was a grouping around the duke d'Orléans and the *abbé* Dubois. The latter promoted his own family and entered the Council of the Regency in March 1717. In this cabal there were those who had links with the aristocracy as well as the *robe* of the Parlements, governmental finance and the world of letters – the examples would include Canillac, Nancré, Nocé, Rémond and the Chavignard brothers. Actively opposing this cabal were to be found the 'appreciated pedants' of the old Court, amongst whom Huxelles, Villeroy, the Noailles, and then Torcy, constituted a quartet, then a quintet, of disgruntled opponents. The *abbé* Dubois became, on the Regent's behalf, the official leader of the group at the heart of the Council of the Regency. He abandoned any pretence at reserve, at masking his authority. In January 1718, he was overjoyed at the disgrace of his enemies d'Aguesseau and the duke de Noailles. The enlargement of the triple alliance with the adhesion of the Empire in August 1718 cemented the abbot's authority and he already looked forward to his cardinal's hat.

There remains the decisive experience of the Regency, the John Law affair. It had its basis in the economic recovery which had begun in 1715. In its turn it further stimulated the recovery which would be translated in due course into a solidly based and productive economic recovery which would accompany the whole of the reign of Louis XV through to 1774 and even beyond. Politically, the contradictions generated by the system of John Law brought to a swift end the 'liberal' phase of the Regency and inaugurated, in the summer of 1718, its 'authoritarian' phase – although this would never become a return to the specific restraints imposed by, or the particular tensions generated within, the Louis XIV régime and its superficial glory.

Law was Scottish by origin. He was initially in the service of the English ambassador Stair, himself an Orléanist of a kind. From 1715 onwards, and particularly after the creation of his bank in May 1716, he became one of the key figures amongst the Regency government, at first in cooperation, then later in competition with Dubois. Besides stimulating the economy, the issuing of banknotes by Law created political and social conflicts which provided the impetus to the transition from liberalism to authoritarianism in 1718. Law's predecessors as ministers of finance between 1713 and 1718 (Desmarets, Noailles, Argenson), followed financial orthodoxy and wanted to revalue the *livre tournois* in the interests of the *rentiers*.[9] However, the hugely increased circulation of paper money provoked a savage deflation in May 1717, one of the most abrupt in French history. Although such an act of expoliation would occasion few surprises to those living in the late twentieth century, the holders of fixed capital were aghast at it; creditors and *rentiers* were hit by the sudden surge in inflation which ate into the value of the loans which they had placed. The excessive liquidity, represented by the paper currency which had been issued, encouraged those with debts to repay their loans. Their lenders, who were used to stable receipts on the basis of usurious rates of interest, were mortified. On the other hand, the huge amount of money in circulation led to a decrease in rates of interest which threatened the whole profitability of the credit market. The Parlement of Paris, however, was composed of magistrates who were *rentiers* and lenders of capital. They would be amongst those most compromised by the System of John Law and, in consequence, they threatened him with fire and brimstone. The higher nobility at court remained, however, much more sanguine and it is easy to understand why. They were hugely encumbered with debts and so John Law represented manna from heaven for them. Agricultural production became highly profitable since agricultural prices moved in step with the inflation generated by the System. Finally, Philippe d'Orléans paid his senior courtiers in banknotes. Delighted, they rushed to convert this huge mass of paper into gold.

Law was undoubtedly responsible for the resulting devaluations and the *parlementaires* did not spare their criticism. In June 1718, they registered a vigorous protest against the Scots' inflationary policies. A blistering *lit de justice* in August 1718 put an end to their little Fronde. Maine and Louis XIV's bastards were caught up in the protest but to the ultimate benefit of

---

[9]   Marc René de Voyer de Paulmy, Marquis d'Argenson (1652–1721) was responsible for the overall administration of finance from January 1718. Michel Antoine, *Le Gouvernement et l'administration sous Louis XV; dictionnaire biographique* (Paris, CNRS, 1978), pp. 247–8.

the peerage. The old Louis XIV court was humiliated by the escapade. The Regent's party emerged with its grip on the levers of power the more solidly entrenched. He gained support amongst the technocracy, the House of Condé and the relics of the reforming groups left over from the previous reign. The summer and autumn of 1718 thus marked, as has already been noted, the point of transition from the 'liberal' Regency to the 'authoritarian' Regency. There was no need, however, to return to the excesses of the Louis XIV pattern of rule. The Philippists were, in fact, merely concerned to remove all those from the old court who held positions of influence. It is in this respect that the authoritarianism of the second phase of the Regency is more marked. Philippe d'Orléans also grew somewhat impatient of the Augustinian religious tendencies which had marked the first years of the Regency. He used a good pretext in September 1718 to dissolve the Council of Conscience, and then to abandon almost all the polysynodical councils. The English ambassador was involved in this shift. It removed the most anglophobe and hispanophile (Huxelles, Villars) from power in Paris.

The transition to the more authoritarian phase of the Regency in August/September 1718 was thus a profound social shift. It involved not only financial matters (Law) and religion (the Jansenist question), diplomacy and cultural affairs (openness to English influence), but also the question of social ranks and dynastic matters (dukes versus illegitimate royal sons) and the structure of government (the end of polysynodical councils). It was at the same time a technocrats' coup. The secretaries of state, the universal medicine to the bureaucratic ills of the Ancien Régime, regained their former status. The great ministerial families (the Phélypeaux and the Le Peletier) found themselves returning to the newly refashioned portfolios. They had formerly worked for Louvois and Desmarets; now they would serve again under Philippe d'Orléans and Dubois. With a fine sense of timing, Dubois would become, in September 1718, secretary of state for foreign affairs.

D'Antin was disgraced along with the rest of the *Conseil des affaires*. According to him, his fall from power was part of a move to follow the methods of Louis XIV and expel, this time for good, the great nobility from power. D'Antin was not entirely mistaken but the court aristocracy and prelates would, in fact, hold on to or retake several of the ministerial posts which they had been given at the beginning of the Regency. This would have alarmed Louis XIV who, with only a few exceptions, preferred the *robins* as his ministers. Although they were excluded from the majority of the key positions in government, however, the aristocracy were the gross beneficiaries, and by millions, from Law's System. The Regent and Dubois treated the portfolios of state like empty milk bottles, putting them outside the front door the night before to wake up to the fresh milk of an imaginative political agenda the following morning.

This imaginative political agenda was, first and foremost, the creation of Law. His System reached its climax in 1719, and then crashed in 1720. A brief summary of the background to the event is thus easily given. The whole Law experiment took place in the context of an economic recovery which had already begun in 1713. It also had its international context. In England, a similar attempt at a paper currency also took place at the same time as the bank of John Law. It would also come to grief in 1720 in the wreckage of the South Sea Bubble.

In any case, the results of the John Law scheme were very positive. Thanks both to it and the favourable economic climate, the state was able to pay its debts and to fund the wages of its servants and the pensions of its courtiers. The navy was also re-established, the receipts to the Treasury were buoyant, those with debts found them amortized and the agricultural sector was given a boost. At the same time, unemployment was reduced and the willingness to work was intensified, the money economy was stimulated and so was trade and manufacture. The principal victims, on the other hand, were to be found amongst the lending organisms – the monastic communities and the hospitals. There were generally fond memories of Law's System – its collapse did not leave too many casualties in its wake – but this was not universally the case. It has been said that its collapse would prevent the creation of a central bank in eighteenth-century France; but would the kingdom have been able to support such an institution? In reality, Law laid out the path towards the stabilization of the *livre tournois*. His achievement would be consolidated in 1726 and, with the exception of the short period of the *assignats* during the French Revolution, it would last for almost a further two centuries. Law's paper currency managed to survive a good deal better than the paper money circulated by Desmarets during the 1700s and it worked much better than the French Revolution *assignats*, both of which were experiments which were carried out in the teeth of profound national crisis and war.

Which social groups, particularly amongst the élite, benefitted from the System of John Law, and which did not? The Parlement remained its most determined opponent. The Regent followed up the coup against the *parlementaires* of 1718 with the wholesale exile of the assembly *manu militari* to Pontoise in July 1720. At the old court, meanwhile, the attitude to Law's System was always somewhat ambivalent. With the sole intention of assisting Law, Philippe d'Orléans dissolved the polysynodical councils in September 1718 to the detriment of the old crocodiles of the Maine-Maintenon clan with its accumulated mitres and titles. From 1715 to 1718 they had wallowed in the creeks of government until drained of water by the Regent. But to a dark cloud there is often a silver lining and what the grand seigneurs of the old court lost in offices and synodical portfolios they made up in banknotes which Philippe d'Orléans and Law generously distributed in their direction. Thanks to this, some of the best-placed aristocrats such as d'Antin and Bourbon-Condé were able to make and remake real fortunes. In his usual imperious and immoral fashion, Orléans showered his friends and enemies alike with gratifications with the only

LE DIABLE D'ARGENT

L'argent, en bonne foy est si rare et chacun forme
que l'homme descendroit au fond du Mo humét
s'il y creoit trouuer quelque besace pleine
de ce diuin Metal, dont il en perdre l'haleine
pour la rapporter en ce lieu
Ou on l'estime plus qu'un dieu

A Coups d'espee a Coups de Pique
et de Mousquets chacun se pique
de tirer ce Diable d'argent
Mais ce demon par sa rubrique
a tant qu'ils sont faysant la nique
ne leur donneroit pas un escu seulement

Luy seul va toute a vous

Chacun tire a ce Diable d'argent

Par rue St Jacques
a Grand St Remy

En fin pour temoigner l'humaine resuerie
de s'attacher aynsi a cette diablerie
S'efforçant de tirer ce diable par la queue
Luy dent on alonger plus grande d'une lieue
Ne lairoit de sa bource tomber pas un denier
quand tous en sa presence denier enrager

Plate 15   *The Devil Money*   Contemporaneous with the disruption and final stages in the discrediting of Law's System (1720), this engraving points the accusing finger at '*Le Diable d'Argent*' (The Devil Money), an object of attack from all quarters which, as the figure on the left of the engraving says: 'is going to have everything'. Yet there is no mention in the engraving of banknotes, the essential feature of Law's expansion of credit.
Paris, Bibliothèque nationale, cabinet des Estampes

stipulation being that they had to belong to the élite. In this way he reduced the risk of dangerous conspiracy or civil war. The new equilibrium which was established after the transition of August 1718 thus rested on a subtle balance of forces. The Orleanist group was set to work, was forced to coexist one with another (Law and Dubois, both rivals of each other), the Parlement's influence on events was amputated for the moment but not abolished for good, the old court was cashiered but well-rewarded for its pains.

That the suppression of polysynodie was not, as has sometimes been alleged, purely and simply a return to the state of affairs before 1715 is well demonstrated by the 'Cellamare affair' and the 'Spanish question'. The strategies of the cabals during these two events, and their standpoints in foreign affairs, were worlds away from those which had existed under the elderly Louis XIV. The conspiracy of Cellamare was discovered by Dubois in December 1718. It was made up of opposition elements which included the bastard sons of Louis XIV and various figures in the higher French nobility as well as some Spanish and Italian support, the latter ultramontane by definition. Philippe did not have much difficulty in rallying the hispanophobe and Jansenist sentiments of the Parlement, which some months before he had snubbed, against this comic opera of a conspiracy, which was readily dubbed 'pro-Jesuit'. A blow to the left was matched with one to the right. The Regent earned himself the approbation of adherents to the Jansenist 'left-wing', whom he had previously offended, by offering them the entertaining spectacle of humiliating the ultramontane 'right-wing'. Divide and rule: the cut and thrust of the Regent's politics was adroit. Dubois was increasingly the master of the operation and becoming the Regent's *éminence grise*. Law retained the simple role, however, as a technical supremo of the state's finances and Jackanorry to the Regent. The division of responsibility between Dubois and Law eloquently reveals where the true power now lay – inevitably with Dubois, although under the Regent's control and with the material and financial assistance of John Law.

The modest war with Spain launched by France against its Bourbon cousins in Madrid in 1719 was part of a parallel strategy on the part of the Regent and Dubois. Inexpensive and relatively bloodless, the conflict was more of an argument amongst friends. It forced Spain to accept the European system outlined by the English and French ministers (Dubois, Stanhope). The added anti-Spanish and italophobe doses to the public rhetoric were not entirely irrelevant, either, since they provided the means to satisfy the Jansenist or Gallican patriotism of the French élites, including also some of the middling groups in society.

The adroitly anti-Spanish politics of Philippe d'Orléans and Dubois bore fruit also at the beginning of 1720 during the Brittany affair. There were genuine reasons to fear a united aristocratic front in the Breton peninsula leading its autonomous and independent elements. Various components of the Breton nobility would have been prepared to rally against Parisian centralization. The rural squirearchy and the *parlementaires* in Rennes would have been ready to make common cause in defence of the province's privileges, particularly in fiscal matters. But ultramontane Spain openly offered its support to the discontented elements of Brittany and this compromised the cause sufficiently to frighten the *parlementaires* of Rennes, discreetly Gallican in their attitudes if not Jansenist, back into line. Henceforth, at least during the Regency period, they would not swerve from their French loyalism and so the rural Breton nobility found themselves, with their leader Pontcallec, isolated in their rebellion, and then arrested. Four of their leaders were executed by order of a royal court, convoked at Nantes by the normally more indulgent Regent. Once again, the rupture with Spain, which the Regent had shrewdly played on, served to maintain or to re-establish something of a national and provincial consensus around the régime of Philippe d'Orléans.

The end of the Brittany affair in March 1720, followed by the final disgrace of Law in December 1720 marked the supreme triumph of Dubois. The old court party was completely marginalized, despite being joined by the Colbertian Torcy and despite receiving some late overtures from a desperate John Law. Dubois, with the support of his ministerial, pro-English specialists, sought to gain the support of two old Dauphiné families who had become established in Paris. Firstly, there were the Tencin (brother and sister, master and mistress of intrigue) and then, secondly, the Pâris (a quartet of financier brothers who helped the minister to escape from the twitching remnants of the John Law bank, following from its crash). This was the moment, from 1719 to 1721, when Dubois chose to intrigue for a cardinal's hat. Would this former abbot, now archbishop of Cambrai, abandon his pro-English policies and his accommodation with the Jansenists and sacrifice both to the *Unigenitus* bull, to the Jesuits, or to the Papacy, the dispenser of cardinals' hats? To believe Dubois capable of entertaining such a notion would be utterly to misunderstand him. He coldly calculated that he would be able to acquire the cardinal's hat on his own terms. In fact, far from distancing himself from the English, Dubois placed even greater reliance upon them and used their good offices with His Holiness through the intermediary of the Holy Roman Empire and thus gained, in return for the necessary cash, the famous cardinal's hat. Dubois' active opponent during this period was Cardinal Alberoni, the disgraced minister of Philip V of Spain. This ultramontane Italian cardinal had long been in Spanish service and a devotee of ultra-Catholicism *à l'outrance*.

A weary truce! The Regent also recognized when it was necessary to demonstrate a more solid support for the Jansenists. In February/March 1719 he granted the university of Paris, with its Augustinian tendencies, a substantial sum for scholarships and the state funding of its teaching programme. The Regent's daughter, the picturesque abbess de Chelles, was amongst several nuns who launched an appeal to the Regent against the bull *Unigenitus*.[10] However, this was still the time for compromises and

---

[10] Louise-Adélaïde d'Orléans (1698–1743), the Regent's daughter, was Mother Superior of the great Abbey of Chelles. Intelligent, attractive and original, she rejected, both in thought and action, the anti-Jansenism of the established church.

in December 1720 the Parlement of Paris undertook the final, and completely hypocritical, registration of the bull *Unigenitus*, despite their known convictions for a kind of Jansenism and loyalties to the Cardinal de Noailles. The Parlement sought to cover up this hollow, superficial capitulation to the Roman Curia and to ultramontane Jesuitism as best it could. The majority of the judges amongst the assembly, by then sitting at Pontoise, accepted *Unigenitus* despite those of its number such as the *abbé* Pucelles who were diehard Augustinians. But the Parisian magistrates hedged their acceptance with so many qualifications and equivocations that 'they were tantamount to saying that they had not enregistered it' (Marais) or again 'that nothing had happened and that it was all a game' (Barbier).[11] This superficial 'reconciliation' was the reward which the *parlementaires* conceded in return for the disgrace of the detested Law. It was a strange coincidence which saw the Scottish John Law leave Paris on 14 December 1720, a victim of his own unpopularity (albeit this was less widespread than would be later claimed was the case) as well as of the Parlement and the 'Peace of the Church'.

The final withdrawal from the scene of Law as *contrôleur général des finances* represented in itself a major concession to the *parlementaires*, the implacable defenders of *rentes*. They felt that their whole life-work had been undermined by the politics of lowering interest-rates and by Law's tactic of stimulating an incautious but productive bout of inflation. Law was their sacrificial victim and, in return, they saw to the registration of the bull *Unigenitus* in a way in which there was more shadow than substance, and handed this to the Regent, although he was also hardly its warmest supporter. At the same time, the French church saw the formation of a twin coalition. One, a narrow alliance, brought together the opportunistic prelates who were open supporters of Dubois – in particular, Tressan, Bezons and Rohan. These three bishops willingly undertook to carry out the wishes of the chief minister in religious matters and relied on Parabère, the Regent's mistress, for their support. The other was a broader coalition and one with more moral scruples which brought together several bishops and all the French cardinals in favour of a compromise which was along the lines of the wishes of Philippe d'Orléans and Dubois. This compromise involved the construction of a third party half-way between the Jansenists and the ultramontane *zelanti*. The long sought-for church peace would thus be located away from the zealots on both sides.

This settlement of the Jansenist quarrel, although it would not last, coupled with the quest for the cardinal's hat for Dubois, had run its course by 1721. Neither issue had forced Dubois to alter his foreign policy – indeed rather the reverse. That policy was characterized by the overtures which were made towards the maritime and Protestant powers in Europe

---

[11]   Mathieu Marais, *Journal et Mémoires sur la Régence* (Paris, 1863); Edmond-Jean Barbier, *Chronique [ou Journal] de la Régence* (Paris, 1857); for the end of 1720, both these authors are cited by Leclercq, *Histoire de la Régence*, ii, 125.

and by the search for a European concert of powers which would embrace France, England, the Low Countries, the Holy Roman Empire and Prussia. The objective behind France's isolation of Spain, followed by its attack in 1719, was to ensure that, by persuasion or by force, it fully accepted the new world-order and its Anglo-French axis. 'I attack my neighbour (Spain) but it is to embrace him.' Should one regard Dubois in this affair as a 'good European'? The compliment would be wholly anachronistic, but not entirely unmerited, for Dubois' diplomacy was, in some respects, very far from being opportunistic. Undoubtedly, he sought to protect the dynastic interests of his patron Philippe d'Orléans just as his good friends Stair and Stanhope served the interests of the Hanoverian dynasty. Yet the politics of peace pursued by Dubois (even when it was enforced by means of the mini-war with Spain in 1719) represented the inventive and creative application of principle to French foreign affairs. It broke with the traditions of all-out war and frequent diplomatic isolation which had characterized the two centuries of policy under both the later Valois and the early Bourbons. It returned, however, towards the 'protestantophile' diplomacy of Francis I, of Henry IV (much admired by Philippe d'Orléans), of Richelieu and of Mazarin. It reached its elegant heights in a perception of foreign affairs which was not narrowly nationally focused but which was anglo-continental in its considerations. It reflected the ecumenical and pacifist predilections of the Palais Royal and of the Orléans family. These would be represented in the personality of the Regent's mother, Madame the Elder, the Huguenot-sympathizing Germanophile who corresponded with the great Leibniz. Such preoccupations were also personified by the *abbé* Saint-Pierre, the author of a project for perpetual peace, and embodied by the Regent himself who was steeped in the pacifist philosophical outlook of Fénelon. In comparison, the diehard hispanophiles of the old court party cut a poor figure.

The departure of Law exposed the remnants of the old court party which, in seeking its final refuge by coolly offering to support John Law, found itself abruptly exposed and no longer in any state to resist Dubois' firm stamp of authority. He appeared invincible to everything except mortality itself. The sequence of diplomatic events which followed was one in which foreign affairs and domestic politics were closely intermingled, as was always the case under the Regency. From May to July 1721, the mutual alliance between France and Spain was signed, to be followed by the triple alliance between France, England and Spain. Once more, there was never any question of Dubois abandoning his anglophile political stance in favour of a unilateral *rapprochement* with the Bourbons in Madrid. During the negotiations, the French statesman sought to bind Spain more closely to the system of European security which he had devised. The axis of policy remained a Franco-British one.

The project for the Spanish marriages which reached a successful conclusion in July 1721 was to conjoin in matrimony the young Louis XV and the daughter of Philippe d'Orléans with two offspring of Philip V of Spain.

These marriage treaties can also be interpreted as a continuation of the pacifist, paradoxically pro-British, not to mention pro-Protestant, European perspective of French foreign policy. They were perceived as serving to embrace Spain within a western security framework, the centres for which lay in London and in Paris. Dubois would win approval for having sacrificed some minor pawns such as the naval base at Pensacola in Florida, which could not have been retained in French hands in the longer term. He also agreed to the dismantling of the Franco-Spanish monopoly over the Atlantic slave-trade, the *asiento*, and extending it to include the British. Finally, Dubois surrendered the fortifications at Mardick, close by Dunkirk. Dubois did not believe Mardick was worth fighting for. Over the years since his death, some historians hostile to Dubois have accused him, albeit with absurdity and without the slightest proof, of treason and even of having been bought by the British. In reality, the Dubois group had the advantage of an excellent team of diplomats which would contribute to the success of his foreign policy.

Amongst them one should single out the *chevalier* Des Touches, the Jesuit Lafitau, the *robin* Chavigny, the *abbé* de Mornay and even the writer Fontenelle who, from time to time, would write pieces in favour of the minister. Saint-Simon would, in the course of an official posting to Spain, become Dubois' obedient servant. His master took some pleasure in ruining the petty ducal fortunes of Saint-Simon through the excessive costs of being a diplomatic representative. At the same time, he humiliated him by making him a servant in charge of all the fine details of the minister's domestic life. Saint-Simon never forgave the bitterness which resulted from this period. He would exact his own revenge 20 years later in his *Mémoires* where the reputation of Dubois was excoriated. Thus was the reputation of a great French statesmen unjustly tarnished.

It was the case – and here Saint-Simon was correct – that Dubois was not the epitome of honesty, any more than Colbert was. His cardinal's hat cost the French Treasury a small matter of 8 million *livres tournois*, dispensed amongst the entourage of the sovereign pontiff. Yet this was no purely honorific title; on the contrary it was worth its weight in gold. It became for the first minister an effective instrument of power and exclusivity. Thanks to this title, the newly promoted cardinal was *ipso facto* in terms of protocol one of the most senior figures in the Regency Council. By means of his elevation, he was able to exploit etiquette to the disadvantage of his opponents. Dukes and peers and the *maréchaux* of France would never let a mere nobody such as the ex-*abbé* Dubois, the son of a physician or an apothecary – i.e. someone who had come from common stock – take up a place at the Council of the kingdom and assume a rank of precedence over them. However it was impossible to contest his right to do so as a cardinal. Only one solution remained open to the lay, titled aristocracy if they wanted to save face and that was to resign from the Council themselves. This was what happened in February 1722. Thus were removed three of Dubois' worst enemies from the old court party in the shape of

Villars, d'Antin and Noailles. At the same time, Dubois dismissed from their ministerial posts two of his adversaries, Torcy and, for a second time, d'Aguesseau. He promoted in their place his own clients, amongst whom were a couple of principal families who had proven loyalty towards him, the Le Peletier-Armenonville and the Pâris brothers. In these circumstances, the Council of the Regency became something of a simple tête-à-tête between the House of Condé (Charolais and Monsieur le Duc) which, for the moment, was behaving itself; the remaining bastards (the count of Toulouse); and four or five of Philippe d'Orléans and Dubois' friends and henchmen. There were some other exclusions which were accomplished without bloodshed and which eliminated from the Court, by now re-established at Versailles, the remains of the old Louis XIV factions amongst the grand seigneurs and the old ministerial cliques. The triumph of Dubois and of his disciple or patron Philippe d'Orléans was established from that moment onwards until their mutual demise in 1723. Bishop Fleury, having courted political disaster, withdrew from opposition before it was too late. He conserved his forces for a future which, both personally and politically, had everything still in store. He felt himself still to have age on his side and to be relatively inexperienced. He was in no doubt of the affection of his tender and royal pupil, the young Louis XV. He had the luxury of time on his side. He was but 69 years old and it would not be long before he would become Louis XV's first minister when the king entered into his majority. He would remain in post for close on 20 years.

In assessing the Regency, one must be careful to avoid creating a Gilray-style cartoon picture of the period, even in mezzo-tint. These days Orléans is no longer openly criticized for his sexual promiscuity although the latter continues to figure in the sub-text and to motivate the pejorative statements which occur in the studies of the eight years of the Regency. At least no one could ever suppose Philippe d'Orléans to have been a homosexual; indeed his heterosexual exploits figure in a moralizing historiographical tradition which censured his promiscuous behaviour. Yet, and here is the paradox, the same tradition ignores the harem at the court of Henry IV, the king who is the hero of the primary school history books and Lavissian historical ideology.[12] This constitutes the proof that, behind the 'stories of Ladies' and the Regent, there is a further agenda in play, that of Jacobin tradition. In fact, although his sexual licence is hardly mentioned, the Regent is still criticized for his less than robust attitudes towards England, the Parlement and the aristocracy. Such criticism continues to be implicit, but the same critics would not dream of levelling the same charges against the good King Henry IV, who also had his various women and who also had a pre-absolutist attitude to authority, was also pro-English,

---

[12] For the significance of the rôle of Ernest Lavisse's contribution to French academic history, see W.R. Keylov, *Academy and Community* (Cambridge, MA, Harvard University Press, 1975).

protestantophile and open-minded towards change. So we need to provide a more objective assessment of the period.

Measured on their own terms, and by the objectives which the Regent set for himself to achieve, the eight years of power exercised by Orléans represent a success. His overriding objective was evident. Uncle Philippe wanted to transmit royal authority to his nephew Louis intact. At the same time, and in the spirit of Fénelon, he wanted to extricate the government from the improper or pointlessly authoritarian exercises to which it had been committed (perpetual warfare, an overburdensome fiscality, an excessive despotism, popular misery – at times atrocious). Philippe succeeded in achieving this objective, deploying a style of government which was avuncular, yet stimulating of others, a style which was of a piece with his Regency and its empirical modes of operation. He avoided a Fronde or a civil war, which would have been the worst-case scenario. He operated by small steps, each developed progressively in relation to each other like the florid rococo decoration which characterized the Regency style, so different from the rigid geometric neo-classicism of enlightened despotism, which had yet to capture Europe's imagination.

At the heart of things, the Regency was marked by some changes in personnel but these were undertaken without bloodshed; Philippe's entourage, even amongst those closest to him, consisted of Scots, Bordelais, Dauphinois, Rouergats, Périgourdins, Dutch, English, Limousins and Languedocians. Up to a point, those who enjoyed his trust were geographically as well as socially from the periphery, if not the margins. They were from a distinctively different milieu from those who served Louis XIV. For Colbert, Le Tellier, Louvois, the Phélypeaux, Voysin, Chamillart and the Villeroy were also from the *robe*, albeit spruced-up for royal service, but their roots lay in the Paris basin, as did the gothic roots of the centralist French state and, eventually, French jacobinism. This was the heartland which gave French royal strategy its multisecular continuities, including an endless rallying of the state for war to defeat the Dutch and English competitors and the undiplomatic harrying and hassling of neighbouring powers. The approach of Dubois and of Fleury was more flexible. They were both from the French Midi and neither was primarily hyperpatriotic or hypernationalistic in his attitudes. It is clear that, with a different team of ministers, Philippe and his royal nephew were able to forge a policy which was less concerned with 'glory' in the splendiferous sense of the word, and more willing to accommodate the progressive forces which were coming to dominate the horizons of the maritime, capitalist and Protestant powers to the north. To some degree the attitudes which the French adopt towards England, and today towards the United States (or the 'Anglo-Saxons' as they are readily referred to in France), remain in the eighteenth, nineteenth and twentieth centuries, one of the touchstones of French liberalism, albeit but a partial one.

Should Philippe be credited with an earlier version of nineteenth-century 'Orleanism'? The coincidence of the name Orléans and Philippe, occuring at the time of a Regent as a 'citizen-king', is hardly a sufficient criterion for making the comparison. Yet it is nevertheless the case that the cadet branches of the royal family put themselves, with varying degrees of perspicacity, at the head of desires for change in society. This was true of the Condé and the Bourbon-Navarre in the sixteenth century, of Gaston d'Orléans under Richelieu as well as of Beaufort and Condé during the Fronde, of Philippe under the Regency as well as, later, Egalité, and then Louis-Philippe between 1789 and 1840. The cadet lines charted a less dogmatic and authoritarian course than that pursued by the senior Bourbon branch. From this point of view, the Regent may reasonably be taken to be the architect of the first 'Orleanism', although his political style did little to direct the more authentically liberal 'Orleanism' of Philippe-Egalité and Louis-Philippe over a century later.

More directly, the Regency posed the problem already alluded to earlier in the chapter of how to dismantle an excessive authoritarianism; or, at the very least, how to chart a way out of a repressive system of government with all its tensions following the death of the preceeding sovereign. The way forward would be manifested by conservative tradition and by a controlled process of adaptation. Of course, it will not do to compare Louis XIV's hegemony directly with that of modern dictators of the twentieth century, whether totalitarian or not. Yet the harshness of the Sun-King's régime, above all on the eve of, and after, the Revocation, not to mention the ways by which he secured consent from the élite, the interminable wars and the fiscal demands made of the people at large – all these made the succession to Louis XIV a delicate matter for someone who sought to conserve the system of government and preserve as much as possible of its best features whilst removing those which were improper. This was, in truth, the task which Philippe and his collaborators set themselves and the three ways by which they set about it may for simplicity's sake be named 'Saint-Simon', 'Law' and 'Dubois'.

'Saint-Simon' signifies the appeal (albeit somewhat far-fetched) for participation and for a kind of consensus amongst the governing classes, i.e., for the purpose of the exercise, the aristocracy.

'Law' is economic recovery, and thus a measure of relief for the mass of the population. The bank and the ministers endeavoured to help their plight by amortizing their debts and reducing fiscal burdens.

'Dubois' is the foreign policy, already described, directed towards the more liberal and open-minded powers in maritime, capitalist and Protestant Europe, for these purposes, England and the Dutch. The dismantling of authoritarian régimes in Europe and elsewhere in the nineteenth and twentieth centuries would eventually have to use the same three routes – but the individuals involved in the process would be entirely different in each case. It should be added that this pattern of conservative-based transition provides a broad, multisecular typology and it implies *ipso facto* a degree of change amongst the political establishment. But this is not necessarily a violent process, and certainly not of the kind which will have been present in the preceding reign or under the previous ruler. In the course of this process of change, there are necessarily periods of reaction, moments when change had to be slowed down, occasional resorts to a kind of neo-authoritarianism. By these means the ruler sought to prevent the system from becoming caught up and tearing itself apart under the pressures of an excessive liberalization. For the new ruler, the important objective is to reform in order to sustain the system, rather than to destroy it. During the Regency, the operation was successful and the transition achieved without peril such that the system, suitably humanized, could finally be entrusted to a competent manager with a clean record, someone who would look after it without attempting to change things. In France, following the interim of the duke de Bourbon, this rather dull, though far from undignified, role was carried through by the gerontocratic Fleury during the first decades of Louis XV's majority.

By way of conclusion, we may examine the structure, or rather, the genealogy of the exercise of power as we have delineated it so far in the France from the years after the Fronde until the early stages of the reign of Louis XV. Five royal or princely generations and, related to them, seven power-groups, held, or anticipated holding, power. These five generations and seven groups were as follows: *Anne and Mazarin*; *Louis XIV and la Maintenon*; *Monseigneur* (Louis XIV's son); *Bourgogne* (Louis XIV's grandson); *Orléans* (his nephew); *Bourbon* (his cousin); finally, *Louis XV* (his greatgrandson) with Fleury by his side. These groups represented the axes around which the power-networks, and the bids for power, revolved during the years from 1650 to 1730.

Anne and Mazarin, to begin with, left to Louis XIV their servants Le Tellier, Colbert, Lionne and Fouquet (the *first group*). These state servants would hold the fort during the first period of Louis XIV's personal rule, until the 1680s. The disgrace of Fouquet and the retreat of Lionne transformed the ministry into the famous duo of Colbert on one side of the coin and Le Tellier-Louvois, father and son, on its reverse side.

After the death of Louvois in 1691, the king, assisted by Madame de Maintenon, eventually chose his own collaborators (the *second group*). Amongst the succession of ministers who were selected to serve during the second half of the reign, we should single out the Phélypeaux-Pontchartrain, father and son, Chamillart, Desmarets (a Colbert, although by now in the Maintenon camp), and Voysin, allied to Desmarets through his wife. A camarilla of grand seigneurs – Villars, Huxelles, Harcourt and such like – revolved around this power grouping during its period of ascendancy; later, it would become, under the Regency, the principal component of the old court party. It was thus a group with its sights turned towards the past and nostalgic for the latter years of Louis XIV's rule.

A cabal of ambitious men and women (the *third group*) also congregated around Monseigneur, Louis XIV's son. This group, like that converging around Louis XIV and Madame de Maintenon, lay in opposition to those with reformist and pacifist tendencies. Colbert's relatives and cronies formed themselves around the young duke of Burgundy who represented the fourth royal generation during the years from 1700 to 1710. The death of its principal figures marked the end of this Burgundian and Fénelonian constellation (the *fourth group*).

The death of Louis XIV provided the opportunity for the *fifth group* to make its appearance, that of the Palais-Royal and its key figure, Philippe d'Orléans. At first, this Orleanist cabal was composed of little more than the close companions of Philippe and whoever was amongst his older or more recent acquaintances – the names of Dubois, Rémond, Bezons, Saint-Pierre, Law and Saint-Simon come to mind. The group quickly began to gather momentum, however, as the Regent's authority became more asserted and the opportunists amongst its number, and above all the civilian, military and financial specialists, those who would be responsible for the Regency's political success, gradually came to the fore. That success was based upon openness and also on an effective control of events, such that they never entirely got out of control or escaped the vigilant eyes of those in power, even when it was engaged in the productive but wild and badly controlled System of John Law.

The death of Dubois and d'Orléans left the field wide open to the House of Bourbon-Condé, incarnated by Monsieur le duc de Condé, and his mistress Madame de Prye, with the financier Pâris-Duverney at his side (the *sixth group*). Openness was no longer in fashion and a vigorous deflation was instigated, repressive measures once again began to be enforced, at least in theory, against the Protestants. They evoked the malevolent memories of the Revocation, although they did not emulate either its worst nightmares or excesses. Then came the semi-famine of 1725 and, in the following year (1726), Louis XV, by now beyond adolescence, could bring to power his own man, by then in his seventies and shortly to be made a cardinal – Cardinal Fleury.

Fleury governed with the help of the great ministerial *robin* families such as a new generation of Phélypeaux, the Le Peletier (Armenonville and Morville), Orry, Leblanc, Amelot and d'Aguesseau. Putting himself at the head of a *seventh group*, he stabilized the *livre tournois*, unified the tax-farms of the kingdom, let economic growth continue, maintained the English alliance and reunited Lorraine to the French kingdom. Inheriting the achievements of the Regency he consolidated them and prudently avoided taking on new initiatives. His ministry lasted almost 20 years and it was punctuated by the occasional incident of repression which generally characterizes periods of pure consolidation. It was during Fleury's ministry that, under the pressure of renewed persecution, the Jansenists found themselves embroiled in dramatic incidents of demonic possession known as 'convulsions', not to mention doing the splits over the tomb of the deacon Pâris, all of which brought ridicule upon their cause.

* * * * *

We have already said in the course of the first chapter of this book that it is a work which, from cover to cover, concentrates on the political history of the French state, with its own autonomous existence and internal logic. This clear focus should not prevent us, where necessary, from exploring the links which existed between, for example, the mercantilist strategy of a particular minister, the conduct of a particular war (or not, as they case may be) and the economic and demographic context at that particular time. It is like a puzzle with three bodies or entities, all relating in various ways with one another, and each confronting the spontaneous, voluntary and independent decisions of the productive classes beneath them. Such a 'plural' analysis of the 'Philippian' years from 1713–26, one which explores the economic background behind the narrative sequence, is essential, particularly given the wider significance of the period.

The years from 1715 to 1725 represent a decennial, or inter-decennial period when the productive and demographic basis upon which French society rested began to shift.[13] It had remained embedded in a period of relative stagnation since 1560, a stagnation manifested by the ceiling reached by, or the very slow overall growth of, its population as well as its agricultural production (at least of cereal crops).[14] Of course this had not prevented the remarkable, but somewhat unilateral, developments in the cultural, political, administrative and military domains. There were also a number of innovations in various aspects of civil society both in non-agricultural technologies such as in science, in urban life and, up to a certain point, in some specialized areas of agricultural production (brandy, maize, silk, etc.). By contrast, the eighteenth century – after 1700 or 1710, and the date invites debate – was one of demographic growth. The expansion was continuous and regular and it took the 'national' population levels within the conventional frontiers of the French hexagon, from 21.8 million around 1685 to 23.4 million around 1715, 25.3 million around 1745, and to 28.5 million in 1789.[15] There is no doubt that the causes for this expansion were diverse and profound but not least amongst them was certainly the end of long periods of warfare after the Peace of Utrecht, something which constituted an important shift in the life of the entire country, a turning-point which had demographic, and not merely military or diplomatic, significance.

Looking back across the seventeenth century, both the death and birth rates were equally high and this left a noticeably restricted margin for population growth. The fairly regular occurrence of great *mortality crises* eliminated hundreds of thousands, sometimes up to a million or more, from the overall population in the majority of the country through the high death rates and the correspondingly low birth rates. Although the subsequent recovery was doubtless rapidly achieved, the possibility of a sus-

---

[13] 'Inter-decennial' – i.e. 'longer than a decade' in the terminology of Ernest Labrousse, *La Crise de l'économie française à la fin de l'Ancien Régime et au début de la Révolution* (Paris, PUF, 1943).

[14] Jacques Dupâquier, *Histoire de la population française, de la Renaissance à 1789* (Paris, PUF, 1988), ii, 68.

[15] Ibid.

tained, secular increase in the overall population was thwarted. Such demographic crises occurred during the wars of religion, then from 1626 to 1636 (at least in the regions to the east, devastated by the Thirty Years War), then during the Fronde and the civil war which accompanied it (1649–52); and then finally in 1661–2, 1693–4 and 1709–10. Without exaggerating the overall picture, there is no doubt that, in the majority of France's provinces and particularly in the countryside, poverty existed in large measure. This situation, coupled with the inelasticity of levels of production, made compulsory levies such as taxation the less supportable which, in other circumstances, would have been accepted with greater ease. It also diminished the overall levels of income which remained sluggish and insufficient.

The picture should not, however, be exaggerated. The French seventeenth century had, economically, its springtime periods, notably under Henry IV and continuing during the first 15 years of the reign of Louis XIII. It also experienced the Indian summer, as we have already seen, under Colbert, the glow of which would last even after Colbert's death. The harsh winter would only come after 1689 with the savage frosts and famine of 1693–4, and 1709–10, dates rich with symbolism in the medium term. But the feature which most characterized the longer period from the beginning of Richelieu's ministry through to the end of Louis XIV's reign, was the country's weakness in its agricultural production and in the commercialization of that production. This was something which France probably shared with the overwhelming mass of the continent of Europe but it was a weakness which was crippling when it came to establishing a truly sustainable economic expansion, and solving that weakness was one of the keys to all that would follow from sustained economic growth.

One further element needs to be taken into consideration. Twice in the seventeenth century the French economy touched rock-bottom. This occurred firstly from 1633 to 1653 (and, above all, for the period of Thirty Years War/Fronde dislocations from 1648 to 1653). Secondly, there was the 20 to 25-year period at the end of the reign of Louis XIV from 1689 to 1713. However, these difficult years did not prevent some positive developments of great potential and long-term significance for economic growth, especially in the manufacturing sectors, in viniculture, colonization and long-distance trades. The importance of cloth and silk manufacture, as well as of Santo Domingo, have already been alluded to. Against this, however, there were forces preventing change at work, particularly the exactions which were the most productive of economic dislocation in periods of war, and the most volatile – i.e. royal taxation. There is thus no great mystery in the recurrence of antifiscal uprisings in the seventeenth century. These rural and urban rebellions, drawing on popular or semi-élite support, occurred most notably in the period from 1635 to 1675 although there were Croquant disturbances in Aquitaine through to 1707. These popular movements were thus, after their own fashion, a rational response of the harvester to the tax-gatherer, the reactions of people who would not, or could not, pay their taxes to the state.[16] At the same time, such reactions were contrary to another kind of rationality, one which was state-driven, war-orientated and absorptive of taxation. To the latter, the immediate interest of the French population at large did not come first but rather the greatness of the kingdom and its clout, embodied in its military machine and in the apparatus of state at the command of the cardinal-ministers, and thereafter in the hands of the Apollo of Versailles and his *contrôleur général*.

The eighteenth century, by contrast, was in many ways a period of change and of reaching towards both domestic calm (albeit not definitively) and economic growth, all of which was very much in harmony *grosso modo* with the idea of progress which would be enamoured of Condorcet in due course but which had already been popularized by Perrault during the debate between the Ancients and the Moderns. Antifiscal revolt waned after 1713 partly because feverish increases in taxation only occurred very spasmodically, and partly because the gross national product was growing again. In the disturbances of the pre-revolution period from 1751 to 1788, and then again during the French Revolution, there would be renewed agitations against state taxation, but this was within a context in which the protests, uprisings and rebellions were much more diverse and where the question of taxation, although still a live issue, was only one of the many capable of striking a popular chord. During the age of the Enlightenment, the economy diversified and, above all, the population began to increase in a regular fashion, without (as during the Fronde) the increase being wiped out at any stage. This increase took place both in rural and urban France, a double movement which had its own logic since, although agricultural productivity remained low (although there were modest improvements), an additional cohort of cultivators of the soil was necessary to support the increase in urban populations. As a result, the birth-rates of rural France remained high, despite the zest for contraception which spread from the urban to the rural world and which began to make its appearance from around 1760 or 1770.

In the case of death, three of the Horsemen of the Apocalypse (i.e., war, famine and plague) were all, if not routed, at least in retreat. The end of massive famines was linked to the growth in agricultural productivity, which has already been alluded to, as well as to better mechanisms for distribution and sale. And when the money did not reach the rural world, the peasants, particularly from the upland regions, went in search of it in the towns, by means of the temporary or permanent migration of rural labour to take up domestic service, or to work in the construction industry

---

[16] Much has been written about the 'savage' rebellions and 'primitive' rebels in Ancien Régime France. In fact, the introduction of the poll tax in England in 1989 produced street demonstrations and hostile crowd scenes which were in no sense irrational or 'savage'; and they were not so different, and certainly no less violent, than the rebellions recorded in Rouergue, in the Vivarais and at Montpellier in the seventeenth century against the establishment of an eventual capitation tax.

or other industrial enterprises. The propertied classes also, albeit in a different fashion altogether, enjoyed a quasi-urban, quasi-rural existence. The nobility, the senior clergy and the rich bourgeoisie had one foot in the town where they kept their winter residence and another on their domains in the countryside which provided them with a progessively increasing income from rents which grew along with the favourable economic climate during the eighteenth century.[17] Seigneurial dues (whose monetary signifi-cance was small) hardly increased at all; and nor did tithes and taxes. The small peasant cultivator was doubtless the one who suffered both from the sub-division over the years of his small-holding and the progressive and eventually impoverishing wages for day-labour, the rates for which strug-gled to keep up with the increase in prices and which ended up well behind. If the real daily income of an individual tended to diminish, the number of days' work which various members of a family undertook and were paid for increased notably as a result of the certain degree of prosper-ity and the greater volume of work available to be done. So the standard of living in the rural world grew, albeit in a very unequal fashion, during the reign of Louis XV. That of the 'lower' orders also probably tended to grow as well in the course of the century (although to a lesser degree than occurred for others). If it did, then it was at the cost of increased 'elbow-grease' on their part and in the overall context of the continuing existence of a vast mass of rural and urban poverty.

The eighteenth century was thus one of expansion in rural France and this brought with it various breaks with past patterns. Its fundamental institutions (the church, the family, etc.) stimulated amongst rural com-munities the need for basic education and they were assisted by the spontaneous desire for literacy which was to be found amongst the rural élites as well as more generally in the rural world. This could, in turn, have something of a 'boomerang' effect since it eventually fostered a detach-ment from the church amongst the former pupils who had been taught in its primary schools and enjoyed the intellectual benefits, however modest, this had brought. At all events, literacy was more broadly spread out than in the past. Books, amongst which featured the popular or pseudo-popular chapbook literature called the *bibliothèque bleue*, circulated, along with the latest news from Paris and elsewhere, from town to town and from the urban world outwards to the countryside. This led to the emergence of a national market for information, the unforeseen consequences of which would be felt rather later at the time of the Great Fear of 1789. This meant that opinions, accusations and denials spread rapidly in a few weeks from one end of the country to the other; eventually views which were openly challenging and dangerous for the established order also spread with one region imitating another. More routinely, it follows from this perspective

[17] *François Quesnay et la physiocratie* (Paris, Institut national d'Etudes démographiques, 1958), i, 102; 135; ii, 794. See also E. Le Roy Ladurie, *Paysans de Languedoc*, 2 vols (Paris, Mouton, 1966), i, 474.

that the steady extension of the network of made-up roads, thanks to the road engineers of the ministry of state responsible for them (the 'Ponts et Chaussées'), provided the means whereby the transfer of knowledge and the better informing of the people from neighbourhood to neighbourhood could take place.

Although the peasantry displayed a less violent reaction to seigneurial authority than in the past, partly because of the effects of the (still rudimentary) education which was increasingly available, they showed every disposition to dispute it.[18] A twin process of modernization was underway. On the one hand, it affected the seigneurie, the 'manor' or home-farm of which was farmed out to rich, or relatively well-off farmers who knew how to write, count and invest – albeit in a modest way – and who could undertake innovations. There was also, however, a process of modernization which affected, albeit in an entirely different fashion, the peasantry, which found itself more and more in contact with the market, and partially rescued from local obscurity and from misery. The twin effects of these two processes, the one seigneurial and the other based around village communities, were eventually to become two contrary social forces, one seigneurial and the other peasant, in due course to be in conflict with one another. The twin process encouraged in each a heterogeneity whilst the upward demographic movement created a degree of land hunger. This was a recipe for confrontation and this would in due course occur as a result of the effects of these twin processes. To apply a geological metaphor to the situation, the fissures and fault-lines formed and reformed between the huge social 'continental plates' which were moving at different speeds to one another with all the consequent tensions, frictions, ruptures and seismic shudders which can easily be imagined as occuring between village and manor, and vice versa.

As for the towns (defined as conglomerations of a population of 2,000 or more), France witnessed, like the rest of Western Europe, both a relative and absolute increase in urbanization. Around 1600, the urban populations represented no more than 14 per cent of the national population.[19] By 1700, this had risen to 17 per cent; by 1790 it would be 20 per cent. This was a substantial rise, but by no means meteoric growth. It was shaped by rural immigration since the cities were generally insanitary and, in many cases, they were mortuaries for the poor. Immigration became still

---

[18]   The thesis of a reduction in brute violence amongst the peasantry, especially in northern provinces ('from crime to theft') has provoked a good deal of discussion amongst historians. There is no conclusive reason, however, to dismiss the conclusions of Pierre Chaunu's research pupils, according to whom the level of violence progressively decreased in the course of the eighteenth century (B. Boutelet, 'La Criminalité dans le bailliage de Pont-de-l'Arche', *Annales de Normandie* (1962)). See also E. Le Roy Ladurie in G. Duby and A. Wallon (dirs), *Histoire de la France rurale*, 4 vols (Paris, Seuil, 1975–7), ii, 547; 559; 698 n. 218.

[19]   Dupâquier, *Histoire de la population française*, ii, 86–7, tables 2 and 3; the figures proposed in the body of the text by this author present, however, some unfortunate contradictions with the evidence of these two tables.

more essential as urban birth-rates tended to decline under Louis XV and Louis XVI. This phenomenon was the result of the beginning of a modification, or modernization, in sexual practices. At Rouen, for example, it has been calculated that there were 6.9 births per couple in the period 1670–99, but only 4.5 births between 1760 and 1789.[20] This contraceptive 'New Deal' points to a transformation in patterns of behaviour which in turn generated various particular difficulties and what may truly be termed a collective pathological state. Sexual habits became less firmly established and the result was a considerable rise in the amount of urban prostitution and illegitimate births, and a tragic increase in the number of abandoned children (there were up to 6–7,000 foundlings a year in Paris between 1760 and 1780).[21] The children who were sent to be wetnursed away from their mothers died like flies. There was, however, a remarkable decrease in what had been the worst population scourges of the past; plague, war and famine were all in retreat and this affected the towns especially. The *last* great plagues occurred in 1668–70 in northern France and from 1720 to 1722 in Marseille.[22] Famines were replaced after 1710 by food shortages which generated grain riots rather more than death. Finally France was a war-free zone and the absence of military invasions of the kingdom produced an additional advantage. The ramparts which were held to be absolutely indispensable around cities in the seventeenth century were often replaced in the age of the Enlightenment by boulevards planted with trees, with their accompanying greenery and fresh air.

In a general sense, the favourable conditions of the eighteenth century, despite many setbacks, favoured the urban world. The branches of the economy which it was able to control were expanding fast and more rapidly than the overall gross national product. France's trade with the outside world increased five-fold (if measured in nominal prices) and three-fold (if measured in constant prices) between 1716 and 1788, with evident consequences for French cities. The archictecture of Bordeaux, with its stock exchange (*bourse*), its eighteenth-century dock facilities and its theatre, provide extant testimonies to the 'American-style' development of the great Gironde port in the last decades of the Ancien Régime.[23] At the same time, industrial production and French craft manufacture tripled in 80 years (measured by volume), and so did the export of manufactured goods.[24] On the eve of the French Revolution, industrial production in France (including industrial goods, craft manufacture and service) already

[20] Ibid., 386. Jean-Pierre Bardet, *Rouen au XVIIe et XVIIIe siècles; les mutations d'un espace social* (Paris, SEDES, 1983), p. 271.

[21] Dupâquier, *Histoire de la population française*, ii, 396 and 481.

[22] Jean-Noël Biraben, *Les Hommes et la peste en France et dans les pays européens et méditerranéens* (Paris/The Hague, Mouton, 1975), i, 118–122 and 388.

[23] François Crouzet, 'Angleterre et France au XVIIIe siècle, essai d'analyse comparée des deux croissances économiques', *Annales ESC*, 21 (1966), 261.

[24] Ibid., 266 (proposed figures, which are then subjected to discussion and reevaluation in the article).

seemed to have become the equal of agricultural production.[25] This reveals
immediately the extent of the influence felt by the towns within the
economy of France even though they represented at best a fifth of its
population. The urban minority controlled, in all sorts of ways, the destinies of the rural majority, and the more so since the urban population, and
particularly its notables, possessed 50 per cent or more of the land under
cultivation or capable of being cultivated in France.[26] The other half lay in
rural hands – peasants and country squires (*hobereaux*) etc. In England,
this trend was even more pronounced and the peasantry only owned 20
per cent of the soil, less than half the figure for France. Even so, the landed
base which lay in the hands of those in France's cities was huge. Rents and
farm leases were in most cases collected by urban-based groups. In addition, the urban world collected many other resources which originated in
the rural world in the form of taxes, tithes, seigneurial dues and interest
payments on debts. As to the peasant labour dues (*corvées*), exacted in kind
to assist with road construction, the benefits of their work were felt more,
although not exclusively so, by the urban world. It would be realistic to
estimate that a quarter of all agricultural income went to the towns.

In general terms, if the twin sources of profit from agricultural and non-
agricultural sources are put together, then over half of the overall national
income passed through at some stage, or resided in, France's towns, and
this in a country which has often been presented as stuck in its peasant
autarchies and held back by patterns of local self-sufficiency. Instead it was
the towns, through the rich and diverse interplay of demand, which were
gradually reshaping the countryside around them. Even small urban centres set up vineyards around them in the suburbs and immediate locality to
avoid drinking the local and heavily polluted water supply. At a broader
level the examples of cattle-raising in Lower Normandy, viniculture in
Burgundy, cereal specialization in the Beauce or the Brie, the migration of
rural masonry workers from the Limousin to jobs in Paris, are all the
responses of a peasantry which was capable of positive response and

[25]   T.J. Markovitch, 'L'Histoire française de 1789 à 1964', *Cahiers de l'Institut des sciences
économiques appliquées*, 6 (1966), 317–18. If we take into account a degree of native
conservatism, France was 'the primary industrial power in the world' even compared with
England. On the nuances which should be given to the (exact) idea of this comparison
between industrial and agricultural production (2.5 million francs each on the eve of the
Revolution), see Markovitch, ibid., p. 318. For a comparison between this French growth
and Japanese economic growth in the eighteenth century, see Haruhiko Hattori,
'L'évolution économique au Japon et en France au XVIIe siècle' in Hisagasu Nakagawa
(ed.), *Diderot, le XVIIIe siècle en Europe et au Japon* (Nagoya, Kawai Centre for Culture,
1988), pp. 231–42.
[26]   On this subject, see our contribution to G. Duby (dir.), *L'Histoire de la France urbaine*,
5 vols (Paris, Seuil, 1980–5), iii, 347. The cultivated and productive land in France was
divided up (taking very approximate percentages) between the peasantry (41%), the clergy
(7%), the nobility (22%), the bourgeoisie (perhaps 30%) – i.e. 59% in non-peasant hands,
the vast majority of whom belonged to the urban classes and above (taken from Michel
Vovelle, *La Chute de la monarchie, 1787–1792* (Paris, Seuil, 1972), p. 15).

innovation when faced with the demands for milk, wine, bread, butter, meat, cheese and manual labour in the building trades which emanated from a huge and groaning capital city of more than 600,000 people – the population of Paris and Versailles, the one inseparable from the other. Large or small, the town exploited the countryside but it also stimulated it to transform, adapt and modernize.

These processes of stimulation, working from within, from the interior towards the exterior, from the town to the countryside, are also to be found in the cultural domain where, once again, the position of the towns was naturally a preeminent one. Urban levels of literacy in France, as far as we know, grew from 51 per cent in 1683 to 60 per cent in 1770 whilst the corresponding increase for the whole of France, including both the urban and rural worlds, would be 41 per cent. The towns would retain, of course, their higher levels of literacy in comparison with the countryside and this would increase as their population grew; but we can see from these figures that the difference between urban and rural litcracy ratcs was declining, and this facilitated the dialogue between the masses which would be such a feature in 1789 when political revolution in the towns went hand in hand with peasant revolutionary fervour. In addition, female literacy, although less advanced, was no less responsive to the provision of the rudiments of elementary reading and writing. Madame Roland, née Phlipon, would long remember her experience at the hands of the sisters of the Notre-Dame congregation in the *faubourg* Saint-Antoine in Paris. The sisters were not blinkered in their attitudes. The bourgeoisie paid for the education of their children but there were free school places for the children of those who could not afford it. Mother Sainte-Sophie, one of the sisters, 'could write beautifully, do magnificent embroidery, gave good lessons in penmanship, and was no stranger to the study of history'.

Elementary education was continuously pumped into France's urban and rural population but, in contrast, the numbers of students in secondary education appeared to level off at around 50,000 young people from the seventeenth century through to the nineteenth century. To be more precise about the figures, one boy in every 45 attended a secondary school in 1842. In 1789, the figure (above all for urban France), was not that much less: one boy in 52 between the ages of 8 and 18 attended a college (or 48,000 students overall). What is most surprising, however, is that, in the years 1627–9, the equivalent figures were the same if not rather higher. There was a remarkable stability in secondary education from Louis XIII's reign through to Louis XVI's reign and on to that of Louis-Philippe – and this stability followed on from a considerable initial expansion which had taken place in the period from the reign of Francis I to Henry IV. Secondary schools or colleges were the way by which the élites were sustained from one generation to another and the mechanism for social ascension. They 'produced priests and reproduced notables'. It was thus kept strictly under limits whilst primary education was continually expanded.[27]

Malthusian trends were thus evident when it came to the foundation of new institutions of secondary teaching. The eighteenth century saw very few new schools of this kind being founded. Of a sample of 100 various secondary colleges in existence in 1789, only 15 were created after the period from 1600 to 1650. The age of the Enlightenment was beneficent in expanding rural literacy but mean when it came to urban secondary education. Should this be interpreted as a refusal, perhaps in the circumstances with some good reason, to expand excessively the ranks of the élites? Should it also be seen as a consequence of the crisis which began to emerge in 1762 with the expulsion of the Jesuits? In all events, the number of colleges could not have expanded too much since the numbers being taught remained stagnant. This disequilibrium between an increasing proportion of the people in primary education (which would enable them to frame the political demands to advance their own interests) and an élite in secondary education which remained numerically stable would overshadow the later eighteenth century and act as a 'prelude' to the French Revolution. The disequilibrium would grow greater as the primary education sector grew still larger on the eve of the French Revolution.

The lack of any quantitative expansion in secondary education did not prevent a gradual improvement in the quality of teaching being provided in some of these colleges from taking place. The neo-classical period after 1750 was one which witnessed a growing technical awareness amongst the élites, especially among those entering the armed services to spend their lives in garrisons and barracks. The Military School in Paris, the Military Engineering School at Mézières or the Artillery School at La Fère, or the royal military colleges devoted themselves to expanding the range of talent upon which they could draw so that they would no longer be the ghettos of modest poor provincial nobility, albeit of long lineage. Napoleon Bonaparte would be the most extraordinary exemplar. From 1720 to 1820, the methods of teaching put into practice by the Jesuits and the Oratorians, or inherited from them, 'formed' their students into the generation which would project France into being the foremost scientific nation in the age of D'Alembert, Delambre and Laplace.

More generally, the class gradations were standardized in the course of the seventeenth and eighteenth centuries. At Auch from 1598 to 1608 the average age of pupils in each successive class from the Sixth Grade up to Rhetoric remained extremely varied. A hundred years later, young pupils and older students too progressed regularly from class to class, spending about a year in each class before moving on to the next one. The current school curriculum with its progressive steps from the Sixth

---

[27] See below, p. 482 for some qualifications which are required to this proposition in respect of secondary education.

Grade to Philosophy had not been fully worked out under Henry IV but was in place by the reign of Louis XV. Similarly the age of the top class in colleges (the final year or Philosophy Grade) had already become set around 19 years of age on average, i.e. a 'modern' arrangement according to the canons of current educational practice. By contrast, in the period from 1601 to 1606 the average age for those in their final years was 21 years old.

It goes without saying that secondary education was biased in favour of the children of notables. The college was an instrument of social ascension. Yet it operated in accordance with a process of rigorous selection. It allowed the largest possible number to enter at the bottom; at Gisors and Avallon, for example, 'one artisan's or merchant's son out of every seven will rise to become an officeholder or join the liberal professions (advocates especially).'[28] For the sons of artisans alone, the equivalent figure is one in every 25. At the risk of repetition, the key opportunity for social ascension of 'gifted children' from modest backgrounds remained the priesthood. Although this route barred the way to a family and a succession it was still possible for the successful priest to assist financially and culturally with the education of his young nephews who remained the sons of artisans or peasants, enabling them, in their turn, to attempt an intellectual career. This promotional social ascension was like a pair of climbers tackling the sheer face of a mountain, one taking a turn to lead and then helping the other up. In many cases the ascent would require two generations at least. The sons of artisans became merchants or minor officeholders; the grandsons would, in their turn, climb higher up the ladder. Their family connections extended outwards and interconnected from generation to generation like tree branches or the tentacles of creepers. At the college of Avallon, the students reflected this, fathers and sons, uncles and nephews all attending successively the same college. It was even harder, though, for those coming from the rural fastnesses of Avallon to make a breakthrough; yet here too, the farmers who sent their children to college were essentially merchant labourers, the cream of the rural élite. But there would be no children at the college of Avallon from the Morvan peninsula, particularly disadvantaged by its poverty, before 1760. . . . This example from the Morvan indicates a further prototype for how the avenues of social advancement might be opened out. It was a sign that the end of the Ancien Régime was far from being niggardly towards the socially ambitious, as the remarkable careers of star pupils like Rivarol or Chamfort, whose origins were very humble, demonstrate. Yet such individual successes did not satisfy the innumerable frustrations of others which would make themselves felt in the last decade of the century. What is more, those brilliant students who benefitted from the absolutist 'piston' of advancement would be quite prepared, when the moment came, to

---

[28] On all these problems, see the important work of Marie-Madeleine Compère, *Du collège au lycée, 1500–1850* (Paris, Gallimard, coll. 'Archives').

transfer their loyalties to the revolutionary cause. Chamfort's transformation would be typical of many.[29]

If education did not have an egalitarian impact in France, it certainly had a coalescing effect. In peripheral provinces, recently annexed by military force, it completed the processes of more or less forced incorporation by means of the acculturation or assimilation of the young. This phenomenon of integration advanced at a reasonable pace. The hexagonal geometry of the French state was almost in place by the first third of the eighteenth century and it would be officially confirmed by the final entry of Lorraine into the kingdom in 1766. National coalescence was already a process at work, even though no one was being frogmarched into being French as would occur under the Third Republic. The territorial acquisitions of the French monarchy from the thirteenth through to the eighteenth centuries had often been, though not always, harshly and violently carried out and it was the linguistic minorities or peripheral peoples which often had borne the brunt. We need only mention, in this context, the examples of Languedoc, or the *pays d'oc* more generally, equally the cases of Roussillon, of Alsace, Flanders, Lorraine, Brittany and, rather later, Corsica.[30] Despite these unpropitious precedents in the construction of what would become 'the great nation' the relationship between centre and periphery after 1713 did not generate tensions. The Revolution would open up many old wounds but old national identities on the French margins were not amongst them; they did not feed through to Girondin federalism which had rather different roots. Looking more closely at, amongst other examples, the case of the southern French littoral, it is evident that the religious hostility which brought its Huguenot communities into open conflict with the absolutist régime in 1703 evoked huge tensions in comparison with the modest disputes between royal authority and the Catalans in Roussillon (as it was) or the Occitans in Béziers. It is true that royal government was careful in this kind of area to base its actions on an effective blend of sovereign will and more or less partial respect for local institutions. In Roussillon, for example, where central government certainly acted with a heavy hand, the intendants appointed *de facto* all the mayors of important towns. But a 'sovereign council', created by the French authorities ended up becoming a kind of regional parlement with all that this implied in the long-term in terms of the discreet frustration of initiatives from Versailles. A French identity was often proclaimed in the frontier regions of the kingdom by benign institutions such as hospitals, universities, the *ponts et chaussées*, the *maréchaussée*, theatres,

---

[29]   Chamfort (1740–94) was 'humbly' born and had a successful literary career under the Ancien Régime, although this did not stop him becoming, when the moment arrived, a partisan of the Revolution.

[30]   For this, and for what follows, see E. Le Roy Ladurie, 'Les Minorités périphériques; intégration et conflits', in André Burguière and Jacques Revel (ed.), *Histoire de la France* (volume directed by Jacques Julliard and entitled: *L'Etat et les conflits*), (Paris, Seuil, 1989), pp. 459–630.

poor-relief centres etc., or by festivals which had gradually become authentically popular in honour of victories achieved by French armies in the course of a war, or in celebration of a happy event such as a royal birth or a marriage.[31] At the same time, administrators sent out from the 'centre' displayed a certain respect for local customs. 'Do not disturb the local traditions of Alsace' was the message from the office of the *contrôleur général* under Louis XIV; and the same basic approach was also applied *grosso modo* to the whole region between the Vosges and the Rhine. In the hinterland around Dunkirk in Flanders, in the Basque country, in Languedoc and in Provence, the intendant and his subdelegates allowed the institutions which most represented and acted as the incarnation of the localities to survive with Versailles' consent. Thus the Pyrenean assembly known as the *Biltzaar*, or the Flemish meeting known as the *Département* were tolerated alongside, of course, the provincial estates which met from time to time in Montpellier, Aix and elsewhere. In some extreme cases, as in Provence in the latter years of the Ancien Régime, the intendant, the so-called strong-arm of royal authority ended up by being no more than the representative at Versailles of the local populations and élites, whose indigenous institutions he held in high regard.[32] In this instance, one is very far removed, whatever Tocqueville may have thought, from the prefects of Bonaparte's time, or even those of Louis-Philippe. In general, provincial revolts were a thing of the past after 1713 and they would only begin to emerge again after a long period of calm, in the last five years of Louis XVI's life.

The integration of the various élites into a francophone, or semi-francophone 'centrality' did much to cement a sense of national identity in the peripheries. The higher nobilities, even from the more distant provinces, found themselves domesticated under the aegis of Versailles. Such, at least, was what happened, amongst others, to the Montmorency-Robecq from Flanders, the Castries from Languedoc, the Gramont from south-west France.[33] Another outcome was that the formerly fractious local nobility became extinct for various reasons and was replaced by a bourgeoisie or gentry which derived both pleasure and profit from doing business with the smart French from further afield. In other places, part of the regional nobility took up exile in a neighbouring country (Spain, for example) towards which it felt a degree of affinity. In the space thus vacated the bourgeoisie seized its chance, and transformed itself into a neo-nobility and declared its fidelity to the king of France, their sheet anchor and guarantee of statutory promotion. This was what took place amongst the Perpignan élites between the last third of the seventeenth century and the Revolution. In northern Catalonia a resigned and reticent

---

[31]   E.G. Léonard, *Mon village sous Louis XV d'après les Mémoires d'un paysan* (Paris, PUF, 1941; reedited 1984), ch. 2, p. 219.

[32]   François-Xavier Emmanuelli, *Pouvoir royal et vie régionale en Provence au déclin de la monarchie* (Doctoral Thesis, Université de Lille III, 1974), part I, ch. 2 (i, 143–5).

[33]   Gramont, not to be confused with the Grammont who were from Franche-Comté.

attitude towards the region's annexation by France was surpassed by a rather conventional loyalty towards the kingdom until, after 1789, and not without some disputes, it manifested a much clearer adhesion to the national or patriotic ideal. Economic and demographic growth was particularly marked during the eighteenth century in these surrounding regions and this also doubtless assisted in this transition. In the Flemish regions of northern France the intensive agricultural methods *à la chinoise* which had made their appearance a long time previously, became more pronounced with the abolition of periods of fallow, strip cultivation and natural pasture, etc. In Alsace a more intensive agriculture, the spread of potato cultivation and the rise of the textile industry changed for the better the nature of that province's problems in comparison with the disasters wreaked upon it during the military campaigns of previous wars, under Richelieu and then Turenne. In the French Basque country, deep-sea fishing for cod and, to a lesser extent, sardines replaced harpoon fishing for whales when they became too rare. The product was sold in the vast market for fish in the south where it was prized because it contained iodine which gave protection against goitres. The foothills of the western Pyrenees were one of those many sectors which prospered – or at the least struggled out of their former poverty. The Catalan *huerta*, at the other end of the mountains towards the East also continued its economic prosperity under Louis XV, or (in Spain) Philip V and Charles III. This brought benefits not only to Barcelona but also to the Roussillon valleys. Vauban had described them as 'infertile and badly populated localities' but, for the last century of the Ancien Régime, this would no longer be the case. Finally, and more generally, the great cities of southern France (Marseille, Bordeaux, Lyon) and the northern sea-ports (Dunkirk) more than matched the overall urban growth of the eighteenth century. This overall prosperity could have divisive political effects, however, particularly in the form of remonstrances from the parlements, which were, as in Bordeaux, highly regarded by the local population of their areas. Despite such divisions, however, the growing prosperity also favoured the integration, albeit on a partial, elitist basis, of the inhabitants of Dunkirk and Bordeaux into a national community of language, culture and sensibility and even unanimous views about the monarchy. The city-people – more numerous, more active, more affluent too – would be, in time, conscientious citizens, some of them at least, and it would be on that basis that they would turn the Revolution into one which, led by the urban magistracy, would be patriotic and French. But this is to anticipate the story of the fin de siècle, or, at the least, the second half of the eighteenth century.

In French culture, various changes were taking place, some of them massively visible, some of them imperceptible to many contemporaries. In that part of French Flanders which was Flemish-speaking, for example, there were ultra-Catholic developments in baroque art such as those by Jordaens under the influence of the Antwerp school and in the tradition of the Tridentine church. But even here, the spread of true French culture reached as far as the Channel coastline in the Pas-de-Calais, beginning under Louis XIV and *a fortiori* continuing under his two successors. The process was stimulated from on high by royal initiative, of course, but it was also assisted by local trends, both social and intellectual which were at work both on the French side of the frontier (in Lille) and even across the border (at the university of Douai). Such was the 'universality of the French language' at this period that, to take a specific example, it is remarkable that the regions which would become what is now Belgium became French-speaking in the eighteenth century thanks to the Austrian Habsburg administration which communicated and expressed itself in the language of Racine. Thus, surrounded to the east and the south by the *langue d'oil* French-speakers, the Flemish élites in Dunkirk and Bailleul could do little other than submit, continuing to be taught to read and even educated in Flemish but willingly immersing themselves in French ideas and the national culture. At the other end of the kingdom, Languedoc continued to produce excellent writers in its dialect such as the *abbé* Fabre. The theatre in Provence witnessed many remarkably fresh plays during the baroque period and these were written in an ultra-Frenchified Occitan lingua franca which could be understood both by those native to the region north of the Auvergne or the Donzère watershed. And from the dioceses of Nîmes, Rodez and Bordeaux came writers born or brought up in the Midi who wrote brilliantly in French and at various different levels – whether a Montesquieu writing for the courtyard of an educated public, or Rivarol for the theatre-going nobility, or pseudo nobility, or Pierre Prion for those in the gallery.[34] In Roussillon, too, whilst continuing to use Catalan as their vernacular, they also adopted French as the language for formal communication rather than Castilian which had sinister memories and which held few attractions for its intellectuals. Finally, and beyond any linguistic register, we should note the career of the exceptionally gifted Perpignan artist Hyacinthe Rigaud which demonstrates how, both before and after the Regency, it was possible to be from Catalonia and also make a great career for oneself in Paris and Versailles. It was a career whose geographical orientation – from Catalonia to the French capital – prefigured that of his fellow-countryman Picasso.

Finally, we should not leave religion out of this persepctive. The anti-Calvinist persecution in the south generated enormous conflicts but, as we have already indicated, the conflict did not take on any national identity characteristics such as the Huguenot Occitans versus the northern French Catholics. In this respect, the situation was entirely different from that in Ireland which, at precisely the same moment, was being harshly treated and where British oppression had turned into a quarrel which was both religious and national. Except in Languedoc, royal policy had proved to be (and who would have thought it?) remarkably flexible in respect of

---

[34] E. Le Roy Ladurie and Orest Ranum (ed.), *Pierre Prion, scribe* (Paris, Gallimard, coll. 'Archives', 1985).

religious conviction. This was the case in Alsace, for example, where the Revocation, which was aimed against Calvinists, left the local Lutheran congregations alone. The French administration between Mulhouse and Strasbourg merely enforced a *simultaneum* whereby Catholics and Lutherans took it in turns to worship in the local churches and where the former were treated favourably but the latter not eliminated. Elsewhere, in Flanders, Brittany, the Basque country and Roussillon, the French régime was dealing with orthodox Catholic regions where the Revocation caused no offense to either the clergy or their parishioners; rather, the measure put them at their ease and further inclined them to loyalty towards the French monarchy, the faithful supporter of the 'true church'. Again, religion proved to be a factor working towards an integration which was not perfectly realized but which was still ongoing.

The question of the connections between peripheral minorites in the state and the other great powers of Europe should be mentioned at this point. The presence of the Spanish Bourbons on the throne in Madrid during the eighteenth century assisted the good relationships which were fostered between the Catalan minority and the French authorities since on both sides of the Pyrenees the two dynasties were closely related and not far apart in politics and diplomacy either. In the same way, the shift in international alliances made France the new-found friend of the 'old enemy' of the Bourbons, the Austrian Habsburgs, and put paid to what might have become a kind of dalliance between Alsace and various constituent elements of the Holy Roman Empire. Vienna was henceforth tied to Versailles *via* Strasbourg, something which was evident at the time of the marriage of Marie-Antoinette to the future Louis XVI in 1770. As for Prussia, although it would be the focus of attention for all ideas of teutonic national identity in the nineteenth century, it had a long way to go before becoming a major power, although its beginnings had been spectacular enough.

So, during the eighteenth century, the great challenge for the politics of national coalescence (albeit only partial) from the peripheral minorities would come from Brittany. This was not simply a matter of its stubborn linguistic irrendentism around the Celtic or lower-Breton of the western fringes of the peninsula. Perhaps it was also because the economic situation proved to be markedly less favourable towards the Bretons from the middle of Louis XIV's reign onwards. The great province of the west had enjoyed a golden age between 1460 and 1674.[35] A period of decline was to follow, marked by the perhaps excessive burden of military institutions in and around the province, both military and naval, which transformed this huge granite platform into an operational base against England. In addition, the Breton nobility were vigorously active and strongly entrenched in the Parlement of Rennes. Of all the crosses which Louis XV had to bear,

[35]   The Breton revolt against the *gabelles* and the stamp duty took place in 1674 and was repressed. It marked a turning-point, a geological fault in the long history of Brittany.

that posed by Brittany would be the most difficult to endure during the 1760s and just before the Maupeou counter-offensive.[36] The 'Well-Beloved' Louis XV was a noted goldsmith. During his childhood, if not in his adolescence, he had already needed to cross swords with his noble, and not always most faithful, subjects of an ill-tamed Brittany, for whom the recent death of the Sun-King had done nothing other than to excite in them a spirit of conflict.

[36] Cf. below, chapter 10.

8

A Debonnaire Hercules

On 15 February 1710, with Louis XIV still on the throne, the duchess of Burgundy, his granddaughter-in-law, had given birth to a duke of Anjou, christened Louis. A sequence of deaths – Louis XV's grandfather the Dauphin, called Monseigneur, then his father (the next dauphin) and his mother (the seductive duchess of Burgundy), then finally the death of his elder brother, the little duke of Burgundy and third dauphin in succession – led this five-year-old to become the inheritor of the throne and then, in 1715, to be king when Louis XIV 'half emptied the Universe' and passed away. Louis XV was an orphan and a lone boy; soon he would be a lonesome man, intelligent, often taciturn and timid, well educated to the task (although some have claimed to the contrary) by often first-rate tutors.[1] In his earliest years, Louis sheltered under the skirts of his governess, the duchess of Ventadour, *alias* 'Maman'. The mothering she lavished on him protected him from the imbecile and lethal remedies to which the royal physicians wanted to subject him. 'Maman' Ventadour showed him a good deal of affection in these early years, too much some would say. She transferred her store of affections, temporarily unabsorbed in any other directions, towards him; Louis XV, who had secretly been badly affected by events, would be the last to complain.

At seven years old, Louis left 'Maman Ventadour' and was handed over to be looked after by men. Amongst them was his governor Villeroy, an old cavalry officer of good character but not very bright, for whom the routine of the court accounted for thought. In addition there were various clerics and laymen, none of them stupid, who oversaw his intellectual development. Amongst them was the prelate-tutor and eventual cardinal, Fleury, as well as the *abbés* Fleury and Vittement together with various professors of geography and mathematics. They were rarely poor teachers and they included various experts, under whose supervision Louis developed into a fairly rounded individual, well-informed about religion, geometry and

---

[1] For all of what follows, we should note here, once and for all, the indispensable assistance of Michel Antoine, *Louis XV* (Paris, Fayard, 1989).

Plate 16   Portrait of Louis XV   In one of the copies of an original painting by Jean-Baptiste Van Loo in 1727 (and now lost), Louis XV, aged 17, is depicted in military uniform with the blue sash of the Order of the Holy Spirit across his breast-plate and the baton of military office in his right hand.
Chambord, château

earth sciences as well as being stimulated by scanning the night sky in the company of professional astronomers. He had some experience of manual work, too, as a blacksmith and printer. He was keen on sports as well, particularly horse-riding and hunting. Although it has often been said that Villeroy inculcated in him a kind of narcissistic auto-infatuation, in fact he nurtured in him a reaction of distaste towards the rituals of the court.[2] Villeroy was so taken up with the court conventions of the old Versailles of Louis XIV that this bred a hostile reaction in the child-king who was bored to death by them. The family's misfortunes scarred the orphan king to the extent that he was unable to identify himself with the task of kingship to anything like the degree of his magisterial great-grandfather.

Other rites of passage soon awaited the young adolescent Louis. First there was the proclamation of his majority in a *lit de justice* of the Parlement when he was 13 years of age in 1723. Then came his coronation at Reims several months later which projected a cleric-king rather than a sovereign-soldier. Then came the twin deaths in close succession of the Cardinal Dubois in August 1723, followed by that of Philippe d'Orléans in December 1723. Both men, and particularly the Regent, had given the young man, who lacked confidence in himself, a robust political culture. These twin deaths forced Louis to find new collaborators and, because of his youth, they would end up acting the part of patrons, and successive first ministers. The first was the rather second-rate Bourbon, 'a great, tall, lanky good-for-nothing',[3] to be followed by the politically remarkable Fleury. Louis' majority would not, in fact, happen until after 1743 precisely because of the longevity of his old mentor, Hercule de Fleury, who became like a grandfather to him.

Despite the long-lasting hegemony of the cardinal (Fleury was elevated to the cardinalcy in September 1726), this was a king by no means devoid of personality. In appearance, he was a pretty child who became a striking figure of a man. Even aged 44 he could ride dozens of kilometres on horseback on a frozen road, exhausting three mounts under the weight of his 85 kilos of well-toned muscle, little of which had turned to fat. He hunted deer, shot pheasant and kept his physique by sporting activities and a reasonable diet. Physical activity seemed to be indispensable to him, serving as a complement to his conciliar and official business, where the pressures were intense and demanding. Perhaps it was also the case that his passion for hunting acted as a compensation for his lack of warrior pursuits. From Francis I to Louis XVI, the Capetian kings saw their personal intervention in warfare gradually decline. As it did so, they invested still more of their energies in that other typical activity of the gentleman besides warfare – i.e. stalking game, shooting rabbits and sticking boar. Regularly on horseback across the length and breadth of the royal forests, Louis was, after his own fashion, a country gentleman, an overgrown squire. During his countless travels through the country in pursuit of game, he took careful note of what he saw, and described to his friends, relatives and other correspondents, the state of the newly-sown fields and wine harvests in the Ile de France. He thus was able to make something of

---

[2] Saint-Simon, *Mémoires*, ed. A. de Boislisle, 45 vols (Paris, 1879–1930), xxxiii, 53–4 (a rectifying note) and, above all, xxxvii, 131–4.

[3] See his bullying and highly ineffectual policy towards the unfortunate Protestants.

Plate 17   The consecration of Louis XV in 1722 This painting was a kind of painting exercise for Pierre Subleyras, a young painter who had a bright future before him and who was studying in the atelier of Rivalz. Copying (and cleverly adapting) a similar painting by Rivalz, Subleyras portrays Louis XV's consecration in the cathedral at Rheims at the moment when the archbishop anointed the young king with the holy unction. Beyond and to the right, the sword of consecration was held aloft throughout the ceremony.

Toulouse, Musée des Augustins

the grain and wine situation which formed the substance of reports from the intendants from across the kingdom. In the course of his travels and hunting, he showed a lively awareness of the dangers of dearth which haunted his subjects as well as the dramas of unexpected accidents, whether, for example, it was a villager drowning in a pond and crying out one last time 'Long Live the King' as he breathed his last, or a valet whose head was split open in a carriage accident. He was as alive to ecological matters as to human tragedy. He personally saw to the pruning of his trees, or those of his closer friends, with well-aimed, sharp cuts from a well-adjusted bill-hook. Like many aristocrats of his generation, there was in Louis a countryman at heart, a wayfarer, a backwoodsman and a wencher. His outlook on life resembled that of the Sire de Gouberville from the Cotentin peninsula in the sixteenth century;[4] and whilst on the one hand it should not be idealized, nor should it be totally ignored by letting an ideology limit our perspectives.

Louis XV retained throughout his life the profound influence of the strongly Catholic culture he had been imbued with during his childhood. He owed it to the two Fleurys – the prelate Hercule and the *abbé* Claude – as well as to Vittement and other clerics who favoured a broadly-based Christianity in the traditions of St-Sulpice, not inclining to either Jansenist or Jesuit extremes. This included a devotion to the Mass, an obligation to fast on the relevant days of the Catholic calendar and a submission to God and Rome (for Louis XV was far less Gallican in his inclinations than Louis XIV had been). Such royal piety embraced a simple approach to faith and it would have been complete had it been matched by a similar lifestyle; but royal religious obligation applied above, rather than below, the belt. The first mistresses made their appearance in 1732, and they were quickly followed by a series of other ladies. Yet this was just the point, for it was the excessive scruples of the monarch which proved his downfall. Aware of his peccadilloes, Louis no longer attended confessions or communions since this would have been sacrilegious in someone who knew only too well as a conscientious Christian that he would be attending them as someone who would not make a firm promise to sin no more. As he approached his thirties, the king was no longer a confessing or communicating member of the church and so he was obliged to abstain from touching for the King's Evil since this required the toucher to undertake a prior period of sacramental and penitential purification. The fact that he abstained from the Eucharist was swiftly interpreted by his entourage as a sign that Louis, for all his sincerity, was a public delinquent and a sexual miscreant, and this spread through the court, the urban world and to public opinion at large, which was always powerfully influenced by the whiff of scandal. For the king not to heal for the King's Evil was *ipso facto*

---

[4] On Gilles de Gouberville, a Normandy country noble of the sixteenth century, see Madeleine Foisil, *Le Sire de Gouberville; un gentilhomme normand du XVIe siècle* (Paris, Aubier-Montaigne, 1981); see also our *Le Territoire de l'historien* (2 vols, Paris, Gallimard, 1973), i, 187 *et seq*.

Plate 18   Portrait of Queen Marie Leszczynska   Jean-Marc Natier was commissioned to paint this picture of Marie Leszczynska in 1748. She is depicted in 'town dress' rather than court attire, the sign of a new and more domestic sensibility, reflected in the decorations of the private apartments at Versailles.
Chambord, château

to deconsecrate and desacralize the monarchy at the same time, and to be diminished in this way was certainly the last thing that the monarchy needed in the circumstances. The Well-Loved king[5] set himself up before the unforgiving tribunal of public opinion as a depressive and unhappy individual who recognized his own faults and was unable or unwilling to do anything about them. The target was a tempting one and it was taken up in popular songs and cruel jokes at his expense.

In 1725, Louis was engaged in marriage to the Polish Marie Leszczynska, the daughter of a dethroned king. That Europe's premier monarch should stoop, for lack of other suitable candidates, to make a match with a wandering, or at least exiled, princess who dabbled with painting in her spare time was the definition of an unequal liaison. The duke of Bourbon's clan was responsible for concocting the marriage and the young girl in question was stronger in virtue than in good looks. For

[5]   This is the surname which would be given to Louis by popular will in 1744 after his unexpected recovery. Cf. Antoine, *Louis XV*, p. 379.

seven or eight years, the couple nevertheless enjoyed a good relationship, both physically and emotionally. Ten successive pregnancies ended in stillbirth and the queen eventually grew weary – 'Always in bed, always in labour' she would say. Louis sought in Marie, as her portrait readily reveals, a woman who was like his mother, the duchess of Burgundy, who had disappeared so early in his life. After a time, the king's disappointments surfaced and, since he was denied by the symbolic begetter of legitimate children, he set about, as a second-best, finding himself some surrogate sisters to replace those who had died in his own family. The king was a creature of habit, though, and he was attracted to familiar faces. So he liked to spend his time, at least whilst he was a young man, in the familiar circle of his companions. Thus, from 1733 onwards, he embarked upon a trio, or even a quartet, of successive liaisons with the Nesle sisters.

From 1738 onwards, Louis became, albeit with regret, more or less committed to his irregular lifestyle. He gave up communion, confession and touching for scrofula. The three Nesle sisters (Mailly, Vintimille and La Tournelle, the latter being metamorphosed into the duchess of Châteauroux) were in turn treated to royal favours.[6] Two of them died in service. The Châteauroux Affair, which broke in 1744 during the War of Austrian Succession, became something of a scandal. The king fell gravely ill at Metz whilst visiting the front-line troops and undertook public (and temporary) penance for his liaison on what he believed to be his death bed. The suasions of the local bishop were behind a public humiliation of this kind. Once on the road to recovery, the king quickly returned to his 'great affair' with the duchess of Châteauroux, but in the process, the public image of His Majesty had been lastingly damaged by this incident, for which he was set up by the church and the *dévot* party. If public opinion polls had existed at this time they would have reflected this first sharp temporary decline in the popularity of the monarch immediately following a rise in his standing nationally in 1744.

In 1745, Jeanne Antoinette Poisson, later the marquise de Pompadour, became the king's mistress. With her help, the king became emotionally mature. He no longer had need of a pseudo-mother, nor a quartet of sisters, but a friend. For her part, she was pretty, intelligent, cold and ambitious. Born of a father of modest origins who had made himself a fortune (but nothing is absolutely proven as to her true origins), she belonged to the social group of financiers who had recently been ennobled. Her presumed father was, in reality, one of the clients of the Pâris brothers and had held the levers of power in the Bourbon ministry of 1723–6. The Pâris would retain their enormous influence through the rising favour of their protégée. Jeanne's arrival on the scene marked the rise of the *fermiers généraux* and the other tax-collectors. Linked by marriage and various business deals with the upper aristocracy, they helped to bring together

---

[6]   The case of the fourth sister, Lauragais, is less clear, or at least more 'furtive' – Antoine, *Louis XV*, p. 490.

Plate 19   The marquise de Pompadour   Historians tend now to be more favourable in their judgements on Madame de Pompadour, Louis XV's mistress. Her role in the patronage of the fine arts and her support for Choiseul's initiatives constitute the most positive components of her achievements, reflected in this painting of her after Maurice-Quentin de La Tour.
Versailles, Musée national du château

under the banner of a royal favourite the eighteenth-century's new élites. The shapers of opinions, despite all this, were far from being Madame de Pompadour's admirers, particularly when it came to these processes of upward social mobility of which she was one of the beneficiaries and one of the symbols. For his part, the king was henceforth held in suspicion of becoming too close to the milieu of fast women and financiers instead of the great ladies and seigneurs at court whose company had pleased his great-grandfather Louis XIV.

After 1752 the Pompadour liaison grew less intense, becoming simply a mutual friendship, affectionate and sincere, complicated only by the fact of Madame de Pompadour's excessive lust for power, or at least influence. She obtained the tabouret for duchesses in 1752 and then, sublimating her own feelings, she became more or less a female procuress for the king, furnishing to her former concubine a succession of young women and some very young girls as well, who would be lodged at modest expense at the Parc-aux-Cerfs. The very name of this place would send contemporary chroniclers into howls of rage although, in reality, it was no more than the name given to a small corner of the town of Versailles and particularly to one of its town-houses; it certainly would hardly merit the orgiastic connotations which would become associated with it. The result of this sequence of rather squalid encounters which came close to prostitution (which would not stop some of the respected statesmen of the following century from 'sinning' in the same way) was a score of bastards. In this respect, Louis' behaviour was indistinguishable from that of a group of aristocrats whose sexual encounters with the lower orders led to the births of numerous illegitimate children. The king was careful, as a general rule, not to legitimate his natural children, *a fortiori* so that the princes of the blood did not feel outnumbered. He thus avoided the reproaches directed by them towards Louis XIV and his attitudes.

As for nominations, the influence of Pompadour over appointments and dismissals was not always for the best. At least she represented a fairly liberal voice within the monarchical entourage, supporting the philosophes and physiocrats. François Quesnay, the leader of the physiocratic economists, was her personal physician. She opposed the Jesuits who, in truth, had done little to spare her blushes. They had been the ones to discover that she was the royal procuress, hardly an activity likely to accord with the moral principles laid down by St Ignatius Loyola. They had no inclination to be made dupes by her first moves towards a personal conversion (which had perhaps been sincere) to which the marquise briefly committed herself in 1756. The king's companion naturally put her weight against the *dévot* party which provided inspiration to the dauphin and the king's daughters above all, motivated by exasperation with 'Madame Putain'. The ministerial appointment in 1758 of Choiseul, the distinguished representative of ancien régime, latter-day quasi-liberalism, probably owed much to Pompadour's high regard for the Lorraine statesman. Still more important, through her own sense of taste and the delicate discernment she showed in artistic matters (like many aristocrats, even the *parvenus*) she was the source for important decisions in architecture and town-planning. In the latter, her influence was felt through the unsubtle instrument of her brother Vandières, who had been made superintendent of Buildings and marquis de Marigny. Pompadour and Marigny, brother and sister, the latter a business woman of some talent, played an important role in the construction, overseen by Gabriel, of the present Place de la Concorde, formally known as the Place Louis XV, as well as the Ecole militaire and (although it was completed after Madame de Pompadour's death), the Petit-Trianon.[7]

Louis XV's last sexual liaison was with Jeanne Bécu, a former high-class prostitute (she had become the Countess Du Barry through a marriage of convenience to a Languedocian nobleman). It was bound to shock upright observers, and even the less than upright. In another age, more modern and indulgent, it would have made an enchanting story for popular fiction writers. Louis was a widower and a free man (the queen had died in 1768). He set out, not without bravura, to live in true bourgeois fashion with a prostitute whom he had rescued from the 'gutter'. The girl was pretty, not a mischief-maker, and able to adapt to the strange land of the Versailles court! In the eyes of many, however, there was, in 1770 as in 1840, nothing other than inexcusable damage done to the monarch. Choiseul's companions, removed from power in 1771, did not pass up the opportunity of making the facts known, both amongst the royal entourage and to public opinion at large. Everything considered, the fate of Louis and his last mistress was determined in advance of the trial by public opinion. From 1715 to 1790, there was a general upsurge, which turned into outburst from time to time, of politico-pornographic publications which swamped Paris and elsewhere in unprecedented quantities. It had begun in the attacks on the Regent, a ready target, and on his supposedly scandalous daughter, the duchess de Berry. Later on, after a racy interlude involving the Nesle sisters, it was Madame de Pompadour's turn to be vilified in verse and prose, then the plump girls at the Parc-aux-Cerfs, and finally Du Barry herself, at the very least an open target for the satirists. The upsurge would finally sink the sexually faithful Louis XVI through the entirely mythical public persona created for his wife Marie-Antoinette.[8] An extraordinary propaganda campaign originated with obsessional scribblers who turned her into a vaginally voracious vampire, a sexual equivalent of Don Quixote's Maritornes, or the incestuous Messalina, good for nothing save to be whipped, shaved and decapitated. This was the only logical punishment, and it is what would be meted out to the innocent Marie-Antoinette and to Madame Du Barry, although there was nothing whiter than white in her case. Should we not see this kind of political pornography, in the longer term, as little more than 'copycat copulation',[9] one of the by-products of the Enlightenment and of a devalued and adulterated

[7]   Danielle Gallet, *Madame de Pompadour ou le pouvoir féminin* (Paris, Fayard, 1985), pp. 205–6. See also Guy Chaussinand-Nogaret, *La Vie quotidienne des maîtresses du roi* (Paris, Hachette, 1990).

[8]   Chantal Thomas, *La Reine scélérate, Marie Antoinette dans les pamphlets* (Paris, Seuil, 1980).

[9]   The expression is used by J.-M. Goulmot.

Plate 20 Madame Du Barry Louis XV's last mistress, Madame Du Barry, was detested by Choiseul and became the butt of the gutter-press at his behest. Her influence acted in support of absolutism, the 'triumvirate' and the *dévot* cabal. Her lowly origins were scarcely disguised by a good education and intellectual contacts in high places (Crébillon, Guibert and the Prince de Ligny) hinted at in this painting by François Drouais in 1772 of la Du Barry surrounded by the emblems of the Muses.

Versailles, Musée national du château

Christianity? At all events, the sexual frustrations, homosexual encounters, and fornications of the great and good were displayed for all to see when previously they had been kept the close secret of the confessional.[10] 'Sex became a subject for conversation.' It is worth adding simply that the demands of a moral code emanating from the Jansenists as well as the Jesuits led to Louis XV being condemned by many for things which had been tolerated, whether for good or not, in Henry IV, even in Louis XIV. The degree of 'democratization' which took place in the office of the royal favourite did not help matters in the eyes of the Court. Estrées and Montespan were great ladies from titled families. Madame de Pompadour, on the other hand, was described by some as the daughter of a lackey who had narrowly escaped being executed;[11] and Madame Du Barry had nothing by way of a 'presentable' pedigree to shelter behind. Yet they were both 'presented' at court to the Queen and the Dauphine who could do nothing but receive them.

⋆   ⋆   ⋆   ⋆   ⋆

When he was not spending his time with women, or hunting, or being present at a religious service or a function at court, Louis was running the state – a nominal role before the death of Fleury in 1743 but his real task thereafter. The administrative team which, from near and far, undertook with the king the overall responsibilities of state was very extensive. From 1715 to 1774, according to the historian Michel Antoine,[12] there were some 580 individuals, chancellors, ministers of state, secretaries of state, councillors, masters of requests, *contrôleurs généraux des finances*, intendants of finance, of commerce, and provincial intendants.

Contemporary historians estimate, and with good reason, that the 'indigenous' nobility – the court nobility and *noblesse d'épée* – gained, or rather, regained some of their influence within the power-élite during the Louis XV period. This compares with their almost complete lack of influence under Louis XIV, at least in respect of civil administration (an important qualification because in the military sphere the 'indigenous' nobility always retained its primary significance, as the careers of Turenne, Villars, Berwick and Vendôme illustrate). From the statistics, however, it is clear that the socio-political phenomenon of the revival of the old nobility within royal administration should not be overstated. Of some 569 individuals in the power-élite we have to hand details of their fathers' background: 72 came from the court nobility or old *noblesse d'épée*, whilst

[10]   See Michel Foucault, *Histoire de la sexualité* (Paris, Gallimard, 1976), p. 45 *et seq*; Jean-Louis Flandrin, *Le Sexe et l'Occident* (Paris, 1981), p. 251 *et seq.*

[11]   François Poisson, a financier of modest origins, capable of tact and loyalty, had become the object of enquiries in 1727 for financial irregularities (Gallet, *Madame de Pompadour*, pp. 7–15).

[12]   Michel Antoine, *Le Gouvernement et l'administration sous Louis XV. Dictionnaire biographique* (Paris, CNRS, 1978).

351 descended from the *noblesse de robe*, mainly from royal office-holders (only in a small minority of cases did they come from advocates, physicians, university professors, notaries or other bureaucratic posts). A further 93 were descended from fathers engaged in finance and 10 were the sons of government ministers. Twenty-two rose from commerce, industry or the highly skilled artisan crafts. Six were born of those who classed themselves as 'bourgeois' without being more precise, 3 of 'nobles' (again, no precision); 2 were the sons of diplomats and 10 were descended from fathers whose backgrounds have not been identified. The kingdom was thus governed by a power-élite which was 78 per cent descended from the *robe* and financial milieux (where the 'created' nobility were most common, and often interrelated one to another). By comparison, only 13 per cent were descended from the 'indigenous' nobility,[13] whilst a mere handful came from the productive or commercial classes, and none at all from the peasantry. So the fertile soil from which the élite governing classes were cultivated under Louis XV would remain overwhelmingly that of the *robins*. Although Louis XV might, by continuing the initiatives inspired by Saint-Simon begun by the Regent,[14] increase the role played by the 'true' aristocracy, he could not change the fundamental basis of the system which had been in place since at least Richelieu's period and which had been developed to perfection by Louis XIV, Colbert and the rest. By virtue of this system, the *robe* servants on the Council in its legislative, executive and judicial modes emerged directly from the *robe* of the law-courts, flanked by those from the world of royal finance. The weakness of such a method of recruitment was that it provided a very narrow base for the power-élite, one which the Revolution would easily unseat 50 years later only to return in a modified form after the Revolution.[15] The advantage, however, was that France was ruled by several hundred jurists and that it therefore remained in 1750 a 'justice-state', however authoritarian the pretensions which it manifested albeit unsustained by the degree of force which it possessed.

In these circumstances, the personal authority of the king was subjected to various limits which were not all of a judicial kind. He had, of course, his own revenues which he disposed of as he wished, and which were

[13]   This distinction between a 'native' and a 'dative' nobility comes from Charles Loyseau at the beginning of the seventeenth century; see E. Le Roy Ladurie, *The Royal French State* (Oxford, Blackwell, 1994), p. 274; Brigitte Basdevant-Gaudemet, *Aux origines de l'Etat moderne, Charles Loyseau (1564–1627) théoricien de la puissance publique* (Paris, Economica, 1977), p. 266; Charles Loyseau, *Traité des ordres et simples dignités* (Paris, éd. L'Angelier, 1613), ch. 4, p. 27.

[14]   These figures have been extracted from an exhaustive reading of M. Antoine, *Le Gouvernement* . . . , in which there are court nobility (12.7%), *robe* (61.7%), finance (16.3%) – all of whom make up the principal 'sociological' groups. The adjective 'Saint-Simonian' is here meant to refer to the duke de Saint-Simon and not to the famous nineteenth-century socialist theoretician.

[15]   Pierre Bourdieu, *La Noblesse d'Etat, grandes écoles et esprit de corps* (Paris, Minuit, 1989).

distinct from the vast budgetary receipts of the kingdom which were subject to various controls. But the 'pocket-money' which he drew from the Treasury or from other hidden sources, did not exceed a million *livres* a year – the equivalent at most of the average revenue of six *fermiers généraux* added together. In Paris, Nancy, Bordeaux, Valenciennes, Rennes and Rouen, statues and royal squares celebrated the cult of Louis XV's personality. Yet, in this particular case, the personality of Louis was far from being a unified whole, integrated and projected in a universal fashion through an assemblage of images tending in the same direction, and solely to present to and fascinate the 'public' (meaning both 'public opinion' and 'audience' in a theatrical sense). This was the great difference from the Sun-King, who identified himself body and soul with his own monarchical persona. Louis XV, by contrast, was less monotone and had a 'dual' existence. From his great-grandfather he inherited a pronounced taste for authority, for sovereignty. Yet he had objections to this which troubled him and which he had inherited from the Fénelonian influences in his education. It was these objections which restrained him from wars where the bloodshed would be excessive; and, when it happened, he at least showed remorse. Similarly he had no wish to exhaust the country through excessive taxation. In fact, for this reason and for many others too, tax-payers found their burden eased in the period from 1715 to 1775 at the state's expense. The dual personality of the king appeared in other ways, especially in the division between public and private. Louis ordered the construction of *cabinets* and then *petits appartements* in the wide-open spaces of Versailles. He thus provided for his personal life a more enclosed and private space. In this trend he illustrated a current of thinking and behaviour which reflected closely the greater respect for privacy felt amongst the élites in the eighteenth century. This greater degree of 'privatization' did not, however, stop the monarch from getting out of bed each morning and putting on his dressing gown to make his way to the ceremonial bed of his great-grandfather where he would submit himself to the daily ritual of the royal *lever*.[16]

Louis XIV's reign had been politically of a piece overall. Straight line vectors could represent the main aspects of policy: enduring, militant anti-Protestantism, a continuous search for territorial acquisition by conquest both on the continental frontiers of France and overseas, and burdensome fiscality, its corollary. Such conquests were not always undertaken with prudence, but they were often accomplished with foresight and even sometimes moderation. The great king's reign had unfolded to the monotonous sound of a constant military march, with fife, trumpet and drum. Louis XV's reign, however, was more like an interminable symphony in which, despite some dissonance and false notes here and there, the movements developed in mutual and striking contrast one with

---

[16] Jacques Levron, *Louis XV, l'homme et le roi* (Paris, Perrin, 1974), p. 122.

another: allegro, andante, minuet, and then finale.[17] In this respect, Louis
XV's reign may be fitted into the broad continuities of the Capetian
dynasty. Since the dawn of the Renaissance, there were some reigns which
fitted the 'straight-line vector' pattern of Louis XIV, whose policies remained all of a piece, either because of their strategic determination (such
as in the case of Louis XI), or simply because of the relatively short length
of their reign (e.g., amongst those open to change, Charles VIII's and
Louis XII's; and, amongst the more rigid in tendency, Henry II's). Other
reigns, however, were noted for one or several changes in direction in mid-
term. Amongst others, we may cite the examples of that of Francis I, fairly
latitudinarian until 1534 and then more clearly anti-Protestant thereafter,
or that of Henry IV with its numerous, bold and clever changes in direction. Louis XV's reign is in the latter category, one with 'oscillations' or
'alternative strategies'. The sheer length of the reign was favourable to
fundamental changes of direction and modifications of style and rhythm in
government. There were moments of release from the pressures of change;
these would then give way to a new phase of discreetly liberal influences;
and then vice versa, as though the reign was living and breathing. It was
this rhythmical change which Louis XV's great-grandfather, despite his
own tactical flexibility, would probably not have appreciated. . . . In certain respects, too, Louis XV was different (though in a way that he was
entirely unconscious of) from traditional monarchs and should be compared with a modern head of state who, in order to deal with the very
different problems as they arise in the medium-term, has distinctively
different ministerial teams to call upon. Ernest Labrousse would stress the
splendour of Louis XV by presenting, in a marvellous fashion, the achievements of the French economy during this great reign.[18] Splendour; but
also, I would add, suppleness. It was these oscillations and undulations,
resulting from an ability to adapt to circumstances, which are also a feature
of the artistic politics of the king and his entourage. They, too, would be
moulded to meet the needs of tradition as well as the circumstances, the
tastes and the various needs of the moment.

Architecture, town-planning, décor – in each Louis XV and those
around him shifted their approach in line with contemporary trends,
flirting with each in turn. How else should the young sovereign begin his

---

[17]   Two authors writing about authoritarian systems more powerful and more recent than
French absolutism in the seventeenth century have strongly emphasized the importance of
fluctuations and alternatives within the dominant political tendency. They are Alain
Besançon, *Présent soviétique et passé russe* (Paris, Livre de poche, 1980), p. 195 *et seq.*, and Y.
Brossat, *Le Stalinisme* (La Tour d'Aigues, éd. de l'Aube, 1991), pp. 33–45.
[18]   Ernest Labrousse, *La Crise de l'économie française à la fin de l'Ancien Régime et au début
de la Révolution* (Paris, PUF, 1943). The introduction to this book chooses to contrast the
splendour of the Louis XV period with the misery (perhaps exaggerated by the author) of the
reign of Louis XVI, a reign marked, according to Ernest Labrousse, by a interdecennial
crisis (which, in fact, is barely perceptible and only in viticulture, and then not throughout
the period). Labrousse confused a reduction in the prices of grain with a decrease in (cereal)
production, which was much less evident.

career but with the completion of the great building projects of Louis XIV? Ancestral devotion demanded the finishing of the chamber of Hercules (1736) and the basin of Neptune (1741) at Versailles. At the same time, or subsequently, there began to appear the characteristic volutes of the *rocaille* style, a transformation which is often termed *the* 'Louis XV style'. At Fontainebleau, the royal staircase was completed in 1749 with its wrought-iron balustrade, inevitably in the *rocaille* style.[19] At Versailles, meanwhile, the finishing touches were put to the *église* Saint-Louis whose façade, organ-loft and bell-towers were also baroque. And then, although it is too often wrongly associated with *the* 'Louis XVI style', an austere and civic neo-classicism, with its antique associations, made its first appearance. The removal or progressive elimination of rococo foliage during the second half of the reign of Louis XV is apparent in the château of Compiègne, the Petit-Trianon at Versailles and elsewhere. In Paris, meanwhile (using the names given them in the eighteenth century and readopted in the twentieth) there was the place Louis XV, the Ecole militaire, the Mint, the Pantheon (formerly Sainte-Geneviève), the Faculties of Law and Medicine, the place de l'Odéon – all were begun, but not all of them finished, during the periods of Madame de Pompadour and Madame Du Barry's influence on the reign. In all, it was a remarkable achievement for Louis XV, and above all, for the French state. Louis XIV would have been immoderately proud of it all; not so Louis XV, however, who was perhaps less concerned about public image, and who did not vaunt his own accomplishments to excess. Of course it was true that these projects were not achieved by the king alone. He enjoyed the collaboration of great dynasties of creative artists such as the Gabriel in architecture or the Fontanieu in internal furnishings. These were collective efforts which testify to the multi-faceted dispositions of the king and those around him in the face of tradition, transition and change.

The death of the duke d'Orléans in 1723 inaugurated, at least in principle, the personal rule of Louis XV, then 13 years old. The duke of Bourbon (born in 1692) was, in reality if not in law, given the tasks of first minister. Historians will continue to judge this great aristocratic figure harshly. It is true that he was no genius and that financial speculation of various, often scandalous, kinds, had made him a fortune in the period of John Law's System. But should he be held more to account for this than Richelieu, Mazarin, Colbert, Dubois, Saxe, Choiseul or, later on, Talleyrand? At all events, he is an uninspiring figure in comparison with Philippe and Dubois, his predecessors, and with Fleury, the prelate who succeeded him and whose influence in the *Conseil d'en haut* was important from 1723 onwards. A number of the senior *robe* figures in government, themselves also members of the Council, were secretaries of state and worked alongside Bourbon. Amongst them, Armenonville and his son Morville, Dodun, La Vrillière and Maurepas (the latter two

[19] Antoine, *Louis XV*, p. 540.

belonging to the great administrative family of the Phélypeaux-Pontchartrain) should be particularly noted. Amongst the clients, friends and collaborators of Bourbon there were also some financiers, also capable of functioning as important men of state – the Pâris brothers are the obvious case in point. At a less exalted level, there was also the marquise de Prye, Bourbon's mistress and the daughter, like la Pompadour herself, of a financier.

Whatever the mediocrity of the duke of Bourbon it was nevertheless to his credit that there were no irretrievable disasters between 1723 and 1726. Perhaps one should limit oneself to taking account not of the achievements to his name, but the disasters which he avoided! It is true that the anti-Protestant royal declaration of 1724, and which has often been cited against him *a posteriori*, renewed (and to some degree intensified) the ultra-repressive measures which had been promulgated against them under Louis XIV. But in reality there was no return to the terrifying and violent persecution of the period from 1685 to 1703. The letter of the law and the practical reality need to be kept separate and after 1724, although there was a slight eventual rise in the numbers sent to the galleys, the numbers involved were very small in comparison with the heights reached in the statistical totals of 20 or 30 years previously. The anti-Huguenot ordinances of 1724 which were promulgated under the duke of Bourbon's ministry, were above all a symbolic response to the renewal of Protestant assemblies which had occurred in 1723.[20] This renewal did not do much to change the overall decline in anti-Protestant persecution in the longer term. It should be added that Bourbon diplomacy (and, at this date it was doubly Bourbon since both Louis XV and his first minister were from the dynasty) reinforced this overall tendency. Louis XIV had kept to the logic of events because whilst he persecuted the religious minority of his own subjects he also disavowed any Protestant alliances abroad, notably with the English, the Dutch or the German Protestant princes, alliances which Francis I, Henry IV and Louis had each in his own way tried to cultivate in the past. The Orléans-Dubois tandem ministry, by contrast, resurrected these 'heretical' alliances with the maritime power of the north and north-east from 1717 onwards. But, in this area, Bourbon followed stricly in the footsteps of the Regency. In conjunction with Fleuriau de Morville, Dubois' successor as foreign secretary, the new minister-duke concluded the League of Hanover against Austria and Spain in 1725 which included France, England, Prussia, the Dutch Republic, Sweden and Denmark. It would be difficult to conceive of a more complete Franco-Protestant coalition than this! It is thus even easier to understand that, despite the inferences which one might draw to the contrary in the otherwise excellent Lavisse volume on Louis XV, the internal policies of the Bourbons, although theoretically hostile to the native Protestant minority, were only ever applied in a reluctant fashion . . . even by the

[20]   Philippe Joutard, *Les Cévennes* (Toulouse, Privat, 1979), p. 142.

policy's architects themselves.[21] The left hand, with its grip firmly resting on diplomacy, undermined or almost completely crippled what the right hand was rather unenthusiastically proposing to undertake in the Cévennes or in Poitou.

In the financial sphere, and in the wake of the serviceable but risky inflation of the System of Law, the Bourbon team began a phase of experimental projects which lasted several years. The deflation of the *livre tournois* was attempted, albeit without great success. The inspiration for the basic idea came from Pâris-Duvernoy in 1724 and although it was soundly conceived it was put into practice excessively. At the same time, and during the same year, a tax on a fiftieth (the *cinquantième*[22]) of landed revenues (including those of the nobility) was instituted. The *maréchal* de Villars was opposed to it, and his views said a good deal about the rooted objection of the aristocracy towards any invasion of their fiscal privileges. The new fiftieth was mooted at a time when the major powers of Europe were at peace, even though there might have been some storm-clouds on the horizon which, although they were not of great importance, might seem sufficient to justify a modest increase in the tax burden. The fiftieth, as its name suggests, was a tax on 2 per cent of landed revenues; this compared with the 10 per cent involved in Louis XIV's tenth (*dixième*) which was typical of a period of major warfare. The 2 per cent, at least in theory, was to be collected in nature, and thus conformed to the old ideas of Vauban – even though taxes in money were much easier to collect than grain or wine. Yet this notion of collecting taxes in kind conformed to the archaic nature of French agriculture during this period, one in which living off one's own means and truck barter for the rest were often the dominant feature of economic life. The monetarization of the landed economy only spread gradually, albeit still patchily, during the eighteenth century.

The fiftieth turned out, in the end, to be a failure, and one which is very revealing of the fiscal weakness which characterized the administration of the young Louis XV and in striking contrast with the hyperactive fiscality which had been willingly acceded to by Louis XIV. Yet, despite the dismal failure of this nex tax, the *contrôleur général* Dodun did not fail on all counts. He laid the ground-work for, and succeeded in establishing, what would remain a masterstroke and triumph for monetary policy in France through the eighteenth and nineteenth centuries. He effected the definitive stabilization of the *livre tournois* (later the *franc germinal* under Napoleon and afterwards).[23] It would last through to 1914 except for the brief

---

[21]   Henri Carré, *Histoire de France*, dir. E. Lavisse (Paris, Hachette, 1903–14), viii-2 (*Louis XV (1715–1774)*), p. 84 *et seq.*

[22]   Besides, the *cinquantième* symbolized a period of peace because it was a small tax (2%) whilst the *dixième* (tenth) (in principle 10%) represented the penal taxation typical of periods of major warfare.

[23]   The *livre tournois* stabilized from 1726 onwards; the pound sterling achieved a similar stability in the middle of the sixteenth century! (Fernand Braudel, *Ecrits sur l'histoire* (2 vols, Paris, Arthaud, 1990), ii, 133).

disruption as a result of the revolutionary *assignats*.[24] On 15 June 1726 the silver content of the *livre tournois* was fixed at 5.25 grams. The announcement was made shortly after the dismissal of Dodun, who had undertaken all the preparations; so it was his successor as *contrôleur général*, Le Peletier des Forts, who would be given all the moral and political credit for the measure. The silver content would not be changed again for almost two centuries, save for the disturbances of the 1790s. The French kingdom thus became the next, after England, to enter the world of a fixed national parity for its currency. It was a world which created its own social injustices. The fact that there were no trades unions, and no workers' movements or strikes to put upward pressure upon wages and rekindle inflation, was an inseparable component of such stability lasting for almost two centuries. This stability was also linked to the consolidation of fortunes already made; and credit arrangements, which proved such a heavy burden to the debtors, were all handed down without great difficulty from one generation to another, thanks both to the robustness of monetary values and the practice of passing on inheritances *ad hoc*. It remained the case, however, that this endless monetary calm for the *livre tournois* meant that France was spared the problems which always result from an over-frequent resort to savage monetary deflation. It follows that the new period which was about to begin in 1726, and which would prove to last for a very long time, can only be seen in the context of a vigorous French economy which had fully recovered from the trials of the end of Louis XIV's reign.

The vigour in the French economy also explains why France was able to weather the storm of the grain harvest failure of 1725 without too much difficulty. This failure had been caused by the heavy rains during a dreadful summer which had destroyed the crops. In 1661 a similar weather pattern, with a similarly wet summer, had caused a particularly nasty period of famine during the very year of the Sun-King's assumption of personal rule. Despite a good deal of suffering, measured by the high points reached by the indices of prices and death-rates, there was no major disaster comparable with what had occurred in 1661 or 1709.[25] The principal victim of the wet summer of 1725 was the duke of Bourbon himself whose fiscal projects, the fiftieth as well as other taxes, had not been expected to run into conflict with the hostile mood of rural tax-payers who found themselves the impoverished victims of the bad weather in 1725. Bourbon had been supported by the young Queen Marie

---

[24]   During the French Revolution, the *assignats* consisted of a paper money which did not take long to devalue. The 100 *livre tournois* note in January 1791 was not worth more than 3 *sous* 6 *deniers* at Toulouse in July 1796, or a devaluation of over 90% (G. Frêche, *Les Prix du grain à Toulouse* (Paris, PUF, 1967), p. 131). G. Frêche's work also contains (p. 131) a useful table of the value of the *livres tournois* in fine silver following the detailed data collected by Natalis de Wailly, 'Mémoire sur les variations de la livre tournois', *Mémoires de l'Institut, Académie des Inscriptions*, 21 (2nd part) (1857), 348 *et seq.*

[25]   Jacques Dupâquier, *Histoire de la population française* (4 vols, Paris, PUF, 1988), ii, 203–13.

Leszczynska. She owed her marriage and her crown to him. But neither the king nor Bishop Fleury were impressed by Bourbon. The latter had attempted to undermine the elderly prelate who was overshadowing him in the *Conseil d'en haut*. After an initial showdown, the adolescent king and the elderly prelate removed the minister-duke in June 1726 by banishing him to gilded exile in the Condé château at Chantilly.[26] Bourbon was, in fact, to be the last of the princes of Condé (following his great ancestor from the period of the Fronde) to occupy a position of considerable responsibility, or overall authority, within the French state. He did so without any great success to his credit but there was never any question of his attempting to mastermind a Fronde after his fall from power. Louis XIV and the Regent had seen to it that the court-based aristocracy had been gently brought into line, regimented and bought off. It would be the moment for Fleury, the future cardinal, and his long-standing patience would find its reward.

*   *   *   *   *

Hercule de Fleury (he would change his name to the more Christian André-Hercule later) was born in 1653 at Lodève (in what is now the Hérault *département*) of a family of revenue collectors in the diocese of Lodève. His father had been a *receveur* of royal *tailles*. It was a family of provincial financiers, devoted as much to throne as to altar and well connected to the upright *noblesse de robe* families, the landed seigneurs and gentry of Languedoc such as the Ranchin and the Sarret. Like Dubois too, the young Hercule was typical of a pattern for the future, and one which has survived through to our own day. He was a gifted child from the Midi who completed an outstanding educational career in Paris and became, in time and by a meritocratic process, absorbed into the dominant élite of the capital, and thereby of the realm. At the age of six, Hercule benefited, through the influence of his relatives, from the friendship of two influential Languedocian power-brokers with connections at the court of the young Louis XIV – the Cardinal de Bonzi and the marquis de Castries. Hercule thus enjoyed the best educational opportunities Paris could afford, study-ing first at the *Collège* de Navarre on the Montagne Sainte-Geneviève, and then at the *Collège* Louis-le-Grand, and finally ending up at the *Collège* Harcourt, now the *Lycée* Saint-Louis. These were three establishments which Saint-Simon neatly as ever characterized as 'these little finishing schools'.[27] Hercule was destined for the priesthood and became a canon at Montpellier in 1668, thus returning to his native Languedoc. In time, he would make his way back to the Ile de France as the queen's almoner in 1675 through the never-failing support of the Cardinal de Bonzi. He

---

[26]   It was from the day of this disgrace (11 June 1726) that Fleury carried out the functions, in fact, of first minister but with the simple title of minister of state. Fleury was minister of state from February 1723 (Antoine, *Le Gouvernement* . . . , p. 104).

[27]   *leg*: 'ces petits collèges de bon marché'.

Plate 21   Cardinal Fleury   André-Hercule de Fleury (1653–1743) acted as de
facto prime minister of France from 1726 until his death, and his personality,
portrayed here in around 1728 in a painting by François Stiemart after Hyacinthe
Rigaud, dominated the whole period.
Versailles, Musée national du château

gained his theological degree in 1676 and, in 1678, he became one of the
eight almoners to the king. In 1680, he was a deputy at the assembly of
clergy, by which time he was becoming a recognized figure in the best
society. He was noted for being even-tempered and spiritually minded and
he was not a known (at least not to historians) fornicator. He was on good

terms with the great and good of the various factions at court but he never sold out to any one party. He enjoyed good relationships with the Jesuits and was on the closest of terms with the Colbert, the Villeroy, the Harcourt, the Noailles, the Vaylus, the Villars and the Lamoignon-Basville. Too close perhaps, since Louis XIV regarded him as altogether too worldly and would grant him nothing more than the second-rate diocese of Fréjus. His was a career which had begun promisingly and then stalled, although it had not been cut short.

Fleury spent 15 years in his diocese at Fréjus. He was an active bishop and took an active part in the local workhouse (*bureau des pauvres*), the junior seminary, the diocesan synods, and the educations of boys and girls. He took a stand against Jansenism but without excessive zeal. At the other end of the spectrum of Catholic beliefs, he stood apart from excessively *dévot* hispanicism. This made him neither Jansenist nor Molinist and gave him a centrist position which would be where he would remain. In the period from 1707 to 1710, the most hazardous period of the War of Spanish Succession, Fleury would apparently reflect a vigilant patriotism (whatever Saint-Simon might say to the contrary) towards any invaders, whether Savoyards or others. All the same, he was willing to meet enemy soldiers with at least a show of politeness. However, he grew tired of the little town of Fréjus and hoped to make a return to court. At the beginning of 1715, he resigned his bishopric and his departure from the diocese in July was much regretted. Henceforth Louis XIV, at the instigation of Villeroy and Maintenon, showed him high favour and, shortly before his death, appointed the 'former bishop of Fréjus' as tutor to the little Dauphin and future Louis XV.[28] It was one foot on the ladder and, at the age when others contemplate their retirement, Fleury was just about to begin his career. He would have a considerable future ahead of him.

Fleury's role as tutor formally began in 1717, once Louis XV had been 'handed over from the nurses'. The educational principles which he instilled in his student reveal the major planks of the bishop's approach to government which he would put into practice when he became first minister after 1726. Beyond the commonplace recommendations concerning the importance of religious piety was a matching respect for the prerogatives of the Gallican church which encompassed a degree of suspicion towards the papacy, albeit much less marked than would have been the case under Louis XIV.

A good deal of space was devoted to the role of justice including the attention which the king should give to the welfare of his people, much more clearly stated than had been the case in, for example, Richelieu's *Testament politique*. The millions of France's subjects were no longer to be regarded *a priori* as its mules. On the contrary, the king should seek to

---

[28] Fleury assumed his official tutorial functions in April 1716 (Antoine, *Le Gouvernement* ..., p. 53). He exercised them in reality from February 1717 when Louis, seven years of age, left 'women's hands' and responsibility for him was assumed by men.

reduce the fiscal burdens upon them whenever the opportunity to do so allowed it. Finally, the monarchy must know how to project its strength to others, but imperial majesty emphatically did not imply that it was essential to extend in any systematic fashion the territorial limits of the kingdom. Here Fleury reflected the sentiments of Fénelon rather than the military campaigns of Louis XIV who was forever keen to push outwards and increase still further the kingdom's security through the addition (by military conquest, if necessary) of a particular new town or region. That said, Fleury would show considerable ability in accomplishing the sole provincial acquisition for which he would be responsible, namely that of Lorraine.

Aged 73, the former bishop of Fréjus took over overall responsibility for the state in June 1726 when Louis XV, aware of his own inexperience, unhesitatingly handed it over to his old tutor, for whom he retained considerable affection.[29] He became a cardinal in 1726 and since this gave him the right of precedence in the *Conseil d'en haut*, Fleury would retain the essential element of political authority until his death in January 1745. Few European statesmen have had to wait so long, or be of such an advanced age, before taking up office and doing so with such success. The exception is perhaps Konrad Adenauer, chancellor of the Federal Republic of (as it then was) West Germany, and, despite the enormous differences of context, the comparison is not entirely absurd. Both individuals, the one from Languedoc, the other from the Rhineland, devoted their old age to articulating a strategy which sought to benefit 'the common weal' and 'the public good'. Although Fleury has generally been favourably judged by historians of various backgrounds, he has not always received the appreciation which, in retrospect, might be said to be his due. He has even been accused of raping two women and attempting to seduce the queen – and all this from an able writer, Chamfort, from whom one generally expects rather better. It would be difficult to imagine a less plausible accusation to level against Fleury.[30] Chamfort had not even the elements of a case and, on occasions, his work was nothing more than pure gossip.[31]

On the encouragement of its 'patron', the ministerial team and state secretariat around Fleury tended towards a kind of pacifism. Of course some of the higher nobility and marshals of France (Orléans Junior, Conti, Villars and Huzelles . . .) participated in the *Conseil d'en haut* and the *Conseil des dépêches*. But the specialists in charge, and the departmental heads, were all *robins*, at least in the key posts which mattered; and they naturally collaborated with a first minister who was himself from a provincial financial background and who was an ecclesiastical *robin* himself. The

---

[29] The 'scientific' biography of the two great cardinal ministers and men of peace in the eighteenth century, Dubois and Fleury, remains to be written. One can make use of the well-informed Maxime de Sars, *Le Cardinal de Fleury* (Paris, Hachette, 1942).

[30] Chamfort, *Mémoires* (Paris, Gallimard, 1982), p. 254 (maxim 906).

[31] Simone Balayé, *Histoire de la Bibliothèque nationale des origines à 1800* (Geneva, Droz, 1988), p. 359.

Phélypeaux (Saint-Florentin and Maurepas) were responsible for Protestant affairs and the navy. Le Blanc, followed by d'Angervilliers and then Breteuil, were at the War Office whilst Chauvelin and then Amelot held Foreign Affairs. Le Peletier des Forts was at the Treasury, to be succeeded by Orry. D'Aguesseau was Chancellor, backed up by Armenonville and then by Chauvelin. These were all competent individuals who, with the exception of Fleury himself, were young or middle-aged and there was not the shadow of a court grandee amongst them. How readily, therefore, one can understand the great duke Saint-Simon's lack of warmth for Fleury. This was the prelate whose 'gentle and modest' appearance belied a 'proud and implacable' spirit within – and Saint-Simon's judgment was right if we take it to mean that Fleury knew how to establish a (generally pacific) line of conduct and then hold it steadfastly almost up to his death. At all events, Fleury took steps to see that, as soon as it was possible to do so, Saint-Simon was distanced from the court.[32] His lack of trust in him was probably well-judged despite the degree of friendship which existed between the two men.

In foreign affairs, the cardinal's pacifist inclinations were very close to those of Orléans and Dubois and far removed from those of Louis XIV. He had seen a good deal and learnt from his experiences but, despite his age, Fleury accepted the culture of his contemporaries and its often severe judgements on the Sun-King and particularly his bellicose diplomacy. During the Fleury ministry, or a little before it, some intellectuals had begun to voice open criticism of the 'tyrannical, bellicose and annexationist' recent past. Amongst the critics[33] were Count Henri de Boulainvilliers, the *abbé* de Saint-Pierre, the marquis d'Argenson, the Jansenist Duguet and, to a lesser extent, the great writers like Montesquieu and Saint-Simon. Fleury doubtless had not read all these works but his actions were implicitly guided by views very similar to theirs.

In the three decades from 1713 to 1743, Europe was, save for the very end of the period, at peace. This was perhaps the 'Thirty Years Peace'. At all events the contrast with the seventeenth century is a striking one since Europe had been at war somewhere on the continent almost continuously from 1635 to 1713. When the War of Spanish Succession finally drew to a close in 1713, the two kingdoms which were left well provided for at the treaties of Utrecht were France and Great Britain. Two ministers of considerable skill in each saw to it that this state of affairs was sustained and protected. Fleury in France and Walpole in England were both prudent individuals who mutually respected one another's abilities. It was a special relationship evoking others in the past, that between Francis I and Henry VII, for example, or between Elizabeth I and Henry IV, or between Cromwell and Mazarin. Facing the nations which had benefited from

[32] Saint-Simon, *Mémoires*, xli, 305–6 (expulsion); and xv, 201 (enduring friendship, despite all?).
[33] Nicole Ferrier-Cavervière, *Le Grand Roi à l'Aube des Lumières, 1715–1751* (Paris, PUF, 1985).

Utrecht were two dissatisfied powers with unsatisfied claims – Austria and Spain. Their grievances and demands were considerable. At the end of Louis XIV's reign, Spain had lost its former possession in Italy as well as Gibraltar, now in the hands of the British, although the latter played to the gallery periodically by offering one day to return the Rock to its rightful owners; no one, however, was fooled. . . . Queen Elizabeth Farnese, the ambitious, energetic and politically activist second wife of Philip V, hoped to obtain compensation for the territorial losses in Italy. The duchies of Parma and Tuscany should, she thought, be inherited by her son Don Carlos (the future Charles III of Spain). But, here too, there were frustrating delays in the negotiations. Another subject for contention was that King Philip V of Spain, although a Bourbon and the grandson of Louis XIV, had no rights (should his young nephew Louis XV die without a male heir) to accede to the French throne, despite his genealogical qualifications which certainly made him the closest male heir to the French king. But the claim had been formally renouned at Utrecht and, in London, this clause mattered, for reasons which are clear. The prospect of a double Franco-Spanish Bourbon crown brought sweat to a Hanoverian brow. Finally, for their part, the Castilians resented the commercial incursion practised in the Spanish New World by English shipping and the Austro-Belgian fleet of the Company of Ostende and which infringed Madrid's monopoly of trade. For its part, Austria also had its own *desiderata*. Through the commercial company based in Ostende it attempted to foster a nascent Belgian capitalism, now that the Utrecht settlement had transferred Belgium from Spanish to Austrian hands. It thus challenged the English, Dutch, French and Spanish expansion across the oceans and their dominance in world trade. Catholic Flemings and francophone Walloons from the southern Netherlands thus, under Austrian aegis, challenged a formidable quartet of world powers. There was yet a further Austrian grievance, for the Emperor Charles VI had no surviving male heir and he wanted the Habsburg hereditary lands (Austria, Hungary, Croatia, etc.) to be passed on to one of his daughters, one of whom was Maria Theresa. Soon to be renowned, she would, via Marie-Antoinette and Marie-Louise amongst others, be the grandmother to Ancien Régime Europe. Charles VI thus had to gain the recognition of the other powers in Europe for a decision in favour of Maria Theresa's succession, whose cause he robustly advanced and which would provoke numerous problems, particularly in respect of Hungary. He made his decision official in 1713 and then again in 1724 in the form of the Pragmatic Sanction. The question was whether the other states in the concert of European powers would agree to ratify it.

In the light of these various ambitions, a number of strategies emerge as possible. For example, one can envisage an alliance of the states with grievances to be settled such as Spain and Austria. But this would have been to create an extraordinary pantomime horse of an alliance between two long-opposed dynasties – the House of Habsburg in Vienna and the Bourbon branch in Madrid. Yet this was what was put in place, and made to work for a time, by the remarkable efforts of Ripperda who was sent from Spain to Austria and who concluded treaties of peace, friendship and commerce in 1725 which appeared to bind the two Catholic powers to one another. This spectacular reversal in the European alliance patterns did not, however, last long. It succeeded, at least, in demonstrating the continuing vitality of Bourbon Spain. Philip V and his second wife, Elizabeth Farnese, with Alberoni and Ripperda also drew on the favourable economic climate in the eighteenth century which had begun a renewed process of growth in Spanish commerce, production and maritime trade. Whatever the outcome, the recognition, albeit delayed, by Philip V of the Austrian monarchy was a fact of considerable significance which, in past circumstances, would have brought much joy to Louis XIV.

That said, the Austro-Spanish pact was bound to alarm the Protestant and maritime powers of Europe as well as France (which remained by tendency austrophobe despite the efforts of Louis XIV). Straightway, and without hesitation, they all strengthened their mutual agreements by means of the alliance of Hanover in September 1725. The possibility of a war breaking out between the 'Hanoverian-Orléans' and 'Vienna-Madrid' axes was now a real possibility. In February 1727, in fact, Spain put Gibraltar under siege for several months. It did not, however, attempt to storm the Rock and this was because the emollient and conjoint diplomacy of Fleury and Walpole opened the door to an agreement. The details of the complex and cleverly conducted negotiations need not detain us but, from 1729 to 1732, the two were able to conjure into being their irenic objectives, partly by skilful mediation and partly by offering various tempting rewards. For his part, Fleury floated the alluring possibility before Philip V of his being allowed to claim the French throne in the event of Louis XV dying without a male heir. Such a promise cost the cardinal nothing, knowing perfectly well that Louis XV's procreative endeavours with Marie Leszczynska would be likely to yield fruit in due course – and a Dauphin was duly born in 1729. In this respect, however, it is worth remarking further that the rights of the Spanish branch of the Bourbons to succeed to the French throne were not as null and void as they seemed afterwards, more especially as they had been implicitly recognized by the wily cardinal who chaperoned Louis XV.[34] At all events, Queen Elizabeth Farnese and Philip V had every reason to expect more substantial concessions. At length, Austria having signalled its agreement, Don Carlos took possession of Parma thanks to the military occupation of the town by Spanish forces. At the same moment, Carlos advanced his claim to Tuscany. There was a momentary panic when it seemed possible that the duchess of Parma, the widow of the duke of Parma who had died in 1731, might be carrying his child posthumously. Her urge to eat chocolate, typical in a pregnant woman, threw the chanceries of Europe into disarray until it became clear that it was only a nervous simulation of pregnancy. In October 1732,

[34] John Rogister, professor at the University of Durham, has strongly underlined this point.

Carlos was legally installed in Parma with the accord of the great powers. The Emperor Charles VI was not initially welcoming of this new alliance in the Italian peninsula where he had his own interests to further, beginning with Milan. This was settled, however, when he obtained the compensation which was to his satisfaction. In March, and then in July, 1731, England and Spain successively came to recognize the Pragmatic Sanction. The future of Maria Theresa was thus secured.

As for Great Britain, already satiated in 1713, it lost nothing in all these dealings and could even derive both honour and profit from those which had been struck. For Austria agreed that, from 1727, it would freeze the activities of the Company of Ostende for a period of seven years, which would in reality sound its deathknell. Meanwhile, in that same year 1727, Madrid abandoned its brief and spectacular Austrian alliance and made a new pact with London and Versailles. At the same time, Spain returned the English shipping captured in the West Indies and granted English merchants, although heretics, their former privileges in Spain. It was a wonderful example of circular negotiations leading to mutual concessions where each participant, Madrid, Vienna and London, gained something whilst Fleury and Walpole played the honest brokers. The wishes of the *abbé* de Saint-Pierre, who had been such a partisan of European ententes, were thus realized. For his part, Walpole had to resist English popular opinion which was prejudiced against Papist Spain. Fleury, too, had to silence Chauvelin, his secretary for foreign affairs, who was the spokesman for the anti-Austrian faction at the French court, whose influence had been felt in France since the later Valois and Bourbon, certainly since the days of Richelieu and Mazarin. Thus the Anglo-French axis, or Anglican-Gallican, kept war at bay from Western Europe.[35] It was the strategy of Dubois, certainly of Fleury; but also of Louis XIV himself during the most intelligent period of his foreign policy formulation from 1698–1701 when he attempted to construct a peaceful resolution of the Spanish succession question, an attempt which in the end came to nothing. It was also a logical extension of the mental robustness of Louis XIV who, rather

---

[35]   J.O. Lindsay (ed.), *New Cambridge Modern History* (Cambridge, Cambridge University Press, 1957), vii, p. 202 emphasizes these positive achievements in the years from 1731 to 1732, peace in Europe being ensured by the Anglo-French alliance and, in particular, by the friendship of Fleury with the Walpoles, Horace and Robert, the one plenipotentiary in Paris, and the other the almost unshakeable British first minister up to 1742 (on this useful friendship, see Saint-Simon, *Mémoires*, xv, 199–203, text and notes). The English accord was abandoned by France definitively in the 1740s and not without a degree of fickleness. Whatever the responsibilities of the Versailles court in the matter, however, it was also the case that the powerful demographic imperialism of the British in Northern America, working to the detriment of the fragile empire which had been put together recently on the New Continent of America by Louis XIV and Philippe d'Orléans, made this rupture almost inevitable at some stage. It is not at all certain that the second half of the 'second Hundred Years War' (in fact 126 years, from 1689 to 1815) after 1750 could have been avoided. In this respect, the Orléans-Dubois-Fleury-Walpole interlude could only be a long intermission between two interminable conflicts.

later, at the age of 76, foresaw the possibility of a rapprochement with Austria. These various developments culminated in the years 1731–2 and, without over-emphasizing the point, they were a recognition of an elementary kind of social contract between kings and the people's representatives. Both the Hanoverians in London and the Bourbons in Madrid held their crowns, at least in part, by virtue of the English House of Commons and the Spanish Cortes respectively. Even the Parlement of Paris subscribed to the renunciation clauses of the Treaty of Utrecht, albeit with considerable debate. The victorious states had agreed some concessions to satisfy those who had lost out, Spain and Austria. A new international order came together on the basis of a European balance of power. The need for nations to conduct themselves in a civilized way was posed in practice even if it was not always precisely identified in theory. The ministerial, ecclesiastical and cardinalesque emollience of Hercule de Fleury, flanked by Walpole, had a demonstrable efficacy to it. If the seventeenth century was coloured by the sombre hue created by the Thirty Years War, the eighteenth century took on a new look, thanks to a quasi-peace which lasted almost 30 years, nurtured and nursed by statesmen of high quality.

Peace remained a relative concept and under pressure – generally from extremists in Fleury's own camp rather than potential opponents. He could be persuaded of the necessity to declare war, albeit in a very limited and controlled fashion. Military hostilities, within well-defined limits, were for the cardinal (as for Philippe d'Orléans) merely the continuation of peace by other means. Such was the short and rather uncomfortable period which opened up following the death of August II, Elector of Saxony and King of Poland. As early as 1661, the Polish king on the throne at the time had already, in a moment of remarkable prescience, foreseen the menacing prospect that Russia, Austria and Poland would one day 'tear apart' his kingdom and partition it out amongst themselves.[36] His prophecy would not come true until 1772 but already in 1733 the Russians (under Tsarina Anna Ivanovna) and the Austrians (under Emperor Charles VI) were advancing their own candidate for the succession to the throne in Warsaw. This was none other than August III, the Elector of Saxony and son of August II, the deceased King of Poland. The rival candidature of Stanislas Leszczynski, the father-in-law of Louis XV, was supported by a large group of the nobility of Poland. He had already served as king of Poland for the short period from 1704 to 1709. Stanislas' claim to the kingship was recognized in the Diet of September 1733.[37] Some in France were excited by this prospect, declaring themselves favourable to his candidature because they were unhappy at seeing Louis XV married to a commoner and not to the daughter of a truly sovereign dynastic house.

[36] Cited by Ernest Lavisse in *Histoire de France*, vii-2, 201 (a prophetic text, 111 years ahead of its time).

[37] In total, Stanislas would thus be king of Poland twice, from 1704 to 1709 and then from 1733 to 1735.

It became important, therefore, to satisfy these ardent Bourbon supporters to see Louis XV assist his father-in-law Stanislas back onto the throne in his native country and cement a Warsaw-Versailles axis. Fleury, the obedient servant of his now-crowned pupil, went along with this point of view, but did so with a carefully calculated degree of reluctance because he never liked risking a conflict unnecessarily.

The Polish enterprise was a fiasco. Fleury was not prepared to sacrifice the benefits of the alliance, or at least neutrality, of Britain and the Netherlands at any price, an alliance which he had expressly guaranteed in November 1733. Thus he despatched in the spring of 1734 a small armed force to the Baltic which would not have the power to prevent the Russian and Saxon contingents from seizing Danzig during the summer months. Stanislas could do nothing other than take clandestine flight and leave his native 'kingdom'. In reality, the 84-year-old Fleury demonstrated a prudence which is readily understandable in terms over and above that of someone over 80 years of age. The possibility of sending a French expeditionary force to the Baltic in such numbers that it would irritate the maritime powers was difficult to contemplate seriously. Their friendship was accounted essential to France after 1716 by Louis XV's ministers. The scale of France's intervention thus had to be carefully judged so as not to arouse the wrath of the British or the Dutch and it would occur in the Rhineland and in northern Italy, far away from Warsaw and, thus *a fortiori* from Cracow too. Berwick and Villars, the old generals of Louis XIV's high command, were able to secure easy victories against Austria in these sectors relatively close to France's borders. France was able to call on the support of Spain and Savoy and although it briefly appeared to act the part of a 'Herculean super-power', it showed its capacity for military force without using it to excess. French influence could be extended through the territorial acquisitions or the 'iron curtain' of fortresses of the Louis XIV and Vauban period. It would also be advanced through economic expansion and through an intelligent pursuit of national policies devoted to maintaining the peace, as during the period from 1715 to 1734. No longer would the realm be required to fight on three or four fronts at once (at sea, in India, in North America and on the continent of Europe) as had occurred in the last quarter of the seventeenth century.

Starting from these favourable circumstances, the peace, which had been established in reality from 1735, was eventually signed after many lengthy negotiations at Vienna in November 1738. This conclusion to the Polish War of Succession was also one of Fleury's masterpieces, of the kind at which he excelled. There were mutual exchanges, territorial swaps like a game of musical chairs or game of tig. So the House of Austria recovered Parma and Piacenza at the expense of the Spanish Bourbons. Duke François de Lorraine marred Maria Theresa, the inheritor of the Holy Roman Empire. He sacrificed his hereditary duchy at Nancy but received in return, over and above the hope of imperial succession, the grand-duchy of Tuscany which was vacant after the death of the last

Medici in 1737. This marked the end of the Medici (who were Tuscan from old roots) and also the glorious end of the French Lorraine house, now an imperial family.

It also brought a particular Europe to a close. The Spanish Bourbons had by no means done badly since although Don Carlos had sacrificed Parma he also took possession of the realms of Naples and Sicily. A 'neo-Bourbon' régime would thus play a reforming role in southern Italy for a period. For its part, Savoy/Sardinia received various territorial titbits, including Lombardy. On the whole, the entire house of Bourbon (Spanish and French branches) had, with a minimum of campaigning or military investment, gained a good deal from this 'Polish' conflict which had been well-prepared and well-conceived. The initial pretext of the events which had taken place a few years earlier in Poland was completely forgotten. Augustus I of Saxony was able to install himself without difficulty on the Polish throne. In this respect, however, the peace represented a dangerous victory for the pro-Muscovite party in the Polish state, to which it should be added that, for the first time in European history, the army of the Tsar had advanced into western Germany to counter the French. The far-sighted Fleury was much impressed by the brief but deep incursion of these troops from the far East and by the emergence in Europe of Russia, this 'great form in movement'. At the level of the international interests of the House of Bourbon, at all events, and within the essentially dynastic conceptions of the period, which have become so alien, not to say incomprehensible and scandalous to us now, the results which had been obtained were not inconsiderable. The base had been laid for the 'family pact' which would be concluded later in 1761 between the various Bourbons in Madrid, Versailles, Naples and Parma. Although gently treated by Fleury, Austria could hardly feel entranced by the position in which it found itself. The Austrian state suffered from a handicap as a result of the armed incursions from the Turkish empire which threated the south-east flank of its Habsburg possessions. The Ottoman victories in the Balkans in 1737 and 1739 obliged the Emperor to cede northern Serbia and Belgrade to the Ottomans, territories which had formerly been conquered for the Habsburgs by Prince Eugene of Savoy. Besides, French agents, particularly the marquis de Villeneuve, provided decisive assistance to the Sublime Porte in this affair. Instead of 'projecting' its influence into the Baltic, the 'Herculean' France of Cardinal Fleury was thus capable of exercising a degree of influence on the shores of the Bosphorus to the detriment of the Austrian empire. As for Duke François de Lorraine, he was showered with potential largesse at a conjugal and territorial level and therefore had to cede (following the bargaining chain) Lorraine to Stanislas Leszczynski who would in turn retrocede it on his death to his blood-relative, Louis XV. In truth there was barely a pretence of waiting until the death of his unfortunate rival Augustus II of Saxony. Stanislas' Chancellor La Galaizière would spend all his time in Nancy, much as an intendant of a French generality in the Touraine or in Languedoc. It was the case,[38] however, that Chaumont de La Galaizière, Stanislas' 'mayor of the palace', was also the brother-in-law and direct subordinate of Orry, the French *contrôleur général des finances*. By these means, Nancy was operated from Versailles. With the irreversible coalescence of the Lorraine lands into the French system, the French hexagon took on its definitive modern form (despite the interruptions between 1871 and 1945). One can but admire the economy of means, and the elegance of the methods employed by Fleury. They suited the context of a 'less barbarous' Europe where the methods used in international relations were infinitely more subtle than the much more brutal tactics employed in the decades of a Gustavus Adolphus or of a Wallenstein. The three latter years of the cardinal's life (1740–3), contemporaneous with the beginnings of the War of Austrian Succession, were much less impressive. The old Hercules had to relinquish his gentle mace and take up a much-merited retirement; and, at 86 years of age, it was the least which was due to him. But Louis XV liked him . . . and he would not find his equal amongst his successors.

Fleury's endeavours, although strictly speaking a continuation of those of Dubois, the other cardinal, remain, nevertheless, impressive. The son of the tax-collector from Lodève had made a diplomatic pattern all his own which, with the agreement of Protestant powers, would turn out to be both profitable and relatively inexpensive. In this respect, it was a diplomatic pattern which (at least in this one feature) shared common ground with that of all four cardinal-ministers: Richelieu, Mazarin, Dubois and Fleury. It was as though, in order to secure a durable entente with the heretic powers, it was important to secure, either to begin with or *en route*, oneself from attack from behind by reinforcements from the church in Rome. And what better assurance was available, in reality, than that of a cardinal's hat on a ministerial head to reinforce oneself during contacts with Protestants which, in the eyes of others, would be seen as smacking of heresy.

It might be objected that foreign policy was thus being forged without any consultation of the popular will but simply in terms of the interests of princes and ruling dynasties. Just so, and it was difficult to envisage other procedures being adopted at this period. Nevertheless, within this 'outmoded' environment, some qualifications have to be made. Firstly, peace (in the way in which Fleury conceived of it) was, at all events, worth having for the broad masses of people for whom war was almost always something to endure, either fiscally or physically. As for the annexation of Lorraine to France, thanks to a legitimizing agreement to which the last local dynast (Duke François) had consented, it proved to be enduring in particular because the majority population of this province was already French-speaking. The transfer from principality to being part of an authentically national community, the latter being founded on a shared linguistic identity, would be the more easily accomplished when it came to 14 July 1790,

---

[38]   See Michel Antoine, *Le Dur Métier de roi* (Paris, PUF, 1986), p. 181.

which would constitute the symbolic date of the feast of the Federation celebrated on the Champ-de-Mars.

Was it not also the case that Fleury used a similar kind of tact when confronting, in order to resolve (at least in a provisional fashion), the various Jansenist tergiversations during his long ministry? After the unfortunate *Unigenitus* bull of 1713, followed by the Regency, France had witnessed[39] a close fusion between three disparate elements. First, there was old-fashioned *Jansenism*, a theology of grace. Secondly, there was *Richerism*, a political and synod-based reaction amongst rural priests, successors of Christ's Apostles, and against an episcopacy which appeared to them too aristocratic. Thirdly, there was *Gallicanism*, a particular model of the church, simultaneously steeped in national and patristic roots. This triple synthesis diverged *a priori* from the confrontational stance of the Roman system which was suspected by an influential section of opinion in France of rococo Jesuitism, the Jesuits being seen as suppliant to powers such as the papacy which seemed feeble. *Unigenitus*, in the eyes of Gallicans and Jansenists, represented nothing more than the personal view of the late Clement XI, and one which was not particularly well-founded. It had not the status of a dogma, merely that of a *doxa*[40] against which a determined campaign would be mounted, and which would result in 1762 in an official *Kulturkampf*.[41] And so long as *Unigenitus* had not been officially received by the clergy of France, expressly enjoined to do so, it could not carry the force of law. The anti-popery of the Augustinian wing of the church (which should not be confused with the rabid anti-popery of the Huguenots or the Anglicans) is represented by the *abbé* Pucelle or by the Parlement of Paris; equally, on a European level, by the noted canonist Van Espen at Louvain, as well as in the works of the advocate Pietro Giannone in Naples and, rather later, in the writings of Justinus Febronius, the suffragan bishop of Trèves.[42] Meanwhile in France, a fraction of the senior and lesser clergy, seculars and regulars (with the exception of the Jesuits) were infected by the Richer-Gallican-Jansenist ideology. So, too, was a proportion of the juridical bourgeoisie from the court ushers right up to the senior judges and including the notaries and advocates. But some of these groups controlled a substantial part of central and local authority through the office-holding classes. The positions adopted by the jurists in favour of a degree of religious heterodoxy was bound *a fortiori* to risk weakening royal instituions. In 1682, at the height of his glory, Louis XIV had made use of the Gallican

---

[39] See Jacques M. Gres-Gayer, 'The *Unigenitus* of Clement XI: a French look at the issues', *Theological Studies*, 69 (1988), 259–82.

[40] *Doxa*: i.e. a received or self-evident opinion (even one with rational, veracious or scientific basis) within the context of a dominant culture.

[41] Cf. below, ch. 10.

[42] Zeegers Van Espen (1646–1728); Pietro Giannone (1676–1748); Justinus Febronius (1741–90). Cf. *New Cambridge Modern History*, vii, 119–21.

clergy against Rome; in 1685, the parlements, hostile to all forms of heresy, had been 'given their head' under the auspices of the Sun-King against the Huguenots. This was a sign of just how efficient were his strategies for élite coalition and integration in a clerical, *parlementaire* and national context.

Yet, gradually the Bourbon dynasty earned all the favours from the Vatican after 1695 (with royal concessions on its former Gallican positions towards the papacy, who had no sympathy towards Gallicanism at all), and after 1715 (*Unigenitus*), when the Bourbon dynasty earned all the favours in the Vatican. This was an authentic change of strategy within a continuously sought-after objective of hegemony. Louis XIV, and then Louis XV, sought (as always) to impose their 'leadership' over the French church but now (and here was the novelty) did so with the willing compliance of Rome. As a result, they also sacrificed two precious allies: the Gallican clergy firstly (so numerous amongst the priesthood and even the episcopacy); and, secondly, the *parlementaires*. The latter had only wanted their anti-Calvinist sentiments to be exploited in the express circumstances of their having the right (a right which was now being refused them) to flirt with Jansenism and Gallicanism. And both of these 'isms' had an aura of heterodoxy around them, the first well-established, the second of more recent vintage. This was a highly dangerous evolution for the long-term vitality of the French monarchy. In effect, it lost a number of allies who had formerly appeared to be consubstantial with it amongst the clerics and the Gallican magistrature. The same was also true for the vitality of the church; for how could one prevent anticlericalism from creeping into its debates? It made its presence felt against the Jesuits and against the majority of the French bishops, suspected of colluding with royal power, suspected also of substituting a religion of proud domination for a religion of evangelical humility. The perils in the diffusion of deism, less sophisticated than the anti-ritualistic Jansenism, should also be noted. And, more elementary still, an overall antipathy towards revealed religion of all kinds (held to be conflict-ridden or even ridiculous) was spreading. This antipathy was typical of that part of the Enlightenment which detested both the 'hypocrisy' of the Jesuits and the rigorism of Jansenism. To this, we should add that the eighteenth century was also a period of decline in the political and material authority of the Vatican. By insisting on *Unigenitus*, the Vatican acted as though it sought compensation for this decline in its temporal authority by requiring adherence to additional and more rigid dogmas and rituals (as would Pius IX at a later date . . .). Failing to impose its will on the Emperor or the king of Spain, the Vatican turned its attentions to the Jansenists and sought to make the French royal state complicit in its actions, to which it had, somewhat naively, lent its agreement.

In August 1720, after several tergiversations which were typical of the 'compromise period' of the Regency, Philippe d'Orléans agreed to the terms of the *ad hoc* 'Declaration' by which the constitution of *Unigenitus* would be observed throughout the realm. As a result, under the Bourbon ministry, Fleury would be responsible for ecclesiastical matters to the Council of Conscience. He would assume *ex officio* the responsibility for carrying out the 1720 'declaratory' act of Philippe d'Orléans. The anti-Jansenist position of the former bishop of Fréjus turned out to be both firmly based and flexibly applied. The firmness came first from his point of view; later events would confirm the fact that what had begun in purely Augustinian terms to disturb the fabric of the French church alone would eventually enfeeble the absolutist structures of the state in their entirety (and, on this point, Louis XIV had perceived the situation correctly and with a keen eye on future developments). At the same time, and herein rested the habitual flexibility of the individual, Fleury remained attached, like many of the bishops of his generation, to the inheritance of Bossuet, and an irreducible set of Gallican principles. He thus forcefully refused, for all that he was a cardinal, to surrender to the restrictions proposed by Rome merely for the pleasure of destroying the lintels and stamping on the reliquaries of Port-Royal once more.

In this situation, Fleury's erosive responses to Jansenism were at first limited, prudently local and *ad hominem*. Well before the ex-Jansenizing Cardinal de Noailles had capitulated to royal authority in 1728, carefully conceived pressure obtained the condemnation, and then the expulsion (in September 1727) of Bishop Soanen, bishop of the tiny diocese of Embrun and known throughout France for his foolishly audacious Augustinianism. The Soanen affair threatened a full-scale reaction. At the end of 1727, it resulted in 50 Parisian advocates favourable to the dismissed prelate meeting in 'consultation', a meeting which was soon followed by concerted action from a dozen bishops. The purely formal pretext for their meeting was that they wanted to stand in solidarity with their dismissed colleague from Embrun. Well might the young Louis XV (18 years old) rail against these forces, for they would henceforth make good use of the power of clandestine publishing. In 1728, the *Ecclesiastical News* (*Nouvelles ecclésiastiques*) was shrewdly compiled and then secretly printed and distributed. It spearheaded the 'good cause' of the invisible church of the saints, miraculously healed by Jansenism, against the leading figures of the official clergy and the visible church. There thus developed the phenomenon of propaganda and the manipulation of public opinion which would be of the first importance for the rest of the eighteenth century. The techniques of secrecy exploited by the compilers of the *News* were used to perfection. Its meetings were recorded, its contact networks between correspondents who were unknown to each other were firmed up. . . . Against the clandestine spread of the *News* what could the authorities, led by Fleury, do? The cardinal had a double responsibility to respond to what was happening – both ministerial and ecclesiastical. He sought to remove the last Jansenist elements from the episcopacy and the abbacies to purify or isolate the last Augustinian remnants who still held responsibility within the church.

In March 1730, Fleury transformed *Unigenitus*, which was already official policy for the clergy, into a state law! This was the high-point of Fleury's political offensive against Jansenism. As a result he was confronted with the vigorous opposition of the Parisian *parlementaires* with their Jansenist tendencies. He reacted to this by exiling them, albeit to somewhere close by the capital and with comfortable quarters. In August 1731, it was the turn of the Parisian advocates to copy the senior judges and to declare a strike, irritated by a sharp injunction from by Mgr de Vintimille, the new Archbishop of Paris who was much more under the thumb of the government. Noailles, who had for so long obstructed the Jesuits, had died in May 1729 and been succeeded by Vintimille.

In the end, Fleury stopped these attempts at repression in mid-track. They had not touched the hard core of the Jansenist movement; nor had they incurred deaths or imprisonment of the opposition on a large scale. In August 1732 the king was able to issue a fairly crude declaration which forbade the Parlement from repeated remonstrances against edict. It also proscribed strikes amongst the pro-Jansenist judicature. It also limited the competence of the Parlement to intervene in religious matters. A sword waved in the air or a façade of a measure, to be replaced by a later agreement? At the end of 1732, in fact, an accord was realized between Versailles and the *parlementaires*. Fleury lifted the exile imposed on the magistrates whilst they agreed, with varying degrees of sincerity, to submit to royal authority. Meanwhile, the chancellor, on the order of the cardinal, proclaimed the *surséance* (or 'suspension') of the decrees of August 1732. This compromise between opposites was arrived at for various motives. The Jansenists found themselves ridiculed in the eyes of many following a recent 'convulsionary' incident at Saint-Médard. The standing of the Jansenist sect, although still enormous, was certainly affected by it. But the 'suspension' also drew on a degree of moderation on the part of Fleury, congenital to the make-up of a prelate who had been formed after the fashion of a southern politician or a Languedocian notary. Taking everything into consideration, the cardinal had no desire to see things go too far (as would occur after his death, after 1750), and certainly not to see the Augustinian activists denied the sacraments. For 15 years after 1733 this would not be a major issue, save in isolated cases. There would be no major ideological battles in the French church. The rule of silence would hold good for a period and Fleury (along with Joly de Fleury, the *procureur général* in the Parlement), would preside over the ensuing calm. The (not invariably sweet) malleability of the Lodève cleric who had made it many years previously to Paris, proved of enduring worth in these circumstances as well. It was the same force which had, with the compliant friendship of Walpole, resolved the Anglo-Hispanic tensions, just as it had untangled the imbroglios surrounding the successions to Poland or Lorraine.

This said, the Jansenist crisis, which was *ipso facto* a *parlementaire* crisis brought to the surface a new (or revivified) principle. It was not the only group to raise the issue, however, which concerned the proper role of the nation, 'represented' (or *soi-disant* represented) by the Parlement, in the framing of legislation in conjunction with the king. It was not yet an affirmation of national sovereignty but it was a claim to the separation of two of the three essential powers of sovereignty (legislative, judiciary and executive). Such, at any rate, was the lesson to be drawn from the pamphlet entitled *Judicium Francorum* which was produced in 1733 at the moment when the excitement generated by the 'hyper-Augustinian' events of the years from 1729 to 1732 was dying down – at least on the surface if not more fundamentally. It was thanks to the adroitness of Hercule de Fleury's ministry that such a degree of calm had become possible.

The cardinal managed, at least for the time being, to appease Jansenist agitations. At the same time, he and his colleagues in government managed to avoid exasperating Protestant groups in France or driving them to desperation, and this despite the fact that discriminatory persecution continued to persist towards them to some degree. However limited such hostility was, it nevertheless caused manifest pain to the Huguenot churches, and to their self-esteem, and they lost no time in documenting it amply for posterity. The chronology of the traumatic incidents inflicted upon them in this way is at once unpredictable and nuanced.

We should examine, first, the years from 1725 to 1726, which correspond to the transition from the Bourbon ministry to Fleury and which followed the dramatic legislation of 1724[43] promulgated by Bourbon to repress (in principle) the Calvinists. Yet, during these two years, which one might imagine to have been 'fearful' for 'heresy', not *one* Protestant[44] was condemned to the galleys! This goes to show how important it is to distinguish between the (menacing) letter and the (more indulgent) events in practice – something which historians like Carré,[45] systematically hostile to Louis XV, have tended to ignore. They put the emphasis exclusively on the letter of the law and not on the radical failure to apply it in practice. By contrast, the second year of Fleury's ministry (1727) was marked out by 13 condemnations of 'heretics' to the galleys. A gross and distressing statistic! But, throughout the whole ministry and beyond, from 1728 to 1744 (17 years), there were only 30 Protestants condemned to the galleys – *less than two a year*! This was two too many . . . but equally it is far fewer than under Louis XIV when the equivalent figure had easily exceeded *a hundred per year*. From 1745, shortly after the death of the cardinal, a temporary hardening of attitudes was registered – which testifies *a contrario* to the relative moderation of the Fleury years. The Fleury period corresponded to a new efflorescence, sometimes quasi-legal simply because of the relaxation in tension, in Languedoc Protestantism. As Philippe Joutard notes: 'In the heart of the Cévennes after 1740, it was as

[43] See above, p. 334.
[44] Lavisse, *Histoire de France*, vii-2, 845.
[45] A. Zysberg, *Les Galériens, vie et destin de 60,000 forçats sur les galères de France, 1690–1748* (Paris, Sevil, 1988), pp. 382–3, *annexe 1*.

though the Revocation had never happened.'[46] The Huguenots breached the rules governing abstinence laid down by the Catholic church with impunity. Protestant inn-keepers, landlords and butchers worked, sold and ate meat on the days of Catholic abstinence (Friday, Lent, etc.). The first Protestant parish registers, eventually parish accounts,[47] made their appearance in 1744. Protestantism had become a quasi-public 'heresy'. . . .

★   ★   ★   ★   ★

From the economic and, above all, the financial point of view, the transfer from Bourbon to Fleury was marked, primarily, by the reduction in a certain degree of ministerial amateurism and a conscious support for the phase of (relative, of course) prosperity. The latter was 'in the air' since Law, even since the Treaty of Utrecht. The Bourbon ministry had put in train a number of unfortunate experiments. There had been a diplomatic willingness to take France to the brink of a possible war (the Franco-English war against the Austro-Spanish) which would have required financing. To this should be added the imposition of the *cinquantième*, not in itself a heavy tax (only 2 per cent of revenues), and other extraordinary taxes, deflationary measures which were followed by efforts at reinflation! All of this was laid to one side by the pacifist Fleury in favour of the implementation of a gentle but firmly ascendant line of policy correlated to monetary stabilization, which was achieved definitively for the *livre tournois* in 1726. Agriculture, above all cereal production, which remained the basis for the rest of the system, took up a rhythm of gentle but incontrovertible[48] growth. Following on from the very real famine of 1709, some major crop failures would also occur in the two or three succeeding decades; but they remained minor in comparison with the notorious catastrophes at the end of Louis XIV's reign. Certainly the excessive rainfall of 1725 threatened somewhat the quality of the harvest that year. Above all, 1740 was a bad year, more than 12 months in succession of cold, wet weather, no matter what the season, which did nothing for the harvest. But this is the point where one can appreciate the degree to which

---

[46]   Philippe Joutard (ed.), *Les Cévennes* (Toulouse, Privat, 1985) p. 142. Very important from this point of view are the notarial annotations collected by Alain Molinier, who has the benefit of a remarkable knowledge of these archives. In an article in the *Bulletin de l'histoire du protestantisme français*, 130 (1984), he points out that, from 1743 onwards in the Huguenot Vivarais, fines (which had been heavy) ceased to be levied for the absence of Protestant children from Catholic schools. After 1755, the practice of taking Protestant children away from their parents and placing them in Catholic foster-care was stopped. Such details are small, but essential.

[47]   P. Joutard, p. 142.

[48]   Whatever one makes of the systematically careless calculations on this point proposed by Michel Morineau and our critical remarks; see Michel Morineau, *Les Faux Semblants d'un démarrage économique* (Paris, A. Colin, 1981); and E. Le Roy Ladurie in *Histoire, économie et société*, 3 (1985), 435 *et seq.*

this was a different period. In the seventeenth century, the Parisian basin had often been the theatre for terrible tragedy when profound dearth was accompanied by a massive increase in the death-rate.[49] Yet in 1740 this same region avoided this accompanying mortality which had been the consequence of dearth, a sign of new crop facilities, and of a profound and radical improvement, depending on the circumstances, in the levels of yield, in transport and eventually in imports. The government favoured the latter when the need arose; it consisted of grain convoys for the Parisians, who preferred white bread; and of barley and rice for the poor people of the rural hinterland who thus were able to make do somehow. Fifty or a hundred years earlier they would, in similar circumstances, have died.

On these more solid foundations, a well-conceived financial policy became possible, and particularly since peace (despite the bellicose moments which accompanied the Polish Succession) made things much easier. It would continue to make things easier *grosso modo* until 1792. If we put on one side the conflicts which were, in reality, *minor* – at least in terms of the intensity of their military operations – such as the War of Devolution, the micro Franco-Spanish conflict of 1719, or the War of Polish Succession, we are left in fact with the *great* or 'terrible' wars such as the Thirty Years War, the Dutch War, the War of the League of Augsburg and the War of Spanish Succession. These accounted for 54 years in total out of 85 years from 1635 to 1715 and they were both longer and more intense under Richelieu and Louis XIV than the only two important wars of the Louis XV period, i.e. the War of Austrian Succession and the Seven Years War: 16 years out of a total of 59 years, the chronological percentages in each case amounting to 64 per cent and 27 per cent respectively.

The first *contrôleur général des finances* of the Fleury period was related by marriage to the great Lamoignon family. He was thus a relative of the intendant Lamoignon de Basville, for long the 'uncrowned king' of Languedoc from the Revocation through to May 1718. His son-in-law, known as Le Peletier des Forts, took on his own shoulders, as his father-in-law had done, the hostility of the public and thus spared both the king and the cardinal-minister. An excessively lenient contract to farm taxes[50] was, for example, agreed to in 1726 with the farmers of the *gabelles* and the other indirect taxes. The farmers were then required to agree to a more equitable deal – but they remained no less vilified (albeit very unjustly) in

---

[49] Principally in 1626–31; 1636–8; 1651–3; 1661–2; 1693–4; 1709–10. The favourable periods were situated, on the other hand, during the 'chicken in the pot' years of Henry IV and the immediately post-Henrician period (1595–1625); equally in the Colbertian and post-Colbertian years (1663–91); then, of course, after the Treaty of Utrecht and the death of Louis XIV. The crises of the 1740s were much less intense than those of the Richelieu or Louis XIV epoques (Dupâquier, *Histoire de la population française*, ii, 192–213; this important section of Dupâquier's work was due to J-N. Biraben and Alain Blum).

[50] This was the Carlier contract (Antoine, *Louis XV*, p. 312 *et seq.*; Lavisse, *Histoire de France*, viii-2, 96) so-called from the name of the sieur Carlier who had taken the overall responsibility for the farm on behalf of an important group of *fermiers généraux*.

the eighteenth century. Le Peletier was also subjected to a similar unpopularity for some time as a result of this ill-judged tax-farm contract. In other respects, he attempted to reduce the interest payments servicing the larger *rentes*, a doubtless justifiable economy measure but one which was ill-received by the élites of Paris who were generally-speaking *rentiers* in their own right. Then came the scandal of speculation in the shares of the Company of the Indies in 1730. Le Peletier wanted to stimulate the situation and thought it would be a good idea to raise the market-price of 'Indian' shares by secret purchases without himself intending to gain by the operation. But the wave of hostility in public opinion which followed the unmasking of this little affair was sufficient to send Le Peletier, a convenient scapegoat, packing in 1730. As for his successor, Philibert Orry, he had lived in the shadow of his father, who had been the manager of Philip V's finances in Spain from 1701 to 1706 and then from 1713 to 1715. Philibert Orry had then, still a young man, enjoyed an itinerant career as a provincial intendant. This gave him a good knowledge of the kingdom from Flanders to Roussillon. The Orry-Fleury duo would thus constitute a remarkably efficient team. A wily old politician needs a good financier to rely on. The two men were characterized by a degree of honesty as well as an attitude of relatively scrupulous disinterest. Both signal the welcome evolution towards the great public servants of our own day, devoted to the service of the state and expecting no more than modest personal comfort for themselves. The contrast could hardly be clearer with individuals like Richelieu, Mazarin, Colbert and Dubois[51] for whom it was normal practice (following the model of the cardinal nephews, dear to the Roman pontiffs) to enrich themselves greatly from their service to the king.[52]

To return to Le Peletier, and then Orry, although they were the ministers with overall responsibility, the role played by their immediate subordinates should not be entirely forgotten. The activities of the *intendants des finances* as *de facto* under-secretaries of state should not be underestimated. Some of them stand out particularly, especially the d'Ormesson (father and son), Fagon, the son of one of Louis XIV's physicians, and Trudaine, who would distinguish himself in the transport ministry.

Agricultural changes and improvements to the food supply in the eighteenth century were inseparable in fact from the establishment of a road network for which the personalities of Orry, Trudaine and various others

---

[51] We should note, in fact, within this context the main revenues (if not the overall fortune) of Cardinal Dubois, based on abbeys and ministerial emoluments and other posts, and which totaled some 575,000 *livres tournois* of revenue per year. The figure put Dubois above Colbert but below Mazarin and even Richelieu. On the main revenues of Dubois, see Saint-Simon, *Mémoires*, xli, 193–5 and xxxiv, 302. The suggestions of Saint-Simon, Duclos and d'Argenson about an English pension of 960,000 *livres* received each year by Cardinal Dubois are mere calumny.

[52] From Dubois to Fleury, from 1723 to 1726, there was, in this respect, an interesting transition towards our modern conceptions of public service.

were both an inspiration and a representation of a tendency. It was in 1738 that Orry, drawing on his experience as an intendant, drafted a circular on the *corvées*. It was typical of the administrative monarchy since it had no legislative basis nor regulatory framework.

The word *corvée* was particularly ill-conceived, without any feel for 'public relations'; it evokes an essentially Carolingian feudalism, and yet no comparison could be less apt. In fact, true to the spirit of Vauban, Orry proposed a tax in kind (collected in the form of work). It was to be levied on the populations adjacent to (and at some distance from) the main roads, and thus mainly on the rural world. The roads which were thus constructed or improved were of benefit to the peasantry but they bene-fited the urban world proportionately more. The idea was to create new high-speed roads, not *autoroutes* but *hipporoutes*.[53] They doubled the average pace of a carriage to the speed of a galloping horse. Henri Carré,[54] who never misses a trick, supposes in his contribution to Lavisse's *Histoire de la France*, and against all the evidence, that these *corvées* were imposed 'above all on the poor'. This is a familiar strain, a hoary old myth about the Ancien Régime. In fact, beyond the inevitably privileged classes, the exemptions from the *corvée* normally only applied to the masters of free-schools, post-masters etc. The obligation to provide work-service, on the other hand, mobilized in proportion to the demographic balance of the population (excepting a statistical majority of hand-labourers who were effectively without money resources) all those who had horses and plough-oxen – i.e. the middle or relatively well-off classes of country peasant-proprietors who, in principle, were far from being 'down on their uppers'. The results of the *corvée* were dramatic; road-building continued under official sponsorship up to the Revolution. In England, by contrast, it was generally the private sector which was, in the same period, charged with the construction of the major toll-roads. In 1782, after half a century of the Orry (and post-Orry) system, France could count on 30,000 kilometres of new carriageways. Traffic could spin along at a reasonable pace and pass.[55] The enduring nature of the changes, lasting four decades or more, ensured their positive contribution. Orry and his successors (for the formidable *contrôleur général* was dismissed from power in 1743, although this changed virtually nothing) had the century on their side. They were not (like their predecessors, Sully, then Colbert) reduced to impotence by the apearance of a regent (as in the case of the *grand voyer* Sully, whose efforts were finally brought to naught by Marie de Médicis who patroned other projects) or by the coming of a major military conflict (such as the Dutch War, and then the War of the League of Augsburg), which absorbed all the available

[53] Guy Arbellot, 'La Grande mutation des routes de France au milieu du XVIIIe siècle', *Annales ESC*, 28 (1973), 765 et seq.
[54] Ernest Lavisse, *Histoire de France*, viii-2 (*Louis XV*), 102.
[55] All this follows Guy Arbellot, 'La Grande mutation', p. 765 et seq. See also the unpublished thesis of Christophe Studeny, pupil of the late lamented Jean-Paul Aron, on 'La Vitesse en France du XVIIIe au XXe siècle' (Ecole des Hautes Etudes, 1991).

resources, and which had enfeebled the Colbertian and post-Colbertian programme of road-building.

The economic (and wider) significance of roads, gradually constructed in the course of the eighteenth century, became immense. They liberated regions, and exorcised famine (which would only return to France under the Revolution in 1795 as a result of the disruptions which the political troubles created to commercial traffic and agriculture). The major roads facilitated the diffusion of news. They permitted the immediate spread of the Great Fear in the spring of 1789 as had never happened in the past during periods of panic which had remained regional.

In building roads, had the Ancien Régime signed its own death-warrant, a warrant delivered to it by (amongst other messengers of doom) the Great Fear? Whether or not this was the case, the road-works had their own logic. In 1775, Turgot substituted a money tax for work-service for them, a tax destined to pay for the contractors on the royal roads. At this point, historians have willingly pitted Turgot against Orry, the former being the partisan of modern monetary taxes against the arcane extractor of labour services 'in kind' by *corvée*. But an alternative hypothesis is also equally plausible, namely that between 1738 and 1775, an increasing abundance of means to pay, coupled with the increased levels of economic activity, had made a reduction in the degree of subsistence and dealings in kind possible, as well as a more powerful stimulus to the monetarization of commercial activity, and thus an evolution in the techniques for collecting resources and revenues – i.e. the transition from a tax in kind to a tax in money. Vauban was eclipsed by Adam Smith. In these circumstances, the economist Turgot was only superficially the antagonist of the technocrat Orry. In reality, he represented rather more a logical continuation carried on at a rather more elevated level.[56]

Besides, recent historiography has taught us to reevaluate the significance of the road-building effort under Louis XV and Louis XVI. In a work which created a good degree of comment, the American econometrician Robert Fogel demonstrated with statistics, on the basis of 'counter-factual' research, what would have been the effect of *not constructing* the railroads in North America in the nineteenth century, and similarly what would have been the effects of putting in their place a more restricted network of roads and canals and whether it would have stimulated an economic growth of the same phenomenal kind which was, in fact, re-

[56]   It is an entire mental attitude of historians towards the last century of the Ancien Régime which needs, from this point of view, to be changed. The monetarization of the economy (which was progressing) counts for far more than the Enlightenment of economists in an explanation of the transition from taxes (or rents) in kind. At the same time, in a distinctly separate context, the partition of communal lands in the eighteenth century is explained much more than Marc Bloch allowed for by demographic increase and the consequent increasing land-hunger rather than by the spread of new ideas about agrarian individualism. See Marc Bloch, *Caractères originaux de l'histoire rurale française* (Paris, A. Colin, 1988 edition), pp. 242–3.

corded by the United States during the period of railway construction.[57] By comparison, it is difficult to illustrate more effectively the profound effects on the French kingdom of the construction of 30,000 kilometres of roads between 1738 and 1782 – i.e. 31 times the length of France at its maximum extent, and all begun by the initiatives of Orry.

As for the intellectual consequences of this immense network of roads, they were far from negligible. One should begin with the trio composed of Orry himself, the *intendant des finances* Trudaine and then, finally, the geographer and draughtsman, Perronet. These three were all initially trained in the provincial offices of intendancy or cartography. They then 'went up' to Paris, once their competence had been recognized. In 1743, Orry gave Trudaine the responsibility for Roads and Bridges (*Ponts et Chaussées*). Trudaine, after some hesitations, in turn created a School of draughtsmen, cartographers and future engineers of Roads and Bridges in 1747. With his habitual sense of the paradoxical, Michel Foucault saw in this School not a place for the transmission and elaboration of scientific and technical knowledge (such as differential and integral calculus, the preparation of plans etc.), of great use to the realm, but rather an examination system through which 'a ritual of power was constantly played out'![58] Knowledge was trammelled by power. In reality, however, the School of Roads and Bridges represented one of the first milestones towards the French system of *grandes écoles*, the Schools which would be the nursery of talent whose importance (and limitations) for the development of French industry and research is well known. Other technical schools of the first importance (the *Ecole de la Marine*, the *Ecole du Génie de Mézières*, the latter acting as the progenitor for the future *Ecole polytechnique*) made their first appearance between 1741 and 1751. The graduates each year from these new institutions would provide the *corps* of engineers, technicians and functionaries who would soon be at the heart of the originality, or at least the precocity (not to mention 'free-masonry') of French public service. This should be compared with the former state apparatus, relying principally on office-holders, only tangentially on *commis*, themselves 'proto-functionaries' who were generally to be found in less senior ranks of the administration than would be the future 'old boys' of the *grandes écoles*. This 'engineering' élite faced competition from private contractors, builders of metalled roads, often former master-masons who had risen from nothing and who played a vigorous role in extending the provincial road network and thus spread out its 'liberating' effects. The Dauphiné Alps provides a good example, a region where communications were very difficult and where the new roads played a vital and strategic role from the years 1725–30 onwards. The non-native entrepreneurs

---

[57] Robert Fogel, *Railroads and American Economic Growth: Essays in Econometric History* (Baltimore, MD, John Hopkins University Press, 1964).
[58] Michel Foucault, *Surveiller et punir* (Paris, Gallimard, 1975), p. 188; and compare (for the opposite) René Taton, *Enseignement et diffusion des sciences en France au XVIIe siècle* (Paris, Hermann, 1986), p. 358.

(Parisians, Bernois, Piedmontese) who were responsible for deciding where the routes went and for the official building works were gradually eased out by the local Dauphinois, above all by the master pavers and other specialists in 'construction' from Grenoble.[59] Thus a road-based and 'routier' capitalism began to develop in which local firms exploited the more limited horizons which were offered but did so dynamically and creatively.

The extension in the road-way network and the increase in road traffic accompanied the development, the opening-up of continental France. As for the surrounding oceans the rapid growth of the Company of the Indies in the Fleury period should be noted. It first recorded a great profit from its African trade. The profits from the Company's trade with Guinea, for example, tripled from 1730 to 1745. But it was from beyond the Cape of Good Hope and from Asia that the essential components of success would come. The profits from the trade with China alone increased from 1 to 13 million *livres* between 1725 and 1745. The imports of white cottons, muslins, blue and white porcelain from India and China were always the greater. The number of workers employed by the Company of the Indies tripled from 1725 and 1745. At the *Ile Bourbon* (now called Réunion) the number of black slaves increased six-fold during Fleury's ministry, and the tonnage of coffee increased five-fold. The *Ile de France* (now called Mauritius) saw its population multiply by 16 between 1725 and 1740. At Lorient, the leading-port for the Company, the number of baptisms tripled during Fleury's ministry. The sums collected in the town under the *capitation* rose almost five-fold, an indication of increased well-being. In short, 'oriental' maritime France enjoyed a boom. The French caught up with, even overtook, the English and the Dutch in the second third of the century. One can well understand why, once Fleury and Walpole were out of the way, the British government should have become disturbed by the rapid progress of its southerly neighbours and sought to limit it in the Seven Years War.

From such a point of view, the various successes of Colbert, then of Law, founding and then re-founding the initial Company of the Indies appear in retrospect to have been completely justified whatever the criticisms which have been levelled, and which will be levelled, at both statesmen. In the final analysis, however, the continuous and vigorous expansion in French trade in the 'South Seas', unfortunately peppered with various damaging military defeats, encouraged some purely liberal tendencies which wanted French commerce to function henceforth separately from all attempts at territorial hegemony on the Indian subcontinent; hence, from 1769, the suspension, and then the liquidation, of the Company of the Indies.[60]

[59] René Favier, 'Les entrepreneurs de travaux publics en Dauphiné au XVIIIe siècle', *Bulletin du Centre d'histoire économique et sociale de la région lyonnaise* (Centre Pierre-Léon, Université de Grenoble), 1–2 (1988).
[60] On all this, see Philippe Haudrère, *La Compagnie française des Indes au XVIIIe siècle (1719–1795)* (Thesis: Université de Paris-IV and Librairie de l'Inde, 1989), vol. iv.

'Free' trade was more precisely the pattern for France's Atlantic trade, particularly that with Santo Domingo (Haiti) which developed with the speed of lightning – which is not too strong a word for a trade whose spectacular growth took place within conditions which were 'semi-free' rather than 'free' since, in the absence of being controlled by a privileged company, the Antilles were subjected to a Colbertian-devised régime of 'exclusion'.[61] The total trade of Bordeaux (imports and exports) was largely dependent on the Caribbean islands. In 1717, it had an annual value of 13 million *livres*. Following a period of sometimes strong contrasts, but overall continuous increase, it rose to more than 50 million *livres* from 1740 to 1745. The persons and the products carried (the two being bundled together in a horrifying fashion), increased in value (African negroes to the Caribbean, Bordeaux wine to Santo Domingo, sugar from Santo Domingo back to Bordeaux). Bordeaux's commercial increase was around 4 per cent per annum, which was hardly remarkable; but it was not so different from the rates of growth recorded during the 'Thirty Glorious Years' from 1945 to 1975.[62] The ships were ever larger. The annual increase of '+4 per cent' recorded at Bordeaux should also be compared with the comfortable and evidently 'supportable' growth, albeit at a lesser rate, in France's external trade during the eighteenth century of 2.3 per cent per annum. In this respect, too, the Fleury period was not badly endowed; national exports were worth less than 50 million *livres* in 1715; but they accounted for over 100 million in 1720 and 200 million between 1740 and 1745. The five last years of the cardinal's ministry were triumphant for France's exports; they exceeded British exports in absolute value as well as in relative growth.[63]

Turning to transatlantic matters, Santo Domingo was ceded by Spain to France in 1697 and, at the end of the seventeenth century, was producing neither sugar nor tobacco. But in 1714, the newly annexed colony produced 7,000 tonnes of sugar annually; in 1720, this had risen to 10,000 tonnes; in 1743, it stood at 43,000 tonnes, the leading location by far for sugar production in the world.

Once more, the 'balance-sheet' on the 'Fleury period' (to use his name to delineate a chronological period) appears to have been substantially positive. And even beyond the death of the ministry, the growth remained impressive, with 65,000 tonnes of sugar being produced in 1767 and 86,000 tonnes in 1789, all coming from the French part of Haiti.

---

[61]   The Colbertian régime of 'exclusion' was copied from the Spanish colonial system; the colonies (the Antilles in the French case) were required to buy and sell only from metropolitan France's ships and traders. Fraud was extensive – the counterpart to 'exclusion' was interloping. The 'exclusion' régime, however negative its effects on free competition, did not prevent the amazing development of Haiti in the eighteenth century; equally, the development of the Lesser Antilles was very swift, especially after 1770.

[62]   Jean Fourastié, *Les Trente Glorieuses ou la Révolution invisible, de 1946 à 1975* (Paris, Fayard, 1979).

[63]   On all this, see François Crouzet, 'Angleterre et France au XVIIIe siècle: essai d'analyse comparée de deux croissances économiques', *Annales ESC* (1966).

Table 8.1   Sugar and slaves on Santo Domingo

Year	Number of sugar factories	Number of black slaves
1686	–	3,000
1713	138	–
1720	–	47,000
1730	339	80,000
1740	–	–
1754	430	–
1789	–	463,000

Some statistics on the number of sugar-mills and slaves on Santo Domingo confirm the overall picture[64]: see table 8.1.

To begin with, these figures are particularly telling of the far-sightedness of someone of the calibre of Louis XIV who boldly annexed Santo Domingo in the immediate aftermath of the War of the League of Augsburg, a war about which later commentary has generally been limited to describing it as wholly disastrous for France. Equally, beyond the 'good' years of the Fleury ministry, the figures provide a measure of the extraordinary and explosive powder-keg which was being stored up in this colonial ergastula.[65] There would be almost half a million slaves on Santo Domingo by 1789. Haiti would be the only important place in the black slave world to witness a slave rising like that of Spartacus, unsparing and merciless. Neither Brazil nor the southern United States would experience anything like it. On the other hand, it was the case that these large continental regions were not affected by the ultra-specific developments in metropolitan France and in its island colonies of the French Revolution.

We have already referred to Colbertian 'exclusion'. France owed a good deal of the prosperity of its Antilles islands to that policy; for it rested in substantial measure on the re-export from France's Atlantic ports of Haitian sugar to other countries in Europe, particularly northern Europe. Without the policy of 'exclusion' a good part of this fruitful traffic would have avoided French ports and traded directly with the other ports of northern Europe. The reason for this is simply the fact that freight costs remained lower for English and Dutch ships than French ones.[66]

---

[64]   The figures on French foreign trade are drawn (notably by François Crouzet) from Emile Levasseur, *Histoire du commerce de la France* (Paris, A. Rousseau, 1911), i, 512–18 and from Ruggiero Romano in *Studi in Onore di Armando Sapori* (Milan, 1957), vol. ii.

[65]   I.e. a prison for slaves in Antiquity; by extension the term is applied to slave territories in this period.

[66]   On all of which, and particularly the population of Haiti, see Pierre Pluchon, dir., *Histoire des Antilles et de la Guyane* (Toulouse, Privat, 1982), pp. 113–14 and *passim*. See also the contribution of François Crouzet to Charles Higounet, dir., *Histoire de Bordeaux*, vol. v (*Bordeaux au XVIIIe siècle*, directed by F.-G. Pariset (Bordeaux, Fédération historique du Sud-Ouest, 1968)), pp. 195–200 and Crouzet, 'Angleterre et France au XVIIIe siècle'.

As for the industrial policy of Orry, it would excite *post festum* a good deal of criticism. Henri Carré, for example, representative of a rather unthinking economic liberalism, would hardly be able to find words to condemn the craze for regulation which led the *contrôleur général des finances* towards the 'fixing of every detail of manufacture, even preventing the cleaners of cloth from using Spanish chalk', etc. These are the familiar sounds of the Lavisse school of history (no matter how great the merits of its masters). In fact, Orry (as Michel Antoine has reminded us[67]), oversaw the production of quality products, those likely to lead to sustained exports. Serious investigations *in situ* provided the background to strict controls on quality which were carried out by the manufacturing inspectors. The results were the more impressive when the economic trends were favourable and the spirit of manufacturing enterprise sufficiently developed. At the end of a period of rapid manufacturing growth, through the whole of the eighteenth century (a rise of just over 1 per cent per annum in France's industrial production as compared with 1.17 per cent in England), the period from 1715 to 1743 (the 'Regency' and 'Fleury' periods) figured as particularly significant. There was a doubling of the manufacture of woollen cloth at Amiens between 1715 and 1750, and a tripling of the same at Beauvais between 1724 and 1755. The overall increase in woollen manufacture across France between 1726 and 1751 was .84 per cent per annum, or the greatest increase recorded in the whole period from 1708 to 1778. The production of cotton goods at Rouen tripled between 1732 and 1749. The sale of glassware from Saint-Gobain doubled between 1725 and 1739[68] and so too did the activity of the Lyon silk-workers between 1720 and 1760.[69] Thus there was a gathering pace in the rapid growth of French industry after 1730, and just at the moment when British industry was somewhat (temporarily) stagnating.[70]

'Give me a good economy and I will give you a good royal financial policy and make significant budgetary savings.' This is almost what Le Peletier des Forts, followed by Orry, would have said at the time. The expansion in French GDP (gross domestic product), substantial in industry and perceptible in agriculture, coupled with the dynamism of foreign trade, made the task of successive chancellors easier. The trends of the period were towards good budgetary management, and the more so as the ambitions of the state were scaled down. From the beginning of the Regency through to around 1740, the 'committed expenditure' of the monarchy remained constant at around 800 tonnes of silver-equivalent per

[67]   Antoine, *Louis XV*, p. 319.
[68]   Claude Pris, *La Manufacture des glaces de Saint-Gobain, 1665–1830, une grande entreprise sous l'Ancien Régime* (Doctoral Thesis: Lille, Atelier des thèses de l'Université de Lille-III, 1975), ii, 804. See also Jean-Pierre Daviet, *Une multinationale à la française. Saint-Gobain, 1665–1989* (Paris, Fayard, 1989), p. 36 (same tendency, with slightly lower figures).
[69]   André Latreille (ed.), *Histoire de Lyon et du Lyonnais* (Toulouse, Privat, 1975), p. 236.
[70]   Crouzet, 'Angleterre et France au XVIIIe siècle'.

annum,[71] whilst the same expenditure committed by the Louis XI state during the War of Spanish Succession had increased brazenly to 1,500 or 1,600 tonnes, well above the net revenues to the Treasury. The difference was financed in gross measure by borrowing since taxes did not cover it. The administration directed by Fleury cut expenditure in comparison with its predecessors pre-1713. True, he was no longer beset by major wars to fight, but only by smaller-scale conflict. Herein, though, lay simultaneous benefits, for the Fleury state extracted more from many of its subjects without squeezing them dry since, in the interval, they had grown richer, or at least less impoverished. Louis XV (or those who acted in his name) succeeded in increasing the net revenues from taxation (not including extraordinary revenues such as borrowing, office-sales . . .) to 700, 800 and then to 900 tonnes of silver-equivalent per annum[72] in around 1739. In comparison, under Louis XIV the equivalent figure had fallen to 300 tonnes of net revenue per annum at the nadir of ruined France's fortunes in 1709–10, and had only painfully crept up to 800 tonnes per annum at the peak of its performance in the years 1688–90.

Orry even succeeded in balancing the budget in 1739 and 1740 with a slight surplus on receipts. This miracle had not occurred since the early years of the 'great' Colbert. It would not occur again in such a clear and sustained fashion until the days of Louis XVIII![73] Of course, the War of Austrian Succession would pose fiscal problems in the 1740s, but they bear no comparison with the pressures of fiscal exaction in Louis XIV's reign. In the middle and long term, the weakness of fiscal exactions[74] (9–10 *livres tournois* per head of the population under Fleury), whilst they stimulated the economy in peacetime, would have grave consequences for the state and for the kingdom at large. England had a heavy tax burden (equivalent to 20 *livres tournois* per year per inhabitant at the same period), clearly more burdensome than France's. Georgian England was strengthened, however, by the national consensus endowed by the nation to its Parliament; and strengthened too by its per capita wealth which was greater for the 'average' Englishman than the 'average' subject of Louis XV. This was how Great Britain was able to win its wars against the Versailles Bourbons and steal their colonies, especially since it only had to fight on the maritime front, unlike the French kingdom which had to finance a great fleet and army at one and the same time.[75] At a rather later date, the smaller French tax-base, resulting too from the fiscal exemptions granted to the privileged, would bring about the collapse of the Ancien Régime when it could no longer service the enormous debts resulting from

---

[71]   Alain Guéry, 'Les Finances de la monarchie française sous l'Ancien Régime', *Annales ESC* (1978), 227.

[72]   Ibid.

[73]   Antoine, *Louis XV*, p. 317.

[74]   Jean Meyer, *Le Poids de l'Etat* (Paris, PUF, 1983), p. 63.

[75]   Paul Kennedy, *Rise and Fall of the Great Powers* (London, Unwin Hyman, 1988; reprinted Fontana, 1989), pp. 116–18 (from the Fontana edition).

the (albeit victorious) American War. But such matters were not on the agenda yet in the days of old Cardinal Hercule.

A further, and negative, legacy of the Fleury years was the weakness of public credit. It is a commonplace that the System of Law, whatever its merits in stimulating the economy, demonstrated (or epitomized) for a long time thereafter, the impossibility of France creating a great state Bank such as the *Banque de France* would become in the nineteenth century. A decade after Law, in March 1730, the scandal of Le Peletier's handling of shares in the Company of the Indies (albeit well-intentioned on his part) cast a shadow over stock market dealings in forward transactions and futures. A Council decision (*arrêt*) of 19 March 1730 (issued on the same day as the dismissal of Le Peletier) forbade both kinds of transactions. Thus 'not only the development of a good credit market, but also that of a stock-exchange capitalism in eighteenth-century France'[76] was inhibited.

Thus the under-development of the Bourbon régime in comparison with the English system began to become manifest, an under-development which the Fleury team, less imaginative than that of the Regent, did not really seek to remedy. At London, the Bank of England was in place from 1694, the national debt had been consolidated whilst the stock exchange and the country banks were flourishing and paper money was widely in use without being engulfed by inflationary pressures. In short, the beneficent effects of the arrival of Mexican silver and Brazilian gold on the world economy, so typical of the eighteenth century, were gradually being injected equally into the more sophisticated financial structures of Great Britain and into France. But, for the latter, there would be a heavy price to pay, at least in comparative terms. For, during the War of Austrian Succession, the British government would finance its armed forces with loans whose rates of interest would be no more than between 3 and 4 per cent, half the rates applying in the days of Marlborough. At the end of the American War of Independence, whose financial consequences would be disastrous for the French monarchy, the national debt would be roughly of the same order in both France and Great Britain; but the annual interest payments of the French national debt would be double those paid north of the Channel.[77]

By no means everything would be stagnant or archaic in Paris and Versailles. In matters of state finance,[78] the internal mechanisms for tax-collection were tending to change. Louis XIV, for example, had bridged the vast deficits in the annual accounting 'exercise' by the systematic sale

[76] Antoine, *Louis XV*, p. 319.

[77] All this follows Paul Kennedy, *Rise and Fall of the Great Powers*, pp. 109–11.

[78] According to John Bosher, *French Finances, from Business to Bureaucracy, 1770–1795* (Cambridge, Cambridge University Press, 1970), pp. 41–2, Ancien Régime France did not have a budget. The same opinion had already been recorded by Marcel Marion, *Dictionnaire des institutions de la France* (Paris, Picard, 1989 edition), p. 58 (art: 'Budget'). Michel Antoine, *Le Conseil du Roi sous le règne de Louis XV* (Geneva, Droz, 1970), p. 452 is less categorical and willingly agrees to use the term. We follow Antoine on this point.

of office. 'Every time Your Majesty creates an office, he finds a fool to purchase it' remarked Chancellor Pontchartrain. Apparently the number of fools declined in the eighteenth century. At all events, the value of venal offices fell. The price of a post as councillor in the Parlement of Paris[79] was worth in the region of 100,000 *livres* in about 1720. This figure declined fairly steadily to 45,000 *livres* in 1743, the year of Fleury's death, and would not recover from this decline before 1771, the date when the parlements were dissolved and when venality of office would disappear for several years. Were the *parlementaires* the authors, in the event, of their own decline? This is possible; the enduring conflict which pitched them against the régime from the exile of the sovereign court in 1720 up to 1732, the most critical year of this first phase of antagonism in the eighteenth century, rendered the prices of their offices less attractive investments.[80] The devaluation in office-prices was, for the rest, in line with the growth in state *commis* and functionaries whose numbers had increased in tens of thousands, the rational, modern state, the precursor of the administrative patterns of our own day. At all events, the number of office-holding posts levelled off at around 50,000 under Louis XV and remained similar under Louis XVI. In these circumstances, the attempts of ministers to sell offices as had happened under the Sun-King were bound to fail; and it was a failure which could be contained relatively easily within the state budget, given the absence of gross fiscal bulimia during this period of quasi-peace and healthy tax receipts. Office-sales would continue, at least until around 1740. Orry certainly attempted in the edict of November 1733 (as previously in 1692) to 'venalize' municipal posts (mayors, aldermen and consuls). The new town-hall offices thus created by the *contrôleur général* turned out to be unsaleable in the real world; and municipalities would thenceforth have a tendency to become more elective, particularly following a new more liberal phase[81] in the kingdom between 1764 and 1771. In the light of this failure,[82] where could one turn for money when a fairly costly war occurred such as the War of Austrian Succession? Would the key to the problem be found in the provinces?

---

[79]   This decline is true for the offices of *conseillers* in the Parlement of Paris; by contrast, recent research would tend to suggest that the offices of *procureurs*, *avocats* in the *Conseil du roi*, and the posts of *secrétaires du roi* (which ennobled their holders) saw their value continue to increase in the eighteenth century (William Doyle, 'The Price of Offices in Pre-Revolutionary France', *Historical Journal*, 27 (1984), 831–60).

[80]   François Bluche, *Les Magistrats du Parlement de Paris au XVIIe siècle* (Paris, Les Belles Lettres, 1960; republished in 1986), p. 167.

[81]   Marcel Marion, *Dictionnaire des institutions de la France* (Paris, 3rd edition, 1984), art: 'Municipalities'.

[82]   As so often in history, research is proceeding apace. That of William Doyle (see above, n. 79) has recently come to our attention which questions somewhat the idea of a decline in the prices of office, especially in the province. If this idea is substantiated, the liberal reform of the municipalities due to L'Averdy in 1764 would be explained more in terms of highly respectable principle (the liberal tendencies in Choiseulism) and, to a far lesser degree, in terms of motives of financial opportunism.

From 1742 onwards, Orry borrowed significant sums of money via the provincial estates, particularly those of Languedoc, whose credit was better than the king's since it rested solidly on the 22 diocesan areas which made up this southern province. At Béziers, as at Carcassonne, the middling classes knew the provincial estates to be reliable at paying dividends and did not hesitate to lend them money which then made its way to Paris and Versailles in the form of second-generation loans, agreed to on a short-term basis by the estates. The Languedoc assembly thus became, in the absence of a true banking system along English lines, a kind of regional bank. In acting in this fashion, the *contrôleur général* put an end to the future suppression of or constraint upon these great representative institutions of France's peripheral zones, such as had been attempted by Richelieu and Mazarin, the vanquishers of (amongst other victims) the estates of Normandy. As a consequence of the new borrowing policy, which Orry put into practice on this regional basis, absolutism thus encountered its own limits, being itself prevented from putting further into practice the 'major leaps forward' to the detriment of provincial representation, to which it had formerly committed itself during the seventeenth century.[83]

There was a similar moderation when it came to indirect taxation. After a brief period of direct government management of the collection of indirect taxes as a result of the shocks delivered to the financial system from the Law System, Fleury (the son of a financier) restored tax-farming in 1726, the year of his elevation to being first minister. 40 *fermiers généraux* combined toegher in an overall farm offering the king 80 million for farming the salt taxes, the *aides*, the *traites*[84], etc. The sum was too low and created a scandal. The 'residual' benefits accorded the tax-farmers had been estimated at an excessively high level in the conditions of the treaty. The already tarnished reputation of the financiers did not recover, although this was very unjust, given their intelligence and the efficiency of their methods of tax-collection. The following contracts, at all events, were revised upwards[85] to take into account the growing wealth of the country and to correct the initial errors made in 1726. The value of the tax-farms reached 91 million *livres* in 1738; 102 million in 1750; 110 million in 1755; 138 in 1773. The relative gentleness of this rise in relation to the increase in France's national revenue, particularly in the Fleury period, should be noted. In the period of peace (1726), these indirect taxes accounted for 46 per cent of the budgetary receipts as against 43 per cent coming from direct taxes with the rest deriving from other ancillary

---

[83] François Furet, *Revolutionary France* (Oxford, Blackwell, 1992), p. 9.

[84] The *traites* were composed of various indirect taxes whose collection was farmed out to the *fermiers généraux*. These included the *gabelle* (the tax on salt), the *aides* (taxes levied on the trade in drink, oil, soap, playing cards etc.) and taxes paid (like customs duties) on the transport of goods between one province and another.

[85] Figures in Guy Chaussinand-Nogaret, *Financiers de Languedoc* (Paris, SEVPEN, 1970), p. 237.

sources. The modest levels of taxation encouraged, rather than prevented, the improvement in methods of collection. During the second quarter of the eighteenth century, the organization (too often misrepresented) of tax-farms employed some 25,000 agents and staff (rising to 29,000 in 1760) with modern rules for their remuneration, promotion and retirement. Thus a model was to be found, located in a sector which paradoxically was only semi-public (the financiers remaining, in certain respects, men of business); a model of the growth of clerks and quasi-civil servants which had occurred also in the state – i.e. the elaboration of the finance-state in comparison with the old Justice- and Offices-State. The tax-farms administration employed on its own account in the eighteenth century half as many people again as held offices at the beginning of the reign of Louis XIV.[86] This already represented the appearance of functional modernity within the old *bric-à-brac* of the system of resignable, hereditary and titled offices. It should be added that a new extension would complete the system in 1730. Drawing its lessons from the temporary disgrace of the Pâris brothers, the government of Cardinal Fleury offered the monopoly for the sale in France of tobacco imported from the English colonies in North America out to farm. A huge organization would be formed and mobilized as a result of this decision. Tobacco alone, within the general tax-farm, would bring together in 1782 around 20,000 guards and officers as well as 43,000 privileged outlets, the latter being the retailers of what would still be known today as 'tobacco kiosks'.[87]

At the conclusion of this economic and financial survey, we would have liked to have painted an optimstic picture of the Fleury period. But in the suburbs of the towns, and amongst the day-labourers of the river-plains, *a fortiori* in the moneyless Massif Central, a pocket of misery if ever there was one, a mass of poverty was to be found, particularly during years when bread was dear. A degree of under-nourishment during these periods was evident in the Auvergnat mountains where, as the intendant wrote in 1728; 'The only nourishment comes from oats mixed with foul grains and vegetables.' There was suffering also to be found in the Blesle region in 1731 'where people's faces are emaciated and leaden' and where the inhabitants live off 'milk products and herbs which they collect from the fields' whilst a good proportion of the population had left the place to seek its fortune in less afflicted provinces. In 1740, a particularly bad year in France's vast 'under-developed'[88] regions, the priest of Bort near Billom

[86] I.e. 25,000 agents, of whom 600 were employed in the central offices in Paris, and all of whom enjoyed in reality the status of civil servant *avant la lettre* (Antoine, *Louis XV*, p. 313). From the point of view of bureaucratic modernity, the superficial and trivial character of the violent attacks mounted against the tax-farmers in the eighteenth century needs to be appreciated. The criticisms of Courteline against the civil servants of the Belle Epoque were no more impressive.

[87] The figures refer to 1782 and are doubtless slightly higher than those at the time of Louis XV; see Jacob M. Price, *France and the Chesapeake; a History of the French Tobacco Monopoly, and of its relationship to the British and American Tobacco Trades, 1674–1791* (2 vols, Ann Arbor, University of Michigan Press, 1973), i, 434–5.

[88] Dupâquier, *Histoire de la population française*, ii, 215.

confirmed that in his parish the 'miserable' (but which of them were not?) ate fern roots (the classic 'nourishment' during periods of dearth in fact) or buckwheat hash, cooked in pure, unsalted water. Again, in 1751, the inhabitants of the western mountains of the Low Auvergne were short of bread. The *subdélégué* Ribeyre described them as 'poor starving creatures looking like ghosts and who are completely lacking in energy and unable to work'. At the same time, there was the increasing use (but it was an ersatz which was not particularly catastrophic) of oat-bread in the *élection* of Issoire. Abel Poitrineau,[89] the historian of the Auvergne, to whom we owe these carefully balanced examples taken from the archives, points out that the high prices for cereals and all the signs of the beginnings of a subsistence crisis in the Massif Central did not result in a huge death rate. In the administrative correspondence, so rich in concrete detail as we have just seen, it was never a matter in this period of famine as such. Here was the difference, and advantage, in comparison with the seventeenth century, no matter how undoubtedly bleak were some of the descriptions concerning the conditions in the eighteenth century.

We should now attempt to go beyond the particular case of the Auvergne and to generalize, with all the habitual reservations, to France as a whole. Almost everywhere there was the continuance of a multifarious pauperism which became particularly acute in periods of grain shortage. But however vast this poverty was, it affected a smaller proportion of the population. Between 1726 and 1743 the three sectors (primary, secondary and tertiary) of the economy were undoubtedly released from previous constraints, albeit to varying degrees. The middling and lower-middling classes saw their position improve. Millions of individuals had escaped from the miserable poverty in which their ancestors had vegetated, leaving what may have been[90] around ten million or so men, women and children to continue the fight at the (not too generous) heart of the kingdom. In this situation, through their various initiatives, sometimes useful, sometimes useless, some *dirigiste* and some liberal, those in power, principally the governments of Philippe d'Orléans and Fleury, proved the accuracy, through their daily practice, of the unpretentious precept formulated a few

[89]   Abel Poitrineau, *La Vie rurale en Basse-Auvergne au XVIIIe siècle: 1726–1789* (Paris, Université de Paris, Faculté des Lettres, 1965), pp. 92–3 (published subsequently by the Publications de la Faculté des Lettres de Clermont-Ferrand, 1966 and in a facsimile edition (Marseille, Lafitte, 1979)).

[90]   The nominal daily wages of Parisian master-masons increased by 50% between 1727 and 1785; those of building labourers by 44%. Prices went up by 60%. The resulting 'impoverishment' of day labourers was nothing in comparison with the scale of that which occurred between the end of the fifteenth and the end of the sixteenth centuries; and there was some compensation from the fact that there were some wage increases per head. But the levels of standards of living of such workers remained very low, even if they had the 'consolation' (although they would be unconscious of it) of no longer being the victims of the mega-mortality as had their predecessors in the seventeenth century (see the fundamental work of Yves Durand, 'Recherches sur les salaires des maçons à Paris au XVIIIe siècle', *Revue d'histoire économique et sociale* (1966), p. 468 *et seq.* (notably the tables)).

decades later by Adam Smith: 'To bring a state to the highest degree of opulence from the most profound barbarism, there is only the need for peace, taxes which are not too high, and a proper administration of justice.'[91] Through excess military and conquering dynamism, Louis XIV ended up ignorant of this simple precept, just as it would escape the ultra-bellicose Frederick II of Prussia later on in the eighteenth century. The administration and government of the young Louis XV, on the other hand, were, in contrast to those of his predecessor as king, motivated by a more pacific tendency which emerged from a Fénelonian background. They grew naturally, like roots to water, in the direction of the common sense which was embodied by the Scottish founder of political economy. For this reason, albeit not only this one (for one must take into account the favourable European and world climate as well), a trend towards progressive dis-impoverishment was set in place within a society which, from most points of view, remained still a society of suffering poor.

Over and above certain elements of progress in the economy of daily life lay the well-known and admirable flowering of French culture in the century of the Enlightenment under Philippe d'Orléans and Fleury. It is not the direct object of this book to analyse such matters, save in respect of the impact which they had on French political and socio-political history and vice versa. In reality, the cultural initiatives of those in authority, which were on occasions aimed in a liberal direction, were never less than significant and sometimes important.

Books provide a striking example. Jacques Bernard Chauvelin was the cousin of Germain Louis Chauvelin who, from 1727 was both Secretary of State for Foreign Affairs and Keeper of the Seals. However, this same Jacques Bernard, with his highly placed connections, found himself appointed Director of the Book-trade, i.e. in charge of censorship, between 1729 and 1732, under the aegis of the Chancery and the Keeper of the Seals. Jacques Bernard had all the time in the world to concoct a fruitful system of censorship known as 'tacit permission'. This legalized *grosso modo*,[92] and under various pretexts, some of the initially clandestinely published editions. It was an open breach in the ramparts of a system of censorship which had never in fact been completely impregnable. Elsewhere, the *abbé* Bignon, the royal librarian (in other words the administrator of what is now the *Bibliothèque nationale*) doubled as a result of his enthusiastic commitment the number of works contained in his institution.[93] More generally, the collection of books put together by Bignon by means of copyright deposit (*dépôt légal*) represented 78 per cent of French printed materials. The whole collection of printed works of all kinds in the

[91]   Adam Smith, cited by Albert O. Hirschmann, *The Strategy of Economic Development* (New Haven, CT, Yale University Press, 1959), p. 203.
[92]   Antoine, *Louis XV*, p. 345.
[93]   Simone Balayé, *La Bibliothèque nationale*, pp. 147 and 200 (the numbers of printed works in the collection increased from 70,000 in 1719 to 155,000 in 1742).

royal library became accessible to Parisian readers. It was Bignon who divided it up into the various divisions, many of which still survive today (manuscripts, engravings, printed books, etc.). It was one symptom amongst many.

The desire for knowledge was still more evident in the upper échelons of the state. It was in the name of this desire for knowledge in both its theoretical and practical forms that various administrative and scientific enquiries were launched. One might mention the chequered but ultimately successful expedition of La Condamine to Peru in 1735. It was encouraged by Maurepas, the secretary of state at the Navy, and was destined to verify, thanks to the measurement of various degrees of the meridian, Newton's hypothesis concerning the flattening of the earth at the poles and its enlargement at the equator. Geographical exploration was also well represented. In 1733, the general mapping of the kingdom began, an operation which was entrusted to Cassini II and his family. Thus would be born the 'Cassini map', an erudite ancestor to the military maps of today.

In law, on the other hand, the initiatives of Chancellor d'Aguesseau, the greatest French jurist of his generation, resulted in (on the basis, once more, of huge enquiries) placing on the statute book legislation concerning wills, legal beneficiaries,[94] parish registers, etc. The legislation which was formulated would generally find itself incorporated, without much change, in the law-code constructed by Bonaparte's legislators at a later date, and which would then be followed by other régimes in the nineteenth century.

In the domain of public health, finally, the medical establishment, which tended towards sclerosis during this period, received the first and auspicious impetus for change when Louis XV himself (flanked by several innovative physicians from the medical faculty in Montpellier) created in 1731 the academic assemblies of surgery. These would eventually lead on to the establishment of a proper Academy of Surgery in 1748. This echoed and amplified the first 'fillip' given by Louis XIV when he declared the separation of the surgeons from the barber-hairdressers in 1692. The surgical profession, whose success in our own day has been so prodigious, was just beginning to emerge from its humble origins which had seen it for too long mixed up with hairdressing and shaving. In general, the Fleury triptych (relative peace and half-collusion with international Protestantism; semi-liberalism within France; economic and cultural expansion) developed along some of the logical lines experimented with firstly by Henry IV, ones which had been reinvented subsequently by the 'Philippian' Regency whilst all the while adapting them to the infant Enlightenment period. This 'triptych' would not be able to survive intact the death of the Languedoc cardinal who was at once its promotor, its

---

[94] I.e. the technique of passing a legacy from one individual to another through the agency of a third party, trust, or *fidéicommis*.

initiator and simply the name to give to this collection of policies. Many of its positive elements would, however, remain.

9

Reaction and Retraction

Emperor Charles VI of Austria died in 1740. His death immediately whetted the appetites of a number of powers, among them Spain, Prussia, Bavaria, Saxony and Savoy, on the look-out for lands and titles which they could steal from Austria. War broke out in December 1740, when Frederick II invaded Silesia, but this was a conflict from which Louis XV and Fleury wished to remain aloof. The king and the cardinal would have liked to 'retire to Mont Pagnotel', a hill in the forest of Halette where hunters could stand and so be present at the kill without enduring the perils of the chase. But Belle-Isle, grandson of the ill-fated Fouquet, headed an informal anti-Habsburg party, supported by a public opinion conditioned by a century of austrophobia. Belle-Isle was an attractive personality and a good soldier, but a mediocre politician. Fleury, now nearly 90 years old, was in no condition to counteract the various forces which, both among the élites and in the country as a whole, were urging intervention in the fighting. The radical novelty was that diplomacy would from now on have to contend with public opinion, the rise of which is normally dated to 1750–2, associated with the Jansenist and *parlementaire* affairs, but which as far as diplomacy and war are concerned made itself felt rather earlier. The first result of this was the absurd spectacle of Louis XV's armies marching through Bavaria and Bohemia, providing thoroughly useless reinforcements for Charles Albert, Elector of Bavaria. The latter had just been hollowly elected Emperor in January 1742, thereby theoretically supplanting (and to great rejoicing among the deluded French) the in truth immovable Habsburgs of Vienna. By this action, Belle-Isle saved the skin of Frederick II of Prussia who, having seized Silesia from the Austrians, retired satisfied from the fray. Above all, Louis XV, under the influence of Belle-Isle, found himself in the same situation as had Louis XIV between 1700 and 1713. Like his great-grandfather, he was in effect allied with Catholic Spain against the Protestant powers, the United Provinces and Great Britain, themselves flanked by 'papist' Austria. The felicitous system of Philippe d'Orléans and the early Fleury, inherited from Francis I and especially Henry IV and

Richelieu, based on friendship with the Protestants to the north-east and the north, was abandoned, with unfortunate consequences for the security of France. It is true that the kingdom was now stronger than it had been in Louis XIV's time, consolidated by economic expansion and by the qualitative and quantitative strengthening of the frontiers, as fortified and expanded by the Sun-King. If the armies of Louis XV lost battles, these were at least far distant from France; it was no longer a question in 1743 (as it had almost been in 1708) of losing the war within the hexagon itself.

So where was this war to be fought? 1744–5 saw a revision of French strategy. Pointless excursions towards the east, the futility of which had been shown in the preceding years, were discarded in favour of an active military presence in the north, as in the days of Condé, Luxemburg and Villars. It fell to the *maréchal* de Saxe, a pupil of Prince Eugene, a great believer in the use of artillery and the last great French strategist (though of foreign origin) of the Ancien Régime to defeat the Anglo-Dutch forces at Fontenoy in May 1745 and then at Raucourt in 1746 and Lawfeld in 1747. Saxe thus took control of the Austrian Low Countries, then drove into Dutch territory at Berg-Op-Zoom and Maastricht in 1747–8. The exploits of 1672 lived again. The prestige thus gained was undeniable. But the material territorial results were limited if not non-existent. For Louis XV knew, or thought he knew, just how far he could go; he had learnt the lessons of the misadventures of his great-grandfather. Louis XIV, after the errors he had made during the Dutch War, had put his ideas into order and clarified them. Rejecting the dreams of his youth, he had given up any notion of annexing the Austrian Low Countries, even less any part of the United Provinces, knowing full well that any such action would leave him a prey to perpetual counter-offensives from the Dutch, the Austrians, the British, and so on. This lesson in European balance was still valid in 1748, after and in spite of the victorious operations led by Saxe, and Louis XV knew it full well. Furthermore, the still youthful king was, by virtue of his education, of a Fénelonian turn of mind, a peace-loving individual. He was no annexationist. As a rule, he hated death, especially violent death: he loved life as he loved women. Fénelonian irenicism was deeply rooted in his being, even in the context of alliance with Bavaria and enmity towards Britain and Austria, evoking the warlike propensities of the age of Louis XIV. So we have a bizarre, even dysfunctional marriage between a diplomatic conjuncture which recalled the epoch of the Sun-King, and a king whose mentality recalled that of the 'swan' (Fénelon) of Cambrai. Louis XV, following the example of his master, Fleury, considered that the French 'hexagon' (which was not yet so named) was complete. He had no desire to incorporate any further provinces.

The Treaty of Aachen in April 1748, therefore, constituted a sort of stand-off, and even in the eyes of certain observers a goal-less draw. This greatly displeased the new goddess of public opinion, all too readily chauvinistic and expansionist, and followed in this by a number of historians, left-wing and right-wing.[1]

This treaty seemed to mark (this was Voltaire's opinion) the international apogee of Louis XV, as the Peace of Nijmegen had marked that of Louis XIV. In the context of a general return to the *status quo ante*, typical of the Peace of Aachen, with restitution of conquests by all sides, France recovered the strategic Canadian fortress of Louisbourg, which had been seized by the British in 1745. Quebec was to remain in French hands. Compared with the Franco-Canadian catastrophe 15 years later in 1763, such an outcome was not negligible. In this fragile domain, faced with the heavy and even overwhelming presence of the British colonists of North America, not losing was a victory: it maintained territory along the Saint Lawrence and gained time, or at least a decade and a half. From a dynastic point of view, the Bourbons of Spain were installed in Parma, which represented a stronger presence on a European level for the French royal house (or a house of French origin).

And yet disputes, in Europe and across the Atlantic, were growing ever more worrying. In the east, Russia, whose southern border had in October 1739 moved closer to the Black Sea as a result of a treaty with the Ottomans, had extended her *de facto* protectorate over Sweden and Poland. She was becoming ever more influential in the fortunes of Christendom. Prussia, now mistress of Silesia, had become a formidable military power, at the heart of international affairs. She had inched her way into the exclusive club of the great powers. The pro-Hohenzollern policies of Belle-Isle, then of the Marquis François d'Argenson, Secretary of State for Foreign Affairs between 1743 and 1747, may be judged through the benefit of hindsight as imprudent. They had both egged on Frederick II against Austria. France would pay a heavy price for this, from Rossbach (1757) to Sedan (1870) and beyond.

Austria had revenge on her mind: the Empress Maria-Theresa clung to the vain hope of recuperating Silesia, at the risk of losing everything.[2] Yet her husband, François of Lorraine, nephew of the late Charles VI, was now recognized as Emperor under the name of Francis I. Thus transferred to the east and 'Habsburgized', the former ducal family of Lorraine lost all interest in the province of which it bore the name and from which it had drawn its original identity. The French hexagon, by reason of this *a posteriori* legitimization of the annexation of Lorraine, was consolidated in one of its most important corners. Great Britain, now free (with the ultimate complicity of Versailles) of the disagreeable prospect of any

---

[1] E. Lavisse and A. Rambaud, *Histoire générale du IVe siècle jusqu'à nos jours* (13 vols, Paris, 1890–1901), vii (*Le XVIIIe siècle*), 204, deplores the French surrender of its grip on Maastricht as well as the expulsion of the Stuart pretender from its territories, comparing the defeat, with some degree of contrasting nostalgia, to the early victories of Bonaparte. Similar regrets are also expressed in Gabrial Hanotaux, *Histoire de la nation française* (Paris, Plon, 1929), ix (*Histoire diplomatique*), 311–13.
[2] Jean Bérenger, *Histoire de l'Empire des Habsbourg* (Paris, Fayard, 1990), p. 745.

possible restoration of the Catholic Stuarts, continued to threaten the French possessions in America: Canada, Louisiana, and between them the fragile cordon of military and missionary posts between the Ohio and the Mississippi basin. The rapid rise of the Anglo-Saxon population in the New World still constituted a permanent danger to the vast swathes of French territory built up under Richelieu, Colbert and the Regency between the Atlantic and the great plains. The 'Second Hundred Years War', which had started in 1688, was still smouldering, despite the provisional respite provided by the Treaty of Aachen. This 'Second War' would only end in 1815 with the almost total defeat of France.

French historiography in the tradition of Lavisse here laments the fact that Louis XV did not profit from the success of the *maréchal* de Saxe and grab a large chunk or at least a juicy morsel of Belgium and Holland. Such jeremiads show the habitual contradictions of a school of historians[3] who cherish at one and the same time the democratic humanism of the Constituent Assembly and the territorial expansionism of the Jacobins: 1789 and 1793 'harmoniously' melded. After all the Revolution is all of a piece, if we are to believe Clemenceau! Let us stick, however, to the domain of *Realpolitik*: the terms of the Treaty of Aachen were decided in a few weeks during the spring of 1748 as a result of bartering between Lord Sandwich and Saint-Séverin, representing Louis XV. It was a matter of give and take. Among other *de facto* bargains, the French emissary San Severino (he was of Italian origin) whispered in the ears of the English lord: 'I won't take Belgium if you let me keep America, that is Louisbourg and Cape Breton.'[4] It was a deal! America for Belgium. In the long term, the trade-off thus concluded was not absurd, as is shown by the still vigorous French identity of Quebec; it could have been the origin of a North American (Canadian) Frenchness much more extensive than it is today. But in the medium term, the transatlantic defeats of the Seven Years War would discredit retrospectively in 1763 the negotiators like San Severino to whom Louis XV had delegated his powers in 1748. Why make sacrifices in Belgium and elsewhere for the sake of recuperating a position in Quebec which would be lost 15 years later? Any judgement on this question depends of course upon the historical perspective of the judge. All the blame cannot be laid at Louis' door. French public opinion, very anti-Austrian in 1740, pushed the king into a war which he should have had the courage to resist. But this same public opinion was wrong again in 1748 in deriding the stand-off peace, which it considered to be 'stupid' ('*bête comme la paix*'), but which could hardly have been bettered from the French point of view. Going to war had been a mistake, but once involved, France extricated itself with as little damage as possible in the Treaty of Aachen. The only other possibility would have been to go on fighting and

[3] Ernest Lavisse, *Histoire de France depuis les origines jusqu'à la Révolution* (Paris, Hachette, 1903–14), viii-2 (*Louis XV*), 166. Lavisse and Rambaud, *Histoire générale*, vii, 204.

[4] Michel Antoine, *Louis XV* (Paris, Fayard, 1989), p. 400; Lavisse, *Histoire de France*, viii-2, 165.

so improve the final treaty at the cost of crippling the country with taxes, as Louis XIV would have done. But times had changed, at least from this viewpoint: the taxpayers, hard-headed and with support from the parlements, were not the docile sheep waiting to be shorn that they had once been. Never again before 1789 would France be capable of raising an army of 300,000 men, as she had done in 1710.[5]

In any case, the Peace of Aachen was only a truce. The emergence of the two Protestant powers, Britain and Prussia, one maritime, the other continental, *a priori* destabilized international affairs. The outbreak of the Seven Years War, which followed that of the Austrian Succession, was preceded by a spectacular 'diplomatic revolution'. This inversion of alliances assumed its definitive form after a game of 'musical chairs' among the powers. This game did not lead, at it had in Fleury's time, to a consolidated peace, but to war. This circle was vicious, not virtuous.

First movement: the Anglo-Russian agreement of September 1755. The British were trying to break from east to west through the north–south line of military posts which marked out the feebly populated lands of French America along the Ohio valley, and this to facilitate the *Drang nach Westen* of their compatriots from the formerly Puritan colonies on the east coast. In 1754 the Anglo-French war, without being officially declared, flared up again along the western crest of the Alleghenies. Versailles was particularly horrified by the murder of the French officer Jumonville, killed in cold blood by the soldiers of George II. In Europe George was anxious to preserve his dynastic possessions in Hanover against any threat from France or Prussia, for the moment allies. The London government, looking for an insurance policy, therefore made sure, for a fee, of the friendship of Russia, as protection for Hanover. The Tsarina Elizabeth was only too happy to lend a hand because she envisaged the expansion of Russian power towards the west and into the states along the shores of the Baltic, Prussia included. The Prussians in turn were alarmed by the appetite of the new Muscovite giant. In return for a large subsidy in pounds sterling, the Russian government promised to place an armed force of 55,000 men at the disposition of its new British friends.

Second movement: the Anglo-Prussian alliance of January 1756. Frederick II felt himself to be totally isolated in the face of the hostility of Austria and Russia, now both allies of Britain. He knew full well that the friendship of France would not go so far as to provide reinforcements in Berlin against an invading Russian army. Paris was simply too far from Brandenburg. The king of Prussia, therefore, looked towards Britain and signed an alliance with her in January 1756, promising to defend Hanover; by sleight of hand he took the place of the Russians in the role of loyal friend to the English. *Ipso facto* the Russian threat to Berlin diminished, because they could no longer use the defence of Hanover as a pretext for trampling over Frederick's lands and subjects en route.

---

[5] André Corvisier, *Armées et sociétés en Europe de 1494 à 1789* (Paris, PUF), p. 126.

Third movement. The Anglo-Prussian entente acted as a spur to developments which had been taking shape in France and Austria for some time. We have seen how Louis XIV, whose prophecies proved accurate on this point, had foreseen an alliance with Austria. After 1713 the Empire, now turned towards the east, was no longer the menace it had been in the days of Richelieu or Pontchartrain, when the crowns of Vienna and Madrid were both in the hands of the Habsburgs. Versailles had come to accept the Austrian conquest of Hungary. It is also true that in 1750 the devout Catholicism of Vienna made Austrian friendship the more precious to Louis XV, whose government had been engaged for some years in a series of pro-episcopal, even pro-clerical, because anti-Jansenist and anti-*parlementaire*, actions. Statesmen and stateswomen of varied calibre stepped forward to seal the Austro-French rapprochement. Kaunitz and Ambassador Stahrenburg acted on behalf of Maria Theresa. At Versailles around Louis XV, Madame de Pompadour and the *abbé* de Bernis took charge.[6] Bernis, a court priest with the extrovert style of a secret agent, was sharp and astute, though somewhat lacking in breadth of vision and perspective. A solid, amusing and diverse culture and a long noble genealogy would assure, though with ups and downs, the fortune of this writer and diplomat who was attractive to women while not being unattractive to the church.

In these conditions, the Anglo-Prussian entente of January 1756, formed by Uncle George and his nephew Frederick, precipitated the finalization of a counter-alliance between the Seine and the Danube, which had previously only existed in outline. Louis XV had lost an unreliable friend, but an ally all the same, in Frederick II. Now isolated, the king of France had to find new partners in Europe, and all the more urgently because since 1755 Britain had been waging a fierce if undeclared naval war against French shipping, both military and commercial, in the Atlantic. The only alliance available of any weight was with Austria, despite the fact that anti-Austrian cabals were still active in France. Public opinion would sustain these up to the decapitation of Marie-Antoinette, and far beyond, even up to 1918, when Clemenceau, *volens nolens*, would put Austria-Hungary out of its misery.[7] In the immediate short-term, alliance with Vienna nevertheless represented the wisest option. It was given concrete form by the first Treaty of Versailles in May 1756. By the terms of this agreement, the two parties were bound to provide help if the other was the victim of a land offensive by a third power (for example, an ally of Britain if France was the injured party). But it was not an equal

---

[6] François Joachim de Pierre de Bernis (1715–94), born in the Vivarais of good military lower-Languedocian noble stock, had become a canon in 1739, ambassador in Venice in 1752, minister of state in 1757, disgraced . . . before being made cardinal in October/ November 1758 and French chargé d'affaires at the Vatican from 1769 to 1791. Protected by Fleury in his youth, Bernis enjoyed subsequently a beguiling career as a mediator and even a pacifist.

[7] Bérenger, *Histoire de l'Empire des Habsbourg*, p. 727 *et seq*.

partnership. The Austrian guarantee did not include maritime or colonial conflicts, such as had already been raging for two years between the British, who had initiated them, and Louis XV's American subjects. Despite this weakness, the Franco-Austrian axis was formidable. It even engendered a triple alliance: in April 1756 Russia declared herself ready to go to war alongside the troops of Maria Theresa against the Prussians.

Louis XV hoped to use this first Treaty of Versailles as an instrument of deterrence and therefore of peace, even if an armed peace, against Britain. The lightning war launched victoriously in August 1756 by the king of Prussia against Saxony and then Austria showed that a completely different logic was at work. The general staff in Berlin, who instigated this preemptive strike, could boast a 'good excuse'. By getting his retaliation in first, Frederick wished to avoid being overwhelmed by a numerically superior coalition of Austrian and Russian armies. But his Blitzkrieg was an affront to Saxony, and Louis XV could not ignore the fact that his daughter-in-law was of Saxon origin. To offend the daughter-in-law was to provoke the father-in-law. In any case, Louis was obliged to go to the help of Austria, which was in danger of collapsing under the Prussian assault, thereby depriving France of essential support on the continent against the insolence of the British. The second Treaty of Versailles, against Prussia and entirely her own fault, was therefore signed in May 1757 between France and the representative of Maria Theresa. France reiterated her promise of armed aid for the Empress, but the arrangement was still unbalanced. Austria still showed no inclination to get involved in the Franco-British conflict. She offered the Austrian Low Countries, in two pieces, like gratuities, to Louis XV and his Spanish son-in-law, another Bourbon. These were Belgian fantasies, perhaps, but on a continental level Louis' calculations were not so absurd. The combined forces of the three great states, Austria, France and Russia, the latter wanting to get her hands on the eastern part of Prussia, should have been able to crush Frederick in less than a year. They should, moreover, have been able to assure French control over Hanover, to be used as a bargaining counter with England. France, thus delivered from all cares on land, could then have turned all her resources and her forces, the army and the navy, against the British. The plans of mice and men . . . ! The military genius of Frederick the Great, the excellent morale of the Prussians, the growing power of Great Britain, would deliver a crushing blow to them, however sensible they may have appeared.

Yet the period following the second Treaty of Versailles was far from disastrous for France. In June 1757 Frederick II was beaten by the Austrians at Kollen on the Elbe. By the autumn the French army held Hanover, to the detriment of the duke of Cumberland, son of George II, and was deployed as far as the Elbe, far from its point of departure. Frederick was lying in wait for them there.

Things started to go badly for France and her allies in the final months of 1757. They could not confront with impunity the two strongest military powers of the age, the British at sea and the Prussians on land. At Rossbach in November 1757 a 64,000 strong Franco-Austrian army, commanded by the mediocre Soubise, was defeated by 41,000 of Frederick's Prussians. Prussian training, its soldiers moving like automatons, made possible the 'perpendicular wheeling' of the lines of battle, enabling them to confront an opposing army at points where it thought it could not be attacked. At Leuthen in December Frederick employed the oblique battle order, an even more sophisticated manoeuvre, assuring victory for his 36,000 Prussians over the 80,000 Austrians of Prince Charles. But, for all the military genius of Frederick the Great, he was to win less glory during the next few years. Despite half-successes or even victories such as Liegnitz in August 1760 and Torgau in November 1760, Prussia was wearing herself out against numerically superior enemies. By the end of 1761, bereft of men and money, she experienced misery almost on a par with that suffered by the France of Louis XIV between 1709 and 1713. The death of the Tsarina Elizabeth in January 1762 and the accession to power in Russia of the pro-Prussian Tsar Peter III allowed Frederick to re-establish his position. With the Hohenzollern thus back in the saddle, France, with no better solution in sight, soon envisaged making peace.

But before this could be done, the fate of France had been decided at sea and across the Atlantic. In November 1756 that brilliant and erratic genius, William Pitt, the strategist of marine and colonial intervention, formed a government in London. He could rely on a more reliable system of taxation than that available to his French counterparts. Admiral Anson, who held that the British fleet should use its overwhelming superiority to blockade the western and southern shores of the hexagon, took charge of the Admiralty. In August 1759, at Lagos, off the coast of Portugal, a dozen ships of the Toulon squadron were destroyed by Admiral Boscowen. Further north, Edward Hawke, the old familiar of the shores of Brittany and organizer of the blockade of this province, the 'naval prow'[8] of the kingdom, manoeuvred skilfully through the bays, reefs and storms of the Breton seas. Off Quiberon in November 1759 he struck a decisive blow against the French Atlantic fleet, leaving it a mere shadow of its former self, no longer able to sail to the help of the French in Canada or support any landing on the coasts of England. Seen from London, 1759 was an *annus mirabilis*.[9] George II's troops occupied French outposts in the Ohio valley, as well as the city of Quebec and the island of Guadeloupe, followed in September 1760 by the fall of Montreal and the surrender of Vaudreuil, the French governor of Canada. The intelligent and courageous Montcalm, French commander in America, could only delay the inevitable British victory, so crippling was the numerical inferiority of the 'New

---

[8]   Philippe Haudrère, *La Compagnie française des Indes au XVIIIe siècle* (4 vols, Librairie de l'Inde, 1989), ii, 542; 580; 588; 592 etc.

[9]   Paul Kennedy, *Rise and Fall of the Great Powers* (London, Unwin Hynas, 1988; reprinted Fontana, 1989), p. 147.

French' against the anglophone populations of the east coast colonies, civilians as well as soldiers.

In Madrid the new king, Charles III, was worried about British incursions into Spanish America. Deciding, therefore, to join his military forces with those of France, he came off just as badly! The count of Albemarle took Havana for the British in August 1762, and in October Admiral Cornish captured Manila, as well as its galleons and treasures. Such were the bitter fruits of the 'pacte de famille' formed in August 1761 between the Bourbons of Versailles, Spain, Naples and Parma, a secret clause of which envisaged a declaration of war by Spain against the British, which took place in May 1762. Bitter as it proved at first, this family pact would nevertheless with time contribute to the 30 years of peace on the continent between 1763 and 1792.

With the French and Spanish beaten, George II dead in 1760 and Pitt out of office since 1757, the path to peace lay open. The Treaty of Paris in February 1763 represented the abandonment by the French government, if not of all influence, then of all sovereignty on the continent of America. Canada and the valleys of the Ohio and the Mississippi were abandoned to the British. Louisiana was ceded to Spain as compensation for the miseries she had suffered as a result of the alliance with France and for the transfer of Florida to British control. In the Indian sub-continent France lost all her possessions, except for five trading posts.

The results of this treaty, at first sight catastrophic, were however less clear cut than they may appear. To be sure, taking a long-term view, France was robbed of any hopes of creating an extensive francophone zone in North America, especially in Canada, where the prospects up till now had been reasonably good. The exception, of course, was Quebec, a tremendously hardy perennial, but perpetually battered by the overpowering waves of 'Englishness'. Nevertheless France kept Santo Domingo and its sugar, a rich, if fragile, source of commercial and colonial prosperity. Above all, the conflict had been engaged, from beginning to end, outside the kingdom. France was spared all but a very few real battles on her own soil as well as the kind of unremitting military and fiscal pressures which Louis XIV would have imposed on her under similar circumstances.

France was defeated between 1757 and 1763, among other reasons, because she had created for herself political, administrative, military and naval apparatuses which turned out to be relatively cheap, less costly than those possessed, in their different ways, by Britain and Prussia. In the short-term, the military arm of the French was too short and too feeble (taking into account the mediocrity of its commanders and its archaic methods) to attain victories in the field: it contained the seeds of defeat within it. In the medium-term and looking to the future, the relatively low level of taxation, despite its unfairness towards certain social groups, assured a painless return to economic growth, notably in the 1760s, once peace, no matter how 'dishonourable', had been secured.

Defeat, one might say, had its positive side! But negative factors were also at work: the shortage of bank credit, which had caused battles to be lost, now hindered (at least to a small extent) the expansion of the peace-time economy. The country suffered from weak leadership, not only in military affairs, but also at the political and ministerial level. This deficiency is all the more surprising because at this time the French were accomplishing great things in the intellectual, manufacturing and commercial fields. It may be legitimate to refer, around 1757–63, to a crisis of the aristocracy, sword and *robe*, whose job it should have been to provide the country with high quality military and political leaders: generals, marshals, and ministers. From a psychological point of view, nevertheless, the 'disaster' of the Treaty of Paris was no more dispiriting or depressing than would be, for example, the experience of decolonization between 1954 and 1962, as seen from the *métropole*. Public opinion, as expressed by the philosophes, felt a sense of deliverance from the onerous burden of the snowy wastes of Canada, even if this meant swallowing an insupportable humiliation at the hands of the British. And in these matters public opinion was of crucial importance, even if it may not have been aware of the real, or supposedly real, national interest.

The foreign and war policy of the period 1740–57 followed its own logic, based *grosso modo* (though with less attendant misery and less success) on that pursued by Louis XIV between 1672 and 1715. Reversing the line adopted between 1715 and 1740 by the anglophile trio of Orléans, Dubois and Fleury, after 1740 Louis the Well Beloved and his new agents, from Belle-Isle to Bernis, behaved, consciously or unconsciously, as if they saw Europe as divided between a Protestant bloc (Britain and Prussia) and a Catholic bloc with Orthodox accessories (France, Spain, eventually Austria, and Russia). To be sure, such a logic was also prevalent outside Versailles and France: it became for a moment inherent in the mentality of Europe; if not it would never have carried any conviction. Thus was revived (though without the fanaticism) a conjuncture reminiscent of the religious wars of yesteryear. The Catholic element, whether one liked it or not, regained considerable importance in French diplomacy and her conduct of war. Choiseul[10] would soon sort this out, but in 1757–8 his time had not yet come. When it did, the *abbé* Bernis, the elegant and frivolous promoter of the Austrian alliance, was made a cardinal, a suitable reward for the quasi-confessional coalition he had created. The quadruple axis of Paris, Vienna, Rome and Madrid, openly declared in 1756, could not but be Roman Catholic. In France this external strategy was entirely consistent

---

[10] Etienne-François, Count de Stainville, then Duke de Choiseul, began his career as an army officer. He then became French ambassador in Rome (1753) and was patroned by Madame de Pompadour. The contribution which he made during his service at Rome to the moderate stance of Pope Benedict XIV towards the anti-Jansenists (the moderate encyclical *Ex Omnibus* of 1756) gave him a foot on the ladder. In March 1757, he became ambassador in Vienna. In December 1758, he was secretary of state for foreign affairs and minister of state.

with internal policy. A wave of clericalism, or more precisely of episcopal activism, swept over Paris and nearby places, culminating after 1750 in much sound and fury. It was linked with the offensive against Jansenism and the Parlement, against a backdrop of an insufficiently realized fiscal reform, itself reined in by the powerful lobby of bishops. Everything fits together, by virtue of logical and quasi-structural correlations.

Analysis of this new 'hard-line' tendency, in its fully fledged form, may begin conveniently with the arrival in power of Machault d'Arnouville, named as *contrôleur général des finances* in 1747. He was the product of an old *robe* family, one of whose members had been nicknamed *tête de fer* ('Iron Head'). Cold and tough, pragmatic and clear-headed, the taciturn Machault was a politician of the hard breed, a Percheron of finance, firm in character, blunt in spirit. Appointed to office a year before the end of the War of Austrian Succession, he financed the tail-end of the conflict from day to day, using loans and the same kind of subtle stratagems long employed by his predecessors. With the Treaty of Aachen prepared in April 1748 and signed in October, Machault was obliged, in time-honoured fashion, to fill the financial deficit caused by the vast expenses of the war. He envisaged achieving this by using the methods of 'enlightened despotism' before the term had been coined. Orry had already shown the way, salutary and authoritarian, in a completely different domain by his construction of roads through the use of *corvées*. Machault, for his part, aimed to re-establish budgetary equilibrium (more or less) by a method which it was hoped would be both equitable and effective. Such was the aim of the edict of 1749 creating the *vingtième*. This new tax replaced the *dixième*, the previous war-tax, but with the intention of only taking a twentieth or 5 per cent of the net revenues of the king's subjects of all classes, *privilégiés* included. The modernity of the *vingtième* is evident: its apportionment or *assiette* was calculated not by officers, but by state servants with direct control over its implementation. We can see once again the gradual creation and growth of a modern civil service, as had already been instituted in other sectors, such as the navy, foreign affairs and the *ferme générale*.

The *vingtième* ran into opposition from actual and potential taxpayers. Sabotage by the parlements was quickly neutralized. In May 1749, the Parlement of Paris, after some initial mincing around, ended up by registering the new tax. The clergy were a different matter. The episcopal faction, mentioned above, girded their loins and fought a valiant battle to protect the claims of the prelates and to extract concessions concerning the *vingtième* from the monarchy. The bishops, despite being the lackeys of Louis XV, affected to impersonate Thomas Becket, resisting Henry II of England in the twelfth century, or Boethius standing up to Theodoric. They were defending the rights of the church against the encroachment of the powers of the state. This was a totally presumptuous comparison: Becket was a saint! But as far as the French servants of God in 1749–51 were concerned, it was first and foremost and quite vulgarly a question of the immense wealth of the church. The self-interest of the clergy, especially the higher clergy, was at stake. It is true that the First Order could argue, in a reactionary fashion, that Machault's enterprise was subversive, if not revolutionary. The *contrôleur général des finances* was in effect acting as a leveller, making (in full conformity with the deepest wishes of Louis XV) the priest, the noble and the *roturier* all equal in the eyes of the taxman.

In order to settle this argument it was necessary to determine whether the church, as 'dispenser of the revenues of inalienable property dedicated to the service of God and the poor', could be subjected to the general law, as it was decreed by an enlightened soveriegn, or would she continue, as far as fiscal matters were concerned, to stand apart from the rest of society, in the cadre of a unique corporate body convoked at regular intervals, the assembly of the clergy. This gathering had up till now bestowed upon the monarch an annual *don gratuit* or 'free gift' of on average 13.5 million *livres tournois*,[11] at least for the period 1742–8.

Faced with this problem, Louis XV at first stood firm and supported Machault. He dissolved the assembly of the clergy which had been in session since May 1750 and which had jibbed at furnishing royal agents with the description of clerical property, landed and other, necessary for fixing the allocation of the *vingtième*. Louis, squaring up to clerical resistance, sent the prelates off packing back to their dioceses. Similarly, the estates of Languedoc, Brittany and other peripheral provinces, also grumbling about the *vingtième*, were brought back into line by the king's emissaries and commissioners. The bishops wielded great influence in these bodies. The idea of sacrificing their fiscal privileges and declaring the true state of their incomes, just like everyone else was obliged to do, was deeply repugnant to them.

At court, a party of the pious supported the church's opposition to the new taxes. The Dauphin, for all his piety, was not deeply involved: the heir to the throne was always conscious of the fundamental duties imposed by his royal status. Marie Leszczynska, on the other hand, who considered that the faith itself was imperilled by taxes imposed on ecclesiastical fortunes, did support the pro-clerical faction. The queen was encouraged in this thought by several bishops, among them Christophe de Beaumont, Archbishop of Paris, and his colleagues from Sens, Amiens and Orléans. In accordance with the rule that such cabals spread their tendrils through the branches of the genealogical tree of the royal family, the king's daughters, notably Madame Adélaïde, joined forces with the cabal of *dévots*, who, incidentally, had hopes of seizing a slice of power for themselves. In the government, that is the *Conseil d'en haut*, and among the secretaries of state, the proclerical group was in the minority. It included Cardinal Tencin, from a Dauphinois family much given to intrigues; the former

---

[11]   Detailed figures in Marcel Marion, *Dictionnaire des institutions de la France (XVIIe-XVIIIe siècles)* (Paris, Picard, 1989; originally published 1923), p. 149.

Bishop Boyer, who had charge of the *feuille des bénéfices*, and Count d'Argenson, Secretary of State for War. At the time of Louis, Duke of Burgundy, the *dévot* party had included some remarkable intellects, headed by Fénelon. Forty years on, this same party had sunk into a self-serving corporatism.[12] In a sense this represents the end of an era, the epoch during which reforming energy had flowed from the clergy itself and its close friends. But now the stream of enlightenment, like so much else, was laicized. Not until the emergence of Archbishop Loménie de Brienne would a reformism of episcopal origin spring up once again, but this time without success.

In marked opposition to the ultra-Catholic group stood the marquise de Pompadour. This was not a question of belief or non-belief, but of position. The good lady was afraid that the *dévots* might lead Louis XV back onto the pious straight and narrow, which would mean dismissal for the royal mistress. The marquise, therefore, by an alliance of convenience, hitched her fate to the coarse and rough Machault, who did not think much of her to begin with and would betray her some years later. But for the moment he represented a kind of insurance policy for her. Machault, in effect Minister of Finance, assured himself of the marquise's good graces by means of some modest monetary gratifications. The anti-*dévot* faction could also count on an active group of ministers, secretaries of state and *grands commis*, notably Saint-Florentin, of the Royal Household and very close to Machault; Rouillé in the Marine; Puizieulx[13] and his successor Saint-Contest at Foreign Affairs; Saint-Séverin (San Severino), diplomat without portfolio; Trudaine at the *Ponts et Chaussées*, and the *intendants des finances*. In short, the 'technocrats' of the time and the majority of the government stood opposed to the minority, in and around the government, of 'clericals'. Finally, at Court the partisans of fiscal reform could count on the *maréchal* de Noailles, aged survivor of the old Maintenon cabal, on the *abbé* de Broglie, and on the *maréchal* de Richelieu. The promoter of the *vingtième*, Machault, 'papist' Catholic though he may have been, did not hesitate in making use of a Jansenist writer to provide favourable propaganda for his new tax in a pamphlet divertingly entitled *Ne répugnez pas à votre Bien* ('Don't be disgusted by your good [or goods]').

To make a success of this new tax, then, Louis could rely on substantial support in the ministries, at Versailles and even among public opinion. From mid-century onwards, opinion was turning against a clergy seen as too attached to their privileges. In such conditions a ruler like Frederick the Great would have forged ahead, counting on the support of the philosophes to overcome the resistance of the clerics. Louis XV on the other hand, turning his back on his supporters, abandoned his original

---

[12] On all this, see Marcel Marion, *Machault d'Arnouville, étude sur l'histoire du contrôle générale des finances de 1749 à 1754* (Paris, Hachette, 1891), ch. 11, p. 303 *et seq.*

[13] On Puisieulx, also written as Puyzieulx or Puisieux etc., see Saint-Simon, *Mémoires*, ed. A. de Boislisle, 45 vols (Paris, 1879–1930), xxx, 306, n. 7.

hard line, and capitulated before an assembly of the higher clergy in December 1751. After secret negotiations with the anti-Machault faction, in the majority among the bishops, Louis agreed to exempt the clergy from the *vingtième*, to which the other 'estates' of the kingdom remained subject. The church of France would be left to establish what taxes it ought to pay and to decide, as it had always done, the size of the *don gratuit* it would consent to make every year to the sovereign. *Plus ça change, plus c'est la même chose.*

How is the rout of the monarchy by the clerical lobby to be explained? One suspect must be the fervent ultramontane rituals of the jubilee of 1751, rich in devotions, penitence and confessions in the churches of Paris and elsewhere. Jubilees, celebrated four times every century, were accompanied by the massive distribution of plenary indulgences and the pardoning of sins, on condition that the sovereign kept his hands off church revenues. Louis XV was a sinner but also a good Catholic; he took seriously, as the king of Prussia would never have done, the theological arguments aimed like darts by the clergy against the fiscal 'aggression' of Machault. Was Louis, in making this major and highly inopportune concession, maintaining the fiscal exemptions of the clergy, trying to redeem the grave faults of his private life? It is true that his sexual sins scandalized public opinion and even the people. The king's popularity had taken a nose dive since the last wave of affection for Louis the 'Well Beloved' at the time of his grave illness at Metz in 1744. An existential divorce between certain sections of the population on the one hand and the church and the monarchy on the other began to make itself felt in the middle of the century. The *vingtième* affair, the tax exemptions unfairly re-established for the benefit of the clergy, the cleverly orchestrated whispering campaign about the king's sexual capers, and finally the anti-Jansenist offensive were without doubt factors in the inception of this breach between 'the people' (or a certain people) and the Ancien Régime.

To this gamut of motives pushing Louis towards making tax concessions to the prelates should be added the aid given by the new archbishop of Paris, Christophe de Beaumont, in the affair of the *Hôpital général* of the capital between 1749 and 1752. Beaumont, a devout Périgordin (like those other great prelates, Fénelon and Belzunce) had helped, despite opposition from the Parlement, in the dismissal of the traditionally Jansenist administration of the largest hospital in Paris. For this he deserved a suitable recompense. Louis, owing Beaumont a favour, showered gold upon the clergy as a whole in the form of exemption from the *vingtième*. This became the genesis of a policy of fiscal amnesty which would one day do great damage to the monarchical régime, which seemed almost incapable of modernizing the tax system in the radical way that was needed. The collusion between church and state also harmed the clergy, accused without trial of being collaborators with the government.

The genesis of a policy thus existed, and also a structure: a structural correlation between external diplomacy and internal politics. French alliance with the Catholic powers against the Protestant nations went hand in hand with the alliance of Throne and Altar, directed against the Huguenots of the kingdom and especially against the Jansenists, an alliance useful for maintaining social order, though not for creating calm on the religious front. But could Louis XIV's old methods of devouring Protestants and then Jansenists be made to work again? Times had changed. The Jansenist tragedy did not repeat itself so much as farce, more as bourgeois drama or sentimental comedy.

In 1746, then, Christophe de Beaumont, in his forties and zealous to a fault, settled in as archbishop of Paris. This combative character succeeded before long in lighting the blue touch paper! From 1752 onwards he brandished anew the weapon of withholding the sacraments, already in use in the diocese of Amiens since 1747. The time had long passed since the Augustinian fellow traveller, the Cardinal de Noailles (deceased in 1729), could deny the sacraments to Jansenist henchmen without the pro-Jansenist Parlement taking any offence. During the second quarter of the century the line-up of forces had been modified. To the starboard we observe the traditionalist portion, probably a majority, of the French clergy, faithful to Rome and the bishops, eager to combat the followers of Jansenius by 'rubbing them out', depriving them of confession, communion and extreme unction. Alongside this powerful pro-episcopal band (the 'axis' of the church, representing much more than a mere camarilla) stood the king and the greater part of his government. Both groups still clung to the old adages of the Sun-King, viewing the Jansenist party as 'republicans in religion and politics'. (This official conception would, however, vary in the coming years, for the wind was turning and Louis XV, like an anenometer, would show himself to be sensitive to the draughts of public opinion, if incapable of mastering them.) On the port side, however, stood the Gallican and Jansenist-sympathizing *parlementaires*, eager to do battle against the right-thinking clergy, who they thought were meddling in affairs of state; they desired also to sound off against the royal government, which had shown too much weakness in facing up to the clergy and granting the exemption from the *vingtième*. The struggle for power within the élite, once united under Louis XIV, now pitched the scarlet against the black, and the *robe* of the Parlement against the *robe* of the Council: these conflicts would not cease until their suicidal conclusion in 1789.

In a more personal way, the Parlement wished to get even with Archbishop Christophe de Beaumont, who had so annoyed the magistrates during the *Hôpital général* affair. As for the Jansenists, fortified by support among the lower and middle-ranking clergy of Paris and the provinces as well as the urban bourgeoisie, they portrayed the debate as a quarrel between two churches, the bad and the good, both sprung from the same religious source, just as in the old days, according to 'figurist' theories, Rebecca had given birth to both Esau and Jacob. The Augustinians identified themselves with Jacob, the faithful son, and his little flock. Esau for his part symbolized a rotten clergy, destined to be killed off by the righteous. Forty years later the Civil Constitution of the Clergy would deliver the final blow, accompanied by loud applause from the dogmatic compilers of the *Nouvelles Ecclésiastiques*. This 'Constitution' of 1790 would claim to be restoring the church to the purity of its origins, depriving the bishops of the opulence which inevitably led to corruption.

From 1747 onwards, and especially after 1752, the question of the refusal of the sacraments, the so-called *billets de confession* affair (named after the papers issued by the ecclesiastical authorities, granting the holder the right to be absolved by a priest after suitable penitence) raised an important doctrinal issue: the right to the sacraments, especially on one's death bed, when they conferred the key to eternal salvation, was held at this time to be inalienable and sacred, as the Rights of Man (liberty, property, etc.) would be later. Furthermore, the Jansenist quarrel invoked the reappearance of a vengeful, predestinating and unforgiving deity, to be set against the more benign God of the counter-reformation. The Old Testament Almighty, on whom Calvin, two centuries earlier, had bestowed such prominence, was back in the saddle. Calvinists and Jansenists resuscitated their exacting, aggressive and loud-mouthed 'Jehovah' with all his 'murderous rigour'.

In Paris, the refusal of communion and the other sacraments occupied centre stage from March 1752 onwards. Devotees of the *longue durée* and facile paradoxes may even date the beginning of the French Revolution (which, according to François Furet, finished around 1780) to this period, for from now until 1789 agitation, first Jansenist, then *parlementaire*, and finally affecting the Third Estate, would never cease. In March 1752, then, Bouettin, *curé* of Saint-Etienne-du-Mont, refused the sacraments to a Jansenist Oratorian priest, who died shortly afterwards. The death of this cleric, deprived *in extremis* of the comforts of religion, provoked a scandal. The Parlement promptly declared war on Bouettin. Louis XV, hesitatingly and less than wholeheartedly, crawled to the aid of the church and took a strong line against the *parlementaires*. In the *Conseil d'en haut*, the marquis d'Argenson and the *dévots* supported the anti-Jansenist *constitutionnaires*, the duke de Noailles backed up his sovereign; while Machault and la Pompadour, still friends at this time (they would fall out later) steered their way between Augustinian rock and Curial hard place. The conflict sharpened during 1752 as a result of litigious affairs concerning Jansenist nuns. Antagonism between the king and the Parlement became so marked that in May 1753 the court went on strike as a protest after Louis XV had turned a deaf ear to remonstrances expressing the magistrates' hostility to the withholding of the sacraments. The king's reply was immediate: the *parlementaires* were removed or exiled from Paris. One of the first presidents was even dispatched, one might almost say 'deported', to the Sainte-Marguerite islands, off the coast of Provence.

This royal repression was nevertheless moderate: none of the victims died. But it only served, as often happens in such cases, to make the opposition bolder. The antigovernment and anti-episcopal, pro-Jansenist and pro-Gallican offensive spread like wildfire through the provincial parlements, to Aix, Bordeaux, Toulouse, Rennes and even Rouen, where the overexcitement of the magistrates gives the lie to the conventional placid and stolid image of the people of Normandy. The *Châtelet* of Paris joined in the movement, as did the *Cour des aides*, where the singular talent of Malesherbes was turned loose against the royal government. In 1750 the Parlement of Paris had even sought allies outside the ranks of the *basoche*. It called for help from the *pairs* of France. Such an alliance would have been reminiscent of the Fronde, that is if the great lords had still possessed the warlike dispositions of their seventeenth-century forebears. Moreover, the situation was double-edged. For civil war, which would have been the worst possible catastrophe, was never a threat in the years following 1750. So the monarchy could not use the necessity of putting an end to fratricidal conflict as an excuse for silencing the Parlement in the interests of maintaining civil peace. In the age of Mazarin and the young Louis XIV the state had often used this form of blackmail, in the supposed interests of public order: the state or anarchy, the court or disorder, Louis or disaster! This tactic was out of the question in 1752. The Sun-King had succeeded in muzzling or winning over the higher nobility, now no longer capable of raising the frayed standard of military insurrection: all of which worked to the advantage of the perfidious irenicism of the magistrates.

Taking a long-term view, already in the 1750s we find the kind of context which Jean Egret, looking at the similar *parlementaire* agitation of 1787, would call politically pre-revolutionary. That at least is what the benefit of hindsight allows us to assert.

When the provincial *parlementaires* showed signs of a rebellious spirit, the government, inspired by Machault, convoked them to Paris so as to give them a good dressing-down. However, the magistrates used the occasion to put their heads together, assembled as they were as a sort of united national Parlement, a new and formidable concept. In these conditions, according to Michel Antoine, Louis XV looked like a teacher baited by his pupils. He still showed more energy and resourcefulness than his grandson, Louis XVI, was to display in similar circumstances. He was capable, if need arose, of demonstrating decisiveness and political skill. He would never completely lose control of the situation. He cultivated the art of adapting to circumstances and choosing capable men at the right moment, by practising a sort of successive double vision: Choiseul would soon appear on the scene, followed later, facing in an almost completely opposite direction, by Maupeou and Terray. For the moment, between 1753 and 1757, the king used an alternative method. To use the obvious metaphor, he alternated the stick and the carrot. The stick in late 1753 took the form of replacement tribunals to break the *parlementaire* strike, anticipating the much more decisive action taken 17 years later at the time of the Maupeou reform. As a carrot for the restive magistrates, in July 1754 the king regretfully dismissed the implacable Machault from his post as *contrôleur général des finances*, while retaining him as *garde des sceaux*.

Machault was in any case politically dead, as a result of his failure to defeat the church over the *vingtième*. Louis was simply signing his death certificate. Now he made further concessions and completely reversed his policy. In September 1754 he recalled and amnestied the Parlement. A new period of reciprocal give and take between the government and the magistrature seemed to be opening.

In chronicling all these ups and downs, we have more than once used the fateful word 'opposition'. Thanks to the Parlements, a political opposition existed for the first time in a continuous, even structured fashion from 1752 onwards. It grew and flourished for four years, until the political trend went into reverse under Choiseul. In this business the *billets de confession* had served as detonators, apparently trivial sparks which nevertheless started the brush fire which would much later set the entire forest ablaze.

The opposition was at first religious, both in theory and in reality. It acted like fermenting yeast in a human dough which remained predominantly Catholic. For religion, it goes without saying, had not suddenly become irrelevant. Nor had the popularity of the crown suddenly evaporated. But the struggle, on the level of the élites, had cost both of them dear. In May 1754, the marquis d'Argenson, conscious of the new age which was struggling into existence, reflected upon a system of spirituality which would get rid of 'all priests, all revelation, all mysteries'. This would, he said, go much further than the 'crude' Lutheran reformation of the sixteenth century, and would culminate in a vague deism, without any priesthood as intermediaries. It is very possible that such a creeping dechristianization was already under way.

It should be remembered that in the years of the Jansenist affair a whole clutch of Enlightenment masterpieces, not all of them reeking of sanctity, emerged into the light of day. Between 1746 and 1758 Diderot published his *Pensées philosophiques*, the *Letter on the Blind* and the first volume of the *Encyclopaedia*, Montesquieu produced the *Spirit of the Laws*, Voltaire his *Century of Louis XIV* and *Essay on Manners*, and Rousseau the two *Discourses* ('Science and Art' and 'Inequality'), both decisive in the formation of the modern ecological and anti-hierarchical personality. Finally in 1758 Quesnay produced his *Tableau économique*. The historian Daniel Mornet went to great lengths[14] to show that these great works did not at the time have any real influence on the public opinion that mattered, and that this would only happen later. But it is not clear that Mornet's thesis is very convincing. Already there were 'cultural intermediaries'[15] transmitting subversive ideas widely in society, though to a lesser degree than they would during the reign of Louis XVI.

[14]   Daniel Mornet, *Les Origines intellectuelles de la Révolution française* (Paris, 1933; republished Lyon, La Manufacture, 1989), p. 524.

[15]   *Les Intermédiaires culturels* (Paris/Aix-en-Provence, Champion/Publications de l'Université de Provence, 1981).

In such circumstances, the armistice concluded between the king and the *parlementaires* in September 1754 was unlikely to be longlasting, especially since it was a three-sided fight, with the archbishop of Paris determined to concede nothing as far as the *billets de confession* were concerned, while the Parlement laid into them tooth and nail. The king was hoping in vain for peace to break out on such a violently contentious matter. During the winter of 1754–5 the king even exiled Beaumont from Paris, to Conflans, then to Lagny. Would this expulsion of the archbishop be enough to quieten the magistrates down? Some hope!

In March 1755 they delivered the supreme insult by declaring that the bull *Unigenitus*, the prime mover of the entire drama, did not possess the status of an article of faith. This represented a considerable encroachment by the Parlement (which after all, even if pro-Gallican, should have confined itself to the purely secular domain) into the powers of the papacy in questions of dogma. The conflict between the king and the Parlement flared up again as hot as ever, which led by boomerang effect to a new consolidation of the tottering alliance between the throne and the altar, so typical of those years. To be sure, attempts at conciliation would once again be made. The king and his ministers even asked for mediation from the Vatican. Pope Benedict XIV reacted in an open-minded and pragmatic manner. Benedict was trying to inject a spirit of detente and realism into the rigid and ossified structures of the Catholic church, rather as Dubois, Orléans and Fleury had tried to do within the narrower confines of French absolutism. Seeking the best way to untangle the confused jumble of Jansenism, the pope conferred with Stainville, the future Choiseul, then ambassador in Rome and who supported making concessions to the *parlementaires*. The result, after long consultations between Versailles and the Vatican, was the papal encyclical *Ex omnibus*, issued in October 1756. This wisely dropped the obligatory nature of *billets de confession*, putting in their place a small number of spiritual demands, inevitably pro-*Unigenitus*, which the priest was ordered to communicate to the dying believer. This macabre compromise was nevertheless too much for the Parlement of Paris and its provincial counterparts, now united by a solidarity of 'classes' and even of class. The magistrates repudiated all attempts, no matter how well meant, at papering over the cracks at the centre of the politico-religious edifice, and went so far as to 'suppress' the encyclical *Ex omnibus* on formal grounds. With papal arbitration thus rejected by the judges, the schism between Louis XV and the judiciary seemed unbridgeable. And in fact the government's response was not slow in coming. In December 1756, a *lit de justice*, with the king in attendance, disciplined the Parlement and considerably reduced its powers, its organization and its offices. Thus emasculated, the *parlementaires* immediately went on strike for the second time in less than four years, refusing to carry out their judicial and political activities. On 5 January 1757 the attempted murder of Louis XV by Damiens revealed dramatically the climate of hatred and conflict which had built up over the previous five years.

Plate 22   Engravings on the attempted crime of Damiens   Robert François Damiens'
attempted stabbing of Louis XV took place on 5 January 1757. The top engraving
depicts his interrogations before an examining magistrate whilst the lower engraving shows his being 'put to the question'. His execution on 28 March 1757 was
also accompanied by torture. Louis XV would have been prepared to grant a
pardon but an exemplary punishment was required by the standards of the age. It
was Louis XVI who would suppress the use of torture in judicial cases.
Paris, Bibliothèque nationale, cabinet des Estampes

At the end of 1756 the protagonists seemed set in their respective dispositions. Louis XV was no longer on top of his form; he was depressed, fed up with life, suffering from growing personal unpopularity, his authority slipping away. The higher clergy for their part continued to support the principle of the *billets de confession*, but had split into two groups: the Cardinal de la Rochefoucauld led the majority, more moderate tendency, known as the *Feuillants*, as opposed to the zealous and hawkish minority of so-called *Théatins* (Theatines).[16]

Confronting the bishops, the *parlementaires*, following Montesquieu, denounced royal 'despotism'. They drew upon a fantastical but inspiratory historiography of the Merovingians, which borrowed themes from obscure theoreticians of the nobility like Le Laboureur and Boulainvilliers.[17] This transformed the magistrates into the direct successors of the long-haired warriors who, according to these chronicles, had acted as advisers to Chlotar, Clovis, Childebert and Charlemagne! This recollection of 'Frankish roots' earned the 'senators' of the parlements the support of a section of the *noblesse de race*, who earnestly fantasized about themselves as descendants of the blonde, blue-eyed, Germanic warriors who had conquered Gaul during the first millennium. Within the parlements militant minorities of ideologues snuffed out the voices of the first presidents and *procureurs généraux*. These latter were in theory the agents of the king, but now they often allowed themselves to be manipulated by the 'base', fearing that if they resisted, their lower-ranked colleagues would banish them from the magistracy. Emboldened by the solidarity of the lawyers (who would one day furnish the cadres of the Revolution and the Republic), the parlements challenged the *arrêts* of the *Conseil du Roi*, which were the very expression of the administrative monarchy. Between 1752 and 1788 the top tribunals became an alternative centre of power, after the fashion of the British Parliament, although with an entirely different structure, and one which the monarchy was forced to take into account at all times. In this perspective, it fell to the *avocat* Louis-Adrien Le Paige (1712–1803) to establish a link between *parlementaires* and Jansenists. Le Paige benefited from a certain immunity, thanks to protection from the prince de Conti, who enjoyed the king's confidence. Maître Louis-Adrien supplied the magistrates with arguments drawn from his remarkable collection of all the printed works relating to the courts and Jansenism. At the same time, under the auspices of the Augustinian sect, he constructed a bridge through time between the convulsionaries of Saint-Médard (whom he

---

[16] The Feuillants were Cistercian monks from the reformed wing of the Cistercian order. The Theatines were an independent religious order (which would disappear, at least in France, during the Revolution). In the Jansenist affair, the Feuillants were so-called after their leader, the Cardinal de la Rochefoucauld, the holder of the 'file' (*feuille*) of benefices. As for the hard-line tendency, known as the Theatines, it owed its name to the fact that its leader, the recently deceased Bishop Boyer, had been a Theatine himself (Lavisse, *Histoire de France*, viii-2, 241).

[17] Harold A. Ellis, *Boulainvilliers and the French Monarchy* (Ithaca, NY, and London, Cornell University Press, 1988), p. 50 *et seq.*

admired) and the Revolution of 1789 (the Gallicanism of which he would shower with praise). The author of a book on *The Essential Functions of the Parlement*, published in 1753, he acted as the shadowy puppet-master of the revolt of the judges.

This judicial rebellion, 'frondeuse' as it may have been, was not violent in any way. It was purely legal, or almost legal, which represented vast progress since the previous century! Paradoxically, however, this made it potentially more dangerous for the monarchy, at least in the long-term, than the real Fronde had ever been. The risings of 1648–55, stirred up by Condé, La Rochefoucauld and other great nobles, had been so costly in human life and wealth that vast numbers of the French had been unwilling to support them. This was not the case with the anti-establishment but pacific movements instigated by the magistrates of the eighteenth century. No drop of blood was shed, and no damage done to the economic prosperity of the kingdom. Furthermore, the opposition addressed a host of problems, going far beyond the question of the withholding of the sacraments.

In 1756, at exactly the same moment that the Jansenist crisis raged in Paris, the affair of the *terrier* of Guyenne, with had nothing to do with religion or the church, mobilized the Parlement of Bordeaux against the new 'hyper-fiscal' decisions of the royal officials. Old reflexes resurfaced, but in a new context. The diverse levies demanded by the state aroused strong criticism. The intendants of Bordeaux wanted, using any means necessary, to recover the land and regalian rights attached to the royal domain, rights which had been eroded by the recent planting of vineyards by the *parlementaires* on the alluvial deposits of the Gironde, which belonged, from a juridical point of view, to the king. In this affair, the Parlement was directly challenging the authority of the intendant Tourny, who had been responsible (not that the judges cared) for the brilliant reconstruction of the city of Bordeaux. In 1756, in Guyenne as elsewhere, this antagonism was aggravated by a judicial strike launched by the *parlementaires*, an action which caused their counterparts in Rouen, more than a hundred leagues away, to come out in sympathy. And all this at the precise moment that war, especially the naval war, against the British was intensifying, a war which demanded the raising of new taxes and all manner of revenues for the royal treasury. One does not get the impression, on this occasion, of a great gale of patriotism blowing through the Palace of Justice and penetrating the offices of the tribunals! This judicial indifference to the fate of the nation was all the more damaging because the king's ministers, incapable of properly 'communicating', had no idea of how to explain their political and strategic decisions to the public, while this same public was easily influenced by the numerous publications of the parlements and so espoused the magistrates' cause as their own.

The Parlement of Bordeaux, then, assaulted the king's domain. Another offensive opposing the *fiscus*, in the broad sense of the original Latin, was launched against *corvées*, the work levies demanded from the peasants.

Their legitimacy was debatable, even if they produced the admirable benefit of gradually equipping the kingdom with a superb network of roads suitable for vehicles. The *Cour des aides* of Montauban, possibly in all sincerity, used the unpopularity of the *corvées* as a pretext for attacking Lescalopier, intendant of the *généralité* of Montauban, and grand master of road construction in his district. Through him, the fiscal and road-building work of Orry, Machault's predecessor, was called into question, while in the affair of the *terrier* of Guyenne, the Parlement of Bordeaux was attacking the demands of Machault's successors.

The administrative monarchy could flex its muscles aggressively from time to time in internal affairs, against the Jansenists and so forth. In this first year of the Seven Years War, it was nevertheless frustrated at Montauban. In 1756 the *Cour des aides* of Montauban succeeded in having Lescalopier removed and 'promoted' to the intendancy of Tours. This was an ingenious way of getting rid of an unpopular administrator by having him kicked upstairs. He was dispatched north of the Loire (admittedly to a more prestigious position) as a result of his demand for *corvées* for road-building. The magistrates of Montauban scored a point over Lescalopier and by implication over the king as well.

Agitation at the beginning of the third quarter of the century was thus polarized around two subjects: the religious problem (with its political fall-out) and defiance over taxation. In this second sector, the growing and arguably debilitating influence of public opinion made itself felt through the 'waltz of the *contrôleurs généraux*', who came and went in quick succession after the sacking of Machault (who nevertheless survived as *garde des sceaux* for several years). His place was taken first in 1754 by Moreau de Séchelles, who, worn out by fatigue, ceded his position to his son-in-law Peyrenc de Moras, who lasted until August 1757, to be succeeded in turn by a whole stream of *contrôleurs*. The time had passed when a Colbert or an Orry could take root in this great financial office for 15 or 20 years, or even in some cases for life. This was one of the early signs of the destabilization of the political system, which would only become worse in the course of the next 30 years.

Faced with finance ministers of unprecedented weakness, victims of ministerial instability, the anti-tax ferment used and abused the situation, inventing new motives for anger and activism. Of course, the end of the War of Austrian Succession, the return of peace in 1748, and the economic vigour of the kingdom, all allowed the deficit caused by warfare to be diminished. In 1755 and the first half of 1756 the budget even came close to a positive balance. But during 1756 the outbreak of the Seven Years War after almost a decade of peace forced the government to demand new sacrifices from the tax-payers to finance rearmament. In July Louis XV decreed a second *vingtième* for this purpose. This managed, with difficulty, to overcome the first obstacle of registration by the Parlement of Paris, but encountered strong opposition within the provincial parlements, notably at Rouen, Toulouse, Besançon, Grenoble and Nancy. It was as if

France was living, not under a parliamentary regime (which no-one would haved dared to assert), but under a multiparliamentary system which served to make the government's life even more complicated!

The magistrates' protests were responding to two concerns. First, corporate egotism prompted them to denounce the imposition of taxes on noble land (at Toulouse for example), which in theory was exempt from taxation. But the judges were not so vulgar as to to be thinking only of themselves. They were civic-minded to boot! The high courts, therefore, at Besançon as at Grenoble, also relayed the grievances of other social groups, including *roturiers*, who were complaining about their share of the taxes being increased. This double motivation, selfish and altruistic, is clearly visible in the case of Montauban. Here, the members of the *Cour des aides* flew to the aid of their farmers 'pressured' by *corvées*, but they were also looking after their own interests, because less frequent and less intense *corvées* on building the king's highways meant more work for the benefit of the judges who leased the land and more crops in the warehouses of the honourable gentlemen of the *Cour des aides*.

At Rouen, old and new habits of opposition were bound together. The militant antifiscalism and Jansenism of the local *parlementaires* simmered, here as elsewhere, throughout the 1750s. At a popular level, a serious food riot in 1752, one of the ten large-scale revolts of this kind in Rouen between 1661 and 1789, was punished by five hangings and one condemnation to the galleys. In general terms, a slow detachment from the traditional culture of the past (a detachment which should not be exaggerated) was shown in the capital of Normandy during this period by a modest growth of religious indifference and decisions by married couples to have fewer children.[18]

In Dauphiné antifiscal agitation did not stem solely from the parlement. It generated the plebeian epic of Louis Mandrin,[19] the chivalric smuggler and Robin Hood of his age, who successfully fought pitched battles against tax-farmers and royal troops, at times reducing the central regions of eastern France to a state of popular and military turmoil. At a time when the officer ranks in the royal army were mostly reserved for the nobility, Mandrin showed the wealth of tactical and strategic talent to be found among the 'inferior classes', the very classes which would provide several remarkable generals for the armies of the Revolution. Cheap pamphlets known as *mandrinades* (soon to be posthumous) immortalized the exploits of the big-hearted contrabandist for the general public, and their publication coincided with the Jansenist and *parlementaire* crisis of 1754–5.

[18]   Jean-Pierre Bardet, *Rouen aux XVIIe et XVIIIe siècles. Les mutations d'un espace social* (Paris, SEDES, 1983), p. 318. Michel Mollat, *Histoire de Rouen* (Toulouse, Privat, 1979), pp. 263 and 266.

[19]   On Louis Mandrin (1724–55), the pugnacious smuggler and notorious bandit, a generous-hearted Dauphinois law-breaker, see E. Le Roy Ladurie's contribution in Georges Duby and A. Wallon (dirs), *Histoire de la France rurale*, 4 vols (Paris, Seuil, 1975–7), ii, 545 and 550.

Plate 23   Louis Mandrin   Louis Mandrin, depicted here in an engraving of 1755 after Jacques-André Treillard, was born of Dauphiné peasant stock in 1724. At 18 years of age he joined the army transport corps for provisioning required across the Alps by the French army in northern Italy. He went bankrupt, however, and he and his brother were condemned to death, Louis for killing someone in a quarrel, and his brother for false coinage. With nothing to lose, Mandrin joined a band of smugglers engaged in fiscal fraud between Savoy and France. The years 1753–4 marked the high-point of their contraband trade before the officers of the *Ferme générale* succeeded in organizing his capture in Savoy and repatriation to France. He was condemned and executed at Valence in May 1755, but not before he had become a kind of Robin Hood.

Paris, Bibliothèque nationale, cabinet des Estampes

In Paris, five years before the execution of Mandrin, the so-called 'abduction of children' affair of 1750 had revealed, even before the worsening of the Jansenist crisis, a certain malaise among the *menu peuple*. Since the high rises in grain prices of 1747–8 the city had, whether it liked it or not, become a magnet for young vagabonds. The police, just for once, showed no subtlety in dealing wth them, making arrests without bothering about mere details, and in the process even imprisoning young people of good family, uncontaminated by the crime of having no fixed abode. This triggered off popular disorders, protesting against this kind of injustice, whether real or imagined. The authority of the commissioners of police and the city authorities was called into question during the long hot summer of 1750. An absurd rumour spread that they were covering up for the bizarre dealings of a leprous nobleman who was trying to cure his sick body using a rejuvenating cure, the main ingredient of which was the blood of kidnapped children.[20] It was a 'gigantic false report', like the later 'famine pact', the queen's necklace or the Great Fear of 1789. The return to high prices in 1756–7, following a momentary fall in the price of grain, did nothing to settle matters.

The 'basochienne' agitation of 1752–6 had taken root at an early date within those courts which were trying to support the 'persecuted' Jansenists. It then turned against its own foundations, or certain among them, even calling into question, without trial, the powers of a judicial institution as important as the *Grand Conseil*. In 1755 a dispute over jurisdiction broke out between the *Châtelet* (a second-rank tribunal in Paris) and the *Grand Conseil*, which claimed supreme authority. Since the sixteenth century, the Council had been claiming for itself the position of supreme appeal court of the kingdom, over and above the parlements, which in theory only held that power in their respective provinces or in Paris. The aversion felt by the other magistrates towards these inordinate demands may easily be imagined. They showed it by the use of procedural chicanery, while in retaliation Louis XV declared his support for the *Grand Conseil*, which had become the scapegoat for the parlements' hostility towards absolutism. This may seem another minor matter, but it was instrumental in once more binding together the 'classes' of the magistrates of the sovereign courts against the *Grand Conseil* and by implication against the sovereignty of the dynastic state. Furthermore the *parlementaires* appealed once more to the princes of the blood, who were in theory members of the Parlement of Paris by right. Thus did the ducal family of Orléans, sires of the future Philippe-Egalité, enter the opposition stage as leading actors for the first time, taking their place alongside the *robe*. The liberal tradition of Orleanism, interrupted since the death of the Regent, was revived. It would now blossom continuously until the Revolution, and even up to the age of Louis Philippe and beyond.

---

[20]   Arlette Farge and Jacques Revel, *Logiques de la foule; l'affaire des enlèvements d'enfants à Paris en 1750* (Paris, Hachette, 1988).

Through these various episodes, and especially between 1752 and 1756, public opinion had made a remarkable breakthrough. For six decades, let us say since the close of the seventeenth century or the end of the League of Augsburg, the sovereign had communicated badly with the nation. Where now were the celebrations of the cult of personality around Richelieu, Colbert, not to mention Louis XIV? Was their disappearance due to the difficult wars of the later years of his reign or to an overdue outbreak of humility on the part of a Sun-King who in his youth and maturity had been anything but humble? Villars, the skilful and loyal strategist, was not granted a tenth of the glory bestowed upon Turenne, who had been a traitor to the state during the Fronde. As for Louis XV, his popularity had naturally gone up and down during the first 40 years of his reign, first under the Regency and then under his personal rule. It seems that his popularity was at its height just after 1743–8, at a time when the still young king, aided by Maurice de Saxe, took a personal part in the glorious victories of his armies during the War of the Austrian Succession.[21] But thereafter, public opinion, which was becoming more and more important, thanks notably to the rise of the periodical press, felt duped by the Treaty of Aachen, even if it had brought peace to France. It was widely considered a dishonourable piece of chicanery. It had led Louis XV's agents to expel the Stuart pretender, a great friend of France, from the kingdom. And, despite success on the battlefield, no new province had been annexed to the east or north of the hexagon. Many in Paris and elsewhere regretted the fact that the king had foregone territorial expansion, which was doubtless in conformity with the general spirit of equity of the Treaty, but which would never have been agreed to by a Louis XIV at the height of his power. Furthermore, the king's liaison with la Pompadour, excessively and universally vilified as an avaricious bourgeois harpy, was more and more criticized. The kidnapping of children, this 'slaughter of the innocents', no matter how much truth there was in it, saw the king reviled as a 'new Herod', in the image of his great-grand-uncle Henry III. It is reminiscent of the fate of the Jews in the age of medieval anti-Semitism, accused of ritual murder and infanticide. In 1750, His Majesty, drawing the inevitable conclusions from this debasement of his image, built the 'road of revolt'. This led directly from the palace of Versailles to the château of Compiègne, passing through the tiny city of Saint-Denis and by-passing Paris itself, where Louis now feared he might have to endure the anger of hostile crowds. It only remained for what Jules de Goncourt would later call the 'engravers of turds' to unleash an unbridled campaign of lampoons and pamphlets against the sex maniac of Le Parc-aux-Cerfs. In short, in the few brief years between 1748 (the 'stupid peace' of Aachen) and 1756 (the beginning of the Seven Years War), a decisive step was taken towards divorce between the monarchy and the affections of the nation. And in fact, the idea of the Nation was itself the crux of the

[21]   Antoine, *Louis XV*, p. 601.

problem. By concluding a peace without annexations at Aachen, Louis had offended the chauvinism of his subjects, or at least of the most politicized among them. In undermining the Jansenist party he was damaging the fibres of Gallicanism, in other words a sort of Frenchness dear to the hearts of the *parlementaires* and their numerous henchmen (lawyers and the like). Louis XIV, by contrast, had known how to humour this anti-Roman tendency at the assembly of the clergy of 1682 over the question of the Four Articles. The monarchy of 1755 thus suffered from a dual 'national deficit', the result of the 'objective alliance' between a disappointed chauvinism and a devious Jansenism.[22] The identification between royalty and patriotic consciousness, so well constructed by the Sun-King[23] was losing its energy, and the defeats of the Seven Years War would do nothing to make matters better. The public figure of Louis XV was challenged far more than it had been during the first part of his reign. The man, luckily for him, had strengths in reserve. He would confront, come what may, and even surmount a new series of political trials. His grandson, after 1774, would show far less capability in this domain.

It was perhaps inevitable that the pro-Catholic and 'Protestantophobic' tonality of French diplomacy between 1740 and 1757 would lead to renewed harassment of Huguenots within the kingdom, notably in the Cévennes. And in fact several episodes show this. The numbers sent to the galleys for Calvinist heterodoxy rose somewhat during several years after 1745. This little 'hump'[24] in the graph of Huguenot convicts cannot, however, be compared with the extraordinary summits scaled by the figures on the same graph just after the Revocation or during the Camisard war. This new 'hump' coincides roughly with the execution of a small number of pastors in southern towns between 1745 and 1752, continuing until 1762, notably at Grenoble, Montpellier and Toulouse. The final wave of forced rebaptizing of children of so-called 'New Catholics' in the region of Nîmes[25] dates from 1752, but it was to be the last. In any case, the Protestants of the Midi could no longer be intimidated by these outbursts of physical or symbolic violence. They continued imperturbably

[22]   See, in this respect, the fascinating work of the theologian-sexologist Uta Ranke-Heinemann, *Eunuchen für das Himmelreich* (Hamburg, Hoffmann, 1988), ch. 22.

[23]   At least up to 1693, the date when Louis XIV accepted that the clergy should renounce the Gallican Four Articles of 1682 in return for various concessions from Pope Innocent XII in respect of the *régale* and episcopal investitures. The 'deal' was a finely-balanced one (Madame de Maintenon having seemingly had a hand in it); but it indicated a certain realignment of the Bourbon monarchy on the side of the Vatican, an alignment which opened up the way for *Unigenitus* – see J.-P. Labatut, *Louis XIV, roi de gloire, (1638–1715)* (Paris, Imprimerie Nationale, 1984), pp. 280–1. Labatut made use of the work of M. Langlois, 'Madame de Maintenon et le Saint-Siège', *Revue d'histoire ecclésiastique*, 25 (1929).

[24]   A. Zysberg, *Les Galériens, vie et destin de 60,000 forçats sur les galères de France, 1690–1784* (Paris, Seuil, 1988), pp. 104 and 382–3.

[25]   Emile Léonard, *Mon village sous Louis XV* (Paris, PUF, 1941, republished 1984), pp. 256–68 (in the 1984 edition).

with their baptisms, marriages and funerals in the Genevan manner. After 1756, the relative softening of the official attitude towards the Huguenots (moderation in practice if not in law) is explained by the installation of a certain tolerance in accord with the spirit of the age. The picture should not be made too rosy: the Calvinists were spared, relatively speaking, because episcopal and even royal repression was for the most part directed against the Jansenism which was now its principal target. The Huguenots benefited to an extent from the sufferings of others. But this suffering would not last long: a few years later the Augustinians would wreak a harsh revenge on the Jesuits. Thus turns the wheel of fortune.

The great conflicts of the War of the Austrian Succession and the Seven Years War did not exhaust French resources in men and money in the way that the League of Augsburg and the Spanish Succession had ruined the country. Warfare in the eighteenth century was in some ways a most peculiar business! The winners could be bled white, like Frederick the Great's Prussia, severely depopulated at the end of the Seven Years War, while the vanquished, like Louis XV's France, emerged in excellent economic health. Under Louis XIV things had been very different.

Admittedly, the burden on French taxpayers was heavy. The *dépenses engagées* of the state, at their highest during the Seven Years War, amounted annually to the equivalent of 1,800 tonnes of silver, that is to say more than the 1,600 tonnes spent annually at the worst moments of the War of Spanish Succession.[26] Extensive recourse to loans was therefore necessary, since the standard revenues of the monarchy, raised from direct and indirect taxation, were insufficient to cover the increase in outlay. That said, the nation, though having to pull in its collective belt, confronted the trials of war gallantly. Of course, some sectors suffered: the commercial activities of the Company of the Indies collapsed, as was predictable,[27] between 1743 and 1747, then again between 1759 and 1763. The colonial commerce of Bordeaux, only slightly affected during the War of Austrian Succession, was disastrously depressed during the Seven Years War. But if we consider foreign trade in general, and not only colonial commerce, the overall impression is less pessimistic. To be sure, the figures for French exports fell during the two conflicts, reaching a low point of 170 or 180 million *livres*, instead of the 240 million between the wars in 1754–5. But at no time did they plummet to the depths of the last years of Louis XIV. And then, after the solid re-establishment of peace in 1764, they rose vigorously to beat all previous records. In any case, the losses in external trade were caused by the collapse of exchange with the colonies. For the rest, most sectors held steady: the export of wine from Bordeaux, for example, remained healthy during the Seven Years War. So agricultural and wine production in the country as a whole held firm,

---

[26] Alain Guéry, 'Les Finances de la monarchie française sous l'Ancien Régime', *Annales ESC* (1978). We should note that Louis XV's France, much richer than that of his predecessor as king, could sustain such a tax without so much difficulty.

[27] Haudrère, *La Compagnie française des Indes*, ii, 436 (graph).

despite being scarred by the damage caused by the British navy to oceanic commerce, carrying goods to and from French possessions in the tropics. The internal market stood up well: if we look at the figures for salt consumption,[28] and especially at 'voluntary' buying (which is a good reflection of consumer behaviour, because beyond the reach of the fiscal arms of the state), we find that the Wars of Austrian Succession, in marked contrast to the disasters of the Fronde, the League of Augsburg and the Spanish Succession, had no depressing effect on the nationwide consumption of salt, which continued to rise. Even the Seven Years War saw only a slight lowering of between 5 and 6 per cent in 'voluntary' sales. In the long term, the resolutely ascending 'saline' or *gabeleuse* figures between the chasm of 1710 and the summit of 1780 were hardly affected by this weak negative fluctuation around 1760.

As far as agricultural production is concerned, the movements of tithes and rents, calculated in real monetary terms or paid in kind, provide information not only for the long term, but also for the medium term, for specific periods of war, peace and between wars. The War of Austrian Succession was marked, here and there, by minor problems over cereals. But it would appear that the far greater conflict, the Seven Years War, far from damaging agrarian production in France, acted as a stimulus to it.[29] Cereal production in particular remained in rude good health between 1757 and 1763: it even rose markedly in certain regions for which we possess statistics, including the Lyonnais, Anjou and Lower Normandy, where the high prices maintained during the war, in particular as a result of purchases by the intendancies, helped stimulate agricultural enterprise and production. Again this is in marked contrast to its collapse during the much more damaging wars of the later part of Louis XIV's reign. In the Cambrésis, the Paris region, Burgundy, Maine, Brittany, lower Languedoc and the south-west, agricultural production remained buoyant or rose slightly during the Seven Years War. The same picture applied in Alsace. Finally, a more confused impression emerges in the Auvergne,[30] where tithes in cereals rose in some places and fell in others. In this second third

[28]   E. Le Roy Ladurie and J. Field-Récurat, 'Sur les fluctuations de la consommation taxée du sel dans la France du Nord aux XVIIe et XVIIIe siècles', *Revue du Nord* (Oct.–Dec. 1972). The curve plotted by this salt consumption over two centuries is reproduced in *Histoire de la France rurale*, ii, 362.

[29]   If famine had been spirited away after 1715 in comparison with the Richelieu and Louis XIV periods, this was not only because of the (modest) increase in agricultural production during the eighteenth century, but also because it did not decrease as much, or did not decrease at all, during the periods of major war. The War of Austrian Succession and the Seven Years War were, in this respect, in happy and complete contrast to the 'Thirty Years Fronde' as well as the wars of the League of Augsburg and the Spanish Succession. All these three conflicts had been very damaging (from every point of view, including excessive exactions) for agricultural producers.

[30]   On all this, see the research which E. Le Roy Ladurie conducted or directed in collaboration with Joseph Goy, and which has often been cited in these pages, in the three volumes relating to tithes and peasant dues.

of the eighteenth century, the French had to deal with a relatively mild form of warfare in which production did not have too bad a time; the tax burden was certainly heavy, but not crippling. The resistance of the parlements, reprehensible though it may have been from a patriotic point of view, with its antifiscal guerilla actions, at once lawful and non-violent, may have been partly responsible for this. The hexagon had become a sanctuary, its population spared the slaughter of warfare and the passage of contending armies. The partial maritime blockade of the French coasts by the British fleet encouraged the overland transportation carried out by peasant wagoners. This provided a new way for rural people to make money, even if maritime and colonial commerce suffered badly. Enrichment possibly provided some consolation for the inevitable suffering.

No tears need be shed either for the urban economy during the two major conflicts of the mid-eighteenth century. We need only consider the sometimes undulating but unstoppable movement in Parisian rents between 1741 and 1762. If Louis XV lost his second great war against Pitt and Frederick, this was in no way due to French economic weakness. Rather it was because the taxation system, the willpower of the political class, and the competence of the army and navy were lacking in vision and unity at decisive moments. The economic success of the kingdom compensated somewhat for the financial and logistical shortcomings of the armed forces, which led to failure in combat. This was in contrast with the seventeenth century, when atrocious conflicts which left the kingdom exhausted were waged with considerable success on the battlefield. Between 1756 and 1763 the military expeditions launched by the French regularly misfired, but this did not impose unimaginable suffering on the civil population. This was some consolation. Some people even talked, with excessive optimism, of *la guerre en dentelle*, a polite, rational and 'civilized' warfare.

This picture had its light and shade. On the negative side, the woollen industry remained stagnant during the warlike quarter of a century between 1740 and 1763. Production figures did not descend to the lows of the beginning of the eighteenth century, they were even fairly buoyant, but they were sluggish as far as basic production was concerned, with sales growing in value as a result of the long-term rise in the price of fabrics. The tardy expansion of the woollens sector would only make itself felt after 1763, during the years of peace, and especially during the 1780s, which can no longer be seen, as Ernest Labrousse saw them, as a period of pre-revolutionary 'crisis' in textile manufacture. On the positive side, despite the loss of India and Canada, the revival of the colonial trade after the return of peace from 1764 onwards was little short of remarkable. In the words of Pierre Chassaigne: 'admittedly the colonial market was disrupted and paralysed by the first rumours of war [the Seven Years War]. But at the same time the vitality and potential of Santo Domingo should not be forgotten. For the real golden age of the island began after 1763, from the end of the Seven Years War, which had been an extremely difficult period for the colony.'[31] This new and powerful 'take-off' is easily explained, because the prosperity of the island depended on the cultivation of tropical plants, the production of which was not seriously affected in times of war. 'There was a large reserve [of sugar] ready to be sent to France as soon as circumstances permitted.' In the age of the Enlightenment, periods of warfare did not lead *a priori* to economic disaster: 'Rather they were parentheses, gloomy to be sure, but during which the economic factors were not changed in a structural fashion'. This could not be better expressed: in Santo Domingo, but also and above all in France herself, there is a transition from the catastrophic wars of the long seventeenth century (1589–1713) to wars of a new type, experienced as parentheses, difficult to live through but not necessarily disastrous from the economic point of view, during the *belle époque* of the Enlightenment.

[31] Pierre Chassaigne, 'L'Economie des îles sucrières, l'exemple de Saint-Domingue', *Histoire, économie et société*, 7 (1988), 102.

10

Public Opinion's First Successes

The years 1752 and 1753 could well be taken as the period when, at least according to the marquis d'Argenson's[1] notes, what may readily be called anticlerical activism commenced. 'The priests', wrote the marquis, 'hardly dared to show their faces in the streets without being booed. No one dares speak up any more in favour of the clergy. In polite company they are regarded as not far removed from the familiars of the Inquisition.'[2] In 1753, he noted the decrease in the number taking communion as more than a third (?), as well as the emptying of the Jesuit colleges; the appearance of bishops, abbots, monks and nuns in increasing numbers at carnival-time, each with their masks. . . . Hatred against the priesthood and the episcopacy was on the increase in certain quarters. It was the beginning of something of major significance for a certain sort of French sensibility which, until the present, would be often distinctively marked out by its anticlericalism.

Such sensibility, purely Jansenist in other instances, could also nourish a hatred for Louis XV. On 5 January 1757, Robert-François Damiens, a former lackey, wounded the king by striking him with a dagger. The assailant had taken seriously the opposition talk which he had heard at the lodgings of his patrons. Amongst the latter, some (like Bèze de Lys) were pro-Jansenist *parlementaires*, hostile to royal power and to the *dévot* party.[3] The regicidal act of Damiens, although it did not succeed, marked a turning-point. From 1740 onwards, above all from 1752, Louis had given

[1] I.e. René de Voyer de Paulmy, Marquis d'Argenson.
[2] According to Michel Antoine, *Louis XV* (Paris, Fayard, 1989) p. 238. Daniel Mornet, *Les Origines intellectuelles de la Révolution française* (A. Colin, 1933, republished Lyon, La Manufacture, 1989) *in fine* thought that d'Argenson was exaggerating at this point. Mornet was undoubtedly not entirely wrong to 'soft-pedal' it, But Argenson was the more intelligent and he was always excellent at indicating a tendency, or the reversal of a tendency, even when, as elsewhere, he exaggerated the phenomenon in question.
[3] Dale K. Van Klay, *The Damiens Affair* (Princeton, NJ, Princeton University Press, 1984), esp. pp. 88–92. As lackey, Damiens had served numerous Jansenist masters, amongst whom were various *parlementaires*, notably Bèze de Lys; their conversations may well have incited him to act.

Plate 24 Portrait of Louis XV This painting of Louis XV is a copy of the original (now lost) by Louis-Michel Van Loo. Diderot had much admired it in an account of 1761, around the time when it was painted: 'The king is beautifully painted, very fine, and it is said that it is very life-like.' He remarked on the ermine mantle which the king is portrayed as wearing, and which gave him something of 'the dignity of the *président* of the Parlement'. Diderot unconsciously revealed something which would become the theme of the decade for Louis XV with his attempts to placate the political machinations of the magistrates and their presidents by means of Choiseulian concessions.

Versailles, Musée national du château

in to the demands of a policy which sought to replicate (without always succeeding in its objectives) traditional absolutism and pro-episcopal religiosity. Disturbed by having just been the target for an assassination attempt and faced by the active resistance of the sovereign judges, he decided in the end to retreat and offer concessions. He gave in to the implicit and insistent dislike which he sensed to exist almost everywhere against the ministry. In February 1757 he dismissed two of his leading ministers, Machault and the count d'Argenson, the one disliked intensely by the Parlement, and the other allied to the *dévot* faction. In the course of the following summer, he recalled the exiled or disgraced *parlementaires*, the same individuals against whom he had hoped, towards the close of the previous cycle of opposition in December 1756, to deliver a knock-out blow. A phase of decisive concessions to the *parlementaire* opposition, a 'U-turn', followed the ministerial disgraces and the recall of the Parlement. The pendulum swung once more towards more receptive attitudes and towards taking more account of the wishes of the juridical élites, if not of the nation. Choiseul and his group embodied this different direction which, in various respects, returned French politics to the suppleness of Fleury's years, and away from the interlude of the 'reactionaries' after the style of Belle-Isle and the Count Pierre d'Argenson.

This new and more 'relaxed' attitude which was instituted post-1757 and above all post-1763 (when the burden of military conflict was lifted) would last through to 1770. It would correspond to the 'third phase' of Louis XV's reign[4] after the first Orléans-Fleury phase (quasi-liberal), and then the Belle-Isle-d'Argenson phase (more strictly Catholic and authoritarian).

The new direction, which might also be described as quasi-liberal, was particularly clear between the Treaty of Paris (1763) and the coming to power of an evidently more 'robust' triumvirate (Maupeou, Terray and d'Aiguillon) in 1770. The action of Choiseul dominated the decade of the 1760s. The group in power, besides the Choiseul clan, included the *contrôleurs généraux* Bertin and L'Averdy, and then Louis XV himself. Finally, playing the part of a chanting or lamenting chorus to a Greek tragedy, came the *parlementaires*. All these individuals and groups, with the more or less gracious accord of the Choiseulists, contributed to the construction of a common policy, the result of a parallelogram of forces which explains this period of a decade and more.

The policy which was thus articulated consisted of three points. Firstly, there were major concessions to the élites, and particularly the magistrates, to the extent that they claimed (and not without some justification) to represent the national will. The relaxation in policy invited the Jansenist judges to discriminate against, and suppress, the Jesuits. The second panel

---

[4] On the various phases – decennial (more or less) 'shifts' – through which, in many cases a long reign evolves, see Fernand Braudel, *Ecrits sur l'histoire* (2 vols, Paris, Arthand, 1990) ii, 229–30.

in the triptych consisted of putting alongside the vigorous economic growth (which, at all events, had occurred spontaneously) an orchestrated legislative programme with liberal overtones, inspired by the physiocrats. It was a precocious effort at 'laissez-faire' state voluntarism. Thirdly, far from being pacifist in the rather lamenting fashion of Fénelon, or even Fleury, the government proceeded to a huge effort to constitute the state's armed forces, both military and naval. This firm attitude flattered the French nationalism which was the lay equivalent of pro-*parlementaire* Gallicanism of the Choiseulists; Gallican ideology, aimed against Rome, struck a chauvinistic chord. Bouts of patriotism (of all kinds) nevertheless had their limits. Raising the standard of the military machine had to be restricted within the overall pacifist limits of a diplomacy which remained attached to the maintenance of the continuum of good relations abroad. This corresponded to the wishes of His Majesty who had been, after all, educated by distinguished tutors in the Fénelonian mould during his youth.

Following on from Philippe d'Orléans, Fleury and d'Argenson[5] and coming before Maupeou, Choiseul was one of those individuals who provide a marking-point to the successive phases of Louis XV's reign. From a great Lorraine family which had good connections with the neighbouring kingdom, Choiseul had initially been a distinguished officer in the French army from 1730 onwards, and then an ambassador in Rome and Vienna. His family name was Stainville until, becoming noticed by the king and court, he became duke de Choiseul in the summer of 1758. He subsequently became first minister between December 1758 and December 1770. In tandem or alternately with one of his cousins, Choiseul-Praslin, he held the key posts as minister for foreign affairs, war and the navy. For his part, Louis nominated him to be governor of Touraine and superintendent of the postal service. He was also colonel in chief of the Swiss (*colonel général des Suisses*), a handsomely rewarded post. In short, in the 1760s, he was put 'in overall charge of the shop'. Ginger-haired, devoid of good-looks or large fortune, Choiseul enriched himself by gifts from the state, even though he was a spendthrift and became heavily indebted. He hated avarice, the incarnation in his mind (as for many aristocrats) of an anti-social vice *par excellence*. In this respect, Choiseul was closer to Fouquet than Colbert. With his turned-up nose, his vivacious personality and his real sense of friendship, he went round acquiring for himself without too much difficulty the good connections in high places which his breeding, tact and impetuosity attracted to him. His biting wit ensured that Choiseul had the respect of, and gave pleasure to, the salon-world as well as the court. His wallet and his cosmopolitan culture had gained him ready access to or knowledge of the Austrian monarchy, the smaller German princely courts, the Turkish army, Chinese architecture, Flemish painting and gardens *à l'anglaise*. A philosophers' friend, he was

---

[5] I.e. Marc-Pierre de Voyer de Paulmy, Count d'Argenson.

Plate 25 Etienne-François, Duke de Choiseul-Stainville Etienne-François, Duke de Choiseul-Stainville (pictured here in a painting by Louis-Michel Van Loo in 1763) was the more renowned of the two brothers from the Choiseul family whose careers took them to elevated heights in the service of the Bourbons. The family had its origins in Champagne and Lorraine and had already seen distinguished military service in the seventeenth century. Etienne-François, born in 1719, was a *maréchal de camp* in 1748 before becoming an ambassador in 1753, and then secretary of state for foreign affairs and minister of state in 1758. He was the architect of a series of imaginative political initiatives both at home and abroad which included the Franco-Austrian alliance, a compromise with Jansenism and the *parlementaires* and a degree of liberalism in the grain trade. His brother, César, served as a lieutenant-general in the armed forces before himself becoming a foreign secretary and minister for the navy.
Versailles, Musée national du château

no *dévot* and demonstrated a degree of tolerance towards religious heterodoxy, whether Jewish or Protestant. He was an indefatigable worker and an
insatiable lover, who found his feminine conquests (unlike Louis XV) from
among the ladies of the aristocracy. Nevertheless, he did not hesitate to
offer his sister as a mistress to the French king or to spy on his pretty young
cousin. In the game of Versailles politics he relied on La Pompadour, and
then forgot her once she was dead – a case of the habitual ingratitude of the
ineveterate politician? At the beginning of his military career, he had been
the protégé of the duke de Noailles who himself had begun life serving as
a nephew by marriage and client of la Maintenon. From one marquise to
another – Choiseul had all the contacts! The logic of his 'factional' and
pompadourien position led him to oppose the *dévot* party represented by the
Dauphin and his servant La Vauguyon, entrusted with the education of the
future Louis XVI. Choiseul was an all-rounder. In the army, he had been
much apreciated as a staff-officer before joining the high command. Yet he
was not a war-monger. A diplomat who blended suppleness and authoritarianism, he was able to extract from Pope Benedict XIV in 1756, who
was happy to oblige, a suitably bland statement on the question of anti-
Jansenism (*Ex omnibus*). Choiseul's wife, whom he loved and duped, was
born a Crozat. She was related to the world of high-finance and Choiseul's
opponents linked him (not always in good conscience, for he was a noble
de race) with upstart financiers. If you believe the purists, what's bred in
the bone, even on the wife's side, will come out in the flesh. A semi-
physiocrat in his old age, disgraced by his king, Choiseul kept a herd of
Swiss cows on his acres at Chanteloup. In political economy, he had, in
fact, generally placed in the forefront the destinies of trade, and especially
the 'gentle commerce' of overseas trade. In their honour he sacrificed
Quebec, the territorial remains, for the lucrative interests of export trades
in Santo Domingo and the cod-fishermen of Newfoundland. In short, he
fostered a 'phoenician'-style French expansion. He preached a version of
Gallican and quasi-liberal nationalism tinged with anti-Jesuit hatred and
pro-*parlementaire* sympathies. This was all a good deal different from his
predecessor d'Argenson and his successor Maupeou – an enlightened
despotism after the French manner perhaps, post-baroque, or (at least)
post-rococo in style.

The attack on the Jesuits, with the passive, even active, compliance of
the duke de Choiseul began in a tortuous fashion in the last years of Pope
Benedict XIV. His Holiness embodied the Catholic *tiers parti*, balanced
midway between the Jansenists and the Molinists.[6] Within a wholly French
environment, Le Paige[7] and his supporters orchestrated the attack, using
their good contacts with the Parlement, within the French government,

---

[6]　The Molinists, partisans of the Jesuits and of anti-Jansenism, took their name from the
Jesuit theologian Louis Molina (1553–1600), author of highly subtle theories which attempted to reconcile divine grace with human liberty, ones which would be challenged by
the supporters of Jansenius in the course of the following centuries.

[7]　See chapter 9 above, pp. 393–4.

and at Rome. They secretly concocted the text of a bull which their friends amongst the clergy would then persuade the pope to approve and sign. If it had been promulgated, it would have overturned the doctrinal positions taken up in the old bull *Unigenitus*. The death of Benedict XIV (May 1758) put an end to this manoeuvre, in which one can already detect the secret and manipulative techniques of societies of thought (Jansenist in this instance). In their lay forms, these societies would constitute one of the anchor-points of the beginnings of the French Revolution. Damiens' assassination attempt on Louis XV also provided some pseudo-arguments in favour of the Augustinian Jansenists to Le Paige, the indefatigable politician of the corridors of power. Le Paige was amongst those who peddled the rumours that (falsely) attributed the failed regicide attempted by Damiens to Jesuit intrigue. The latter were, so it appeared, desirous of having the king assassinated in order to see his son, the Dauphin, crowned in his place since he was more favourable than his father to the *dévot* party and to the Jesuits. It was nothing more than a current rumour and a slanderous one! Damiens had felt the influence, in fact, of the Jansenist magistrates, the sworn enemies of Jesuitism. But the calumny stuck. . . .

The death of Benedict XIV in May 1758 brought the curtain down on all this. In July, Clement XIII was enthroned and he refused to annul the *Unigenitus* bull. And then, to leap ahead a few months to September, Joseph I, King of Portugal, was himself the object of an assassination attempt, a crime which was, of course, also attributed to the Jesuits who were currently in dispute with the Portuguese king. Confronted with these new facts, Le Paige and the supporters of his sect dramatically revised their project of attack. *Unigenitus* was forgotten!

Jansenist aggressiveness was now directly aimed against the Jesuits who, in 1760, condemned the work published by Le Paige and Coudrette on the general history of the Jesuit order. Montesquieu had criticized, albeit without incurring too many risks, an oriental despotism – a respectable distance from France, in distant Asia for example. Now it was the more specific 'despotism' of a religious order within the realm itself which was the object of polemic. It was equally the case that a pre-revolutionary mechanism began to be put into operation. They were hitting closer to the target. Taking the uncompromising reflections composed by Montesquieu in the *Esprit des Lois*, put together in his ivory tower amidst the vineyards of the Bordelais, they transformed these meditations into war machines put into battle in the internal politics of the kingdom between Rouen and Bayonne,[8] between Rennes and Aix-en-Provence.

It is quite likely that Choiseul had given his willing consent to the contorted plans conceived by his new Jansenist friends. Politics, even religious politics, makes strange bed-fellows. Choiseul ('Le Lorrain') had

[8] Dale K. Van Klay, *The Jansenists and the Expulsion of the Jesuits from France* (New Haven, CT, Yale University Press, 1975), pp. 229–36; Antoine, *Louis XV*, pp. 578–92.

no love for the Jesuits. It was a subtle game that was being played since he wanted to win over the *parlementaires* so that they would the more willingly accept, or at least agree to without too much complaint, the heavy taxation necessary to pay for a continuation of the ill-conceived military conflict in the Seven Years War. He thus hoped to strengthen royal authority and earn Louis XV a happy old age. In this respect, Choiseulism was apparently a shift in the strategies of those in power towards the centre, or even towards the left. Choiseul distanced himself (without completely breaking off contacts with them) from his former Jesuit and episcopal close companions. He sought new allies amongst the magistrature and the church. La Pompadour had helped her friend Choiseul up the ladder to the heights of power in the state. She never forgot, however, the severe harassment unleashed against her by the Jesuits, great enemies of her illegitimate liaisons with the king. She would be only too willing to assist Choiseul in bringing about the collapse of the Jesuits. For their part, the Jansenists acted as persecuted-persecutors. They began a long cycle of offensives against the regular clergy on the basis of anti-Jesuitism which would be continued, amplified along a broad anticlerical front, and well beyond the issue of the Jesuits, during the French revolutionary period.

For the moment, during the Louis XV period, a paltry little affair set things alight (a similarly minor incident such as the *curé* Bouettin's refusals to hear some indviduals' confessions had been the torch which had lit up the first conflicts). From 1741, Antoine La Valette, a Jesuit father, carried on a profitable business in Martinique, with sugar cane plantations, purchasing slaves and dealing in currency and bills of exchange with metropolitan France. But, in 1755, at the outset of the war, the English fleet captured the Jesuit's boats and cargoes on the high seas. They had been destined to meet the huge debts which he had incurred from a commercial organization based at Marseille. Once the Marseillais gathered what had happened, manipulated by a Jansenist lawyer, they took their legal case to the Parlement of Paris. In May 1761 the *grand-chambre* of the Parlement condemned the Jesuit order (and not just La Valette) to pay a million and a half *livres tournois* to the plaintiffs from Marseille. The latter would never see the colour of their money but an unstoppable engine had been set in motion.

The *abbé* Chauvelin, a sworn adversary of the Company of Jesus, denounced the despotism of the Jesuits before the Parlement in April 1761. He demanded that the constitutions of the Jesuit order be examined before the Parisian tribunal. The Jesuit fathers were caught head-on in this affair and suspected of being, as we would put it, a 'fifth column' of the Vatican. The trial would last over four months. France was at war with the English but this was the least of the worries of the sovereign court judges. They were much more concerned about matters of internal or religious policy than the destiny of armies which barely interested them. The factions active in Paris fanned out from right to left as though upon an imaginary semi-circular stage. The chancellor Lamoignon was a firm supporter of the

Jesuits. Amongst the royal judicial officers some moderate Gallicans such as the *procureur général* of the Parlement, Joly de Fleury, tried to produce a compromise solution. From the Augustinian side, Le Paige gave a good impression of outrage, something which suited his taste for polemical exaggeration. At the margins of this faction there were also the hard-line Augustinian extremists represented by such individuals as L'Averdy, a *conseiller* in the Parlement. He was, however, a man of parts and some years later in 1763 he would be appointed to the key post of *contrôleur général des finances*. Through this remarkable nomination, Choiseul once more demonstrated his desire to lure the Jansenist flock within the enchanted circle of power so that he could use them for his own ends. In the course of the summer of 1761, after the Parlement of Paris had thwarted various attempts at conciliation emanating from the *Conseil d'en haut*, they enthusiastically adopted the conclusions of the judge who was but a mere *conseiller* in the Parlement, L'Averdy. This was the August injunction (*arrêt*) by virtue of which[9] the Parlement prohibited the Jesuits from recruiting novices and taking vows from new recruits. Their congregations and provinces were dissolved; their colleges were ordered to close within a set period of several months or up to a year. L'Averdy would later come the victim of a French Revolution, to the preparation of which in the long-term he had unwittingly contributed. He would face the guillotine in 1793; thus did the Revolution devour its own parents.

The injunction of 1761 might still have been suspended; but the provincial parlements each passed a series of definitive injunctions in 1762 which also led to the suppression of the Jesuits. The unity of the Nation, which the monarchy for its part was far from having completely realized, was thus articulated at an entirely different level following provincial initiatives, coming 'from below', and directed against the sole enemy, the Jesuits. Scapegoats? Or, rather, foil and demon. . . . In this respect, the parlements were in a much more favourable position than Pope Clement XIII in Rome and Ricci, the General of the Jesuit Order, who both refused to make any concessions, however insignificant, on the doctrinal position and regulatory framework of the Company. Yet they would perhaps have disarmed the anti-Jesuit offensive by softening the intransigence of the Augustinian magistrates, their colleagues and accomplices, an intransigence which was reinforced by an almost total corporate unanimity amongst the parlements and advocates.

Confronted with such intransigence at the Vatican, Louis XV and Choiseul ended up by being, or seeming to be, sick of the whole affair. They abandoned the Company of Jesus to its sad fate. The king let them become fodder for the *parlementaires*, so urgent was his need to gain their consent to new fiscal measures. He washed his hands of the whole affair, leaving the Dauphin, Lamoignon and the *dévot* party to their own devices. Louis XV even went so far as to lend his support, despite his own

---

[9] D. Van Klay, *The Jansenists*, p. 135.

Plate 26   Crime Punished   The decisions in 1761–2 of the Parlement of Paris and the provincial sovereign courts were a bitter blow to the Jesuits. The *arrêt* of 6 August 1762, the subject of this engraving, was particularly severe. It suppressed the Jesuit order in France, sequestered its property and dispersed the Jesuit fathers.

Paris, Bibliothèque nationale, cabinet des Estampes

fundamental convictions, to the Jansenist victory. In 1764, a royal edict brought the existence of the Jesuit order in the French kingdom to an end. Louis XVI, equally, would ratify various edicts later on which went against his own conscience. At least his grandfather, Louis XV, had managed to remain more or less the master of the political situation until his death. In 1767, the Spanish and Neapolitan Bourbons would imitate Versailles' example and proscribe the Company in their own lands too.

There were clearly various factors behind the Jesuit 'affair'. The government needed, for purely political reasons, to put in place a compromise with the old Augustinian opposition in the Parlement and did so on the back of the Jesuit issue. There was also the uncompromising attitude of the pope who refused to budge an inch despite the conciliatory efforts of Versailles. There was also the growth of a vast public opinion, still a minority in the country but very 'vocal' and hostile to the old régimes of the church whether in their Ignatian or Tridentine forms. France was not totally, or equally, affected by this 'mood'. At the periphery of the kingdom, in those provinces recently attached to it (the French Low Countries, southern Alsace, Franche-Comté – i.e. the three annexations undertaken by the Sun-King), the members of the parlements and the sovereign courts did not take to adopting the reforming and anti-Jesuit zeal which overtook their colleagues in the sovereign courts in the 'interior' of the country, the old Capetian heartland which had been the most profoundly affected by the 'Enlightenment' and by the successive waves of changes and thus was most up in arms against entire sections of the old Catholic edifice.

Overall, the episode which destroyed the Jesuits is far from being an inexplicable enigma. It was a kind of Revocation in reverse, in miniature, far less grave and traumatic than the act of 1685, of course, but still pregnant with significance. The persecution, albeit more gentle, had merely changed its target, no longer aiming at the various fringe minorities but at the centre, or close by, of the counter-reformed church. This went to the heart of the *dévot* cause. In 1682, royal Gallicanism had sought to subordinate the church to the state and ended up three years later by acting on the margins and eradicting the minority Huguenot community. The *parlementaire* Gallicanism of 1762 which was more or less adopted, and for political reasons, by the monarchy and the ministry in power, remodelled the church in its innermost recesses. The years from 1762 to 1790 constituted less than a generation which would culminate in the civil Constitution of the clergy, itself the fruit of juridical Gallicanism, a typical product of the Constituent Assembly. So, over and above the Jesuits, it would end in a rather brutal fashion in the last decade of the century with the questioning of the whole Roman influence in the French church. The whole process was not without a certain logic and it would last for over 30 years from the elderly Louis XV to the mature Louis XVI; but the magistrates and the monarchy which had initiated it would in the end, from

1789 to 1793, be destroyed by it, like sorcerer's apprentices, consumed in the maelstrom which they had themselves conjured up.

As for the Jesuits, they represented absolutism in the church and the sovereignty of the Vatican over the church, a sovereignty which was 'indivisible as the point in geometry'. Their collapse was a foretaste for the fall of absolutism in all its forms a quarter of a century later. To put it more prosaically, the clearing away of the living branches of the Company of Jesus was a prelude shortly afterwards to grubbing up all the old dead wood. Political authority, learning from the experience, would not want to be outdone by its former opponents the Jansenists. It took the lead and stole its clothes. In 1766 it created a commission on the regular orders, composed of archbishops and councillors of state. The commission suppressed nine religious orders and over 400 monastic houses whose utility, existence even, no longer appeared to be self-evidently justified. Colbert had happily criticized monks for their laziness and he would have applauded this measure. But the introduction of utilitarian criteria into ecclesiastical politics was but one more sign of the beginning of a laicization of mentalities which would constitute an enormous threat to the traditional order. . . .

More precisely, the closure of the Jesuit colleges forced the royal state to intervene in secondary education, with which it had hitherto little to do. The typical French pattern of national state examinations (the *concours d'agrégation*) was created for this reason in 1766. Educators,[10] even if they were secular priests, had to be found to replace the defunct Jesuit colleges. In the long-term, the expulsion or suppression of the Jesuits in Europe – they had been expelled from Portugal in 1759, from France in 1762, and from the entire Catholic world in 1773 corresponded to a 'great movement experienced in various states in which each wanted to play a much greater part in the responsibility for public education'.[11] *Kulturkampf* had arrived *avant la lettre*.

At the purely French level, the victory of the Jansenists appeared in certain respects suicidal. Theologically, the Jansenists survived as a kind of religious revival, common to Europe at this period, whether Protestant or Catholic, Augustinian, Wesleyan or Pietist. But politically the distant descendants of Jansenius were henceforth figures from the past. In suppressing their old rivals they had cut off the ideological and polemical branch on which they themselves had comfortably sat since the glorious days of Antoine Arnauld and Blaise Pascal. After slaying the Jesuit Beast there was not much else for them to do but disappear like the heroic

---

[10]   It was in 1766 that the University of Paris instituted the *concours d'agrégation* for the establishments in its region. The examination's illustrious history up to the present day is well-known (Louis-Henri Parias, *Histoire générale de l'éducation en France* (Paris, Nouvelle Librairie de France, 1981), ii, 544).

[11]   Marie-Madelaine Compère, *Du collège au lycée (1500–1850)* (Paris, Gallimard, 1985), p. 135.

Beowulf once he had slain the fire-spitting dragon.[12] Their services were literally no longer required! In the conflict which was brewing against the contemporary political system, they would henceforth cede the preeminent place to the philosophical and encyclopaedist currents of thought with which they had some leaders in common. La Chalotais, for example, was much respected by the Augustinians. He also enjoyed the support of the anticlerical intellectuals who, nevertheless, had no time for theories of grace, efficacious and sufficient or not.

For Louis XV, however, all things considered, it had not worked out too badly. On both fronts, Jesuit and Jansenist, he had shed surplus baggage and the king had henceforth a free hand to engage in a process of transformation which would be purely lay and political such as that which would be launched in 1770 by the new ministerial triumvirate.

★   ★   ★   ★   ★

Those who professed to be Gallicans also proclaimed themselves to be patriots. Choiseul had challenged the Jesuits, too Roman in their loyalties in his opinion. He equally wanted to reform the king's army, discredited by the defeats of the Seven Years War. Choiseul's team professionalized it through education and training initiatives. The Military School, actually founded by d'Argenson at the middle of the eighteenth century, received strong encouragement from the following ministry, and the school at La Flèche, which nurtured many future officers, was installed significantly in the former Jesuit college there. This process of professionalization affected essentially the nobility which retained its quasi-monopoly on the officer-corps for combat troops. But the ministers sought now to recruit future officers from amongst the gentry who had a military vocation, however poor they might be, rather than recruit operetta colonels from amongst the dregs of the aristocracy of the court or high finance, as had too often been the case during the last war from 1757 to 1763. Choiseul was thus in line with the ideas proposed by the Chevalier d'Arc in his book *Military Nobility* (*Noblesse militaire*), which had appeared in 1756.

The artillery was, in turn, rendered more adaptable to the different forms of war through the reforming attentions of Gribeauval. He subdivided the weaponry into campaign pieces, siege engines, coastal and fixed cannon. Ten of the armament factories, particularly those for cannon, were 'royalized' (i.e. 'nationalized'?) and much expanded. Finally, troops were transferred to barracks and no longer lodged on the inhabitants as before, with all the abuses which that had generally entailed.

The modernization of the military apparatus was inseparable from an increasing briskness in national life, which would make its full appearance

---

[12]   C.L. Wren and W. Bolton (eds), *Beowulf* (University of Exeter, 1988), verse 2,669 *et seq.* (p. 196 *et seq.*).

in the revolutionary period. In 1763–4, there was an air of needing to take some revenge against the English and, tangentially, against the Prussians, whose military methods (camps for great military manoeuvres, 'automization' of the soldier in his individual physical manifestation as well as collectively in his corps) were nevertheless much admired and imitated.

In the navy, the monopoly of the nobility on the officer-corps in combat units was not abolished either, however necessary it had become. But the scientific and educational training was improved, as the activity of the naval academy at Brest demonstrated. Under Choiseul and Praslin, 165 ships were constructed, of which 66 were large vessels, amongst the most modern in the world. The high command of the fleet remained dominated by a gerontocracy of admirals amongst whom the merits of the great sea captains of the War of American Independence (Guichen, De Grasse and Suffren) stand out still more remarkably. Equally astonishing was the enterprise of one Admiral Bougainville who, in 1768, discovered (or, rather, re-discovered) the island of Tahiti, with considerable philosophical consequences. The intellectuals in Paris (beginning with Diderot) turned this island into a philosophical and libertarian paradise, an enchanted isle, peopled by surprising phantasms purely of their own imagining.

Overall, the Choiseulian period, putting aside the irreplaceable loss of Canada, witnessed the encouragement of a twin development in the public and the private sector, the royal navy and the merchant navy, both rapidly expanded as a result of the efforts both of the state and of private individuals. In comparison with England, France retained in maritime affairs all its options and it would require the Revolution and the Empire wantonly to throw all the key cards away. . . .

The initiatives of Gribeauval, the achievements of the naval academy at Brest, the progress in naval construction were all evidence, amongst other indications, of the rise of a high degree of technical competence in the upper spheres of the military and naval 'establishment'. There was a widespread tendency towards greater sophistication in the Choiseul period, which grew out of previous initiatives. The *grandes écoles*, the flagships of the latest technical and scientific methods, made spectacular advances in the years from 1762 to 1771. This was true of the School of Bridges and Roads (*Ecole des Ponts et Chaussées*), the Royal School of Engineering (*Ecole royale du génie*) at Mézières, the School of Mines and the Naval Academy, and also of the newly founded Veterinary Schools at Lyon and Alfort, created in 1762 and 1766 respectively. Nor should the attempt to found a kind of agricultural college, part farm-school part model-farm, a project dear to the heart of the secretary of state Bertin and sadly still-born be forgotten. As to the Cabinet of Charters (*Cabinet des Chartes*), installed in the king's library for political reasons above all, it became, in 1762, the home and seed-bed for profound and, in the end, objectively pursued erudition.

The proliferation of these senior intellectual institutions in the wake of the Treaty of Paris, whether with explicitly pedagogic, or peri-pedagogic, objectives, puts the destruction of the Jesuit order in a less unfavourable light. The suppression, or at least the change in status of 106 Jesuit colleges might appear at first as a catastrophe. But the growth of important teaching and research establishments, controlled by the state, indicated generally a will on the part of the ruling élite (ministers and *parlementaires*) towards a relative laicization of a society still dominated by the church but one into which Enlightenment ideas were already percolating. . . . Laicization, which has had such an extraordinary impact on the long-term destinies of France, thus made its discreet or implicit entrance on the educational scene; a century and a half later it would have become an almost overwhelmingly dominant force. The twin initiatives of Choiseul and his supporters, suppressing the Jesuits on the one hand and encouraging the *grandes écoles* (whether military or civil) on the other, would be vastly extended during the revolutionary years. It was in the course of the Revolution that the old clerical Sorbonne would be destroyed (although it had not always been unworthy of its prestigious reputation); but the *Ecole polytechnique* would be created which would favour the development of French society during the later period. Decadence and innovation went hand in hand. . . .

In principle, the Choiseulian state sought to stimulate (the navy, the *grandes écoles* . . .) and to liberate (the grain trade, the economy in general . . .). Of course, the daily reality of the country, which retained in so many ways its routines, refused to conform in every respect to the good intentions of the régime. The latter was able to engineer substantive results, however, in the malleable sector of the colonies, a sector which was closely related to naval matters (both remained the responsibility of the secretary of state for the navy, a post which was firmly controlled by the Choiseul clan). In strategic terms, the state during the 1760s bid farewell to its hopes for a continental-based colonization; but it pinned its hopes more than ever on the broader ocean horizons and sought to give priority to exploiting the islands which it possessed (Bourbon, *Ile de France*, and, above all Santo Domingo, which was incomparably the black jewel in the crown of France's colonial trades, whose overall dynamism was increasing). The islands were precious as sources of tropical produce and, at sea-level, as supply ports for the navy. Elsewhere, a certain degree of action remained possible at the transoceanic and continental level on the coastal margins, despite the disappointing outcome of the Treaty of Paris. Thus the western seaboard of Africa in the latitudes of the Gambia and Goré remained accessible to French enterprise, essentially geared towards the export of slaves. A blind eye has to be cast over the catastrophe of the authoritarian and failed colonization of Guyana in South America. In general, the maritime and colonial policy of the Choiseulians after the Treaty of Paris witnessed some successes since it simply relied on the remarkable spontaneous growth in French external trade (particularly its tropical trades), a growth which reached its highest levels between 1763 and 1778.

This considerable progress was accompanied by the second component of Choiseulism, namely a movement towards liberalization in common with the period as a whole. The Company of the Indies, having accomplished its historic mission, saw its trading privileges suspended[13] by a decision in Council of August 1769. The king's subjects were henceforth, in principle, free to trade beyond the Cape of Good Hope. This govermental decision mirrored the wishes of Choiseul himself. The ground-work for it had been deeply laid by the action of various groups, including the clans of Marseille and St Malo business men, convinced free-traders. The privateer Jacques Montaudouin became the spokesman for the lobby hostile to the Company of the Indies in 1755. After that date, the economist Vincent de Gournay, the *abbé* Morellet, the physiocrat Dupont de Nemours all expressed themselves forcefully in a string of publications as opponents of any form of monopoly in the India trades. By a remarkable coincidence, economic trends in external commerce were working in their favour and they added their support to the port-lobbyists from Brittany and Provence. Their cause was assisted by the publications of specialists on the economy and Enlightenment writers. Then, in the end, emerged the regulatory edict promulgated in 1769 by the *Conseil d'en haut* which suspended the Company's privileges. It was almost as though Madame de Pompadour, who had been the protector of the physiocrats and who had died in 1764, continued to exercise her influence over events from beyond the grave and to inspire the liberal measures of her former lover Louis XV and her former protégé the duke de Choiseul. The *abbé* Terray undoubtedly sought to resurrect the Company of the Indies after 1770. But it was already a lost cause, just as unhappy as the future for the Company of Jesus. The process of liberalization in the leading sectors of the economy seemed irreversible, affecting *sponte sua* the patterns of individual conduct and conscience.[14]

The systematic strategy of picking off naval bases one by one on the main routes to the tropics in place of the continental conquests which had become too expensive perhaps explains the annexation of Corsica. Under the pretext of maintaining order there on behalf of the republic of Genoa, Corsica became attached to France as an established fact because of the debts owed by the Genoese to the French kingdom, debts which it was known *a priori* could never be reimbursed to the French royal Treasury. A debtor became a giver – Corsica was acquired by means of a diplomatic swindle! The death of Stanislas in 1766 also opened the door to the integration of Lorraine, a neophyte province which showed every sign of being more docile than, at the equivalent period, Brittany was proving to

[13]   Philippe Haudrière, *La Compagnie française des Indes au XVIIIe siècle* (4 vols, Librairie de l'Inde, 1989), vol. iv.
[14]   Ibid.

be, although the latter had been incorporated into the kingdom in the fifteenth and sixteenth centuries. But Duchess Anne of Brittany was still turning in her grave . . . .

In general, Choiseul's France retained a low profile. Henceforth, Versailles preferred to make sure of a possession close at hand (Lorraine) rather than reach out for a transatlantic colony (Louisiana) without really having the means to control it, or pretend to a zone of influence far from its frontiers. Hence the progressive weakening of the support for that old ally, the kingdom of Poland, since it was calculated that France could no longer prevent the Russians, nor for that matter the Prussians, both with advance guards close at hand, from tightening their omnipotent grip over the unfortunate country. The Choiseulians were adjusting to the fact that a decisive change in the balance of forces had taken place in central Europe with the rise to power of Russia and Prussia after Peter the Great and Frederick. Eastern Europe could no longer be seen as the exclusive reserve for the French. Here was one more reason to concentrate more clearly on France's own territorial integrity. At best, France could seek, as in billiards, to aim for an indirect shot. Louis XV's agents such as Vergennes, the ambassador in Constantinople, worked on France's Turkish ally to launch an attack from the rear against the Muscovites whose provocations furnished the Ottoman Turks with ample pretexts. This strategy of 'third party risk' cost France little but its results were either zero or unimpressive. In 1770, the ill-fated soldiers of the Sultan were roundly defeated by the Russian army. For the French government, the last word had been said. Yet, some years later, from 1778 to 1783, it would make use not of the Turks but, and at huge cost, the American insurgents against the British crown. The operation would end in a resounding success (with the British conceding defeat in 1783), but it was a success which would be translated a few years later into a financial cataclysm, since the government of Louis XVI had taken on debts up to the hilt to pay for the American war. The collapse of the Ancien Régime beckoned.

But we should not anticipate the story since, under Choiseul, prudence was the order of the day. In Sweden, the party of the Hats, anti-Muscovite and francophile, was pensioned by the Versailles government. The Hats had to give way in 1769 to the cabal of the Bonnets which, supported by the English and the Russians, sought to clip the wings of the Swedish monarchy in Stockholm. We should not, however, overstate the scale of this French 'defeat' in the north. Louis XV's influence amongst the Scandinavians (who were closer to France, in terms of the length of time of a voyage, than the Catholic Slav populations of Eastern Europe) remained sufficiently strong to contribute to the maintenance of Swedish independence, in contrast to that of Poland, ignominiously partitioned in 1772. At best, the agents of Louis took note of the build-up of Russian forces on the shores of the Baltic, compared to which France could only offer the Nordic powers a capacity for arbitrating their differences and a modest capacity to counter-balance the various powers.

So much for the north! To the east, the significance of the Austrian alliance should not be overestimated. Of course, it remained the ultimate and uttermost hope, the corner-stone of French foreign policy from 1756. But even if one takes into account the betrothal pact finally concluded in 1766 between Marie-Antoinette and the future Louis XVI (a marriage which would remain completely barren for several years thereafter) it should be noted carefully that the Austro-French alliance, as a general rule, brought with it few concrete benefits. It remained a platonic affair. Louis XV envisaged that this Viennese liaison would help to maintain the internal equilibrium of the German principalities, thus avoiding the total predominance of any one great state, Prussia, of course, but also Austria . . . .

To the south, France was linked by the family pact of August 1761 with the Spanish Bourbons and collaterally with Parma and Sicily. In principle, this Iberian connection was more essential to those in power; at all events, more vital than that with Austria. It was seen as a means of counter-balancing the British menace and even as a way by which revenge could eventually be meted out to the London government. At an ideological level it would be wrong to envisage the Franco-Spanish alliance against England between 1761 and 1770 as a reworked version of the Catholic coalitions of the past, particularly the alliance concluded by Louis XIV and his grand-son Philip V north and south of the Pyrenees in concert against the Protestant powers (England and the Dutch). Such a caricature of 'Reaction' against 'Progress' was already only half true for the period of the War of Spanish Succession and it would be wholly false for the Choiseulian years. The Bourbon king of Spain, Charles III, was, in reality, an enlightened despot, a philosopher king who hardly identified with any of the exaggerated devotions of a Philip V. As for Britain, it was not the incarnation of modern liberty which it had been in the past, a fact which would be highlighted in a more emblematic way during the revolt of the American colonies. Already in 1769, the count de Broglie, a good prophet of the future, had predicted that King George III would experience difficulties with the inhabitants of New England.[15] So the Bourbon family pact was not a holy alliance of despotism against constitutional monarchy. It should be added that it had nothing of the character of an offensive alliance either. After 1763, the France of Louis XV, although it was undertaking a degree of reasonable rearmament, still followed in the ways *de facto* of a certain pacifism which Fénelon would have approved of.

Choiseul provided the proof of this pacifism. In 1766, he acted as a calm mediator in a bitter Anglo-French conflict over the enormous monetary debts which Madrid was due to reimburse to the Treasury in London. Then, in a further episode, Choiseul calmed Spain's manifest irritation, ready to break off relations with the British for having suddenly occupied the minuscule archipelago of the Falkland Islands (the Malvinas). Four

---

[15]   Antoine, *Louis XV*, p. 885.

years later, in 1770, a new crisis erupted. This time it was Choiseul who seemed to have transformed into the 'hard-liner'. Did he feel strengthened by the recent rearmaments of France? At all events, this time, he was the war-monger. He incited Charles III of Spain and Grimaldi, the Spanish foreign secretary, to resist the British, with military force if necessary. The cause for Choiseul's robust attitude was, once more, the Falkland Islands, which Britain persisted in holding onto, despite the fact that the Spanish in Buenos Aires sought still more actively to reconquer them. This time it was the turn of Louis XV, acting more prudently than his minister, to salvage peace. In December 1770, His Majesty, who was adamant in opposing a war, eventually disgraced Choiseul and ordered him to retire to the country seat which he owned at Chanteloup in the Touraine. From 1763 to 1770, official French policy had demonstrated, by the successive, and sometimes contradictory, efforts of Choiseul (and then of Louis XV), its desire for non-belligerence. There was no question of the French kingdom letting itself become embroiled in anti-British conflict, even in the name of its Spanish alliance, however much that friendship counted for the Bourbon in Versailles.

In general, the Choiseulian period, including the final episode which ejected from power the man who gave his name to the period, was characterized by two tendencies. Firstly, there was a reinforcement of the national 'centre' by the renewal of France's military institutions. At the same time, moderation carried the day at the periphery. Alliances which were too far off (Poland, Turkey, even Sweden) were allowed to drop, or at least, weakened. Friendships closer to home (Austria, Spain) remained active but not to the point where peace would be imperilled in support of them. The foolish projects for an invasion of England, cultivated in the secret recesses of the king's entourage by the preposterous Chevalier d'Eon, were lampooned after 1768. As for future alliances with the English colonies in North America, they were, in effect, foreshadowed but not put into practice.

In sum, there was a truce on the home front with the régime's traditional opponents (the Jansenists and the *parlementaires*). Abroad, there was a pacifism with external powers, which did not exclude the maintenance of a well-armed vigilance. Finally, there was expansion and liberalism in the economy. In this outstanding and arduous decade is to be found one of those periods of triple expansion, certainly of relative relaxation, periods for which the Bourbon monarchy showed itself to be prodigal, whether it was a question of Henry IV and Sully, of Philippe d'Orléans, or of the Cardinal de Fleury. The Choiseulian period, had, of course, its own distinctive, or original, components, with its strong concentration on national (Gallican, or simply military) identity. But, to repeat, this process of concentration occured without its leading to over-extended external commitments which would risk the French government becoming involved where it did not want to to commit itself. Peace abroad remained the watch-word.

* * * * *

Relatively conciliatory on various fronts (diplomatic, Jansenist, *parlementaire*), Choiseulism, as a collective entity, tended to be reforming and liberal in respect of grain policy. Of course, such a policy was not conceived out of nothing. It was possible because it was based on a reality which had already been established for two generations, namely, the end of famine in France. To move on from this fact to unlock the controls over cereal traffic, since this new phase seemed suitable to contemplate such an audacious further step, would be difficult, but tempting, to undertake.

On the end of famine, to repeat, the recent work of demographic and economic historians leaves no doubt. In the eighteenth century, except in individual cases or particular regions with extraordinary problems, death no longer occurred physically from famine either in the countryside or the towns. During the periods of great grain shortage, beginning with that of 1709, increased misery increased *ipso facto* the risk of epidemics, which were the great killer. But the price of grain, however high, was not, of itself, the decimator of the population. The poorest in the community were often assisted quite effectively by royal and municipal authorities. They often unearthed bread rations (even though deficient from a dietary point of view) which enabled people to survive until the next typhoid attack which their weakened body resistance could not fight off. The *mercuriales*[16] declined in their significance but the problem of epidemic disease continued apace. This was already the case in 1709–10. At Angers and Bordeaux, during the two years in question, their populations were much afflicted by grain shortage but the (numerous) deaths came about as a result of dysentery and, again, typhoid. The 1740 crisis resulted from a cold year which created a grain shortage. But the most evident causes of death, strongly in evidence in Paris, Auch and Caen during these years, seem to have arisen from attacks of bronchial pneumonia which were exacerbated by the cold weather and the under-nourishment of the 'lower classes'.[17] The high death-rates, recorded above all in the hospitals and suburbs of Bordeaux, Auch and Montpellier in 1747, immediately preceded and closely mirrored the grain-crises which were recorded that year, but did not coincide with them.[18] It goes without saying that this consoling picture, according to which 'no one died of famine any more' under Louis XV ought not to encourage one to paint too rosy a picture of this reign as a whole. In fact, in the particular conditions of the Ancien Régime, where

---

[16]   *Mercuriale* – register where grain prices were inscribed and which, by extension, signified the degree of freedom of control of the market in grain and its repercussion, good or bad, on the lives of consumers.

[17]   M. Bricourt, M. Lachiver and J. Queruel, 'La Crise de subsistance des années 1740 dans le ressort du Parlement de Paris', *Annales de démographie historique* (1974), pp. 281–333.

[18]   Jean-Pierre Poussou, 'Les Crises démographiques en milieu urbain: l'exemple de Bordeaux (fin XVIIe-fin XVIIIe siècle)', *Annales ESC*, 35 (1980), 244.

the consumer society was but a dream for large numbers, the less famine killed, the more survived in poverty, at least amongst the most disadvantaged urban and suburban poor who were growing more numerous because of the relatively more favourable demographic circumstances. And we should not imagine that the bread-winner, or *gagne-denier*,[19] was automatically the more ecstatic to learn that, because grain was in less short supply, he would not die of starvation, unlike his great-grandfather, buried in the famine of 1661.

In any case, 'cyclical' grain shortage remained a phenomenon of primordial importance in eighteenth-century towns. Famine, however, was a terrible memory which stretched back to the previous century. As Steve Kaplan[20] has put it, in this respect 'the eighteenth century seems placid.' This was sufficiently true for the state to carry out an experiment with the liberalization of the grain trade in the 1760s (the 'Choiseulian' period). In some places it would assist, in others disrupt, the urban consumers. Up to around 1760, an explicit or implicit agreement, a *covenant*, linked the king and his good citizens. The latter would ensure a reasonable degree of social tranquillity and obedience in their towns so long as he saw to it, to the extent that it lay within his power, that food supplies, particularly grain, arrived without difficulty on their doorstep. These reciprocal responsibilities constituted what was called the *police urbaine*.

The latter was particularly hostile towards grain merchants, suspected of being 'monopolists'. In a period still dominated by ecclesiastical concepts, trade was held in almost the same degree of suspicion as fornication. It is readily conceivable how a complete freedom of commerce in grain would have been difficult to put into practice. Yet this liberty, little by little, began to see the light of day. The justifications for the control of the market, those which also underpinned the prohibition on the export of grain, were increasingly questioned. Why should peasants within a radius of ten leagues around Paris be required to sell their produce at the capital's markets? Why should they not be allowed to sell it in retail samples (*'sur échantillon'*) from farms and inns? These were the questions asked by, amongst others, the Normand Boisguilbert (under Louis XIV); and (under Louis XV) the *fermier général* Dupin, then the Bordelais Herbert.[21] The initial studies of Dupré de Saint-Maur, the Meuvret[22] of the Ancien Régime, on the general history of prices (1746) reinforced in advance such kinds of argument. His statistics tended to 'show' (with greater or lesser degrees of accuracy . . .) that the urban control over the grain trade tended

---

[19] A *gagne-denier* was 'the name (under the Ancien Régime) of someone who gains his living by manual (and law-paid) work without having a particular craft' (Littré, *op.cit.*) – and thus a manual labourer or *manouvrier* in an urban context.
[20] Steven Kaplan, *Le Complot de famine* (Paris, A. Colin, 1982); *Le Pain et le roi* (Paris, Perrin, 1986); *Les Ventres de Paris* (Paris, Fayard, 1988).
[21] Claude-Jacques Herbert, *Essai sur la police générale des grains* (London, 1753).
[22] Jean Meuvret was, until recently, one of the great historians of French prices – see, e.g., his *Etudes d'histoire économique* (Paris, A. Colin, Cahier des Annales, 1971).

to make prices rise, under cover[23] of making them lower! Other thinkers like Forbonnais and the agriculturalist Duhamel de Monceau, the direction of whose thought was, at the very least, quasi-liberal, took up the cudgels from the vacillating hands of Claude-Jacques Herbert. The school of thought, or sect, of Quesnay and the physiocrats transformed these early refrains into a more orchestrated demand, albeit not without countersquawks which would soon make themselves heard. The Parisian élite spread these liberal opinions. The provincial towns provided such views with an indispensable and substantial basis from which to operate, particularly the ports like St Malo, Vannes or Nantes, whose prosperity depended on the possibility of their being allowed to export grain. The free-trade lobby was equally given a hearing in that great entrepôt of grain in southwest France, Toulouse, which exported more than it consumed in this respect. In contrast, it was not so clear that the shortest road to absolute free-trade lay either through Paris or Rouen. These huge towns were situated close to the productive grain-growing regions whose great landed proprietors resided in their aristocratic districts. They had every interest in freeing the grain trade from its administrative tutelage. But they also accounted for tens of thousands or, in the case of Paris, hundreds of thousands of consumers. For them, the regulation of grain seemed like a vital necessity, without which neither their daily sustenance nor public order could be assured in future – or this, at least, was what Parisians sincerely and truly believed.

However, an initial edict of 1763, and above all the edict of July 1764, drafted by the *contrôleur général* L'Averdy, suppressed all impediments to the free trade in grain with the exception of the capital city and its immediate hinterland, allowing for the fact that, on the other hand, the import and export of grain from France itself still remained regulated. The English model (the British had been the great victors of the Seven Years War in 1763) had been decisive, just as similar profound frustration would impel the French élites to be inspired by the Prussian system after the defeat of 1870. The good harvests and the (relatively) low prices of the four years from 1760 to 1763 helped to make the decision viable. It was no longer conceivable, or an attempt had been made to forget, in 1764 that the lean years were over for good under the Ancien Régime and that there were only good years to come. Some old fogeys at the time expressed their scepticism at this. Joly de Fleury, the advocate general of the Parlement of Paris, let it be known that the lot of the urban poor, always vulnerable to the unfettered upward movement in wheat prices, had been ignored. . . . An urban jacobinism based on taxation was already forming in opposition to a girondism based on the liberalization of food-supplies and this became evident in Bordeaux, Toulouse, Aix and Grenoble amongst other places.

[23]   Nicolas-François Dupré de Saint-Maur, *Essai sur les monnaies, ou réflexions sur le rapport entre l'argent et les durées* (Paris, Coignard, 1746).

The urban population, for its part, reacted more stubbornly than the 'upper' classes and the intellectuals. It had initially been caught unawares by the suppression of the regulations guaranteeing, as it imagined, the arrival of its daily bread. In scores of towns and villages, numerous bread riots were sparked off between 1764 and 1777; the preceding years, by contrast (when the regulation of grain supplies was in force) had been fairly calm. Women carried sharpened knives and sounded the tocsin against the grain merchants. The authorities discovered with stupefaction that if a quarter of the population sold grain to the market (and profited from the liberty to do so where and when they wished), the remaining three quarters were consumers of grain, in the town and, still more, in the countryside. The 'police' (lesser urban magistrates etc.) were often accomplices in these popular uprisings against a freedom to trade which put them out of a job. Faced with this resistance, the authorities were astonished by it and uncomprehending of it. The *contrôleur général* L'Averdy did not want to made concessions on his *laissez faire* measures, so recently introduced and so poorly understood. But, on his own, he cut a poor figure as their only guarantee of success since, for his obduracy to be worth something, he would have required a strong state (which was contrary to liberalism) and a good surplus stock of grain. He could offer neither. At the end of September 1768, Louis XV and Choiseul dismissed the courageous L'Averdy, for grain prices had greatly increased from 1763 to 1768 and free-trade had done nothing to act as a brake on rising prices.

Anti-liberalism emerged at the beginning from amongst the urban masses and from the old regulatory régime. Thereafter it would find eminent intellectuals and quasi-economists to defend such a stance, amongst whom one finds Galiani, Necker and Sébastien Mercier. It now seemed scandalous that grain was traded and trafficked in all over the place, except at the old, traditional market-place at the town centre. The market-place was an institution as ancient and respectable as the cathedral and the town belfry. Once freedom to trade had been granted from 1763–4 onwards, the traffic in food-stuffs had spread everywhere, in small-town inns, in farm granaries, in abbeys, and along the way-sides and river-banks . . . the liberation in the grain trade stimulated the great agricultural potential of the rich labouring-farmers, who were swiftly dubbed exploiters by the poor city-dwellers. Royal authority, despite being often efficient in its ways of working, was feeble in questions of public relations. It had forgotten that France was made up *also* of 19 million consumers. Ugly rumours began to abound to exactly the same rhythm as that created by the furious and excited women who attacked the shops of bakers, categorized as starvers of the people. You would need, it was said, 'teeth of gold to eat bread this winter'.

Then again, liberalization had a positive impact, if not in social terms, at least at the strictly economic level. In scores of towns, a teeming world of petty grain merchants grew up, profiting from the new *laissez faire* conditions in the course of the 1760s. They were former barbers, farmers, foreigners or obscure nobodies. One might have imagined oneself back in the far-off days of John Law when businesses rose up like mushrooms; but the ultra-mobile sack of grain had replaced the old banknotes of the Scot. Social ascension certainly had its day in the 1760s. Almost a fifth of the new grain merchants were illiterate, a sure sign that they had come from amongst the 'lower' orders. In general, they were not 'capitalists'. Only a very small minority of them had partners or formed 'companies'. The overwhelming majority of the neo-traders were salesmen who traded in grain around the inns where this retail trade had formerly been forbidden, alongside prostitution. But, in truth, French economic growth[24] in the eighteenth century was made in large measure by small tradesmen, much more than by the activities of authentic capitalism. They were to be found crawling all around Meaux, for example, the queen of the grain trade, in 1770. . . .

Free-trade in grain was suppressed by Terray in 1770. The harvests were decidedly too low and the panic psychology of the urban masses defeated the ambitions of the physiocrats.[25] It would have to await the arrival of Russian and American wheat, and even tractors and fertilizers, to make the spectre of grain-shortage disappear. The spectre would consistently return with each major war. The decades of the 1760s and 1770s nevertheless provided the conditions for implementing various remarkable socio-economic innovations. Mills were modernized. A royal grain-store was created under the auspices of erstwhile financiers who had left the ranks, such as Malisset and Domerc. An able and manipulative individual, the paranoid Le Prévost de Beaumont, exploited all this to launch against the minister and the king the accusation of a *famine pact* (consisting, he said, of lucrative speculative dabbling through official purchases of grain stocks). The accusation against Louis XV was as empty as the *Protocols of the Elders of Zion* for the Jewish communities but, sadly, as effective in certain quarters. It was one of the important pretexts for the destabilization of the monarchical system in the last third of the century. Le Prévost de Beaumont found himself in prison and was only released during the revolutionary years, during which time he returned once more to his dangerous silly talk.

The liberalization of grain prices (1764) had been premature. Grain, a respected prisoner, was not yet in a position to be given its freedom. But

[24]   Denis Richet, 'Croissance et blocages en France du XVIe au XVIIIe siècle', *Annales ESC*, 23 (1968), 759–87.
[25]   This chronology closely corresponds with that proposed elsewhere by Louis Dumont: 'Le mouvement physiocratique, selon Weulersse, a son origine autour de 1756 et sa fin en 1770 . . . Après un engouement passager et une dizaine d'années d'influence notable dans les sphères gouvernementales, la partie est perdue et le mouvement se disperse en 1770. Le trop bref passage de Turgot au contrôle générale des Finances (1774–6) n'est qu'un épilogue tardif' – Louis Dumont, *Homo hierarchicus* (Paris, Gallimard, 1977), p. 58. To this it should be added, of course, that the pre-French Revolution of Calonne and after would itself also have recourse to physiocratic and liberal notions as the inspiration for its measures.

the experiment had, nevertheless, indicated some things clearly. The seventeenth century had truly seen the end of the real famines (1661, 1694, then 1709) which had assailed the French population. If two alternatives henceforth presented themselves as conceivable (a partial free-trade in food-supplies after 1764; then a return to 'policing' grain supplies and an authoritarian suppression of this liberty after 1770), then this was because the margin for manoeuvre had become greater. But the towns still did not have sufficient grain to dispense with grain-trade regulation altogether. They were, however, already sufficiently provided to be out of the shadow of killer-famines and to experiment over a number of years with new and more liberal regulations as opposed to the good old policing framework which had been inherited from more difficult times.

⋆　⋆　⋆　⋆　⋆

The period of political reaction which followed the attempted assassination by Damiens was thus marked out by concessions to more 'enlightened' opinions, particularly of the economists but also of the Jansenist magistrates (and others). These concessions were manifest, in particular, in the suppression of the Jesuits and the liberalization of the grain trade. For a decade or more, France lived under a monarchy which was still vaguely absolute, and which was held in check by certain philosophe constraints. 'A monarchy tempered by the philosophes' was how Goncourt would put it. In general, and in contrast to the period pre-1757 which had been demonstrably more authoritarian, a degree of openness was exercised towards the *noblesse de robe* and its élite sitting in the Parlement in Paris. In 1758, Louis XV gave them satisfaction on matters relating to the *Hôpital général* in the capital, and on the rights to summon the peerage of France which they claimed to have. The king also resisted the temptation to have his illegitimate offspring legitimized by the Parlement, a move which, in truth, he had never taken very seriously. He did not imitate his predecessors who made legitimized princes of their bastard sons. Under Henry IV, this 'legitimating' move had not provoked much surprise but in the more moralistic period of Louis XIV's reign, the vivid manfistations of the sexual 'excursions' of the king, whether in the form of the duke du Maine, the count de Toulouse or the rest, scandalized the Parlement and public opinion more generally. Such would have been *a fortiori* true of Louis XV's reign; but he resorted to a degree of dissimulation by way of precaution, something which was necessary because of the increasing prudery (more in theory than in practice) of his contemporaries and the internal conflicts which his Christian conscience provoked in him.

When it came to the royal prerogative (which no doubt existed at this time), there was still much which could be done. By a series of conciliatory gestures, calculated withdrawals, small gestures, the king and his ministers sought to conciliate the sovereign courts. These included the 13 regional parlements (amongst which stood the Parlement of Paris, which covered a good third of the kingdom), the four *Cours des aides* which dealt with appeals from tax-assessments, and the 12 *Chambres des comptes*. All of them, but the parlements in particular, acted as courts of law and of appeal, with 'rights of registration and remonstrance, and responsibilities in respect of overall police matters, rituals, corporations, poor-relief, food-supplies, transport, taxes and education'![26] The office-holders in these corporate bodies were often cantankerous and disputatious. These 1,200 *parlementaires* and over a thousand other office-holders in the other sovereign courts were the object of royal attention and overture. These sovereign courts were imbued with a sense of 'magisterial' representation (for want of any better)[27] of society in general in contrast to the august solitude (in theory, at least) of Louis' powers. At all events, these bodies provided the best guarantees of what was wanted, namely, a limited monarchy, which (by virtue of their existence) found itself unable to sustain its often rather exaggerated pretensions to absolutism. Since power is constrained *by* authority, the sovereign courts made possible, at the very least, a 'bridled absolutism', limited by powerful juridical constraints. The remonstrances of the sovereign courts, once they were published and broadcast, refuted by the fact that they were distributed the complaints of despotism heaped in steady streams by the courts at the door of monarchical power. The latter possessed no really effective means of censorship which could prevent the spread of such remonstrances by the written and printed word amongst the literate laity of the provinces. Thanks to the corporations of senior office-holders, Louis XV (who might have otherwise passed for a candidate for the accolade) did not come across as a tyrant. French monarchy can thus be defined 'as legalist, and as receptive of the pacific expression (via the *parlementaires*) of the discontent of its subjects'.[28]

The indubitable support for the Parlement from the bourgeois and popular elements, at least of the towns, made the sovereign court into a 'means of ensuring confidence' and even, paradoxically, a legitimizing mechanism for the monarchy, a mechanism which, on some occasions, had been (the Fronde) or would be (the pre-Revolution of 1787) destabilizing for royal power.

The magistrates of the parlements thus functioned sometimes in harmony with, and sometimes in opposition to, the royal Council. The latter exercised, in reality, certain judicial functions as the collective embodiment of the sovereign will. This made the royal Council a competitive body to the professional judges and a source of irritation to them. Besides, there was no lack of occasions for antagonism such as the *vingtième* tax (1749) or the *billets de confession* affair (1752) to develop between monarch and sovereign courts from around 1750 onwards. Such conflicts generated insuperable obstacles and chains of vicious circles. Even though it was

---

[26] François Lebrun, *Le XVIIe siècle* (Paris, A. Colin, 1988).

[27] Christian Jouhaud in *Le Monde* (9 February 1990).

[28] William Doyle, *The Oxford History of the French Revolution* (Oxford, Clarendon Press, 1989), p. 39.

mitigated by a degree of flexibility in the Choiseulian exercise of power, the debate between king and Parlement rested on a tangled knot of contradictions. For their part, the magistrates were fairly representative of popular opinion but they defended their corporate and noble privileges in an egoistical fashion, particularly in fiscal matters. By contrast, royal authority was often enlightened; but however popular it became at certain periods, it could not pretend, as such, to 'represent' 20 to 25 million individuals. Hence there was, simultaneously, a *parlementaire* obstacle to the path of progress on the one hand and, on the other, a monarchy deficient in its ability to represent its subjects.

Overarching the Jansenist debates, fiscal discontent served to provide a real pretext, and a sincere motive, to the militant attitudes of the red robes in the sovereign courts. The state had to ensure that the wartime expenditure incurred during the Seven Years War was recouped and the arrears created by the conflict sorted out. In 1759, the *contrôleur général* Silhouette, who came from a family of administrators and financial specialists, entered the government. He had about him an aura of competence and he proposed an edict creating a 'general subvention' (*subvention générale*) by means of an increase in, or continuance of, direct and indirect taxes. Some of these taxes, such as those on servants and on luxury horses, affected the privileged order; but the majority of the proposal was burdensome to the broad mass of tax-payers. The *Cour des aides* published well-judged remonstrances against the Silhouette proposal. A looming bankruptcy brought the minister down in November 1759 and, in a way unthinkable under the immovable Colbert, *contrôleurs généraux* came and went in torrents as they became more often sacrificed on the altar of public opinion.

Exit Silhouette. Enter Bertin! The latter became *contrôleur général* from 1759 to 1763. The demands of war, even a war which could not be won, had not changed. Of course, Bertin abandoned the term 'general subvention' used by his predecessor. But he proposed almost the same kinds of tax increases, both direct and indirect, notably a supplementary *vingtième*, and a shilling in the pound (*sol pour livre*) on the general tax-farm, which Silhouette had tried to introduce, albeit in vain. The new *contrôleur général* also wanted to introduce a cadastral-based tax, after the fashion of the *taille réelle* in Languedoc, which would tax the privileged. It was easy to foresee that this would certainly create discontent. The parlements of Besançon, Grenoble, Toulouse, Bordeaux, Rouen, not to mention Paris, treated the king's representatives, military governors, commanders of their various provinces, as 'targets' for their discontent in a distasteful way. This was what happened to, amongst others, Bourgeois de Boynes at Besançon, Du Mesnil in Dauphiné, Fitz-James in Toulouse, Harcourt in Rouen and the intendants Tourny in the Gironde and Etigny at Pau.

The well-judged concessions of Choiseul, always the diplomat, in 1761, and particularly in 1763, defused the conflict. But there was a price to pay. The state ingloriously sacrificed Bourgeois de Boynes and Tourny who had been its loyal and devoted servants. Unhappily for them, however, during this first phase, they had shown a degree of zeal in standing up to the magistrates in comparison to the eventual moderation of Choiseul himself. Being placed in the firing line, they found themselves still more vulnerable *a posteriori*. In 1763 it was Bertin's turn to be relieved of the post of *contrôleur général*. Leaving by the front door, he returned by the back, however, since he was given a consolation prize by his personal friend, Louis XV – that of a fifth and newly created secretaryship of state, made to measure for him, and given responsibility for economic matters. The post even became known as 'the secretaryship of M. Bertin'! L'Averdy was made *contrôleur général*, a carefully chosen Jansenist and *parlementaire*. Here was nothing less than an Augustinian in charge of affairs! Louis XIV, from beyond the grave, would not have approved. . . . This fact alone speaks volumes for the liberal and innovative direction of Choiseulian politics. It was an appeasing gesture towards the magistrature, whose outer flank was still influenced by the successors of Port-Royal.

In addition, there was another source for appeasing conflict in the end of the war. The increase in taxation and the creation of a cadastral-based tax could be abandoned. The annual state expenditure reached 1,800 tonnes in silver-equivalent by 1763, falling back after the peace to 1,500 tonnes. It would fall again to 1,200 tonnes by 1770–5. As for the net revenues coming in to the state, they followed a contrary, and upward, trajectory. They stood at 700 tonnes during the Seven Years War, and increased to almost 800 tonnes when the relative prosperity of the peace-time period had been consolidated in around 1770–5. Despite the budgetary deficit which remained and which continued to increase the debt, the two accounts, revenue and expenditure, otherwise known as the 'scissors', were tending to converge. As a result, the urgency provoked by the fiscal problem was less pressing under the auspices of L'Averdy, and during peacetime, than it had been in Bertin's period and in wartime. Besides, the magistrates were not entirely mindless of the gestures on their behalf by the duke de Choiseul in January 1764. Du Mesnil and Fitz-James, the military commanders at Grenoble and Toulouse respectively, were recalled to Versailles in semi-disgrace.

The *Grand Conseil*, the *bête noire* of the parlements, decided on its own dissolution in April 1765. The humiliation of the Company of Jesus had given a good deal of pleasure to the majority of the *parlementaires*, or at least the most hard-line amongst them. Free-trade in grain (which did not go down well in Rouen and Paris) was remarkably popular elsewhere amongst the provincial magistrature, many of whom were landed proprietors and whose hearts lay in the good prices the grain produced by their own farmers would fetch. In general terms, and except for Brittany which remained in a state of perpetual agitation, *robe* discontents were disarmed and kept within limits which the régime could regard as tolerable. The conciliatory tone adopted by Choiseul had borne fruit. The intendants and Parisian commissioners even succeeded in 1765 in mastering the parlement at Pau which had taken it into its head to resist a disciplinary ruling which it had itself registered 17 years previously! At most, and in the realm of principle, the remarkable formulae adopted by the Parlement of Rouen should be noted. They were far-reaching, stretching forward to a future which no longer seemed quite so far off. The sovereign court of Normandy in effect proposed already the idea of a contract between ruling king and obedient people. The idea (even taking into account the respectful terms in which it was drafted) blew a hole in the concept of a divinely ordained absolutism. In a more concrete fashion, the Rouen parlement also sought in 1760 the reinstatement of the estates of Normandy, which had been abandoned in the seventeenth century under the rod of the cardinal-ministers. A desire for a return to the more temperate monarchy of pre-Richelieu days was thus expressed on the banks of the lower Seine. It was a desire which would run through from Choiseul to Loménie de Brienne. The Normandy judges also proposed in 1760 the device *Un Roi, une loi, un Parlement*. It was a triad which, in the long term, perpetuated other formulae of a similar kind: see table 10.1.

The vertical axis of column C in table 10.1 (faith – country – parlement) is, nonetheless, of interest. It gives *ipso facto* the national and quasi-religious component to the union of the judicial power, or *parlementaire*, 'classes'.

Despite these conceptual leaps, *parlementaire* agitation in the Choiseulian decade, would have left few lasting memories had it not been for the Breton affair. The latter was, as we would say now, 'inevitable'. Firstly, Brittany was not fully integrated into the central sovereign institutions and it thus was different from the Touraine, or even from Normandy. The synthesis between the two regional institutions, the provincial assembly of the estates and the Parlement of Rennes, of the province allowed

Table 10.1 Patterns of politico-religious unity

A	B	C	Source
one sole seigneur	one sole baptism	one sole faith	St Paul (Ephesians)
one king	one law	one faith	Guillaume Postel and the Catholic party at the beginning of the wars of religion[a]
one king	one state law	one country	Jean de Serres; a moderate Protestant in 1597
one king	one law	one parlement	The Parlement of Rouen in 1760[b]

[a] The references for this and the following line of the table are to be found in E. Le Roy Ladurie, *The Royal French State, 1460–1610* (Oxford, Blackwell, 1994), p. 285.
[b] M. Antoine, *Louis XV* (Paris, Fayard, 1989), p. 758.

them both to resist royal legislation all along the line. In Paris, by contrast, the *parlementaires* found opposition much more difficult than their colleagues in the Breton peninsula. They had no image of an institution directly representative of the people, or simply of the regional élites, *a fortiori* the nation, such as existed elsewhere in the provincial estates.

In addition, personal factors played a certain part in the Breton capital. Louis-René de Cardec de la Chalotais, the *procureur général* of the Parlement of Rennes, acted by virtue of his 'procuration' as the king's agent, or at least in theory. In reality, La Chalotais was an intellectual, which had both positive and negative consequences. A man of the Enlightenment, he published works on education (in which he expressed rather 'retrograde' ideas) and wrote works on the grain trade (which evoked a liberal response from him) and on the Jesuits, an order which he bitterly detested. Having becoming a systematic opponent of the régime, and particularly of the duke d'Aiguillon, the military commander of the province, the *procureur* at Rennes was both a writer and a politician. He had no scruples in contemplating blackmail against Louis XV himself, if he could, to make his own views prevail. In the end it was he himself who would be submerged. It is not with impunity that one meddles with the background notions contained in a secret and sensational set of documents such as the private correspondence between a sovereign king and one of his current mistresses, Anne Couppier, called Mlle de Romans.

In many respects, La Chalotais reminds one of another *arriviste*, who would also end up in prison, i.e. John Wilkes, the ferocious and poisonous adversary of George III. But Wilkes utilized English nationalism, the modernity of the House of Commons and the freedom of the press to achieve his ends. Taking all into account and despite the many scrapes, including imprisonment, which Wilkes found himself in, he had all the advantages in comparison with La Chalotais who was, by contrast, although the darling of the Parisian *salons* from time to time, only a provincial politician, reduced to make do with the rather archaic institution of the Parlement of Rennes to oppose the king. Is it right, therefore, in these circumstances to compare this Breton agitator of a preceding generation with Mirabeau? La Chalotais found himself placed at a paradoxical moment when the juridical élite, Jansenism and the Enlightenment conjoined, an individual with his own integrity, forging his own role, true or false, as an 'honest and virtuous magistrate, the champion of Breton liberties'. Mirabeau, on the other hand, was the typical classless paragon of the Bohemian intelligentsia who would carve out for himself an importance, a preeminence even, in the coming of the Revolution.

The polemics concerning the life and activities of La Chalotais rolled on through 1764 and 1765 and around the opposition which the parlement at Rennes put up against the fiscal measures which had been announced by Bertin and which had been continued with a minimum of alterations by L'Averdy. Louis XV found it difficult to put up with the Breton sovereign court's determination and its *procureur* (who soon found himself in prison).

The king found himself still more irritated by the solidarity which was shown by the other 'classes' of magistrate in the realm and in favour of their colleagues at Rennes.

The king's patience was pushed to the limit and Louis XV, assisted by the *conseiller d'état* Gilbert de Voisins and several other members of the *robe* in Council, drew up and then delivered before the assembled Parlement of Paris on 3 March 1766 the speech known as the Flagellation (from the name of the feast-day). The speech acted as a premonition for the Maupeou *coup de majesté* of five years later and demonstrated that a 'hard core' of royalist theory had not been tamed even though its practical expression changed from time to time. Absolutism was reaffirmed: 'The magistrature does not constitute a corporation or an order separate from the three orders of the realm. It is my person alone wherein resides the sovereign power whose very character is the spirit of counsel, justice and reason.' Elsewhere, in a letter to Charles III, King of Spain, Louis spoke of 'this sovereign power which wc hold from God alone'. Unswerving on the principles, the king remained flexible when it came to judging, in the same year as the Flagellation declaration, an individual case, a provincial and, in the end, a rather marginal matter. In December 1766, Louis simply dropped all the proceedings against La Chalotais. It was a far cry from the violent proceedings (decapitation, etc.) which had been used by Richelieu, if not Louis XIV (the latter would certainly have despatched La Chalotais to the 'simple' punishment of perpetual imprisonment in a fortress). But the former accused *procureur* of 1765 fared better; he found his name *de facto* cleared by royal initiative, and he discreetly left the Bastille in December 1706. In due course, La Chalotais would be relegated, albeit without suffering further affront, to the town of Saintes. He would remain there until the end of the reign, awaiting the day when Louis XVI, once on the throne, would restore him to his post as *procureur* in the Parlement of Rennes in 1775.

In Brittany, one affair followed another. After La Chalotais, and in consequence of the affair, it was the turn of d'Aiguillon to experience a notoriety which the duke in question would find extremely irksome. The Duke Emmanuel d'Aiguillon, a relative of the Richelieu and Phélypeaux families, was commander in chief of the province of Brittany. A competent administrator and a courageous soldier, he had driven the English into the sea after their landing in the bay at Saint-Cast in 1758. He was responsible for the construction of many roads in Brittany, with much benefit to its commerce. But these roads irritated the local people and the magistrates because of the *corvées* which were indispensable to the completion of the work, *corvées* which were identified with despotism by those who formed public opinion. As a result of the La Chalotais affair, the commanding duke d'Aiguillon faced the concerted obstruction (for antifiscal and other reasons too) from the estates, the *parlementaires* and even from his own Breton supporters and he resigned from his post in August 1768. It seems to have been the case that Choiseul, always ready to run with the hare and

hunt with the hounds and in cahoots with the *parlementaires*, offered
d'Aiguillon only modest support during the Breton crises which led to his
retirement. Choiseul had perhaps even cut the ground from underneath
his feet. The duke de Duras who succeeded his colleague in command in
Brittany proved himself, Choiseul and Louis XV having helped him to do
so with concessions, much more favourable to the local *parlementaires*. The
latter found themselves re-established in their rights and functions in July
1769. This was, after several years, the end of a Breton revolt, but there
would be a second phase of it in 1788 which, from the point of view of the
excited crowds of Rennes, would be much more successful. Meantime, the
magistrates of Rennes accused d'Aiguillon of having implicated La
Chalotais in fabricating false accusations against him. The duke had even,
apparently, attempted to poison the poor *procureur général* in his own gaol!
For his part, the former commander in chief of the province sought to
answer the accusations which had been levelled against him. His trial,
which he himself had actively solicited, was heard before the Parlement of
Paris in the spring of 1770. Once again, Louis XV adopted a solution of
mediating prudence and wisdom. No fuss; a low profile! At the end of a *lit
de justice* in June 1770 he declared the case brought against d'Aiguillon null
and void and reqired the various interested parties to agree to remain
absolutely silent on the whole affair. It was a delaying and conciliatory
tactic. D'Aiguillon did not end up a hero and the affair which looked set
in other respects to become a camouflage for the *parlementaires*, entirely
hostile to the former commander-duke, was brought to an end. Methods
which played for time succeeded well in the old king's hands. His successor could have done with learning the same lesson during the scandalous
affair of the collar which poor Louis XVI found incapable of sweeping
under the carpet.

In the end, though, Louis XV would not have the final word. A complete change in the government's attitude to the *parlementaires* was just
round the corner. Active complicity (of a Choiseulian kind) or gentle
playing for time (allowed up to 1770) would no longer be allowed. The
time for repression, pure and simple, would soon arise. 1771 would see
the *coup de majesté* dreamt of by Maupeou. But he would first have to see
to the removal of Choiseul. This 'tight-rope walker' in the eyes of the king
would soon be regarded as a 'humbug' (as Michel Antoine called him) or
simply as a master of illusions.

11

Order, Authority, Realm

Choiseul and his cousin were dismissed from the government under pressure from the king in December 1770. Louis held the pair to account for their bellicosity during the Falkland Islands (the *Malvinas* in the South Atlantic) affair. Perhaps Choiseul thought that, having not so far played the military adventurist, it was time to show that he was indispensable by the rattle of sabres. Whatever his motives, the fact is that, by pretending to commit France to war in 1770, the French minister nudged Spain into a military and naval conflict with the English which was aimed to help Charles III retain the Falkland Islands, then being hotly disputed between the London and Madrid governments. But for his part, Louis XV remained a pacifist, his Fénelonian tendencies once more in evidence. He let himself also be guided by an objective view of the European situation. In his attitudes to the British government, the French king had lost, if he had ever had it, the swaggering attitude of a Napoleon III towards Bismarck. He knew that France was still ill-equipped to wage a successful war, despite Choiseul's reform of the army and navy. Choiseul was dismissed in the first place because he was accused of becoming too adventurist in his foreign policy.

That said, there were deeper explanations for the dismissal of Choiseul which went beyond these superficial explanations. It was the internal situation which fundamentally determined Louis XV's action and here the circumstances were reversed. The minister-duke who had become too audacious in diplomatic affairs was presented at home, by contrast, as a moderate within the kingdom, in every way a mediator towards the parlements, the opposition and public opinion.

But over several years, the innermost recesses of Louis XV's attitudes had *hardened* towards the opposition. He was a good Catholic and he disliked their anti-Jesuitism. He did not accept the compliance of Choiseul and his team towards the parlements. Over the preceeding 12 or 13 years, there had been attempts to find a compromise with the *parlementaires* and obtain their reluctant consent to measures of fairly heavy taxation in order to secure its acceptance in the country at large. This compromise had been

Choiseul's master-stroke. But after seven years of peace, the financial situation had much improved. The budgetary deficit, as the graphs of Alain Guéry demonstrate,[1] was clearly reduced. Expenditure was decreasing and receipts were up. The somewhat surly political neutrality of the magistrates as fashioners or interpreters of public opinion was no longer something that royal authority was prepared to purchase at any price. To restore order to royal finances could now be obtained by by-passing the permission of the *parlementaires*; for the realm was much more robust and prosperity, despite the serious problems of food-supplies, had greatly increased.

After a long period of rising bread prices of some 35 years on the basis of a vigorous growth 'cycle', these prices reached a dangerous maximum in 1770, during precisely the same year which saw the downfall of Choiseul materialize. These high prices favoured the large producers of cereal crops but they sowed the seeds of grain riots on the streets. In these conditions, the politics of grain-trade liberalism such as had been carried forward by Bertin and, above all, L'Averdy, appeared to many as entirely inappropriate. This was one more reason for the king to be discontented with some of his ministers.

Finally, a certain reordering of the factions had taken place at Versailles since the death in 1764 of la Pompadour, Choiseul's protector. The *dévot* cabal (which defended traditional religion and which supported royal authority against the parlements) had become more entrenched in its position. It included the duke d'Aiguillon, the *maréchal* de Richelieu, an old friend of the king's, the *abbé* de Ville (the first secretary in foreign affairs), Terray, the *contrôleur général* after 1769, and Maupeou, the chancellor after 1768. Under the wings of la Du Barry, the official royal mistress after 1768, the pious cabal coalesced and it lacked neither motives nor candidates prepared to unseat him.

So, towards the close of 1770, the minister fell from power. It was in vain that he developed a vast campaign of satirical pornography against la Du Barry (whom he detested). That campaign failed but the idea would have a promising future when, a few years later, the target changed and Marie-Antoinette took the place of la Du Barry, i.e. when Louis XV's mistress was replaced by the young and vulnerable wife of his successor. It was this successor whose hold on power Louis XV sought now, from 1771 onwards, to consolidate. The elderly Louis XV became preoccupied henceforth with his grandson, the future Louis XVI. He was still young and inexperienced and Louis XV wanted to leave him a state whose administrative components would no longer be repeatedly challenged by the sovereign courts. This constituted one more reason at the end of the reign for the 'triumvirate' coup.

---

[1] Alain Guéry, 'Les Finances de la monarchie française sous l'Ancien Régime', *Annales* ESC (1978).

The years of openness, albeit discreet ones, were thus at an end and the crown once more set itself on a more 'robust' course. This was indicated after 1771 with the suppression, or at least the *diminutio capitis*, of the parlements. However archaic the latter were, they provided, for want of something better, a 'channel' of communication by which the public could influence the government and, moreover, there was no other way by which the élite of the sovereign court judges could influence the process of decision-making 'from on high'. The moment when Louis XV bid farewell to the parlements, even if only temporarily (for Louis XVI would re-establish them in 1775), is a good opportunity to survey briefly the machinery and means of expression of political authority in France as the time of the Maupeou initiatives.

In around 1770–1, the *Conseil d'en haut* was made up of 'ministers of state' and it had become the instrument *par excellence* for monarchical dominance. It had benefited from the chink of light, socially speaking, which had been let in by the slightly more relaxed 15 'Choiseulian' years. Senior ecclesiastics and also court aristocrats (Bernis, Choiseul, Praslin, Belle-Isle, and soon, d'Aiguillon and Monteynard . . .) were given access to positions as ministers of state which Louis XIV would have refused to their forebears. They rubbed shoulders with the traditional *robins* who were as assiduous in their presence as always. In the first ranks of the list of ministers the chancellor recovered, under Louis XV, his prestige and even his authority. Colbert had banished the chancellor from the *Conseils d'en haut* and thus advanced the Finance-State at the expense of the Justice-State. But the chancellor, as head of the judicature, would recover his primacy under Louis XV as a result of the *parlementaire* disputes. What is more, thanks to the talents of the two individuals who served as chancellor, they exercised considerable power. D'Aguesseau, the legislator *par excellence*, was the 'Solon' of the Ancien Régime's last century. Maupeou, in 1771, forced a 'coup' which profoundly shaped the end of the reign. He was not, however, a Bonaparte; or at least, not exactly. . . .

The *contrôleur général des finances* retained a good deal of the administrative responsibility which his predecessors had acquired and then shamelessly exercised under Louis XIV between 1661 and 1715. The instability which undoubtedly affected the office after Machault, as a result of the increased instability of public opinion, decreased the respect in which it was held. But the *abbé* Terray, who held the post from 1769 to 1774, lent a certain prestige to the *contrôle*. Besides, the latter was given new freedom of manoeuvre thanks to the, by then traditional, presence of five or six *intendants des finances* at his side: Trudaine at the *Ponts et Chaussées*, d'Ormesson at the revenue, etc. Indefatigable, competent and well-informed, they owned their offices, benefiting from a longevity much greater than their patrons would enjoy; for the latter, Bertin, L'Averdy and Maynon d'Invault, only exercised authority on the basis of a simple revocable commission. Such longevity would be the envy of the current under-secretaries of state, the successors to the former *intendants des finances*. The intendants of finance remind one more of the immovable *directeurs des grandes services* in the ministry of finances under the Third Republic. Above all, however, the *contrôle*, seen as an overall entity (including the *intendants des finances*), remained in charge of a considerable fraction of the instruments of state despite the personal vicissitudes of the holders of the office of *contrôleur général*. They were responsible for almost half the expenditure of the senior government bureaucracy in Paris and Versailles (597,813 *livres* for 'finance' as compared with 617,000 *livres* for the secretaries of state and the chancellery). The *contrôle* equally employed[2] almost 50 per cent of the staff in the senior échelons of the bureaucracy which accounted for overall about 500 employees. This is a figure which indicates, by the way, the efficiency of these personnel, both financial and otherwise, in comparison with the enormous numbers salaried staff of all kinds to be found in the Parisian ministries of our own day.

Taking everything into account, and particularly the preponderant place of the financial structure within the government overall, the position of justice, and particularly the chancellery, was somewhat paradoxical. The chancellor, however vigorous the personality of a d'Aguesseau or a Maupeou, remained, after Colbert, excluded from the *Conseil d'en haut*. By contrast, he remained *ex officio* a member of the *Conseil des dépêches* which recovered, or increased, its importance under Louis XV after its eclipse under Louis XIV. This second Council was responsible for internal matters (parlements, book-sellers and even the colonies) whilst the *Conseil d'en haut* specialized in external affairs, in other words, diplomacy and war.

The increasing power of the *Conseil des dépêches* reveals one of the distinctive characteristics of Louis XV's reign, during which matters of opposition at home (*parlementaires*) increasingly eclipsed matters of war and peace, hitherto fundamental. The *Bien-Aimé* divided his time between these two supreme Councils, the *Conseil d'en haut* which looked (but with an increasingly uncertain eye) towards adventures abroad; and the *Conseil des dépêches* which was more introspective, dealing with internal matters, although coupled with colonial affairs. It was as though the Council of ministers or Cabinet of a modern government was divided in two like a roundabout in two semi-circles, one of which was responsible for national defence and foreign policy, and the other for justice, internal affairs, the economy and the *Dom-Tom*,[3] etc. This government division was not entirely illogical but it would not find favour with posterity, which would be increasingly concerned with internal affairs and which would thus see the reintegration of a Council of ministers as a whole as logical and natural. The Council would thus become concerned with problems which were

---

[2]   Michel Antoine, *Le Conseil du Roi sous le règne de Louis XV* (Geneva, Droz, 1970), p. 317.

[3]   'Dom-Tom'; i.e. the overseas dominions of France according to the common parlance of the French government in 1990.

more specifically French rather than those of France in Europe and in the world. This reintegration had been long foreshadowed. Already in Louis XV's time, there was a committee of ministers which brought together informally the members of the two Councils (*d'en haut* and *des dépêches*) in order to prepare or harmonize their respective decisions on internal and external affairs. The principal figures involved from both Councils brought together about half a dozen individuals. They included the chancellor and the *contrôleur général des finances* as a matter of course; also involved were the four secretaries of state (which became five with the accession of Bertin[4] to the post in December 1763). These ministers were supported by additional permanent secretariats and larger office-staffs. It was one way of indicating that ministers, although they were officers, had become politicians, who needed an entourage and who were subjected to processes of obsolescence (sometimes rather rapidly) which subjected them to the often hostile pressures of public opinion. Eventually (beyond 1789 and during the nineteenth century) the establishment of representative and elected assemblies would occur which would submit the government to severe inspection. Then the secretariats of ministers would become, by the force of circumstances, ministerial cabinets which would keep a weather-eye out for political storms ahead. In 1770, the government was a long way off from such an arrangement. The king, for his part, did not even have a proper personal secretariat. He drafted his own letters and replies himself. . . .

At the top, the ministerial Councils (*des dépêches* and *d'en haut*) remained very active. But at the level immediately below them, the other Councils, acting as points for 'collective' deliberation, became clearly less robust in the maturity of Louis XV's reign. The Council of conscience (*Conseil de conscience*), the Royal Council of finances (*Conseil royal des finances*) and the Council of trade (*Conseil de commerce*) either disappeared or simply ceased to meet. The *Conseil d'Etat et des finances* fell into desuetude. The bureaucracy, *Monsieur le bureau*, tended everywhere to become more dominant, a non-deliberative and hierarchical form of decision-making. Alone amongst these older 'discursive' organs for decision-making to retain more or less its power lay the *Conseil d'Etat privé* or *Conseil des parties*, made up of councillors of state, *intendants des finances*, masters of requests and the *contrôleur général*. This Council 'oversaw respect for the legislative process, examined questions of contested judicial decision-making or the quashing (*cassation*) of legal decisions . . .' and acted as a kind of Supreme Court.[5]

The *Conseil des parties* aside, the 'conciliar' structures, hitherto supreme, of the state *stricto sensu* had been gradually put to sleep, or gently allowed to wither away. This process of creeping euthanasia had begun under

---

[4] Michel Antoine, *Le Gouvernement et l'administration sous Louis XV, Dictionnaire biographique* (Paris, CNRS, 1978) (article on 'Bertin'), p. 34.
[5] Michel Antoine, *Louis XV* (Paris, Fayard, 1989), p. 125.

Louis XIV; but in many respects, it had been continued, or even inaugurated under Louis XV. But, between 1770 and 1774, a shorter-term brutality in the process was set in train. The authoritarian-state, with its bureaucracy and what remained of its conciliar structure, set itself up energetically against the old collective structures of the state which had become burdensome, turbulent, controversial and tribune-like in their tendencies. The sovereign courts, and, in particular, the parlements which had shown such activity in the years from 1749 to 1770, thus found themselves fundamentally challenged. In periods of quasi-liberalization, these sovereign courts had become the personification of criticism, legalism and privilege, each paradoxically associated with one another. They had become, in the other political phases of the recent past, the *bêtes noires* of the monarchy when the latter, seeking to increase its authority and sharpen its attack, attempted to recover, in 1771 and afterwards, all or part of the ground which it had gradually lost to the magistrates.

The Choiseulian laxist compromises had become no more than a memory. Freed of his Lorraine rival, and once *de facto* head of the Council, René-Nicolas de Maupeou acted with the speed of a Napoleon, reconstructing institutions and cutting a swathe through new ground. The (farfetched) comparison with the future Emperor is less implausible than one might think since Lebrun, the future secretary to the 'triumvir' Chancellor Maupeou, would become in 1799 the third consul to Bonaparte, and in charge of the huge administrative question. From the 'triumvirate' to the 'triumconsulate' . . . !

Brought up as a *parlementaire*, nourished in the bosom of the judiciary, Maupeou's intelligence and abilities were outstanding and added lustre to the chancery. But he would use the post to bring down the magistrature and reinforce the royal prerogative. From the summer of 1770 through to the winter of 1771, led by the d'Aiguillon affair, there would be a succession of moves and counter-moves, of monarchical edicts and *parlementaire* remonstrances, strikes of judges and advocates, and then, finally, royal *lettres de jussion* which sought to recall the *parlementaire* gentry back to royal obedience. The princes of the blood, in the main, made common cause with the *robe*. But the era of the Great Condé, that manipulator who turned the agitation amongst the lawyers to his own advantage, was long past. In an opposite sense, the lawyers now attached the prestigious names of the old princely houses – Orléans, Condé, etc. – to their cause, rather than vice versa.

The monarchical blade fell in February 1771 and brought these battles to a provisional conclusion. Venality of offices was suppressed – a significant turning-point! The judges remained salaried by the government but were no longer the owners of their offices. Justice ceased to be a matter of payment. The enormous area of jurisdiction which had been served by the Paris Parlement was divided between six superior courts. By acting in this way, Maupeou had tackled a dangerous adversary in a fashion which none of the predecessors of Louis XV had dared to risk since Charles VII. Even

Plate 27 René-Nicolas de Maupeou, Chancellor of France René-Nicolas de
Maupeou, here portrayed in a painting attributed to Jean-Joseph Taillasson, was
the son of a Parisian *parlementaire* who became successively a councillor and then
a *président* in the court in his turn. His father briefly exercised the post of chancellor
before resigning it to his son in 1768. Maupeou had already, as *premier président* of
the Parlement, acted as the spokesman for the government before the increasingly
hostile Parlement, a role which prepared him perhaps for his later task of foreclos-
ing upon the Parlement entirely.
Versailles, Musée national du château

Louis XIV had balked at the prospect, humiliating the Parlement but not contemplating its disintegration. Then, shortly afterwards, judges, in principle newly established, were recruited and then installed in the six courts replacing the Paris Parlement placed at, for example, Lyon, Poitiers, Clermont-Ferrand, Arras. . . . The men who were chosen to serve had been employed before as advocates or, more often, in the offices of former magistrates, officers or *parlementaires*. In the opinion of these newly-promoted judges, the posts which Maupeou had peremptorily established, were, on reflection, worth the taking. In the provinces, or outside the former jurisdictional area of the Paris Parlement, the whole operation was quickly carried out. The Parlement of Toulouse, for example, was dissolved; it would become transformed into two courts, one remaining in the rose-red city of Toulouse, and the other taking up residence in Nîmes. From the beginning of 1772, the whole judicial landscape had been completely transformed. Maupeou's initiative was successfully implemented. After a guerilla campaign lasting half a century, the parlements were rationalized, split up, and transformed. It would take the death of Louis XV to bring them back.

The efforts of the 'triumvirate' did not end there – or, more precisely, those of the 'duumvirate' of Maupeou and Terray (for d'Aiguillon, the Secretary of State for Foreign Affairs, was ancillary to these other two, and the more so since he had not been a party to their first political action). In economic and fiscal matters, the *abbé* Terray (who was tonsured but not a priest) was *contrôleur général des finances* from 1769. He was efficiency writ ecclesiastically large. Intelligent, plain-speaking, hard-working and rich, he acted like a Colbert but did not forsake his amorous encounters for his work. The only problem was that he lacked the time to act – he was minister for barely five years, as against the quarter of a century enjoyed by his predecessor Colbert. Not only was time not on his side, however, but more significantly, nor were the times – the fashion for commercial, manufacturing and philosophical liberalism was in the ascendant. Except for the fact that he died rather too soon, Louis XV gave lavish support to the *abbé* Terray. Besides, there was no war to disturb his five years in office, in contrast with the Dutch War which disrupted Colbert's achievement. In the grain trade, Terray remained *dirigiste* like his forebears who had served as ministers under Louis XIV. He disavowed the profitable but perilous propositions of Bertin who had supported a freedom of trade for grain. This had led to numerous problems for the king after 1763, which was when the initial decision for freedom in the grain-trade had been decreed by Bertin and L'Averdy and which the *abbé* Terray revoked. In his economics, as in his politics, Terray was, albeit without fanaticism, antiliberal. He would have found the remarks of Michelet on the 'captivity' of grain[6] almost a century later grotesque in the extreme. By two proclamations (*arrêts*) of July and December 1770, issued at a time of great grain

---

[6] 'Il y avait en France un misérable prisonnier, le blé, qu'on forçait de pourrir au lieu même où il était né. Chaque pays tenait son blé captif.' Jules Michelet, *Histoire de France, Louis XV et Louis XVI* (Paris, Chamerot, 1867), pp. 206–7.

shortages it is true, Terray suspended the export of grain to other countries (August) and then attempted to retain (December) a relative degree of liberty of commerce in grain within the realm. In fact, this second measure was suggested to him by the beginnings of a relaxation in the position of grain supplies, and which began to feed through at the end of the year in 1770 after the disastrous spring and summer. Historians have been mistaken in regarding these authoritarian measures of control, particularly that of the summer of 1770, as a dead-letter. They have not taken the elementary methodological precaution of testing their pronouncements against a reading of the grain-price statistics. The fact is that these prices declined continuously after 1770 and up to the death of Louis XV. There was, therefore, no sense in which the *abbé*'s actions could be regarded objectively as a failure. At worst it was a psychological failure in the sense that Terray proved unable to 'sell' his food-supply policy to public opinion (a failure he shared in general with the old monarchy). The semi-*dirigiste* measures which he inaugurated did nothing, of course, to shape the pattern of cereal prices post 1770 where plentiful supplies made prices favourable to the consumers of bread. However the trends in prices discreetly accompanied his measures. What is more, from May 1770 onwards (significantly, in the midst of rising prices) the *abbé* began various measures of administrative contingency planning. He asked the intendants to send him a report on the 'likely condition' of the forthcoming harvest by 15 June each year. This action (besides its immediate utility) would provide later historians with a remarkable series of documents.

In questions of financial policy, Terray began by increasing the lease for running the postal services. He accomplished some economies in the state by reducing the interest payments to the *rentiers*. He reduced pensions and sold to office-holders the revalorization of their wages. He increased the return from the royal rights over mortgage specifically by creating the post of 'registrars of mortgages' (*conservateurs des hypothèques*) which would remain a permanent fixture in France. He perpetuated or continued the various *vingtièmes* and attempted, often with success, to make their collection more equitably based and better related to the revenues of the taxpayers. To achieve this, he even created various schools for the training of *contrôleurs* of the *vingtième*, a forerunner, perhaps, of the modern French *écoles des impôts*. He improved the receipts from the Parisian capitation by means of an exact survey of the dwellings in the capital and ensuring that it reflected *grosso modo* the revenues of its inhabitants. This was, once more, the application of the method of enquiry and equity, to which Terray, like Machault, was attracted. It was designed above all to produce an exact 'evaluation' of the contributive valency of individuals in order to increase fiscal resources without excessively burdening any of the numerous groups of those liable to pay the *capitation*. Terray also increased the levy of tariffs from the taxes on commercial traffic (by 2 *sols* in the *livre*[7] or

---

[7] There were 20 *sols* or *sous* to the *livre tournois*. To increase the levy by 10% was thus, in other words, to increase it, using the contemporary expression, by 'deux sols pour livre'.

10 per cent). The overall revenues from the tax-farms on these taxes immediately increased by 15 per cent if one compares the leases of 1774 with those of 1768. This increase was the result of the rises in tariffs, of course; but it also came about because of the buoyant state of French commerce during this period.[8]

In general terms, the fiscal results of Terray's period in office were encouraging. The Treasury was satisfied with the fact that the expenditure to which the state was committed clearly decreased between 1770 and 1775 (the dates which encompassed *grosso modo* the five-year tenure of Terray). They declined in this period from 277 million to 234 million *livres*. Although the government[9] thus became less prodigal, this was only right because prices (or, at least, cereal prices) decreased for almost all the decade after 1770, which altered accordingly the value of the taxes collected. The latter, in any case, greatly increased. This rise was the result of two linked phenomena; the vigorous growth in the economy and, linked to that, the increase in the tax thresholds which the *abbé* Terray had brusquely introduced. The gross revenues of the state increased from 318 million to 377 million *livres* between 1770 and 1775. Net revenues (once all the interest payments had been paid, and what was left to pay for committed expenditures) increased from 169 million to 213 million *livres*. As a result, the deficit decreased substantially. It stood at 247 million *livres* in 1760 during the Seven Years War, the war itself adding to the enormous size of the debt. Once peace had returned, the size of the debt fell progressively to 180 million *livres* in 1765; to 108 million in 1770 . . . and to under 25 million in 1775. These creditable results were, in the final analysis, partly the result of the 'Terray effect'; the latter was an able financier who had emerged from the long and favourable post-war period, just as, later, Poincaré would in 1926, and Pinay in 1952. . . . But the *abbé* would not be able to lay claim to the popularity of the latter two individuals. We should not seek, however, to rehabilitate his reputation too much by over-stressing his personal impact. Peace and economic growth played the prime role in refloating, like a favourable wind and a rising tide, the beached budget. Like a good pilot, Terray had the simple merit of having pointed the ship in the right direction to make the most of these positive trends to ensure that they could act almost spontaneously upon it. There remains one note of criticism.[10] The servicing of the royal debt retained an excessive place in the budgetary disposition of 1775. For the moment, however, the payment of interest on the debts entered into by the state, or

---

[8]   François Crouzet, 'Angleterre ét France au XVIIIe siècle: essai d'analyse comparée de deux croissances économiques', *Annales* (March–April 1966), p. 262, with data on foreign trade.

[9]   This, and what immediately precedes it, is taken from Michel Antoine, *Louis XV*, pp. 943–9; cf. Crouzet, 'Angleterre et France', and Alain Guéry, 'Les Finances de la monarchie française', p. 239.

[10]   Michel Morineau, 'Gestion des finances royales au XVIIIe siècle', *Revue historique* (1980), p. 315. And Alain Guéry, ibid.

the repayment of capital, remained within reasonable limits. It was a long way from the delirious, impetuous and tempestuous levels of debt which, after the death of Louis XV, would accompany the War of American Independence and the ministry of Necker. This would destroy the basis of public finance and bring down the Ancien Régime.

★ ★ ★ ★ ★

The 'third man' of the team, d'Aiguillon, was in charge of diplomacy and more closely supervised by the king. He did not have such a difficult task for, during the five last years of the reign of Louis XV, the men in power in Versailles had no desire to begin a military conflict. The bipartite world, in which the Habsburgs had confronted Richelieu alongside the Protestant powers, had totally disappeared from the world scene. Diplomacy functioned along the lines of multi-polar axes (England, France, Spain, Austria, Prussia, Russia).[11]

To the east, the ground was fully taken up by the three great powers of Austria, Prussia and Russia. France could do little . . . unless it was prepared to commit itself to the huge and formidable military investment which Napoleon would put towards it and with the all-too-familiar results. The result was that, in the period from 1770 to 1775, the French would quietly let go of two important allies on the eastern flank, i.e. Turkey and Poland. In fact, having been conquered by the Russians in 1774, the Turks signed the most humiliating treaty in their whole history at Kutchuk Kainardji. It involved great territorial losses, at once symbolic and religiously significant. Versailles recognized its impotence in the face of events and did nothing. Two years before that, Poland had been partitioned by Russia, Prussia and Austria in 1772. Louis XV's France had to look on as a friendly power was dismembered. On the other hand, as we have already noted,[12] Louis XV was in a better position to exercise some influence in Sweden, since the maritime routes connected France to Scandinavia directly without any continental interposition. The French king could thus act to dissuade Prussia, Denmark and Russia from attacking the Stockholm régime. Gustavus III had carried out a sort of *coup d'état* in Stockholm in 1769 with the assistance of the faction of the Hats (francophiles) and thus brought to an end the pro-Russian efforts of the Bonnets and their 'anarchic parliamentarianism' or, as one might see it, crypto-liberalism. In the far North, there thus would be established a régime of a semi-absolutist, albeit enlightened, tinge which sought to limit old 'Swedish liberty' without destroying it altogether. A Scandinavian Maupeou? Of the

[11]   The appearance on the European power scene of Prussia and Russia after 1750 had considerably complicated the 'game' which between 1700 and 1740 had been, depending on the circumstances, either tri-polar or, at most, penta-polar (England-The Dutch, France-Spain, The Austro-Hungarian Empire).

[12]   See above, chapter 10.

Plate 28   The Kings' Cake   This engraving from 1773 depicts (from left to right) Tsarina Catherine the Great of Russia, King Stanislas August of Poland (holding an uncertain crown on his head), Emperor Joseph II of Austria (who is looking the other way) and Frederick the Great, King of Prussia, deciding how to cut the '*gâteau des Rois*' of Poland.
Paris, Bibliothèque nationale, cabinet des Estampes

alliances with Turkey, Poland and Sweden, Louis would retain *grosso modo* only the latter.

With Bourbon power excluded from the East, it could henceforth concentrate its efforts more modestly on the Atlantic rimlands (from Sweden to Spain), and on the western Mediterranean. The alliance with Madrid remained, in this respect, the essential component as was normal in a phase involving a return to political Catholicism for which the expulsion of the Jesuits was a closed book. The lines of friendship with the Vatican had become strained in the Choiseul period. Stubbornly hostile to the Jesuits, Choiseul had flirted with the anticlericals. D'Aiguillon, on the other hand, secretary of state for foreign affairs alongside Maupeou and Terray, had no pressing reason at all to preserve such an anti-Roman 'chill'. In April 1774, Avignon and the Comtat Venaissin (held in royal hands since 1768 as a reprisal for the measures which the pope had taken against the sovereign duke of Parma, an enemy of the Jesuits and Louis XV's grandson) were returned to His Holiness.

Towards England, the principal enemy, the policies of Louis XV remained pacific, despite some underlying menace. Some years later (in 1778), France would become the supporter of a more robust Protestantism in Anglo-Saxon lands (the puritanism of the Boston colonists) against the softer Protestantism (of Anglican England). Was this not a return to the 'heresophile' stance of Francis I, Henry IV, of Richelieu and of Dubois? At all events, this was something which would only mature under Louis XVI with the rise in the ruling élites of a patriot and pro-*philosophe* party, and one which was favourable towards Benjamin Franklin and the insurgents of the future United States of America. In contrast, four or five years before that, in his latter days, Louis XV was more hispano-papal in his heart-felt convictions than ever. The king reasoned, nevertheless (in the wake of the aborted Falklands intervention of 1770) that he should not break with England. Louis XV knew all too well that he would regret such a rupture; the lessons of the disastrous Treaty of Paris (1763) had not been forgotten.[13]

The undoubtedly authoritarian politics of the 'five-year triumvirate' were thus held in fairly reasonable check where necessary. Of course they bore down heavily on, and to the disadvantage of, the *parlementaires* (and much more so than had been the case under Louis XIV); but this would not last long – the four years from 1771 to 1774 would quickly pass. In opposition to the measures taken by Maupeou, the magistrates had their backs to the wall but they revealed themselves to be more garrulous (or more ideological) than dangerous. The sovereign judges were no longer capable of starting a Fronde. Of course, when it came to it, 15 or 18 years on, they would find themselves in a position of setting a Revolution alight;

---

[13]   For his part, Louis XVI would not have such a long memory. The war against England, a limited one it is true, would be fatal to him both financially and ideologically – see below, Conclusion.

but they could in no sense be seen as its leaders. Rather, it would quickly engulf them. In other respects, royal policy maintained a degree of Colbertian *dirigisme* in economic matters and questions of grain supply. In this respect, it is important not to exaggerate things. Terray would make his administration apply a degree of control over the integrity and quality of manufactured products, even so far as to certify officially the authenticity of Vichy water-bottles. But he would not revive the Company of the Indies which Choiseul had suppressed. Instead, he loyally pursued to its logical conclusion the final break-up of this association. The techniques of rationalization and increases in taxation carried forward by Terray lie firmly within the traditions of *contrôleurs généraux* from the Louis XIV period, whether Colbert or Pontchartrain. The burdens inflicted on the tax-payers were, all things considered, infinitely less in around 1775 than they had been in the seventeenth century with its perpetual wars. The administration of the triumvirate proved to be, on the whole, positive and suited to a period of peace – somewhat heavy-handed, but with measures which were often rational. The country benefited from the maintenance of public order. It profited from the rising value of the *livre* on the international market. It was gradually working its way more or less out of poverty, with, or without, the help of the state.

But an objective analysis of the government's actions is one thing; the psychological and political effects which these actions had in people's minds is entirely distinct from the factual results, often broadly favourable, which the 'triumvirate' had achieved in terms of administration, diplomacy, economy and fiscality. The embryos of a representative system, such as it had existed before 1770, were not to be suppressed with impunity, even if they happened only to exist in the form of these 'rotten boroughs' called parlements. The abolition which Maupeou had called for was regarded as definitive, even though it would turn out to be provisional, from 1771 to 1775. At all events, it was not well received by public opinion, or at least, not by the public opinion which counted.

To do it justice, the government, in the shape of Maupeou, went some way to make its policies acceptable to the people who thought, and the public opinion which counted. At least a hundred books and pamphlets, inspired by the government, were published.[14] They favoured the royalist line rather than the *parlementaire* one. The circumstances in which they were produced was distinctive for its gallocentrism and they took no account of the European experience in terms of public liberty. At best these pamphlets referred here and there to cross-Channel examples. The ablest talents, with the odd exceptions, took little part in such battles in support of the ministry. In fact, the contacts of individual and ideas between government agents and the philosophe faction were of little importance. Here lies the enduring difficulty for those responsible for

---

[14] On all that follows, see the important work of Durand Echeverria, *The Maupeou Revolution in France* (Baton Rouge, Louisiana State University Press, 1985).

order in France when they try to approach the world of thought. . . . The ideas of those who are called, in a rather over-simplified fashion, the 'royalists' (it would be rather better, technically, to call them the 'maupeouists') were, however, far from being stupid. Let us admit, they said, that the country needs reform, in which case this can certainly not be provided by the aristocrats, nor the feudal elements, nor the parlements nor even the Estates General. The incapacity of the latter would end up being demonstrated in the near future when the Estates General, to take just that one element, would become totally transformed in 1789 and give birth to a hitherto unknown form of Constituent Assembly which would, in turn, prove incapable of mastering the situation! The royalists were aware of such institutional constraints. They readily invoked the spectre of 'republican' anarchy which would result in the installation in the corridors of power of this or that privileged order, or even of the three orders together. An enlightened despot would be more suitable for the task in hand according to these 'right-wing' pamphleteers. They would propose and promote the practical and structural changes which would be in the common interest. Who, other than a paternalist king, absolute and benefi-cent, would, so they said, embody the sovereignty and unified will of the people and who else would better protect the social body (organically conceived) from its own excesses, its own poisons, in order to fit it to the vacillating circumstances of a changing world? In this sense, royal sover-eignty was conceived in a Bodinian sense as one and indivisible. The idea of the separation of powers, dear to Montesquieu, was rejected. It her-alded, albeit expressed in less harsh terms, the one and indivisible Repub-lic of the revolutionary period. The monarchy was thus conceived by its most ardent supporters as resting on the three pillars of custom, divine right (albeit less emphasized than it had been in the seventeenth century), and, finally, the needs of authority and utility – for it was the monarchy which would protect property, safety, security and civil liberty. The latter was conceived as a liberty 'not to be oppressed by the great, to enjoy one's honour and one's property, great or small, to establish a family and to raise children'. There thus emerged under the auspices of a tutelary state which was objectively popular (in such a conception), the idea of an organic and effective liberty, effective in contrast to the theoretical 'pseudo-liberties' of an opposition which, in the other camp, were being dreamt of by the theorists of a democracy, and who were still in search of it. The more the monarchical régime was directive, guided from above, working with firmness towards the common good, the more it would achieve the peo-ple's well-being. No doubt such patterns of thought would be disqualified after 1789; but they would remain, despite everything, attached to certain ways of thinking, and traces of them would appear in the thoughts of Bonaparte and de Gaulle. We should note, finally, how numerous histo-rians from both the right and the left have, up to our own day,[15] vigorously

[15] Antoine, *Louis XV*, p. 903.

defended the Maupeou reforms on the (not entirely mistaken) grounds that they rid the state of a surplus gangue or an unnecessary feudal accretion.

In terms of practical results, Charles-François Lebrun, Maupeou's collaborator, reckoned in 1769 that monarchical authority which was thus defined as indivisible, and which was modernized, had, before all else, to achieve some important and emancipatory tasks such as the extension of public education or the abolition of feudal justice. These would be good ways to attack the structural archaism in France as well as the excessive authority of its grandees. But Lebrun was only a high-level secretary and, in the event, an idle dreamer. The true power belonged to his master, Maupeou, who preferred to concentrate his efforts on the more immediate task of a brutal consolidation of royal authority. In other respects, the thoughts of Lebrun and his royalist friends, the supporters of enlightened despotism, were probably seen by the chancellor as no more than utopian dreams. He perhaps did not care a fig for them; behind the ideologies of the reforms, whether royalist or absolutist, lay the solid realities, those of the full powers accorded the king, with no great pretensions to remodel profoundly the whole of society.

Whether writers or simple scribblers, the partisans of the royalist thesis were, in general, obscure and ill-qualified. There was, however, one exception: Voltaire. Favourable to the triumvirs, Voltaire was somewhat influenced by the considerations extended to him by the French authorities, who came to the aid of the Swiss clock-manufactory which the philosophe-entrepreneur controlled. Voltaire knew well how to modify his successive loyalties to suit the interests of the moment. Careless of contradictions, he supported Choiseul; then, when the moment came, Maupeou; and then finally Turgot. Despite these *volte-face*, he was held in suspicion by the monarchy because of the attacks which he had formerly launched against the church. But (sweet revenge) the partisans of the anti-absolutist cause also had their suspicions of the philosopher from Ferney after 1770, so compromised had he become with the Ministry.

Voltaire's position had, in the circumstances, a certain logic. The great writer was always hostile to the privileged 'corporations' and, above all, to the parlements, which he characterized as egoistical, with an oppressive or feudal outlook and a backward-looking bigotry. We should add that, beyond the political agitations of the magistrature, the author of the *Lettres anglaises* was devoted to his revenue income and feared that a wave of anarchy, albeit *parlementaire*, would be unleashed which would not be at all in the interests of the state's *rentiers*. 'I have no taste for the Fronde war, seeing that the first shots did not fail to maim those who paid the *rentes*; and, what is more, I would prefer to obey a good lion, born stronger than myself, than 200 rats of my own kind.'[16] Others would put the same

---

[16]   Letters to Saint-Lambert, 7 April 1771, in *The Complete Works of Voltaire* (Banbury, The Voltaire Foundation, 1975), vol. cxxi, 350.

Plate 29   Voltaire in his study   In the course of his huge career, Voltaire cam-
paigned successfully against intolerance and bigotry. His anti-Catholic deism
sometimes over-simplified issues despite his manifest social conservatism. Here, in
a painting of the eighteenth-century French School, he is depicted at work in his
study. *Paris, Musée Carnavalet*

sentiments thus: five pigs cost more to fatten than one. Voltaire, a pessi-
mist, feared that egalitarianism and democracy would degenerate into
grave troubles (the French Revolution would not undermine the proposition). He also doubted that the people would be sufficiently rational to

fabricate its own good fortune by itself. 'We are a nation of mutinous infants, who need both the stick and the sweet.'[17] His hostility to the education of the masses also contributed to making all ideals of popular auto-emancipation suspect in his eyes. In the end, the admirer of Henry IV, the friend of Frederick II, always returned to the paternal ideals embraced in an 'enlightened despotism' which would fight against superstitious customs. A strong monarchy, in his view, would be freer in its movements; it would discover without too much difficulty the necessary means to adapt, thanks to which the fundamental values of 'liberty and property, this cry of Nature' would survive. Such fundamental values as the right not to be a serf and not to lose the family fortune through the application of the archaic right of *mainmorte* which backward seigneuries continued to enjoy in Franche-Comté were sustained by the monarchy. The now absolute monarchy had brought honour upon itself by its support for the abolition of serfdom in the eighteenth century. Voltaire strongly urged it to continue in this liberating vein by forcing, where necessary, the hands of the masters of the soil. In sum, the patriarch of Ferney sustained energetically the various objectives along the line: hostility towards the parlements, towards anarchy, and towards serfdom.

The philosophe knew, however, that he was playing with dangerous paradoxes. He sustained the prerogatives of the king and yet His Majesty had scant regard for him so long as he remained hostile to the church. Voltaire made light of the alliance between Throne and Altar but it was the latter which would provide, despite their transitory quarrels, the generic law of the Bourbon monarchy. Conscious of the *cul de sac* into which he had stumbled through his support for Maupeou between 1770 and 1774, Voltaire would be only too happy, a little later, to return to his natural inclinations and rally around Turgot. He took, nevertheless, the elementary precaution of waiting until the 'iron chancellor' was definitely disgraced. One cannot be too careful!

Simon Linguet, like Voltaire, wrote in support of Maupeou, although he was not a member of the chancellor's coterie. An able pamphleteer and an advocate, a somewhat marginal figure however, Linguet would pay dearly for his expressed views, or at least those imputed to him afterwards. The Revolutionaries would not neglect him and he would be guillotined in June 1794. For him, as for Nietzsche later on, humanity was divided into two groups: the lazy, exploitative governors and the naive subjects who are without hope of liberty. From this axiom, which he held to be irrefutable, Linguet did not draw conclusions which were hostile to the lesser subjects. According to him, the so-called inferior classes did not have rights to public education, which would merely increase the number of embittered and frustrated individuals; but they did have the rights to exist, to public

---

[17]   Letter to the duke de Richelieu, 29 April 1771 (ibid., p. 374). It is true, however, that the letters of Voltaire to this particular duke, a friend of Louis XV's, were particularly obsequious.

esteem, to pity, and to the minimum vital means to survival, to small pockets or patches of property which would guarantee their individual survival. In order that these tasks of social protection were carried out, a strong executive (like Maupeou?) was needed who was alone capable of reforming the laws.

Once again an organic conception of power was presented. It had its roots deep in the past, and particularly in Christian or medieval conceptions which revolved around the 'mystical body' and the 'political corpus'.[18] Society, in Linguet's view, was like a human body which grew and metamorphosed itself. Society thus had to change its clothing, lose its old skin, and (above all) provide itself with a (royal) head if it could. Things being as they were, Montesquieu's separation of powers was merely a trap, destined to serve the interests of those (magistrates, notables etc.) who would advocate such a separation and use it to the detriment of the lesser folk. It is easy to understand why Maupeou should be attracted to Linguet's propositions, even if he did not use him as a direct agent. Linguet even took to praising oriental or Asiatic despotism in order to 'startle the older brethren' on the grounds that they were more favourable to the lower orders than the relatively moderate monarchies which were to be found in the West. Voltaire upheld the royal lion against the *parlementaire* rats. Linguet also supported a unique and leonine power, but this time against the aristocratic tigers with their sharpened teeth.

However sophisticated Linguet and the consort of writers who supported Maupeou proved to be, their arguments always had the same weakness. They emptied the idea of national representation of almost all meaning at a time when all the political evolution of the eighteenth and nineteenth centuries would force it more and more onto the political agenda. Can the same be said of the physiocrats and others whom it is tempting to present also as Maupeou's partisans?

The great period for the flowering of physiocratic thought had been before the government of the 'iron chancellor'. The disciples of Quesnay had enjoyed a good period under the notably 'open' Choiseul period when the liberty for the grain trade was legalized between 1763 and 1769. Following the return to *dirigisme* in corn-trading put into effect by Terray, the physiocrats' star was waning, but this is the moment when Quesnay emerges, along with Mirabeau (the elder), the *abbé* Baudeau, Dupont de Nemours, even Turgot (close to the principles of the physiocratic school but not its tactics). This is tantamount to saying that the links of the physiocrats to Maupeou were perhaps more a matter of partial coincidence in their ideas (both professed a superficially similar respect for absolutism); but there was not active complicity, nor momentary agreement, since there was a disjuncture which separated the physiocrats from the triumvirate at the time.

---

[18] Ernst Kantorowicz, *The King's Two Bodies* translated as *Les deux corps du roi* (Paris, Gallimard, 1989), p. 155 *et seq.* (in the French translation).

We should note, in this context, that the ideological system which provided the inspiration to the economists had little to do with the Christian religion; yet it was the latter which remained the buttress to the authentic absolutism *à la* Maupeou. Quesnay's thought was profoundly lay, peppered with philosophic notions. His cardinal values were *Nature* (the physiocrats would call it the 'desirable domination of natural laws over the economy'), *Reason* (quasi-Cartesian in form), *Utility, Property, Justice* (rather than Catholic charity, to the point where the strict notion of a salary maintained at the strictest minimum which would then be the means for the increase of business profits and net production seemed entirely logical to the partisans of physiocracy, however brutal it might appear to the lower orders).

The economists would only agree with Maupeou on highly particular matters, essentially governmental ones. According to the physiocrats, the underlying sense of collective, and even individual, interests, had to be translated into the hands of a paternalist monarchy which would be, in various ways, absolute, by means of a transfer of sovereignty. The proposition was one with which the Louis XV of the Flagellation and the later years of the reign would find little to disagree. The king which this transfer of sovereignty had thus installed and 'absolutized' would embody *ipso facto* (at least this was what the physiocratic theorists imagined) the general will, expressive of common interests. It was not, however, a matter of a translation of power from the people to the ruler, a power which was authentically democratic, and thus revocable – such as Jean-Jacques Rousseau would envisage in *The Social Contract*. The tutelage advocated by the physiocrats was a 'legal despotism' (much less violent, of course, than the Asiatic despotism which had drawn paradoxical praises from Linguet). That such a system would be grist to the triumvirate mill was far from clear, however. In fact, the *sui generis* absolutism of the physiocrats was trammelled by all kinds of protective guards. Some of the latter had already given Louis XIV and even Louis XV pause for thought, and these two monarchs had been hardly dictatorial (in the contemporary sense of the adjective) at all. Amongst the protective guards which would somewhat limit the arbitrariness of the 'legal despot' were the forces of Nature and Reason, but also, in more concrete terms, the municipal assemblies which would be elected by and from the propertied classes. They would play a consultative role vis à vis the monarch, answering the wishes of Turgot which had, in fact, envisaged such bodies in a *Memorandum* on the municipalities.[19] The future minister was, on this point, close to the municipal agenda formulated by Dupont and Mirabeau the elder. Dupont even went so far as to propose the setting up of Estates General which, this time, would have compromised absolutism from beginning to end – but only for North America! In Europe, legal despotism would remain viable

---

[19]   Douglas Dakin, *Turgot and the Ancien Régime in France* (New York, Octagon Books, 1965), p. 274 *et seq.*

or would become more flourishing; it was nevertheless held to be important to reduce its own bureaucratic apparatus to the minimum. A solid
state – yet a modest one. Maximal power; minimal administration. Within
these limits the so-called absolute Prince would thus be prevented from
abusing his powers of intervention in the lives of individuals and constrain-
ing the free dynamism of its native subjects (*régnicoles*) within their business lives and within the economy. In sum, the kind of king strongly
preferred by the physiocrats would be 'omnipotent' (for this 'Auriga'
would reject the separation of powers and hold all the reins of power of his
three 'steeds', legislative, executive and judicial) yet remain imbued with
benevolence. He would be the vigorous, yet attentive, president of a
society of landowners and himself a landowner. For the king was the
beneficial tenant and it was an indispendable function of sovereignty that
a certain proportion of net production should flow towards him for the
effective discharge of the function of the police-state. The monarch was
thus the guardian of a society of vast fixed and landed investments as
broad as the realm itself. His Majesty should restrict himself to applying,
and with the usual rigour (but no more), the regulations regarding police
and joint ownership. The sovereign might sometimes act with a heavy
hand; but, even so, he would leave the landowners in peace on their own
domain, and completely free to act to secure the most profitable exploitation of their labour-force and their lands. The same was to be applied for
the preferences of landowners in matters of religion and thought. Such an
extension of personal liberty would, of course, sit ill alongside an erosion
of political liberties. But individual initiative was at least given free rein,
and from this fact would emerge (for example) a press without constraints,
the suppression of colonial monopolies, the freeing of slaves and even the
abolition *tout court* of colonization as such. In these various respects, the
physiocrats were 'libertarians' and innovators, despite their indifference to
the lot of the people, whose aim was just to survive if they could not
struggle to become richer.

Physiocracy wanted to allow free rein to these various liberties and thus
had various reservations about equality. The physiocratic school regarded
the fact of individual equality as contrary to the Nature of things. In
contrast, the economists willingly conceded the equality of rights as between individuals, a typical Enlightenment position. They looked for the
day when the differences and privileges which distinguished the true
gentlemen (of ancient lineage) and the nobility of dignity (established on
the basis of an office, the latter profoundly disturbed by Maupeou) from
common mortals. They advocated the fusion of the élites and an equality
which, for want of a better term, they would call natural and which would
take place within the landowning class, all orders of the Ancien Régime
being merged into it and their identities submerged within it. They willingly held tithes and seigneurial dues up to derision. They expected
economic growth to reduce social inequality and, in certain cases, to
abolish misery when it became a scandal. These rarefied notions were

hardly compatible with the practical, day-to-day needs of a vulgar propaganda to support the few steps attempted by Maupeou, however original and vigorous had been his solemn attempts to cut a swathe through the 'gothic' undergrowth of old institutions. At most there was a degree of pro-absolutist convergence which provided a common denominator between the thoughts of the physiocrats and the actions of the chancellor. In reality, the ideas of the Quesnay school, by their support for legal despotism (a good deal more legal than despotic!) and by the prescience with which they could foresee a future world taking shape from a *tabula rasa* or on the basis of an unshackled human enterprise, tended rather to encourage the free operation of factions which criticized the heavy-handed authoritarianism of the triumvirate. The latter consisted of 'patriotic' cabals alongside *philosophe* groups who were even more audacious than the 'patriots'.

Maupeou's *coup de majesté* acted, in reality, like a 'litmus test', or benchmark. It fostered allergic (but not reactionary) responses and retrospective nostalgia as well as the development (if not the appearance, for it was already in evidence) of opposition alliances, notably (first of all) the 'patriot' coalition. The latter supported the *parlementaire* cause in their (often ephemeral) writings as against the royal cause. Some of them were true gentlemen such as the viscount d'Aubuisson and the duke de Brancas. Others were magistrates from the Parlement and elsewhere, either nobles (Malesherbes) or the offspring of judges (Augeard). The could also be clerics (like the *abbé* Mey), who incidentally was a Jansenist and an advocate; or, again, they could just be advocates by virtue of a professional and civic tradition which would become more widespread under the Revolution and continue throughout the nineteenth century. Amongst these lawyer-patriots, there were, for example, André Blonde, Elie de Beaumont and Target, the future delegate at the Constituent Assembly who was already close, as he would be henceforth, to the philosophes. To these one should add the names of three extremists: Marivaux,[20] Morizot and Saige. The last of the bunch was inevitably the journalist or 'novelist' Pidanzat de Mairobert. Overall, they were a coalition 'across the classes' based around the enlightened nobility and the garrulous world of the law; both groups embodied the active majority of public opinion, this new 'flagship' of French political conflicts, freshly launched from the growth-points of the century – the increase in publishing, in journalism, in the urban population, in the literate classes and in the administrative and judicial world. Since the time of Richelieu and the *Gazette* launched by Renaudot, the state had had the time to inculcate a political culture in French society which would, in turn, duly transform, and then dissolve from top to bottom, the state-like structures, or at least the forms which they had manifested during the Ancien Régime.

The views which counted, from this point of view, emerged from the civic groups (both noble and non-noble) who were the most educated, the

[20]   I.e. the publicist J.C. Martin de Marivaux, the partial namesake of the famous dramatist.

best-trained in terms of law, power and Enlightened views. These groups, however important they considered themselves to be, constituted a small minority amongst the 27 million 'French' but this hardly mattered since, despite a considerable degree of progress, the majority of Louis XV's subjects remained barely literate and politically silent, at least for the immediate present. The opinion of such a numerous population had not been asked for in the past by the king, and they would not be called on to voice one now by public opinion. The pamphleteers writing in support of the patriot party were lesser authors but their works reached the educated minority and down towards an already amply and thoughtfully aware French readership and brought them the systems of thought of the principal authors whose major works (*The Social Contract*, for example) had adorned the second third of the eighteenth century.

After 1770, the patriotic party would also take up with the Jansenists who had become afflicted by a kind of pernicious anaemia once the expulsion of the Jesuits had deprived them of their hereditary enemy and left them up in the air. Some of the authors such as Le Paige and the *abbé* Mey attempted to build bridges between the two factions, the Augustinian and the patriotic. Of course, the favourite target was no longer the Molinism of the Catholic church[21] but the Molinism of the state, which was how the authoritarian characteristics of the Maupeou system were presented. That said, however, in the house of the opposition to the régime there were many 'mansions' and the links which drew pro-*parlementaire* patriots towards Jansenism did not prevent various members of the opposition from developing a penchant for philosophe views. Amongst these mediators figured, for example, Pidanzat de Mairobert as well as the duke de la Rochefoucauld d'Enville. The latter was a grand seigneur, the friend of princes of the blood who also, in turn, turned to support the magistrates. He was also, however, a friend of certain philosophes as a result of the 'free-masonry' of common acquaintance. Both patriots and philosophes joined together in praise of the memory of Fénelon whose reputation, by contrast, remained blackened in the eyes of the government. Patriots and philosophes were both responsible for a rather tedious theatrical play called *The Druids* which made fun of Madame Louise, Louis XV's daughter, who had recently entered the Carmelite order. The official censors contributed, without wanting to, 'consolidating' the opposition factions by not discriminating in their censorship of works between those which they judged to be subversive, and those which (for all their patriotism) had their roots in philosophe thinking.

The patriots thus became professionally the defenders of the sovereign court judges and their courts which Maupeou had suppressed at the stroke of a pen. In consequence they were drawn to reflect on the problems of corporate France, its constituted bodies, and 'corporations' whether representative and/or privileged, such as the Estates General or the

---

[21] Cf. above, chapter 10.

parlements. . . . How was royal sovereignty to be transferred into the hands of institutions with a greater degree of representation? How should it be transmitted to assemblies of the three orders or, in their place, to the *parlementaire* gatherings which had the role of controlling, or of modifying monarchical power? In 1771, Maupeou had wanted to alter the old *corporate-absolutist* state into one which was more purely absolutist – or, at least, he had begun to set about the task. Patriots, by complete contrast, wanted to transform the quasi-absolutism which Maupeou had succeeded in putting into practice into a *corporate-representative* system.

Such an approach implied firstly that they had in mind a certain ideal of the French 'constitution'. In principle the constitution rested, according to these publicists, on the old traditions of the kingdom – for the former parlements were of great antiquity and their existence attested from the thirteenth century onwards. Their constitutional ideas were also derived from the law of Nature and the law of Reason, a law which, whilst originating with God, set them at a distance from official Catholics. They also were developed from the notion of utility, or rather, of 'public well-being'. *Salus populi, suprema lex*, or 'the well-being of the people is the supreme law', taught the Roman law. But there was a twin peril facing the patriots from their line of thinking. Firstly, there was a conservative trap, which meant that some of them sought to maintain or to resurrect at all costs (as against Maupeou's simplifying and rationalizing programme) the *bric-à-brac* of the Ancien Régime's institutions which had slowly accumulated and matured over the centuries without any great sense of order, one on top of another. On the other hand, there was also the opposite (Cartesian) trap, which afflicted the more forthright of the patriots – the trap of what to reconstruct on the basis of a clean sheet all France's national institutions. Having become involved in constitutional issues, patriotism equally invoked the fundamental laws of the kingdom, which had been set down since the dawn of time. Historical research in the eighteenth century had, however, demythologized them, penetrated all their mysteries, and the patriots did not shrink from completing the process. They included amongst these fundamental 'laws' various measures to protect *parlementaire* offices whose integrity Maupeou had challenged. They also equally sought the maintenance, or rather the calling into being, of the constituted bodies or the 'corps' of the realm such as the parlements or the Estates General. The former had been dissolved by the triumvirate; the latter had not been summoned since the last session in 1614/5.

In the majority of cases, however, the patriots faced a precise objective. They sought to juxtapose, or replace concepts of monarchical sovereignty or divine right with notions of national sovereignty and further, drawing on Rousseau, notions of the general, or common, or national, will. The endpoint of this process of substitution (which remained, for the moment, purely intellectual) lay in the theoretical figure of the king which, although it did not disappear completely, would be outshone, and overshadowed by that of the *Patrie* and of the *citoyen*.

The Nation which was thus envisaged, and even promoted over and above the sovereign ruler, remained (for the moderate patriots of the Miromesnil persuasion) a hierarchical society, slightly feudal, composed of orders and 'estates'. In the minds of some extremists, like Marivaux, it would be transformed under the cloudless skies of a utopian vision into a collection of free men, pure and simple. This was a dream which would only begin to be realized, at least in the political arena, 15 or 20 years later.

The idea of the 'contract' which Rousseau had not invented but which he had elaborated, acquired strong resonances amongst these patriot writers. They saw it not as some vague theoretic pact but as a real act such as, for example, the charters, articles and privileges accorded to newly conquered Normandy by Philip Augustus in 1204. By virtue of their existence, Normandy, the great province of the west, was 'guaranteed'[22] against the arbitrary rule of the Capetian king. This contract, in the minds of the patriots, remained a revocable act in cases when the ruler who had signed it in the presence of the people did not satisfactorily fulfil it. The contract was conditional in the sense that it was dedicated to the well-being of the realm's inhabitants, a well-being which must be confirmed as the prime objective of His Majesty's activities. In the end, the contract was nothing more than a simple commission issued to the sovereign, a commission which, inverting the normal relationship between sovereign and commissioner, made the king himself the commissioner. His Majesty (and was the king still 'His Majesty' in these circumstances?) had to act in the best interests of 20 or 30 million inhabitants . . . and be able to be sacked if their discontent was found to be justified.

The patriots also had a great respect for the law which, according to them, would be at once above the Prince and equal to all, whatever the unequal circumstances in which every individual found himself. Law remained, in principle, above the attempts to sway it, the manipulative desires of governing authorities. In short, their perception of law was entirely separate from the 'arbitrariness' for which the patriot publicists endlessly castigated Ancien Régime institutions, incidents of which had occurred under Maupeou and even before him. The respect accorded by the patriots to the 'repository of laws' (a synonym for the defunct Parlement) came close to superstitious reverence. 'Sacred are they (the laws) for no one shall lay a finger on them.' Patriotic and systematic in its patterns of thought, the opposition was not, however, constructive in its attitudes. It refused to follow in the chancellor's footsteps in his justified attempts to reform and simplify French institutions which he attempted to instill in the heart of French provinces. It would require, however, nothing

---

[22]   Michel de Bouard, *Histoire de Normandie* (Toulouse, Privat, 1970), p. 195.

less than a Bonaparte, with all the discretionary power which he would enjoy, with Lebrun at his side, the former collaborator of Maupeou, to achieve the unification of the law with the final drafting of the Civil Code. The opposition was only at its best in performing a negative role, 'being against' but not feeling much like wanting to be constructive! Then one word had a shock effect on the opposition, galvanizing their energies and uniting them in hostility towards the established authorities, a united group which refused to give way. That one word was *despotism*. Through its use, concepts which had been given credence in the seventeenth century such as Reason of State and divine right became henceforth detested and attacked without remission.

There were, at best, those patriots (and they were numerous) who retained a strong sense of religious conscience for whom divine right might have survived on its own by means of a reinvestment of its legitimacy by stressing the initiating role of the people, beyond all kinds of consecration, conceived in a strictly royal sense. In this sense, the voice of God would bless and confirm the voice of the people: *Vox populi, vox Dei*. There was also an anti-bureaucratic element which made itself public in the writings of a renowned representative of the patriots, Malesherbes, the *président* of the *Cour des aides* of Paris.[23] He opposed the 'tyranny' of royal administration, its 'agents', the *intendants des finances* and the commissioners of all kinds, particularly the provincial intendants. This seemed, it is true, a lost cause. The rise of bureaucracy would be one of the great social facts over the two centuries following Maupeou's coup. The controversy in which Malesherbes played a leading part had, however, the advantage of highlighting one of the important points in a pattern of thought which was hostile to centralization, a pattern which would be given the purest expression 60 or 80 years later by Tocqueville, whose forebear and family relative was the *président* in the *Cour des aides*. Adopting an air of false naivety and portliness, Malesherbes became the Socrates of the enlightened magistrature in the latter days of the Ancien Régime. Sent to the guillotine in 1794 as a defender of Louis XVI, he reinforced, through an execution which he approached with dignity, his lifelong fidelity towards the ideal of resistance to uncontrolled power. Sadly, poor Malesherbes would find himself confronted by Montagnard persecutors who would be far harsher than ever Louis XV and Maupeou had been. In 1770, and again in 1775, Malesherbes was not infused with the corporate egoism of those who hoped that the parlements and other sovereign courts would be empowered afresh with functions to resist royal power and with the attributes of a national quasi-representativity. In reality, as with a number of the patriots, Malesherbes was also capable of a breadth of vision and would call for the summoning of the Estates General (after 160 years in cold storage) to act as correctives to the excesses of central authority.

[23]   Elisabeth Badinter, *Les 'Remonstrances de Malesherbes', 1771–1775* (Paris, UGE, 1978), p. 114 *et seq.*

The assembly of the three orders of the realm, according to Guillaume Saige, one of the better writers of the patriot party, would act as an organism of legislative authority against the royal executive. However it is at this point that corporatism, having been ejected by the front door, re-enters by the back. In the absence of the Estates General, the Parlement, according to Jacques Augeard, could take over, in a provisional or definitive fashion, the role of representative of the Nation. Similarly, according to Jacques Mey and the duke de Brancas, the Parlement ('a kind of attenuated and small-scale three estates') should, in the absence of the Estates General, take action as the political administration of the kingdom and its legislative authority. The Carolingian edict of Pistes, dated to 864, was even adduced in support of this hypothesis, an edict which willed that one of the ways in which laws should be made was with the consent of the people. Thus was handed on, as in a game of pass-the-parcel, and under the wrapping of medieval phraseology, the enormous weight of the people's choice to the slender protection of the Parlement.

It was the same pattern for consent to taxation. Malesherbes, followed by Augeard, Brancas and Target, wanted to give such authority to the Estates General, or rather, to restore such powers to it. Yet since the estates were not, for the present, able to be summoned, there was no other solution except to vest the powers in the Parlement! Such a position had already been envisaged by Mey, Blonde and by the sovereign courts of Normandy and Franche-Comté in 1771. From such a position, the main lines of force of decentralizing notions flowed through to those who wanted the provincial parlements each to be entrusted with preserving the customs and privileges of their respective region. This was far from starting from scratch, which was how the Constituent Assembly, the putative heir to the Estates General of 1789, would pretend to reconstruct, in place of the various parlements, the whole country's political structure. But this is to ignore the intervening stages; the baton of authoritarian centralism would remain in Maupeou's hands before he then passed it on to the Jacobins and Bonaparte – when the time came.

In all these patriot notions, there remained, nevertheless, an essential insight. In some shape or form, it was, according to them, a corporation, a company, an assembly, a collective and representative entity which would assume the totality (or, at the least and in the opinion of the moderates amongst the cabal, the overwhelming degree) of legislative power and capacity to make protests against the abuses of an over-zealous executive authority. Such a notion had great value and the experience of the following six or seven generations would fully confirm its validity even if the organism to which one should assign such a task (parlements, Estates General) would be shown to be ill-adapted to the task, and to the extent that, following the years 1789/1791, a formula for new assemblies to accompany the representative and critical tasks had to be found.

Also worth noting is the degree of anti-aristocratic sensitivity displayed by the patriotic party, a party which remained, however, dominated by the *robe* nobility, no enemies to the princes of the blood. The prodigious effects of this allergic and principled hostility against the noble order 15 or 20 years later needs no underlining. It is almost as though, over and above the particular influence exercised by one individual or social group, there was a new political culture taking shape which proclaimed the Revolution, and which was dawning in the last years of Louis XV in the various writings of different individuals.

Hated 'despotism' leads one, by antithesis, to the other word, liberty, which was exalted to the skies in the Maupeou period. The word would become still more important a few years after the death of the 60-year-old king in 1774, when the tremendous movement for solidarity with the American colonists began to take shape during their revolt. Liberty meant, paraphrasing Montesquieu *grosso modo* 'the right to do anything that (just) laws allowed'.[24] On this point, patriotic thought was richly embellished. Following Huguenot and Jansenist approaches, it advocated liberty of conscience, a concept of considerable importance to Pidanzat de Mairobert, Saige, Blonde and Target. This included the freedom of the press, which was pressed for by the viscount d'Aubusson. It embraced a notion of personal liberty in opposition to *lettres de cachet*, even when such instruments were issued by the royal authorities 'in the interest of families'.[25] It meant the liberty to choose one's place of abode, one's profession, one's friends, and on all these points there was a wonderful passage in the *Maximes* written by Mey. Then there was the right to life, an elementary form of emancipation emphasized in the *Catéchisme du citoyen* of Saige. At the group level there was also an idea of 'national liberty' which would become identified with the sovereign destiny of the vast national conglomerate when the latter had recovered its own self-determination. In other words, it would become part of the general will which was (some clear-thinking individuals excepted) not yet conceived as something which would, come 1793, become the destroyer of liberty.

Liberty also became linked, and in a way which is somewhat surprising these days, to the notion of property (in all its various guises). The latter did not merely extend to the material goods and landed property such as we imagine it to consist of today; it also involved, as the *parlementaires* of Besançon proclaimed in 1772, all that was dear to a man: his customs, his liberties, his life, his passions, and (of course) his belongings and his inheritance.

The patriots were rather more timid when they approached the question

---

[24] Montesquieu, *Esprit des lois*, ch. 11, section 3.
[25] Arlette Farge and Michel Foucault, *Le Désordre des familles: lettres de cachet des archives de la Bastille* (Paris, Gallimard, 1982).

of equality. Despite the anti-aristocratic foibles to which they were attached, they sought to defend the privileges of the *parlementaire* nobility. At best, the patriots admitted that each citizen had an 'equal' right to integrate into a national community, duly vested with an autonomous will (but not endowed with any possibility of universal suffrage to embody that right, equal or individual, in practice!). In other words, knowing who would be the true deciders of national destiny, and who would be the electors of those who decided such a matter in a great 'liberated' country such as France remained an open question, still up for discussion. The habits of informality across the social divide acquired in the masonic lodges tended to break down, however, amongst these 'opinion-formers', the rigid divisions which once had separated the social orders one from another.

The patriots should not be regarded at all as revolutionaries. Many of them were conservatives in the Burke mould. They did not want profoundly to change the social order which they believed to have been instituted across the centuries of the past. They simply wanted to put an end to the disorder which they thought absolutism had created. They were strongly in favour of regional institutions which had stood the test of time. In this respect they were closer to the views of Tocqueville than Sieyès. The only model of revolution of which they had any knowledge, and that through reading about it, was the Glorious Revolution in England in 1688. The majority of the patriot writers could conceive of no more than passive, or non-violent, resistance to 'arbitrary will' such as the French parlements had practised from 1750. Among some of the patriots, however, such as Pidanzat de Mairobert, there was a rather isolated and rhetorical appeal to overturn the tyrant, which could well be taken to mean, some day or other, an invitation to renewed violence. But such verbal audacity did not yet reflect the opinions of the patriot group as a whole.

Besides the (pro-Maupeou) royalist and the (pro-*parlementaire*) patriots, the 'rainbow' of political shades of opinion revealed a third colour, itself a mixture of several others. These included the independent and radical voices, the creative and innovative minds of the period. They had no love for refined, robust absolutism (despotic) nor for the Parlement, which had been responsible according to them for a burdensome past history of successive truces with oppressive authority and particularly with the church, albeit a Gallican church. These individuals (sometimes they were women) corresponded to the older and now well-matured generation of philosophes, *encyclopédistes*, along with other tangential, younger, personalities at their side. Some of them, the gentler brethren such as Necker and the *abbé* Galiani, would be content to live under a well-tempered absolutism, one which put a stop to the excessive and gratuitous arbitrary will which had been exercised by, as they saw it, Louis XIV or (later) Maupeou. As for Turgot, he directed his sharpest criticism against royal despotism and also against the *parlementaire* 'paper-tigers'; but he also knew well enough that, when faced with participating in government, pragmatic realism and practical reform constituted the only reasonable, and thus *a priori* moderate, solution.

Most of the philosophes and their acolytes went further, however, whether we look at Diderot, d'Alembert, Helvetius, d'Holbach, Mably' Condorcet, the *abbé* Raynal or Grimm, Madame d'Epinay and Mirabeau the younger. In opposition to despotism, the undoubted common enemy, against this Gargantua of a monarchical state devouring, like the monster in an old engraving, cows and pigs in their thousands and plate-loads of fruit and vast slices of bread, they summoned the forces of the Enlightenment, the natural law, the imperative demands of the emotions and the human spirit, the irrepressible quest for collective and individual happiness, and even the democratic (if that was truly what they had been) and representative traditions of the French going back to the Merovingians and the Carolingians. They feared (and with a degree of paranoid exaggeration) a general increase in absolutism across Europe. In this respect, they cited Maupeou, of course, but also the *coup de majesté* of Gustavus III in Sweden and Count von Struensee in Denmark. They could scarcely find words harsh enough to condemn despotism (again that word) and superstition. But they felt no corresponding desire to rush to support the *parlementaire* gentry which they detested almost as cordially as they did governmental tyranny.

By contrast, liberty, once more, constituted one of the positive themes which forcefully characterized this group of intellectuals. Some of them, like Diderot, saw liberty as an end in itself. Others regarded it as a way forward to some higher, eventually transcendent, Good such as justice (Condorcet, Turgot), virtue (Mably) or simply happiness (d'Holbach). Thus defined by these various parameters, liberty led on to the equally classic and disparate domains of freedom of action, freedom of religious choice, freedom of the press and freedom of speech.

Despite the liberally-minded anglophile and empirical leanings which were to be encountered in various ways around the group as a whole, its leading innovative figures demonstrated, when the occasions arose, a certain ideological rigour, more clearly present than amongst the patriots. They sincerely sought a degree of religious tolerance for Protestants; but they did not exclude from the back of their minds that, one fine day, they would say goodbye to the Catholic church.

The freedom of the press, in d'Alembert's case, for example, was less an end in itself, than a means by which Enlightenment could be advanced and superstition defeated. It was a far from sophisticated approach, but it would become more widespread during the revolutionary years, and wth consequences which were, as we know, unforeseen or even dangerous. The teachings of Jean-Jacques Rousseau were not forgotten, either, and the innovative group, in general, preached equality before the law through the writings of d'Alembert, Diderot and d'Holbach. They all also upheld the fundamental notion of popular sovereignty, albeit with different emphases when it came to examining the nature of the basic political and social contract which had to be struck between ruler and ruled. The contractual principle is formulated by authors as diverse as Diderot, Mercier, Morellet, Condorcet, d'Alembert, Mably and even Turgot. Once realized, popular sovereignty would have be embodied within a legislative and national body of representatives who would be elected, nevertheless, on a restrictive franchise determined by those who owned property; such at least, was the 'property qualification' supported by Turgot, d'Holbach, Condorcet, Diderot and Morellet. But Sébastien Mercier preferred to go a stage further and envisage a quasi-republican constitution, qualified only by the retention of a nonentity as a king whose presence would be largely symbolic. Held personally responsible for his actions before the country's judges, this monarch would be the more willing to accept the propositions of the sovereign people. The new régime established on this basis would be, in any case, governed by a legislative Chamber which would have the essential power to consent to taxes.

For its part, worse was to await the church, or so it seemed, once these master-thinkers ever achieved power. The Revocation of the edict of Nantes, seen in the long-term, and still more *Unigenitus* had, in effect, 'moored' the church alongside the temporal powers that be. Provided with wealth aplenty in this world, the clergy, and above all the higher clergy, found itself threatened by the designs of the philosophes in its property, its tithes, its revenues of all kinds, and in its papal and episcopal hierarchy. The Jansenists, alongside Choiseul, had already made a breach in the defences with the expulsion of the Jesuits. Now the philosophe storm-troopers could engulf the church through the gap which had been formed. For the principal attackers (Diderot, d'Holbach, Helvetius, Condorcet, the *abbé* Raynal and Mably) it was a matter of crushing the Beast, not merely guaranteeing an indispensable and legitimate right of toleration to minority faiths (such as the Huguenots). It would require a clear-sighted individual, however to foresee the distant and future prospect where the welcome freedom of the Jews and the Calvinists would be finally achieved only to begin an equally prolonged period of oppression of Catholics faithful to the sovereign pontiff in Rome. At all events, some bishops, and Louis XV as well, were aware of the danger.

And, in the wake of the clergy, what fate did the philosophes have in store for the court nobility, and the *noblesse de race, d'épée* and *de robe*? They too had opposed absolutism, particularly the *noblesse de robe*. Some of the great reforming writers, especially Condorcet, were gentlemen born and bred. But the second order did not feature prominently amongst the opinion-formers who, on the whole, believed that too many aristocrats benefited too much from the grace and favour of the court. The latter may have been less profligate than its opponents made out, but it still disqualified its courtiers by domesticating them. It hardly mattered that the court was open to only a relatively small minority of the nobility (barely more than 5–10 per cent of the total). The discredit heaped on this small fraction reflected upon the whole of the nobility as a group, which was already additionally unpopular by virtue of the fiscal privileges which it enjoyed. The complaints lodged against the aristocracy were often far from coherent. The philosophes were easily able, and without risk of contradiction, to accuse the nobility of being lazy; and, at the same time, to accuse them of monopolizing all the government posts which, in a great monarchy, required of their holders a minimum of work and commitment. In the end, the nobility and the priests were the butt of equivalent, if not similar, accusations. Both groups, or at least some of their number, were accused of having compromised with absolutism, even in its enfeebled and chastened post-Louis XIV form. In reality, the state had become, after the Colbertian reforms, the source and confirmation of all noble privilege and this connection attracted to the nobility the common aversion felt towards the state and the nobility. At all events, the hereditary principle did not find favour in the age of the Enlightenment. Diderot, d'Alembert, d'Holbach and Mercier criticized the hereditary succession of social status which, they said, could in no way motivate the privileged. No doubt it would be impossible to abolish the fact of inequality as between one individual and another. But this should not provide an automatic justification for the presence or otherwise of a social pedigree determined on the basis of a genetic patrimony possessed by this or that individual. Social gradation should be sustained by talent, industry and virtue. Over and above the sought-after removal of the remaining 'feudal' entities and seigneurial rights, they thus sought to erect a society which would properly reward merit; and such aspirations would eventually find their expression in the real world in terms of our own meritocracies.

Beyond that, the revolutionary radicalism which would be so clearly expressed by a Condorcet was readily accessible. The sky was the limit! Why not summon before the tribunal of Reason those various strange entities whose existence had historical justifications alone, such as the nobility, the church, the monarchy. . . . All of these institutions were at risk of being declared old-fashioned and to be abolished once the philosophes applied their exacting critical standards to them. The most outlandish amongst them, Raynal, Mercier and Mably, had no hesitation at all in setting off a torrent of hostility towards wealth, and a complete justification for the rights of the poor. A whole new political synthesis, albeit heterogeneously composed and from disparate sources, was perhaps in the process of being formed. If this was the case, then it was situated somewhere midway between an organizational realism and a creative (or destructive) utopianism, between Terray and Turgot, between paradise and practicality. It would combine the forthright authoritarianism of a Lebrun (although not a Maupeou) and the anti-despotism of the patriots. It would set the agenda for the refashioning of all the social institutions of the Ancien Régime to the prejudice of the king, the church, the nobility and even, eventually, the propertied classes.

Conclusion

Louis XV died in unpopularity at the age of 64 on 10 May 1774. The king's death brought the epoch covered by this volume to a close and this conclusion is thus a 'postface' to the two volumes on *The Royal French State* and *The Ancien Régime* which have covered the period from 1460 to 1774. The following reign, that of Louis XVI from 1774 to 1792, coincided with the liquidation of the royal system. Over some 20 years, there was a decline into final catastrophe when the 'heir of St Louis' reached his end under the executioner's blade. The Most Christian King ascended into Heaven. This terminal 'cesura' requires an assessment of the period as a whole and this entails a retrospective evaluation of the periodization of France's political history over the several centuries from 1460 to 1774.

Such an evaluation has to be undertaken at three levels. Firstly, and in the very long-term, there was the growth of the state which can be illustrated by some figures which have already been cited. There were five million office-holders in around 1515, as compared with 46,000 in around 1665 and 51,000 in the last years of the Ancien Régime.[1] To the latter figure should be added, during the eighteenth century, a whole host of *commis*, precursors of our modern civil servants, with at least 30,000 of them serving in the general tax-farm (the *ferme générale*) service alone. In principle, this considerable increase in the number of individuals who were directly in the service of the state apparatus should not have created a trend in the state towards a particular form of government, liberal, democratic or 'despotic', at any particular point in time. The French republic in 1986 would have 1,990,000 servants in the public sector and it would still

---

[1] William Doyle, *The Origins of the French Revolution* (Oxford, Oxford University Press, 1980), pp. 43–4. Doyle uses the figures provided by Necker himself for the late eighteenth century which, as he admits himself, were likely to have been conservative estimates. As for the numbers of office-holders in the earlier period, see E. Le Roy Ladurie, *The Royal French State* (Oxford, Blackwell, 1994), p. 17. According to Doyle, the nobility occupied scarcely 10 per cent of these offices, although it was the case that these were amongst the 'more senior' posts.

be a democracy. On the other hand, in the particular context of the Ancien Régime, when there was a considerable increase in the number of office-holders between the sixteenth and the eighteenth centuries, the result would be the creation of a state which was clearly more authoritarian, and in a way which would be described *a posteriori* as 'absolutist'. The development was long in the making but one possible date for its emergence is that of 1624, when Richelieu finally took his seat at the *Conseil d'en haut*, with Mazarin following in succession to him. Louis XIV gave the absolutist system (or the system which was presented as such) its finishing touches, whose dominant themes (not always applied in practice) would be those of *order*, *authority* and *realm*. During the eighteenth century, when absolutism was fully developed, it began to show signs of strain; or, rather, it became more flexible whilst retaining the essential aspects which the cardinal-ministers and the Sun-King had given it in the period from 1624 to 1715. The most revealing aspect, the 'acid test', the most characteristic feature of this politico-administrative arrangement which developed, matured and then decayed in the period from 1624 to 1788, was, despite the survival and flourishing of some provincial and local assemblies, the long absence of any convocation of any form of representative body of the 'estates' which made up the realm, the country as a whole. The last meeting of the Estates General had taken place in 1614; the final assembly of notables occurred in 1627. Between these two dates it can be said that absolutism was still 'in the balance'. After 1627, the path was 'chosen' or, at least, definitively laid down (as it would remain, in formal terms, until 1787, the date of the next and final assembly of notables). This French pattern of government would coexist with other régimes in Europe of a similar kind, for example that of Prussia, but it was a Europe where there also functioned different systems on a semi-representative basis (as in the case of England) or an oligarchic/republican model (such as the Protestant Swiss cantons or Catholic Venice).[2]

That said, the emergence of a more highly developed state sector, more generously provided with tens of thousands of office-holders and *commis* and the putting in place of an absolutist system of government did not, of itself, prevent other political developments between 1460 and 1774. In the more medium-term periodization (a decade or sequence of decades) we can determine in a remarkable fashion the phenomenon of 'alternation'[3] with an unequal rhythm between modes of government which were either more 'open' or more 'authoritarian' depending on the period. There were authoritarian periods such as the reigns of Louis XI and Henry II and, of course, the whole period of the emergence and apogee of absolutism between 1624 and 1715, leaving aside the five or six years of the Fronde.

[2] Ernst Hinrichs, *Einführung in die Geschichte der Frühen Neuzeit* (Munich, C.H. Beck, 1980), p. 178 *et seq.*
[3] A good analysis of what may be seen as the 'openness' or, alternatively, a more marked degree of 'authoritarianism' in ancien régime France (in its ideological valency) may be found in Fénelon, *Oeuvres* (2 vols, Paris, Gallimard, 1983), i, 298–300.

In contrast were the periods of relative openness, such as the Regency of
Anne de Beaujeu, followed by the reigns of Charles VIII and Louis XII;
and the reign of Francis I, at least up to the Affair of the Placards in 1534.
Thereafter, there were the 'compromising' impulses towards religious
coexistence which coincided with Catherine de Médicis' periods in power,
and later with those of Henry III, albeit that they took place in the
horrifying context of the wars of religion, followed by the 'fanaticism' of
the League. More marked and successful flexibility was to characterize the
reign of Henry IV and, much later, the regency of Philippe d'Orléans. The
whole period of Louis XV's reign was marked by signs of a relaxation of
the exercise of authority during a period of often outstanding civilization.
But even during his reign, the oscillatory patterns of openness and authoritarianism continued like the to-and-fro sculling of a boat from the stern.
The ministry of Fleury up to around 1740 or 1743 was characterized by
the relaxation of the old Louis XIV tensions, a relaxation which had been
begun by Orléans, Law, Dubois, Saint-Simon and the Cardinal de
Noailles. By contrast, the period from August 1742 to February 1757
corresponded to the years when Pierre de Voyer de Paulmy, Count
d'Argenson served in the ministry.[4] He did not always play a dominant role
in affairs (for Fleury would have no worthy successors, and at best was
replaced by substitutes) but he was a 'bench-mark' figure who can serve
for historiographical purposes to symbolize in a convenient fashion a
decade and a half of political reaction and relative authoritarianism. It
would not, however, be the case (and it almost goes without saying) that
there could be a return to the apogee of absolutism such as it had been
practised for over 50 years by King Louis XIV. From 1758 to 1770, the
ministry of Choiseul reversed the direction towards a quasi-liberal policy,
which breached the old monarchical paternalism by introducing the freedom of trade in grain. It also eroded ultramontane clericism by the
suppression of the Jesuits. At the same time, it sketched out, in the years
1764 and 1765, a representative system through the creation, albeit temporary, of partially elective municipal government. Finally, between 1770
and 1774, came, by way of balance, a reaction. The Maupeou-Terray-
d'Aiguillon 'triumvirate' returned strongly towards the path of authoritarianism with the dissolution of the parlements which was something which
Louis XV had never contemplated in his wildest dreams. Despite this, and
various other succeeding exploits, Maupeou and his friends could not, and
did not want to, drag the administrative structures, let alone the politico-
juridical corporations of France, back to the patterns of authority and,
complementary to them, of blind obedience, such as had broadly characterized these corporations and administrative units under the Sun-King.
History could not be turned back a whole century. In the end, following
1774 and the death of Louis XV, the fracture of this pattern was complete
and the antiphony between openness and authority, the amoeba-like tens-

---

[4]   M. Antoine, *Le Gouvernement et l'administration sous Louis XV; Dictionnaire biographique*,
(Paris, CNRS, 1978), p. 250.

ing and relaxation of the muscles of authority, fell into desuetude and terminal turbulence. Nevertheless, the preceeding centuries had made the most of periods of fairly continuously directed political energies.[5]

How was it that a political régime which had displayed a remarkable capacity to adapt in this oscillatory fashion (almost like a pendulum) should become 'deconstructed' after 1774? The system which was over-thrown was systematically 'taken apart' in the 15 or 20 years, depending on whether one dates the final collapse as occurring in 1789 (the 'official' beginning of the French Revolution) or in 1793 (the execution of Louis XVI). How did this come to pass? The answer to that question belongs essentially to François Furet, author of the following book in this series, who provides the logical complement, and one of the first importance, to these two volumes.[6] At all events, the revolutionary, and pre-revolutionary events, can now be deciphered without too much difficulty thanks to both well-established and more recent research, and also to the retrospective enquiries stimulated in particular by the recent occurrence of the bi-centenary of the Revolution in 1989.

If the French monarchy found itself in travails, slipping and then finally collapsing, then it was, firstly, the result of an unprecedent economic and cultural growth which had occured through the greater part of the eight-eenth century, particularly from 1715. In social terms, there had been, alongside these phenomena, the growth of an Enlightenment élite,[7] critical both of authority and of itself. It was made up of a component of the legal bourgeoisie, which would eventually become office-holders and property-owners, practising the liberal professions and often highly educated. It also was made up of the liberal nobility, the enlightened aristocrats of old roots, as well as, in many instances, the *parlementaire* magistrates and others.[8] Seen in this aspect, the nobility appears as a competent and professional

---

[5] See, in this context, E. Le Roy Ladurie, 'La Monarchie française d'Ancien Régime; un système ouvert', *Revue de la Bibliothèque nationale*, 27 (1988), 3–14.

[6] This conclusion owes much to the thought of François Furet who could well have been cited more often than opportunity has afforded. See, notably, his volume in this series on *Revolutionary France, 1770–1880* (Oxford, Blackwell, 1992). See also François Furet, *Penser la Révolution française* (Paris, Gallimard, 1978).

[7] On the élites, see Denis Richet, 'Autour des origines idéologiques lointaines de la Révolution française. Elites et despotisme', *Annales ESC*, 24 (1969), 1–23; also Guy Chaussinand-Nogaret, *Une histoire des élites, 1700–1748* (Paris, Taillandier, 1975). The concluding remarks to this volume have not explored the Marxist (in reality, Marxist-Leninist) theories on the French Revolution. It is presented as one contribution to the triumph of the bourgeoisie, and the means of capitalist production. The latter, however, was rather more constrained than stimulated by the Revolution! The main lines of argument of these theories are presented in Albert Soboul, *La Révolution française* (Paris, PUF, 1967) as well as in Soboul's other works. See also Claude Mazauric, *Sur la Révolution française. Contribution à l'histoire de la Révolution bourgeoise* (Paris, Messidor, 1988). It is, of course, undeniable that these theories have had considerable importance in the elaboration, in the short or the medium term, of a particular historiography of the French Revolution.

[8] Christian Jouhaud expressed it well in *Le Monde* (9 February, 1990) when he said that the parlements of this period 'prennent, faute de mieux, valeur d'institutions représentatives'.

class,[9] recruited on quasi-hereditary lines (the military regulation of 1781 accentuating still further for the officer ranks the characteristic requirement of noble birth). This latter 'class' retained almost all the posts of important responsibility (in the army, the magistrature and the senior public service, in finance etc.). It had a tendency towards exclusivity despite the entry into it of a number of newly ennobled individuals; but it was not overall a parasitic class since, in many cases, the heads of the families worked hard at their tasks. Yet it was threatened, or at least jealously regarded, by the commonality of the Third Estate which resented the idea that the essential functions of the state should thus become monopolized by a narrow group, albeit one which was active and well-educated, and composed of some tens of thousands of families. The nobility, the privileged 'Estate' *par excellence*, did not take very seriously the jealousies directed towards it by the Third Estate. It concerned itself with matters which were less 'general' and less likely to arouse passions. The nobility felt, in fact, a responsibility for the state for, after 1749, it paid more in taxation, in particular through the *vingtièmes* (in the preceeding period, it had only been charged under the capitation[10]). From the end of the seventeenth century, the nobility regarded themselves as guardians[11] for the absolutism which, from Richelieu to Maupeou, had accomplished (over the century and a half from 1624 to 1774) its historical mission. The absolutist system of government had, in reality, done much to rationalize the state administration, but the task had only been half completed. It thus remained, in the eyes of these new rationalist thinkers, a 'gothic monster'. In the process of the modernization of state and society, however, absolutism had encouraged (in a way which had not always been of its own volition) the first beginnings of equality between individuals, the latter still remaining subjects, having not yet become citizens. Equality, or at least equalization, thus proceded from the processes of Justice which, in principle, was the same for all. It also resulted from the creation of new taxes which were designed to weigh on all tax-payers alike, privileged or not, noble or commoner. Amongst these new taxes should be included the *capitation* from 1695 to 1782, then the *dixième*, and then, above all, the

---

[9] On the professionalism of the Ancien Régime nobility, see the most outstanding recent study (appearing after that of Guy Chaussinand-Nogaret) by David Bien in the article 'Aristocracy' in François Furet and Mona Ozouf (eds), *Dictionnaire critique de la Révolution française* (Paris, Flammarion, 1988) p. 640 *et seq.* As for the possibilities for the political reemergence of the nobility, see Montesquieu.

[10] The *capitation* (a direct tax, notionally paid by everyone) was established in 1695, then abolished with the return of peace in 1698. It was re-established in 1701 after the outbreak of the War of Spanish Succession and would continue until the Revolution. In principle, it was paid, despite numerous exemptions, by the nobility as well.

[11] Montesquieu specifically envisaged that 'revolutions' provoked by the nobility would replace 'Despotism' (as he called it) with a monarchy, controlled or limited by the 'intermediary authority' of the nobility; see Montesquieu, *De l'Esprit des lois*, book III, ch. 9 and Arlette Jouanna, *Le Devoir de révolte, la noblesse française et la gestation de l'Etat moderne, 1559–1661* (Paris, Fayard, 1989), p. 399.

vingtièmes.[12] By these means, absolutism had unintentional consequences and effects which threatened its own survival. To the degree that it undermined the society of orders, privileged or not, and corporation, it increased the discontents felt amongst some of the nobility which, with the best of intentions, wanted, as we have already indicated, to participate more directly in political decison-making. Above all, it would end up, in some degree, with destroying the aggregates of society, some of which were still very much alive. These aggregates included the 'estates' and the 'corporations', those bodies which had formerly been constituted and 'shepherded' together under the old-fashioned monarchy of the Valois and the first Bourbon. Their substitute would lie in the rubble of a society already individualistic and heavily atomized, a process which was already well under way, albeit not yet completed, by 1774 or 1788. Was it not the case that absolutism, because of its individualizing effects, tended to isolate itself and cut itself off from its social roots? The residence of the monarchy at Versailles, isolating, separating or separatist, did nothing to help matters. The nobility itself, because some of its number had become a rich minority serving as 'insects of the court', was tainted to some degree by the disdain in which the courtiers' lifestyle was held, considered (rightly or wrongly) as parasites and transformed into scapegoats. More seriously still, although it was less and less the object of popular respect, this did not prevent the court of Louis XV or Louis XVI from lashing out from time to time, mocking the king, the queen and the ministers in songs and pamphlets. What a difference from the well-tamed courtiers of Louis XIV's day!

That said, rather than the isolation of absolutism (and, after all, well into the eighteenth century, the system still knew how, thanks to the provincial intendants, to nurture solid links[13] with the rural village world and against the rural seigneuries, who had few friends amongst the legists), rather than splendid isolation pure and simple, should we not rather speak of an erosion of absolutism's principle of legitimacy? This principle had functioned well, by contrast, in the more favourable conditions (even though administrative and centralizing rectitude languished) when the three Valois of the Renaissance, followed by the first Bourbon, governed the state more gently, in spontaneous symbiosis with the 'gothic' structure of its constituted corporated bodies, and in symbiosis with its social 'estates' which were not at all threatened by the later processes of atomization.

History is full of subtle nuances and, during the subsequent, at times atomizing, phase, absolutism would be able to generate its own antibodies; for it was the monarchy itself which, under Louis XIV and Louis XV,

---

[12] On the *capitation*, see glossary. The *dixième* was inaugurated in 1710 and would be abolished and then reinstituted several times in wartime. The *vingtième* made its appearance in 1749 and it would subsequently become a replacement for the *dixième*. From the point of view of the equitability of its collection, it was a highly modern tax.

[13] Hilton Root, *Peasants and King in Burgundy* (Berkeley, California University Press, 1987).

would encourage the rise, for fiscal reasons, of craft guilds and associations which grew up in the protective shadow of the state. But this was precisely what Turgot abolished when he did away with the corporations in 1776, thus cutting off the branch astride which the two Bourbon predecessors of Louis XVI had sat. As a result, a king in 1789 with absolutist pretensions, and reigning over a mass of individuals with increasing lack of differentiation between one another, and with whom he could have, because of their huge numbers, nothing approaching a personal relationship, was less assured of his power-base than a 'temperate' monarch in 1540 who prided himself on embodying in himself, in his 'political corpus', however out-of-date, the structural components of an effective 'corporate' structure in the state.[14] In such conditions, the royal 'fruit' on the topmost branch seemed ripe and ready to drop by the last quarter of the eighteenth century. The élites who had 'unleashed' absolutism on France, or their predecessors who had launched it and tended it, now looked to collect the 'fruits' of its decay and place them firmly in their grasp. This had already been the case in England post-1688 (to a considerable degree, although not completely so). The French élites regarded themselves as capable of carrying out the various political and 'gubernatorial' functions of the state directly in addition to the judicial, administrative, seigneurial, military and financial roles which they had already been discharging for some time. How could they not be interested in recovering power from the hands of an exhausted absolutism, and which was theirs for the taking and which it might eventually ask them to assume? The latter was almost what would occur in 1788 when the king would ask his 'faithful subjects' to enlighten him on the most propitious ways and means to reassemble the Estates General.

This was a way forward which, nevertheless, lay thick with peril. We have already indicated the envious frustrations of a militant fraction of the Third Estate towards the nobility, whatever its professional competence, and which led those without noble privilege to oppose the privileged on principle. But the nobility itself, with numerous internal splits, was hardly in better shape. The *Mémoires* of Saint-Simon are one of the great works of literature of the eighteenth century, contemporary (in terms of their composition, but not in terms of their publication which would be later) with the influential works of Rousseau, Montesquieu, Voltaire or Diderot.

---

[14]   The process of 'auto-erosion' within the Ancien Régime was extremely complex after 1750 or 1780. On the one hand, the monarchical state introduced the seeds of equality into society (through its judicial institutions and other social aspects) which could serve to destabilize the (corporative) existing hierarchy. On the other hand, by creating new corporations and taking already existing corporate bodies under its wing (by, for example, nominating new nobles, or bishops, or developing the craft guilds), the state became accused eventually of authoritarianism, even by those within these corporate, or neo-corporate, entities. As a result, its own unpopularity was thereby increased. At the same time, it created the sense of these corporate bodies being compromised by established authority, and this undermined the prestige enjoyed by these *corps* in the eyes of the public, a public which was itself becoming more dominant in the years after 1750.

However these *Mémoires* underline amply, albeit *a posteriori* (for, evoking Louis XIV's reign through the writings of someone like Saint-Simon was, in itself, a way of attacking Louis XV indirectly) the divisions, diversities and fissiparous nature of the nobility, both within the order and towards the other élite groups in society. Its fissures were even encouraged by the monarchy, for it liked to give substance to nobodies, and readily developed games of precedence at Court and elsewhere in order the more readily to reign. By exploiting the incontestable hierarchical logic within the nobility, the monarchy could set a duke against a simple gentleman, a sword nobleman against a magistrate, the favourite of the day against the the disgraced favourite of yesteryear. Envy, vanity and jealousy and any number of mutual misunderstandings; these would be capital resources for group psychology amongst the élites on the eve of the Revolution as during the nineteenth century.[15]

From this point of view, the major element, or at least the essential product of the 'divisibility' within the élites and (of course) between the élites and the rest of society, was the desire for equality, a compensatory mixture of envious frustration and philosophe ideology. At the very least it involved a desire for equality in rights or civil equality, a desire nurtured by Graeco-Roman culture; but, apart from some of the early forerunners of socialism, the vast majority of theorists were agreed in recognizing that an *absolute* equality between individuals, in terms of wealth, talents, and ability to deploy both, was a dangerous, utopian dream. The desire for equality of rights was at first (which is hardly surprising) the preoccupation of the non-privileged, at the heart of which (and amongst the topmost representatives of whom) social jealousy towards those endowed with a title, a status and a seigneurie, was evidently the most strongly felt. But this desire was also to be found amongst the liberal elements of the nobility, breathing in the contemporary air for it, expressing their soul's generous longings, or hoping to make it to positions of power by assuring themselves of easy popularity amongst the commoners. These liberal elements readily flirted with the chimera of abolishing privileges, so long as some distinctions were maintained. Egalitarianism also found its source, or one of its sources, in certain currents or patterns of Christian thinking. All men are equal before the Eternal Father, being only distinguishable from one another by their capacity to lose their soul or, vice versa, to gain everlasting life. It hardly mattered from this perspective whether such people were monarchs, nobles, commoners, labourers or beggars. Within the French church, Jansenism, which was widespread amongst the clergy, did much to reinforce such a tendency. It established a direct link between Christians and their God; it sapped the role of the episcopal, the priestly intermediary. It substituted Jacob for Esau, the invisible church of the pious for the official church, which was seen as fallen into the hands of Satan. It tended

---

[15] Edmond and Jules de Goncourt, *Journal* (Paris, Robert Laffont, 1989 edition), i, 462–3; 475.

to devalue in an egalitarian fashion the hierarchy of prelates (themselves recruited from amongst the nobility) as well as the decorums of rituals and sacraria.

Beyond religion we must also mention as factors the (at least contributory) role at the social level of taxation in its new forms and the importance of Justice. Even when the latter appeared to be arbitrary to the world of the poor (and this was not always the case) the instruments of justice, at least in theory, applied the law impartially to the clients appearing in its courts, from whatever group in society they came, high or low. This undermined the existence of the divisions of rank and noble privilege, whilst consolidating their existence in the name of the law. Saint-Simon was very conscious of it, extremely unhappy too, and complained when the *présidents* of the Parlement of Paris refused to raise their bonnets when asking for the judgements of the dukes and peers.

In matters of customary law, besides, a progressive modernization had taken place since the sixteenth century and decisive progress had been made in terms of the equal subdivision of inheritances, all the offspring of a single father being granted a portion without discrimination or gradation in favour of the eldest. This equitable arrangement applied so far as the vast majority of commoner families were concerned, but it did not affect the nobility, of course, which would continue to cultivate their right of primogeniture. 'All the offspring' meant all the male heirs, and sometimes both the male and female heirs, particularly in the Paris basin, and the regions of the Loire and in Brittany. But this excluded the Midi d'Oc, still imbued with the 'inequality' of Roman law.

★   ★   ★   ★   ★

If we look more specifically at the eighteenth century and its 'cradling' of revolutionary developments, then its successive generations were witnesses and participants in the rise of a veritable 'public space'[16] different from other traditional forms of space. This was distinct from what is properly regarded as the 'public sector', in other words the state and the court, where royal commands and aristocratic hierarchy prevailed, the latter being held in ridicule, of course, but (at the same time) exalted to a grotesque degree by the minute demands of precedence imposed by the daily duties of the courtier. The *public space* or 'public sphere' in question should equally be distinguished from the 'private sphere',[17] particularly the world of the family which itself was subject to a particular form of indi-

---

[16]   Roger Chartier, *Les Origines culturelles de la Révolution française* (Paris, Seuil, 1990), p. 32 *et seq.* Jürgen Habermas, 'The Public Sphere, an Encyclopedia Article' in *The New German Critique*, 1 (1974), 49–55. Above all, from the same author (trans. M. de Launay), *L'Espace public* (Paris, Payot, 1978).

[17]   See Roger Chartier (dir.), *L'Histoire de la vie privée*, vol. iii (*De la Renaissance aux Lumières*) (Paris, Seuil, 1986).

vidualism, at least in the case of the nuclear family,[18] which continued to make its presence felt more insistently from the end of the Middle Ages up to the Enlightenment. Public space and private sphere both delineate the third entity, the state, which, although expanding, was held within strict limits which were difficult for it to breach. And, above all, it was the first of this trio of terms which enjoyed a relative freedom of judgement, accounted to nobody for its actions (although this did not render it *a priori* infallible). This 'public space' began to make itself felt, beginning tentatively under Louis XIV and then proceeding apace under Louis XV and his successor. It occupied the salons and the academies,[19] which quadrupled in number in the provinces from 1710 to 1789, with their rise being particularly marked between 1715 and 1760. It was taken up by the reading rooms and philosophical societies, the libraries, the cafés and the clubs. It lodged in the masonic societies[20] which grew up in spectacular fashion, influenced from across the Channel in their initial burst of enthusiasm during the 1740s.

These institutions and entities were highly diverse, at once both levelling and also manipulative of individuals. They exemplified horizontal sociability and rendered the old vertical chains of hierarchical structure and superior authority obsolete, at least when that authority was expressed (even if it did not turn out to be so in reality) in absolutist terms. In general these new entities and exemplifications were tolerated by those in power, even though it was sometimes with a rather ill grace. The powers that be had even, in Richelieu's generation, tried, through the creation of the *Académie française*, briefly to control such developments by providing directive organisms for Taste and Thought. But, in due course, these would become emancipated, either partially or fully, from royal control and thus seize the intellectual high ground on their own account in a way which the ministries of state could hardly contradict. The learned and bookish debates which they conducted gradually turned towards politics which rapidly took on an oppositional flavour. After 1750, this criticism of the government had become a recognized fact. 'Public space' saw itself expanding, with all kinds of informal leaders, men and women, who directed its salons and other collectivities. They expressed the responsibility for moral leadership and opinion-forming which, in the seventeenth century, had been undertaken by the court, by the pulpit, by the confessional and by the literary cliques. However, in the public sphere which was thus emerging, the values of equality tended, reflecting the heat of the

---

[18]   Emmanuel Todd, *L'Invention de l'Europe* (Paris, Seuil, 1990), p. 29 and *passim*.

[19]   Daniel Roche, *Le Siècle des Lumières en province, académies et académiciens provinciaux, 1680–1789* (Paris, EHESS, 1978), esp. ii, 477.

[20]   Ran Halévi, 'Les Loges maçonniques dans la France d'Ancien Régime: aux origines de la sociabilité démocratique', *Cahiers des Annales, ESC* (Paris, A. Colin, 1984), esp. p. 45; see also E. Le Roy Ladurie in Georges Duby (dir.), *l'Histoire de la France urbaine* (5 vols, Paris, Seuil, 1980–5), iii, 520–1.

Enlightenment, to become (in intellectual terms) sovereign. Of course the 'public', or, more exactly, the literate public, would continue to be made up of the privileged in large measure. But as soon as it became a matter of establishing one's competence, or making one's opinions count in a debate about a matters of taste or learning, or arbitrating on the degree of depth in this or that remark or aesthetic opinion, birth counted for little. In other words, and contrary to what Beaumarchais wrote, 'it did not suffice merely to have the trouble of being born.' In the literary sector narrowly defined, the orders of society, nobles and others, counted for nought from the desks in colleges onwards; or rather, such orders found themselves reaching out beyond their normal zones of competence. The essential question, in the world of letters, whether one had a title or not, was, first of all, to be recognized by one's peers, i.e. by one's *equals*, as able to produce a view which was capable of commanding universal approval, or at least a minimum degree of consensus from amongst other cultivated persons. In these circumstances, it hardly mattered that the 'public', circumscribed in this fashion, was not the same as the 'people', and still less (to use the disdainful term of contemporaries) the 'populace'. The collection of views, *alias* opinions, which emanated from, or were in common usage amongst the public made up what one might call public opinion. The latter acted rather like money and credit, other instruments of equalization of social differences, other means for the abolition of the hierarchies of rank on the basis of social status alone. Public opinion gained a quasi-sovereign importance after 1748, 1750 or 1760, in the realms of religious debates, diplomatic affairs, grain-trade, financial matters and fiscal policy.[21] In each case, the opinion-formers were placed on a level footing with each other, just as were the receivers of such opinions. They were not classified according to a system of social hierarchies which was now considered in this respect as old-fashioned and 'out of date'. Equality's scythe made a harvest of all kinds of opinions, salon views and fireside conversations, *ex cathedra* pronouncements, rumours and printed texts which, when bundled together, effectively constituted 'opinion'. The levelling effect was still more pronounced when it came to printed materials. There was no 'trickle-down' of social contempt to separate out and organize the communication of concepts and fashions which worked their effects in the intimate heat of discussion round the family dinner table or in the smoke-filled atmosphere of the lecture room.

In such matters, the overwhelming, enriching, refreshing overabundance of literacy played a huge role. Literacy had its classic age and, in a later phase, its neo-classic revival. To know how to sign one's name, how

---

[21] The increasing weight of public opinion (which, of course, had existed at an earlier date) was very evident in the chauvinism displayed during the War of Austrian Succession. It became also very evident post 1750 in the affair of the *billets de confession* and the antifiscal campaigns of the *parlementaires*. It is in the case of the latter (and in this respect alone) that one can conclude that the antifiscal revolts of the seventeenth century already heralded, albeit in the most distant fashion, the coming Revolution.

to read and write, no matter how badly . . . the various flows in elementary
education chased one another in a race towards literacy. The countryside
began to catch up some of the gap in its literacy rates in comparison with
the city. The Midi sought to overtake the North, although it would not
succeed. The towns retained their lead on the basis of the facilities for
public education which had been laid down in the Renaissance and even
earlier, in the Late Middle Ages. The national level of literacy increased,[22]
including the rates amongst women.[23] An increasing minority amongst
these literate readers and writers could thus, as a result of this trend, have
access to the greater degree of information made available by the editors of
newspapers and other periodicals, as well as the books printed by publishers whose production in terms of the numbers of titles and the numbers of
pages increased in the course of the century. If we take merely the number
of periodicals published in France (and exclude those French publications
which were printed in the Netherlands and elsewhere to avoid French
censorship), the number of periodicals went up more than six-fold between the beginning of the eighteenth century and 1765. The first Parisian
daily newspaper appeared in 1777. There was thus an effervescent turmoil
and even explosion of information which, alongside other factors, tended
to make a political change of massive proportions inevitable.[24] It would
soon be the case that, in such conditions, one could no longer govern the
country as in the past.

The triumph of print (or manuscript) over oral culture, from custom to
'written law' – it is easily said, but the changes were far-reaching. At all
events, the book popularized things, familiarized ideas. It defeated censorship,[25] especially thanks to the imports of books from Switzerland and

---

[22]   Figures taken from François Furet and Jacques Ozouf, *Lire et écrire. L'Alphabétisation des
Français de Calvin à Jules Ferry* (Paris, Minuit, 1977), p. 38 *et seq.*

[23]   On the increasing provision of education for girls, particularly in Paris, during the
eighteenth century, see (despite the habitual, and possibly indispensable, accompanying
feminism) Martine Sonnet, 'L'Education des filles à Paris au XVIIIe siècle' in *Problèmes
d'histoire de l'éducation* (the proceedings of a seminar organized by the French School at
Rome and the University of Rome in January–May 1985) (Rome, Ecole française de Rome,
1988), pp. 53–78, esp. p. 55; in Paris, the elementary schools for girls could accommodate
one in three or four of those of school age.

[24]   William Doyle, *Origins of the French Revolution* (Oxford, Oxford University Press, 1980,
2nd edition 1988). Daniel Mornet, *Les Origines intellectuelles de la Révolution française* (Paris,
A. Colin, 1933, new ed. Lyon, La Manufacture, 1989), p. 397 *et seq.* (on the growth of the
provincial press). See also Claude Bellanger *et al.* (ed.), *Histoire générale de la presse française*
(Paris, PUF, 1969), i, 159 *et seq.*

[25]   The reality of censorship remained, however, in place, at least in principle, and (up to
a point) in practice, too, under Louis XVI. See William Doyle, *Origins*, p. 68 (where he
concentrates on the evidence for a 'relaxation' in censorship); and Robert Darnton, 'Le
Livre français à la fin de l'Ancien Régime', *Annales ESC*, 28 (1973), 741 *et seq.* (a fascinating
article not only about the problems of censorship and the contraband book trade but also
about the proposition of a 'defused Voltairianism' amongst the French reading 'public' in
around 1779) which the author advances. See also Robert Darnton, 'Reading, writing and
publishing in eighteenth-century France: a case-study in the sociology of literature',
Daedalus (1971), pp. 232–7.

elsewhere. Books appeared in folio volumes, then in octavo, and then finally as pocket-books. They were taken up and then thrown away, carried around in pockets, ready for discussion. A respectful contemplation of what they contained was replaced with an avid consumption of what they had to say. Even the parlements themselves 'tuned the presses' to popularize their remonstrations and criticisms of the government. The latter, with varying results, also turned to employing hack writers to try and render its policies acceptable. Nor was it merely the 'top-of-the-range' print formats which were used. The spread of revolutionary or pre-revolutionary ideas, or 'objectively revolutionary' notions also took place through prints; through paintings, engravings, collections, pornography, contraband literature, songs, festivals and Nonconformist sermons. Grain riots acted as tutorials in class struggle. There were endless conversations in inns and restaurants as the world of taverns, cafés and coffee-shops endlessly spread.[26] It is superficial to regard such polymorphic popularization as subordinate to books proper, 'recognized'[27] works, too dear for the common purse and frustratingly inaccessible to many. We should, of course, take account of book culture in its traditional literary forms, and particularly for the history of ideas. But, at the same time, we should consider the long period of socio-cultural gestation, which laid the groundwork for the revolutionary events which were to come. In this area, patterns of thought, drawing on concepts and pure ideas, became gradually and more generally corrosive. One example of the process is provided by the printing press at Neuchâtel which published both d'Holbach's works and also a refutation of them. What was significant in the process, as the objective factor in destabilizing the existing order, was the debate on his ideas, for and against them, which had been created and which the publisher incidentally hoped would bring in a profit for him. It is this process, rather than the Holbachian ideas themselves, however explosive they might appear at first sight to have been, which mattered.

Within the limits of the pre-revolutionary 'public space' (in its broadest sense) the expansion in elementary education through 'new primary schools' was willingly undertaken by a Catholic church which was, in this respect, enlightened. Unwittingly, however, it thus became a 'sorcerer's apprentice' for change. In contrast, the number of pupils at secondary schools seems to have been stagnant throughout the period from Louis XIII to Louis XVI (a bizarre phenomenon which is, however, based on

[26]   Henry M. de Langle, *Le Petit Monde des cafés et débits parisiens au XIXe siècle; évolution de la sociabilité citadine* (preface by Pierre Chaunu) (Paris, PUF, 1990), p. 14. The number of cafés increased five-fold in Paris between 1723 and 1793 (by which date, there would be 1,800 of them). The Goldoni play *Le Café* was put on by the Comédie Française in October 1990 and it gave an excellent idea of the popularization of this kind of establishment and the positive regard for café proprietors in the public mind.
[27]   Denis Richet in *Le Nouvel Observateur* for 30 September 1988. See also Roger Chartier and Daniel Roche in their introduction to T. Barbier and C. Jolly (eds), *Livre et Révolution* (a colloquium organized by the Institut d'Histoire moderne et contemporaine at the Bibliothèque Nationale, Paris, on 20–22 May 1987) (Paris, Amateurs du Livre, 1988).

statistics which are open to discussion). It was, above all, the increasing variety in teaching establishments and the changes in the quality of the teaching offered more than the numbers of 'schoolboys' put through the mill (which did, in any case, eventually rise) which had its impact and which mattered when it came to the impact of the educational system in destablizing the Ancien Régime. In this respect, the expulsion of the Jesuits in 1762 and their replacement by the Oratorians,[28] by priests, or by lay teachers contributed to decreasing the weight of conservatism in the knowledge transmitted to the young high school students. As for higher education, it displayed classic and more predictable changes than those in secondary education. From the universities, and particular the law faculties, the number of intellectuals[29] which were produced was increasing but the job market for them did not always grow at an equivalent rate. The buoyancy in the increasing numbers of students entering for law-degree courses and graduates from faculties of law is eloquent in this respect. As a result there was a place (if not a job) for a growing rank of frustrated and proletarianized intellectuals, hack-writers ready to sell their talents to the highest bidder. They would sometimes be known as the 'literary scum', and even the 'gutter-Rousseau'[30] and they would be there at a later date, ready and waiting to mobilize and energize the revolutionary crowd. In this respect, the faculties of law created semi-marginal figures amongst society. At the same time, however, it also had its fair share of those who integrated successfully into society;[31] but, they too, in certain circumstances could also turn against the Ancien Régime! The forces for destabilization were, indeed, complex. We find amongst these new jurists, fresh from law schools and destined to play a role in the French Revolution, numerous advocates who had begun a successful provincial law career under Louis XVI (for example, Robespierre). Many of them became office-holders in the *bailliages* and elsewhere.[32] They would be the ones who would write out in the traditional language of the lawyers and the customary law-codes the socio-political demands which would emerge from their electoral region,

---

28   In fact, many of the Oratorians would readily subscribe to the civil constitution of the clergy, influenced (as many of them were) by their Jansenist convictions.

29   Roger Chartier, *Les Origines culturelles.*

30   'Canaille littéraire' and 'Rousseaux du ruisseau'; Robert Darnton, *Bohème littéraire et révolution* (Paris, Gallimard/Seuil, 1983), pp. 17–41. See, as an example of one such individual, semi-marginal and much preoccupied, the case study of the librarian Carra in Française Bléchet, '1789 à la Bibliothèque du Roi', *Dix-huitième siècle*, 20 (1988), 151–60, especially 151–2.

31   Emile Léonard, *Mon village sous Louis XV* (Paris, PUF, 1941), p. 91 *et seq.* and *passim*, esp. *in fine*. In this village, the destiny of the Batifort family, whose members studied to become able lawyers and local judges, is particularly relevant from the particular point of view which we are exploring here. Having been conformist, they then became more critical of the established order at the end of the period. Cf. E. Le Roy Ladurie and O. Ranum, *Pierre Prion* (Paris, Gallimard, coll. 'Archives', 1985), pp. 30–2.

32   Roger Chartier, *Les Origines culturelles*, p. 102. Robert Darnton, *Bohème littéraire et révolution*, p. 32 *et seq.* Alexis de Tocqueville, *L'Ancien Régime et la Révolution* (Paris, Gallimard, 1952), part III, ch. 1.

or those which they chose to represent, in the spring of 1789. Their formulations would find their way into the drawing-up of the *cahiers* for the Estates General. The same individuals, the lesser law-officers and legal clerks of the middle classes, would in due course turn up, lined up in serried ranks and dressed in black, at the Constituent Assembly of the Third Estate on 5 May 1789 at Versailles when what became the National Assembly was first opened. Over and above these various categories, the 'gutter Rousseau' and the small-town *robins*, the intellectuals and writers had become the leaders of public opinion and they were, above all, the instigators of ideologico-political initiatives amongst an enlightened public opinion, or one which regarded itself as such. They had taken over the role of the priests and other clerics in holy orders but they were not obliged to adhere, as they were, to the conservative-tending beliefs of divine revelation. So, instead, they leaned towards the chimeras and more abstract notions and all the more readily since, in comparison with England, they were excluded from the solid realities of power. From the time of Richelieu and the beginnings of the administrative monarchy, in fact, the ruling classes (whether noble or, *a fortiori*, commoner-born) found themselves isolated from the world of decision-making, which was limited to a few dozen great office-holding and *commissaire* families belonging to the *robe* on the royal Council. Since they were not obliged to be responsible for decisions, the 'Public' was thus constrained to dream, to live in the clouds, amidst rational or utopian speculation. Only too willing to distill the quintessence of such speculation, only too eager to make a fresh start at constructing a new society from a *tabula rasa*, based only on the foundation of the dictates of reason and in defiance of history, the coterie of intellectuals and authors who were ambitious for national regeneration, became the directing forces for the thoughts[33] of an élite. But it was not the whole élite for, in the provinces, there were still to be found groups of magistrates who rather distrusted philosophy and were perfectly content.[34]

In 1790, *post festum*, there would be the first reckoning. Judging on the basis of what he read from this critical and radical intelligentsia, and the Constituents who were enthralled by it, Edmund Burke, the English writer, polemicist and politician, was aghast. He was an advocate of a kind of old-fashioned (in the best sense of the word) empiricism and he was much saddened by all the things which were being held up to ridicule, by the destruction carried out in the early years of the revolution, the loss of various components which had been hallowed by the past, the nobility, the clergy, and soon the monarchy. For Burke, such things, to use his familiar

---

[33] This situation would have a long and important future before it. In Russia in the nineteenth century (leaving the Third World of our own day to one side) the intellectuals would play a rather analogous role as an 'intelligentsia', albeit in a rather different context. Alain Besançon, *Les Origines intellectuelles du léninisme* (Paris, Calmann-Lévy, 1977); and *Education et société en Russie dans le second tiers du XIX siècle* (Paris, Mouton, 1974).

[34] Maurice Gresset, *Gens de justice à Besançon* (Paris, Bibliothèque nationale, 1978), ii, 668.

expression, 'could still serve', even in the new more equitable structures devised by the Revolution. To Burke's profound regret, the levelling[35] egalitarianism of the Revolution constituted one of the essential ingredients of this total overthrow of everything, theoretically starting again from nothing, and from absolute first principles. It is true that a *tabula rasa*, a society without genealogy, a fraternity without paternity[36] (and eventually consumed, according to its supporters, by that strange and violent emotion which is self-hatred[37]) had its supporters. Was it not Turgot, minister to the Most Christian King, who was the first amongst those in the corridors of power to outlaw the use of the famous *tabula rasa* lest it should gain disciples (Condorcet, for example) who might prove more daring than its master? Was it not the marquise de Merteuil who, in *Dangerous Liaisons* (*Liaisons dangereuses* (1782)) affirmed that no one had fashioned her but herself: 'When have you seen me', she wrote to Valmont, 'depart from the rules which I have proscribed for myself or fail to live up to my principles? I call them my principles, and I do so by design, for they are not, as with other women, chosen by chance, received without scrutiny or followed by habit. They are the profound result of my own thoughts. *I have created them and I may say that I am my own product.*'[38] Ten years later, the Revolution would define itself in the same fashion.

Well before the last decade of the century, the *public arena*, progressively exploited *by* the monarchy (with egalitarian consequences) and *against* the monarchy (which was pictured as tyrannical), furnished a fertile area for a particular social milieu which would become increasingly receptive to the demiurges of equality as a driving force for the creation of things *ex nihilo*. The milieu welcomed such ideas and this helps to explain the easy and fashionable success which they enjoyed. Jean-Jacques Rousseau, the most outstanding from this point of view amongst numerous other authors, a *primus inter pares*, published his *Discourse on the Origins and Foundations of Inequality amongst Mankind* (*Discours sur l'origine et les fondements de l'inégalité parmi les hommes*) in 1755. Inequality was something which, of course, he opposed at every point in his thinking, even (and above all) when he had to be more accommodating and more flexible in applying his simplifying theory to the complexity of the real world and to social realities. In his *Discourse*, Rousseau argued that the third and last condition of inequality 'was the change from legitimate power to arbitrary power'.[39] The levelling struggle became thus associated with the fight against 'des-

---

[35] Edmund Burke, *Reflections on the French Revolution*.

[36] Lynn Hunt, *Politics, Culture and Class in the French Revolution* (Berkeley, California University Press, 1984), pp. 31–2.

[37] 'I'll join with black despaire against my soul,
And to myself become an enemy.' (Shakespeare, *King Richard III*, Act II, Scene 2).

[38] Laclos, *Oeuvres complètes* (Paris, Gallimard, 1979), p. 170 (*Liaisons dangereuses*, Letter no. 180).

[39] Jean-Jacques Rousseau, *Oeuvres complètes* (Oeuvres philosophiques et politiques) (Paris, Seuil, 1977), ii, 241.

potism'. In the same way, Rousseau believed 'that it was evidently against the law of nature, however one defines the latter, that a handful of men should enjoy every luxury while the famished multitude lack the bare necessities of life.' The expression was somewhat irresponsible for a period where, on the contrary, the increasing levels of production, of commercial traffic, and of the administration (*alias* the police) of the grain-trade, although they were influences which had not banished poverty, had gone a good way to exorcise the demon of famine. But then, doubtless one cannot expect the kind of objectivity from an armchair theoretician which only close contact *in situ* with farmers, traders, provincial intendants, and grain-merchants would have given him. At all events, the author of the *Discourse* made a strong link between the theme of equality and two other characteristic phenomena of the period: élites against despotism; masses against the hoarding of essential foodstuffs. The overcharged tirades launched by Rousseau, Mably and others in favour of equality[40] and which would be regarded as banal today, did not simply reflect the frustrations of the Third Estate, or the wounded honour of the bourgeoisie, tired of being lorded over (as they saw it) by the nobility. Their invective was also symptomatic of a new mentality, an egalitarian tendency, which had spread widely through part of the élites and would soon do so amongst the masses as well. It was the moment when the 'providential' movement (as Tocqueville would call it) in favour of democratic egalitarianism took shape; and it would sound the death-knell from then until the present day of older mental attitudes with their aristocratic and hierarchical assumptions.

There thus existed a three-fold constellation of portents which boded ill for the Ancien Régime. Absolutism was, if not isolated, at least enjoying less legitimacy since it was attacked, and with passion, for being despotic. The élites took up the question of national representation, dropped since 1614 or 1627 and absent from the political agenda. They wanted to use it to establish their own power, in the manner of the English, the Bordelais, or Montesquieu, and juxtapose it with the prerogatives of the king, the latter now being considered as arbitrary when exercised on their own, or seeming to be so exercised. The monarchy had exercised its authority (with decreasing efficiency) through vertical chains of command, the élitist model. Now this pattern no longer seemed to work. Well-informed contemporaries, influenced by the century's growth, wanted now to 'horizontalize' power and diffuse it amongst the superior strata of the élites, and even amongst the Nation in general. Independently of all this, last but not least, there was, thirdly, the successful popularization of an abstract and egalitarian ideology, more amply endowed with rationality than reasonableness. This was a series of three factors – to which should be added, on a more substantive level, the growing popular unrest, its

---

[40] André Delaporte, *L'Idée d'égalité en France au XVIIIe siècle* (Paris, PUF, 1987), esp. ch. 3 (pp. 237–324).

antagonisms either loudly proclaimed or expressed *sotto voce*, when compared with the preceding period pre-1750 or pre-1700. The urban masses were periodically disturbed by the cyclical dearth of food-stuffs, even though (and above all, because) the threat of famine had disappeared. The thresholds of tolerance had decreased and, in the rural world, the peasantry refused to accept (not everywhere, of course, but in many regions, particularly in Burgundy and Provence[41]) the seigneurial régime, or what remained of it, a régime which was more vulnerable and which had decayed and lost its teeth. The time had long gone when the medieval fortress protected *grosso modo* the peasant from attack. Under the early Bourbons, and still more so during the eighteenth century, the Justice State had assumed this protective function and it had a full complement of legal specialists to rely on. The parlements, the *présidiaux*, and the other official courts were only too keen to take over the judicial functions of the seigneurial courts which, from this point of view, had ceased to be competitive. Seigneurial justice was left as an exposed hang-over from the past. Rural disturbances gradually changed its characteristics. They had been antifiscal under Louis XIII and Louis XIV, especially in the south-west. Without necessarily losing this older characteristic, they became antiseigneurial under Louis XV and Louis XVI, especially in the north. What is more, discontented villagers made greater use of legal chicanery themselves, and with greater effectiveness, rather than have recourse to the violence of the micro-revolts or major rebellions of the past. All this formed part of a more general process of acculturation, and equally a softening of attitudes, which took place in the last century of the Ancien Régime,[42] a softening process which would be brutally reversed with the reappearance of the violence of 1789 and the succeeding years. The attack on seigneurial justice represented a challenge to the traditional masters of the soil, inherited from ages past. The state, by means of the intendants, sought to sustain the broad mass of its tax-payers and its fiscal base, and so it was the more prepared to take the side of the village against the seigneurs, thus encouraging the former at the expense of the latter.[43] This process tends to make the theory which has been supported through thick and thin and which regards the Bourbon state as an instrument of 'feudalism' look even more fragile. The peasant contemporaries of d'Argenson

---

[41] See the E. Le Roy Ladurie volume (vol. ii) of Georges Duby (dir.), *Histoire de la France rurale*, ii, 561 *et seq.* Also E. Le Roy Ladurie in *Annales ESC* (1974), pp. 6–22. Cf. E. Baratier, *Histoire de la Provence* (Toulouse, Privat, 1987), p. 402.

[42] The bibliography related to this 'softening of attitudes' ('*adoucissement*') is to be found in E. Le Roy Ladurie's volume in Duby (dir.), *Histoire de la France rurale*, ii, 561 *et seq.*, and also his article in *Contrepoint* (1973). Michel Foucault, *Surveiller et punir* (Paris, Gallimard, 1975), pp. 77–80, has rightly annotated (including bibliographically) the phenomenon; but his ideological interpretation eventually leads him away from the facts about what he rightly terms in this respect 'the Pierre Chaunu School'.

[43] Hilton Root, *Peasants and King in Burgundy. The Agrarian Foundations of French Absolutism* (Berkeley, California University Press, 1987), pp. 193–202.

and Necker found themselves in ever greater contact with urban culture, itself destabilizing of the Ancien Régime.

Such developing contacts drew on greater degrees of migration from the rural to the urban world, and the closer links between the rural economy[44] and the urban market, or the semi-urban world which surrounded it and which was becoming more diverse. It also grew up around the more noticeable presence in the countryside of a group of small-time lawyers, educated in the towns in their college or university days and now the suppliers of the ideological weapons, and above all the legal know-how for the village community against the manor. Here was a further way by which rural recourse to law was fostered. The seigneurs themselves were not adamantly opposed in principle (and the night of 4 August 1789 would amply demonstrate the fact) to the 'defeudalization' of agricultural domains. This was more especially the case since the 'capitalist' revenue which the latter produced, itself a consequence of the demands of the urban market-places, had become larger and more secure than the archaic and often miserable little returns collected by the seigneur and his agents from the so-called 'feudal rights'.[45] The attempted 'feudal reaction' by some individuals does nothing to change this fact.

As for the church, a further supporter of the established régime (although it was also much more than that), it could rely, of course, on the regular Sunday and Easter observances which had become almost unanimous for over a century, whether it was Sunday mass, Easter communion or the annual confession. But various 'tangential' indications suggest a less optimistic picture. Amongst these, there was the increasingly habitual refusal to pay tithe on the part of the peasantry.[46] There was also a crisis, or at least a mini-crisis in ecclesiastical recruitment, particularly for the monastic orders. There was a decreasing output of religious books.[47] Then there was the growth, particularly in the urban world, in the use of contraception (*coitus interruptus*) despite the Biblical and Roman Catholic injunctions to the contrary. The decline in the fecundity of married

---

[44] Contrary to a widely-held prejudice, agriculture which is not highly productive (such as, *grosso modo*, that of France in the eighteenth century, despite its more productive sectors and localities) was not, *a priori*, autarchic. In reality, particularly when the towns were growing fairly rapidly (as was the case under Louis XV and Louis XVI) they were bound to lure the marginal producers (since there were not the ultra-productive great farms of the twentieth century to be found) and attract an increasing number of small rural suppliers to sell their produce *inta muros*. Hence the closer ties and 'teeming' contacts between town and countryside.

[45] For one seigneurie and its experience of 'infant capitalism' in the course of the last 50 years of the Ancien Régime, see Gérard Aubin, 'La Seigneurie en Bordelais au XVIIIe siècle, d'après la pratique notariale (1715–1789)', *Le Gnomon*, 70 (1980), 20–3 and the same author's complete thesis, published by the University of Rouen (no. 149).

[46] Georges Frêche, *Toulouse et la région Midi-Pyrénées au siècle des Lumières vers 1670–1789* (Paris, PUF, 1967), p. 539 *et seq.* (for the increasingly contentious anti-tithe disputes and related lawsuits post 1750 and, above all, post 1775).

[47] François Furet, 'La Librairie du royaume de France au XVIIIe siècle' in François Furet (ed.), *Livre et société dans la France au XVIIIe siècle* (Paris/The Hague, Mouton, 1965).

women in Rouen from the end of the seventeenth century onwards has already been referred to.[48] Such varying, but convergent, phenomena, tend to demonstrate that the church no longer exercised the strict control over its flock which it had done in the period of the Catholic reformation in the previous century. The anti-Protestant, and above all the anti-Jansenist tensions played, one way and another, a particular role in these developments. Jansenism, for its part, affected the authority of the clergy and contributed to the formation amongst both clergy and laity of virtual batallions of free-thinkers, emancipated from the internal divisions and authoritarianism which a 'persecuting' church had sought to exercise. Above all, it was the monarchy which, by its attack on Augustinian Gallicanism, sawed off the 'national' branch on which it had so comfortably sat for so many centuries. The militant anti-Protestant attitudes, for which the papacy, the bishops, priests and the king were so reproached, provided certain obsessional images which were detached from them to become part of the propaganda hostile to Catholicism. What provoked the greater criticism was not, in this context, the revocation of the edict of Nantes and the massive expulsion *de facto* of Protestants from France in 1685, but the massacre of the Huguenots at St Bartholomew,[49] the effects of which were somewhat exaggerated.

Finally, the endless insistence of Voltaire and his disciples in the field of philosophe and Encyclopaedic literature carried an entire sector, an important part, of public opinion with him. His views were firmly anti-Christian, albeit not always anti-religious. The philosophe at Ferney doused Catholic fervour in the icy waters of cultural relativism. Why was it, he intimated, that the outworn texts of a tiny minority (the Jews), dispersed to the four corners of the known world, should be accorded more weight by a young reader now than the teachings of the philosophers of Greece, India or China? Such reasoning took no account of either historical precedent or common sense, for a small minority, after all, might well have been able to acquire access to some additional, or 'testamentary' grain of truth, in comparison with the sages of great empires. But in a period when inter-continental travel literature was popular, Voltairian scepticism, with its various echoes of Montaigne, appealed by virtue of its very simplicity and flattered the common sense of its numerous readers, who were quickly converted to it.

The church was thus faced with a triple assault. There was, firstly, a degree of relativism coming from the great geographical discoveries and from the Renaissance of Graeco-Roman civilization. Then, secondly, there was the recovery (by Lutherans, Calvinists and Jansenists) of the works of

[48] J.-P. Bardet, *Rouen aux XVIIe et XVIIIe siècles. Les mutations d'un espace social* (Paris, SEDES, 1983).

[49] Diego Venturino, in Keith Baker and François Furet (eds), *The French Revolution and the Creation of Modern Political Culture* (vol. ii, ed. Colin Lucas), pp. 13 and 29. See also, in this context, Mona Ozouf's article on 'Voltaire' in François Furet and Mona Ozouf, *Dictionnaire critique de la Révolution française* (Paris, Flammarion, 1988), p. 917.

St Paul and St Augustine, the proponents of insistent theories on Faith and Grace, theories which their adherents judged incompatible with the theological and ritualist 'line' of the Vatican. Finally, there was the rise of scientific rationalism in the wake of the fraternal enemies, Descartes and Newton, the latter being widely popularized on the continent thanks to Voltaire. Such rationalism, transmuted by the eighteenth-century philosophers from the pure sciences to the religious and politico-social domains, was hardly supportive of the 'gothic' structures of the state and the clergy. A church organized on an 'English' basis, despite its lack of European universalism or planetary pretensions, would have been more locally structured, and more open to change from its local base. It would, no doubt, have adapted better to the coming torrents than the French priesthood. That said, the latter would display a good deal of energy in defending themselves after 1789; for they were strengthened by their corporate experience (unlike the nobility, which had no right of national assembly, the assemblies of the clergy had been regularly convened after 1561). They also relied on the enthusiasm, sometimes habitual, sometimes sincere, which emanated from the masses and from part of the élites (and not merely the women). Following the French Revolution, the clerics would reemerge anew with a much greater degree of solidarity than that salvaged by the lay élites from the old and newer nobility. The latter was destroyed as a specific 'estate' in society; its status would survive on an individual and familiar basis alone. It remains the case, however, that the church represented the most formidable obstacle to the torrential changes which overcame France post 1790. It was, after all, no small endeavour proposed by those who had conjured forth that change, to undertake a wholesale overturning of things amidst a great Catholic country. The Dutch had been Calvinists for ages, England was already Anglican or Puritan Protestant; and both had emerged unscathed from their revolutionary experiences by the end of the sixteenth century; or rather from the middle years of the seventeenth century. By contrast with the experience of the maritime powers, however, the French hexagon was being invited to absorb two revolutions at one and the same time. One of these was, predictably, political; the other was the religious revolution which had been attempted in sixteenth-century France in Paris, Lyon or Toulouse, but which had not finally succeeded. So France faced a twin set of demands and a Herculean labour. However, the time of crisis (as Rousseau said) would crystallize at one moment or another, and it did so crystallize in France in the latter years of the eighteenth century. It is at the level of the events of that period that one has to look to bring together in a coherent picture, and around a precise date (1789), all the various clinical signs of that crisis which, up to that point, had remained dispersed. Once assembled together, the established order was fairly speedily consigned to oblivion, however familiar and indestructible it seemed to some contemporaries.

The first episode to provide a matrix for the 'unexpected force of events' was the American conflict. Neither Louis XV, whose Fénelonian prudence became stronger as he became older, nor Turgot, the *contrôleur général* at the beginning of Louis XVI's reign, had any real desire to see France involved in the hornet's nest of the American War of Independence, however alluring the international scenario may have made it seem. Turgot explicitly warned his young sovereign king against such an adventure, regarding it as likely to sound the (financial) death-knell of the monarchy. It was true that the circumstances surrounding such an involvement could appear superficially attractive. One would be allying with liberal, even democratic, voices on the east coast of North America which supported French public opinion. By a fortuitous coincidence, the French kingdom was in the process of acquiring a more welcoming face. It was opening itself up, or re-opening itself, to religious minorities and also giving a voice to its provincial and regional élites. It would soon be the time when the Huguenot Necker could be a minister of the crown, and when provincial assemblies, decided upon by Necker himself, took shape. These assemblies would not, however, be very representative and would remain more or less associated with the decisions taken by the central government. Finally, the economic situation of France was probably not as bad as Ernest Labrousse estimated it to be.[50] Foreign trade, the textile industry, and the agricultural sectors of the economy (with the exception of wine) remained buoyant, despite some contrary indicators, particularly in artisanal crafts.[51] The real economic depression would not begin until 1785/1786, and not in earnest until the summer of 1788, which was distinguished by bad harvests with the catastrophic consequences which they would bring in their wake in 1789 (a fear, albeit exaggerated, of dearth; the springtime Great Fear, etc.). On the whole, then, if one surveys

[50] Ernest Labrousse, *La Crise de l'économie française à la fin de l'Ancien Régime et au début de la Révolution* (Paris, PUF, 1943). If we set aside the undoubted crisis in viticulture which affected several years around 1780, the other conclusions of this work concerning the existence of a crisis are much more debatable. This has not stopped them being piously repeated for almost half a century by various historians who have not taken the trouble to check the validity of the main thesis upon which they are so respectfully laying their trust. See, for example, Theda Skocpol, *Etats et révolutions sociales; la Révolution en France, en Russie, et en Chine* (Paris, Fayard, 1985), pp. 169–70, particularly in respect of the so-called 'intercycle of contraction' (in which some prices may have declined, but not necessarily the economy). The initial date of this 'intercycle' shifts from 1770 to 1778 within the space of a few lines! The 'proof' offered by Ernest Labrousse for the crisis in viticulture is particularly unconvincing. In reality, the prices for wine were particularly erratic and therefore, by definition, it was a 'lottery' as to whether producers or consumers were caught by high and low prices (see, on this subject, Jules Milhau, *Etudes économétriques du prix du vin en France* (Montpellier, Causse, 1935), p. 77 and *passim*). It proves nothing as to the effective reality of a general malaise in the French economy under Louis XVI, at least before 1786 or 1788. Was this not, perhaps, why Labrousse left his great thesis incomplete?
[51] Alain Belmont, *Les Artisans ruraux dans le Bas-Dauphiné du XVIe au début du XIXe siècle* (Unpublished thesis, EHESS, 1990).

the two decades pre-1789, it seems reasonable to conclude with Jacques Marseille[52] that the French Revolution did not begin, was not marked out by, a long-term economic crisis, although it certainly was affected by a short-term crisis.

Returning to the war-years of 1778–83, it should be noted that, in terms of strategy and the balance of military forces, as well as in terms of the pattern of warfare, the War of American Independence was intelligently pursued by the French, despite various reverses on the naval side which were more temporary than definitive to the result. Louis XVI, a determined advocate of maritime power, and Vergennes, the foreign minister from 1774, were careful to avoid the classic trap of a war on two fronts, both in continental Europe and at sea. Such wars had ruined, but not defeated, Louis XIV; and they had defeated, but not ruined, Louis XV.

From 1778 to 1782, the war was essentially a maritime one (in the Atlantic or the Indian Ocean) and a transoceanic one (on the territory of the North American colonies). The tactics of the French navy, which had been thoroughly modernized, were put to the test and generally (but not always) proved successful. First-rate admirals (Suffren, La Motte-Piquet, De Grasse, d'Estaing) achieved victories off the coast of India and the New World. With inadequate forces, the expeditionary force of Rochambeau which landed at Rhode Island, nevertheless succeeded at Yorktown (October 1781) alongside Washington and De Grasse in a brilliant combined operation which deployed, besides the artillery forces of Gribeauval, only some 10,000 French soldiers. The small British army was captured. This was a long way removed from the costly combats of the period 1672–1763; and equally distant from the extermination wars typical of the Revolutionary and Napoleonic periods. In the end, a magnanimous and victorious peace was achieved at Versailles in 1783 which guaranteed the tender flower of American liberty and 'avenged' the French defeats of the Seven Years War.

The balance-sheet thus seemed a positive one. But the later impact of the military alliance with Washington and Franklin would eventually turn out to be difficult if not for 'France' itself (which became the long-lasting ally of the United States) at least for the Ancien Régime, burdened with the financial weight of the naval and landed warfare which it had incurred. The war did not ruin the national economy but it did drain the exchequer and weaken public credit in a country where privilege had created a financial paradise which prevented the king from 'paying his way' and gaining from his subjects (especially those in the privileged élites) a rapid settlement for the costs of the military engagement.

The financial situation which Louis XVI had inherited from his predecessor in 1774, before the American war, had, however, been reasonably

---

[52] Jacques Marseille, 'L'Economie française à la veille de la Révolution; blocage ou dynamisme'; unpublished lecture delivered at the Université de Paris-Dauphine, 17 May, 1989.

healthy. In 1770, at the end of Louis XV's reign, the *abbé* Terray could reflect on his brutally honest foresight, the vigorous resources released by a buoyant French economy and the period of peace which had already lasted almost 15 years, all of which had contributed to refilling the coffers of the state. The haemorrhage of resources caused by the deficit budgets from 1757 and the beginning of the Seven Years War were a thing of the past. After the death of Louis XV, Terray was dismissed and Turgot was appointed by the new king as *contrôleur général*. He came into office to find a well-resourced Treasury which could but assist in his experiment at 'philosophic monarchy'.[53] What is more, Turgot did not prejudice this favourable situation. The simple fact of his refusal to undertake any war (until his fall from power in May 1776) accounts for his preservation of monarchical finance. No doubt Turgot can be criticised for his *tabula rasa* rationalism and his lack of a sense of history and the accumulated wisdom of the past. In this respect, he was like his putative offspring, the later revolutionaries who would equally, but in their own ways, be committed to wholesale reconstruction. The spirit of finesse, the kind of Beauvillier mentality which would take into account the infinite nuances of the social world, would be replaced by the spirit of geometric abstraction, the Chevreuse mentality, which measured and took the scissors to the real world without any sense of having, one day, to put it all back together again.[54] But, then again, and independently of these more distant dangers, Turgot's reforms, such as the abolition of the *corvée* and the suppression of the corporations, were either justifiable or, in every case, inoffensive and, at the end of the day, not extreme measures. Only one reform turned out to be a failure, and this was the attempt of the *contrôleur général* to introduce, as had already been tried in 1764, free trade in grain. The unfortunate experience of Choiseul and L'Averdy in this respect should have given the new philosophe-minister pause for thought. At a time when the system of food supplies remained always at the mercy of a bad harvest, was it a good idea to open it up to free-market conditions? The people at large, or those who took to the streets in their name in 1775 around Paris in a series of riots known as the 'Flour War' (*guerre des farines*), readily perceived the problem. The riots were noisy but their intentions were merely preventative since no real dearth threatened at that moment and the trend in grain-prices from 1770 had been towards a decline. In a period of declining prices, Turgot's naive rectitude thus succeeded in achieving a small masterpiece, namely, the spectre of popular agitation over grain shortage, a spectre which one might imagine had been put to rest by the ending of the Choiseulian system of liberalism in the grain trade after 1770. Yet the troubles which were provoked in 1775 were not signs of an imminent danger to the Ancien Régime. The parlements, which had

---

[53] François Furet in Yann Fauchois, *Chronologie politique de la Révolution* (Alleur (Belgium), Marabout, 1989), p. 6.
[54] Saint-Simon, *Mémoires*, xix, 30.

been recalled into being in November 1774, did not attempt to exploit, at least not yet, the popular agitation. In fact, the savage blow dealt them by Maupeou had left them cautious, enfeebled, even after their recall. The fall of Turgot (1776) and the reintroduction of grain control would calm matters. And, so long as no exterior conflict threatened to overturn things, the finances of the monarchy remained stable, and the outlook favourable.

With France's entry into the War of American Independence in the summer of 1778, it was a different story. From October 1776, Necker, a Protestant banker of Genevan origins, became director of the Treasury. He subsequently was made director of Finances and in charge of the latter, even though his religion disabled him from attending the *Conseil d'en haut*. Money, credit, public opinion, and the trend towards new and quasi-revolutionary values, propelled Necker to prominence. He did not emerge from the traditional *robe du Conseil*. It was a sign of the times that his career had been in banking, and not in the general tax-farms or the normal circle of tax-farmers (*traitants*).[55] Consistent with his professional background, Necker financed the American war by borrowing. In this respect there was at least a partial innovation when one compares this with the methods which, from 1635 onwards, had been used by previous kings when dealing with the costs of the huge conflicts which they had faced or launched against their foreign enemies. Richelieu, Louis XIV and Louis XV had certainly made a habit of borrowing money as and when they needed to. But they equally had recourse, and with a degree of harshness, to taxation, to turning the financial screws, as was clearly evident in 1640, 1692 and 1704. Necker, on the other hand, besides his 'banking' background, also had the excuse of only having to finance a war on one, oceanic and transoceanic, front. It was not the case that the national territory was endangered. Necker could legitimately argue for a war without painful financial consequences,[56] financed by borrowing rather than by taxation. He could further argue that the English did precisely the same when faced with the American War, financing everything by borrowing. But they could allow themselves that luxury because the credit mechanism of George III was more firmly established than that of Louis XVI, thanks to the existence of the Bank of England which, after the relative collapse of Law's System, remained without an equivalent on the other side of the Channel.[57] Connected to this reality was the fact that interest rates were lower in London than at Paris or Versailles. For various reasons, historians

---

[55] Furet, *Revolutionary France, 1770–1880*, pp. 35–6.

[56] R.D. Harris, 'Necker's Compte Rendu of 1781: A Reconsideration', *Journal of Modern History*, 42 (1970); also 'French Finances and the American War, 1777–1783' *Modern History*, 48 (1976). Harris has since published various works on Necker, *viz.*, *Necker: Reform Statesman of the Ancien Régime* (Berkeley, California University Press, 1979) and *Necker and the Revolution of 1789* (New York, Lanham, 1986).

[57] Philippe Haudrère, *La Compagnie française des Indes au XVIIIe siècle (1719–1795)* (4 vols, Librairie de l'Inde, 1989), iv, 184–5.

have not been entirely mistaken[58] in considering Necker's policy one of financing the war without recourse to new taxation nor to other fiscal means but merely on the basis of credit as imprudent. The facts speak for themselves. From 1777 to May 1781, the date when Necker fell from power, he had borrowed 520 million *livres*.[59] From May 1781 to the end of 1782, additional loans to meet army and navy requirements accounted for an additional 252 million *livres*. Overall, the American War cost France a total of a billion *livres*.[60] Later loans to finance the interest payments on these debts and fund the post-war expenditures would be, under Calonne as *contrôleur général des finances* from November 1783, some 422 million *livres* between 1783 and 1787. The overall borrowing between 1777 and 1787 would thus be around 1,194,000,000 *livres*. Calonne himself would calculate the figure as 1,250,000,000 *livres* for the years from 1776 to 1786. These should be put in the context of the normal revenues of the state which, in 1786, stood at 475 million *livres* as against 587 million *livres* of expenditure that same year, expenses *ipso facto* expanded by the service charges on these huge debts. Clearly, although the country was better off, the state was bankrupt and living beyond its means. The annual deficit which, at the time of Louis XVI's accession in 1774, stood at 40 million *livres* or less, and which would fortunately decrease still further over the following two years, would, under the aegis of Turgot, having almost been reduced to nothing, increase once more[61] to 112 million *livres* under the impact of war and the immediate post-war pressures[62], as compared with the 22 million *livres* in 1776. It is true that Necker, with Turgot and Terray continuing the same policy, had the signal merit[63] to reform the central administration of finance, simplify it, and outlaw the sale of office, superfluous offices, and judicial gratuities (*épices*).[64] He thus presaged the

---

[58] R.D. Harris gives some excellent insights into the Neckerian credit arrangements; but, despite his attempts, he is unsuccessful in refuting the classic propositions of other historians, hostile to Necker's imprudent financial politics. It was evidently the case that the anti-fiscal sabotage carried out by the Parlements successively since the middle of the eighteenth century turned out to be sufficient to persuade Necker away from the raising of new taxes. In this sense, the gradually undermining effects of the *parlementaires* from 1750 onwards must be seen, in the long-term, as one of the reasons behind the paralysis in the monarchy's fiscal initiatives. Hence the need to find something later on which would bridge the yawning financial gap which would engulf the Ancien Régime.

[59] R.D. Harris, *Necker: Reform Statesman*, p. 136 writes of 530 million *livres*.

[60] Ibid., p. 118. This amount (one billion *livres*) was not, in itself, insurmountable. It would only become so in the context of the inadequate fiscal and monetary structures and their inadequacy relative to the policies which they were required to support.

[61] This follows William Doyle, *Origins of the French Revolution* (Oxford, Oxford University Press, 1980). See also his *Oxford History of the French Revolution* (Oxford, Clarendon Press, 1989), pp. 66–70.

[62] Harris, *Necker: Reform Statesman*, p. 124.

[63] John Bosher, *French Finances, from Business to Bureaucracy* (Cambridge, Cambridge University Press, 1970), pp. 142–66.

[64] Calonne would be *contrôleur général des finances* from November 1783.

great administrative reforms which would take place in the kingdom's financial affairs after Calonne and which would be carried through by Brienne and by the governments of the Revolution. It remains the case, however, that the damage done to the Ancien Régime by Necker, and the war, by his borrowing policy, and continued in full spate by Calonne, is undeniable.

Such damage would not have been irremediable in the days of Colbert or Philippe d'Orléans. Louis XIV, to take but one example, had confronted similar difficulties and in a France which was much less well endowed than it was by the end of the eighteenth century. At the very least, a Chamber of Justice (*Chambre de justice*) would have sufficed, as it had done in 1661, or in 1716–17, to persuade the corrupt financiers (and the honest – there were some – ones as well, but that was not the problem) to cough up.[65] After the ritual of a Chamber of Justice, the state would have proceeded to declare a partial bankruptcy such as had occurred in 1720 when the complete devaluation of Law's banknotes and the 'crash' of the Law System took place.[66] With Calonne as minister, however, such brutal ways of proceeding, *à la* Colbert or Law, were no longer a realistic possibility any more than they had been under Necker. For state credit, even though it struggled to meet its obligations, deserved better and, henceforth, the public debt had become sacrosanct.[67] It would be the Revolution (and after) which would bring about a return to more blunt methods of proceeding, with the creation (and then the devaluation) of the *assignats*, which would, in due course, be followed a few years later by the guillotining of the financiers (such as Lavoisier in 1794). In the preceeding period, however, these same tax-farmer contractors and financiers under Louis XVI (and the situation was already true under Louis XV) belonged well and truly to the cream of the aristocracy by the simple fact of the unification of the country's élites. Their social status had considerably increased since the days of Louis XIV, or since the appearance of the *Turcaret* of Lesage (1708) which had held them up to public ridicule. There was no longer any possibility of treating such individuals, now considered as honourable and part of high society, as though they were rogues (whether it was the truth or merely a pretence) and turning them into diabolic public enemies, such as had occurred in the cases of Fouquet and Semblançay in the past.[68] The consolidation of the aristo-financial élite made such a broad sweep 'witch-hunt', and one which might have saved the Treasury and, with it, the French monarchy, henceforth impos-

---

[65] Bosher, *French Finances*, pp. 18–19.

[66] Dom H. Leclercq, *Histoire de la Régence pendant la minorité de Louis XV* (3 vols, Paris, Champion, 1921), iii, 477. For the state bankruptcy, declared by Mazarin in July 1648, see Pierre Goubert, *Mazarin* (Paris, Fayard, 1990), pp. 248–52.

[67] Doyle, *Origins of the French Revolution*, pp. 46–7.

[68] On Fouquet, see above, chapter 4; Semblançay was the *surintendant des finances* under Francis I who was hanged on the king's orders in 1527 following a series of accusations concerning irregularities in the accounts and his personal enrichment.

sible. The monarchy was now more civilized, and thus more vulnerable. As for the *livre tournois*, its value remained stable from 1774 to 1788, just as it had done more or less from 1726. This too had become something which was almost sacred in a social system where the *rentier* classes occupied a solid position within it. It was no longer a question of an unscrupulous devaluation of the national money of account to enable the state to pay its debts. This was what had happened in the past and would occur again after 1789 and then again in the twentieth century. In the latter years of the Ancien Régime such, however, was not the done thing; it was not 'seemly' and the *rentiers* would never hear of it! It was a remarkable state of affairs when French money held its value and French credit was at its lowest ebb! The only important measure which Necker could devise to improve things gradually was to transform the country's financial administration by better management and make it more efficient. In this way it would (paradoxically) be transformed from *business* to *bureaucracy*.[69] It would be metamorphosed into a more modern structure, thanks to the partial elimination of the semi-private agencies (the tax-farm contractors and the financiers) which had a hand in state finance. The financiers could no longer be hanged, but their activities could still be short-circuited. It was also a matter of abolishing venal offices, such posts being henceforth replaced by *commis*, more like the modern civil servants of our own day. Such reforming impulses should be properly credited to Necker; he followed the attempts of Terray and Turgot, both of them modernizers of the financial system in the same mould. But such measures could not, however, yield immediate results. They would be, in any case, curtailed by the fall of Necker in 1781 and would remain to serve in no other way than to reinforce his own reputation later on. Although this may have been a just outcome, the American War, and the heavy borrowing which it left behind it, left French state finance as leaky as a sieve.

In terms of the French kingdom itself, the American War had, in the strict sense of the particular (not to say specious) interests of the monarchy, a considerably less positive impact than might at first sight have been imagined. In terms of territory, it had 'resulted' in almost nothing. All that had been acquired or repossessed were some small islands in America and some factories in Senegal. The essential injustice of the Treaty of Paris, i.e. the annexation of francophone Quebec by Britain was not addressed and, in reality, there was never any question of its being so. The eastern part of Canada would remain, as before, attached to the British monarchy as part of the 'Britannicization' of the St Lawrence seaway.[70] The politics of Louis XVI, following on from that of Louis XV, did have a certain logic to it, however. As for the English, commerce remained the key preoccupation. The kernel of French strategy in the New World remained centred on Haiti, the pearl of the Antilles, the primary sugar producer in the world,

[69] Bosher, *French Finances*, especially p. 307.
[70] Jean Hamelin (dir.), *Histoire du Québec* (Toulouse, Privat, 1976), ch. 8.

and the key to the growth in France's colonial traffic. If one looks at the Treaty of Versailles (1783) in this context, it is clear that the Bourbon monarchy gained nothing from it, but it also lost nothing either, and this in a period when the sugar and slave trades were enjoying an enviable prosperity. And the fact remained that, in North America, it was the French who had contributed a good deal to the freeing of Britain's American colonies. . . .

This conclusion merits, however, some further reflection. The British colonies already benefitted from the libertarian régime *à l'anglaise*. If they had been defeated by the armies of George III, it would not, in the long term, have changed many of the modern features of their public life, their administration and electoral arrangements. They remained committed to an ingrained English liberalism. In fact, by lending assistance to the United States to achieve its independence, the French navy and its army above all contributed to the leonine distant Anglo-Saxon world hegemony which has been experienced in the twentieth century. That hegemony would be broadly benefical to Humanity at large but, from the 'revanchist' perspectives of Vergennes and the ministers of Louis XVI this would have appeared *a posteriori* as more than a little paradoxical.

The important fact, and the one which should count as more significant amongst these prospective (or retrospective) conclusions is that this war would serve to put a torch to the 'gothic' superstructure of the Ancien Régime, fragile and fossilized as it had become. For it created an intellectual debate which was filled to the brim with the decisive ideas of the American Revolution, both its more moderate notions (such as 'no taxation without representation' and 'checks and balances') and its more radical as well (equality, popular sovereignty, the democratic spirit, the political triumph of Reason, the regeneration of society, the rights of man, and the autonomy of the individual, the inseparable concomitant of a particular egalitarianism). All these notions were brought back to France in the baggage of the younger liberal nobles such as La Fayette and his consorts. They spread abroad also in a wave of pro-American pamphlets which proclaimed the 'Birth of a Nation' on the basis of principles which were presented in France (although it was an exaggeration) as purely rational. The philosophes were quick to draw out the major conclusions from it all. Liberty should no longer be regarded as an aristocratic privilege, however invaluable the latter might be.[71] It acquired, henceforth, the nature of a founding principle with a universal valency.[72] The philosophes

---

[71]   Catherine Secrétan, *Les Privilèges, berceau de la liberté: la révolte des Pays-Bas. Aux sources de la pensée politique moderne (1566–1619)* (Paris, Vrin, 1990).
[72]   See the contribution of Philippe Raynaud on 'Révolution française, Révolution américaine' in François Furet, *L'Héritage de la Révolution française* (Paris, Hachette, 1989); and the same author's, 'Révolution américaine' in François Furet and Mona Ozouf, *Dictionnaire critique . . .* , p. 860 *et seq.*

thereby heralded the beginning of the age of Democratic Revolutions on both sides of the Atlantic Ocean.[73]

The American War thus created the stresses and strains of the dramatic events to come. It was responsible both for the financial crisis and for the ideology which would envelop the Ancien Régime. Calonne seems to have realized the scale of what was happening rather late in the day (to be precise, in August 1786, when, as *contrôleur général*, he was finally in a position to measure the scale of the deficit) and to draw his own conclusions.

Calonne was inspired by the distant example of Vauban and Pâris-Duvernoy, the duke de Bourbon's financier who, in 1725, invented the tax known as the *cinquantième*. He also drew on the examples of his more immediate predecessors, Turgot and Necker, and conceived of an overall plan to simplify the state[74] and even society too, using the techniques of the *tabula rasa* beloved of Turgot[75] and the philosophes. He proposed the measures which he regarded as essential for a solvent state Treasury. There was to be a new 'land-tax', the main weight of which would be borne by the privileged orders. It would replace the *vingtièmes* and would provide the *ad hoc* resources on the sought-after egalitarian basis of fiscal justice, since it would be proportional to the wealth of each and every individual. In a somewhat bizarre detail, this 'subvention' would (at least according to the official pronouncements) be paid in kind. This was reminiscent of the royal tithe scheme of Vauban, albeit revised and altered by the physiocrats. The pill which was to be administered would be sugared, however, by the granting of physiocratic measures which had already been anticipated by public opinion. These included the abolition of the *corvées* which, after the fashion of Turgot, were to be replaced by a tax in money; and the suppression of internal customs tolls which acted as a constraint on the volume of trade and, thus, on the revenue from indirect taxation itself.

An assembly of notables, made up of an élite of the privileged, was assembled in February 1787, in order to discuss (and, most importantly, to ratify) these proposals. Dominated by the upper clergy and nobility, the very fact that this assembly was summoned put the first, gaping, hole in absolutism's side. By this late date, its existence had already become more theoretical than real. At all events, this was the first time since the assembly of notables in 1626–7[76] 160 years previously, or since the Estates General of 1614, that an appeal had been launched for national representation *per se* (even though it would be, in the event, rather hamstrung) to approve or

[73]   Robert Palmer, *The Age of Democratic Revolution: a political history of Europe and America, 1760–1800* (2 vols, Princeton, NJ, Princeton University Press, 1967–9), i, ch. 1, p. 3 *et seq.*
[74]   Jean Egret, *La Pré-Révolution française, 1787–1788* (Paris, PUF, 1962), p. 6 *et seq.*
[75]   On the 'doctrinaire' stance of Turgot, see Lucien Laugier, *Turgot* (Paris, Albatross, 1979), p. 11 *et seq.*
[76]   Jeanne Petit, *L'Assemblée des notables de 1626–1627* (Paris, Margraff (Clavreuil), 1936).

reject a monarchical proposal. It was unfortunately foreseeable, however, that the assembly of 1787 would reject Calonne's schemes. Its refusal was a reflection of its corporate egoism as well as its greater attentiveness to public opinion, which would remain entirely unpersuaded of the merits of the fiscal measures unilaterally proposed by Calonne. To be more precise, the assembly of notables accepted Calonne's principles but refused him the means to put them into practice. The *contrôleur général* thus lay at the mercy of public opinion, the notables and the privileged orders. From all quarters he was criticized for his attempts at reform, despite their egalitarian and redistributive tendencies, and his fiscal measures which threatened a virtual bankruptcy. Although in terms of the dangerous possibilities which reform beckoned, Necker was as guilty or responsible as his successor, the Genevan banker always remained popular whereas Calonne attracted all the unpopularity. In 1787, he was as unpopular as it was possible to get and he was reluctantly dismissed by Louis XVI.

The king replaced him in May 1787 by Loménie de Brienne (archbishop of Toulouse, and then of Sens), a deist *philosophe* and, until his appointment, a leading figure in the assembly of notables. His nomination had the support of the queen, and it accorded a degree of influence to the concept of national representation, at that point vested after a fashion in the notables of 1787. In this sense, the appointment of Brienne as minister was one more step towards the takeover by the élites or by one of their highly-placed agents of the destiny of France with the disgruntled accord of the monarchy. The Revolution had not yet perhaps begun, but the pre-Revolution[77] was well under way, and Brienne was an energetic reformer.

Brienne was intellectually able[78] and full of good intentions, although he was handicapped by some weaknesses of mind and body. He succeeded, nevertheless, in summarizing in his not insubstantial presence half a dozen of his predecessors in office, i.e. Bertin, Choiseul, Maupeou, Turgot, Necker and even Calonne. Like Choiseul, and with the assistance of Guibert,[79] Brienne set about professionalizing the army, and 'Prussianizing' it,[80] whilst limiting on the grounds of economy the excessive numbers of senior officers. This had positive results in the long-term (in the military victories of the Revolution and the Empire); in the short-term, however, it led to grumbling in the ranks and discontent. This frustration would reduce the efficiency of the soldiers and officers when they were called on, without much success, to attempt to put down the first revolutionary uprisings in 1789. The modernization of the defence

---

[77]   Egret, *La Pré-Révolution française*, p. 80 *et seq.*
[78]   Ibid., pp. 53–5.
[79]   Jacques Guibert (1743–1790), was secretary to the *Conseil de la guerre* in 1788, and one of the great innovators in military tactics of the French army and in Europe in the reign of Louis XVI. See the entry in the *Dictionnaire d'art et d'histoire militaire* by André Corvisier (Paris, PUF, 1988).
[80]   Egret, *La Pré-Révolution française*, p. 55 *et seq.*

forces did not mean that Brienne was a war-monger. On the contrary, the archbishop, like Turgot, was committed to peace, and refused to commit France to the kinds of ruinous 'errors' which had led to French intervention in North America. He avoided committing the country to a new war when, in 1787, the patriots and Dutch bourgeois opposed the 'despotism' of the Orangist Stadholder, William V. The latter had the support of Russia and the English navy but, despite the efforts of the *marechaux* Ségur and Castries, Brienne decided that peace was the wiser course of action and, above all, the less expensive in the circumstances of a major national deficit. So much for national prestige! The French superpower which had put forces on the east coast of North America, was now as shrivelled as a dry chamois leather.

Following Turgot and, before him, Bertin, the archbishop attacked the *corvée* as well as the impediments to the free-trade in grain. In the case of the latter, his success seemed, initially, complete. But the bad harvest of August 1788 would deal him a rebuff in the following spring, a rebuff which had its precedents. Like Necker, whose disciple at this point he was (and almost as misunderstood), Brienne suppressed a large number of the parasitic offices at the heart of the financial system.[81] He reorganized the royal Treasury and created 'the unified Exchequer' in order to centralize all receipts and disbursements.[82] The administrations of the period from 1790 to 1799 would also be the subject of 'Tocquevillian recentralization' and 'bureaucratic change' and they thus had merely to continue the work which had been begun.[83] They would complete the unification of the Treasury whilst suppressing a good many of its staff in a series of measures which would become irreversible. Like Calonne, the minister-archbishop also attempted to establish a land tax on egalitarian lines. Then, when this failed through being rejected by the Parlement, he attempted to use the *vingtièmes* whilst making this tax more equitably distributed amongst the contributors or supposed contributors from the three estates. Brienne also modernized the judicial system in suppressing the use of 'the question' (i.e. torture) to confirm the testimony of witnesses. Like Maupeou, too, he sought to subdue the Parlement and exiled it, hoping thus to deprive it of its 'dangerous' prerogatives, *viz.* its powers to enregister royal edicts and its rights of remonstration. He hoped to succeed in this through the creation (thanks to an edict of May 1788) of a court of plenary jurisdiction composed of the most senior magistrates, dignitaries who would thenceforward be invested with these twin functions exercised formally by the Parlement. The difference between Brienne's proposal and that of

---

[81] Bosher, *French Finances*, p. 309.

[82] Egret, *La Pré-Révolution française*, p. 106; Bosher, *French Finances*, p. 24.

[83] John Bosher, *The French Revolution* (New York, Norton, 1988), p. 245 *et seq.* The appearancee of the word 'bureaucracy' between 1785 and 1787 in the writings of Sébastien Mercier and Jean-Louis Carra is significant in this respect (ibid., pp. 245 and 325). See also, on this subject, Clive Church, *Revolution and Red Tape. The French Ministerial Bureaucracy* (Oxford, Oxford University Press, 1981).

Maupeou remained, however, very considerable. Brienne had good intentions. Unlike Maupeou, who had wanted to re-establish 'odious absolutism' in a more efficient form, Brienne, by contrast, appealed over the heads of the parlements, which he had put into retirement, to the Nation. He asked it for support by means of a series of three measures: the restoration of the provincial estates, the creation of municipal and provincial assemblies which would emasculate the majority of the powers of the intendants,[84] and finally the summoning of the Estates General. The latter was seen as a counter to be used in November 1787 against the parlements in the forlorn hope that the *parlementaires* would, in return, accept the government's plans for financial reform and change. Its summoning was promised initially for 1792; then brought forward to the fateful year, 1789. Was this a return to a *Ständestaat* or 'State of estates' of the kind which had existed under the Valois or first Bourbons, a return to an institution called the Estates General which would mean leaping back over the intervening absolutist phase (1624–1774)? This would be one way amongst many of presenting it. In reality, however, the debate was taking place in a new context and this was underlined in particular by the appearance of the provincial assemblies, closer to the ideas of Fénelon, Saint-Simom, Montesquieu, Turgot and Necker, than Francis I or Henry III. L'Averdy had already attempted in 1764–5 to establish elected municipalities on the basis of a relatively restricted franchise.[85] Turgot and Dupont de Nemours[86] had dreamt of establishing municipal and provincial representative institutions through assemblies which would be elected by property-holders (this remained the physiocratic ideology, transcending the older divisions of a society of orders by the concept of property). For his part, Necker had gingerly begun to create provincial assemblies, half nominated, half co-opted, in Berry and in the region covered by the intendancy of Montauban. Calonne opened the way forward to national representation with the assembly of notables, which was to be complemented by a project to establish provincial assemblies, elected on a vari-

---

[84] François-Xavier Emmanuelli, *Pouvoir royal et vie régionale en Provence au déclin de la monarchie* (service de reproduction des thèses d'université de Lille III, 1974), ii, 899, regards the intendant (following P. Ardascheff, *Les Intendants* . . . (Paris, 1909)), at least for the region which he has studied, as a decentralized kind of administrator, very different from the future Napoleonic prefects. In fact, setting to one side the rather particular example of Provence, it seems more correct to regard them rather as Tocqueville did, as the effective (albeit flexible) agents of centralization. This was why they were so compromised by the decentralized measures introduced by Brienne (Cf. John Bosher, *The French Revolution*, pp. 67 and 307; Maurice Bordes, SEDES, *L'Administration provinciale et municipale en France au XVIIIe siècle* (Paris, 1972), ch. 6, p. 156 *et seq.*

[85] Maurice Bordes, *La Réforme muncipiale du contrôleur général L'Averdy et son application (1764–1771)* (Toulouse, Publications de la Faculté des Lettres de Toulouse, 1968), summarized in M. Bordes, *L'Administration provinciale*, ch. 9, p. 45 *et seq.* See also, for a regional example, Bruno Teyssier, 'Le Pouvoir et les groupes de pression locaux en Vivarais', *Bulletin du Centre d'histoire économique et social de la région lyonnaise*, 4 (1987), 22.

[86] Douglas Dakin, *Turgot and the Ancien Régime in France, 1770–1774* (New York, Octagon Books, 1965), p. 272 *et seq.*

ously graded property franchise.[87] These assemblies were intended to provide the owners of land (particularly the nobles), thus summoned to participate in regional power, with a counterpart to the fact that the state now wanted to tax them on the basis of the revenues from their landed domains. In other words, increased taxation meant enhanced responsibility in the state . . . it was an idea whose time had come. For his part, Brienne picked up the idea of creating a generalized system of local and provincial representation and using it to limit (now that it was manifestly in decay) absolutism's prerogatives, and restrict the intendancies which relied on it.[88] It was in this respect that a first revolution was being nurtured under Louis XVI, from 1774 to 1788, from Turgot to Brienne *via* Necker and Calonne. There were changes occurring in the depths of the body politic as a result of the regional, and then national, participation which was being summoned into existence. It had begun by seeming old-fashioned; but an opening up of French politics had occurred and its increasing effectiveness was undeniable. The summoning of the Estates General represented the culmination of these processes of association which had been widely begun; at the same time, as would only become clear a little later, the alarm-bells for the final *débâcle* were sounding.

In other ways, the accord of civil status to the Huguenots in 1787 was a spectacular way of declaring the revocation of the edict of Nantes to be null and void. It was no longer a matter, as it had been over the preceeding 20 years, of casting a blind eye over whether someone was a Huguenot or not, of treating the issue with benign neglect. The official status of Protestants was henceforth improved. This first measure of toleration was also designed, once again, to secure their compliance for fairly drastic fiscal measures.[89] At the same time, it underlined an irreversible change in people's mental attitudes on religious matters, or rather in matters of religious scepticism both at the ministerial level as well as amongst the parlements and in public opinion at large.

In a general sense, Brienne cut a figure as a statesman who was both traditional and modern; not far removed from the 'populist' kings of the past (Francis I, Henry IV) but also able to be placed alongside the moderate revolutionaries of the following few years. The archbishop sought to appeal to the 'Commons', at all events to the Third Estate and the liberal nobles, over the heads of the privileged orders (whether clerical or lay) who opposed his liberal measures. Hence his manoeuvring[90] in July 1788 which Tocqueville regarded as politically naive and which was rather more a crafty ruse with rather lasting effects. The ruse consisted of leaving the question of deciding, or helping to decide, in what form the Estates General should be recalled to suggestions coming up from below. It would

[87]   Egret, *La Pré-Révolution française*, p. 20 *et seq.*
[88]   Ibid., pp. 103 *et seq.*, 117.
[89]   Ibid., p. 185, citing Talleyrand, *Mémoires* (Paris, Calmann-Lévy, 1891), i, 185.
[90]   Egret, *La Pré-Révolution française*, p. 306 *et seq.*

be left to public opinion and antiquarian erudition as to how, if possible, the body should be revised to make it compatible with Enlightened views. It was a ruse which Brienne only half believed in himself. One thing is clear; he was the opponent of the parlements. He rejected out of hand the advice which they would shortly proffer, to the effect that the assembly of the Estates General had to be summoned in the 'barbarous and feudal' forms which it had in 1614, when the Third Estate was still overawed by the other two superior orders.

The range of reforms announced, and in many instances speedily carried through by Brienne, was admirable. But the circumstances were less favourable than ever to his eventual success. By the beginning of August 1788, there was a crisis in state finance. The Treasury was exhausted and only 400,000 *livres* remained to settle the annual expenditure of the state, estimated at 580 million *livres*. It was tantamount to saying that he should clear his desk, since the surgically precise solution of a bankruptcy had been, as we have already seen, rejected out of court. Exit the archbishop from power that same month (August 1788).

At the moment of Brienne's fall, the degree to which the financial leukemia of the state had become the catalyst[91] and then the detonator for the cycle of pre-Revolution, or 'primary' Revolution events during the two 'fateful' years from August 1786 to August 1788 is much more evident. The financial question repeatedly raised that of the participation of the élites, then of the people at large, in government, a matter which had a response in contemporary cultural assumptions. It had been the growing realization of the problems of the Treasury by Calonne in August 1786 which had, firstly, led to the convocation of the assembly of notables. It was then the (perhaps fallacious) prospect of a financial improvement in the course of the following five years, which led Brienne and Louis XVI in November 1787 to hold out the hope of convoking the Estates General in 1792 in order to stimulate the parlements not to put further obstacles in the path of reform. Finally, it was the collapse in public credit (with, it is true, the 'finishing touch' being provided by the rising known as the *journée des tuiles*[92] in Grenoble in June 1788) which broke the Brienne ministry in August of the same year, opening the way to the unlimited expression of the national will, as the forthcoming Estates General would be entitled to describe itself, in less than a year's time. And, behind all that, there was the costly spectacle of the American War, the writing on the wall of monarchical destiny, chalked up involuntarily thanks to the efforts of the American faction in France, to Vergennes, Franklin and La Fayette, from 1776 to 1783. Terray, and even Turgot, saved the royal finances. Necker and Calonne spent it all even before Calonne attempted in vain to mount a rescue package. It did not take longer than five terms of office for Brienne

---

[91]   This is also the view of William Doyle, *Origins of the French Revolution*, p. 53 *et seq.*
[92]   Vital Chomel (ed.), *Histoire de Grenoble* (Toulouse, Privat, 1976), p. 222 *et seq.*; Egret, *La Pré-Révolution française*, p. 261 *et seq.* and sidenote.

(from May 1787 to August 1788) to gallop round the whole course again, and cover the same ground as that paraded in over a decade by the ministers from the latter years of Choiseul through to the first ministry of Necker.

At the end of August 1788, Necker returned to power. The Huguenot banker was unrepentant and he carried the confidence of the lenders to the government with him. This time, however, the monarchy and Necker himself let things take their course. In the seemingly justified hope that confidence and credit would revive, Necker decided to play his last card. Whether through sincere or feigned optimism, he presented the general will (in reality the body to be convoked under the title of the Estates General in 1789) with a blank cheque and invited the sovereign nation to take in hand the reorganization of the country in the course of the following year. *Tabula rasa* was the order of the day and, as soon as the authorities realized what was planned, they recognized that, for the period from the end of the assembly of notables to the beginning of the Estates General, they merely provided an interim government. In the deliquescent state of absolutism, they could hardly be said to represent much. In a period of weeks at the end of 1788 and the beginning of 1789, 'the public debate changed tack' as a result of the 'cold shoulder' from the apparent 'turn to the right' of the *parlementaires* who remained firmly wedded to the old formal arrangements for Estates General 'as in 1614'. Such outdated forms were rightly detested by the spokesmen for the Third Estate, the advocates and others, including the leaders of the liberal nobility, represented in the 'Committee of Thirty'.[93] Once more the scene on which the events were unfolding 'was transformed' or 'shifted through a half turn'.[94] The battle against despotism which had unified the opposition, gave way to a battle for juridico-political equality. It would soon be for social equality. Both issues divided the opposition and it splintered, or split assunder. It was one passion chasing the other. The 'struggle of the classes' (the term specifically used by Tocqueville in this context), or, at the least, the struggle between the orders of society was taking shape, the bourgeoisie massing against the aristocrats of varying degrees, nobles whom Sieyès would depict as parasites and, *a priori*, guilty. The militant egalitarianism of the Third Estate would enlarge the unifying concept of Nation, and

---

[93] The so-called *Société des Trente* was given its name *a posteriori* and, in reality, it corresponded to the 'Société réunie chez Duport' (Adrien Duport was a *conseiller* in the Parlement of Paris). It included the younger *parlementaires* (those between 30 and 50 years of age), dukes, dukes and peers, a young prelate (Talleyrand) and a clutch of publicists, commoners and others, who were 'formers of opinion'. This Committee represented the outer flank of liberal élites, amongst whom were many from the nobility (Egret, *La Pré-révolution française*, p. 326 *et seq.*).

[94] Furet, *Revolutionary France*, pp. 43–4. For the citation from Mallet du Pin, ('Le débat public a changé de face'), see Jean Egret, *La Pré-Révolution française*, p. 366, with the complete text as follows: 'Le débat public a changé de face. Il ne s'agit plus que très secondairement du Roi, du despotisme et de la Constitution. C'est une guerre entre le Tiers Etat et les deux autres ordres' (*Journal de Mallet du Pin*, January 1789).

wrongly identify it exclusively with the third estate of the kingdom. The newly nascent Nation-Third Estate would then give way to the fully fledged nation-state when the moment for it came. The aristocracy, in the scrupulously enlightened hands of the *abbé* Sieyès, became an unsalvageable mechanism, to be ignominiously and symbolically excluded from the nation which was rapidly and successfully emerging. That nation was one whose destinies, over the following quarter of a century, would be prodigious. What was more, the risks[95] of a poor harvest (as occurred in 1788) heightened the awareness of the urban and rural masses in the Great Fear of the following spring (1789). The 'people' (for want of a better term) were mobilized into crowds by the rising price of bread, and the latter were politicized (a new feature) through the rhythm of local election meetings. The grain riot became the basis for a schooling in street agitation and even a mass seminar in class warfare.[96] The pace of events was quickening and the long-term factors were being overlaid by the more frenetic rhythms of the short-term events.

The clubs and philosophical societies, the 'laboratories of equality' pulled the strings as to who was chosen to be a candidate for the Estates General.[97] Sometimes the strings were all too evident; at other times they were barely visible or hardly existent. They even had a major part in the drawing up of the *cahiers*. The wheels were set in motion and, with them, the springs and triggers which would launch the Revolution, the 'complex whirlwind' which was at once creative and destructive, and impossible to stop, let alone drive back.

By May 1789, everything was caving in. Royal sovereignty had begun to crumble, prior to its total destruction. The society of orders was being liquidated. The Rights of Man were being proclaimed. Religious minorities were being emancipated. Feudalism, whether agrarian-based or not, was being destroyed or disbanded. Also being disbanded was the old army,[98] which became incapable of repressing the overwhelming force of events. There were also the (at first) gentle, and then progressively more brutal, attacks on the church. It was threatened in its tithes, its wealth, its power-bases and its structure, and fundamentally compromised by having in the past supported the old system. This was despite the old-fashioned opposition to authority which it had displayed in May 1788, and which would prove to be suicidal. The sense that the church was compromised was not far from the truth; for it would have been difficult to break with the absolutist or ministerial 'despotism' of the Ancien Régime in all its de-

---

[95]   J. Neumann and J. Dettwiller, 'Great Historical Events that were significantly affected by the weather during the year leading to the Revolution of 1789 in France', *Bulletin of the American Meteorological Society*, 71 (1990), 33–41.

[96]   E.P. Thompson *et al.*, *La Guerre du blé au XVIIIe siècle* (Paris, Editions de la Passion, 1988), p. 122 *et seq.* and *passim*.

[97]   The work of Ran Halévi will make these connections more precise, using the studies of Augustin Cochin and François Furet.

[98]   Bosher, *The French Revolution*, p. 66.

crepitude, more despised than truly odious, unless at the same time, a sacrilegious and destructive hand was also laid on the other two principal pillars or products of the Ancien Régime, namely the church and the nobility. After all, it was the king who, as a collective entity, ensured the choice of the bishops, verified the nobles, and created new nobles.

These initial episodes during the turmoil of the two years from 1789 to 1790 led with a frightening regularity, under the active influence of the new Paris 'sections', to the clubs and factions outbidding one another for ideological purity, each enamoured of the abstract concept of egalitarianism. Common, too, were the successive exclusions from their ranks, dehiscences and interminable explosions of controversy, which would only be brought to an end by the disgust and rejection of the Thermidorian Reaction of July 1794. At the same time, and concomitantly, there was a realignment of activists and the radicalized masses, whether manipulated from above or spontaneously rallying together, whether acting on abstract principle or concrete political issue, around a national and popular agenda. It would eventually become overwhelmingly a popular agenda, and it was hardly of great significance if this categorization was often sociologically inexact. The 'agenda' in question would henceforth progressively lead to the expulsion of the aristocrats, then the moderates, then the rich, and then a bit of everybody, from Danton to Hébert, and from Cloots to Desmoulins. Opportunists and other chameleons could do nothing other than conform and follow the movement; otherwise they risked losing their popularity, or worse, their heads.[99]

Patriotic unanimity was the other side of the coin from an ever-present sense of suspicion and betrayal which created its own paranoias and obsessional fears. Such fears fed and reinforced those who were newly in power, and who wanted to find scapegoats for their actions. The monarchy would pay dearly for the 'national deficit' (over and above the financial deficits) which was charged to its account. Was it not the monarchy which had lost the war with England in 1763 (the American victory had not changed a great deal)? Was it not the French monarchy which had long ago sold out to the ultramontanes, in collusion with the Vatican and at the expense of old French Gallicanism which Louis XIV, by contrast, had carefully protected, at least up to 1693? The latter-day efforts of Choiseul, dissolving the Jesuit order, hardly sufficed to purify the régime from the stain of the infamy which it incurred. More recently still, was it not Brienne who had let the Dutch Patriots down ignominiously? Despite the wise financial precautions which lay behind the decision, the Patriots were the traditional maritime allies of France against the pro-Prussian Stadtholder despotism.

---

[99] A good example of subtle adaptability to the unfolding events is provided by Rétif de la Bretonne, who was very much a 'trimmer' as it turned out. See, in this respect, Mohammed Bakkali-Yedri, 'Rétif et la Révolution', *Etudes rétiviennes*, 10 (1989), 19–38. Alternatively, read Rétif himself, the apologetic Rétif, in his *Nuits révolutionnaires* (Paris, Editions de Paris, 1989).

But Nationhood, as an ideal which combines paradoxically in it both patriotism and universality, is also and always more than just the Nation. On the basis of the dissolution of the monarchies, 'mass democracy'[100] literally exploded, or rather, extravasated beyond the borders of the hexagon during the four summers from July 1789 to August 1792. The conflict began in April 1792 and then rapidly spread. It was a war fought against the old Europe and at the same time for the new creed of the Rights of Man. It was a war fought with an 'eschatological impulse'[101] which would replace for better or worse the old religion. The war was fought for the Montagnards and the defence of the *patrie*; it would soon be fought for the huge pillage which was undertaken at the expense of foreign nations who would be freed by the 'armed missionaries' of the Revolution. It would all cost millions of lives in the various battlefields and it would last for over 20 years. Within France, on the other hand, the Terror would, even including the Vendée, 'only' lead to some hundreds of thousands of victims, many of them decapitated one after another 'like cabbage-heads' (Hegel). The Terror began its existence without any great ceremony in 1789 in the consecutive lynchings which took place after the seizure of the Bastille. Some years later the Terror would have developed its own endogeneous dynamic and be fully deployed and protected by its own justifications on the basis of external 'circumstances', justifications which hardly stood up at all to critical or impartial examination.[102] The phenomenon has all the marks of a witch-hunt.[103] It was the Thermidorian and the post-Thermidorian (Directorial) Reaction which would serve to release France from the bloody *cul de sac* of 'terrorism' and the revolutionary government.

Striking the overall balance is awe-inspiring and it requires nuance. If it is looked at as a whole, the opening phase of change which was gently inaugurated by Turgot in 1774 and then pursued passionately, but inconsistently, through to 1789 and beyond carried grave risks of leading to disintegration and anarchy from the force of its own attack. The result was that an authoritarian reaction was bound to occur at some stage. The forces of continuity were also not slow to make themselves felt, sometimes in a rather unpredictable fashion. Monarchical centralization *à la Bodin* was implicitly refashioned *à la Rousseau* by the theoreticians of the one and indivisible national will, led by Sieyès.[104] This same centralization, secular in its origins now, would be explicitly practised, albeit in different fashions, by the Conventions, by the Consulate and by succeeding régimes in the

---

[100]   The expression comes from William Doyle, *Origins of the French Revolution*. It is particularly relevant to the period from August to September 1792 (the anti-monarchical *coup* of August, followed by the massacres of the following month).

[101]   The expression is taken from Chartier, *Les Origines culturelles*.

[102]   Furet and Ozouf, *Dictionnaire critique* (art. 'Terreur').

[103]   J. Laplanche, *Vocabulaire de la psychoanalyse* (Paris, PUF, 1973), p. 372.

[104]   On the various tendencies, all implicit in the philosophy of Rousseau, towards 'spiritual despotism', 'absolute liberty', 'libertarian fanaticism' and *tabula rasa*, with the resulting condemnation of intermediary bodies, a rejection of pluralism and even the conjoining of the two heads of the eagle (God and Caesar), see Raymond Court, 'La Liberté et les libertés, J.-J. Rousseau et la Révolution', *Etudes*, 373 (1990), 27–41.

nineteenth century. The administrative machinery of the national, centripetal state, whose numbers of salaried officials continued to grow from the end of the eighteenth century onwards, would emerge reinforced and modernized from the Revolution which had seemed to want to, or to have to, destroy it.[105] This impression had been a mistaken one, however, and the centralist ship of state seemed briefly to sink along with the nobility; but, a little while later, it surfaced again and, like a mastodon, it reemerged unencumbered by the refined tastes of the aristocracy. Hence the long-recognized 'Tocquevillian' continuity between the Ancien Régime and the Revolution over the longer term. It was on this democratic, but centralizing base, paradoxically, that the Republic would end up, a century later, forging the legitimacy which it took almost all of three generations to set in place. Such were the continuities between Turgot and Gambetta.[106]

★ ★ ★ ★ ★

Was the fall of the Ancien Régime inevitable? According to Guglielmo Ferrero, the 'modern' transition from monarchical or (as he puts it) 'aristo-hereditary' legitimacy to democratic legitimacy (such as ours now is) almost inexorably involved a painful and dangerous change, a 'time of troubles' or convulsions which might last several decades and bring with it terrible autocratic and dictatorial side-effects.[107] This was the case for England with its twin revolutions in the seventeenth century (1640, 1688), and, in between, the temporary dictatorship of Cromwell. It was also the case for France, from 1780 to 1880; and later, it would also be true in the other great European nations, Germany, Italy, Spain and Russia, up to our own difficult and sometimes distressing century. As Michael Walzer has shown,[108] there was much to be gained from having at one's disposal well-

---

[105] The agents of the state (office-holders, *commis*, etc.) do not appear to have exceeded 100,000 in 1789 (excluding the armed services). In around 1900, the equivalent figure had exceeded half a million functionaries and employees of the state (J-P. Rioux in *Le Monde*, 28 July, 1990). In 1990, this would have risen to 1,990,010 functionaries and 287,564 additional non-permanent civil servants in the same categories (*Le Monde*, 26 July, 1988). John Bosher (*The French Revolution*, p. 245 *et seq.*) writes of the first bureaucratic revolution as having taken place in the public services in the years immediately following 1789.

[106] Furet, *Revolutionary France*.

[107] Guglielmo Ferrero, *Pouvoirs: les génies invisibles de la cité* (Librairie Générale Française, 1988). On the idea of decisive moments of change in history and (historical) ideology, see the interesting, if rather out-dated, reflections of Etienne Balibar, *Ecrits pour Althusser* (Paris, La Découverte, 1991), p. 9 *et seq.*

[108] Michael Walzer, *The Revolution of the Saints* (Cambridge, MA, Harvard University Press, 1965). Between the Puritans and the Jacobins, the missing link might well be, in Denis Richet's view, the Jansenists. Imbued with Augustinian theology similar to the Calvinists, they would provide, in the latter years of the eighteenth century, a certain number of devoted adherents to revolutionary causes, such as the *abbé* Grégoire. See Catherine Maire (dir.), *Jansénisme et Révolution* (Paris, Chroniques de Port-Royal, 1990), an excellent collective volume (esp. p. 211 *et seq.* on the *abbé* Grégoire and p. 103 *et seq.* on the 'image' of the convulsionaries of Saint-Médard as a theatrical transition between the religious Jansenism of the Louis XIV period and the political Jansenism of the Louis XV period).

trained and determined groups, factions capable of making the first breach (sometimes an atrocious task) and terrifying the opposition with their energetic determination. Such a group was provided by the Puritans in England, and still more so, by the French Jacobins or the Russian Bolsheviks. In this respect, given that France was the most modern country in continental Europe, it was no doubt bound to experience a very long 'time of troubles' several generations after England had done so. It all began, in effect, under Louis XVI; and it would end with the violent death of the king in 1792 and even well beyond that date. The chronology of the key set of episodes which took place in 1789 was a matter of particular circumstances. One can imagine them happening several decades later in a less brutal fashion but it would be risky to speculate further than this.

At all events, there is one definite point which can be made, which is that the revolutionary events which took place had been predicted and prophesied by some clear-sighted individuals. No doubt, the word 'revolution' was only used in a general sense of 'political and social upheaval'.[109] In whatever words they expressed such sentiments, their clear-sightedness remains impressive. In 1757, for example, Friedrich Melchior Grimm underlined the contrast between the illusions of Enlightenment and 'the disordered imagination of the multitude'. 'I am very far from imagining', he wrote, 'that we have reached the century of Reason and I do not believe that it would take much for Europe to be threatened by some sinister revolution.'[110] Six years later, in July 1763, the *sieur* Labatte, the priest of St-Eustache in St-Marguerite's parish of the *faubourg* Saint-Antoine in Paris, criticised the suppression of the Jesuits from his pulpit. 'Sooner or later', he declared, 'Revolution will threaten a realm where the sceptre and the censer are in endless conflict with one another. The crisis is violent and Revolution cannot be far off.'[111] The following spring, it was Voltaire's turn to play the prophet; but his sentiments were the opposite to those of Labatte. He reflected anticlericalism, hostility towards the Jesuits, and a (relative) optimism was the order of the day: 'All that I see around me', wrote the philosopher, 'are the seeds of a revolution which will inevitably occur and which I will not have the pleasure of witnessing. The French are late for everything; but they get there in the end. The taper has been widely passed from hand to hand and, at the first opportunity, there will be such a blaze. Young people are so lucky; they will see wonderful things.'[112]

---

[109]   Alain Rey, *'Révolution', Histoire d'un mot* (Paris, Gallimard, 1989), p. 106.
[110]   Baron Friedrich Melchior Grimm, *Correspondance littéraire* (Paris, Furme, 1829–31), ii, 81 (letter of 15 January, 1757).
[111]   E.F.J. Barbier, *Journal* [otherwise called *chronique* by contemporaries] . . . *du règne de Louis XV* (Paris, Charpentier, 1857), iii, 90 (July 1763).
[112]   T. Bestermann (ed.), *Correspondance de Voltaire*, xxvii (1973), 315 (Voltaire to Bernard-Louis Chauvelin, 2 April 1764).

In 1762, Jean-Jacques Rousseau, for his part, would propose the concept of a state of crisis and a century of revolutions in the coming decades: 'I believe it is impossible that the great monarchies of Europe can last much longer. They have had their moments of brilliance, and now they are in decline.' In Rousseau's text, the word revolution had progressively lost its old cyclical meaning (revolutionary movements of planets around the sun, or revolutionary decline of a society, which would then be followed by its renaissance) to express more cogently the idea of an irremediable divide. 'All that Man has made', wrote the author of *Emile*, 'Man can destroy. It is only Nature which can impart indelible characters to things; and Nature does not make princes, rich men, or great seigneurs.'[113] In a preceding passage in the same volume, Rousseau had already remarked how: 'Up to now, I have drawn no distinctions as to the estate, rank or fortune of an individual, and I will scarcely make any such distinctions in what follows. For man is the same whatever his rank. A grandee is not greater than a commoner. Mankind's natural needs are everywhere the same, the means for him to satisfy them ought also, everywhere, to be equal . . . You put your trust in the current ordering of society without imagining that this ordering is subject to inevitable revolutions and that it is impossible for you to predict or to foresee what your offspring will see. The Great will become small, the rich will become poor, the monarch will become the subject. . . . *We are approaching the state of crisis and the century of revolutions.*'

Premonitions of a similar kind can be found in many other authors, even though the German authors of a recent collection of such texts have done little credit to the customarily high standards of German scholarship by presenting us with a hotchpotch of false references and inexact quotations.[114] It remains the case, and this is the essential point, that the potential for a vast revolution was evidently fermenting in the period between 1750 and the first generation of the nineteenth century. The chronology of events supports, at this point, the literary evidence. In the first weeks of 1789, there was no doubt on the matter, and the anonymous author of an *Examination of the Memorandum of Princes* (*Examen du Mémoire des princes*), published at the beginning of that crucial year, found himself saying: 'Yes, certainly, an important revolution is in preparation but we should not let ourselves attribute it to giddiness in people's brains. We would be doing the princes a grave disservice not to recognise that they had the greater hand in it.'[115] If we were to follow the author of this *Examen*, we should be congratulating Louis XVI, who is presented as an entirely just king, for the coming of the Revolution. And, in reality, the

---

[113] J.-J. Rousseau, *Emile* (Paris, Gallimard, 1969), iv, 468–9 (Book 4). *Emile* was published in 1762 but the text was obviously written rather earlier.

[114] H.J. Lüsebrink and R. Reichardt, 'Révolution à la fin du XVIIIe siècle. Pour une relecture du concept clé au siècle des Lumières', *Mots*, 41 (1988), 35–68.

[115] *Examen du Mémoire des princes, présenté au Roi* (BN, anonymes, Lb 39–874 [microfiche available]).

behaviour of Louis XVI,[116] his openness to justifiable progress, would play its part in destabilizing the Ancien Régime, by his desire to reform it. Through the desire for reform, he would precipitate the Ancien Régime's eventual demise in a period when absolutism, already enfeebled, had begun to sense its own mortality. John Bosher has properly reminded us of the last Bourbon's own responsibilities for its fate. The king had plenty of good intentions and wanted to be a beneficent ruler. He loved, as one would have said in those days, sensibility, liberty, reason, humanity. Louis was a statesman who was thoughtful, well-informed, conscientious and faithful to his wife. He was very concerned to choose a team of reforming ministers to serve in his government: Turgot, Necker, Brienne, Lamoignon, Malesherbes and Calonne. Their bold initiatives helped to precipitate the final collapse of the Ancien Régime by undermining an already fragile structure. A despot, enlightened or otherwise, a strong hand and a steady head, might perhaps have delayed (although perhaps not avoided altogether) might have tamed or domesticated the Revolution. Louis XVI, on the other hand, became one of its handmaids; a not entirely involuntary midwife to Revolution. He was responsible not for its profound causes but, at least in part, for its chronology, particularly in its initial phase.

The preparations which had thus been laid down for the revolutionary process ought not to be judged merely in terms of the distinctive features which it displayed or of the remarkable effects which it would have on politics, culture, ideology and society (the end of the hierarchy of orders, egalitarianism, etc.). The process would also carry forward in the longer term the decline in France's fortunes which had already been engendered four decades earlier in the Seven Years War, followed by the Treaty of Paris in 1763. It was at this moment, the *annus mirabilis* for the English, that the realm of France divested itself of the status of being a world superpower which it had acquired under Richelieu, Mazarin, and, above all, Louis XIV. It had managed to maintain this status without too much difficulty in the beguiling earlier part of Louis XV's reign, from 1720 to 1755. After 1763, the kingdom, once the loss of its American and Indian colonies had sunk in, let itself sink to the slightly lower rank (but still prestigious) of being one great power amongst many. It was still a European, and, indeed, an extra-European, power. The revolutionary quarter of a century, despite the Napoleonic fireworks, would endow the French hexagon with a more modest rank amongst the European powers, and one which it would retain throughout the nineteenth and twentieth centuries. After 1815, France remained an energetic maritime and continental state

---

[116] For François Furet (*Revolutionary France*, pp. 27–31), Louis XVI was a sacrificial victim of his own defects, of his congenital incapacity to rule. For John Bosher, on the other hand (in *The French Revolution*, p. 67 *et seq.*), it was those same qualities of Louis XVI, but viewed in a more positive light (especially his remarkable determination upon reform), which determined his failure. The diagnosis differs, depending upon the historian; but, in both instances, the prognosis is similarly pessimistic.

with prodigious artistic and intellectual accomplishments, paradoxically lay and Catholic at one and the same time. The achievements of the French economy would also remain remarkable or, at least in certain sectors, certainly capable of sustaining a substantial degree of economic growth. But, in terms of world history, the French hexagon would progressively contract to the status of a medium power. There would, nevertheless, be some brutal moments (1870, 1940) when this 'power' would become, at least briefly, the object, rather than the subject, of world history.

Appendix 1: Chronological Table

27 September 1601	Birth of Louis XIII.
17 April 1607	Richelieu consecrated bishop of Luçon.
14 May 1610	Henry IV assassinated by Ravaillac.
15 May 1610	Marie de Médicis declared Regent of France by *arrêt* of the Parlement of Paris.
July 1610	Concini, the Regent's favourite, becomes councillor of state; his wealth and power are thus confirmed and strengthened.
17 October 1610	Coronation of King Louis XIII at Reims.
January 1611	Having fallen from favour, Sully resigns from his post of superintendent of finances. He stands for the old group around Henry IV which is now in decline.
January 1612	The declaration of the Spanish marriages: Louis XIII is betrothed to Anne of Austria, daughter of Philip III of Spain, and Elisabeth, Louis XIII's sister, is to be married to the future King Philip IV of Spain, son of Philip III.
November 1613	Concini, the Regent's favourite, promoted *maréchal de France*.
Winter–Spring 1614	Discontent, but not open rebellion, amongst the Condéen princes.
October 1614	Opening of the Estates General, the last session in the Ancien Régime before May 1789.
May 1615	Conflict between Marie de Médicis and the Parlement of Paris over the *remonstrances* presented by the latter to the policies of the Regent. The various movements of opposition, Condéen and *parlementaire*, coalesce.
September 1615	Conjunction of the interested parties of the opposition reinforced.
28 November 1615	Marriage of Louis XIII and Anne of Austria.
May 1616	The Peace of Loudun apparently reconciles Condé

	and his supporters to the régime, at least for the moment.
November 1616	Richelieu becomes secretary of state for foreign affairs and war.
24 April 1617	Concini is assassinated at the instigation of Louis XIII who personally takes charge of the affairs of state. Richelieu is disgraced.
May 1617	Marie de Médicis is exiled to Blois. Richelieu follows her there. Power lies in the hands of Luynes, Louis XIII's favourite.
December 1617	Assembly of notables at Rouen. This is the penultimate occasion for the summoning by the French king of a body with some pretence to being representative and on a national basis before 1789. French absolutism is close at hand.
23 May 1618	The 'Defenestration of Prague', the prelude to the Thirty Years War.
February 1619	Marie de Médicis escapes from the château in Blois (where she had been held under surveillance) and goes toward Angoulême. The first (benign) 'war' between mother (Marie) and son (Louis).
April 1619	Peace of Angoulême. Marie is forgiven by Louis and given charge of the government of Anjou.
July–August 1620	Second war between mother (Marie) and son (Louis) which culminates in her defeat at Pont-de-Cé (7 August) and, almost immediately thereafter, her reconciliation with the king.
October 1620	Entry of Louis XIII into Pau, followed shortly after by the integration of Béarn into France and the restoration of Catholicism to this province, hitherto under the almost total control of the Protestants.
April–November 1621	Military campaigns by Louis XIII against the French Huguenots of west and south-west France.
November 1621	Louis XIII disappointed in the siege of Montauban which, after several months, he is constrained to abandon.
15 November 1621	Death of Luynes.
April–October 1622	New military campaigns by Louis XIII against the Huguenots in the western and south-western provinces and lower Languedoc.
18 October 1622	The peace of Montpellier concluded with the Huguenots confirms royal 'hegemony' but leaves the Protestants a specified number of security strongholds (*places de sûreté*).
February 1623	A defensive/offensive alliance signed between France, Savoy and Venice over the Valtelline pass.
April 1624	Richelieu enters the *Conseil d'en haut*.

June 1624	France agrees (by the treaty known as the Treaty of Compiègne) to provide subsidies to the United Provinces in their war against Spain.
August 1624	The *surintendant des finances* La Vieuville is arrested and Richelieu becomes head of the *Conseil d'en haut*.
November 1624–February 1625	Occupation, or 'liberation' of the Valtelline by French troops to the detriment of the Papacy and Spain.
January 1625	Beginning of a new Protestant uprising in Poitou (under Soubise) and in Languedoc (under Rohan).
May 1625	The marriage (by proxy) of Henrietta-Maria, Louis XIII's sister, to Charles I, King of England.
5 February 1526	The compromise accord with the Huguenots at La Rochelle.
February 1626	Royal edict against duelling.
August 1626	Execution of Chalais for conspiracy against the king and the cardinal.
December 1626	The meeting of the assembly of notables, the last of its kind in the Ancien Régime before 1787.
March 1627	Treaty of friendship between Spain and France directed against England.
June 1627	Execution of Montmorency-Bouteville and Des Chapelles for duelling.
August 1627	Initial implacements of the royal army taking up positions ready to besiege La Rochelle.
October 1628	The capitulation of La Rochelle.
January 1629	The (enforced) registration by he Parlement of a reforming legal code conceived by the *garde des sceaux* Michel de Marillac and generally known as the Code Michau.
June 1629	The edict of peace or the 'grace of Alais' puts an end to the violent confrontations in the French Midi between the Protestants and the French state, and grants the former their liberty of conscience but orders the destruction of their fortress strongholds.
November 1629	Richelieu becomes the 'first minister of state.'
January 1630	The first meeting between Mazarin (a modest envoy from the Holy See and as yet unknown) and the Cardinal de Richelieu.
March 1630	French troops seize Pignerol, the key stronghold of the important region of Piedmont.
May–July 1630	French expeditions leave Dauphiné for operations in Savoy and Piedmont.
July 1630	Louis XIII gravely ill.
October 1630	French negotiators sign the Treaty of Ratisbon, favourable to the Holy Roman Empire. A disgruntled Richelieu disavows their signature.

10–11 November 1630	The Day (or Days) of Dupes, when Richelieu is apparently disgraced and dismissed by the king, only to find himself the victor over the queen mother, Marie de Médicis.
12 November 1630	The arrest of the *garde des sceaux* Michel de Marillac and the defeat of the *dévot* party, the supporters of peace with Spain and opposed to the increase of taxes which they equated with the waging of an eventual war against Madrid.
23 January 1631	By the Treaty of Bärwalde, Gustavus Adolphus (financed by Richelieu) agrees to maintain a substantial army in Germany and not to sign a separate peace with the emperor.
January–May 1631	Split between Gaston d'Orléans, known as Monsieur, and his brother Louis XIII. Gaston will henceforth embody, not always to best advantage, the opposition to the régime.
January 1632	Marriage (one which does not suit the 'binomial' perspectives of Louis XIII and Richelieu) between Gaston d'Orléans and the sister of the duke of Lorraine.
January/June 1632	Treaties of Vic and then of Laverdun which split Lorraine off from various territories to the advantage of France.
May 1632	End of the trial and highly criticized execution of the *maréchal* Louis de Marillac, a supporter of Marie de Médicis, herself an enemy of Richelieu.
July 1632	Revolt of Henri de Montmorency, governor of Languedoc.
September 1632	Montmorency defeated at Castelnaudary.
30 October 1632	Montmorency executed at Toulouse by decree of the Parlement in session there.
16 November 1632	The death of Gustavus Adolphus at the battle of Lützen.
April 1633	The beginnings of an alliance between Sweden, Wallenstein, France and numerous German princes against the Emperor.
September 1633	Louis XIII annexes Nancy 'to secure his rearguard'.
25 February 1634	Wallenstein assassinated.
March 1634	Renewed rapprochement between France and the United Provinces.
5–6 September 1634	Defeat of the Swedes at Nördlingen.
October 1634	Gaston d'Orléans, whose hostile activities against Richelieu had failed, returns to France where Louis XIII greets him warmly.

February–April 1635	Defensive and offensive alliance between France and the United Provinces which threatens the destabilization of the Spanish Low Countries.
28 April 1635	A Franco-Swedish entente signed at Compiègne.
May 1635	'Open war' officially declared upon Spain by France.
11 July 1635	The treaty of Rivoli brings together the dukes of Savoy, Parma, Modena and Mantua with France and against Spain.
October 1635	A treaty of alliance and subsidy is concluded by France with the strategist and military enterpriser Bernard of Saxe-Weimar.
June 1636	The beginnings of the *Croquant* revolt which scars the provinces of the west and south-west.
August 1636	The Spanish take Corbie, thus unleashing a patriotic response by way of reaction in Paris.
October 1636	New manoeuvres by Gaston d'Orléans against Richelieu.
November 1636	The French retake Corbie and eject the Spanish garrison there.
December 1636	Declaration of war by the Emperor against Louis XIII because of the intervention of French troops in Franche-Comté.
February 1637	Death of Emperor Ferdinand II; his son Ferdinand III succeeds him.
August 1637	The affair of the secret correspondence between Anne of Austria and the Spanish authorities; the queen's confession.
December 1637	*Père* Caussin, the king's confessor, an opponent of Richelieu's protestantophile diplomacy, forced to leave the court.
3 March 1638	Victory of Bernard of Saxe-Weimar at Rheinfelden.
5 September 1638	Birth of the future Louis XIV.
4 October 1638	Death of the young duke of Savoy, François-Hyacinthe, and the beginnings of a delicate regency in the duchy.
18 December 1638	Death of *père* Joseph.
19 December 1638	Bernard of Saxe-Weimar seizes Breisach.
14 April 1639	The Swedish general Baner defeats the forces of Saxony at Chemnitz.
7 June 1639	French defeat at Thionville.
29 June 1639	Seizure of Hesdin by the troops of Louis XIII.
December 1639	Military repression led by Gassion of the *Nu Pieds* revolt in Normandy.
March 1640	Royal declaration creating the *louis d'or*.
August 1640	The capture of Arras by the French, thus opening up the 'Northern Road'.

18 September 1640	Turin capitulates before the French army led by the count d'Harcourt.
21 September 1640	Birth of Philippe, the younger son of Louis XIII and Anne of Austria.
December 1640	Accession of Frederick-William as elector of Brandenburg (the 'Great Elector') after the death of his father George-William. Death of Bullion, the *surintendant des finances* in France who had amassed a substantial fortune from the profits of office.
January 1641	The Cortès of Catalonia depose Philip IV and place, themselves under the authority of Louis XIII, proclaimed by them 'count of Barcelona'.
February 1641	Edict limiting the 'opposition' powers of the parlements.
March 1641	French accord with the duke of Lorraine who loosens his tics with the declining Spain but retains his remnants of dislike for Richelieu.
20 May 1641	Death of Baner, the formidable Swedish general, pupil of Gustavus Adolphus and reinforcer of the French armies in Germany.
December 1641	Mazarin is made cardinal; death of Sully.
17 January 1642	Guébriant, one of the most capable generals in Richelieu's service, secures the military victory at Kempen.
March 1642	Secret treaty between Gaston d'Orléans, alongside other plotters, and the Spanish government.
26 March 1642	Defeat of the French forces under the count de Guiche, Richelieu's nephew by marriage at Honnécourt by the Spanish army in the Low Countries.
12–13 June 1642	Discovery of the conspiracy of Cinq-Mars (and Gaston). Monsieur le Grand (Cinq-Mars, the *grand écuyer*) and his friend François de Thou are arrested.
3 July 1642	Death of Marie de Médicis at Cologne.
9 September 1642	Capture of Perpignan; Roussillon 'turned' towards France.
12 September 1642	Execution of Cinq-Mars and de Thou at Lyon, both found guilty of plotting with Spain.
4 December 1642	Death of Richelieu.
5 December 1642	Mazarin joins the king's Council. Military warfare continues. Various individuals disgraced under Richelieu reappear in politics.
14 May 1643	Death of Louis XIII and the succession of his eldest son, Louis XIV.
18 May 1643	The Parlement of Paris, 'steered' by the Regent, readily overturn the terms of Louis XIII's will.

19 May 1643	Victory at Rocroi for the French forces under the duke d'Enghien (soon to be the 'Great Condé').
October 1643	Potier, Bishop of Beauvais, a highly placed member of the government, is disgraced along with other members of the *cabale des importants*.
March 1644	Edict of the *toisé* tax which hits the owners of houses illegally constructed on the outskirts of Paris.
August 1644	The duke d'Enghien ('Condé') becomes the weary victor of the battle at Freiburg-im-Breisgau.
3 August 1645	Turenne and Condé defeat the forces of Mercy at Nördlingen in Bavaria.
September 1645	A *lit de justice* held in which the Parlement is required, despite their opposition to the measures, to register various edicts increasing taxes.
March 1646	Mazarin becomes superintendent of the king's education.
July 1647	Particelli d'Emery, the *contrôleur général des finances*, becomes the *surintendant des finances*.
15 January 1648	A *lit de justice* designed to crush the opposition amongst the magistrates to tax increases leads the opposition elements in the Parlement to voice their discontents.
30 January 1648	The 'secession' of the Netherlands from their alliance with France and the concluding of a separate peace with Spain.
13 May 1648	The *Arrêt d'Union*, in accordance with which the Parlement of Paris makes common cause with the other sovereign courts against absolutism; the beginnings of the Fronde *parlementaire*.
17 May 1648	Turenne and the Swedish commander Wrangel defeat the Imperial forces at Zusmarshausen.
16 June 1648	The Parlement of Paris confirms the *Arrêt d'Union*.
First week in July 1648	The conjoined sovereign courts draw up the '27 articles' of protest.
20 August 1648	Victory of Condé over the Spanish at Lens.
26–8 August 1648	The arrest of the veteran magistrate Broussel, a popular figure in Paris. The 'Day of Barricades'.
28 August 1648	The release of Broussel.
13 September 1648	The Regent, alarmed, leaves Paris for Rueil, accompanied by the royal family.
22 October 1648	The Regent gives in to the demands of the *parlementaires* and returns to Paris at the end of the month.
24 October 1648	The Treaties of Westphalia bring the Thirty Years War to a close in its Franco-Imperial phase.
5–6 January 1649	Anne of Austria and the young Louis XIV once more withdraw from Paris.

30 January 1649	Execution of King Charles I in England.
February 1649	Skirmishes around Paris between royal troops and Parisian 'soldiers'.
April 1649	'Peace' between Paris and the royal court.
July 1649	The printer Morlot hanged after a sham trial.
18 August 1649	Triumphal Entry (or re-Entry) into Paris of the young boy-king Louis XIV.
18 January 1650	Arrest in Paris at the Palais-Royal of the Condé princes (Condé, Conti and Longueville). The beginnings of the princely and provincial Fronde.
June 1650	The beginnings of the Ormée in Bordeaux.
October 1650	Peace of Bordeaux.
December 1650	The hispano-condéen forces of Turenne, temporarily in revolt, are defeated by the ultra-loyal *maréchal* du Plessis-Praslin.
January–February 1651	The rapprochement and even uniting of the political forces of the old Parisian Fronde (under Gondi) and the princely Fronde (led by the Condés).
6 February 1651	Mazarin flees from Paris into exile.
9–10 February 1651	The Paris mob invades the Palais-Royal and thereby humiliates the Regent and the young Louis XIV.
6 March 1651	Turenne is reconciled with the crown and pardoned by Louis XIV.
7 September 1651	Proclamation in a *lit de justice* of the majority of Louis XIV. The end of the Regency of Anne of Austria.
January 1652	Return of Mazarin from exile to join the royal family at Poitiers.
19 February 1652	Pope Innocent X grants a cardinal's hat to Paul de Gondi (who becomes henceforth the Cardinal de Retz).
2 July 1652	Following the skirmishes at the Porte Saint-Antoine, Condé enters, or retires to, Paris with his rebel forces.
4 July 1652	Condéen or crypto-Condéen riots in Paris culminate in the burning of the *Hôtel de Ville*.
21 October 1652	Entry of Louis XIV to Paris where calm is restored.
19 December 1652	Retz arrested at the Louvre and imprisoned in Vincennes.
February 1653	Mazarin returns to Paris; Fouquet becomes *surintendant des finances*.
3 August 1653	Entry of the royal army into the hitherto rebel Bordeaux. The end of the Girondin Fronde.
21 March 1654	Death of Jean-François de Gondi, archbishop of Paris, whose ecclesiastical post will (theoretically) revert to his nephew, the former Frondeur, now the Cardinal de Retz.

7 June 1654	Coronation of Louis XIV at Reims.
8 August 1654	The Cardinal de Retz escapes from prison and takes up refuge in Italy.
13 April 1655	*Lit de justice* during which Louis XIV is supposed to have said (but, in reality, never did): 'L'Etat c'est moi'.
14 April 1655	The Sorbonne condemns the activities of the journeymen's fraternities.
November 1655	Oliver Cromwell allows himself to be lured by the prospect of an alliance with Catholic France against Spain.
24 March 1656	The 'Holy Thorn' miracle at Port-Royal.
April 1656	Foundation of the *Hôpital général* in Paris.
July 1656	Condé forces Turenne to raise the siege at Valenciennes.
25 September 1656	Cardinal de Retz threatens to put the diocese of Paris under an interdict to put pressure on Mazarin.
27 September 1656	The capture of La Capelle by Turenne's forces.
March 1657	Military alliance against Spain between Mazarin and Cromwell.
7 August 1657	The capture of Montmédy in the presence of Louis XIV.
October 1657	Turenne takes Mardyck and delivers the stronghold to the English.
14 June 1658	The Battle of the Dunes. Turenne is victorious over the forces of Condé and Don John of Austria.
25 June 1658	The capture of Dunkirk by French troops.
July–September 1658	French military success at Bergues, Furnes, Dixmude, Gravelines, Oudenarde, Menin and Ypres.
14 February 1659	Risings at Aix-en-Provence against the *premier président* of the parlement there.
2 March 1659	Aix occupied by the military forces of the duke de Mercoeur, governor of Provence.
13 August 1659	First Franco-Spanish peace talks on the Ile des Faisans; further negotiations will continue until 12 November.
7 November 1659	The Peace of the Pyrenees concluded between France and Spain which puts an end to the so-called Thirty Years War.
10 November 1659	The last synod of the reformed churches of France.
18 January 1660	The arrival of the royal court at Aix-en-Provence.
20 January 1660	The troops of Louis XV occupy Marseille.
2 February 1660	Death of Gaston d'Orléans.
March 1660	Marseille becomes practically under the tutelage of central government.

9 June 1660	The 'Franco-Spanish' marriage of Louis XIV and Maria-Theresa. The Toulousains celebrate the occasion by burning a huge effigy representing 'heresy'.
26 August 1660	The formal entry of the royal couple into Paris.
September 1660	Louis XIV orders the public executioner to burn copies of Pascal's *Lettres Provinciales*.
February 1661	The assembly of the French clergy agrees to the idea of an anti-Jansenist Formulary to be signed by all clerics.
8 March 1661	Colbert becomes *intendant des finances*.
9 March 1661	Death of Mazarin and beginnings of Louis XIV's personal rule.
1 April 1661	Marriage of Henrietta of England with Monsieur, the king's brother.
17 August 1661	A magnificent feast hosted by Fouquet at Vaux-le-Vicomte provides the stimulus to some mordant reflections *in petto* of Louis XIV.
3 September 1661	Arrest of Fouquet.
15 September 1661	Suppression of the *superintendance des finances* and creation of the *Conseil royal des finances*.
1 November 1661	Birth of the Dauphin Louis, who will be generally known as Monseigneur.
14 February 1662	Retz resigns from the archbishopric of Paris.
24 February 1662	Louvois is given powers to act as secretary of state in place of his father during the latter's absence through illness.
April 1662	Treaty of Paris establishing a temporary alliance between France and the Netherlands. Louis XIV thus hopes to have a free hand in dealing with the Spanish Netherlands.
October 1662	England cedes Dunkirk and Mardyck to France in return for cash.
July 1663	Decision to annex the Comtat Venaissin and Avignon announced by the parlement at Aix.
September 1663	Treaty of Nomeny by which Charles IV, Duke of Lorraine, cedes the region around Marsal to Louis XIV.
January 1664	Colbert becomes *surintendant des bâtiments*.
May–August 1664	The establishment by Colbert of various royal factories and companies of the Indies (which will have somewhat mixed fortunes).
September 1664	Protectionist trade tariffs announced. Although at reasonably modest rates they provide the 'touch-stone' for French commercial rivalry with the Netherlands.
December 1664	Fouquet is condemned to perpetual banishment, a

	punishment which Louis XIV commutes to life-imprisonment.
17 September 1665	Death of Philip IV of Spain.
25 September 1665	The court of justice known as the *Grands Jours d'Auvergne* arrives at Clermont.
October 1665	New royal manufacturies created (for mirrors and fine drapery).
20 January 1666	Death of Anne of Austria.
26 January 1666	France declares war on England to assist its ally the Netherlands.
March 1666	The beginnings of a '*recherche de noblesse*' which puts the nobility 'down on paper' and makes it more dependent on the state.
December 1666	The installation, thanks to Colbert's efforts, of the Academy of Sciences.
March 1667	Creation of the post of *lieutenant de police* in Paris for its first incumbent, Nicolas de la Reynie.
April 1667	Increase in the protectionist trade tariffs aimed against the Dutch.
May 1667	The beginning of the War of Devolution. Turenne invades the Spanish Netherlands.
June 1667	The capture of Tournai.
August 1667	The capture of Lille after a siege undertaken by Vauban.
November 1667	Edict which gives final shape to the royal manufactury of crown furnishings established in the Gobelins' factory.
January 1668	Secret treaty between France and the imperial court at Vienna for the partition of the Spanish succession if the Spanish king, Charles II (the Habsburg on the throne in Madrid) has no children.
January/February 1668	Preparations for conquest, followed by the annexation, of Franche-Comté by Condé who has returned to royal favour.
May 1668	Peace of Aix-la-Chapelle under which France surrenders the territory in Franche-Comté but retains Lille, Douai and Armentières.
September 1668	The Bull of Pope Clement IX which establishes for over 30 years the 'peace of the Church' with the Jansenists, Louis XIV being henceforth engrossed by the anti-Protestant struggle.
June 1669	Creation of the *Compagnie du Nord* which, however, fails to energize Franco-Baltic trade to any substantive degree.
August 1669	The *Ordinances des Eaux et Forêts* which regulate forest rights, clearance and lead to the mapping of French forests.

February 1670	A Catholic entente between Louis XIV and the Elector of Bavaria against the danger of a Protestant 'triple alliance' (England, the Netherlands, Sweden).
31 March 1670	Birth of the duke du Maine, illegitimate son of Louis XIV by Madame de Montespan, destined to become a celebrity thanks to the writings of Saint-Simon.
September 1670	Bossuet becomes the tutor to the Dauphin. Intelligent absolutism becomes the pedagogic theme for his pupil who is not particularly gifted.
May 1671	Death of Sébastien Bourdon, who had 'come up' to Paris from the French Midi (like Rigaud). He is the last of the great French painters of Protestant origin in the seventeenth century.
September 1671	The 'Jansenist-tending' Pomponne becomes secretary of state for foreign affairs.
November 1671	Monsieur, the king's brother, marries the Palatine Princess who will be the gently acute chronicler of Louis XIV's great reign.
January 1672	The death of Chancellor Séguier marks what might be seen as the final decay of the 'justice state' in comparison with the 'finance state'.
April 1672	Louis XIV 'announces' (rather than 'declares') war on the Dutch.
June 1672	The French army crosses the Rhine near Schenk.
July–August 1672	William III, the charismatic Orangist leader, avowedly hostile to Louis XIV, seizes power in the Netherlands.
September 1672	Turenne penetrates the middle Rhine despite the Imperial and Brandenburg military forces ranged against him.
10 February 1673	The *régale* is extended to the dioceses of the French Midi in an act of national integration, comparable in this respect with that of the Revocation a little later.
17 February 1673	Death of Molière marks the end of the period when Louis XIV, through his hostility to the *dévot* party, retains a degree of sympathy for some elements of 'critical' drama and thought.
August 1673	The continental, Protestant and Catholic 'Grand Alliance' formed against Louis XIV.
November 1673	The Imperial army recaptures Bonn from the French.
January 1674	Denmark and various German princes join the 'Grand Alliance'.
April 1674	Stamp duty ('papier timbré'), with a fleur de lys stamp, becomes requisite for registering various official acts – in reality, a fiscal measure to help finance the war.

11 August 1674	A bloody 'victory' gained by Condé at Seneffe.
August–September 1674	Deaths of Philippe de Champaigne and Arnauld d'Andilly which mark the end of the distinctive Jansenism of the first and second generations whilst laying the groundwork for the succeeding period.
December 1674	The 'Grand Alliance' fails in its efforts to halt at Mulhousen the Alsatian campaign of Turenne.
Night of 15/16 January 1674	Birth of Louis de Rouvroy, later duke de Saint-Simon.
June 1675	An extraordinarily cold early summer.
27 July 1675	Turenne killed by a stray bullet at Sasbach.
11 September 1675	Sudden collapse of the Lorraine army following the death of the elderly Duke Charles IV at the moment when he hoped to return to his duchy.
18 September 1675	Disarmament of the parish of Maël-Carhaix in Brittany after the revolt of the 'Red Bonnets' ('*Bonnets rouges*') against taxation, and against some of the seigneurs; 48 muskets and 3 pistols are seized.
January–April 1676	Naval victories in the central Mediterranean as a result of the organization and strategy of the French fleet under Duquesne.
17 July 1676	Execution of Brinvilliers, the mistress of poison: 'I would like to be burned alive to make my sacrifice the more meritorious.'
September 1676	The Cardinal Odescalchi, descendant of a family of rich men of business, is elected pope under the name of Innocent XI.
March 1677	Capture of Valenciennes by the French.
11 April 1677	Victory of Monsieur, Louis XIV's brother, at Cassel against the troops of William of Orange, a victory which will be his (military) swan-song.
29 October 1677	The elderly Le Tellier becomes chancellor – the equivalent of a marshal's baton for his services.
November 1677	Marriage of William of Orange to Mary, daughter of the duke of York, himself the future King James II. William thus takes out his first stake, at least implicitly, in the English throne.
Mid-November 1677	The capture of Freiburg-im-Breisgau by Créqui.
March 1678	The success of French troops at Ghent and Ypres.
June 1678	The beginnings of the rumoured 'Popish Plot' leading to a witch-hunt of Papists in England, the counterpoint to anti-Huguenot repression in France.
August–September 1678	Treaties of peace at Nijmegen between France, the Netherlands and Spain.

February 1679	Peace of Nijmegen between France and the Holy Roman Empire.
May 1679	New developments in the English writ of Habeas Corpus, the guarantee of individual liberties and the shape of things to come for continental Europe.
June 1679	The French treaty of Saint-Germain-en-Laye with Brandenburg, which will henceforth be humiliated by Louis XIV.
July 1679	New legislative challenge aims to destroy the *chambres mi-parties* which judge law-suits between Protestants and Catholics.
November 1679	The Colbert clan, led by the plain-speaking Croissy, seizes the secretaryship for foreign affairs from the hands of the Pomponne family and its Jansenist tendencies.
January 1680	Bossuet, the symbol of Gallican absolutism, becomes the Dauphin's chief almoner (*premier aumônier*).
March 1680	Monseigneur, the next in line to the throne, marries a Bavarian princess by virtue of the enduring, although somewhat fluctuating, alliances between the two Catholic states.
August 1680	Death of the cleric Jean Eudes, one of the French paragons of the seventeenth-century counter-reformation or 'century of saints'.
November 1680	Death of the sculptor and architect Bernini. He had incarnated the Italian baroque, a style which failed to penetrate the building projects at the Louvre and Versailles.
January 1681	Secret treaty by which Louis XIV seeks to maintain Brandenburg within the French alliance.
March 1681	Louvois informs Marillac, the intendant in Poitou and one of the inventors of the *dragonnades* designed to 'convert' the Huguenots, of the imminent arrival of a regiment of horse in his province.
28 June 1681	Death of Mlle de Fontanges, the last significant mistress of the king. Not long after this date, Louis XIV marries la Maintenon and thus joins the ranks of the monogamous Bourbons (Louis XIII, Louis XVI) in contrast with the entrenched polygamists (Henry IV, Louis XV).
September 1681	The 'Reunion' (in fact a forced annexation) of the city of Strasbourg to France.
February 1682	The Emperor joins the 'anti-French' League already formulated between Sweden and the Netherlands. A new 'ecumenical' (i.e. Catholico-Protestant) coalition begins to coalesce against the French kingdom.

March 1682	The assembly of French clergy proclaims the declaration of the Four Gallican Articles and thereby defines a brand of Catholicism which is amicable to political and national sovereignty.
6 August 1682	Birth of the duke of Burgundy, the grandson of Louis XIV and the father of Louis XV. An opposition grouping, intelligent, *dévot* and inspired by Fénelon, will later crystallize around this prince.
July 1683	A Turkish army appears at the walls of Vienna. It removes the threat of imperial forces from the French frontier and Louis XIV has his hands free from endless vigilance on the landed frontier of the kingdom.
30 July 1683	Death of Queen Maria Theresa. This conceivably allowed Madame de Maintenon to exercise more influence.
6 September 1683	Death of Colbert. His policies of national economic development, particularly of manufacturing, will remain in place, however, up to the eve of the War of the League of Augsburg. Thereafter the régime is obliged to reorientate everything to meet the heavy fiscal demands of war.
October 1683	Spain, goaded by France in the Low Countries, declares war on France. Swift victories by Louis XIV's armies.
June 1684	Créqui and Vauban capture Luxemburg.
August 1684	The truce of Ratisbon marks the high-water mark of Louis XIV's system in Europe.
October 1684	Death of Corneille, birth of Watteau, mark the end of seventeenth-century macho heroism.
March 1685	Despatch of a French embassy to Siam with, amongst its envoys, the *abbé* de Choisy.
October 1685	Revocation of the edict of Nantes and of a religion which was summarily judged to be the 'enemy of Sovereignty' (La Bruyère).
End October/ early November 1685	Death of the chancellor Le Tellier. The reversion of the office of state is granted, however, to the young Barbezieux, Louvois' son. There is thus a continuity (through to the end of the century) in the ministerial dynasty of the Le Tellier.
November 1685	The edict of Potsdam. The Protestant state of Brandenburg welcomes French Huguenot refugees and thus acts in accordance with the dictates of its own logic.
March 1686	The inauguration of the *place des Victoires* in Paris. Penultimate demonstrations of Louis XIV's cult of personality at its zenith.

July–August 1686	Aggressive formal alliances of the League of Augsburg against France signed by the Emperor, Spain and some German princes from both religious confessions.
11 December 1686	Death of the Great Condé, once the saviour of France, then a rebel, and then (once returned to royal favour) the disillusioned absolutist courtier.
April 1687	Declaration of Indulgence issued by James II imposing toleration of non-Anglicans and as ill-received in England as the intolerant Revocation of the edict of Nantes had been warmly greeted in France.
October 1687	The book-seller Michallet granted the rights to publish the *Caractères* of La Bruyère. The work contains an over-flattering portrayal of Louis XIV but, overall, it gives a highly detailed and precise picture.
November 1687	A new 'Gallican' challenge from Louis XIV towards Innocent XI over the extraterritoriality of the 'privileges' which should be accorded the French embassy in Rome.
February 1688	Death of Abraham Duquesne, a great Huguenot seaman both under Richelieu and Colbert. Duquesne knew how to trim his sails at sea but found it more difficult to do so on land and the Revocation did nothing to change his fundamental religious convictions.
June 1688	Death of the francophile Elector of Cologne, leaving the problem of how to maintain French influence in the middle Rhine region. This is a destabilizing component which leads, eventually, to the war which is looming, the War of the League of Augsburg.
September 1688	French troops, already on a war footing, amass on the Rhine.
November 1688	The landing of William of Orange in England, the prelude to the Glorious Revolution. Grain prices in Paris reach their lowest point in the century before they began to climb again in the last decade as a result of the war and its demands.
January 1689	First performance of Racine's *Esther*, in which Esther (Maintenon) gets the better of the 'judeophobes' (the Protestants?).
February 1689	In London, the Bill of Rights limits arbitrary royal government.
May 1689	Under the pretext of a naval incident, William III declares war on France. The beginning of the 'second Hundred Years War'.
October 1689	Election of Pope Alexander VIII. He will try, without great success, to produce a thaw in diplomatic

	relations between the Vatican and Louis XIV after the tensions under Innocent XI.
February 1690	Death of Charles Le Brun, state-painter and artist of the régime and its presentation.
1 July 1690	Important military success at Fleurus by Luxembourg but a prudent Louis XIV refuses to exploit the strategic opportunity created by the victory.
10–11 July 1690	Naval success of Tourville at Beachy Head (Béveziers); but the Irish and James II are defeated at the Battle of the Boyne. Louis XIV retains his preeminence on the continent but can no longer sustain the pretence of extending it *in situ* to the British Isles.
17 October 1690	Death of the mystic Marguerite-Marie Alacoque who had been the inspiration behind the Sacré-Coeur devotions which created strong opposition among the Jansenists.
8 April 1691	Capture of Mons (now in Belgium) by Luxembourg in the presence of Louis XIV. This was a military reverse for William of Orange who was a good strategist but an inept tactician.
May 1691	Election of Fontenelle to the French Academy. The eighteenth century makes its début in academic circles a decade early.
12 July 1691	Election of the new pope Innocent XII. Devout and charitable, he will heal the rift between the Vatican, Louis XIV and the French church . . . at the risk of 'degallicanizing' the latter.
16 July 1691	Death of Louvois. His ministerial empire will be split up and the way opened up gradually to negotiations with the 'League of Augsburg'.
18 February 1692	Louis XIV offers the hand of his 'bastard' Mlle de Blois to his brother's son, Philippe d'Orléans, the future Regent. In a marriage for which the future is not rosy, the hierarchy of rank in the royal family is thus challenged in a revolutionary fashion.
2 June 1692	Naval defeat of Tourville at La Hougue.
1 July 1692	Capture of Namur after a siege in the presence of Louis XIV.
October 1692	The intendant of the Auvergne predicts widespread famine for 1693 and 1694.
November 1692	Death of Tallement des Réaux who, understandably bitter about the Protestant persecution, became the merciless critic of the 'papist' high society of his generation in France.

April 1693	Institution of the military order of Saint-Louis (the red ribbon), forerunner of the Legion of Honour.
May 1693	Death of Madame de la Fayette, the instigator of the modern French novel and a great diarist.
June 1693	At 55 years of age, Louis XIV takes his well-earned retirement from accompanying his armies on campaign.
July–August 1693	Beginning of the period of widespread famine, as registered at the grain market of Paris.
11 October 1693	Capture of Charleroi by French troops, who consolidate their grip on the Sambre to the south-west of Namur.
June 1694	Jean Bart recovers a convoy of ships from the Dutch navy at the Texel, the convoy being loaded with Polish grain destined for starving France.
July 1694	The English fleet bombs Le Havre and Dieppe causing great destruction of the Norman half-timbered houses in those towns.
August 1694	The establishment of the Bank of England to assist in the raising of war-finance. In France, the notaries often act as surrogate banks.
November– December 1694	Death of Puget; birth of Voltaire – the death of the Baroque and the beginnings of the Enlightenment.
4 January 1695	Death of Luxembourg, a general who had never been defeated. Villeroy, who succeeds him, will be barely competent and this will become a factor making for peace!
21 January 1695	Royal declaration creating the new *capitation* tax is registered in the Parlement of Paris.
June–September 1695	Military successes of William of Orange, who compensates for his tactical incapacity with the abundant resources generated for the war by the Bank of England.
August 1695	Fénelon takes possession of the archbishopric of Cambrai, a 'country diocese' which the quietist 'Swan' of Cambrai regards as something akin to disgrace since he had wanted to be made archbishop of Paris.
17 May 1696	Death of Antoine d'Aquin, the former first physician of Louis XIV and the grandson of a rabbi from Avignon.
28 July 1696	Death of Colbert de Croissy, the aloof secretary of state for foreign affairs. His disappearance from the scene increases the possibilities of moves towards peace.

August 1696	Publication of the Treaty of Turin by which Savoy deserts the Grand Alliance and rejoins the French. Catholic states begin to distance themselves from the anti-Louis XIV coalition.
November 1696	Louis XIV and Madame de Maintenon lavish attentions on the very young Marie-Adélaïde de Savoie following her arrival at Versailles. She is destined to marry the duke of Burgundy, the Sun-King's eldest grandson.
April 1697	The accession to the Swedish throne of Charles XII, who will become in due course, through his ill-considered and lavish escapades, the instrument by which the new strength of Russia will be manifest.
May 1697	The expulsion of the Parisian company of Italian actors, accused of satirical mockery of Maintenon and the clergy.
August 1697	The military talents of Vendôme are reinforced by his capture of Barcelona.
September– October 1697	Peace of Ryswick.
May 1698	Tsar Peter I (Peter the Great) leaves Paris for Vienna during his European tour.
August– September 1698	The military camp at Compiègne where the army parades before the court to demonstrate the fact (and it is not entirely a fabrication) that France has not been exhausted by the preceding war.
October 1698	Louis XIV is in negotiating mood. A treaty is concluded at The Hague for the partition of the Spanish Succession.
12 May 1699	Pope Innocent XIII condemns the *Maxims of the Saints* (*Maximes des saints*) of the Quietist Fénelon.
September 1699	Death of the chancellor Boucherat. Pontchartrain, who had been the *contrôleur général des finances*, will succeed him. In the resulting game of musical chairs, Chamillart becomes the *contrôleur général*, where he is more competent than later historians will make him out to be.
October– November 1700	The will of Charles II of Spain in favour of the duke of Anjou, Louis XIV's grandson. Anjou becomes Philip V, King of Spain.
26 October 1700	Death of Rancé, the *abbé* de la Trappe. He offered the élites of his generation the option available to them of renouncing the affairs and cares of this world.
20 November 1700	Victory of Charles XII over the Russians at Narva; but will David always be able to defeat Goliath?

January 1701	Chamillart, the *contrôleur général des finances*, is also made secretary of state for war. He thus becomes Colbert and Louvois, all rolled into one – at least in theory. . . .
5–6 February 1701	First half-steps towards war as a result of the new Franco-Spanish alliance. The Dutch garrisons in the Spanish Netherlands are expelled by Louis XIV's troops.
June 1701	Death of Philippe d'Orléans, the king's brother. That branch of the family thus loses its titular head but the Orléans line of Bourbons will live on in the person of the cadet Philippe, the future Regent, and his successors.
September 1701	The Grand Alliance (the Empire and the maritime powers) becomes realized in the Treaty of The Hague against the Catholic bloc (France and Spain, but not Austria).
May 1702	Death of William III; yet England and the Netherlands continue to remain the enemies of the French kingdom. The 'second Hundred Years War' continues.
May–July 1702	(Reciprocal) declarations of war; France sets itself up in opposition to the bloc composed of England, the Emperor and the Netherlands.
October 1702	Villars, one of the best French military strategists of the early eighteenth century, demonstrates his prowess in his first victory at Friedlingen.
December 1702	The duke of Burgundy joins all the Councils of the government as a full participating member.
January 1703	Small and debilitating civil war waged by the Camisards in the Cévennes; 'Huguenots against papists'.
May 1703	Treaty of Methuen by which Portugal is allied to England. As a result, the latter will benefit in due course several years later from the first shipments of Brazilian gold.
16 May 1703	Death of Charles Perrault and the end of the 'Perrault age' when the two brothers, Claude and Charles, had occupied dominant positions in architecture, art, fashion and fable.
September 1703	Birth of Boucher whose artistic work, by turns sensuous and *dévot*, will exercise a powerful effect on eighteenth-century France.
12 April 1704	Death of Bossuet and, with it, the withering of a particular absolutist ideology.
August 1704	The two strategic giants of the Grand Alliance, Marlborough and Prince Eugene, destroy a Franco-

	Bavarian army at Blenheim. Gibraltar is captured by the English fleet under the command of Admiral Byng and the prince of Hesse.
January 1705	Villars leaves the Huguenot Cévennes. They had been 'pacified' before his arrival by violent means; he used gentler methods.
July 1705	The Papal Bull *Vineam Domini* opens up once more the royal (and papal) campaign against Jansenism.
August 1705	Following a battle at Cassano on the Adda, Vendôme does what he can to harry the troops of Prince Eugene, thus strengthening the impression of a 'stalemate' or strategic blockage which affects all the military operations during 1705.
May 1706	Louis XIV's attempts at an overall offensive end catastrophically in the defeat of Villeroy by Marlborough at Ramillies.
June 1706	The (temporary) seizure of Madrid by forces hostile to Philip V. He retains, however, both for himself and for his Bourbon successors, the loyalties of Catholic Spain.
October 1706	Death of Ninon de Lenclos, courtesan and woman of the world.
March 1707	Death of Vauban, shortly after the publication of the *Royal Tithe* (*Dîme royale*). The opposition grandees begin to make their presence felt (Vauban, Chevreuse, Beauvillier) towards the end of the reign and well before Louis XV's reign.
May 1707	The Union of England and Scotland creates the 'United Kingdom of Great Britain'.
August 1707	The allies retreat from Toulon which they had temporarily beseiged.
February 1708	Desmarets, a member of the Colbert clan and an important financier, becomes *contrôleur général des finances*.
May 1708	Death of the architect Jules Hardouin-Mansart; the church at the Invalides was one of his masterpieces, completed a few years before his death. Its hierarchically decorated façade recalled the traditions of the society of orders.
July 1708	Vendôme defeated at Oudenarde (present-day Belgium).
August–December 1708	The army of Prince Eugene besieges and captures Lille.
January–February 1709	A terrible winter freezes the land and prevents the sowing of grain and is the presage of a famine which lasts two years.

September 1709	The bloody and indecisive battle at Malplaquet, where Villars confronts both Eugene and Marlborough. But the allied offensive against France is halted in its tracks.
October 1709	The beginnings of the dispersal and (in due course) destruction of the monastery at Port-Royal-des-Champs.
15 February 1710	The duchess of Burgundy gives birth to a duke Anjou, the future Louis XV.
October 1710	The Parlement of Paris registers the new tax known as the *dixième*.
December 1710	The victory of Vendôme at Villaviciosa plays its part in rectifying the strategic balance in favour of France – although the kingdom is half-exhausted by the struggle.
March 1711	Death of Boileau – the 'last dying breath' of the 'classical' seventeenth century.
14 April 1711	Death of 'Monseigneur' the Dauphin. His son, the duke of Burgundy, provides a focus for the reforming group which gathers around him.
September 1711	The small last victory of Marlborough at Bouchain.
December 1711	In London, the new Tory government, less hostile to France, recalls Marlborough and brings his military career to a close.
January 1712	The opening session of the Congress of Utrecht leading to peace.
18 February 1712	Death of the duke of Burgundy. The hopes for reform rest henceforth on the shoulders of Philippe, Duke d'Orléans, the future Regent.
28 June 1712	Birth of Jean-Jacques Rousseau, the philosophic and even prophetic precursor of the French Revolution.
July 1712	By his victory at Denain, Villars and his army decisively extricate Louis XIV from the military stalemate.
April 1713	Treaties of Utrecht which bring the War of Spanish Succession to a close. They establish for close on 25 years a degree of European balance of power.
September 1713	The anti-Jansenist Bull *Unigenitus*. It divides the French church into two opposing factions with incalculable consequences.
November 1713	The two 'heroes' of the war, Prince Eugene and Villars, meet to discuss peace between France and the emperor.
February 1714	A grand masked ball at Sceaux where the duchess du Maine criticizes the excesses of aristocratic social life.

July 1714	Edict declaring the legitimized princes (the 'bastards') capable of succeeding to the French crown. Louis XIV thus reverses the previously accepted degrees of princely rank.
September 1714	French forces under Berwick seize Barcelona. Philip V thus becomes the master of Spain.
January 1715	Death of Fénelon whose Quietist thought, with its humanist, pacifist and constitutional (even socialist) elements will continue to intrigue many in the eighteenth century.
1 September 1715	Death of Louis XIV.
2 September 1715	Louis XIV's will set aside; the Regency is granted by the Parlament of Paris to the duke of Orléans.
3–15 September 1715	Creation of the polysynodical councils.
December 1715	James Stuart ('James III'), King James II's son and Pretender to the English throne, sets sail from Dunkirk for Scotland. The expected Franco-English rapprochement is thus delayed.
January 1716	Despite his relatively modest social origins, Dubois is nominated *conseiller d'Etat*.
March 1716	The Council of the Regency unanimously approves the establishment of a Chamber of Justice (*Chambre de justice*) to bring financiers suspected of peculation to justice.
May 1716	Letters patent establishing the Bank of Law.
October 1716	Defensive treaty of alliance between England and France which interrupts for a few decades their rivalry.
January 1717	Triple alliance (defensive) between France, England and the Netherlands. The realm of the young Louis XV opens itself up to influence from the Protestant, liberal and 'capitalist' nations.
March 1717	Dubois appointed to the Council of Regency.
May 1717	The already inflationary circulation of banknotes by the John Law bank.
August 1717	Suppression of the *dixième* tax. Creation of the *Compagnie française d'Occident* (for colonies); the post-war period begins to bear fruit.
October 1717	By a royal declaration, the Regent attempts to bring about a (difficult) compromise with the Jansenizing faction in the church.
January 1718	A small shift 'to the right' with the replacement of the chancellor d'Aguesseau by Marc René d'Argenson, who will himself die in 1721. The latter is held to be favourable to the Jesuits.

May 1718	Inflation in the money of account and devaluation during a period of economic recovery and growth. The new *louis d'or* will be worth 36 *livres tournois* instead of the previous 18 *livres*.
August 1718	Dubois becomes secretary of state for foreign affairs.
September 1718	Law obtains the contract for the tobacco farm. Polysynodical councils are mostly abandoned.
December 1718	The Madrid government becomes a double target, both through the (French) repression of the conspiracy of Cellamare and through the declaration of war against Spain by England.
January 1719	France enters a minor set of hostilities against Spain.
May–August 1719	Law takes progressively greater control of the French companies of foreign and colonial trade as well as of the currency and the general tax-farms. His eyes are perhaps bigger than his stomach. . . .
October 1719	Letters patent creating a Chamber of Justice to judge the Breton 'conspirators'.
December 1719	Fall and exile of Cardinal Alderoni, one-time head of the Madrid government and then disgraced by Philip V. This is the price for Spanish defeat by the armies of France and England in their recent minor hostilities against the Spanish.
February–May 1720	Philip V adheres to the Quadruple Alliance of which the strongest component is the accord between the English and the French. He renounces his claim to the French throne.
May 1720	A ship from the Levant brings the last major incidence of plague in modern times to Western Europe.
May 1721	Election of Pope Innocent XIII. He attempts to match the spirit of the times by being a pontiff for peace, working to lessen the conflicts between the major Catholic powers.
July 1721	Dubois is made cardinal. The incessant efforts which he has deployed towards international détente are thus rewarded, albeit accompanied by some very Parisian mockery directed at his efforts.
August 1721	The Peace of Nystadt, achieved with the modest mediation of Louis XV's agents. Sweden is weakened and Russia confirmed in its neo-status as a great European power. From a French perspective, this choice has its consequences. Should it choose to import skins from Russia or furs from Canada?
November 1721	The 'bandit' Cartouche, who had been recently arrested, is tortured. The welcome progressive liberalization of the Regency period has its negative

	elements, including an increasing degree of insecurity on the highways.
February 1722	The 'crocodiles' of the old Louis XIV court – d'Antin, Noailles and Villars – retire from the Council of the Regency.
August 1722	Dubois is nominated 'first minister'.
October 1722	Coronation of Louis XV.
February 1723	Death of Cardinal Dubois.
November 1723	Louis XV begins an intensive phase of personal training in equestrian sports which are seen as indispensable to the serious business of hunting.
December 1723	Death of Philippe d'Orléans. Louis-Henry, Duke of Bourbon (Condé) becomes first minister. He is far from impressive.
February 1724	The economic circumstances of peace alongside a period of relative growth allow a degree of (somewhat ill-judged) revaluation of the currency.
May 1724	An abrupt royal declaration against the Huguenots. It has more bark than bite and thus differs from the Revocation of 1685.
October 1724	The duke of Bourbon (first minister) and some of his close advisers decide to send home the Spanish Infanta who was supposed to marry Louis XV. The French government thus maintains its pro-British orientation. The Infanta was also too young to give France the essential Dauphin quickly.
July–August 1725	A wet summer, disastrous for the grain harvest. Grain riots. In Paris, there is a procession of the relics from Sainte Geneviève to implore the end of the rainy spell.
September 1725	Louis XV marries Marie Leszczynska, a remarkable girl and daughter of a Polish king who is currently technically out of office. She was put through a tremendous ordeal during which almost a hundred princesses were considered as possible candidates for the king's hand.
December 1725	Like Louis XIII with Concini, or Louis XIV with Fouquet, Louis XV is a 'night-killer' – albeit a pacific one. Following a secret decision on his part he disgraces the duke of Bourbon who will soon be replaced by Fleury.
June 1726	Louis XV consigns the duke of Bourbon to a gilded 'exile' at Chantilly. Fleury becomes *de facto* first minister. The money of account (the *livre tournois*) is stabilized and will remain practically at the same value through to 1914, leaving aside the turmoil of the

	assignats during the French Revolution.
August–September 1726	The auction of the indirect farms concludes with the *Ferme générale*. These tax-farm contracts will gradually become linked to the prosperity of the economy, albeit not without some profits for an efficient operator.
May 1727	The burial of the Jansenist deacon Pâris in the cemetery at Saint-Médard in Paris. Miracles begin to occur around his grave.
June 1727	Death of King George I of England; succession of his son George II.
July 1727	Eventual suppression of the recent tax of the *cinquantième* which had proved difficult to collect and useless in the context of international peace.
September 1727	Condemnation (for Jansenist tendencies) of Soanen (the bishop of the tiny diocese of Senez) by decision of a provincial council of the church.
October 1728	Cardinal de Noailles decides to accept the bull *Unigenitus* and disavows his own Jansenist past – a small pantomime before his death. . . .
March 1729	Heavy-handed treatment of Soanen and the Jansenists by the bishop of Orléans. Fleury, worried by the possibility of future conflicts, attempts to defuse the issue.
May 1729	Death of the Cardinal de Noailles. The former 'Jansenist bishop' had no great following but the *convulsionnaires* from a much less exalted social circle will take up where he had left off.
November 1729	Spain, rebuffed by the Emperor, rejoins France and England and signs the Treaty of Seville with them, a treaty in which Madrid gives some concessions to the other two powers.
February 1730	Death of Pope Benedict XIII. His successor, Clement XII, is almost in his eighties. A few years later he will promulgate the first papal condemnation of the freemasons.
March 1730	Following a financial scandal, Le Peletier des Forts, the *contrôleur général des finances*, resigns. His successor, Philibert Orry, a great technocrat, will remain in post for over 15 years. The contrast will be very evident with the financial and ministerial instability of the last 35 years of the Ancien Régime, already evidently in decline.
November 1730	Conflicts between the pro-Jansenist advocates of the Parlement and the royal Council. Fleury, as usual, displays a degree of moderation.
March 1731	The Treaty of Vienna confirms the prospects for (European) peace amongst the great powers in accordance with Cardinal Fleury's wishes.

August 1731	A paralysed girl, Mlle Hardouin, is healed of her illness at the tomb of the deacon Pâris – and she is not the only one.
November 1731	The Parisian *parlementaires* exploit their hostility towards *Unigenitus* and, squeezing into 14 carriages, take themselves off to Marly to bare their consciences to Louis XV. The king tells them that he has nothing to say to them.
January 1732	Closure of the cemetery at Saint-Médard whose miraculous ambience has begun to cause the government some concern.
April 1732	Mgr de Vintamille, Archbishop of Paris, threatens to excommunicate the readers of the *Nouvelles ecclésiastiques* (*Ecclesiastical News*), a Jansenist and clandestine periodical.
August 1732	Pierre Jean François de la Porte, an *avocat du roi* at the Châtelet (the law-court for the Paris region) and son of a *fermier général* is nominated *conseiller* at the Parlement of Paris aged 22. This is the beginning of a career which will take him to becoming a master of requests. From 1740 to 1761, La Porte will be intendant in Moulins and then in Dauphiné. Thus is formed the conciliar group from the *robe* nobility.
December 1732	The calming down (for some time) of the Jansenist, Gallican and *parlementaire* crisis, just as the 1668 'peace of the Church' had done. The magistrates offer their submission and, in return, the government retracts the disciplinary measures which it had promulgated in August against the Parlement.
February 1733	Death of the extrovert Augustus II the Strong, Elector of Saxony and King of Poland.
September 1733	Stanislas Leszczynski, the father-in-law of Louis XV, is elected king of Poland . . . and soon has to flee his new throne and take up refuge in Danzig.
October 1733	France declares war on Austria which is in opposition to Stanislas.
November 1733	To finance this (small) war of Polish succession, the *dixième* is resurrected.
June 1734	Death of the octogenarian Berwick, killed by a bullet from a canon at the siege of Philippsburg. This death leaves far fewer traces than the similar disappearance of Turenne. Berwick, the illegitimate son of the king of England, will thus not figure in the pantheon of French national imagery.
July 1734	Death of the octogenarian Villars, after a victorious campaign in Lombardy. He was the last of the great military chiefs of the Louis XIV period.
September 1734	Militant Jansenism is in a state of hibernation. But 'convulsionary' Jansenism is far from dead. One

	woman, the widow Thévenet, drinks water containing fragments of dust from the deacon Pâris. Her contacts amongst other poorly women lead them to turn towards convulsion in October.
April 1735	Stanislas Leszczynski accepts the idea of abandoning the Polish pipedream in favour of more substantial real, albeit more prosaic power in Lorraine.
October 1735	The 'preliminary talks in Vienna' foreshadow the end to the War of Polish Succession. Concessions are made from both sides which (amongst the main) leave Lorraine to Stanislas Leszczynski and then to France . . . and Tuscany to François de Lorraine.
April 1736	Jean-Louis de Bernard de Vaux, son of a *prévôt des marchands* of Paris, the grandson of a councillor in the *Grand Conseil* becomes *conseiller* in the Parlement of Toulouse. He will become in turn a master of requests, a *président* in the *Grand Conseil* and, for 20 years, an intendant.
May 1736	Stanislas Leszczynski leaves retirement at Koenigsberg to set up court at the château of Meudon.
September 1736	Convention of Meudon. Stanislas will enjoy all the trappings of rule in Lorraine whilst France will have its hands on all the levers of power and will facilitate its transition from a ducal régime to a French province.
February 1737	Disgrace of Chauvelin, secretary of state for foreign affairs. Fleury used Chauvelin's talents to prepare peace with Austria and then abandoned him because of his excessively anti-Austrian stance.
November 1738	Exchange of protocols ratifying the Treaty of Vienna. Besides the settlement of the Lorraine question, as a result of which the final piece of the French 'hexagon' is set in place in the north-east, the foothold of the Bourbons in southern Italy (where Don Carlos became king of the 'Two Sicilies') should be noted.
March 1739	Louis XV, unfaithful spouse and conscientious Christian, ceases to exercise the Royal Touch for scofula. Monarchical symbolism is permanently affected in consequence.
September 1739	Treaty of Belgrade. Thanks to the involvement of a French emissary, Turkish interests are safeguarded against the Austrians. The 'alliance of opposites' thus becomes something of a rejuvenation for the Turks.
October 1739	The British push the Madrid government into declaring war on them by attempting to extend their share of the market in Spanish America. There are inevitable resulting tensions between the Hanoverians and the Bourbons, both in Versailles and in Madrid.
Winter 1740 *et seq.*	Cold weather; a bad year for cereal production. The

problems with grain supply are, on the other hand, less serious than they had been in 1693 or 1709.

February 1740   Death of Pope Clement XII. A long conclave, lasting two semesters, will elect as his successor Benedict XIV, a great pontifical innovator.

May 1740   Death of Frederick William I of Prussia. Accession of Frederick II (Frederick the Great).

December 1740   Frederick II invades Silesia.

March 1741   The *maréchal* de Belle-Isle attends the imperial Diet at Frankfurt where he exceeds the pacific instructions issued to him by Cardinal Fleury to the point of adopting an aggressively austrophobe posture.

June 1741   French alliance with Frederick II under the responsibility of Belle-Isle who has barely consulted Versailles on the matter.

August 1741   Renewed imposition of the *dixième* tax to finance the war.

November 1741   A French army under Belle-Isle seizes Prague. The French are now strongly involved in the war known as the War of Austrian Succession.

February 1742   The British prime minister, Robert Walpole, the old friend and partner of Cardinal Fleury, falls from power.

June 1742   By the treaty of Breslau, Frederick II gains Silesia at Austrian expense. He then withdraws from the coalition which had united him (particularly) to France. Furious reactions in France.

August 1742   Cardinal de Tencin and the count d'Argenson, both from the *dévot* clan and adversaries of Fleury, enter the *Conseil d'en haut*.

October 1742   Duke Adrian de Noailles, former protégé of Madame de Maintenon, gradually insinuates himself into the position of leading adviser to Louis XV. Return in force of a 'crocodile' of old courtiers from the Louis XIV-Maintenon days.

December 1742   Brilliant retreat, but a retreat nonetheless, by Belle-Isle. Harried by the Austrian army, he succeeds in retiring from Prague and making his way towards the Rhine.

January 1743   Death of Fleury in his nineties. The bellicose influences of the Tencin-Noailles-Argenson trio will have the upper hand through to 1756–7.

March 1743   Noailles becomes minister of state. This marks (provisionally) the end of the long parenthetic period of greater openness which had lasted through the periods of Duboi, Orléans and Fleury.

June 1743   Noailles is defeated by George II and by the Anglo-

	Hanoverians at Dettingen. This is the last moment when a British monarch accompanies his armies to battle.
October 1743	Isolated by the rest of continental Europe and Britain, as had occurred before during the years 1703–13, France and Spain conclude a new 'family pact' which once more evokes the friendly relations which had existed between Louis XIV and Philip V.
December 1743	New fiscal edicts to sustain the war are registered with difficulty by the Parlement of Paris. The period when the Parlement will passively resist war or post-war taxation will occur a few years later.
March 1744	Louis XV officially declares war on Great Britain. The 'second Hundred Years War' recommences.
May 1744	Louis XV leaves Versailles to take command of the army of Flanders. In the course of his journey he stops to pray before the miraculous Virgin of Cambrai.
August 1744	French troops cross the Rhine.
August– September 1744	Scandal at Metz. Louis XV falls gravely, although only briefly, ill there. The chief almoner of the court and the bishop of Metz widely publicize the inevitable royal 'death bed' parting with the duchess of Châteauroux, the king's mistress. In the long-term, the symbolic damage inflicted upon the monarchy by irresponsible clerics is very serious.
November 1744	Triumphal (as it turns out) return of His Majesty of Paris. Despite the Metz affair (which was more of a time-bomb) Louis remains very popular, strengthened by the 'image' cultivated in his youth and by the martial successes of his armies.
February 1745	Marriage of the Dauphin with the Infanta Maria Theresa of Spain confirms the Latin and Catholic nature of an alliance directed against Great Britain and secondarily, against the Empire.
March 1745	Liaison between Louis XV and Madame de Pompadour becomes effective.
May 1745	Victory of *maréchal* Saxe (and Louis XV) at Fontenoy. Saxe is the last truly great French military leader (of the Ancien Régime).
December 1745	Machault d'Arnouville, an intendant whom Louis XV knew and valued during the movement of his armies in the north of France, becomes *contrôleur général des finances*. He will be responsible for financing the war and for the post-war fiscal reforms.
February 1746	Brussels captured by *maréchal* Saxe.
March 1746	Successive French reverses in Northern Italy in the face of Austrian-Sardinian offensives.

April 1746	The Young Pretender Charles Edward Stuart, having landed in Scotland the preceding year, is completely defeated at Culloden. This is the final defeat for the hopes of the Stuart dynasty in England.
October 1746	In the Low Countries, the victory of *maréchal* Saxe over the Austrians at Raucoux.
January 1747	Disgrace of the marquis d'Argenson, secretary of state for foreign affairs. He is particularly accused of hispanophobia. But the overall 'trend' of the régime, fairly hard-line from around 1743, is increasingly laid down by the count d'Argenson, the brother of the marquis d'Argenson.
April 1747	Preliminary negotiations for peace between the belligerents which have been going on for some time at Breda are disbanded on the initiative of the French government which hopes to exploit its strategic advantage in the Low Countries.
July 1747	French attempt to invade Piedmont repulsed.
March 1748	Beginning of the peace negotiations of Aix-la-Chapelle.
May 1748	Louis XV writes to Ferdinand VI of Spain to tell him than he wants a peace without annexations, in short a 'Fénelonian' peace. Such magnanimity will be ill-received in France and *a fortiori* in Great Britain.
October–November 1748	Peace of Aix-la-Chapelle concluded. It maintains the status quo. The peace marks the (fragile) apogee of French power, just as the Peace of Ratisbon had done in 1684, but within the pattern of a system of balance of powers in Europe. For French popular opinion, however, these hardly spectacular results are 'incomprehensible'.
April 1749	Maurepas, an oustanding minister for the navy, is sacked for some satirical remarks which he had made against la Pompadour.
May 1749	Edict typical of the brusque style of Machault. It establishes the *vingtième* tax on all revenues without distinction of birth or title. The cause of equality was advanced by monarchical will (through the tax-system).
June 1749	Machault invites some bishops to let the relevant authorities have a declaration of all the wealth, revenues and properties of the clergy on a diocesan basis.
October 1749	The summoning of an extraordinary meeting of the Estates of Brittany. It grows out of provincial opposition to the new *vingtième* tax, opposition which is paralleled by similar disquiet amongst the clerical

	and *parlementaire* milieux towards Machault and, eventually, Louis XV himself.
February 1750	The assembly of the Estates of Languedoc which attempts to reject the *vingtième* and which is dissolved by the king's commissioners.
May 1750	After some initial reticence, the Parlement of Paris registers the *vingtième*.
September 1750	The assembly of the clergy, having issued some protests against the *vingtième*, is similarly dissolved on royal orders by M. de Saint-Florentin (a Phélypeaux), secretary of state. In general, the *vingtième* edict sustains the opposition of part of the kingdom's élites.
January 1751	Edict creating the Military Academy (*Ecole militaire*).
February 1751	The representatives of the clergy by no means comply with providing declarations of their wealth for the collection of the *vingtième*.
March 1751	Royal declaration sought to reform the *Hôpital général* of Paris, considered as a hotbed of Jansenism.
December 1751	Royal circular offers a compromise to the clergy over the *vingtième*. A government climb-down.
February 1752	A Council decree (*arrêt*) ordering the suppression of the *Encyclopédie*.
March 1752	Bouettin, the *curé* of Saint-Etienne-du-Mont, refuses the sacraments to a Jansenist Oratorian on the point of death.
October 1752	Louis XV grants Madame de Pompadour the honour of a duchess's stool (*tabouret*) for use in formal royal occasions.
November 1752	A new scandal in Paris after the refusal of the sacraments to various Jansenist nuns.
May 1753	The (benign) exile of the *parlementaires* by royal decree from Paris.
May–June 1753	Secret negotiations between the king and the *parlementaires*, who have taken up residence at Pontoise.
September 1753	The chancellor reminds an agitated Parlement of Normandy of the essential (absolute) principles of the monarchy.
May 1754	Demographic and other pressures from the English colonies in North America lead to pressure on the fragile line of contact via Ohio and the Mississippi which links French Canada to Louisiana. An officer named Jumonville is killed during an 'incident' with an armed platoon led by the young George Washington which leads to reprisals from the soldiers of Louis XV.
July 1754	The British government authorizes the governor of Massachusetts to attack some of the French forts.

	Moreau de Sechelles succeeds Machault as *contrôleur général des finances*. This is the beginning of the 'controller generals' quadrille', a period of chronic ministerial instability, a specific sign of the problems of the Ancien Régime which will become more evident.
October 1754	The British cabinet decides to despatch regiments of troops to North America.
February 1755	Death of Montesquieu who, more than any other, predicts or 'signals' (after his own fashion) the growing significance of the élites within the French political system.
March 1755	The Parlement (which seems to be giving itself the powers of a national council) declares by decree (*arrêt*) that the bull *Unigenitus* no longer has the status of an article of faith.
April 1755	A decree of the Council reverses this *parlementaire* decision.
May 1755	Opening of the assembly of the clergy in which a hard-line minority makes its views known in favour of a rigid interpretation of the bull *Unigenitus*.
December 1755	The British government has seized hundreds of French vessels and seamen. Louis XV therefore issues an ultimatum requiring them all to be restored, failing which there will exist a state of war between the two countries.
January 1756	Defensive Anglo-Prussian pact concluded at Westminster.
May 1756	Reversal of the alliance pattern in Europe. A treaty, concluded at Versailles, predicts 'friendship and secret and consistent union' between France and Austria. The initial Franco-British hostilities begin at Minorca.
October 1756	Pope Benedict XIV promulgates, with discreet collaboration from the Versailles government, the encyclical *Ex Omnibus*, hostile to Jansenism but moderate in tone.
December 1756	*Lit de justice* by which Louis XV seeks to 'discipline' the Parlement.
3 January 1757	Damiens stabs Louis XV who survives the attack but is left emotionally depressed.
February 1757	The dismissal of the count d'Argenson, a friend of the Jesuits. His departure from the government acts as a prelude to the Choiseulian period of French politics.
May–September 1757	Briefly sidelined by the Damiens assassination attempt, the provincial *parlementaires* once more adopt a hostile attitude towards royal fiscality, thus demonstrating their solidarity with their Parisian colleagues.
November 1757	Rout of the Franco-Austrian forces at Rossbach by Frederick II.

May 1758	Death of Pope Benedict XIV who will be succeeded by Clement XIII, a paragon of hard-line politics and pro-Jesuit. European governments, by contrast, will increasingly regard the Jesuits as an easy target.
September 1758	Attempted assassination of Joseph I, King of Portugal. Portuguese Jesuits are placed beyond the law being accused of complicity with those who had undertaken the assassination.
November 1758	The British take Fort Duquesne on the site of present-day Pittsburgh and thus cut off Louisiana from Canada.
December 1758	Choiseul becomes secretary of state for foreign affairs. Quasi-liberalism and the old sword nobility take up the reins of power – a twin blow for the old Louis XIV traditions of the monarchy.
April 1759	Frederick II is 'routed' by the Russians at Kunersdorf.
August 1759	Death of Ferdinand VI of Spain. Accession of Charles III, a 'good Bourbon' and one of the 'enlightened despots' of the eighteenth century who lived up to his name.
September 1759	Capitulation of Quebec to the British.
November 1759	Bertin becomes *contrôleur général des finances*.
January 1760	The Parlement of Paris sets in train various measures designed to destroy the Jesuit congregations in France.
September 1760	Under British pressure, the town of Montreal capitulates. The end of French Canada; the beginning of francophone Quebec.
October 1760	Capture and sack of Berlin by Austro-Russian troops. Death of George II; accession of George III in Great Britain.
January 1761	The British take Pondichéry and Karikal in the East Indies from the French.
March 1761	Opening stages before the Parlement of Paris of a lawsuit initially begun by businessmen from Marseille against the Jesuits.
August 1761	Family compact between the Bourbons of Versailles, Paris, and soon of Parma and Naples, following up similar previous alliances which had been concluded in the wars of Polish and Austrian Succession.
October 1761	Closure of the Jesuit colleges in the Paris region in accordance with the preceding decree of the Parlement of Paris.
November 1761	Trial of the Calas family, begun initially before the city aldermen (*Capitouls*) of Toulouse.
January 1762	Death of the Tsarina Elisabeth, the prussophobe princess, which means that Frederick II lives to 'fight another day'.

February 1762	The Parlement of Rouen issues a final decree disallowing the vows utilized by the Jesuits.
March 1762	Execution of Jean Calas in Toulouse.
May–October 1762	Decrees by various provincial Parlements against the Jesuits.
November 1762	Signature of the preliminary protocols at Fontainebleau which will lead to the Treaty of Paris.
February 1763	Treaty of Paris. France loses the greater part of its colonies in the Far East, in Africa and in America; but it retains its 'black pearl', Santo Domingo.
April 1763	Bertin decrees fiscal measures designed to liquidate the heavy financial burden which the previous war had left behind it. These measures will evoke a strong degree of hostility, especially from Brittany.
August 1763	Death of Augustus III of Poland who will be succeeded by Stanislas Poniatowski, supported by the Prussians and Russians. French influence is weakened.
December 1763	L'Averdy, the new *contrôleur général*, issues his first ordinance liberalizing the trade in grain from province to province within France.
January 1764	Wolfgang Amadeus Mozart, aged eight, plays on the organ in the chapel at Versailles. The 'open-minded' government of Choiseul readily gives in to *parlementaire* pressure and recalls the marquis Du Mesnil, lieutenant-general in Dauphiné and the bête noire of local magistrates.
April 1764	Death of Madame de Pompadour, which will, at least in the medium-term, have a negative impact on the fortunes of Choiseulian quasi-liberalism.
July 1764	Edict liberalizing the grain trade, albeit with qualifications.
November 1764	Louis XV, seeking to capitalize on *parlementaire* support, promulgates an edict which bans the Jesuits from the whole of France. The king seeks, however, to 'limit the damage' and retains *in petto* a degree of sympathy for ex-Jesuits.
March 1765	Rehabilitation of the memory of Jean Calas. Louis XV and the queen display great consideration, including financial recompense, for the family of the unfortunate citizen of Toulouse.
April 1765	The *Grand Conseil*, the frequent upholder of the monarchy amongst the magistracy goes into voluntary hibernation after the attacks directed towards it by the Parlements and a degree of lack of royal support for it.
August 1765	Death of Emperor Francis II. Joseph II succeeds him, like Charles III of Spain the model of an 'enlightened despot'.

December 1765	Death of the Dauphin.
February 1766	Accidental death of the almost ninety-year-old Stanislas Leszczynski. As predicted, Lorraine becomes (albeit without a fuss) simply one more French province.
March 1766	Louis XV orders the speech known as 'The Flagellation' to be read out before the Parlement of Paris: 'Sovereign power resides in my person alone and its essential character is the spirit of counsel, justice and reason.' An ambitious but old-fashioned definition of an absolutism which is attempting to be enlightened.
December 1766	Careful to avoid any scandal, Louis XV covers up the affair of La Chalotais, the most determined member of the Breton opposition.
May 1767	The Marquis Antoine d'Argenson (son of René d'Argenson, known cruelly as 'Argenson the Beast') is nominated ambassador at Venice – a regular stage in the career of this well-placed *robin*, an *avocat du roi*, then a *parlementaire*, who became in 1747 a master of requests and who will finish up in 1774 as the queen's chancellor.
April 1768	A periodical called the *Courrier du Bas-Rhin* reports some of the exploits of the marquis de Sade who had lured to his house at Arcueil a poor woman to subject her to ill-treatment and force her on Easter Sunday to commit blasphemous acts.
May 1768	France purchases from the Genoese republic the *de facto* right of sovereignty over Corsica.
June 1768	Louis XV creates a superior council at Bastia for judicial affairs in Corsica. Death of the queen.
July 1768	An (unconsummated) marriage between Guillaume Du Barry and the woman who will become la Du Barry and who, against the will of Choiseul, will enjoy rank at court.
August 1768	The duke d'Aiguillon, harassed by the Parlement of Brittany at Rennes, tenders his resignation as commander in chief of the province.
September 1768	Maupeou becomes the chancellor. This is the beginning of the final 'ascendancy' of the 'hard-liners' under Louis XV.
February 1769	Death of Pope Clement XIII. His successor, Clement XIV, will conform to contemporary trends and cultivate an image of (moderate) anti-Jesuitism and thus try to rebuild relations with Louis XV and other enlightened despots.

April 1769	Madame Du Barry is presented at court with scandalous reactions amongst the Choiseulists.
15 August 1769	Birth of Napoleon Bonaparte.
December 1769	The *abbé* Terray becomes *contrôleur général des finances*.
May 1770	Marriage of Marie-Antoinette of Austria and the future Louis XVI. The accord between the Habsburgs in Vienna and the Versailles Bourbons which this represents cuts across the austrophobe traditions of French political and diplomatic culture.
November 1770	Choiseul contemplates revenge against the British. He calls for war before the *Conseil d'en haut*. Calls for war are echoed elsewhere, in Spain and in England.
December 1770	Terray, who, because of the grain shortages, had suspended the freedom of trade in grain announced by his predecessor, reintroduces various elements of trade in food-stuffs between French provinces whilst not returning to a position of liberalism, pure and simple. Choiseul is dismissed by Louis XV because of his war-mongering! The way is thus open for what will be called later on the 'triumvirate' of Maupeou, Terray and Aiguillon, which will be hostile to the parlements, and to the very tenatative liberalization of the Choiseulian period.
January 1771	Exile of the Parlement of Paris.
February 1771	*Remonstrances* of the *Cour des aides*, drafted by its *premier président* Malesherbes. The sovereign courts are depicted in this document as the equivalent institutions to the Estates General, and thus invested with a degree of national representation.
April 1771	The establishment of the new Parlement of Paris on the basis (notably) of a suppression of the venality of offices.
January–February 1772	The partition of Poland between Russia, Prussia and Austria. A Catholic nation, which had been the ally of France, is thus eliminated from the map of Europe for a century and a half.
June 1772	Revenge of the anti-Jansenists, or ex-Jesuits. A royal declaration gives an amnesty to the priests who had previously been condemned for having refused the sacrament to the Jansenists.
August 1772	Urged on by Louis XV, Gustavus III, king of Sweden, carries out a pro-absolutist coup d'état which gives some comfort in Versailles after the Polish débâcle.
July 1773	Pope Clement XIV proclaims the papal bull *Dominus ac Redemptor*, in the name of which the Jesuit order is suppressed throughout the world.
December 1773	The 'Boston Tea Party' provides the signal for the

	beginning of the revolution and war of independence in North America.
April 1774	In return for various papal concessions, the Vatican recovers Avignon and the Comtat Venaissin. The French government had seized both of these territories in 1768 under the pretext of fighting against contraband trade which had become considerable in these regions.
10 May 1774	Death of Louis XV.
July–August 1774	Turgot becomes secretary of state for the navy, *contrôleur général des finances* and minister of state.
May 1778	Death of Voltaire.
July 1778	Death of Jean-Jacques Rousseau.
July 1784	Death of Diderot.

Glossary

Following are some brief, non-technical descriptions of French Ancien Régime terms used in the course of this work.

Arrêts Decrees of the sovereign courts and the royal Council.

Bailliages Subordinate judicial courts.

Cahiers (de doléance) Engrossed demands from each locality, which accompanied elected deputies to the Estates General. The latter then proceeded to draft an accumulated *cahier* for each order at the estates for presentation to the crown. A similar procedure was adopted at the provincial estates.

Capitation A new tax introduced in 1695 which consisted of a levy on heads of families graded according to 569 social ranks. It lasted through to 1697 and was then reintroduced in 1701.

Chambres des comptes Sovereign courts in Paris and various provincial centres to audit the accounts of financial officials.

Chambres de l'édit Judicial courts established by the pacification of Nantes (1598) to hear lawsuits involving Protestants and staffed by a proportion, sometimes half (*mi-partie*), of Protestant judges.

Chambres de justice Sovereign judicial courts commissioned on an occasional basis to investigate the peculation of financiers and *traitants*.

Châtelet Subordinate court for the Paris region.

Comptants Money distributed on account (*comptant*) for various purposes by the king or the *Conseil des finances* and which only had to be accounted for in summary fashion before the *Chambre des comptes*.

Conseil des dépêches One of the royal councils in which matters relating to the provinces and internal affairs were discussed.

Conseil des finances One of the royal councils in which matters relating to fiscal and financial matters were discussed.

Conseil d'en haut The inner council of the king.

Contrôleur général des finances Although the title had existed from the middle of the sixteenth century, it was only following the suppression of the *surintendance des finances* in 1661 that the *contrôleur général* became significant as the administrative head of the French financial system. Included within his responsibility was oversight of the work of the four *intendants des finances*, the *intendant du Trésor royal* and the *intendant du commerce*. The placing of these functions in the hands of one individual, who was sometimes also a minister of state in charge of the navy or of the army, gave the *contrôleur général* enormous powers in the Ancien Régime post-1661 and an almost impossible brief to sustain adequately in the second half of the eighteenth century.

Corvées Although the royal *corvée* was not unknown in the later seventeenth century, it was around 1730 that it was extended throughout the realm. It consisted of an obligation placed upon the local population to spend a certain number of days each year in the maintenance and construction of the major highways. Frequently criticized from various quarters, it nevertheless ensured the construction of a remarkable set of roads in eighteenth-century France.

Cour des aides Sovereign court with the power to oversee the tax system (although not all new taxes) and to hear appeals against decisions made by the local financial tribunals (particularly the *élections*) and to try cases of fiscal fraud. There were courts in Paris and 12 other provincial locations.

Dixième A war-time tax on income from property which was introduced firstly towards the end of 1710.

Dragonnades The *dragons* (dragoons) were companies of mounted infantry armed with muskets (later equipped with bayonets) and pikes. The *dragonnades* were one of the instruments used by the crown in the campaign against French Protestants on the eve of the Revocation of the edict of Nantes. It involved billeting such troops on the local Protestant population which was then required to pay for their lodging and sustenance and put up with their indiscipline, to which the authorities were (in this instance) prepared to turn a blind eye. The idea was attributed to the intendant in Poitou, Marillac, who certainly made considerable use of it from around 1680.

Elus (élections) Local financial officers in the *élections* who carried out annual visitations to each locality to ensure that the distribution of the tax-burden, especially the *taille*, was fair and in accordance with royal edicts. Many of their functions were taken over by the provincial intendants.

Ferme Générale, fermiers généraux Farming out the revenues of the king to syndicates of tax-collecting financiers was a regular practice under the Ancien Régime. The multiplicity of different tax-farms for each locality became, however, disliked by both the crown and the tax-farmers. There was, thus, a tendency to group the various tax-farms together into *fermes générales*. From 1669 onwards, the *fermes unies* included the *gabelles*, the *cinq grosses fermes* (which was an earlier accumulation of tax-farms for central France), the *aides* etc. From 1726 onwards, when there was a greater degree of stability in the financial systems of the Ancien Régime, the *ferme générale* became one of the most important institutions of the French monarchy. Contracts were signed up every six years by the syndicates of *fermiers généraux* for very large sums of money. The *fermiers* ran major organizations of tax collection throughout the kingdom and advanced large sums in cautions to the monarchy as part of their contracts.

Gabelles Indirect taxes; principally the salt tax, which was levied at differential rates in five areas, a sixth region being exempt from salt tax altogether.

Généralités Financial area under the jurisdiction of an office of *trésoriers de France*. There were about 20 at the beginning of the period covered by this volume.

Grand Conseil A branch of the Council of State established as a separately functioning court in 1497. Its essential task was to judge matters in which it would be impossible for the parlements to provide the necessary impartiality.

These included ecclesiastical benefices to which the king made nominations, contentious legal judgments between the parlements and matters involving the religious orders. The court increased in size markedly during the Ancien Régime. Its jurisidiction was often contested by the parlements, especially during the eighteenth century, and it was briefly suppressed in 1771 although it was re-established once more in 1774.

Grands Jours   Extraordinary sessions of the sovereign courts on commission held in a particular place within their jurisdiction to hear the complaints of inhabitants against those who might be obstructing the pursuit of justice, including local judicial officers and the nobility.

Grand Prévôt   The head of the royal court's services of police and justice.

Hôpital Général [de Paris]   The famous hospital established in Paris in 1656 whose considerable resources and responsibilities were made up from the ten previous hospitals or houses of correction of the capital. In 1662, there was an attempt to extend the principles behind the Paris General Hospital more widely in France.

Lettres de cachet   Royal letters despatched under the privy seal and containing a particular order to a named individual or specific group. Although the magistrates complained at the indisciminate use of *lettres de cachet* to protect royal favourites and other individuals against justice, in most instances they appear to have been issued not for political motives but at the instigation of families who were concerned to prevent their family name from being affected by a scandal involving one of their number.

Lettres de jussion   Royal letters addressed to a court instructing it to proceed to the registration of an edict or ordinance. If the court still refused and the king wished to have the edict legally enforced, he had to have recourse to a *lit de justice*.

Lit de justice   Formal ceremony by which the king personally enforced the registration of a controversial edict upon the parlements or other sovereign courts or otherwise formally registered his solemn will with the judges.

Livre tournois   The French money of account in the Ancien Régime, worth 20 *sous* or 240 *deniers*.

Maîtres des requêtes   Prestigious and powerful officials attached to the royal Council and employed to undertake preliminary investigations of matters coming up before the Council. Many intendants became masters of requests.

Noblesse d'épée (de race)   The older hereditary nobility, claiming privilege (traditionally) on the basis of its military valour.

Noblesse de robe   The nobility of the *robe* which served in offices which carried with them exemption from payment of the *taille*. In accordance with the rules governing the *taille*, three successive generations of office-holding within a family entitled it to exemption in perpetuity and this constituted one of the bases by which members of the *robe* entered the old nobility. Some senior offices, however, granted personal nobility from the first generation.

Paulette   Payment, initiated in 1604, when office-holders could choose to pay to ensure their rights to transfer their office to their descendants or to another purchaser.

Pays d'états   Provinces in which taxes were levied in accordance with amounts negotiated by the local elected estates, and sometimes through their tax-collectors. The main examples were the peripheral provinces of Languedoc, Brittany, Burgundy, Provence and Artois.

Ponts et Chaussées The organization having responsibility for the maintenance and construction of highways and bridges. In the seventeenth century, this responsibility tended to be shared between local authorities and the central administration with influential finance ministers like Sully and Colbert playing a more dominant role than most of their counterparts. In the eighteenth century, however, the overall responsibility for highways and bridges was assigned (under the Regency) to the marquis de Berenghen. This post disappeared in 1736 but it remained a distinctive responsibility for one of the *intendants des finances*. The *Ecole des Ponts et Chaussées* was formed in 1747 to train construction engineers for the service.

Président (premier président) Presiding magistrate in the parlements and other sovereign courts.

Prévôt des Marchands The nominal head of the municipal government of the city of Paris.

Procureur général One of the king's law officers in a sovereign court, responsible for prosecuting lawsuits involving the crown.

Recherches de faux nobles The 'search for false nobles' was instituted by the crown under the earlier Bourbons, beginning in 1598, to minimize the numbers falsely claiming tax exemption on the basis of assumed nobility, and which led in the course of the seventeenth century to a nobility which was more clearly, and legally, defined and demarcated.

Régale Royal privilege to take the income from vacant bishoprics during the interregnum between incumbents.

Rentes, rentiers A means of borrowing at interest which was accepted as lawful under the canons of the Catholic church because the interest payments were theoretically based on land or landed income. It became extended to the crown which issued *rentes* nominally through other institutions, especially the city of Paris, the clergy and other subordinate institutions whose credit-worthiness was accepted by the public at large. *Rentiers* included *parlementaires*, widows, nobles and any who had capital which they were prepared to commit in return for a (theoretically) regular return in fixed annual or quarterly payments.

Robe, robin See 'Noblesse de robe'.

Roturiers Commoners who paid the *taille*.

Surintendant des finances The administrative head of the French financial administration, with authority over the *trésoriers de France* and over the treasurers at the Exchequer (*l'Epargne*) and who issued orders of payment (*assignations*) to authorize disbursements from the various provincial receipts. At various times, during the first half of the seventeenth century, the post was in abeyance and its powers vested in the Council of Finance. The post was abolished in 1661.

Taille(s) The principal direct tax, levied in areas of *taille personnelle* on the basis of an individual's ability to pay as decided by local collectors of tax. In areas of *taille réelle*, limited to Languedoc, Provence, parts of Guyenne, Artois, Hainault and Flanders, the *taille* was raised as a land-based assessment.

Toisé New tax, introduced in 1644, equivalent to a year's worth of rent, on all property illegally constructed on the outskirts of the capital. Its introduction led to widespread opposition amongst Parisians.

Traites (traitants) Contracts reached with the crown to sell offices, undertake monopolies or raise taxes. *Traitants* were the financiers who formed associations to negotiate the contracts and run the resulting enterprises. It was also a term of abuse for financiers suspect of peculation at the public expense.

Trésoriers de France   Senior financial officials who were organized into *bureaux des finances* in each *généralité*. They were responsible for repartitioning taxes around the various *élections*. Like the *élus*, their duties were largely taken over in the later seventeenth century by the provincial intendants.

Vingtième   New tax, based on the *dixième*, which Louis XIV had introduced in 1710 as an emergency war-time measure and which theoretically aimed to collect a tenth of the landed and other revenues of the kingdom. Although it was withdrawn in 1717, the *dixième* reappeared during the War of Polish Succession (1733–6) and then again during the War of Austrian Succession (1741–9). In 1749, however, the *dixième* was replaced by the *vingtième*, a tax along similar lines although it was introduced in peace-time and aimed to collect only 5 per cent of all revenues. Thereafter, the *vingtième* remained a regular and vital part of the fiscal structure of Ancien Régime France, with two or even three *vingtièmes* being levied in certain years.

Select Bibliography

The bibliography for the French edition of this work has been substantially incorporated into the notes attached to each chapter. Therefore only the principal works cited there have been included in this select bibliography. It only includes items published since 1945 and has been amplified with a number of recent English works. These often provide good avenues of introduction to the immense bibliography in French on the subjects covered in this book but they are in no sense substitutes for the rich and varied French historiography which is available and accessible to students of the period and which the following suggestions for further reading aim to reflect.

Adams, T., *Bureaucrats and Beggars. French Social Policy in the Age of Enlightenment* (New York and Oxford, 1990).

André, L., *Louis XIV et l'Europe* (Paris, 1950).

—— *Michel Le Tellier et Louvois* (Paris, 1942; republished Geneva, 1974).

Antoine, M., *Le Conseil du roi sous le règne de Louis XV* (Geneva, 1970).

—— *Le Conseil royal des finances au XVIIe siècle et le registre E3659 des Archives Nationales* (Geneva, 1973).

—— *Le Dur Métier de roi* (Paris, 1986).

—— *Le Gouvernement et l'administration sous Louis XV. Dictionnaire biographique* (Paris, 1978).

—— *Louis XV* (Paris, 1989).

—— (et al.), *Origines et histoire des cabinets des ministres en France* (Geneva, 1975).

Apostolidès, J.-M., *Le Roi Machine; spectacle et politique au temps de Louis XIV* (Paris, 1981).

Asher, L., *The Resistance to the Maritime Classes. The Survival of Feudalism in the France of Colbert* (Berkeley, CA, 1960).

Aujol, J.-L., *Le Cardinal Dubois, ministre de la paix* (Paris, 1948).

Badinter, E., *Les 'Remontrances' de Malesherbes, 1771–1775* (Paris, 1978).

Baker, K.M., *Condorcet, from Natural Philosophy to Social Mathematics* (Chicago, 1975).

—— *The French Revolution and the Creation of Modern Political Culture* (Oxford and New York, 1987).

—— (ed.), *Inventing the French Revolution* (New York, 1990).

Bardet, J.-P., *Rouen aux XVII et XVIII siècles. Les mutations d'un espace social* (Paris, 1983).

Barry, J., *Versailles, passions et politique* (Paris, 1987).

Bayard, F., *Le Monde des financiers au XVIIe siècle* (Paris, 1988).

Beik, W., *Absolutism and Society in Seventeenth-Century France* (Cambridge, 1985).

Bely, L., *Espions et ambassadeurs au temps de Louis XIV* (Paris, 1990).

Bercé, Y.-M., *Peasant Rebellions* (Ithaca, NY, 1989).

Bérenger, J., *Turenne* (Paris, 1987).

Bergin, J., *Cardinal de La Rochefoucauld. Leadership and Reform in the French Church* (New Haven and London, 1987).

—— *Cardinal Richelieu. Power and the Pursuit of Wealth* (New Haven and London, 1985).

Bergin, J. and Brockliss, L. (eds), *Richelieu and his Age* (Oxford, 1992).

Bernier, O., *Louis XV the Beloved. The Life of Louis XV* (New York, 1984).

Bertière, S., *Retz* (Paris, 1990).

Bien, D., *The Calas Affair* (Princeton, NJ, 1960).

Black, J. (ed.), *The Origins of War in Early Modern Europe* (Edinburgh, 1987).

Blet, P., *Les Assemblées du clergé et Louis XIV (1670–1693)* (Rome, 1972).

—— *Le Clergé de France et la monarchie* (Rome, 1950).

Bluche, F., *Dictionnaire du Grand Siècle* (Paris, 1990).

—— *Louis XIV* (Oxford, 1992).

—— *Les Magistrats du Parlement de Paris au XVIIe siècle* (Paris, 1960; republished 1986).

Bluche, F. and Solnon, J.-F., *La Véritable Hiérarchie sociale de l'ancienne France* (Geneva, 1983).

Bonney, R.J., *The King's Debts. Finance and Politics in France, 1589–1661* (Oxford, 1981).

—— *The Limits of Absolutism in ancien régime France* (Aldershot, 1995).

—— *Political Change under Richelieu and Mazarin, 1624–1661* (Oxford, 1981).

—— *Society and Government in France under Richelieu and Mazarin, 1624–1661* (London, 1988).

Bordes, Maurice, *L'Administration provinciale et municipale en France au XVIIe siècle* (Paris, 1972).

Bordieu, P., *La Noblesse d'Etat; grandes écoles et esprit de corps* (Paris, 1989).

Bosher, J.F., *The French Revolution* (New York, 1988).

—— *French Finances; from Business to Bureaucracy* (Cambridge, 1970).

Bossenga, G., *The Politics of Privilege. Old Régime and Revolution in Lille* (Cambridge, 1991).

Boutant, C., *L'Europe au grand tournant des années 1680. La succession palatine* (Paris, 1985).

Braudel, F. and Labrousse, E. (dirs), *Histoire économique et sociale de la France*, vols i (2 parts) and ii (Paris, 1970).

Briggs, R. *Early Modern France, 1560–1715* (London and Oxford, 1977).

Brunel, Y., *Marie-Adélaïde de Savoie, duchesse de Bourgogne* (Paris, 1974).

Burke, U.P., *The Fabrication of Louis XIV* (New Haven and London, 1992).

Butler, R., *Choiseul, Father and Son, 1719–1754* (Oxford, 1980).

Cameron, I., *Crime and Repression in the Auvergne and the Guyenne, 1720–1790* (Cambridge, 1981).

Carmona, M., *Les diables de Loudun, sorcellerie et politique sous Richelieu* (Paris, 1988).

—— *Marie de Médicis* (Paris, 1981).

—— *Richelieu; l'ambition et le pouvoir* (Paris, 1983).

Castan, N., *Crime et répression en Languedoc au siècle des lumières* (Paris, 1980).

Chaillou, M. and Saltiel, M., *La Petite Vertu. Huit années de prose courante sous la Régence* (Paris, 1980).

Chartier, J.-L., *De Colbert à l'Encyclopédie*. Vol. i (*Daguesseau, conseiller d'Etat*) (Montpellier, 1988).

Chartier, R., *The Cultural Origins of the French Revolution* (Durham, NC, 1990).

—— *The Cultural Uses of Print in Early Modern France* (Princeton, NJ, 1987).

Chartier, R., Compère, M-M. and Julia D., *L'Education en France du XVIe au XVIIe siècle* (Paris, 1976).

Châtellier, L., *The Europe of the Devout* (Cambridge, 1989).

Chaunu, P., *La Civilisation de l'Europe classique* (Paris, 1966).

—— *La Civilisation de l'Europe des Lumières* (Paris, 1971).

Chaussinand-Nogaret, *The French Nobility in the Eighteenth Century* (Paris, 1986).

Chevallier, P., *Louis XIII* (Paris, 1979).

Church, W.F., *Louis XIV in Historical Thought from Voltaire to the Annales School* (New York, 1976).

—— *Richelieu and Reason of State* (Princeton, NJ, 1972).

Cole, C.W., *Colbert and a Century of French Mercantilism*, 2 vols (New York, 1939).

Collins, J.B., *Classes, Estates, and Order in Early-Modern Brittany* (Cambridge, 1994).

—— *The Fiscal Limits of French Absolutism* (Berkeley, CA, 1970).

—— *The State in Early Modern France* (Cambridge, 1995).

Constant, J.-M., *Les Conjurateurs. Le premier libéralisme politique sous Richelieu* (Paris, 1987).

—— 'La Noblesse et la Fronde', *L'Histoire*, 95 (1988), 26–34.

Corvisier, A., *La France de Louis XIV (1645–1715). Ordre intérieur et place en Europe* (Paris, 1979).

—— *Louvois* (Paris, 1983).

Cottret, M., 'Le Républicanisme janséniste: mythe de l'Eglise primitive et primitivisme des Lumières', *Revue d'histoire moderne et contemporaine*, 26 (1984), 99–115.

Crow, T., *Painters and Public Life in Eighteenth-Century Paris* (New Haven and London, 1985).

Dakin, D., *Turgot and the Ancien Régime in France, 1770–1774* (1939; republished New York, 1965).

Darnton, R., *The Literary Underground of the Old Regime* (Cambridge, MA and London, 1982).

Daviet, J.-P., *Une multinationale française; Saint-Gobain* (Paris, 1989).

Dessert, D., *Argent, pouvoir et société au Grand Siècle* (Paris, 1984).

—— *Fouquet* (Paris, 1987).

—— *Louis XIV prend le pouvoir. Naissance d'un mythe* (Brussels, 1989).

Dethan, G., *Gaston d'Orléans, conspirateur et prince charmant* (Paris, 1959).

—— *Mazarin, un homme de paix* (Paris, 1981).

Doyle, W., *The Origins of the French Revolution* (Oxford, 1980; revised 1988).

—— *The Oxford History of the French Revolution* (Oxford, 1989).

Duby, G. (dir.), *Histoire de la France urbaine*, vol. iii (*La ville classique . . .*) (Paris, 1981).

Duby, G. and Wallon, A. (dirs), *Histoire de la France rurale*, vol. iii (*Apogée et crise de la civilisation . . .*) (Paris, 1976).

Duchêne, R., *La Fontaine* (Paris, 1990).

—— *Mme de Sévigné ou la chance d'être femme* (Paris, 1982).

Dulong, C., *Anne d'Autriche, mère de Louis XIV* (Paris, 1981).

Dupâquier, J., *Histoire de la population française, de la Renaissance à 1789* (Paris, 1988).

Durand, Y., *Les fermiers généraux du XVIIIe siècle* (Paris, 1971).

Echevarria, D., *The Maupeou Revolution. A Study in the History of Liberalism, France, 1770–1774* (Baton Rouge, LA, 1985).

Egret, J., *Louis XV et l'opposition parlementaire* (Paris, 1970).

Elias, N., *The Court Society* (Oxford and New York, 1983).

Elliott, J.H., *Richelieu and Olivares* (Cambridge, 1984).

Emmanuelli, F.-X., *Etat et pouvoirs dans la France des XVIe–XVIIIe siècles. La métamorphose inachevée* (Paris, 1992).

—— *L'Intendance du milieu du XVIIe siècle à la fin du XVIIe* (Aix-en-Provence, 1981).

Engel, C.-E., *Le Régent* (Paris, 1969).

L'Etat baroque (dir. H. Méchoulan, including contribution by E. Le Roy Ladurie and preface by André Robinet) (Paris, 1985).

Favier, R., 'Les Entrepreneurs des travaux publics en Dauphiné au XVIIIe siècle', *Bulletin du centre d'histoire économique et sociale de la région lyonnaise*, 1–2 (1988).

Favre-Lejeune, C., *Les Secrétaires du roi de la Grande chancellerie de France. Dictionnaire biographique et généalogique (1672–1789)*, 2 vols (Paris, 1986).

Federn, C., *Mazarin, 1602–1661* (Paris, 1978).

Ferrier-Caverivière, N., *Le Grand Roi à l'Aube des Lumières, 1715–1751* (Paris, 1985).

Fogel, M., *Les cérémonies de l'information dans la France du XVIe au milieu du XVIIIe siècle* (Paris, 1989).

—— *L'Etat dans la France moderne de la fin du XVe au milieu du XVIIIe siècle* (Paris, 1992).

Ford, F., *Robe and Sword* (Cambridge, MA, 1953; New York, 1965).

Fierro-Domenech, A., *Le Pré carré, géographie historique de la France* (Paris, 1986).

France et l'Italie au temps de Mazarin (dir. Jean Serroy) (Grenoble, 1986).

François Quesnay et la physiocratie (dir. Institut national d'Etudes démographiques), 2 vols (Paris, 1958).

Frêche, G., *Prix des grains à Toulouse* (Paris, 1967).

La Fronde en questions (Actes du colloque du Centre méridional de rencontres sur le XVIIe siècle) (Aix-en-Provence, 1989).

Fumaroli, *L'Age de l'éloquence* (Geneva, 1980).

Furet, F., *Revolutionary France, 1770–1880* (Oxford, 1992).

Furet, F. and Ozouf, M., *Dictionnaire critique de la Révolution française* (Paris, 1988).

—— *Lire et écrire. L'alphabétisation des Français de Calvin à Jules Ferry*, 2 vols (Paris, 1977).

Gallet, D., *Madame de Pompadour ou le pouvoir féminin* (Paris, 1985).

Garrioch, D., *Neighbourhood and Community in Paris, 1740–1790* (Cambridge, 1986).

Garrisson, J., *L'Edit de Nantes et sa révocation. Histoire d'une intolérance* (Paris, 1985).

Golden, R.M., *The Godly Rebellion. Parisian Curés and the Religious Fronde, 1652–1662* (Chapel Hill, NC, 1981).

Goubert, P., *Mazarin* (Paris, 1990).

Goubert, P. and Roche, D., *Les Français et l'Ancien Régime*, 2 vols (Paris, 1984).

Goy, J. and Le Roy Ladurie, E., *Prestations paysannes, dîmes, rentes foncières et mouvement de la production agricole à l'époque préindustrielle*, 2 vols (Paris, 1982).

Gres-Gayer, J., 'The *Unigenitus* of Clement XI: a French look at the issues', *Theological Studies*, 49 (1988), 250–82.

Gruder, V.R., *The Royal Provincial Intendants: A Governing Elite in Eighteenth-Century France* (Ithaca, NY, 1968).

Guéry, A., 'Etat, classification sociale et compromis, sous Louis XIV. La capitation de 1695', *Annales ESC*, 41 (1986), 1041–59.

—— 'Les finances de la monarchie française sous l'Ancien Régime', *Annales ESC*, 33 (1978), 216–39.

Guth, P., *Mazarin* (Paris, 1972).

Habermas, J., *The Structural Transformation of the Public Sphere* (Cambridge, MA, 1989).

Hanley, S., *The Lit de Justice of the Kings of France. Constitutional Ideology, Legend, Ritual and Discourse* (Princeton, NJ, 1983).

Hanlon, G., *L'Univers des gens de bien* (Bordeaux, 1989).

Hatton, R., *Louis XIV and Absolutism* (London, 1976).

—— *Louis XIV and Europe* (London, 1976).

—— 'Louis XIV et l'Europe: éléments d'une révision historiographique', *XVIIe Siècle*, 31 (1979), 109–35.

Haudrère, P., *La Compagnie française des Indes au XVIIIe siècle (1719–1795)*, 4 vols (Paris, 1989).

Hazard, P., *The European Mind, 1680–1715* (Harmondsworth, 1964).

Hildesheimer, F., *Richelieu; une certaine idée de l'Etat* (Paris, 1985).

Hufton, O., *The Poor of Eighteenth-Century France* (Oxford, 1974).

Jackson, R., *Vive le Roi! A History of the French Coronation from Charles V to Charles X* (Chapel Hill, NC, 1984).

Jouanna, A., *Le Devoir de révolte. La Noblesse française et la gestation de l'Etat moderne, 1559–1661* (Paris, 1989).

Jouhaud, A., *Mazarinades; la Fronde des mots* (Paris, 1985).

Kaplan, S.L., *Bread, Politics and Political Economy in the Reign of Louis* XV, 2 vols (The Hague, 1976).

—— *Provisioning Paris; Merchants and Millers in the Grain and Flour Trade in the Eighteenth Century* (Ithaca and New York, 1984).

—— *Work in France: Representation, Meaning, Organization and Practice* (Ithaca and New York, 1986).

Keohane, N.O., *Philosophy and the State in France; the Renaissance to the Enlightenment* (Princeton, NJ, 1980).

Kettering, S., *Judicial Politics and Urban Revolt: the Parlement of Aix, 1629–1659* (Princeton, NJ, 1978).

—— *Patrons, Brokers and Clients in Seventeenth-Century France* (Oxford, 1986).

Klaits, J., *Printed Propaganda under Louis XIV* (Princeton, NJ, 1976).

Kleinmann, R, *Anne of Austria, Queen of France* (Columbus, Ohio, 1985).

Knachel P.A., *England and the Fronde. The Impact of the English Civil War and Revolution in France* (Ithaca and New York, 1967).

Knecht, R.J., *Richelieu* (London, 1991).

Konvitz, J., *Cartography in France, 1660–1848. Science, Engineering and Statecraft* (Chicago, 1987).

Kors, A.C., *D'Holbach's Coterie and Enlightenment in Paris* (Princeton, NJ, 1976).

Kossman, E., *La Fronde* (Leiden, 1954).

Labrousse, E., *La Crise de l'économie française à la fin de l'Ancien Régime et au début de la Révolution* (Paris, 1943).

—— *Essai sur la révocation de l'édit de Nantes; une foi, une loi, un roi* (Geneva and Paris, 1985).

Laurain-Portemer, M., *Etudes Mazarines* (Paris, 1981).

Lebrun, F., *Le XVIIe siècle* (Paris, 1988).

—— 'Les crises démographiques en France aux XVIIe et XVIIIe siècles', *Annales ESC*, 35 (1980), 205–34.

Leclercq, H., *Histoire de la Régence pendant la minorité de Louis XV*, 3 vols (Paris, 1921).

Le Goff, T., *Vannes and Its Region in the Eighteenth Century* (Oxford, 1981).

Le Roy Ladurie, E., 'Longue durée et comparatisme: révocation de l'édit de Nantes et glorieuse révolution d'Angleterre', *Revue de la Bibliothèque Nationale*, 29 (1988), 3–17.

—— (dir.), *Les Monarchies* (Paris, 1986).

—— *The Royal French State, 1460–1610* (Oxford, 1994).

Le Roy Ladurie, E. and Field-Récurat, J., 'Sur les fluctuations de la consommation taxée du sel dans la France du Nord aux XVIIe et XVIIIe siècles', *Revue du Nord*, 54 (1972), 385–98.

Le Roy Ladurie, E. and Ranum, O. (dirs), *Pierre Prion, scribe* (Paris, 1985).

Levron, J. *Choiseul, un sceptique au pouvoir* (Paris, 1976).

—— *Les Inconnus de Versailles* (Paris, 1974, republished 1988).

—— *Louis XV, l'homme et le roi* (Paris, 1974).

Lévy, C.-F., *Capitalistes et pouvoir au siècle des Lumières*, 3 vols (Paris, 1969–80).

Lizerand, G., *Le Duc de Beauvillier, 1648–1714* (Paris, 1933).

Ljublinski, V.S., *La Guerre des farines* (Grenoble, 1979).

Malettke, K., 'Les relations franco-prussiennes sous Frédéric-Guillaume I jusqu'à la paix de Stockholm', *Critica storica*, 20 (1988), 489–518.

Mandrou, R., *Louis XIV et son temps* (Paris, 1973).

Maréchal, M., 'Aspect de la crise de 1693–1694 dans la généralité de Moulins', *Revue d'histoire moderne et contemporaine*, 31 (1984), 537–70.

Marie, A. and J., *Versailles au temps de Louis XV, 1714–1745* (Paris, 1984).

Marin, L., *Le Portrait du roi* (Paris, 1984).

Marion, M., *Dictionnaire des institutions de la France* (republished Paris, 1989).

Markovitch, T., *Histoire des industries françaises. Les industries lainières de Colbert à la Révolution* (Geneva, 1976).

—— 'Le triple centenaire de Colbert', *Revue d'histoire économique et sociale*, 49 (1971), 305–24.

—— 'L'évolution industrielle de la France au XVIIIe siècle', *Revue d'histoire économique et sociale*, 53 (1975), 266–88.

Martin, O., *La conversion protestante à Lyon, 1659–1787* (Geneva, 1986).

Merrick, J., *The Desacralisation of the French Monarchy in the Eighteenth Century* (Baton Rouge, LA, 1990).

Mettam, R., *Power and Faction in Louis XIV's France* (Oxford, 1988).

Meuvret, J., *Etudes d'histoire économique* (Paris, 1971).

Meyer, J., *Colbert* (Paris, 1981).

—— *La naissance de Louis XIV* (Brussels, 1989).

—— *La Noblesse bretonne au XVIIIe siècle*, 2 vols (Paris, 1966).

—— *Le Régent* (Paris, 1985).

Minois, G., *Le Confesseur du roi. Les directeurs de conscience sous la monarchie française* (Paris, 1988).

Moote, A.L., *Louis XIII the Just* (Los Angeles, 1989).

—— *The Revolt of the Judges. The Parlement of Paris and the Fronde, 1643–1652* (Princeton, NJ, 1971).

Morineau, M., *Les Faux Semblants d'un démarrage économique* (Paris, 1971).

—— 'Budgets de l'Etat et gestion des finances royales en France au XVIIIe siècle', *Revue Historique*, 264 (1980), 289–336.

—— *Incroyables gazettes et fabuleux trésors* (Cambridge/Paris, 1984).

Mornet, D., *Les Origines intellectuelles de la Révolution française* (republished Lyon, 1989).

Mosser, F., *Les Intendants des finances au XVIIIe siècle. Les Lefèvre d'Ormesson et le 'Département des Impositions' (1715–1777)* (Geneva, 1978).

Mousnier, R., *The Institutions of France under the Absolute Monarchy, 1589–1789*, 2 vols (Chicago, 1979–82).

—— (dir.,) *Un nouveau Colbert* (Paris, 1985).

—— 'Quelques raisons de la Fronde; les causes des journées révolutionnaires parisiennes de 1648', *XVIIe siècle*, 1 (1948), 33–46.

—— (dir.), *Richelieu et la culture* (Paris, 1987).

—— *La Vénalité des offices sous Henri IV et Louis XIII* (republished Paris, 1971).

Muchembled, R., *L'Invention de l'homme moderne. Sensibilités, moeurs et comportements collectifs sous l'Ancien Régime* (Paris, 1988).

Murat, I., *Colbert* (Paris, 1980).

Naudé, G., *Considérations politiques sur les coups d'Etat* (Paris, 1988) – an edition of the text with an introduction by Louis Marin.

Néraudau, J.-P., *L'Olympe du Roi-Soleil* (Paris, 1986).

Nichols-Barker, N., *Brother to the Sun King, Philippe, Duke of Orléans* (Baltimore, MD, 1989).

Norberg, K., *Rich and Poor in Grenoble, 1600–1815* (Berkeley, CA, 1985).

Parker, D., *The Making of French Absolutism* (London, 1983).

—— 'Sovereignty, Absolutism and the Function of Law in Seventeenth-Century France', *Past and Present*, no. 122 (1989), pp. 37–74.

Petitfils, J.-C., *Mme de Montespan* (Paris, 1988).

Piat, C., *Le Père Joseph; le maître de Richelieu* (Paris, 1988).

Pillorget, R., *Les Mouvements insurrectionels de Provence entre 1596 et 1715* (Paris, 1975).

—— *Nouvelle Histoire de Paris: Paris sous les premiers Bourbons* (Paris, 1988).

Poitrineau, A., *La vie rurale en Basse-Auvergne* (Aurillac, 1965).

Porchnev, B., *Les soulèvements populaires en France avant la Fronde, 1623–1648* (Paris, 1963).

Poussou, J.-P., 'Les Crises démographiques en milieu urbain; l'exemple de Bordeaux (fin XVIIe-fin XVIIIe siècle)', *Annales ESC*, 35 (1985), 235–55.

Price, J.M., *France and the Chesapeake. A History of the French Tobacco Monopoly, 1674–1791, and of its Relationship to the British and American Tobacco Trades* (Ann Arbor, MI, 1973).

Pris, C., 'La Manufacture royale des glaces de Saint-Gobain, avant la révolution industrielle', *Revue d'histoire économique et sociale*, 52 (1974), 161–72.

Ranum, O., *The Fronde* (New York, 1994).

—— *Paris in the Age of Absolutism* (New York, 1979).

—— *Richelieu and the Councillors of Louis XIII* (Oxford, 1963).

La Régence (dir. Centre aixois d'études et de recherches sur le dix-huitième siècle) (Paris, 1970).

Richelieu et le monde de l'esprit (Exhibition catalogue from an exhibition held at the Sorbonne – dir. Chancellerie des Universités de Paris) (Paris, 1985).

Richet, D., 'Autour des origines lointaines de la Révolution française. Elites et despotisme', *Annales ESC*, 26 (1969), 1–23.

—— 'Croissance et blocages en France du XVe au XVIIIe siècles', *Annales ESC*, 25 (1968), 759–87.

Riley, J. *The Seven Years' War and the Old Régime in France* (Princeton, NJ, 1986).

Roche, D., *The People of Paris* (Berkeley, 1986).

—— *Le siècle des lumières en province. Académies et académiciens provinciaux, 1680–1789* (Paris, 1978).

Romano, R., 'Documenti e prime considerazioni introna alla "Balance du Commerce" della Francia dal 1716 al 1780' in *Studi in Onore di Armando Sapori*, 2 vols (Milan, 1957), ii, 1265–1300.

Ronzeaux, P., *Peuple et représentations sous le règne de Louis XIV* (Aix-en-Provence, 1988).

Roosen, W.J., *The Age of Louis XIV. The Rise of Modern Diplomacy* (Cambridge, MA, 1976).

Root, H., *Peasants and King in Burgundy. Agrarian Foundations of French Absolutism* (Berkeley, CA, 1987).

Rule, J.C., *Louis XIV and the Craft of Kingship* (Columbus, Ohio, 1969).

Schwartz, R., *Policing the Poor in Eighteenth-Century France* (Chapel Hill, NC, 1988).

Scoville, W.C., *Persecution of the Huguenots and French Economic Development, 1680–1720* (Berkeley, 1960).

Shennan, J.H. (1979), *Philippe, Duke of Orléans, Regent of France (1715–1723)* (London, 1979).

Smedley-Weill, A., *Correspondance des intendants avec le Contrôleur-général des finances (1677–1689). Naissance d'une administation*, 3 vols (Paris, 1989–91).

Solnon, J.-F., *La Cour de France* (Paris, 1977).

Soriano, M., *La Brosse à reluire sous Louis XIV* (Paris, 1989).

Soulié, M., *Le Régent (1674–1723)* (Paris, 1980).

Taton, R., *Enseignements et diffusion des sciences en France au XVIIIe siècle* (Paris, 1986).

Thomas, C., *La Reine scélérate, Marie-Antoinette dans les pamphlets* (Paris, 1989).

Thomson, J.K.J., *Clermont de Lodève, 1633–1789* (Cambridge, 1982).

Vaillot, R., *Le Cardinal de Bernis* (Paris, 1985).

Valensise, M., 'Le Sacre du roi: stratégie symbolique et doctrine politique de la monarchie française', *Annales ESC*, 41 (1986), 543–77.

Van Cruysse, D., *Madame Palatine* (Paris, 1988).

Van Kley, D., *The Damiens Affair and the Unravelling of the Old Régime* (Princeton, NJ, 1984).

—— *The Jansenists and the Expulsion of the Jesuits from France, 1757–1765* (New Haven and London, 1975).

Vauban, sa vie et son oeuvre (Saint-Léger-Vauban, 1984).

Vovelle, M., *La Chute de la monarchie, 1787–1792* (Paris, 1972).

Walton, G., *Louis XIV's Versailles* (Chicago, 1986).

Williams, A., *The Police of Paris, 1718–1789* (Baton Rouge, LA, 1979).

Wolf, J.B., *Louis XIV* (New York and London, 1986).

Zeller, G., *Histoire des relations internationales. Les Temps Modernes,* vol. iii (*De Louis XIV à 1789*) (Paris, 1955).

Zysberg, A., *Les Galériens – vie et destin de 60,000 forçats sur les galères de France, 1690–1748* (Paris, 1988).

Index

This index does not include references to the glossary or the chronological table.